D0192094

T H E
CATHOLIC
SOURCE BOOK

Third Edition

Rev. Peter Klein

The cover photo depicts the south rose window
in the Cathedral of Saint Louis, Missouri.
The window, which features a Greek cross design,
is crowned by mosaics of gold vines.

BROWN-ROA

A Division of Harcourt Brace & Company

BROWN-ROA

A Division of Harcourt Brace & Company

Our Mission

The primary mission of BROWN-ROA is to provide the Catholic and Christian markets with the highest quality catechetical print and media resources.
The content of these resources reflects the best insights of current theology, methodology, and pedagogical research.
The resources are practical and easy to use, designed to meet expresses market needs, and written to reflect the teachings of the Catholic Church.

Nihil Obstat
Rev. Richard L. Schaefer

Imprimatur
✠ Most Rev. Jerome Hanus, O.S.B.
Archbishop of Dubuque
April 28, 1999

The Imprimatur is an official declaration that a book or pamphlet is free of doctrinal or moral error. No implication is contained therein that anyone who granted the Imprimatur agrees with the contents, opinions, or statements expressed.

ISBN 0-15-950653-0

10   9   8   7   6   5   4   3   2

Contents

CHAPTER 1: **PRAYERS**   1

Traditional Prayers, 1; Litanies, 18; A Sampling
of Saints' Prayers, 31; The Psalter, 35; More Old
Testament Prayers, 39; New Testament; Prayers, 43;
Other Blessings, 58

CHAPTER 2: **AN OVERVIEW OF THE TRADITION**   61

A Catholic's Faith, Tradition, and Practice Known
by Heart, 61; God, 63; Conversion, 70; Orthodoxy,
73; Virtues, 75; Gifts, 79; Fruits of the Spirit, 81;
Commandments, 81; The Demands of Social
Justice, 92; Blessings, 93; The Three Notable Duties:
Prayer, Fasting, and Almsgiving, 94; Sin, 105; The
End and Eternity, 111

CHAPTER 3: **SCRIPTURE**   129

Revelation, 129; The Book, 133; The Vernacular
Bible, 138; The Old Testament, 156; The
Relationship Between the Old Testament and the
New Testament, 182; The New Testament, 193

CHAPTER 4: **CHURCH**   213

The Nature of the Church, 213; Historical
Development of the Church, 218; The Episcopacy,
222; The Papacy, 227; Coats of Arms, 236; Mottoes,
237; Insignia, 239; Religious Life, 241; Rites of the
Catholic Church, 249; Protestantism, 254; Places
and Practices, 258

CHAPTER 5: **LITURGY** 275

Background Information, 275; The Seven
Sacraments, 277; The Sacraments of Initiation,
278; The Sacraments of Healing, 301; The
Sacraments of Mission, 308; The Liturgy of
the Hours, 316; Sacramentals, 318

CHAPTER 6: **THE LITURGICAL YEAR** 325

Time, 325; The Church Year, 331; Holidays and
Anniversaries, 342; General Roman Calendar, 345;
The Jewish Calendar, 365

CHAPTER 7: **DEVOTIONS IN CATHOLIC TRADITION** 367

An Overview, 367; Devotion to the Eucharist 369;
Devotion to the Sacred Heart, 374; Devotion to
the Passion, 377; Devotion to the Infant of
Prague, 383

CHAPTER 8: **VENERATION OF SAINTS AND HEROES** 385

The Nature of Veneration, 385; Devotion to
Mary, 386; Devotion to St. Joseph, 399; The
Twelve Apostles, 400; Church Fathers, 408;
Doctors of the Church, 412; The Saints, 415;
The Good News Meets Polytheism, 436

CHAPTER 9: **CATHOLIC SYMBOLS** 441

Cross, 441; Other Symbols, 447; Sacred
Monograms, 461; Numbers and Their
Significance, 464; A Glossary of Common
Terms, 468

CHAPTER 10: **WORD AND PHRASE ORIGINS** 493

Words and Phrases with a Biblical Origin or
Allusion, 493; Words and Phrases with a
Church Origin or Allusion, 515

Prayers

Traditional Prayers

Common Prayers

Part Four of the four-part *Catechism of the Catholic Church* is "Christian Prayer" (#s 2558–2865).

Sign of the Cross

In the name of the Father, and of the Son, and of the Holy Spirit. Amen.

The Lord's Prayer   (Latin, *Pater Noster*) (See CCC #s 2759–2865.)

Matthew 6:9–13; Luke 11:2–4. The Latin name for the Lord's Prayer, *Pater Noster*, means "Our Father." For many years, Catholics referred to the Lord's Prayer as "the Our Father." The seven petitions of the Lord's Prayer are a synthesis of faith and a statement of values. Part of the doxology "for thine is the kingdom . . ." dates back to *The Didache* (mid-first or second century). It was originally a liturgical ending. "Thy will be done," *Fiat voluntas tua*, is the familiar petition from the Lord's Prayer in Latin.

Traditional wording:
Our Father, who art in heaven,
hallowed be thy name;
thy kingdom come,
thy will be done on earth as it is in heaven.
Give us this day our daily bread;
and forgive us our trespasses
as we forgive those who trespass against us;
and lead us not into temptation,
but deliver us from evil.
  Amen.

Hail Mary   (Latin, *Ave Maria*)

The Hail Mary is a composite of the angel Gabriel's greeting (Luke 1:28) and Elizabeth's greeting (Luke 1:42), both to Mary. It has been a popular prayer since the eleventh century. The name *Jesus* was added in the thirteenth century. Various versions of the Holy Mary emerged in the fourteenth century and were in general use by the sixteenth century.

Hail, Mary, full of grace!
The Lord is with you;
blessed are you among women,
and blessed is the fruit of your womb, Jesus.
Holy Mary, Mother of God,
pray for us sinners,
now and at the hour of our death. Amen.

The Lady of the Lake

In 1825, Franz Schubert set to music some of Sir Walter Scott's verses in "The Lady of the Lake." It was later discovered that the Latin text of the Hail Mary, "Ave Maria . . . ," could be sung to the same music. There are those who believe that it was this prayer, and the Blessed Lady herself, that originally inspired Schubert to compose one of the greatest pieces of devotional music ever: the "Ave Maria."

Glory to the Father   (Latin, *Gloria Patri*)

This is the Lesser Doxology (Greek: *doxa*, "glory"), the Greater being the "Gloria" of the Mass. The Lesser Doxology is said at the end of psalms in the Liturgy of the Hours. The wording of the first verse is ascribed to St. Basil, and of the second to St. Telesphorus, a second-century pope. Probably adapted from Jewish blessings, the "Glory Be" was influenced by the Trinitarian Baptism formula (Matthew 28:19). It was forbidden by English Puritans as unscriptural.

Glory to the Father,
and to the Son,
and to the Holy Spirit:
as it was in the beginning,
is now,
and will be forever. Amen.

Creeds

(See CCC, "The Creeds," #s 185–197.)

Apostles' Creed

The Apostles' Creed is the epitome of Christian doctrine. In twelve articles, it contains the truths taught by the apostles. It has existed essentially since the second century and was first referred to in the fourth century. The earliest text dates from the eighth century. Developed by early Church councils, it was adopted in its present form in the eleventh century. Since the early centuries of the Western Church, catechumens were required to learn and recite it before Baptism.

I believe in God, the Father almighty,
creator of heaven and earth.
I believe in Jesus Christ, his only Son, our Lord.
He was conceived by the power of the Holy Spirit
and born of the Virgin Mary.
He suffered under Pontius Pilate,
was crucified, died, and was buried.
He descended to the dead.
On the third day, he rose again.
He ascended into heaven,
and is seated at the right hand of the Father.
He will come again to judge the living and the dead.
I believe in the Holy Spirit,
the holy catholic Church,
the communion of saints,
the forgiveness of sins,
the resurrection of the body,
and the life everlasting. Amen.

Nicene Creed

The Nicene Creed was a response to the Arian heresy, which denied the divinity of Christ. It takes its name from Nicaea, city of an ecumenical council in A.D. 325. Subsequent to the meeting in Nicaea, the original creed underwent some changes—at meetings in Constantinople in 381 and Chalcedon in 450. The Nicene Creed is the only Christian creed accepted in common as authoritative by the Catholic, Orthodox, Anglican, and major Protestant Churches.

We believe in one God,
the Father, the Almighty,
maker of heaven and earth,
of all that is seen and unseen.

We believe in one Lord, Jesus Christ,
  the only Son of God,
  eternally begotten of the Father,
  God from God, Light from Light,
  true God from true God,
  begotten, not made, one in Being with the Father.
Through him all things were made.
For us men and for our salvation
  he came down from heaven:
by the power of the Holy Spirit
  he was born of the Virgin Mary, and became man.
For our sake he was crucified under Pontius Pilate;
he suffered, died, and was buried.
On the third day he rose again
  in fulfillment of the Scriptures;
he ascended into heaven
  and is seated at the right hand of the Father.
He will come again in glory
  to judge the living and the dead,
  and his kingdom will have no end.
We believe in the Holy Spirit, the Lord, the giver of life,
  who proceeds from the Father and the Son.
With the Father and the Son he is worshiped and glorified.
He has spoken through the Prophets.
We believe in one holy catholic and apostolic Church.
We acknowledge one baptism for the forgiveness of sins.
We look for the resurrection of the dead,
  and the life of the world to come. Amen.

Athanasian Creed

This creed receives its title from the fact that it embodies Athanasius's theology of the Trinity. Composed by Hilary, bishop of Arles (fifth century), it is common doctrinal ground (along with the Apostles' and Nicene Creeds) for Catholics and Anglicans. It is also characterized by its extraordinary length and its anathemas against any who would deny the doctrines it professes. Its Latin title is its opening word, *Quicumque* ("He who with this . . ."): "If anyone wishes to be saved, before everything else he must hold the Catholic faith."

A Profession of Catholic Christianity

I, N., enlightened by divine grace,
profess the Christian faith as it is taught and practiced in the Catholic Church.
I believe in God, the Father almighty,
   creator of heaven and earth;
and in Jesus Christ, his only Son, our Lord,
   who was conceived by the Holy Spirit,
   born of the Virgin Mary,
   suffered under Pontius Pilate,
   was crucified, died, and was buried.
   He descended into hell;
   the third day he rose again from the dead;
   he ascended into heaven,
   sits at the right hand of God, the Father almighty;
   from thence he shall come to judge the living and the dead.
I believe in the Holy Spirit,
   the holy Catholic Church,
   the communion of saints,
   the forgiveness of sins,
   the resurrection of the body,
   and life everlasting.
I believe that this Church
   is the Church in which the fullness of God's revelation
   through his Son, Jesus Christ, abides.
I believe that her college of bishops,
   with the pope, the bishop of Rome, presiding at its center,
   continues to exercise in the world the authority
   for teaching and moral guidance
   given by Jesus Christ to his apostles for the salvation of all.
I further believe in seven sacraments,
   signs of worship through which
   the grace of the death, resurrection,
   and ascension of Jesus Christ is communicated.
They are: Baptism, Confirmation, Eucharist,
   Penance, Anointing of the Sick,
   Holy Orders, and Matrimony.
I promise, through prayer,
   participation in Church life and worship,
   and continued efforts to understand the tenets of my faith,
   to form my conscience in such a way
   as to live according to the doctrines and practices
   which the Catholic Church prescribes
   for the individual and common good of her faithful.

Other Mass Prayers

Kyrie Eleison (Greek)

This prayer is still frequently prayed in Greek. It originated in Greek liturgies and became part of the Latin Rite in the fifth century. It is essentially a response to a litany. The Trinitarian interpretation (Lord . . . Christ . . . Lord) was a later development. Until 1969, each line was prayed or sung three times; after 1969 each line was sung or prayed (by a leader or choir) and then repeated (by the assembly). While the prayer can be included in the penitential rite, since it implores the Lord's mercy, it is above all a prayer of praise to the risen Christ in litany form.

Kyrie eleison.	*Lord, have mercy*
Christe eleison.	*Christ, have mercy*
Kyrie eleison.	*Lord, have mercy*

Confiteor ("I Confess")

Mea culpa, "through my fault" (or "It's my fault"), is a phrase in any Confiteor, particularly the one sometimes used during the penitential rite of the Mass. (*Maxima culpa* is "grievous" fault, from the Latin *maxima* meaning "greatest"— in this case "most serious.")

I confess to almighty God,
  and to you, my brothers and sisters,
  that I have sinned through my
  own fault
  in my thoughts and in my words,
  in what I have done,
and in what I have failed to do;
and I ask blessed Mary, ever virgin,

all the angels and saints,
  and you, my brothers and sisters,
  to pray for me to the Lord our God.

Glory to God in the Highest
(Latin, *Gloria in excelsis Deo*)

This is the Greater Doxology (Greek, doxa, "glory"), the lesser being the "Glory Be" or "Glory to God" prayer. The Greater Doxology is the familiar "Gloria," spoken in unison or sung at Mass. Because it echoes the song of the angels at Bethlehem (Luke 2:14), it is called the "Angelic Hymn."

Glory to God in the highest,
  and peace to his people on earth.
Lord God, heavenly King,
almighty God and Father,
  we worship you, we give you
  thanks,
  we praise you for your glory.
Lord Jesus Christ, only Son of the
  Father,
Lord God, Lamb of God,
you take away the sin of the world:
  have mercy on us;
  you are seated at the right hand of
  the Father:
  receive our prayer.
For you alone are the Holy One,
you alone are the Lord,
you alone are the Most High,
  Jesus Christ,
  with the Holy Spirit,
  in the glory of God the Father.
Amen.

Holy, Holy, Holy Lord

(Latin, *Santus and Benedictus*)

These texts are based on two Scripture references: Isaiah 6:3 and Mark 11:9–10 (Jesus' entry into Jerusalem). The prayer was probably first used in the East, but it was quickly incorporated into the Eucharist in the West. It is prayed at the beginning of the Eucharistic Prayer.

> *Holy, holy, holy Lord, God of*
> *   power and might,*
> *heaven and earth are full of your*
> *   glory.*
> *   Hosanna in the highest.*
> *Blessed is he who comes in the*
> *   name of the Lord.*
> *   Hosanna in the highest.*

Lamb of God (Latin, *Agnus Dei*)

This is a litany prayer that accompanies the breaking of the consecrated bread at Mass. It became part of the liturgy in the West in the seventh century. Ending the last petition with "grant us peace" (*dona nobis pacem*) became common during the tenth and eleventh centuries. The reference to Jesus as the Lamb of God comes from John 1:29, Revelation 5:6–13, and other Scripture passages.

> *Lamb of God, you take away the*
> *   sin of the world:*
> *   have mercy on us.*
> *Lamb of God, you take away the*
> *   sin of the world:*
> *   have mercy on us.*
> *Lamb of God, you take away the*
> *   sin of the world:*
> *   grant us peace.*

Other Traditional Prayers

Act of Faith

> *O my God, I firmly believe that you are one God in three divine Persons, Father, Son, and Holy Spirit; I believe that your divine Son became man and died for our sins, and that he will come to judge the living and the dead. I believe these and all the truths which the Holy Catholic Church teaches, because you revealed them, who can neither deceive nor be deceived.*

Act of Hope

> *O my God, relying on your infinite goodness and promises, I hope to obtain pardon of my sins, the help of your grace, and life everlasting, through the merits of Jesus Christ, my Lord and Redeemer.*

Act of Love

> *O my God, I love you above all things, with my whole heart and soul, because you are all good and worthy of all love. I love my neighbor as myself for the love of you. I forgive all who have injured me, and I ask pardon of all whom I have injured.*

Act of Contrition (traditional)

O my God, I am heartily sorry for having offended you, and I detest all my sins, because of your just punishments, but most of all because they offend you, my God, who are all good and deserving of all my love. I firmly resolve, with the help of your grace, to sin no more and to avoid the near occasion of sin.

Act of Contrition (contemporary)

My God, I am sorry for my sins with all my heart. In choosing to do wrong and failing to do good, I have sinned against you whom I should love above all things. I firmly intend, with your help, to do penance, to sin no more, and to avoid whatever leads me to sin. Our Savior Jesus Christ suffered and died for us. In his name, my God, have mercy.

Leonine Prayers (Prayers after Mass)

Formerly, these prayers were said after Mass. They were ordered universally by Pope Leo XIII. They consist of three Hail Marys, the Hail Holy Queen, a prayer to God for sinners and the Church, and the Prayer to St. Michael the Archangel. The prayers ended with a threefold invocation to the Sacred Heart (added by Pope St. Pius X). The Leonine Prayers were formally abolished in 1964.

O God, our refuge and our strength, look down in mercy on your people who cry to you; and by the intercession of the glorious and immaculate Virgin Mary, Mother of God, of St. Joseph her spouse, of your blessed apostles Peter and Paul, and all the saints, in mercy and goodness hear our prayers for the conversion of sinners, and for the liberty and exaltation of our holy mother the Church. Through the same Christ our Lord. Amen.

Holy Michael, the Archangel, defend us in battle; be our safeguard against the wickedness and snares of the devil. May God rebuke him, we humbly pray; and you, Prince of the heavenly host, by the power of God, cast into hell Satan and all the evil spirits, who wander through the world seeking the ruin of souls. Amen.

St. Michael the Archangel

Angelus ("The Angel")

Honoring the incarnation, the *Angelus* is named for its first Latin word (*Angelus Domini*, "the angel of the Lord . . ."). Since the sixteenth century, the church bells (one of the community's clocks) tolled the *Angelus*, at six A.M., twelve noon, and six P.M. The evening call probably began as a curfew bell, a call for Evening Prayer. The six A.M. call was originally a prayer for peace. Formerly, the noon prayer was said only on Friday. In the Easter Season, the *Angelus* is replaced by the *Regina Caeli* ("Queen of Heaven").

V. The angel spoke God's message to Mary,

R. and she conceived of the Holy Spirit.
Hail, Mary. . . .

V. "I am the lowly servant of the Lord:

R. let it be done to me according to your word."
Hail, Mary. . . .

V. And the Word became flesh,

R. and lived among us.
Hail, Mary. . . .

V. Pray for us, holy Mother of God,

R. that we may become worthy of the promises of Christ.

Let us pray.
Lord,
fill our hearts with your grace:
once through the message of an angel
you revealed to us the incarnation of your Son;
now, through his suffering and death
lead us to the glory of his resurrection.
We ask this through Christ our Lord.
Amen.

Queen of Heaven (Latin, *Regina Caeli*)

This prayer replaces the *Angelus* during Easter time.

V. Queen of heaven, rejoice, alleluia,

R. For Christ, your Son and Son of God,

V. has risen as he said, alleluia.

R. Pray to God for us, alleluia.

V. Rejoice and be glad, O Virgin Mary, alleluia,

R. For the Lord has truly risen, alleluia.

Let us pray.
God of life,
you have given joy to the world
by the resurrection of your Son, our Lord Jesus Christ.
Through the prayers of his mother, the Virgin Mary,
bring us to the happiness of eternal life.
We ask this through Christ our Lord.
Amen.

Regina Caeli (Latin)

Regina caeli laetare, alleluia,
Quia quem meruisti portare, alleluia,
Resurrexit sicut dixit, alleluia.
Ora pro nobis Deum, alleluia.

The Trinity crowning Mary

Te Deum

This is an ancient (fourth century) hymn, given its name by its first two words. It is ascribed by some to St. Ambrose who, it is said, prayed it while baptizing Augustine in 386, hence it is also called the "Ambrosian Hymn." The traditional and popular hymn "Holy God, We Praise Thy Name" is an English translation (Walworth, 1820–1900) of a free translation (Franz, 1719–1790) from Latin into German of the *Te Deum.*

You are God: we praise you;
You are the Lord: we acclaim you;
You are the eternal Father:
All creation worships you.
To you all angels, all the powers of
*   heaven,*
Cherubim and Seraphim, sing in
*   endless praise:*
*   Holy, holy, holy Lord, God of*
*   power and might,*
*   heaven and earth are full of your*
*   glory.*
The glorious company of apostles
*   praise you.*
The noble fellowship of prophets
*   praise you.*
The white-robed army of martyrs
*   praise you.*
Throughout the world the holy
*   Church acclaims you:*
*   Father, of majesty unbounded,*
*   your true and only Son, worthy of*
*   all worship,*
*   and the Holy Spirit, advocate*
*   and guide.*
You, Christ, are the king of glory,
*   the eternal Son of the Father.*
When you became man to set us free
*   you did not spurn the Virgin's*
*   womb.*

You overcame the sting of death,
and opened the kingdom of heaven
*   to all believers.*
You are seated at God's right hand
*   in glory.*
We believe that you will come, and
*   be our judge.*
Come then, Lord, and help your
*   people,*
bought with the price of your own
*   blood,*
and bring us with your saints
*   to glory everlasting.*
Save your people, Lord, and bless
*   your inheritance.*
Govern and uphold them now and
*   always.*
Day by day we bless you.
We praise your name for ever.
Keep us today, Lord, from all sin.
Have mercy on us, Lord, have
*   mercy.*
Lord, show us your love and mercy;
for we put our trust in you.
In you, Lord, is our hope:
and we shall never hope in vain.

The Jesus Prayer   (See CCC #s 2666–2668.)

This ancient Eastern Christian contemplative prayer invokes the name of Jesus, the only name in the world given us by which we are to be saved (Acts 4:12; also 2:21; 9:14, 21, for example). Developed by the Desert Fathers, it consists of short phrases from the Scriptures which are repeated interiorly with attention to Christ's presence until prayer becomes one with breathing and the Lord makes a house within (John 14:23, Revelation 3:20).

The most popular phrase combines the christological hymn of Philippians 2:6–11 with the cry of the tax collector (Luke 18:13) and of the blind man begging (Luke 18:38–39): "Lord Jesus Christ, Son of God, have mercy on me, a sinner."

God has given Jesus a name to be exalted (Philippians 2:9–11) with a saving power that is sign and source of the Spirit within (1 Corinthians 12:3). The Jesus Prayer especially invites a person to assume a conscious prayer position, to become centered mentally, and to breathe rhythmically (in with the first phrase, out with the second, and so on).

Morning Offering

This dedication of the day to the Sacred Heart originated with members of the Apostleship of Prayer (League of the Sacred Heart).

O Jesus, through the Immaculate Heart of Mary, I offer you all my prayers, works, joys, and sufferings of this day, for all the intentions of your Sacred Heart, in union with the holy sacrifice of the Mass throughout the world, in reparation for my sins, for the intentions of all our associates, and for the general intention recommended this month.

Prayer Before Meals

Bless us, O Lord, and these your gifts, which we are about to receive from your goodness. Through Christ our Lord. Amen.

Prayer After Meals

We give you thanks for all your gifts, almighty God, living and reigning now and forever. (And may the souls of the faithful departed, through the mercy of God, rest in peace.) Amen.

Prayer to the Guardian Angel   *(Traditional)*

Angel sent by God to guide me,
be my light and walk beside me;
be my guardian and protect me;
on the paths of life direct me.

Angel of God, my guardian dear,
to whom God's love commits me here,
ever this day be at my side,
to light and guard, to rule and guide.
Amen.

Eternal Rest

Eternal rest grant to them, O Lord,
and let perpetual light shine upon them.
May they rest in peace. Amen.

Prayer Before a Crucifix

Good and gentle Jesus,
I kneel before you.
I see and I ponder your five wounds.
My eyes behold what David prophesied about you:
"They have pierced my hands and feet;
they have counted all my bones."
Engrave on me this image of yourself.
Fulfill the yearnings of my heart:
give me faith, hope, and love,
repentance for my sins,
and true conversion of life.
Amen.

A crucifix

Why the Robin's Breast Is Red

This is a story from the life of the Irish saint, Columba (521–597), the abbot of Iona, off the coast of Scotland. One morning he woke from sleep in his little hermitage to find a robin perched on the window sill. "Have you a song for me?" he asked, and in reply the robin sang a song of Good Friday, and how its breast was reddened: From its nest among the moss, the robin saw the Lord of all upon a cross, and the Lord saw the brown, yellow-beaked bird. Christ called and the robin lighted upon him. As the crowds taunted, the robin sang "Holy, holy, holy," with its breast against Christ's bloody brow. Mary's voice then was heard, "Christ's own bird you shall be!" And so the robin has the proud story of its red breast from the day it saw Christ die.

The Divine Praises

The Divine Praises were traditionally recited after the Benediction of the Blessed Sacrament. They were composed possibly about 1800 in reparation for profanity and blasphemy. Invocations 5, 6, 10, 11, and 13 are post mid-nineteenth century additions.

1. *Blessed be God.*
2. *Blessed be his holy name.*
3. *Blessed be Jesus Christ, true God and true man.*
4. *Blessed be the name of Jesus.*
5. *Blessed be his most Sacred Heart.*
6. *Blessed be his most Precious Blood.*
7. *Blessed be Jesus in the most holy sacrament of the altar.*
8. *Blessed be the Holy Spirit, the Paraclete.*
9. *Blessed be the great Mother of God, Mary most holy.*
10. *Blessed be her holy and immaculate conception.*
11. *Blessed be her glorious assumption.*
12. *Blessed be the name of Mary, virgin and mother.*
13. *Blessed be St. Joseph, her most chaste spouse.*
14. *Blessed be God in his angels and in his saints.*

Come, Holy Spirit

This simple and direct prayer to the Holy Spirit evolved in the antiphons and hymns of every liturgical tradition, especially the Pentecost sequence.

V. Come, Holy Spirit, fill the hearts of your faithful
R. And kindle in them the fire of your love.
V. Send forth your Spirit and they shall be created.
R. And you shall renew the face of the earth.
Let us pray.
Lord,
by the light of the Holy Spirit
you have taught the hearts of your faithful.
In the same Spirit
help us to relish what is right
and always rejoice in your consolation.
We ask this through Christ our Lord.
Amen.

Veni, Sancte Spiritus ("Come, Holy Spirit")

This prayer, the "Golden Sequence" of Pentecost, was probably written by Rabanus Maurus (776–856). This translation is by Edward Caswell (1814–1878). Long a part of the Liturgy of the Hours, and called the most popular of all hymns, it is used at papal elections, episcopal (bishop) consecrations, priestly ordinations, counciliar/synodal gatherings, and church dedications.

> Come, thou Holy Spirit, come!
> And from thy celestial home
> Shed a ray of light divine!
> Come, thou Father of the poor!
> Come, thou source of all our store!
> Come, within our bosoms shine!
> Thou, of comforters the best;
> Thou, the soul's most welcome
>   guest;
> Sweet refreshment here below.
> In our labor, rest most sweet;

> Grateful coolness in the heat;
> Solace in the midst of woe.
> O most blessed Light divine,
> Shine within these hearts of thine,
> And our inmost being fill!
> Where thou art not, we have naught,
> Nothing good in deed or thought,
> Nothing free from taint of ill.
> Heal our wounds, our strength
>   renew;
> On our dryness pour thy dew;
> Wash the stains of guilt away.
> Bend the stubborn heart and will;
> Melt the frozen, warm the chill;
> Guide the steps that go astray.
> On the faithful, who adore
> And confess thee, evermore
> In thy sev'nfold gift descend.
> Give them virtue's sure reward;
> Give them thy salvation, Lord;
> Give them joys that never end.

The Rosary

The rosary is called the *Psalter of Mary* because all fifteen of its mysteries, with their 150 *Aves*, correspond to the number of the psalms. Praying all fifteen decades at once is called the *Dominican Rosary*. The Rosary is the most well-known and used form of chaplet (a devotion using beads; from a French word meaning "crown" or "wreath"). There are other chaplets, such as those in honor of St. Bridget of Sweden and in honor of Mary, the Immaculate Conception.

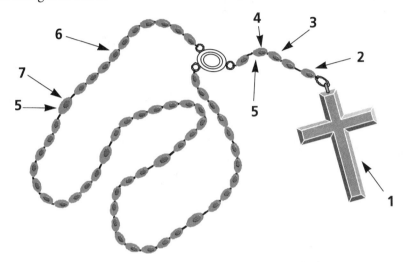

1. Sign of the Cross and Apostles' Creed
2. Lord's Prayer
3. Three Hail Marys
4. Glory to the Father
5. Announce mystery; Lord's Prayer
6. Ten Hail Marys
7. Glory to the Father

Repeat last three steps, meditating on the other mysteries of the rosary.

The Fatima invocation (recommended by Mary to the children at Fatima in 1917) is sometimes recited between decades: "O my Jesus, forgive us our sins. Save us from the fires of hell, and bring all souls to heaven, especially those who most need your mercy."

Hail, Holy Queen (Latin, *Salve, Regina*)

One of the most ancient Marian antiphons in Western Christendom, the *Hail, Holy Queen* was used for centuries in the Liturgy of the Hours. It is most often regarded as anonymous (though it was probably composed by Hermannus Contractus, d. 1054). Its finale, "O clement . . . ," though attributed to St. Bernard, is found in manuscripts that pre-date him. Traditionally, it is sung as the last prayer of Compline, the Church's liturgical night prayer.

Hail, holy Queen, Mother of mercy,
hail, our life, our sweetness, and
* our hope.*
To you we cry, the children of Eve;
to you we send up our sighs,
mourning and weeping in this
* land of exile.*
Turn, then, most gracious advocate,
your eyes of mercy toward us;
lead us home at last
and show unto us the blessed fruit
* of your womb, Jesus:*
O clement, O loving, O sweet
* Virgin Mary.*

Salve, Regina ("Hail, Queen")
Salve, Regina, mater misericordiae,
Vita, dulcedo et spes nostra salve.
Ad te clamamus exsules filii Hevae.
Ad te suspiramus, gementes et flentes
* in hac lacrimarum valle.*
Eia ergo, Advocata nostra,
illos tuos misericordes oculos ad nos
* converte.*
Et Jesum, benedictum fructum
* ventris tui,*
nobis post hoc exsilium ostende.
O clemens, o pia, o dulcis, Virgo
* Maria.*

The Mysteries of the Rosary

Including recommended scriptural meditations

Joyful Mysteries (Mondays and Thursdays)

1. The Annunciation (humility)
   Isaiah 7:10–14; Luke 1:26–38

2. The Visitation (charity)
   Isaiah 40:1–11; Luke 1:39–45; John 1:19–23

3. The Nativity (poverty)
   Micah 5:1–4; Matthew 2:1–12; Luke 2:1–20; Galatians 4:1–7

4. The Presentation (obedience)
   Luke 2:22–35; Hebrews 9:6–14

5. The Finding of Jesus in the Temple (piety)
   Luke 2:41–52; John 12:44–50; 1 Corinthians 2:6–16

Sorrowful Mysteries (Tuesdays and Fridays)

1. The Agony in the Garden (repentance)
   Matthew 26:36–46; Mark 14:26–42; Luke 22:39–53; John 18:1–12

2. The Scourging at the Pillar (purity)
   Isaiah 50:5–9; Matthew 27:15–26; Mark 15:1–15

3. The Crowning with Thorns (courage)
   Isaiah 52:13–53:10; Matthew 16:24–28, 27:27–31; Mark 15:16–19;
   Luke 23:6–11; John 19:1–7

4. The Carrying of the Cross (patience)
   Mark 8:31–38; Matthew 16:20–25; Luke 23:26–32; John 19:17–22;
   Philippians 2:6–11

5. The Crucifixion (self-renunciation)
   Mark 15:33–39; Luke 23:33–46; John 19:23–37; Acts 22:22–24;
   Hebrews 9:11–14

Glorious Mysteries (Sundays, Wednesdays, and Saturdays)

1. The Resurrection (faith)
   Matthew 28:1–10; Mark 16:1–18; Luke 24:1–12; John 20:1–10;
   Romans 6:1–14; 1 Corinthians 15:1–11

2. The Ascension (hope)
   Matthew 28:16–20; Luke 24:44–53; Acts 1:1–11; Ephesians 2:4–7

3. The Descent of the Holy Spirit Upon the Apostles (love)
   John 14:15–21; Acts 2:1–11; 4:23–31; 11:15–18

4. The Assumption (eternal happiness)
   John 11:17–27; 1 Corinthians 15:20–28, 42–57; Revelation 21:1–6

5. The Coronation of Mary (Marian devotion)
   Matthew 5:1–12; 2 Peter 3:10; Revelation 7:1–4, 9–12; 21:1–6

Franciscan Crown or Seraphic Rosary

This rosary of seven decades was introduced among the Franciscans in 1422. Two
Hail Marys were added since then, to total seventy-two, the traditional age of Mary
at her assumption. This rosary commemorates the seven joys of the Blessed Mother:

1. Annunciation
2. Visitation
3. Nativity
4. Adoration of the Magi
5. Finding in the Temple
6. Appearance of the Risen Christ to His Mother
7. Assumption and Coronation.

Memorare (Latin, "remember")

The Memorare is ascribed to St. Bernard of Clairvaux (1090–1153). It was
popularized by Claude Bernard, the "Poor Priest" (1588–1641).

Remember, most loving Virgin Mary,
*   never was it heard*
*   that anyone who turned to you for help*
*   was left unaided.*
Inspired by this confidence,
*   though burdened by my sins,*
I run to your protection
*   for you are my mother.*
Mother of the Word of God,
*   do not despise my words of pleading*
*   but be merciful and hear my prayer.*
*   Amen.*

Litanies

Since Vatican II (1962–1965), these are the formally indulgenced litanies: Holy Name, Precious Blood, St. Joseph, Sacred Heart, Blessed Virgin, and All Saints. Other litanies not indulgenced but approved for the faithful number over a hundred. Each begins with an invocation of the Trinity.

Litanies and Rogation Days

A litany (from the Greek *litanos,* "entreaty") is a prayer consisting of a series of supplications and responses said alternately by a leader and a group. A rogation was essentially the same. Rogation Days were the three days of prayer for the Lord's blessing of a successful harvest from fields and gardens. These days were the Monday, Tuesday, and Wednesday before Ascension Thursday. They were penitential days, including a Mass and procession. Because the Litany (rogation) of the Saints was invoked, Rogation Days were also called litanies, specifically, the "Lesser Litanies" ("lesser" because they are later than the ancient "Greater Litanies," which were a similar observance that originated as a Christian replacement for a pre-Christian procession on April 25 that propitiated Robigus, the god of frost).

The origin of Rogation Days is interesting: Believers have always given thanks to God for sun and soil, water and air. In the beginning, these believers knew themselves as stewards, not just consumers, and they had constant reminders of their dependence on the merciful Lord, who creates and provides and who owns the earth. At times, it seems the very elements conspire against a regular harvest, sometimes even causing prolonged periods of fruitlessness and hopelessness. It is particularly at these times that the call goes out to a provident Lord to restore the earth's bounty.

That is what happened in France, some 1500 years ago, around the city of Vienne. Earthquake, fire, and inclement weather combined to cause crop failure and widespread hunger. Mamertus, the bishop of Vienne, called for penance and prayer on the three days preceding Ascension Thursday. The people responded to the call, and the Lord responded to the prayer.

Throughout France, and ultimately beyond, word of this litany, this rogation, spread, finding a readiness in the hearts of believers. As the years went by, the same three days of penitential prayer were observed annually, and by the eighth century, universally.

Gratitude, an awareness of God's power and earth's bounty, and human dependence on both—these are no less real today. Now week-long, the penitential prayer is now included in the ecumenical Soil and Water Stewardship Week. It is still the spirit and style of prayer called for by St. Mamertus, while, at the same time, we take responsibility for creative conservation and considerate management.

Litany of the Sacred Heart

This litany was authorized for recitation in the universal Church by Pope Leo XIII in 1889. Many of its invocations go back to the seventeenth century.

Lord, have mercy.

Christ, have mercy.

Lord, have mercy.

God our Father in heaven,

> *Have mercy on us.* (after each invocation)

God the Son, Redeemer of the world

God the Holy Spirit

Holy Trinity, one God

Heart of Jesus, Son of the eternal Father

Heart of Jesus, formed by the Holy Spirit in the womb of the Virgin Mother

Heart of Jesus, one with the eternal Word

Heart of Jesus, infinite in majesty

Heart of Jesus, holy temple of God

Heart of Jesus, tabernacle of the Most High

Heart of Jesus, house of God and gate of heaven

Heart of Jesus, aflame with love for us

Heart of Jesus, source of justice and love

Heart of Jesus, full of goodness and love

Heart of Jesus, well-spring of all virtue

Heart of Jesus, worthy of all praise

Heart of Jesus, king and center of all hearts

Heart of Jesus, treasure-house of wisdom and knowledge

Heart of Jesus, in whom there dwells the fullness of God

Heart of Jesus, in whom the Father is well pleased

Heart of Jesus, from whose fullness we have all received

Heart of Jesus, desire of the eternal hills

Heart of Jesus, patient and full of mercy

Heart of Jesus, generous to all who turn to you

Heart of Jesus, fountain of life and holiness

Heart of Jesus, atonement for our sins

Heart of Jesus, overwhelmed with insults

Heart of Jesus, broken for our sins

Heart of Jesus, obedient even to death

Heart of Jesus, pierced by a lance

Heart of Jesus, source of all consolation

Heart of Jesus, our life and resurrection

Heart of Jesus, our peace and reconciliation
Heart of Jesus, victim for our sins
Heart of Jesus, salvation of all who trust in you
Heart of Jesus, hope of all who die in you
Heart of Jesus, delight of all the saints
Lamb of God, you take away the sins of the world
have mercy on us
Lamb of God, you take away the sins of the world
have mercy on us
Lamb of God, you take away the sins of the world
have mercy on us.
V. Jesus, gentle and humble of heart.
R. Touch our hearts and make them like your own.
Let us pray.
Father,
we rejoice in the gifts of love
we have received from the heart of Jesus your Son.
Open our hearts to share his life
and continue to bless us with his love.
We ask this in the name of Jesus the Lord. Amen.

Litany of the Holy Name of Jesus

This litany is of unknown origin, though ascribed to St. Bernardine of Siena and St. John Capistran. It was given papal attention as early as 1588 and universal recommendation by Pope Leo XIII in 1886. The Holy Name Society was founded as early as the thirteenth century, by a Dominican, to promote reverence for Jesus' name.

Lord, have mercy. (repeat)
Christ, have mercy. (repeat)
Lord, have mercy. (repeat)
God our Father in heaven,
have mercy on us. (after each invocation)
God the Son, Redeemer of the world
God the Holy Spirit
Holy Trinity, one God
Jesus, Son of the living God
Jesus, splendor of the Father

Jesus, brightness of eternal light
Jesus, king of glory
Jesus, dawn of justice
Jesus, Son of the Virgin Mary
Jesus, worthy of our love
Jesus, worthy of our wonder
Jesus, mighty God
Jesus, father of the world to come
Jesus, prince of peace
Jesus, all powerful
Jesus, pattern of patience

Jesus, model of obedience
Jesus, gentle and humble of heart
Jesus, lover of chastity
Jesus, lover of us all
Jesus, God of peace
Jesus, author of life
Jesus, seeker of souls
Jesus, our God
Jesus, our refuge
Jesus, father of the poor
Jesus, treasure of the faithful
Jesus, Good Shepherd
Jesus, the true light
Jesus, eternal wisdom
Jesus, infinite goodness
Jesus, our way and our life
Jesus, joy of angels
Jesus, king of patriarchs
Jesus, master of evangelists
Jesus, courage of martyrs
Jesus, light of confessors
Jesus, purity of virgins
Jesus, crown of all saints
Lord, be merciful

Jesus, save your people. (after each
invocation)

From all evil
From every sin
From the snares of the devil
From your anger

From the spirit of infidelity
From everlasting death
From neglect of your Holy Spirit
By the mystery of your incarnation
By your birth
By your childhood
By your hidden life
By your public ministry
By your agony and crucifixion
By your abandonment
By your grief and sorrow
By your death and burial
By your rising to new life
By your return to glory to the Father
By your gift of the holy Eucharist
By your joy and glory
Christ, hear us.
 Christ, hear us.
Lord Jesus, hear our prayer.
 Lord Jesus, hear our prayer.
Lamb of God, you take away the sins
of the world,
 have mercy on us.
Lamb of God, you take away the sins
of the world,
 have mercy on us.
Lamb of God, you take away the sins
of the world,
 have mercy on us.

Let us pray.
Lord,
may we who honor the holy name of Jesus
enjoy his friendship in this life
and be filled with eternal joy in the kingdom
where he lives and reigns for ever and ever.
Amen.

Litany of the Precious Blood of Jesus

This litany was approved for the universal Church by Pope John XXIII (1881–1963).

Lord, have mercy.
> *Lord, have mercy.*

Christ, have mercy.
> *Christ, have mercy.*

Lord, have mercy.
> *Lord, have mercy.*

God our Father in heaven
> *have mercy on us.* (after each invocation)

God the Son, Redeemer of the world

God the Holy Spirit

Holy Trinity, one God

Blood of Christ, only Son of the Father
> *be our salvation.* (after each invocation)

Blood of Christ, incarnate Word

Blood of Christ, of the new and eternal covenant

Blood of Christ, that spilled to the ground

Blood of Christ, that flowed at the scourging

Blood of Christ, dripping from the thorns

Blood of Christ, shed on the cross

Blood of Christ, the price of our redemption

Blood of Christ, our only claim to pardon

Blood of Christ, our blessing cup

Blood of Christ, in which we are washed

Blood of Christ, torrent of mercy

Blood of Christ, that overcomes evil

Blood of Christ, strength of martyrs

Blood of Christ, endurance of the saints

Blood of Christ, that makes the barren fruitful

Blood of Christ, protection of the threatened

Blood of Christ, solace of the mourner

Blood of Christ, hope of the repentant

Blood of Christ, consolation of the dying

Blood of Christ, our peace and refreshment

Blood of Christ, our pledge of life

Blood of Christ, by which we pass to glory

Blood of Christ, most worthy of honor

Lamb of God, you take away the sins of the world,
have mercy on us.
Lamb of God, you take away the sins of the world,
have mercy on us.
Lamb of God, you take away the sins of the world,
have mercy on us.
V. Lord, you redeemed us by your blood.
R. You have made us a kingdom to serve our God.
Let us pray.
Father,
by the blood of your Son
you have set us free and saved us from death.
Continue your work of love within us,
that by constantly celebrating the mystery of our salvation
we may reach the eternal life it promises.
We ask this through Christ our Lord.
Amen.

Litany of the Blessed Virgin (Litany of Loreto)

The litany was approved and indulgences were attached in 1587 by Pope Sixtus V. It is a simplified version of more ancient Marian litanies common even in the twelfth century. Several of the invocations are additions by popes since Sixtus.

Lord, have mercy.
Lord, have mercy.
Christ, have mercy.
Christ, have mercy.
Lord, have mercy.
Lord, have mercy.
God our Father in heaven,
have mercy on us. (after each invocation)
God the Son, Redeemer of the world
God the Holy Spirit
Holy Trinity, one God
Holy Mary,
pray for us (after each invocation)
Holy Mother of God
Most honored of virgins
Mother of Christ
Mother of the Church

Mother of divine grace
Mother most pure
Mother of chaste love
Mother and virgin
Sinless Mother
Dearest of mothers
Model of motherhood
Mother of good counsel
Mother of our Creator
Mother of our Savior
Virgin most wise
Virgin rightly praised
Virgin rightly renowned
Virgin most powerful
Virgin gentle in mercy
Faithful Virgin
Mirror of justice
Throne of wisdom

Cause of our joy
Shrine of the Spirit
Glory of Israel
Vessel of selfless devotion
Mystical rose
Tower of David
Tower of ivory
House of gold
Ark of the covenant
Gate of heaven
Morning star
Health of the sick

Refuge of sinners
Comforter of the troubled
Help of Christians
Queen of angels
Queen of patriarchs and prophets
Queen of apostle and martyrs
Queen of confessors and virgins
Queen of all saints
Queen conceived in grace
Queen raised up to glory
Queen of the rosary
Queen of peace

Lamb of God, you take away the sins of the world,
have mercy on us. (after each invocation)
Lamb of God, you take away the sins of the world
Lamb of God, you take away the sins of the world
V. Pray for us, holy Mother of God.
R. That we may become worthy of the promises of Christ.
Let us pray.
Eternal God,
Let your people enjoy constant health in mind and body.
Through the intercession of the Virgin Mary
free us from the sorrows of this life
and lead us to happiness in the life to come.
Grant this through Christ our Lord.
Amen.

The Mystical Rose

> *"I grew tall . . . like rosebushes in Jericho."*

"I was exalted like the rose plant in Jericho." So says the book of Sirach (24:14). Rendered with five petals, this celebrated symbol signifies Mary's five joys (the five joyful mysteries of the Rosary). Also, backed by a five-pointed star, it represents the five major Marian feasts (all pertaining to the divine motherhood): (1) Annunciation, (2) Maternity, (3) Visitation, (4) Nativity, (5) Purification.

Litany of St. Joseph

The Litany of St. Joseph was approved for the universal Church by Pope St. Pius X on March 18, 1909.

Lord, have mercy.
> *Lord, have mercy.*

Christ, have mercy.
> *Christ, have mercy.*

Lord, have mercy.
> *Lord, have mercy.*

God our Father in heaven,
> *have mercy on us.* (after each invocation)

God the Son, Redeemer of the world
God the Holy Spirit
Holy Trinity, one God
Holy Mary
> *pray for us* (after each invocation)

St. Joseph
Noble son of the House of David
Light of patriarchs
Husband of the Mother of God
Guardian of the Virgin
Foster father of the Son of God
Faithful guardian of Christ
Head of the holy family
Joseph, chaste and just
Joseph, prudent and brave
Joseph, obedient and loyal
Pattern of patience
Lover of poverty
Model of workers
Example of parents
Guardian of virgins
Pillar of family life
Comfort of the troubled
Hope of the sick
Patron of the dying
Terror of evil spirits
Protector of the Church

Lamb of God, you take away the sins of the world,
> *have mercy on us.* (after each invocation)

Lamb of God, you take away the sins of the world
Lamb of God, you take away the sins of the world
V. God made him master of his household.
R. And put him in charge of all that he owned.

Let us pray.
Almighty God,
in your infinite wisdom and love
you chose Joseph to be the husband of Mary,
the mother of your Son.
As we enjoy his protection on earth
may we have the help of his prayers in heaven.
We ask this through Christ our Lord.
Amen.

SAINT JOSEPH

Litany of the Saints (traditional)

This is believed to be the most ancient of the Church's litanies. It was mentioned by St. Basil in the fourth century (in a slightly different form) and prescribed by Pope Gregory the Great in 590 for a public procession of thanksgiving after a plague that had ravaged Rome. Traditionally, versions of this litany have been used at the Easter Vigil, on Rogation Days, on the feast of St. Mark (April 25), in the Mass of Ordination, before the conferring of major orders, during the Forty Hours' devotion, and during religious profession. The words "pray for us" are, in Latin, the familiar *ora pro nobis*.

Lord, have mercy. *Christ, have mercy.*
  Lord, have mercy.
Christ, hear us. *Christ, graciously hear us.*
God, the Father of Heaven,
  have mercy on us.
God, the Son, Redeemer of the world,
  have mercy on us.
God, the Holy Spirit, *have mercy on us.*
Holy Trinity, one God, *have mercy on us.*

Holy Mary,
  pray for us. (after each invocation)
Holy Virgin of Virgins
St. Michael
St. Gabriel
St. Raphael
All holy angels and archangels
All holy orders of blessed spirits
St. John the Baptist
St. Joseph
All holy patriarchs and prophets
St. Peter
St. Paul
St. Andrew
St. James,
St. John
St. Thomas
St. James
St. Philip
St. Bartholomew

St. Matthew
St. Simon
St. Thaddeus
St. Matthias
St. Barnabas
St. Luke
St. Mark
All holy apostles and evangelists
All holy disciples of the Lord
All holy Innocents
St. Stephen
St. Lawrence
St. Vincent
St. Fabian and St. Sebastian
St. John and St. Paul
St. Cosmas and St. Damian
St. Gervase and St. Protase
All holy martyrs
St. Sylvester
St. Gregory
St. Ambrose
St. Augustine
St. Jerome
St. Martin
St. Nicholas
All holy bishops and confessors
All holy doctors
St. Anthony
St. Benedict

St. Bernard
St. Francis
All holy priests and Levites
All holy monks and hermits
St. Mary Magdalen
St. Agatha
St. Lucy
St. Agnes
St. Cecilia
St. Catherine
St. Anastasia
All holy virgins and widows
All holy saints of God, *intercede for us.*
Be merciful, *spare us, O Lord.*
Be merciful, *graciously hear us, O Lord*
From all evil,
    deliver us, O Lord. (after each
    invocation)
From all sin
From your wrath
From sudden and unprovided death
From the snares of the devil
From anger, hatred, and all ill will
From all lewdness
From lightning and tempest
From the scourge of earthquakes
From plague, famine, and war
From everlasting death
By the mystery of your holy incarnation
By your coming
By your birth
By your baptism and holy fasting
By your cross and passion
By your death and burial
By your holy resurrection
By your wondrous ascension
By the coming of the Holy Spirit, the
    Advocate

On the day of judgment
We sinners,
    we beg you to hear us. (after each
    invocation)

That you spare us
That you pardon us
That you bring us to true penance
That you govern and preserve your
    Holy Church
That you preserve our Holy Father
    and all ranks in the Church in holy
    religion
That you humble the enemies of Holy
    Church
That you give peace and true concord
    to all Christian rulers
That you give peace and unity to the
    whole Christian world
That you restore to the unity of the
    Church all who have strayed from
    the truth and lead all unbelievers to
    the light of the gospel
That you confirm and preserve us in
    your holy service
That you lift up our minds to heavenly
    desires
That you grant everlasting blessings
    to all our benefactors
That you deliver our souls and the
    souls of our brethren, relatives,
    and benefactors from everlasting
    damnation
That you give and preserve the fruits of
    the earth
That you grant eternal rest to all the
    faithful departed
That you graciously hear us, Son of
    God

Lamb of God, who takes away the sins of the world, *spare us, O Lord.*
Lamb of God, who takes away the sins of the world, *spare us, O Lord.*
Lamb of God, who takes away the sins of the world, *have mercy on us.*
Christ, hear us. *Christ, graciously hear us.*
Lord, have mercy. *Christ, have mercy.* Lord, have mercy.

Let us pray.

From you, Lord, come holiness in our desires, right thinking in our plans, and justice in our actions. Grant your children that peace which the world cannot give; then our hearts will be devoted to your laws, we shall be delivered from the terrors of war, and under your protection we shall be able to live in tranquillity. Amen.

Litany of the Saints (contemporary)

Today, this version is used for solemn intercessions. Sections marked A and B indicate a choice of one or the other should be made. Saints' names (patron, church title, or founder, for example) and petitions may be added at the end of the litany according to the occasion.

I. Petitions to God

A	OR	B
Lord, have mercy.		God our Father in heaven,
Lord, have mercy.		*have mercy on us.* (after each
Christ, have mercy.		invocation)
Christ, have mercy.		God the Son, our Redeemer
Lord, have mercy.		God the Holy Spirit
Lord, have mercy.		Holy Trinity, one God

II. Petitions to the Saints
Holy Mary,
   pray for us. (after each invocation)
Mother of God
Most honored of all virgins
Michael, Gabriel, and Raphael
Angels of God

Prophets and Fathers of our Faith
Abraham, Moses, and Elijah
St. Joseph
St. John the Baptist
Holy patriarchs and prophets

Apostles and Followers of Christ
St. Peter and St. Paul
St. Andrew

St. John and St. James
St. Thomas
St. Matthew
All holy apostles
St. Luke
St. Mark
St. Barnabas
St. Mary Magdalen
All disciples of the Lord

Martyrs
St. Stephen
St. Ignatius
St. Polycarp
St. Justin
St. Lawrence

St. Cyprian
St. Boniface
St. Thomas Becket
St. John Fisher and St. Thomas More
St. Paul Miki
St. Isaac Jogues and St. John de Brebeuf
St. Peter Chanel
St. Charles Lwanga
St. Perpetua and St. Felicity
St. Agnes
St. Maria Goretti
All holy martyrs for Christ

Bishops and Doctors
St. Leo and St. Gregory
St. Ambrose
St. Jerome
St. Augustine
St. Athanasius
St. Basil and St. Gregory
St. John Chrysostom
St. Martin
St. Patrick
St. Cyril and St. Methodius

St. Charles Borromeo
St. Francis de Sales
St. Pius

Priests and Religious
St. Anthony
St. Benedict
St. Bernard
St. Francis and St. Dominic
St. Thomas Aquinas
St. Ignatius Loyola
St. Francis Xavier
St. Vincent de Paul
St. John Vianney
St. John Bosco
St. Catherine
St. Teresa
St. Thérèse
St. Rose

Laity
St. Louis
St. Monica
St. Elizabeth
All holy men and women

III. Petitions to Christ

A	OR	B
Lord, be merciful.		Christ, Son of the living God,
Lord, save your people. (after each invocation)		*have mercy on us.* (after each invocation)

From all evil	By your suffering and cross
From every sin	By your death and burial
From the snares of the devil	By your rising to new life
From anger and hatred	By your return in glory to the Father
From every evil intention	By your gift of the Holy Spirit
From everlasting death	By your coming again in glory
By your coming as man	You came into this world
By your birth	You suffered for us on the cross
By your baptism and fasting	You died to save us

You lay in the tomb
You rose from the dead
Your returned in glory to the Father
You sent the Holy Spirit upon your apostles

You are seated at the right hand of the Father
You will come again to judge the living and the dead

IV. Petitions for Various Needs

A	OR	B
Lord, be merciful to us. *Lord, hear our prayer.* (after each invocation)		Lord, show us your kindness. *Lord hear our prayer.* (after each invocation)
Give us true repentance		Raise our thoughts and desires to you
Strengthen us in your service		Save us from final damnation
Reward with eternal life all who do good to us		Save our friends and all who have helped us
Bless the fruits of the earth and of labor		Grant eternal rest to all who have died in the faith
		Spare us from disease, hunger, and war
		Bring all peoples together in trust and peace
		Guide and protect your holy Church
		Keep the pope and all the clergy in faithful service to your Church
		Bring all Christians together in unity
		Lead all people to the light of the gospel

V. Conclusion

A	OR	B
Christ, hear us. *Christ, graciously hear us.* Lord Jesus, hear our prayer. *Lord Jesus, hear our prayer.*		Lamb of God, you take away the sins of the world, *have mercy on us.* (after each invocation) Lamb of God, you take away the sins of the world Lamb of God, you take away the sins of the world

Prayer

A	OR	B
God of love, our strength and protection, hear the prayers of your Church. Grant that when we come to you in faith, our prayers may be answered, through Christ our Lord. Amen.		*Lord God, you know our weakness. In your mercy grant that the example of your saints may bring us back to love and serve you through Christ our Lord. Amen.*

A Sampling of Saints' Prayers

(See CCC #s 2683–2684, 2692.)

Watch Thou, Dear Lord (St. Augustine)

Watch thou, dear Lord, with those who wake, or watch, or weep tonight, and give thine angels charge over those who sleep. Tend thy sick ones, O Lord Christ. Rest thy weary ones. Bless thy dying ones. Soothe thy suffering ones. Pity thine afflicted ones. Shield thy joyous ones. And all, for thy love's sake. Amen.

Holy Spirit Prayer of St. Augustine

Breathe in me, O Holy Spirit,
That my thoughts may all be holy.
Act in me, O Holy Spirit,
That my work, too, may be holy.
Draw my heart, O Holy Spirit,
That I love but what is holy.
Strengthen me, O Holy Spirit,
To defend all that is holy.
Guard me, then, O Holy Spirit,
That I always may be holy.

Peace Prayer of St. Francis (attributed)

Lord, make me an instrument of your peace;
where there is hatred, let me sow love;
where there is injury, pardon;
where there is doubt, faith;
where there is despair, hope;
where there is darkness, light;
and where there is sadness, joy.
Grant that I may not so much seek
to be consoled as to console,
to be understood as to understand,
to be loved as to love;
for it is in giving that we receive,
it is in pardoning that we are pardoned,
and it is in dying that we are born to eternal life.

San Damiano Cross of
St. Francis

The Canticle of Brother Sun (St. Francis)

Most high, all powerful, all good Lord!
All praise is yours, all glory, all honor, and all blessing.
To you alone, Most High, do they belong.
No mortal lips are worthy to pronounce your name.
All praise be yours, my Lord, through all that you have made.
And first, my Lord, Brother Sun,
Who brings the day; and light you give to us through him.
How beautiful is he, how radiant in all his splendor!
Of you, Most High, he bears the likeness.
All praise be yours, my Lord, through Sisters Moon and Stars;
In the heavens you have made them, bright and precious and fair.
All praise be yours, my Lord, through Brothers Wind and Air,
And fair and stormy, all the weather's moods,
By which you cherish all that you have made.
All praise be yours, my Lord, through Sister Water,
So useful, lowly, precious, and pure.
All praise be yours, my Lord, through Brother Fire,
Through whom you brighten up the night.
How beautiful is he, how gay! Full of power and strength.
All praise be yours, my Lord, through Sister Earth, our mother,
Who feeds us in her sovereignty and produces
Various fruits with colored flowers and herbs.
All praise be yours, my Lord, through those who grant pardon
For love of you; through those who endure sickness and trial.
Happy those who endure in peace,
By you, Most High, they will be crowned.
All praise be yours, my Lord, through Sister Death,
From whose embrace no mortal can escape.
Woe to those who die in mortal sin!
Happy those she finds doing your will!
The second death can do no harm to them.
Praise and bless my Lord, and give him thanks,
And serve him with great humility.

My Breastplate ("Lorica") of St. Patrick

Patrick was not a warrior, except in spiritual terms. In 433 he composed a prayer petitioning God's help in bringing Christianity to Ireland. It includes the following verses offered when he presented himself before the Druids at Tara.

Christ with me,
Christ before me,
Christ behind me,
Christ in me,
Christ beneath me,
Christ above me,
Christ on my right,
Christ on my left,
Christ in breadth,
Christ in length,
Christ in height,
Christ in the mouth of everyone who
   speaks to me,
Christ in the heart of everyone who
   thinks of me,
Christ in every eye that sees me,
Christ in every ear that hears me.

St. Patrick

I arise today
Through a mighty strength, the invocation of the Trinity,
Through belief in the Threeness,
Through confession of the Oneness,
Of the Creator of Creation.

Too Late Have I Loved You

St. Augustine, Confessions, 10.27

Too late have I loved you, O Beauty of ancient days, yet ever new! Too late have I loved you! And behold, you were within, and I abroad, and there I searched for you; I was deformed, plunging amid those fair forms which you had made. You were with me, but I was not with you. Things held me far from you—things which, if they were not in you, were not at all. You called, and shouted, and burst my deafness. You flashed and shone, and scattered my blindness. You breathed odors and I drew in breath—and I pant for you. I tasted, and I hunger and thirst. You touched me and I burned for your peace.

Suscipe   ("receive," "accept")

Also called "A Prayer of Self-Offering," it may be compared to the *Suscipiat* of Mass, "May the Lord receive this sacrifice . . . " It is the prayer from the Spiritual Exercises of St. Ignatius Loyola.

Take, O Lord, and receive all my liberty, my memory, my understanding, and all my will, all that I have and possess. You have given all of these to me; to you I restore them. All are yours; dispose of them all according to your will. Give me your love and your grace; having but these I am rich enough and ask for nothing more.

Soul of Christ   (Latin, *Anima Christi*)

This is a fourteenth-century prayer common at communion and in adoration of the Blessed Sacrament. This translation is by John Henry Cardinal Newman (1801–1890).

Soul of Christ, be my sanctification;
Body of Christ, be my salvation;
Blood of Christ, fill all my veins;
Water of Christ's side, wash out my stains;
Passion of Christ, my comfort be;
O good Jesus, listen to me:
In thy wounds I fain would hide,
Ne'er to be parted from thy side;
Guard me, should the foe assail me;
Call me when my life shall fail me;
Bid me come to thee above,
With thy saints to sing thy love
World without end. Amen.

Cross of Triumph

A Prayer of the Curé of Ars, St. John Vianney

I love you, O my God, and my only desire is to love you until the last breath of my life. I love you, O my infinitely lovable God, and I would rather die loving you, than live without loving you. I love you, Lord, and the only grace I ask is to love you eternally. . . . My God, if my tongue cannot say in every moment that I love you, I want my heart to repeat it to you as often as I draw breath.

The Psalter

(See CCC #s 2585–2589.)

Some Notable Psalms

The 150 psalms are the Prayer Book of the Church. When Christians pray the psalms, they often see images of Jesus and the Church in them. Christians must remember, however, that first of all, the psalms are the prayers of the Jewish people, and the Christian interpretation of a given psalm is not the first or only interpretation.

22: Jesus on the cross

23: The Lord is my shepherd.

32: A favorite of St. Augustine's

42: Including *abyssus abyssus invocat* (Latin, meaning "deep calls unto deep"), the roaring sea symbolizing affliction

43: The old prayer at the foot of the altar, now a favorite responsorial

45: Christ and his bride

51: The *Miserere* (Latin, meaning "Have mercy"), David's prayer of repentance, has become the name for a Lenten evening service because this psalm is sung, with a sermon following.

66: *Jubilate* (Latin, meaning "Praise," "Be jubilant,"); see also Psalm 100.

67: Beginning and entitled *Deus Misereatur* (Latin, meaning "May God have mercy") and continuing "and bless us, and cause his countenance to shine upon us"

95: The *Venite Exsultemus* (Latin, meaning "Come, let us exalt"), which daily opens the Church's Liturgy of the Hours

130: The *De Profundis* (Latin, meaning "Out of the depths"), a prayer for the faithful departed

Numbering the Psalms

Formerly the Catholic system used the numbering and divisions of the Septuagint (Greek) translation where Psalm 9 was considered two psalms. Protestant and Jewish (and contemporary Catholic systems) depend on the original Hebrew text.

Catholic (formerly)	Protestant and Jewish (and contemporary Catholic)
1–9:21	1–9
9:22–112	10–113
113	114–115
114	116:1–9
115	116:10–19
115–145	117–146
146	147:1–11
147	147:12–20
148–150	148–150

The Psalter of Mary

Such is an old name for the Rosary, because its fifteen decades—150 Hail Marys with fifteen meditations—is a complete Rosary and includes exactly the same number of Hail Marys as there are psalms in the Psalter (Book of Psalms). It was the laity's desire to share in the Church's daily prayer, the Liturgy of the Hours, that led in the twelfth century to the Rosary prayer form. In those days, many of the faithful were unable to read, so praying the *Aves* from memory took the place of the written prayer texts used by the more educated clergy. The well-known and symbolically powerful beads were adopted simply as a counting aid. Such are the scriptural, liturgical roots of this symbol of prayer: the Rosary.

Classification of the Psalms

The psalms can be divided into five "books," possibly in imitation of the five books of the Pentateuch:

1. Psalms 1–41

2. Psalms 42–72

3. Psalms 73–89

4. Psalms 90–106

5. Psalms 107–150

Categories of Psalms

In form and subject matter, however, the psalms vary greatly. Certain similarities and characteristics suggest some categories:

Royal

2, 18, 20, 21, 45, 72, 89, 101, 110, 132, 144. These are for the enthronement of a king, battle hymns, and thanksgiving for victory. With the fall of the monarchy, many psalms took on messianic overtones.

Messianic

2, 22, 45, 69, 72, 89, 110, 132. These are references to David and the future of his line, references which explicitly or implicitly foreshadow Christ, the messianic king in David's family.

Historical

78, 105, 106, 135, 136. The historical psalms record God's constant involvement with Israel.

Penitential

6, 25, 32, 38, 51, 102, 130, 143. Excluding 25, these are "The Seven Penitential Psalms"; they express sorrow for sin and its results. Traditionally, all were used on Ash Wednesday: the first three (6, 32, 38) at Matins, Psalm 51 at Commination (an Ash Wednesday penitential office in the Anglican tradition in which divine anger and judgment are proclaimed against sinners), and the last three (102, 130, 143) at Evensong.

Imprecatory

35, 52, 58, 59, 69, 109, 137. These are human prayers for vengeance on enemies.

Acrostic

9, 25, 34, 37, 111, 112, 119, 145. These psalms are called this because of the presence of initial letters of successive verses from the Hebrew alphabet, probably a mnemonic device, a method to help one remember.

Theocratic

95, 96, 97, 98. These psalms reflect on the sovereignty of God: messianic overtones are present.

Hallel ("Praise")

These are family songs of Passover night: 113, 114 (beginning of meal); 115–118 (end of meal); and 136 ("The Great Hallel").

Songs of ascent

120–134. These Gradual Psalms, or Psalms of the Steps, probably have this name because they formed the "Pilgrim Psalms" (the pilgrimages to Jerusalem for the great annual feasts). The number fifteen signifies ascent and progression, and is found symbolically in the number of steps of the temple, and in the mysteries of the Rosary.

Protection prayers

34, 52, 54, 56, 57, 59, 140, 141, 142, 143. Some are of David fleeing Saul.

Hallelujah (Alleluia, "Praise the Lord")

146–150. Each begins and ends with this word, common as well in other psalms and a fitting crescendo for the Book of Psalms.

Hymns

8, 19, 29, 33, 46, 47, 48, 65, 67, 76, 84, 87, 92, 93, 95–100, 103–105, 111, 113–115, 117, 145–150. Many of these psalms include an introduction or call to worship, a reason to worship, and a conclusion, which may repeat the introduction, utter a blessing, vow, or brief petition.

Collective lamentation

44, 60, 74, 79, 80. These are said on penitential days and for public calamities, and include a memorial of God's past mercy and an expression of confidence.

Individual lamentation

3, 5, 6, 7, 13, 22, 26, 31, 35. These psalms include an invocation of God for help, a description of need, a petition for deliverance, a reason for granting petition, and an expression of confidence.

Gratitude

9, 10, 18, 30, 32, 34, 40, 41, 65, 66, 67, 75, 103, 107, 116, 118, 120, 124, 129, 136, 138

Praise

7, 8, 19, 29, 47, 93, 96, 97, 98, 99, 104, 146

Meditation

8, 9, 10, 12, 36, 39, 49, 50, 53, 73, 77, 82, 94, 139, 141

Lamentation and intense prayer

25, 32, 33, 44, 74, 79, 80, 86, 88

Wisdom

1, 32, 37, 49, 73, 112, 119, 127, 128, 133, 139

Confidence

11, 16, 23, 27, 62, 63, 91, 108, 121, 125, 131

More Old Testament Prayers

Old Testament Canticles (From Latin, *canticulum,* "little song.")

These sacred chants, besides the psalms, are used in the Liturgy of the Hours. (See CCC #s 2568–2584.)

Moses' song of deliverance, Exodus 15:1–18

Song of Moses: God's benefits to his people, Deuteronomy 32:1–12

Song of Hannah offering up Samuel, 1 Samuel 2:1–10

David's song, 1 Chronicles 29:10–13

Tobit's song of praise, Tobit 13:1–8

Tobit's song of praise (addressed to Jerusalem), Tobit 13:8–11, 13–15

Judith's song of praise, Judith 16:2–3a, 13–15

Solomon's prayer for wisdom, Wisdom 9:1–11

Sirach's prayer for God's people, Sirach 36:1–5, 10–13

Isaiah's song: Zion, city of the messiah, Isaiah 2:2–5

Thanksgiving song of the redeemed, Isaiah 12:1–6

The divine vindicator, Isaiah 26:1–4, 7–9, 12

Isaiah's song: just judgment of God, Isaiah 33:13–16

Hezekiah's song of thanksgiving, Isaiah 38:10–20

Isaiah's song: promise of salvation, Isaiah 40:10–17

A new song to the messiah and Lord, Isaiah 42:10–16

Isaiah's song to the hidden God, Isaiah 45:15–25

Israel renewed, Isaiah 61:10–62:5

Song of joy to the Holy City, Isaiah 66:10–14

Lament over Zion's guilt, Jeremiah 14:17–21

God will gather his people, Jeremiah 31:10–14

Renewal of God's people, Ezekiel 36:24–28

Azariah's song, Daniel 3:26–27, 29, 34–41

The three youths' praise of creation, Daniel 3:52–88

Habakkuk's song of divine judgment, Habakkuk 3:2–4, 13, 15–19

The Old Testament Canticles Prayed by the Church

The Old Testament canticles are arranged by the Church for its Morning Prayer (Lauds) according to their theme. Just as the 150 psalms are distributed over a period of time longer than a single week, so in the revised Liturgy of the Hours the Old Testament canticles are spread over four weeks in each of four series. The canticle is prayed between the two psalms of Morning Prayer. (See CCC #s 1176–1177.)

Week One
Sunday, Daniel 3:57–88, 56
Monday, 1 Chronicles 29:10–13
Tuesday, Tobit 13:1–8
Wednesday, Judith 16:2–3a, 13–15
Thursday, Jeremiah 31:10–14
Friday, Isaiah 45:15–25
Saturday, Exodus 15:1–4a, 8–13, 17–18

Week Two
Sunday, Daniel 3:52–57
Monday, Sirach 36:1–5, 10–13
Tuesday, Isaiah 38:10–14, 17–20
Wednesday, 1 Samuel 2:1–10
Thursday, Isaiah 12:1–6
Friday, Habakkuk 3:2–4, 13a, 15–19
Saturday, Deuteronomy 32:1–12

Week Three
Sunday, Daniel 3:57–88, 56
Monday, Isaiah 2:2–5
Tuesday, Isaiah 26:1–4, 7–9, 12
Wednesday, Isaiah 33:13–16
Thursday, Isaiah 40:10–17
Friday, Jeremiah 14:17–21
Saturday, Wisdom 9:1–6, 9–11

Week Four
Sunday, Daniel 3:52–57
Monday, Isaiah 42:10–16
Tuesday, Daniel 3:26, 27, 29, 34–41
Wednesday, Isaiah 61:10–62:5
Thursday, Isaiah 66:10–14a
Friday, Tobit 13:8–11, 13–15
Saturday, Ezekiel 36:24–28

Other Prayers in the Old Testament

Solomon's personal prayer, 1 Kings 3:5–9
Solomon's public prayer, 1 Kings 8:23–61 (2 Chronicles 6:14–42)
Hezekiah's temple prayer, 2 Kings 19:15–19 (Isaiah 37:14–20)
David's thanksgiving prayer, 1 Chronicles 29:10–19
Tobit's wedding night prayer, Tobit 8:5c–7
Raguel's thanksgiving prayer, Tobit 8:15–17
Judith's prayer, Judith 9:5–14
People's blessing upon Judith, Judith 15:9–10
Job's pious prayer, Job 1:21
Job's pliant, Job 3:3–26
Job's penitential, Job 42:2–6

The sage's prayer, Sirach 39:16–35

Prayer of praise, Thanksgiving, Sirach 51:1–30

Jeremiah's complaint, Jeremiah 15:10–18

Jeremiah's vengeance prayer, Jeremiah 18:19–23

Jeremiah's interior crisis, Jeremiah 20:7–18

Jeremiah's praise prayer, Jeremiah 32:17–25

Other Poems and Songs in the Old Testament

Deborah's song, Judges 5:2–31

David's lament, 2 Samuel 1:19–27

David's victory song, 2 Samuel 7:18–29

David's deliverance song, 2 Samuel 22:2–51

David's song, 1 Chronicles 16:8–36

Solomon's love song, Song of Solomon 2:10–17

Dayenu

"It would have been enough" is the translation for this Hebrew word. It is the refrain of a traditional Passover Seder hymn. True to the folk tradition, it is cumulative, each verse developing the last (as "The Twelve Days of Christmas" does). It builds a prayer of gratitude for God's surprising and wonderful work: "If God had created us and not revealed himself in all his marvelous works, it would have been enough. If God had revealed himself and not made a covenant with his people, it would have been enough. . . ."

Isaiah's Suffering Servant Poems

These "Servant of the Lord Oracles" have been interpreted as descriptions of historical Israel, an ideal Israel or representative of Israel, an historical character before or during the life of the prophet, the prophet himself, and Jesus Christ.

1. Isaiah 42:1–4 (" . . . He will not cry out or lift up his voice. . . . ")

2. Isaiah 49:1–7 ("The Lord called me before I was born. . . . ")

3. Isaiah 50:4–11 ("The Lord God has given me the tongue of a teacher. . . . ")

4. Isaiah 52:13–53:12 (" . . . so marred was his appearance, beyond human semblance. . . . ")

Old Testament Blessings

Mizpah Blessing

"The LORD watch between you and me, when we are absent one from the other."

—Genesis 31:49

Aaron's Blessing

This is also called the "Seraphic Blessing" because it became associated with Francis of Assisi ("the Seraphic Saint") who used a form of it to bless a Brother Leo on Mt. Alverno in 1224.

The Lord spoke to Moses, saying: "Speak to Aaron and his sons, saying . . .
Thus you shall bless the Israelites: You shall say to them,
The LORD bless you and keep you;
the LORD make his face to shine upon you, and be gracious to you;
the LORD lift up his countenance upon you, and give you peace.
So they shall put my name on the Israelites, and I will bless them."

—Numbers 6:22–27

Moses' Final Blessing of the People

"Blessed shall you be in the city, and blessed shall you be in the field.
Blessed shall be the fruit of your womb, the fruit of your ground, and the fruit of your livestock, both the increase of your cattle and the issue of your flock.
Blessed shall be your basket and your kneading bowl.
Blessed shall you be when you come in, and blessed shall you be when you go out."

—Deuteronomy 28:3–6

Solomon's Blessing

"May the LORD our God be with us, as he was with our ancestors; may he not leave us or abandon us, but incline our hearts to him, to walk in all his ways, and to keep his commandments, his statutes, and his ordinances, which he commanded our ancestors."

—1 Kings 8:57–58

New Testament Prayers

Canticles

The Gospel Canticles

1. The Canticle of Mary (See page 44.)

2. The Canticle of Zechariah (See page 45.)

3. The Canticle of Simeon (See page 46.)

Other New Testament Canticles

1. God's plan fulfilled in Christ, Ephesians 1:3–10

2. Christ, firstborn from the dead, Colossians 1:12–20

3. Song of the Paschal mystery, Philippians 2:6–11

4. Song of the mystery of our faith, 1 Timothy 3:16

5. Song of the suffering Christ, 1 Peter 2:21–24

6. Song of the Creator and of the Lamb, Revelation 4:11; 5:9–10, 12, 13b

7. Song of divine judgment, Revelation 11:17–18

8. Praise of God's power, Revelation 12:10–12

9. Song of Moses and the Lamb, Revelation 15:3–4

10. The wedding feast of the Lamb, Revelation 19:1–7

The New Testament Canticles Prayed by the Church

Like their Old Testament counterparts in Morning Prayer, the New Testament canticles are prayed (following the two psalms) according to theme, in a one-week series.

Saturday, Philippians 2:6–11

Sunday, Revelation 19:1–7 (1 Peter 2:21–24 in Lent)

Monday, Ephesians 1:3–10

Tuesday, Revelation 4:11; 5:9–10, 12, 13b

Wednesday, Colossians 1:12–20

Thursday, Revelation 11:17–18; 12:10–12

Friday, Revelation 15:3–4

Mary's Canticle *(Magnificat)* Luke 1:46–55 (See CCC #2619.)

Mary's Canticle is Mary's response to Elizabeth's greeting at the visitation. The canticle's title in Latin, *Magnificat,* comes from the opening words: "My soul magnifies . . ." or "proclaims." The *Magnificat* is prayed each day by the Church as part of its Evening Prayer.

My soul proclaims the greatness of the Lord,
my spirit rejoices in God my Savior
for he has looked with favor on his lowly servant.
From this day all generations will call me blessed:
the Almighty has done great things for me,
and holy is his Name.
He has mercy on those who fear him
in every generation.
He has shown the strength of his arm,
he has scattered the proud in their conceit.
He has cast down the mighty from their thrones,
and has lifted up the lowly.
He has filled the hungry with good things,
and the rich he has sent away empty.
He has come to the help of his servant Israel
for he has remembered his promise of mercy,
the promise he made to our fathers,
to Abraham and his children for ever.

Zechariah's Canticle   *(Benedictus)* Luke 1:68–79

Zechariah's Canticle is also named after its first word in Latin. Zechariah, the father of John the Baptist, is singing in gratitude after John's birth. Zechariah praises God's fidelity to the messianic promise. The canticle is prayed each day by the Church as part of its Morning Prayer.

Blessed be the Lord, the God of Israel;
he has come to his people and set them free.
He has raised up for us a mighty savior,
born of the house of his servant David.
Through his holy prophets he promised of old
  that he would save us from our enemies,
  from the hands of all who hate us.
He promised to show mercy to our fathers
and to remember his holy covenant.
This was the oath he swore to our father Abraham:
to set us free from the hands of our enemies,
free to worship him without fear,
holy and righteous in his sight
  all the days of our life.
You, my child, shall be called the prophet of the Most High,
for you will go before the Lord to prepare his way,
to give his people knowledge of salvation
by the forgiveness of their sins.
In the tender compassion of our God
the dawn from on high shall break upon us,
to shine on those who dwell in darkness and the shadow of death,
and to guide our feet into the way of peace.

The presentation in the temple

Simeon's Canticle   *(Nunc Dimittis)* Luke 2:29–32

Simeon's Canticle is also named after its first words in Latin. It is the song of the old man in the temple at the Lord's presentation with his request for permission to die. It is prayed each day by the Church as part of its Night Prayer.

Lord, now you let your servant go in peace;
your word has been fulfilled:
my own eyes have seen the salvation
which you have prepared in the sight of every people:
a light to reveal you to the nations
and the glory of your people Israel.

Prayers in the Gospel   (See CCC #s 2623–2649.)

The angel's greeting

"Greetings, favored one! The Lord is with you."

—Luke 1:28

Mary's reply

"Here am I, the servant of the Lord; let it be with me according to your word."

—Luke 1:38

Elizabeth's greeting

"Blessed are you among women, and blessed is the fruit of your womb."

—Luke 1:42

Song of the angels

"Glory to God in the highest heaven, and on earth peace among those whom he favors!"

—Luke 2:14

Temptation of Christ

"Away with you, Satan! For it is written: 'Worship the Lord your God, and serve only him.'"

—Matthew 4:10

Nathanael

"Rabbi, you are the Son of God! You are the King of Israel!"

—John 1:49

The leper cured

"Lord, if you choose, you can make me clean."

—Luke 5:12

The centurion at Capernaum

"Lord, I am not worthy to have you come under my roof; but only speak the word, and my servant will be healed."

—Matthew 8:8

The storm on the lake

"Lord, save us! We are perishing!"

—Matthew 8:25

Two blind men cured

"Have mercy on us, Son of David!"

—Matthew 9:27

Peter on the lake near Gennesareth after five thousand were fed

"Lord, save me!"

—Matthew 14:30

Peter at Capernaum

"Lord, to whom can we go? You have the words of eternal life."

—John 6:68

The Canaanite woman

"Have mercy on me, Lord, Son of David! . . . Lord, help me. . . . Lord, . . . even the dogs eat the crumbs that fall from their masters' table."

—Matthew 15:22, 25, 27

Peter's profession

"You are the Messiah, the Son of the living God."

—Matthew 16:16

Peter at the Transfiguration

"Lord, it is good for us to be here; if you wish, I will make three dwellings here, one for you, one for Moses, and one for Elijah."

—Matthew 17:4

The man born blind

"Lord, I believe."

—John 9:38

Praise of Mary

"Blessed is the womb that bore you and the breasts that nursed you!"

—Luke 11:27

The prodigal son

"Father, I have sinned against heaven and before you; I am no longer worthy to be called your son."

—Luke 15:21

The apostles' petition to the Lord

"Increase our faith!"

—Luke 17:5

As obedient servants

"We are worthless slaves; we have done only what we ought to have done!"

—Luke 17:10

The tax collector

"God, be merciful to me, a sinner!"

—Luke 18:13

A rich man

"Good teacher, what must I do to inherit eternal life?"

—Luke 18:18

Martha

"Lord, if you had been here, my brother would not have died. But even now I know that God will give you whatever you ask of him . . . I know that [Lazarus] will rise again in the resurrection on the last day . . . Yes, Lord, I believe that you are the Messiah, the Son of God, the one coming into the world."

—John 11:21, 22, 24, 27

The blind man near Jericho

"Jesus, Son of David, have mercy on me! . . . Son of David, have mercy on me! . . . Lord, let me see again."

—Luke 18:38, 39, 41

Zacchaeus the tax collector

"Look, half of my possessions, Lord, I will give to the poor; and if I have defrauded anyone of anything, I will pay back four times as much."

—Luke 19:8

Triumphal entry into Jerusalem

*"Hosanna to the Son of David!
Blessed is the one who comes
in the name of the Lord!
Hosanna in the highest heaven!"*

—Matthew 21:9 and parallels: Mark
11:9–10, Luke 19:38, John 12:12

The agony in the garden

*"My Father, if it is possible, let this
cup pass from me; yet not what I
want but what you want."*

—Matthew 26:39 and parallels:
Mark 14:36, Luke 22:42

First word on the cross

*"Father, forgive them; for they do
not know what they are doing."*

—Luke 23:34

The repentant thief

*"Jesus, remember me when you
come into your kingdom."*

—Luke 23:42

The death of Jesus

*"My God, my God, why have you
forsaken me?"*

—Matthew 27:46 and Mark 15:34

Passion cross

The seventh word on the cross

*"Father, into your hands I commend
my spirit."*

—Luke 23:46

The disciples at Emmaus

*"Stay with us, (Lord), because it is
almost evening and the day is now
nearly over."*

—Luke 24:29

Thomas

"My Lord and my God!"

—John 20:28

Peter

*"Yes, Lord; you know that I love you
. . . Yes, Lord; you know that I love
you . . . Lord, you know everything;
you know that I love you."*

—John 21:15, 16, 17

Prayers in the Acts of the Apostles (See CCC #s 2623–2624.)

After Peter's release

*"Sovereign Lord, who made the
heaven and the earth, the sea, and
everything in them . . . grant to your
servants, to speak your words with
all boldness while you stretch out
your hand to heal, and signs and
wonders are performed through the
name of your holy servant Jesus."*

—Acts 4:24, 29–30

St. Stephen, the first Christian martyr

*"Look! . . . I see the heavens opened
and the Son of Man standing at
the right hand of God! . . . Lord
Jesus, receive my spirit. . . . Lord,
do not hold this sin against them."*

—Acts 7:56, 59, 60

The Christians of Caesarea

"The Lord's will be done."

—Acts 21:14

Prayers in the Book of Revelation (See CCC #2642.)

The four living creatures

"Holy, holy, holy,
the Lord God the Almighty,
who was and is and is to come."

—Revelation 4:8

All creatures and the universe

"To the one seated on the throne
and to the Lamb
be blessing and honor and glory
and might
forever and ever!"

—Revelation 5:13

A huge white-robed crowd

"Salvation belongs to our God
who is seated on the throne, and to
the Lamb!"

—Revelation 7:10

Angels, elders, and four living creatures

"Amen! Blessing and glory and
wisdom
and thanksgiving and honor
and power and might
be to our God forever and ever!
Amen."

—Revelation 7:12

One of seven angels and the altar

"You are just, O Holy One, who
are and were . . .
Yes, O Lord God, Almighty,
your judgments are true
and just!"

—Revelation 16:5, 7

The New Testament Letters

Prayers

Firm resolution

No, in all these things we are more than conquerors through him who loved
us. For I am convinced that neither death, nor life, nor angels, nor rulers,
nor things present, nor things to come, nor powers, nor height, nor depth, nor
anything else in all creation, will be able to separate us from the love of God
in Christ Jesus our Lord.

—Romans 8:37–39

Infinite wisdom

O the depths of the riches and wisdom and knowledge of God! How
insearchable are his judgments and how inscrutable his ways!
"For who has known the mind of the Lord?
Or who has been his counselor?"
"Or who has given a gift to him,
to receive a gift in return?"
For from him and through him and to him are all things. To him be the
glory forever. Amen.

—Romans 11:33–36

Thanksgiving

I give thanks to my God always for you because of the grace of God that has been given you in Christ Jesus, for in every way you have been enriched in him, in speech and knowledge of every kind . . . He will also strengthen you to the end, so that you will be blameless on the day of our Lord Jesus Christ.

—1 Corinthians 1:4–5, 8

Consolation

Blessed be the God and Father of our Lord Jesus Christ, the Father of mercies, and the God of all consolation who consoles us in all our affliction so that we may be able to console those who are in any affliction with the consolation with which we ourselves are consoled by God.

—2 Corinthians 1:3–4

The peace of God

Grace to you and peace from God our Father and the Lord Jesus Christ, who gave himself for our sins to set us free from the present evil age, according to the will of our God and Father, to whom be glory forever and ever. Amen.

—Galatians 1:3–5

Crucified to the world

May I never boast of anything except the cross of our Lord Jesus Christ by which the world has been crucified to me, and I to the world.

—Galatians 6:14

The power of God in us

Now to him who by the power at work within us is able to accomplish abundantly far more than all we can ask or imagine, to him be the glory in the church and in Christ Jesus to all generations, forever and ever. Amen.

—Ephesians 3:20–21

Glory to God

To our God and Father be glory forever and ever. Amen.

—Philippians 4:20

The King of ages

To the King of the ages, immortal, invisible, the only God, be honor and glory forever and ever. Amen.

—1 Timothy 1:17

The King of kings

He is the blessed and only Sovereign, the King of kings and Lord of lords. It is he alone who has immortality and dwells in unapproachable light, whom no one has ever seen or can see; to him be honor and eternal dominion. Amen.

—1 Timothy 6:15–16

Birth to salvation

Blessed be the God and Father of our Lord Jesus Christ! By his great mercy he has given us a new birth into a living hope through the resurrection of Jesus Christ from the dead, and into an inheritance that is imperishable, undefiled, and unfading, kept in heaven for you who are being protected by the power of God through faith for a salvation ready to be revealed in the last time.

—1 Peter 1:3–5

God glorified in us

Whoever speaks must do so as one speaking the very words of God; whoever serves must do so with the strength that God supplies, so that God may be glorified in all things through Jesus Christ. To him belong the glory and the power forever and ever. Amen.

—1 Peter 4:11

Growth in grace

. . . grow in the grace and knowledge of our Lord and Savior Jesus Christ. To him be the glory both now and to the day of eternity. Amen.

—2 Peter 3:18

Prayerful Greetings from the Letters   (See CCC #s 2636–2638.)

To all God's beloved in Rome, who are called to be saints: Grace to you and peace from God our Father and the Lord Jesus Christ.

—Romans 1:7

The grace of our Lord Jesus Christ be with you.

—Romans 16:20, 1 Thessalonians 5:28

The grace of the Lord Jesus Christ be with your spirit.

—Philemon 25, Philippians 4:23

The grace of our Lord Jesus be with you.

—1 Corinthians 16:23

My love be with all of you in Christ Jesus.

—1 Corinthians 16:24

The grace of the Lord Jesus Christ, the love of God, and the communion of the Holy Spirit be with all of you.

—2 Corinthians 13:13

May the grace of our Lord Jesus Christ be with your spirit, brothers and sisters. Amen.

—Galatians 6:18

Peace be to the whole community, and love with faith, from God the Father and the Lord Jesus Christ.

—Ephesians 6:23

Grace be with all who have an undying love for our Lord Jesus Christ.

—Ephesians 6:24

Grace to you and peace from God our Father and the Lord Jesus Christ.

—1 Corinthians 1:3, 2 Corinthians 1:2, Ephesians 1:2, Philippians 1:2,
2 Thessalonians 1:2, Philomen 3

Grace to you and peace from God our Father.

—Colossians 1:2

Grace, mercy, and peace from God the Father and Christ Jesus our Lord.

—1 Timothy 1:2, 2 Timothy 1:2

*Now may the Lord of peace himself give you peace at all times in all ways.
The Lord be with all of you.*

—2 Thessalonians 3:16

The grace of our Lord Jesus Christ be with all of you.

—2 Thessalonians 3:18

The Lord be with your spirit. Grace be with you.

—2 Timothy 4:22

*May grace and peace be yours in abundance in the knowledge of God and of
Jesus our Lord.*

—2 Peter 1:2

May mercy, peace, and love be yours in abundance.

—Jude 2

Paul's Prayers of Thanksgiving

Paul's letters (and those sometimes attributed to him, such as Ephesians) include the standard address of the day (names of the sender and addressee, and a greeting), but often with additions to describe the apostolic mission. Instead of a secular greeting, Paul includes the wish for the spiritual gifts poured out in Christ. He usually includes a prayer using Christian thanksgiving formulas, sometimes integrating a blessing.

*First, I thank my God through Jesus Christ for all of you, because your faith is
proclaimed throughout the world. For God, whom I serve with my spirit by
announcing the gospel of his Son, is my witness that without ceasing I remember
you always in my prayers, asking that by God's will I may somehow at last
succeed in coming to you. For I am longing to see you so that I may share with
you some spiritual gift to strengthen you—or rather so that we may be mutually
encouraged by each other's faith, both yours and mine.*

—Romans 1:8–12

I give thanks to my God always for you because of the grace of God that has been given you in Christ Jesus, for in every way you have been enriched in him, in speech and knowledge of every kind—just as the testimony of Christ has been strengthened among you—so that you are not lacking in any spiritual gift as you wait for the revealing of our Lord Jesus Christ. He will also strengthen you to the end, so that you may be blameless on the day of our Lord Jesus Christ. God is faithful; by him you were called into the fellowship of his Son, Jesus Christ our Lord.

—1 Corinthians 1:4–9

I have heard of your faith in the Lord Jesus and your love toward all the saints, and for this reason I do not cease to give thanks for you as I remember you in my prayers. I pray that the God of our Lord Jesus Christ, the Father of glory, may give you a spirit of wisdom and revelation as you come to know him, so that, with the eyes of your heart enlightened, you may know what is the hope to which he has called you, what are the riches of his glorious inheritance among the saints, and what is the immeasurable greatness of his power for us who believe, according to the working of his great power. God put this power to work in Christ when he raised him from the dead and seated him at his right hand in the heavenly places, far above all rule and authority and power and dominion, and above every name that is named, not only in this age but also in the age to come. And he has put all things under his feet and has made him the head over all things for the church, which is his body, the fullness of him who fills all in all.

—Ephesians 1:15–23

I thank my God every time I remember you, constantly praying with joy in every one of my prayers for all of you, because of your sharing in the gospel from the first day until now. I am confident of this, that the one who began a good work among you will bring it to completion by the day of Jesus Christ. It is right for me to think this way about all of you, because you hold me in your heart, for all of you share in God's grace with me, both in my imprisonment and in the defense and confirmation of the gospel. For God is my witness, how I long for all of you with the compassion of Christ Jesus. And this is my prayer, that your love may overflow more and more with knowledge and full insight to help you to determine what is best, so that in the day of Christ you may be pure and blameless, having produced the harvest of righteousness that comes through Jesus Christ for the glory and praise of God.

—Philippians 1:3–11

In our prayers for you we always thank God, the Father of our Lord Jesus Christ, for we have heard of your faith in Christ Jesus and of the love that you have for all the saints, because of the hope laid up for you in heaven. You have heard of this hope before in the word of the truth, the gospel that has come to you. Just as it is bearing fruit and growing in the whole world, so it has been bearing fruit among yourselves from the day you heard it and truly comprehended the grace of God. This you learned from Epaphras, our beloved fellow servant. He is a faithful minister of Christ on your behalf, and he has made known to us your love in the Spirit.

For this reason, since the day we heard it, we have not ceased praying for you and asking that you may be filled with the knowledge of God's will in all spiritual wisdom and understanding, so that you may lead lives worthy of the Lord, fully pleasing to him, as you bear fruit in every good work and as you grow in the knowledge of God. May you be made strong with all the strength that comes from his glorious power, and may you be prepared to endure everything with patience, while joyfully giving thanks to the Father, who has enabled you to share in the inheritance of the saints in the light. He has rescued us from the power of darkness and transferred us into the kingdom of his beloved Son, in whom we have redemption, the forgiveness of sins.

—Colossians 1:3–14

We always give thanks to God for all of you and mention you in our prayers, constantly remembering before our God and Father your work of faith and labor of love and steadfastness of hope in our Lord Jesus Christ. For we know, brothers and sisters beloved by God, that he has chosen you, because our message of the gospel came to you not in word only, but also in power and in the Holy Spirit and with full conviction; just as you know what kind of persons we proved to be among you for your sake. And you became imitators of us and of the Lord, for in spite of persecution you received the word with joy inspired by the Holy Spirit, so that you became an example to all the believers in Macedonia and in Achaia. For the word of the Lord has sounded forth from you not only in Macedonia and Achaia, but in every place your faith in God has become known, so that we have no need to speak about it. For the people of those regions report about us what kind of welcome we had among you, and how you turned to God from idols, to serve a living and true God, and to wait for his Son from heaven, whom he raised from the dead—Jesus, who rescues us from the wrath that is coming.

—1 Thessalonians 1:2–10

We must always give thanks to God for you, brothers and sisters, as is right, because your faith is growing abundantly, and the love of everyone of you for one another is increasing. Therefore we ourselves boast of you among the churches of God for your steadfastness and faith during all your persecutions and the afflictions that you are enduring.

This is evidence of the righteous judgment of God, and is intended to make you worthy of the kingdom of God, for which you are also suffering. For it is indeed just of God to repay with affliction those who afflict you, and to give relief to the afflicted as well as to us, when the Lord Jesus is revealed from heaven with his mighty angels in flaming fire, inflicting vengeance on those who do not know God and on those who do not obey the gospel of our Lord Jesus. These will suffer the punishment of eternal destruction, separated from the presence of the Lord and from the glory of his might, when he comes to be glorified by his saints and to be marveled at on that day among all who have believed, because our testimony to you was believed. To this end we always pray for you, asking that our God will make you worthy of his call and will fulfill by his power every good resolve and work of faith, so that the name of our Lord Jesus may be glorified in you, and you in him, according to the grace of our God and the Lord Jesus Christ.

—2 Thessalonians 1:3–12

Some Blessings of St. Paul

May the God of steadfastness and encouragement, grant you to live in harmony with one another in accordance with Christ Jesus, so that together you may with one voice glorify the God and Father of our Lord Jesus Christ. . . . May the God of hope fill you with all joy and peace in believing, so that you may abound in hope by the power of the Holy Spirit. . . . The God of peace be with all of you. Amen.

—Romans 15:5–6, 13, 33

Now to God who is able to strengthen you according to my gospel and the proclamation of Jesus Christ, according to the revelation of the mystery that was kept secret for long ages but is now disclosed, and through the prophetic writings is made known to all the Gentiles, according to the command of the eternal God, to bring about the obedience of faith—to the only wise God, through Jesus Christ, to whom be the glory forever! Amen.

—Romans 16:25–27

I pray that, according to the riches of his glory, he may grant that you may be strengthen in your inner being with power through his Spirit, and that Christ may dwell in your hearts through faith, as you are being rooted and grounded in love. I pray that you may have the power to comprehend, with all the saints, what is the breadth and length and height and depth, and to know the love of Christ that surpasses knowledge, so that you may be filled with all the fullness of God.

—Ephesians 3:16–19

Peace be to the whole community, and love with faith, from God the Father and the Lord Jesus Christ. Grace be with all who have an undying love for our Lord Jesus Christ.

—Ephesians 6:23

And the peace of God, which surpasses all understanding, will guard your hearts and your minds in Christ Jesus. Finally, beloved, whatever is true, whatever is honorable, whatever is just, whatever is pure, whatever is pleasing, whatever is commendable, if there is any excellence and if there is anything worthy of praise, think about these things. Keep on doing the things you have learned and received and heard and see in me, and the God of peace will be with you.

—Philippians 4:7–9

May the God of peace himself sanctify you entirely; and may your spirit and soul and body be kept sound and blameless at the coming of our Lord Jesus Christ.

—1 Thessalonians 5:23

To this end we always pray for you, asking that our God will make you worthy of his call, and will fulfill by his power every good resolve and work of faith, so that the name of our Lord Jesus may be glorified in you, and you in him, according to the grace of our God and the Lord Jesus Christ.

—2 Thessalonians 1:11–12

Now may the Lord of peace himself give you peace at all times in all ways. The Lord be with all of you.

—2 Thessalonians 3:16

Grace, mercy, and peace from God the Father and Christ Jesus our Lord.

—1 Timothy 1:2

Some Other New Testament Blessings

Now may the God of peace, who brought back from the dead our Lord Jesus, the great shepherd of the sheep, by the blood of the eternal covenant, make you complete in everything good so that you may do his will, working among us that which is pleasing in his sight, through Jesus Christ, to whom be the glory forever and ever. Amen.

—Hebrews 13:20–21

. . . the God of all grace, who has called you to his eternal glory in Christ, will himself restore, support, strengthen, and establish you. To him be the power forever and ever. Amen.

—1 Peter 5:10–11

Grace, mercy, and peace will be with us from God the Father and from Jesus Christ, the Father's Son, in truth and love.

—2 John 3

May mercy, peace, and love be yours in abundance.

—Jude 2

Now to him who is able to keep you from falling, and to make you stand without blemish in the presence of his glory with rejoicing, to the only God our Savior, through Jesus Christ our Lord, be glory, majesty, power, and authority, before all time and now and forever. Amen.

—Jude 24–25

John to the seven churches that are in Asia: Grace to you and peace from him who is and who was and who is to come, and from the seven spirits who are before his throne, and from Jesus Christ, the faithful witness, the first-born of the dead, and the ruler of the kings of earth. To him who loves us and freed us from our sins by his blood, and made us to be a kingdom, priests serving his God and Father, to him be glory and dominion forever and ever. Amen.

—Revelation 1:4–6

Other Blessings

And the Word Made His Dwelling Among Us

Among Christians there is an ancient custom of blessing a house on the Epiphany, recalling the visit of the magi. After the blessing—usually by the pastor—the initials of the traditional names of the magi, Gaspar (or Caspar), Melchior, and Balthasar, are inscribed and connected by crosses, with white chalk, on the inside door frame. The numerals of the current year serve as bookends: 20 + G + M + B + __. In the old Roman ritual, there is even a special blessing for the chalk used. The book *Catholic Household Blessings and Prayers* (United States bishops, 1988) provides a contemporary version of the house blessing, including as Scripture text, John 1:1–3, 14.

Godspeed

"May God prosper you." "May God give you good fortune." This was used as a wish to a person starting on a journey, or a new venture, or a new life. The archaic meaning of the word speed is prosperity, success, good luck.

Silver/Golden Wedding Anniversary Blessing

This is the exhortation given before the Mass.

Twenty-five (Fifty) years have passed since that day when, with the blessing of the Church, you plighted troth before the altar of God. In the long space of time which has intervened, many things have come to pass. You have had your full share of happiness but you have perhaps tasted sorrow as well. There may have been dark days as well as bright ones, and now, by the providence of God, a very special privilege is granted you, namely, that of celebrating the silver (golden) jubilee of your wedding, surrounded by those who love you (your children, your grandchildren, and your friends).

With hearts filled with gratitude, you have come to the Church today to thank God for his many favors, to renew in his presence the good avowals made long ago, and to receive the blessing of the Church on the years that remain to you.

In very truth you have cause to thank God. He has not only showered his blessings on you, but his fatherly hand has often protected you from evil, and it is by his mercy that in moments of darkness and discouragement you have been preserved from despair and received courage to persevere. (He has given you children to console and support you as the years come upon you.)

I feel sure, however, there is no further need for me to enumerate the many causes of thankfulness which must be well known to yourselves and of which, on a day like this, you must be well aware. The reasons for gratitude must be deeply imprinted on your memory and in your hearts enclosed.

It is for you, then, to remain faithful to God, and in the time that is left, to serve him with your remaining strength. You have borne the heat and burdens of the day bravely; do not lose now the eternal rest you have earned by your labors. Turn to profit the experience the years have brought you, using such experience to the benefit not only of yourselves but of others. Teach the young people around you how to avoid the shoals and quicksands on which married happiness is so often wrecked; advise them, in particular, how to procure the best interest of their children through Catholic training and education.

Be patient with each other in the weaknesses and failings which sometimes are the accompaniment of advancing years, and let an atmosphere of peace and gentleness increasingly surround you. Should it please God to send one or both of you sickness, do not complain but, uniting your sufferings with those of our divine Savior, say often as he did humbly and patiently, "Not my will, but thine be done." In this way your lives will bring forth the fruit of their maturity unto your lasting profit in eternity.

Speaking now to you, children and grandchildren of these happy parents, I charge you to make those lives bright and happy from which you have derived, by the disposition of God, your own being. Anticipate, insofar as you can, their every wish and avoid anything that would sadden or grieve them. Give them that greatest of all consolations, namely, the knowledge that you are leading good Christian lives so that they will understand their labors and pains on your behalf have not been in vain. By doing this you will earn the special blessing promised by God to those who are good to their parents.

—*Book of Blessings*

Heritage Blessing

May the God of Abraham, Isaac, and Jacob,
May the God of Peter, James, and John,
May the God of us all bless us
in the name of the Father, Son, and Holy Spirit.

Irish Blessing

May the road rise to meet you,
May the wind always be at your back,
May the sun shine warm upon your face,
May the rains fall soft upon your field,
May God hold you in the palm of his hand.

An Irish Blessing

May Christ give to you at this time and for always
His peace in your soul
His presence in your heart
His power in your life.

Ah-Choo

"God bless you." Thank-you, St. Gregory. During a pestilence in which a sneeze was a mortal symptom, It is said St. Gregory originated this blessing and recommended its prayerful use.

An Overview of the Tradition

A Catholic's Faith, Tradition, and Practice Known by Heart

According to the Amendments to the *National Catechetical Directory*, 1977, worthy to be known by heart are ". . . elements of Catholic faith, tradition, and practice which, through an early, gradual, flexible, and never slavish process of memorization, could become lessons learned for a lifetime, contributing to an individual's growth and development in an understanding of the faith."

I. Prayers

    A. The Sign of the Cross

    B. The Lord's Prayer

    C. The Hail Mary

    D. The Apostles' Creed

    E. The Act of Faith

    F. The Act of Hope

    G. The Act of Charity

    H. The Act of Contrition

II. Information, formulas, practices

    A. Scriptural

        1. Key themes of salvation history

        2. Major Old Testament and New Testament personalities

        3. Significant texts expressive of God's love and care

    B. Liturgical/devotional

        1. The parts of the Mass

        2. The sacraments (names and meaning)

        3. The liturgical seasons

        4. The holy days

        5. Major feasts of our Lord and of Mary

        6. Various Eucharistic devotions

        7. The Mysteries of the Rosary

        8. The Stations of the Cross

    C. Moral

        1. The Ten Commandments

        2. The Eight Beatitudes

        3. The gifts of the Holy Spirit

        4. The virtues (three theological and four moral)

        5. The precepts of the Church

        6. An examination of conscience

> ### The Legend of the Sand Dollar
>
> It is said that Christ left the sand dollar as a symbol to help the evangelists teach the faith. The five holes commemorate the five wounds of Christ, while at the center on one side blooms the Easter lily, and at the lily's heart, the star of Bethlehem. The Christmas poinsettia is etched on the other side, a reminder of Christ's birth. According to this legend, if you break the center, five white doves will be released to spread good will and peace.

Major Catechisms in History

The German Catechism and *Small Catechism* (1529)

Written by Martin Luther

Question and answer format

Small Catechism order: Commandments, Creed, Lord's Prayer, Baptism, Confession, Sacrament of the Altar

Creed: three articles rather than twelve

The Heidelberg Catechism (1563)

Reformed doctrine

Question and answer format

Content: Misery of humans and divine law, Redemption (creed, justification), Baptism, The Lord's Supper, Authority, Commandments and prayer

St. Peter Canisius

Three catechisms (1555–1559)—for (1) clergy, (2) children, (3) youth

Catholic doctrine: Faith, hope, and charity; Commandments of God and of the Church; Sacraments and Christian justice

St. Robert Bellarmine (1562–1621)

Suggested as a model for the catechism proposed at the First Vatican Council

Content: Creed, Lord's Prayer, Commandments, Sacraments

The Catechism of the Council of Trent for the Clergy (1566)

Prose, not questions and answers

Content: Creed, Sacraments, Commandments, Lord's Prayer

Catechism of the Third Plenary Council of Baltimore (1885)

Questions and answers

So called because it was approved, in 1884, by the Third Plenary Council of American Bishops at Baltimore

US standard, dominant catechetical tool, for seventy-five years

Catechism of the Catholic Church (1994)

Prose, not questions and answers

Content: Creed, Sacraments, Commandments, Prayer—especially the Lord's Prayer

The Four Pillars of Catechesis (See CCC #s 13–17.)

This is according to the great tradition of catechisms.

1. Baptismal profession of faith: the Creed (God's revelation, our response)
2. Sacraments of faith (the Church's liturgy)
3. Life of faith: the Commandments (our final beatitude and ways of reaching it)
4. Prayer of the believer: the Lord's Prayer (the meaning and importance)

God

Five Implications of Faith in One God (See CCC #s 222–227.)

1. Becoming aware of God's greatness and majesty
2. Living in gratitude
3. Knowing the solidarity and true dignity of all people
4. Making good use of creation
5. Trusting God in every situation

Six Attributes of God

They were traditionally symbolized in the hexagonal base of a chalice.

1. Power
2. Majesty
3. Wisdom
4. Love
5. Mercy
6. Justice

God's Omnipotence (See CCC #s 268–274.)

This is the first divine attribute named in the Creed.

1. God's power is universal.
2. God's power is loving.
3. God's power is mysterious (discerned only by faith).

Heresies about Origins (See CCC #285.)

These heresies testify to the permanent and universal quest for origins.

1. Everything, the world itself, is God (Pantheism).
2. The world is a necessary emanation from God, and returns to God.
3. There are two eternal principles, good and evil, light and dark, in permanent conflict (Dualism, Manichaeism).
4. The physical world is evil, a result of the fall, and to be rejected (Gnosticism).
5. The world is made by God as by a watchmaker who leaves it to itself (Deism).
6. There is no transcendent origin, but merely the interplay of matter that has always existed (Materialism).

Humans and God

Four Points of a Soul's Likeness to God

1. Like God, the soul is a spirit (simplicity).
2. Like God, the soul is immortal (immortality).
3. Like God, the soul can reason (intellect).
4. Like God, the soul can choose (free will).

Powers of the Soul

1. Memory
2. Understanding
3. Free Will

"What Do You Know?"

Francis Bacon would ask instead, "How strong are you?" If it's true that knowledge is power, as Bacon said, then the two questions are the same. The actual thought of Francis, the famous philosopher, was *"Nam et ipsa scientia potestas est"* (For knowledge, too, is itself power)—whence the familiar aphorism.

Trinity

Chief Mysteries of Christianity

The Trinity, original sin, and the incarnation have been called the three greater mysteries.

1. Unity
2. Trinity
3. Incarnation
4. Death of our Savior
5. Resurrection

The Dogma of the Holy Trinity (See CCC #s 238–260.)

1. The Father, Son, and Holy Spirit are one and the same God.
2. The divine Persons are distinct from one another.
3. The purpose of the divine missions of the Son and the Holy Spirit is to bring us to share in the life, light, and love of the Trinity.

Pouring the Ocean Down a Hole

One day Augustine was meditating on the mystery of the Blessed Trinity, strolling along the beach as he pondered. Lost in thought, he encountered a child who had dug a little hole in the sand. With tiny bucket in hand, the youngster had begun making trips to the sea and back, pouring pails full of water into the hole in the sand. Observing this for a while, Augustine asked the child what he was doing. "I'm putting the ocean in a hole." Condescendingly, Augustine said, "But you can never do that." Whereupon, the youngster responded, "And neither can you ever figure out the Holy Trinity." Legend has it that the boy disappeared, because in fact he was an angel.

Symbols of the Trinity

Trefoil   Equilateral triangle   Triquetra   Interwoven circle Circles of fish

Note: These symbols are explained in Chapter 9.

The Atonement of Nagasaki?

Nagasaki. The word, the city, is synonymous with the atomic bomb, and with suffering. The bomb killed nearly eighty thousand people and injured countless more. Nagasaki was an alternative target that August 9, 1945, because of the cloud cover over the intended city. It was also the cloud cover over the Mitsubishi iron works that caused the pilot to fix his target instead on the Catholic Cathedral in Urakami, a district of the city that was home to the majority of Nagasaki's Catholics.

Six days later, on the feast of the Assumption of Mary, to whom the cathedral was dedicated, the war ended: August 15. "We must ask if this convergence of events—the ending of the war and the celebration of her feast—was merely coincidental or if there was here some mysterious providence of God." That's the comment of Dr. Takashi Nagai (1908–1951), dean of radiology at the University of Nagasaki, convert to Catholicism, survivor of the bomb, and "mystic of Nagasaki," in the words of Robert Ellsberg in his book *All Saints* (1997).

In the days after the bombing, after finding the charred remains of his beloved wife in their ruined home, a rosary clasped "among the powdered bones of her right hand," Takashi Nagai responded in a most remarkable way: in gratitude. His words, spoken at an open-air Requiem Mass just days after the bombing are counter-cultural and controversial, insisting on a redemptive meaning for the horrors:

We have disobeyed the law of love. Joyfully we have hated one another; joyfully we have killed one another. And now at last we have brought this great and evil war to an end. But in order to restore peace to the world it was not sufficient to repent. We had to obtain God's pardon through the offering of a great sacrifice. . . . Let us give thanks that Nagasaki was chosen for the sacrifice. . . . May the souls of the faithful departed, through the mercy of God, rest in peace.

Nagasaki, since the early Jesuit missions, had been the center of Japanese Catholicism, and consequently the scene of extensive martyrdom. Was this experience and spirituality the well-spring of Takashi's response, and the power source of his call to witness the cause of international peace?

> ## The Devil's Funeral
>
> In medieval England, Ireland, and Scotland, it was traditional on Christmas Eve, at 11:00, to solemnly toll the bell as if for a funeral and to let it peal until the midnight hour. The legend was that the devil died when Christ was born.

> ## Christmas among the Hurons
>
> ### Huron Carolers
>
> First mention of Christmas caroling in America is in a report on the Huron mission by a Jesuit missionary from Quebec, dated October 1, 1645: "The Indians have a particular devotion for the night that was enlightened by the birth of the Son of God. There was not one who refused to fast on the day that preceded it. They built a small chapel of cedar and fir branches in honor of the manger of the infant Jesus. They wished to perform some penance for better receiving him into their hearts on that holy day, and even those who were at a distance of two days' journey met at a given place to sing hymns in honor of the new-born child. . . . Neither the inconvenience of the snow nor the severity of the cold could stifle the ardor of their devotion."
>
> —From footnote 33, page 86, of *Handbook of Christian Feasts and Customs*, Weiser.
>
> ### Jesous Ahatonnia
>
> The first American Christmas carol was in the language of the Huron Indian, "Jesus Is Born." It was written by the celebrated Jesuit missionary to the Huron, St. John de Brebeuf, who adapted a sixteenth-century French folk song into an Indian Christian hymn. It survived the Iroquois destruction of the Huron mission (John de Brebeuf did not) in 1649; it was preserved by the Huron who settled near Quebec. It was later discovered and published in French, and finally in recent years it was reintroduced into the treasury of American Christmas carols. For the Hurons and other Native Americans, caroling with songs like this one was a sign and source of Christian faith, unlike many early English carols which only praise the pleasures of feasting, reveling, and general good will.

The Four Manifestations of Christ

All are "epiphanies," although the magi visit has taken the title for itself.

1. Nativity
2. Magi visit
3. Baptism
4. Miracle at Cana (the first of Jesus' "signs")

The Three Nativity Gifts (Matthew 2:11)

1. Gold, for the royalty of Jesus
2. Frankincense, for the divinity of Jesus
3. Myrrh, for the passion and death of Jesus

Three-fold Birth of Christ

1. Eternal, in the bosom of the Father
2. Temporal, in Bethlehem to Mary
3. Spiritual, in liturgy and daily living

Three-fold Office of Christ

1. Priest, sanctifying
2. Prophet, teaching
3. King, pastoring

Adoration of the Magi

Three-fold Belief in Christ

1. Christ has died, in history.

2. Christ is risen, in mystery.

3. Christ will come again, in majesty.

Christological Confessions (See CCC #s 464–469.)

1. The Church confessed from apostolic times: God's Son Jesus is truly incarnate, "come in the flesh" (condemning Gnostic Docetism, which denied Christ's true humanity).

2. The Church confessed in the third century: Jesus Christ is son of God by nature and not by adoption (condemning the Adoptionism of Paul of Samosata).

3. The Church confessed in 325 at the first ecumenical council (Nicaea): Jesus is the Son of God, "begotten, not made, of the same substance *(homoousios)* as the Father" (condemning Arianism which claimed God's Son "came to be from things that were not," that he was "from another substance" than that of the Father).

4. The Church confessed in 431 at the Council of Ephesus: "the Word, uniting to himself in his person the flesh animated by a rational soul, became man" (condemning the Nestorian heresy that regarded Christ as a human person joined to the divine Person of God's Son).

5. The Church confessed in 451 at the Council of Chalcedon: Jesus is "the same truly God and truly man . . . consubstantial with the Father as to his divinity and consubstantial with us as to his humanity," an affirmation of Jesus' two natures in a "hypostatic union" (condemning the Monophysite heresy that claimed the human nature had ceased to exist as such in Christ when the divine Person of God's Son assumed it).

6. The Church confessed in 553 at the Council of Constantinople II: "There is but one person *(hypostasis)*, which is our Lord Jesus Christ, one of the Trinity" (condemning the heresy that made of Christ's human nature a kind of personal subject or a separate human person).

Christ as Divine Guru, Missionary as Sannyasi

In Hindu India, Jesus as an avatar, a manifestation of God in human form, was comprehensible. Jesus as an "incarnate" son of God was not. So Roberto de Nobili spoke in terms of Christ as the divine guru. Robert de Nobili (1577–1656) was an Italian Jesuit and a great pioneer in what we today call inculturation. This Christian missionary became also an Indian holy man, or *sannyasi*, complete with robes, sandals, and bamboo stick. Through his intensive study of Hindu religion and immersion in Indian culture, Robert won the respect of Brahmin scholars, but also the criticism and finally condemnation of local Church officials. In the prevailing view, the gospel was not distinguished from the (presumed) superior European culture that carried it. There was no response, seemingly, other than "When in India do as the Romans." Rome, however, saw otherwise and later vindicated Robert de Nobili.

The Holy Spirit

Titles of the Holy Spirit (See CCC #s 692–693.)

By Jesus
Paraclete (he who is called to one's side; often "consoler")
the Spirit of Truth

By Paul
the Spirit of the promise
the Spirit of adoption
the Spirit of Christ

the Spirit of the Lord
the Spirit of God

By Peter
the Spirit of glory

Some Symbols of the Holy Spirit (See CCC #s 694–701.)

Water, anointing, fire, cloud/light, the seal (John 6:27), the laying on of hands (Mark 6:5, 8:23, 10:16, 16:18; Acts 5:12, 14:3), the finger of God (Luke 11:20), and the dove (Genesis 8:8–12; Matthew 3:16 and parallels)

"That's Impossible!"

To which Tertullian (third century) would have said, "That proves it!" As a matter of fact he did say, in *De Carne Christi*, *"Certum est quia impossibile est"* (It is certain because it is impossible). That line may not work every time, but it's still true that the apparent impossibility of a truth of a Christian mystery is not an automatic argument for its rejection. Faith goes beyond reason.

Ten Scriptural Evangelizers

Besides the many who spread the word after miracles by Jesus

1. Mary brings Christ to world (Luke 1–2).
2. John the Baptist points out Jesus (Lamb of God) to disciples (John 1:35–37).
3. Andrew introduces Peter to Jesus (John 1:40–42).
4. Andrew introduces a boy with bread to Jesus (multiplication) (John 6:8–9).
5. Andrew introduces some Greek believers to Jesus (John 12:21–22).
6. Philip introduces Nathanael to Jesus (John 1:44–46).
7. The Samaritan woman (at the well) tells townspeople about Jesus (John 4:28–30).
8. Some people bring a paralyzed man to Jesus (through the roof) (Mark 2:1–12).
9. Mary Magdalene tells Peter and John of the empty tomb (John 20:1–2).
10. Peter and John, other apostles, Paul, and the apostolic Church (Acts).

A Vocation in a Dream

As a boy, St. Patrick was kidnapped and taken from his homeland to Ireland. He later escaped, but he was destined to return of his own free will to where he had been taken against his will. In his *Confessions* he wrote that he returned to the Emerald Isle after having a recurring dream in which the children of Ireland cried out to him, "Come and walk among us once more."

Conversion
(See CCC #s 1425–1429.)

The Two Conversions

"[In the Church] there are water and tears: the water of Baptism and the tears of repentance" (St. Ambrose).

1. Conversion to Christ in Baptism ("The principal place for the first and fundamental conversion").
2. The conversion of the baptized (". . . an uninterrupted task for the whole Church").

Stages of Conversion

This example uses the Scriptures and Peter as a model.

1. Before Jesus (the period under the Law).
2. With Jesus (the period of following Jesus).
3. After Pentecost (the period led by the Spirit).

Conversion Process of Adult Converts

1. Hearing the Gospel

Need for preachers of the word (Romans 10:14, 17).

First believers in Corinth (Acts 18:8).

"Everyone then who hears these words of mine. . ." (Matthew 7:24).

"My mother and my brothers are those who hear the word of God and do it" (Luke 8:20–21).

2. Believing

"And without faith it is impossible to please God . . ." (Hebrews 11:6).

"If you confess with your lips that Jesus is Lord and believe in your heart that God raised him from the dead, you will be saved (Romans 10:9).

"No one can enter the kingdom of God without being born of water and the Spirit" (John 3:5).

3. Repenting sins

Joy over repentance (2 Corinthians 7:10), Paul's discourse to Athenians (Acts 17:30).

Providential calls to penance (for example, the tower of Siloam) (Luke 13:2–5).

Penance for the forgiveness of sins is to be preached (Luke 24:46–47).

Parables of divine mercy (Luke 15:1–32).

4. Confessing Christ

"Everyone who acknowledges me before others . . ." (Matthew 10:32–33).

"If you confess with your lips . . ." (see Romans 10:9 above).

Faith leads to justification, confession to salvation (Romans 10:10).

Regarding Timothy's profession of faith (1 Timothy 6:12–14).

"If we deny him, he will also deny us" (2 Timothy 2:12).

5. Being baptized

The Baptism of Cornelius (Acts 10:48).

After Peter's first discourse (Acts 2:38).

Jesus' post-resurrection mandate (Matthew 28:19, see Mark 16:16).

"As many of you as were baptized into Christ, have clothed yourself with Christ" (Galatians 3:27).

"If we have died with him, we will also live with him" (2 Timothy 2:11).

"No one can enter the kingdom without . . ." (John 3:5).

Paul's telling of his own baptism (Acts 22:16).

Noah's ark and its resemblance to Baptism (1 Peter 3:20–21).

6. Living in trust

"Except you become as little children . . ." (Matthew 18:2–4).

"Consider the lilies . . ." (Matthew 6:25–34; Luke 12:22–31).

"Trust in God; trust also in me" (John 14:1).

7. Living in compassion

"Whatsoever you do . . ." (Matthew 25:31–46).

"Clothe yourselves with compassion" (Colossians 3:12).

"Go and do likewise" (the good Samaritan) (Luke 10:25–37; Matthew 22:34–40; Mark 12:28–34).

"I give you a new commandment . . ." (John 13:34–35, 15:12–13).

". . . we should love one another" (1 John 3:11–24, 4:7–21).

The Three Accounts of Paul's Conversion Experience

Acts 9:1–9, 22:3–16, and 26:2–18 (see also 1 Corinthians 15:8).

One Day While Hunting

Hunters claim Hubert as a patron, and lodges have taken his name because of the circumstances of his conversion. Hubert, a married man, was a courtier serving Pepin of Heristal. After his wife died, he turned to the spiritual life, reputedly while hunting and seeing a crucifix between the horns of a stag. He later became a priest, and then a bishop, distinguishing himself by ending idol worship in his diocese. He died on May 30, 727, near Brussels while on a trip to consecrate a church.

Russian Reconciliation

The Lenten fast became especially strict in Russia during Holy Week, in preparation for an Easter confession and Communion. On Holy Saturday, before going to confession, it was the custom to bow deeply to each member of the household, servants included, speaking the venerable phrase, "In the name of Christ, forgive me if I have offended you," and receiving the response, "God will forgive you." After this preparation in the "domestic church," the penitents would make their way to church for reconciliation on Holy Saturday and Communion on Easter.

Returning from the faith community to family, they again ritualized the relationship between liturgy and life: They would again face their whole household, this time sharing an embrace with smiles and congratulations all around. With flowers decorating the room and table, the entire extended family shared in the joy of the one who had celebrated Easter Communion.

Grace   (See CCC #s 1996–2005.)

Definition: Grace is favor, the free and undeserved help God gives to respond to his call. It is participation in the life of God.

Kinds of Grace

1. Habitual Grace: This sanctifying grace is the permanent and supernatural disposition that perfects the soul itself to enable it to live with God and act by God's love.

2. Actual Graces: This is God's intervention, at the beginning of conversion and in the work of sanctification.

Orthodoxy

Creeds

The Primary, Historic Professions of Christian Faith (See CCC #s 185–197.)

1. The Apostles' Creed ("I believe . . . .")

"The oldest Roman Catechism" is a faithful summary of the apostles' faith and the ancient baptismal profession of the Church of Rome. According to ancient tradition (attested to by the likes of St. Ambrose), the articles of the Creed number twelve, symbolizing the fullness of the apostolic faith found in the twelve apostles. It is the faith of the Church professed personally by each believer, principally during Baptism.

2. The Nicene (Niceno-Constantinopolitan) Creed ("We believe . . . .")

With the authority of the first two ecumenical Councils (325 and 381) from which it came and common to all the great Churches of both East and West to this day, this creed is the faith of the Church confessed by the liturgical assembly of believers.

Various Professions of Christian Faith

Others have been articulated through the centuries, in response to the needs of the different eras.

1. The creeds of different apostolic and ancient Churches (like the Athanasian Creed)

2. The creeds of certain Councils (like Toledo, Lateran, Lyons, and Trent)

3. The creeds of certain popes (like the *Fides Damasi* or Paul VI's "Credo of the People of God")

Unorthodoxy   (See CCC #s 817–819, 839–848, 2089.)

Kinds of Unorthodoxy: Apostasy, heresy, and schism are post-baptismal decisions.

1. An agnostic denies the knowability of God.

2. An apostate totally repudiates the Christian faith.

3. An atheist denies the existence of God.

4. A deist denies that God revealed any religion.

5. A heretic (Greek: one who chooses) is a baptized Christian who denies some of the truths taught by Jesus and proposed by the Church, adopting instead a personal creed.

6. An infidel (Latin: not faithful), formerly referred to any non-Christian; now, if used at all, it refers to a professed atheist or agnostic.

7. A pagan (or "heathen") referred to a person without faith; originally meant a "non-convert," not acknowledging the God of Judeo-Christian revelation; today it is used for an irreligious person. It is incorrect to use the term for people who practice a non-Christian religion.

8. A schismatic (Greek: *skizein*, to cut, split; a division) is a full believer in the Church who refuses submission to the authority of its vicarious, earthly head, the pope.

9. A theist believes in a supreme being who created and sustains all things, but does not necessarily accept the doctrine of the Trinity (the incarnation) or divine revelation.

Vincentian Canon

The widely known three-fold test of orthodoxy, articulated by St. Vincent of Lerins (400–450): "Care must especially be had that that be held which was believed everywhere *(unique)*, always *(semper)*, and by all *(ab omnibus)*." The principles of diffusion, endurance, and universality in this triple norm distinguish a Christian's religious truth (orthodoxy) from error.

Julian the Apostate

Julian was an emperor of Rome (361–363) and a great-nephew of Constantine. Even though his famous relative had legalized Christianity, and even though he had been raised a Catholic, Julian renounced his faith and set about reinstating pre-Christian religion in the Roman Empire. In combating the Church, he made an unsuccessful attempt at rebuilding the Jewish temple in Jerusalem. All his anti-Christian efforts and policies failed. He supposedly spoke from his deathbed, "O Galilean, you have conquered," finally acknowledging Christ's victory in the world.

A Heresy/Schism Distinction

1. Heresy is intellectual (in the mind), opposing religious belief.

2. Schism is volitional (in the will), offending the union of Christian charity.

Prerequisites for Formal Heresy

1. Previous valid Baptism (Otherwise, the unorthodoxy would be paganism or a non-Christian religion.)

2. Persistence of external profession of Christianity (Otherwise, the unorthodoxy would be apostasy.)

3. Moral culpability: knowingly refusing a doctrinal imperative (Otherwise, the unorthodoxy would be material heresy.)

Nihil Obstat Quominus Imprimatur

"Nothing hinders it from being printed." The term is usually seen in two parts: the *nihil obstat*, or the judgment of the censor that there is nothing contrary to faith or morals, nothing "stands in the way"; and the *imprimatur*, the official permission to print, especially from Church authorities or a censor. It represents the approval by a bishop for the publication of a religious work and is for material other than that of the teaching Church itself (like council, synod, or bishop). This judgment of the Church comes from the office of the bishop of either the petitioner's residence or the publisher's location.

Virtues

The Sources of the Morality of Human Acts (See CCC #1750.)

1. The object chosen, that is, the kind of act it is

2. The end in view (intention)

3. The circumstances of the action

Grace Builds on Nature

Aristotle said that sanguine, melancholic, choleric, and lethargic are the four human temperaments or dispositions of nature. We'd probably say cheerful, gloomy, temperamental, and apathetic, and then start naming names. We do say that grace builds on nature. We might even say that those four temperaments are the sow's ear out of which grace makes a silk purse.

Priority of Virtues (Hierarchy of Dignity)

1. Supernatural
   - Theological virtues
     — Faith, hope, and charity
   - Moral cardinal virtues
     — Prudence, justice, temperance, and fortitude
     — Their name comes from the Latin word for hinge (*cardo*), "that on which another thing depends." They are also referred to as the moral virtues, prudence being the queen, since it controls all others, guiding conduct specifically and practically.
2. Natural

Three Elements of Faith

Knowledge, assent, and confidence

Qualities of Christian Faith

Universal, firm, constant, and living

The Evangelical Counsels

Poverty, chastity, and obedience. These three counsels of the gospel have traditionally been undertaken in a solemn way by those committed to religious life, with many monastic communities adding a vow of stability.

St. Francis and Lady Poverty

Francis is well-known for his love affair with Lady Poverty. Francis loved to have nothing. One day he decided to give control of his life entirely to God. He went to his bishop and told him of his determination. Francis laid everything he possessed at the feet of his bishop, including the clothes on his back. With that he was able to dance away naked down the street, completely free and dispossessed.

Corporal Works of Mercy

". . . Just as you did it to one of the least of these who are members of my family, you did it to me" (Matthew 25:31–46).

1. Feed the hungry.
2. Give drink to the thirsty.
3. Clothe the naked.
4. Shelter the homeless.
5. Visit the sick.
6. Visit the imprisoned.
7. Bury the dead.

Spiritual Works of Mercy

Based on Christ's teachings and Christian practice since the apostles.

1. Counsel the doubtful.

2. Instruct the ignorant.

3. Admonish the sinner.

4. Comfort the sorrowful.

5. Forgive injuries.

6. Bear wrongs patiently.

7. Pray for the living and the dead.

St. Martin and the Shirt Off His Back

When he was only ten, Martin decided on his own initiative to become a catechumen. As the son of a military man, however, he was forced into the army against his will when he was fifteen. While he was stationed at Amiens, there was an incident and a vision, well-known in tradition and art, which changed his life.

On a bitterly cold day, Martin met a poor man, hardly clothed, trembling in the cold and begging from passersby at the city gate. The young soldier had nothing but his weapons and his clothes. He drew his sword, cut his cloak in two, gave one half to the beggar and wrapped himself in the other half. Some of the onlookers mocked him, dressed like that; others were ashamed for having ignored the man's misery.

In his sleep that night, Martin saw Christ dressed in the half of the garment he had given away, and heard him say, "Martin, still a catechumen, has covered me with this garment." As a result, the story goes, Martin straight-away "flew to be baptized." (Countless times, people ever since have unwittingly referred to this incident and the renowned cloak every time a certain common word is used. See "Chapel.")

Hospitality in the Scriptures: Stranger and Guest

Abraham and three visitors (the Lord and two messengers)—Genesis 18:1–15

Lot and the two visitors (angels of the Lord)—Genesis 19:1–11

Jacob and a wrestler (an angel)—Genesis 32:23–33

Moses and seven girls (Reuel's daughters, and a future wife)—Exodus 2:11–22

Rahab the harlot and Joshua's two spies—Joshua 2

An exception: Jael hosts Sisera and kills him.—Judges 4:17–22

Gideon and a man (an angel of God)—Judges 6:11–40

Solomon hosts the Queen of Sheba.—1 Kings 10:l–13

Elijah hosts the 450 prophets of Baal.—1 Kings 18:19–46

The Shunammite woman hosts Elisha.—2 Kings 4:8–37

Two disciples going to Emmaus and a stranger (Christ)—Luke 24:13–35

Samaritan woman at Jacob's well and a thirsty stranger (Jesus)—John 4:4–42

Matthew hosts Jesus, tax collectors, and sinners.—Matthew 9:10–13

Zacchaeus hosts Jesus.—Luke 19:1–10

Samaritans refusing hospitality to Jesus—Luke 9:51–53

"Whoever welcomes you welcomes me" teaching—Matthew 10:40–42; John 13:20

"Just as you did to one of the least" teaching—Matthew 25:31–46

"I am standing at the door, knocking. . ."—Revelation 3:20

"And their eyes were opened."—Luke 24:13–35

Divine Ambassadors

The Greeks believed that people in need are the ambassadors of the gods. Stories of dignitaries and deities in disguise are abundant and universal in folklore—indeed, in the Scriptures (Abraham's guests, Genesis 18, for example, and Raphael in Tobit 5:4–22). In the early centuries of Christendom, houses of hospitality, or hospices, were provided as shelter for the various "divine ambassadors": the sick, the poor, the orphan, the old, the traveler, and the needy of every kind. Bishops originally supervised these houses of hospitality, delegating certain priests with the administration of their material and spiritual affairs. Bishops, in fact, were enjoined to have such houses in connection with their churches.

"Many Dwelling Places"

Jesus' own experience of homelessness, beginning in infancy, has given his disciples a sensitivity, as well as many stories and traditions.

"A Refuge for the Holy Family"

It's a tradition in south central Italy each Christmas Eve to leave the door of the house open, have the fire lit, and the table laid. This posture of hospitality was assumed in case the Holy Family, pursued by Herod's minions, should need a hiding place or food.

"Gypsies"

Egyptians is where the word comes from, at least according to a medieval notion. Among many legends about gypsies, this one says that they are people condemned to wander the earth without rest. Since they refused hospitality to Joseph, Mary, and Jesus during their Egyptian flight, these "gypsies" suffered the same rootless fate. Of course, this legend is false, and the mistreatment of gypsies for any reason is wrong.

> ### St. Joseph Table
>
> March 19 is the occasion for a traditional show of hospitality, fittingly on the feast of St. Joseph, patron of charity to the poor, a happy home, and peace. The tradition was brought to our country by Sicilian immigrants and includes inviting to the table all who come to the door. Traditionally, the family table is extended full length and, as the altar used to be, moved against the wall with a statue of St. Joseph surrounded by flowers and candles as the centerpiece of a shrine. Having enjoyed the hospitality, the fruits and vegetables, the breads and pastries, and the artistry of the hosts, guests move on, making room for more guests. Beforehand, the priest has blessed the bounty and, afterward, any offering made by guests is given to the poor.

Gifts

The Gifts of the Holy Spirit

Traditional; according to Isaiah 11:2–3

1. Wisdom *(Sapientia)*

2. Understanding *(Intellectus)*

3. Counsel *(Consilium)*

4. Fortitude *(Fortitudo)*

5. Knowledge *(Scientia)*

6. Piety *(Pietas)*

7. Fear of the Lord *(Timor Domini)*

According to Paul; 1 Corinthians 12:8–10

Expression of wisdom

Expression of knowledge

Faith

Healing

Miracles

Prophecy

Discerning spirits

Speaking in tongues

Interpretation of Tongues

The seven flames represent the gifts of the Holy Spirit.

The Fear of the Lord

This term, a reverence for God, is the Hebrew term for religion (see Job 28:28; Proverbs 1:7, 9:10; Sirach 1:16).

1. The object of fear of the Lord is divine justice. "The fear of the Lord is the beginning of wisdom" (Psalm 111:10).
   - Filial fear (selfless): fear of offending
   - Servile fear (selfish): fear of being punished
2. The object of the love of the Lord is divine goodness. "Perfect love casts out all fear" (1 John 4:18).

Charisms

This word comes from the Greek *charismata*, gifts of grace, and is used by Paul for the extraordinary, supernatural, and transitory gifts given directly for the common good, which is the spiritual welfare of the Christian community. This listing, by category, is from 1 Corinthians 12:1–11, the longest single enumeration of charisms.

Charisms of Administration (Gifts for shepherding God's people)

1. Pastor—Ephesians 4:11, Acts 20:28
2. Administrator—Romans 12:8, 1 Thessalonians 5:12, 1 Timothy 5:17
3. Minister—1 Corinthians 16:15, Romans 12:7

Charisms of Knowledge (Gifts for the mind, to instruct others in faith)

1. Prophet—1 Corinthians 12:28; see Acts 11:27–30, 15:32, 21:10–40; 1 Corinthians 11:5, 14:3, 14:24–25; Acts 21:9
2. Evangelist—Acts 21:8, 2 Timothy 4:5
3. Teacher—Romans 12:7, Ephesians 4:11, 1 Timothy 4:13, 16
4. Exhorter—Romans 12:8, 1 Timothy 4:13, Acts 4:36
5. Proclaimer of wisdom—1 Corinthians 12:8
6. Proclaimer of knowledge—1 Corinthians 12:8

Charisms of Prayer

Gifts of communing with God (see 1 Corinthians 14:2).

Charisms of Service

1. Almsgiving—Romans 12:8
2. Manifestation of mercy—Romans 12:8
3. Helpfulness—1 Corinthians 12:28
4. Leadership—1 Corinthians 12:28

Fruits of the Spirit

The Fruits of the Holy Spirit (Galatians 5:22–23)

Traditional	New Revised Standard Version
1. Charity	Love
2. Joy	Joy
3. Peace	Peace
4. Patience	
5. Kindness	Patience
6. Goodness	Kindness
7. Long-suffering	Goodness
8. Humility	
9. Fidelity	Faithfulness
10. Modesty	Gentleness
11. Continence	
12. Chastity	Self-control

Commandments

The Four Expressions of the Moral Law (See CCC #s 1949–1974.)

1. Eternal law (the source, in God, of all law)
2. Natural law
3. Revealed law: the Old Law and the Law of the Gospel
4. Civil and ecclesiastical laws

The Ten Commandments (Exodus 20:1–17, Deuteronomy 5:1–21)

The division and numbering of the commandments have varied in the course of history. The *Catechism of the Catholic Church* follows the division established by St. Augustine which has become the Catholic (and Lutheran) tradition. The first three concern love of God and the other seven love of neighbor.

1. I am the Lord your God: you shall not have strange gods before me.
2. You shall not take the name of the Lord your God in vain.
3. Remember to keep holy the Lord's day.
4. Honor your father and your mother.
5. You shall not kill.
6. You shall not commit adultery.
7. You shall not steal.
8. You shall not bear false witness against your neighbor.
9. You shall not covet your neighbor's wife.
10. You shall not covet your neighbor's goods.

The First Commandment

Sins against Faith (See CCC #s 2088–2089.)

1. Involuntary doubt—hesitation, or difficulty overcoming objections
2. Voluntary doubt—disregard of or refusal to hold the truth
3. Incredulity—neglect, or willful refusal to assent
4. Heresy—obstinate post-baptismal denial of some truth
5. Schism—refusal of submission to the pope or of Catholic communion
6. Apostasy—total repudiation of Christian faith

Sins against Hope (See CCC #s 2091–2092.)

1. Despair—giving up the hope for personal salvation or for help
2. Presumption
   • Presuming upon one's own capacities
   • Presuming upon God's power or mercy—hoping for forgiveness without conversion, glory without merit

Sins against God's Love (See CCC #2094.)

1. Indifference
2. Ingratitude
3. Lukewarmness
4. Spiritual sloth (laziness)—refusing the joy that comes from God
5. Hatred of God, coming from pride

The Virtue of Religion (See CCC #s 2096–2103.)

The rendering to God what is owed God in all justice

1. Adoration (the first act of the virtue of religion)
2. Prayer
3. Sacrifice (St. Augustine teaches, "Every action done for the purpose of clinging to God in communion of holiness and achieving blessedness is a sacrifice.")
4. Promises—in sacraments, like Baptism, Confirmation, Matrimony, Holy Orders, and in personal devotion, like a certain action, prayer, almsgiving, or pilgrimage
5. Vows—a deliberate, free promise to God about a possible and better good; a devotional act of dedication; especially the evangelical counsels, poverty, chastity, and obedience

Sins against the Honor Due to God (See CCC #s 2111–2117.)

1. Superstition—the deviation of religious feeling and of the practices this feeling imposes

2. Idolatry—divinizing what is not God as well as false worship

3. Divination—practices falsely supposed to unveil the future, like recourse to Satan, demons, the dead. (The *Catechism of the Catholic Church* teaches, "Consulting horoscopes, astrology, palm reading, interpretation of omens and lots, the phenomena of clairvoyance, and recourse to mediums all conceal a desire for power over time, history . . . and other human beings.")

4. Magic and spiritualism—attempts to tame occult powers, to place them at one's service and have power over others is most sinful when done with harmful purpose.

The Main Sins of Irreligion (See CCC #s 2118–2128.)

1. Tempting God—putting God's goodness to the test

2. Sacrilege (Latin: *sacrilegium*)—stealing sacred things; refers to profaning sacraments, liturgical action, persons, things, or places consecrated to God; normally refers to an action—desecration—but also to sacrilegious talk

3. Simony—buying or selling spiritual things (See Acts 8:20.)

4. Atheism (including practical materialism, atheistic humanism)—considering humans as ends in themselves, and theories of economic and social liberation apart from God

5. Agnosticism—a "practical atheism," ideas or indifference that often refrains from formally denying God

The Second Commandment

> ### *A Friend as Far as to the Altars*
> Pericles of Athens is said to have responded with this when refusing to swear falsely for a friend. "A friend as far as the altars" (*"Amicus usque ad aras"* when quoted in Latin) could be a friend to death. It could also be more: Where friendship conflicts with religious beliefs or ethics, the good friend draws the line. This is not an admission of friendship's limit; it is a proof of its depth.

Sins against the Name of God (See CCC #s 2142–2155.)

The Christian begins the day, as with all traditional prayers and activities, with the Sign of the Cross, dedicating the day to the glory of God and calling on Christ's grace. The Divine Praises originated as a reparation for blasphemy and profanity. Likewise, a confraternity of men called *The Holy Name Society* originated at the Ecumenical Council of Lyons (1274), was promoted by the Dominicans, and was dedicated to promoting reverence for the name of God and the name of Jesus, and to discouraging profanity, blasphemy, perjury, and all improper language.

1. Promises—infidelity to promises using God's name, engaging the divine honor and faithfulness, "in some way makes God out to be a liar"

2. Profanity (Latin: *profanus*, outside the temple)—taking the name of God (Lord, Jesus, Christ) in vain (without due regard for its sacred character)

3. Blasphemy (Greek: *blasphemein*, to speak ill of): Trivializing, degrading, affronting God, saints, sacred things

4. Swearing—calling God to witness (both oaths that are disrespectful though not blasphemous, like a misuse of God's name, and false oaths like perjury, which is a lie told under oath)

5. Cursing—blasphemy by calling down evil (damnation)

"O Blessed Tongue . . ."

Thirty years after his death in 1231, St. Anthony's tomb was opened. Although his body had returned to dust, his tongue was found there miraculously preserved. St. Bonaventure, then minister general of the Franciscans (of which Anthony was a celebrated member), in veneration of this symbol of sacred eloquence, said, "O blessed tongue that always praised the Lord, and caused others to bless him, now it is manifest how great your merits were before God." (See "Incorruptibility.")

The Third Commandment

The Lord's Day Requirements

The *Catechism of the Catholic Church* counsels, "The faithful should see to it that legitimate excuses do not lead to habits prejudicial to religion, family life, and health" (see CCC #2185, citing also the CCL, #1247).

1. Worship owed to God

2. Joy proper to the Lord's Day

3. Works of mercy

4. Relaxation of mind and body

The Fourth Commandment

The *Catechism of the Catholic Church* (#2197) notes that the fourth commandment opens the second table of the Decalogue and shows us the order of charity.

The Political Community's Duty to Honor the Family

The *Catechism of the Catholic Church* (#2211) notes the need to assist and ensure especially these seven freedoms.

1. The freedom to establish and raise a family in faith

2. The protection of the stability of the marriage bond

3. The freedom to profess one's faith and raise one's children in it

4. The right to private property, free enterprise, work, housing, emigration

5. The right to medical care, aged assistance, and family benefits

6. Protection of security and health (especially against drugs, pornography)

7. The freedom to form association with other families and to be represented

Relationships Illumined by the Fourth Commandment

The *Cathechism of the Catholic Church* (#2212) teaches that our neighbor is revealed in a personal way, not as a "unit" in the human collective; but as "someone" who by his known origins deserves particular attention and respect.

1. In our brothers and sisters, we see the children of our parents.

2. In our cousins, we see the descendants of our ancestors.

3. In our fellow citizens, we see the children of our country.

4. In the baptized, we see the children of our mother the Church.

5. In every human person, we see the children of God our Father.

The Duties of Parents (See CCC #s 2221–2223.)

The *Catechism of the Catholic Church* cites Vatican II's "Declaration on Christian Education" (#3), "The role of parents in education is of such importance that it is almost impossible to provide an adequate substitute," and in #2221 says, "The right and the duty of parents to educate their children are primordial and inalienable."

1. Creating a home where tenderness, forgiveness, respect, fidelity, and disinterested service are the rule

2. Educating in virtues requiring an apprenticeship in self-denial, sound judgment, and self-mastery; subordinating "material and instinctual dimensions to interior and spiritual ones" (from *Centesimus Annus* 36.2)

3. Giving good example, acknowledging their own failings, correcting their children's failings

Conditions for Legitimate Armed Resistance to Oppression

As part of the fourth commandment and "duties of citizens," the *Catechism of the Catholic Church* (#2243) teaches that, after diplomacy, negotiation, and passive resistance, armed resistance by political authority is justified only under five specific conditions.

1. There is sure, serious, and prolonged violation of basic rights.
2. All other efforts to redress the wrong have failed.
3. Such resistance will not cause more violations.
4. There is reasonable hope of success.
5. There is no reasonable expectation of a better resolution.

The Fifth Commandment

Requirements of the Fifth Commandment (See CCC #s 2258–2317.)

1. Respect for human life
2. Respect for the dignity of persons
3. Safeguarding peace

Major Sins Against the Fifth Commandment (See CCC #s 2268–2283.)

1. Intentional homicide
2. Abortion
3. Euthanasia (mercy killing, assisted suicide)
4. Suicide

Meaning of Respect for the Dignity of Persons (See CCC #s 2284–2301.)

1. The souls of others (scandal: leading another to do evil)
2. Health (cult of the body, excess: food, alcohol, tobacco, medicine, drugs)
3. The person and scientific research (including organ transplants)
4. Bodily integrity (kidnapping, terrorism, amputation, and sterilizations)
5. The dead (honor regarding the dying, the body: autopsies, cremations)

Strict Conditions for Legitimate Defense by Military Force

The *Catechism of the Catholic Church* (#2309) includes these traditional elements of what is called the just war doctrine.

1. The damage brought on the nation or world by the aggressor must be lasting, grave, and certain.
2. All other efforts at resolution have been tried and failed or been impractical.
3. There must be well-founded hope of success.
4. The use of arms must not cause worse disorder than the evil to be stopped (a condition requiring more serious consideration than ever because of the power of modern means of destruction).

The Sixth Commandment
The Three Forms of the Virtue of Chastity

These are the distinctions of St. Ambrose, to which the *Catechism of the Catholic Church* (#2349) adds, "We do not praise any one of them to the exclusion of the others. . . . This is what makes for the richness of the discipline of the Church."

1. The chastity of spouses
2. The chastity of widows
3. The chastity of virgins

The Fruits of Chastity for the Engaged

The *Catechism of the Catholic Church* (#2350) teaches that the expressions of affection that belong to married love ought to be reserved for marriage and recognizes the rewards of this "time of testing":

1. A discovery of mutual respect
2. An apprenticeship in fidelity
3. The hope of receiving one another from God

Sins against Chastity (In addition to adultery; see CCC #s 2351–2357.)

1. Lust (disordered desire for, inordinate enjoyment of sexual pleasure)
2. Masturbation (self-stimulation for sexual pleasure outside of a marriage relationship)
3. Fornication (carnal union between unmarrieds)
4. Pornography (real or simulated sex photographed or filmed for display to third parties)
5. Prostitution (sex for pay)
6. Rape (forcible violation of the sexual intimacy of another person)
7. Homosexual activity (sexual relations between two persons of the same gender)

The Seventh Commandment
The Meaning of Respect for Human Dignity (See CCC #2407.)

1. Temperance (moderate attachment to this world's goods)
2. Justice (preserving neighbor's rights and rendering neighbor's due)
3. Solidarity; see "The Golden Rule."

Sins against the Seventh Commandment (See CCC #2409.)

1. Theft
2. Deliberate keeping of goods lent, objects lost
3. Business fraud
4. Paying unjust wages
5. Forcing up prices

6. Speculation to artificially manipulate prices

7. Corrupt influence of lawmakers

8. Private appropriation and use of common goods

9. Work poorly done

10. Tax evasion

11. Check and invoice forgery

12. Excessive expenses and waste

13. Intentional damage to private or public property

The Three Forms of Justice

1. Commutative justice

The *Catechism of the Catholic Church* (#2411) teaches that this virtue "regulates exchanges between persons in accordance with a strict respect for their rights" without which no other form of justice is possible; that it obliges strictly and "requires safeguarding property rights, paying debts, and fulfilling obligations freely contracted."

2. Legal justice

What the citizen owes in fairness to the community

3. Distributive justice

What the community owes its citizens in proportion to their contributions and needs

The Eighth Commandment

The Virtues Balanced by Truth (See CCC #2469.)

1. Honesty (what ought to be expressed)

2. Discretion (what ought to be kept secret)

The Meaning of Bearing Witness (See CCC #s 2471–2474.)

Martyrdom is the ultimate witness given to the truth of the faith.

1. Professing the faith

2. Witnessing the truth of the gospel

Sins against Truth (See CCC #s 2475–2487.)

Bearing false witness, in the original context of the Decalogue (Exodus 20:16), refers to speaking (bearing) falsely before a tribunal (witnessing). Even well before Christ, it came to mean all telling of untruth. *Libel* (publishing something defamatory) is a legal term with moral implications.

1. Lying, especially in public
   - False witness, when in court
   - Perjury, when under oath

2. Disrespecting another's reputation (slander: verbal defamation)
   - Rash judgment (assuming as true stories about another's moral fault)
   - Detraction (disclosing another's faults, however true)
   - Calumny (lying about another)
3. Encouraging another's dishonesty (by flattery, praise, or compliance)
4. Boasting
5. Irony (disparaging someone by malicious caricature)

The Ninth Commandment

St. John's Three Kinds of Covetousness (1 John 2:16)

1. Lust of the flesh (sensual lust)
2. Lust of the eyes (enticement for the eyes)
3. Pride in riches (a pretentious life)

Requirements in "the Battle for Purity" (See CCC #s 2520–2527.)

1. The virtue and gift of chastity
2. Purity of intention (seeking our true goal, God's will)
3. Purity of vision—external and internal ("avoiding entertainment inclined to voyeurism and illusion")
   - by discipline of feelings and imagination
   - by refusing all complicity in impure thoughts
4. Prayer
5. Modesty (part of temperance)
6. Purification of the social climate

An **obscenity** (Latin: *obscaenitas*, offensiveness, filthiness) is sinfully calculated to arouse sexual pleasure.

The Tenth Commandment

The *Catechism of the Catholic Church* (#2536) quotes the *Roman Catechism* (III, 37): "When the Law says, 'You shall not covet,' these words mean that we should banish our desires for whatever does not belong to us. Our thirst for another's goods is immense, infinite, never quenched. Thus it is written: 'He who loves money never has money enough.'"

The Great Commandment—Matthew 22:37, 39

1. You shall love the Lord your God with all your heart, with all your soul, and with all your mind.
2. You shall love your neighbor as yourself.

Precepts of the Church (traditional)

These duties of Catholic Christians were originally approved by the Third Plenary Council of Baltimore, 1884. The second one includes what was commonly referred to as "Easter Duty" in the days when frequent Communion was not the norm.

1. To keep holy the day of the Lord's resurrection: to worship God by participating in Mass every Sunday and holy day of obligation; to avoid those activities that would hinder renewal of soul and body; for example, needless work and business activities, unnecessary shopping, and so forth.

2. To lead a sacramental life: to receive Holy Communion frequently and the Sacrament of Reconciliation regularly; minimally, to receive the Sacrament of Reconciliation at least once a year (obligatory annually only if serious sin is involved); minimally, to receive Holy Communion at least once a year, between the first Sunday of Lent and Trinity Sunday.

3. To study Catholic teaching in preparation for Confirmation, to be confirmed, and then to continue to study and advance the cause of Christ.

4. To observe the marriage laws of the Church: to give religious training (by example and word) to one's children; to use parish schools and religious education programs.

5. To strengthen and support the Church, one's own parish community and parish priests, the worldwide Church and the Holy Father.

6. To do penance, including abstaining from meat and fasting from food on the appointed days.

7. To join in the missionary spirit and apostolate of the Church.

Precepts of the Church (CCC #s 2041–2046, 2048)

The Catechism quotes the following five precepts, makes a comment on each, and cites the *Code of Canon Law* on each.

You shall attend Mass on Sundays and holy days of obligation and rest from servile labor.

The first precept requires the faithful to sanctify these days by participating in the Eucharistic celebration when the Christian community gathers together on the day commemorating the resurrection of the Lord (citing CCL #s 1246–1248, "Sunday is the day on which the paschal mystery is celebrated in light of the apostolic tradition and is to be observed as the foremost holy day of obligation in the universal Church. . . .), and by resting from unnecessary work and activities. (See "Holy Days of Obligation" in this book.)

You shall confess your [serious] sins at least once a year.

The second precept ensures preparation for the Eucharist by the reception of the Sacrament of Reconciliation, continuing the conversion and forgiveness of Baptism (citing CCL #989, "After having attained the age of discretion, each of the faithful is bound by an obligation faithfully to confess serious sins at least once a year").

You shall receive the Sacrament of the Eucharist at least during the Easter season.

The third precept guarantees as a minimum the reception of Communion in connection with the Paschal feasts (citing CCL #920, "All the faithful, after they have been initiated into the Most Holy Eucharist, are bound by the obligation of receiving Communion at least once a year. This precept must be fulfilled during the Easter season unless it is fulfilled for a just cause at some other time during the year").

You shall observe the days of fasting and abstinence established by the Church.

The fourth precept ensures the times of penance which prepare us for the liturgical feast and help us master our instincts and freedom (CCL #s 1249–1253; see "The Penitential Observance of Lent" in this chapter).

You shall help to provide for the needs of the Church.

The fifth precept states that the faithful are obliged to assist with the material needs of the Church, according to ability (citing CCL #222: "The Christian faithful are obliged to assist with the needs of the Church so that the Church has what is necessary for divine worship, for apostolic works and works of charity and for the decent sustenance of ministers").

The Man in the Moon and the Sabbath Breaker

Some used to say that the man in the moon is leaning on a fork on which is a bundle of sticks gathered on the Sabbath. This is rooted in the Old Testament episode (Numbers 15:32–36) of a man caught gathering wood on the Sabbath. He was put to death. Some versions of this fable include a dog, as in the prologue of *A Midsummer Night's Dream*. Still others call the man in the moon *Cain*, with the thorn bush representing the thorns and briars associated with the Fall of the first humans.

Benedict the Black

Born an African slave in Sicily, Benedict was freed, then became a hermit, then a Franciscan, then a cook, and finally, though he was illiterate, superior of the house because of his holiness. On retirement, he returned to his beloved kitchen. That's probably where he made this comment about fasting that has been repeated ever since: "The greatest mortification is not to fast altogether, but to eat a little and then stop."

> ### Japanese Tempura
>
> Some have suggested that the word *tempura* comes from the Latin *Quatuor Tempora* ("four times"), a name for the Ember Days, penitential days marking the changing of the seasons. The tradition of abstaining from meat on those days each quarter was brought to Japan by Spanish and Portuguese missionaries. When this European Christian tradition met a Japanese culinary tradition, a deep-fried seafood and vegetable dish was born: tempura!

The Demands of Social Justice

The Purpose of the Church's Social Teaching (See CCC #2423.)

1. Principles for reflection   2. Criteria for judgment   3. Guidelines for action

The Relationship of Person and Society in the Human Community
(See CCC #s 1881–1885.)

1. The human person is "the principle, subject, and object of every social organization" (Vatican II, "Pastoral Constitution on the Church in the Modern World," #25.1).

2. Participation in voluntary associations and institutions should be encouraged.

3. Subsidiarity requires that "a community of a higher order should not interfere in the internal life of a community of a lower order, depriving the latter of its function . . ." (Pius XI, *Quadragesimo Anno I*, 184–186).

Principles of Participation in Social Life (See CCC #s 1897–1917.)

1. Authority (the condition by which laws are made and orders are given by individuals or institutions expecting obedience)
   • Originates with God
   • Requires due respect from all
   • Presumes the sovereignty of law instead of arbitrary human will

2. The common good (the social conditions which enable persons and groups to reach their fulfillment)
   • Presupposes respect for the human person
   • Requires social well-being and development
   • Requires a just order that is secure and stable

3. Responsibility and participation (the free and generous involvement in the dynamics of society)
   • Requires personal responsibility
   • Invites active participation in public life
   • Calls for the ongoing conversion of the social partners

Principles of Social Justice (See CCC #s 1928–1942.)

Society ensures social justice by fostering the conditions by which persons and associations receive their due.

1. Respect for persons
2. Equality and diversity of persons
3. Human solidarity—revealed in
   - the just distribution of goods
   - the just compensation for labor
   - the just negotiation of conflicts

Blessings

The Eight Beatitudes—Matthew 5:3–11; see Luke 6:20–26

1. Blessed are the poor in spirit, for theirs is the kingdom of heaven.
2. Blessed are those who mourn, for they will be comforted.
3. Blessed are the meek, for they will inherit the earth.
4. Blessed are those who hunger and thirst for righteousness, for they will be filled.
5. Blessed are the merciful, for they will receive mercy.
6. Blessed are the pure in heart, for they will see God.
7. Blessed are the peacemakers, for they will be called children of God.
8. Blessed are those who are persecuted for righteousness' sake, for theirs is the kingdom of heaven.

The eight points of the Maltese Cross represent the Beatitudes.

The Seven Beatitudes of the Book of Revelation

1. Blessed is the one who reads aloud the words of the prophecy, and . . . those who hear and who keep what is written in it . . . (1:3).
2. Blessed are the dead who from now on die in the Lord . . . (14:13).
3. Blessed is the one who stays awake . . . (16:15).
4. Blessed are those who are invited to the marriage supper of the Lamb . . . (19:9).
5. Blessed and holy are those who share in the first resurrection . . . (20:6).
6. Blessed is the one who keeps the words of the prophecy of this book (22:7).
7. Blessed are those who wash their robes, so that they will have the right to the tree of life and may enter the city by the gates . . . (22:14).

The Three Notable Duties: Prayer, Fasting, and Almsgiving

The pages that follow give information about these three "eminent good works."

Prayer

The Prayer of Jesus

Here are some references to Jesus praying, with an asterisk indicating occasions where the prayer itself is recorded.

After he was baptized (Luke 3:21)

In a lonely desert place (Mark 1:35)

Before choosing the Twelve, all night (Luke 6:12–13)

Often in lonely places (Luke 5:15–16)

Before his invitation "Come to me. . . ." (Matthew 11:25–27*)

Before feeding the five thousand (John 6:11; Matthew 14:19)

After feeding the five thousand (Matthew 14:23)

In seclusion, before eliciting Peter's act of faith (Luke 9:18)

At the transfiguration (Luke 9:28–29)

For little children (Matthew 19:13)

Before the raising of Lazarus (John 11:41–42*)

In Jerusalem at Passover (John 12:28*)

For the disciples (the "high priestly prayer of Jesus") (John 17*)

For Peter and his faith (Luke 22:31–32)

After the Last Supper (Matthew 26:26–28)

In Gethsemane (Matthew 26:39, 42, 44*)

On the cross (Luke 23:34, 46*)

The Three Dimensions of Jesus' Prayer (See CCC #2616.)

According to St. Augustine, whose conclusion is, "Therefore let us acknowledge our voice in him and his in us":

1. He prays for us as our priest.

2. He prays in us as our Head.

3. He is prayed to by us as our God.

Jesus Teaches about Prayer

Pray in these words . . . (Luke 11:1–4; Matthew 6:9–13)

Pray in secret (Matthew 6:6)

Ask and you shall receive (Matthew 7:7)

Pray in readiness for end times (Luke 21:36)

Pray for persecutors (Luke 6:28)

The power of united prayer (Matthew 18:19–20)

Persist (Luke 11:5–13)

Jesus' Three Principal Parables on Prayer (See CCC #2613.)

All are from St. Luke.

1. The importunate friend (teaching urgency) (Luke 11:5–13)

2. The importunate widow (teaching persistent patience) (Luke 18:1–8)

3. The Pharisee and the tax collector (teaching humility) (Luke 18:9–14)

The Seven Petitions of the Lord's Prayer (See CCC #s 2803–2854.)

The first three petitions are more theological, draw us toward the Father's glory, are for God's sake (thy name, thy kingdom, thy will), and are already answered in Jesus' sacrifice. The last four are ways toward God and commend our poverty to his grace (give us, forgive us, lead us not, deliver us).

1. Hallowed be thy name.

2. Thy kingdom come.

3. Thy will be done on earth as it is in heaven.

4. Give us this day our daily bread.

5. Forgive us our trespasses, as we forgive those who trespass against us.

6. Lead us not into temptation.

7. Deliver us from evil.

The Final Doxology (See CCC #s 2855–2856.)

The first three petitions of the Lord's Prayer are echoed.

1. The glorification of God's name: the kingdom

2. The power of God's saving will: the power

3. The coming of God's reign: the glory

A Spiritual Life Dynamic

First: Come (contemplation)

1. A call

— Peter and Andrew (Matthew 4:18–19, Mark 1:16–18, Luke 5:1–11)

— James and John (Matthew 4:21–22, Mark 1:19–20, Luke 5:1–11)

— Matthew (Matthew 9:9, Mark 2:14, Luke 5:27–28)

— See also John 1:35–51.

2. A retreat

— Jesus (Luke 5:15–16)

— Jesus before choosing the Twelve (Luke 6:12–13)

— Jesus and apostles (Mark 6:30–33)

Second: Go (action)

- Apostolic mandate (Matthew 10, Luke 10:1–20)

- Apostles' requirements (Luke 9:57–62)

- Courage under persecution (Luke 12:2–9)

Third: Wait

- "Remain here in this city. . ." (Luke 24:49)

- "You will receive power. . ." (Acts 1:8)

The Prayer of the Church

The New Testament, with its proclamation of the good news of Jesus Christ, contains no lamentation prayers, so common in the Old Testament. (See CCC #2630.)

Kinds of Prayer I

1. Liturgical (see Chapters 5 and 6)

Mass, sacraments, and the Liturgy of the Hours (The Eucharist is the "source and summit" of Church activity and power; see "Constitution on the Sacred Liturgy," 10, Vatican II.)

2. Paraliturgical

Lacking full liturgical form or official significance as determined by the Church

3. Devotional/communal (see Chapter 7)

a. Group—penance services, Lenten devotions, Rosary, Stations, prayer services, and so forth

b. Shared—individual prayer shared, as by Jesus in John 17

4. Personal/private prayer—"in secret," as taught by Jesus in Matthew 6:6

Kinds of Prayer II (See CCC #s 2700–2719.)

1. Vocal (conversing)

- "The need to involve the senses in interior prayer corresponds to a requirement of our human nature."

- "This need also corresponds to a divine requirement. God . . . wants the external expression that associates the body with interior prayer. . . ."

- The form of prayer most readily accessible to groups.

2. Meditation (seeking)

- "Considerations and reasonings on a religious truth" (divine knowledge; self understanding; life direction/meaning)
- Also known as discursive prayer ("reflective"), characterized by reflections of the mind (thoughts).

3. Contemplation (discovering/enjoying)

- "A gaze of faith, fixed on Jesus" (awareness of God with love and admiration)
- Also known as intuitive prayer ("immediately perceptive"), characterized by affective sentiments of the will (feelings).

The Basic Forms of Prayer (See CCC #s 2626–2643.)

1. Blessing and adoration
2. Petition, the objects of which are (in this order):
   - The grace of forgiveness
   - The fullness of the reign of God
   - Every need
3. Intercession (which is asking on behalf of another)
4. Thanksgiving
5. Praise

St. Anthony and the Child Jesus

Once as a guest in someone's home, Anthony was seen through an open window, deep in meditation and communion. He was holding Christ so single-mindedly in his heart that the Christ Child was seen in his arms. Images of Anthony with the child Jesus are common in church windows and statuary.

The Doubting Monk and the Singing Bird

A certain monk of old Hildesheim in Hanover, so the fable goes, doubted how it could be that with God 1000 years are as a day. As he pondered, he listened to the singing of a bird in the woods for three minutes . . . or so he thought, for 300 years had slipped by.

Three Notable Definitions of Prayer

1. St. Thérèse of Lisieux: "Prayer is a surge of the heart; it is a simple look turned toward heaven; it is a cry of recognition and of love, embracing both trial and joy."

2. St. John Damascene: "Prayer is the raising of one's mind and heart to God or the requesting of good things from God."

3. The *Catechism of the Catholic Church* (#2579): "[King David's] submission to the will of God, his praise, and his repentance, will be a model for the prayer of the people."

The Sources of Prayer (See CCC #s 2653–2658.)

1. The word of God

2. The liturgy of the Church

3. The virtues of faith, hope, and charity

The Sequence of Christian Prayer (See CCC #2624.)

From the very beginning, believers "devoted themselves to the apostles' teaching and fellowship, to the breaking of bread and the prayers" (Acts 2:42).

1. Founded on the apostolic faith

2. Proven by charity

3. Nourished by Eucharist

A Process of Prayer

1. Listen: "Speak, Lord, your servant is listening."

2. Reflect: "This is the Lord speaking."

3. Wait: "Your will be done" (Matthew 6:10; Psalms 46 and 130)

4. Receive/respond.

Lectio Prayer

Using the word of God, one is led by the Spirit to the highest levels of communion with God; enshrined in Benedictine spirituality; expressed in the classic wording of Guigo II, a twelfth-century Carthusian abbot in his *Ladder of Monks*, "Seek in reading and you will find in meditating; knock in mental prayer and it will be opened to you by contemplation."

1. Reading (an exercise of the outward senses) provides the subject matter for meditation.

2. Meditation (thinking) is concerned with understanding; it digs for treasure which it finds and reveals, but which is beyond its power to seize.

3. Prayer (responding) is concerned with desire; this prayer lifts itself up to God with all strength and begs for the treasure it longs for.

4. Contemplation (resting) outstrips every faculty; (when it comes) it rewards the labors of the other three, "inebriating the thirsting soul with the dew of heavenly sweetness."

The Motive for Prayer

1. To give (as an end in itself) praise and thanks

2. To receive (as a means) faith, courage, insight, mercy, and so forth

The Principal Difficulties in Prayer

The *Catechism of the Catholic Church* (#s 2729–2731) notes these, as well the remedy "which lies in faith, conversion, and vigilance (custody of the heart)."

Distraction, dryness

Two Frequent Temptations Threatening Prayer

The *Catechism of the Catholic Church* distinguishes these from "difficulties" (#s 2732–2733), defining *acedia* as "a form of depression stemming from lax ascetical practice that leads to discouragement."

Lack of faith, acedia

A Prayerful Glossary

Access Prayers
Formerly, prayers of a priest before Mass

Aspiration ("ejaculation")
Prayerful phrase uttered in one breath

Benediction
Generally, a blessing; specifically, the common term for Eucharistic devotion

Blessing
Praise; scripturally: the desire that good fortune attend a person or a thing, dedication of a person or a thing to God's service; liturgically: a cleric's sanctification of persons or things to divine service, and/or invocation of divine favor upon them

Consecration (Ordinary)
A prayer of commitment of self-giving to God through Christ (like that of St. Ignatius Loyola). Since it only makes more conscious what happened at Baptism–Confirmation, it obliges one no more than ordinary discipleship does. Such prayer should always be related to Baptism and associated with Eucharist (offertory). The classic form is the renewal of baptismal vows. In recent centuries, particular acts   proliferated, often involving the inspiration of some saint because of his or her unique relationship to Christ.

Consecration (Total)
More all-embracing, beyond normal gospel demands, patterning the spiritual life on Mary, totally dedicated to Christ. Originated by Odilo of Cluny (d. 1049) and developed by St. Grignon de Montfort (d. 1716).

Eulogia **(Greek: good speaking)**
Blessing (a benediction, in apostolic days), or sometimes a blessed object (especially bread).

Exorcism
The formal exorcism rite is for driving out evil spirits in cases of demonic possession and consists of a series of prayers, blessings, and commands spoken by a priest/bishop ("exorcist"); rare today, and only with the bishop's permission. Lesser forms, not implying the state of possession, are used in the Scrutinies and in Baptism, in the blessing of certain objects, and even by some in private prayer.

Gregorian chant
The form of musical worship revised and introduced into the liturgy by Pope Gregory the Great (600). It probably derived from Jewish sources, and is the oldest chant in current use. It is a form of "plain song," with no definite rhythm.

Invocation
The prayerful and humble appeal to God for mercy, love, and/or generally divine assistance. It could also be to angels or saints, for supernatural help.

Itinerarium

A prayer for a safe journey

Novena

A prayer with a specific intention offered nine days in a row, originating in the nine (*novem*) days of prayer by the disciples and Mary between the Ascension and Pentecost. Many novenas have been highly indulgenced by the Holy See over the centuries. A "novena of grace" was traditionally in March. A "Christmas Novena" begins December 16 and honors the mystery of Christmas. Today the recommended (and only scriptural) novena is the one before Pentecost.

Trisagion (**try-SAHG-ee-on**), **Greek: three, holy**

A common Eastern Catholic liturgical hymn characterized by a threefold invocation such as: "Holy God, holy and mighty, holy and immortal, have mercy on us" (modeled on Isaiah 6:3).

Fast and Abstinence (See CCC #s 1434, 1438, 2015, 2043.)

Definitions

1. **Fasting** refers to limitations on food and drink. Until 1966, in the modern Church, the regulations for days of fast prescribed taking only one full daily meal, plus breakfast and a "collation" (light meal).

2. **Abstaining**, in this context, means refraining from certain kinds of food or drink, typically meat. From the first century, the day of the crucifixion has been traditionally observed as a day of abstaining from flesh meat ("black fast") to honor Christ who sacrificed his flesh on a Friday.

Obligations

Formerly, fast days consisted of all Lenten days except Sunday. Fast and abstinence days were Ash Wednesday, Lenten Fridays, and Saturdays, Ember Days, the vigils of certain feasts. Current practice reflects the 1966 instructions of Pope Paul VI's constitution *Paenitemini* in which:

1. The meaning of fasting was emphasized.

2. The obligation was restated.

3. The extent of the obligation was changed.

4. The universal fast and abstinence days, Ash Wednesday and Good Friday, were confirmed.

5. Some other act of penance should be followed on Fridays if abstinence from meat is not practiced.

6. Specific regulations were left to bishops in their episcopal conferences (see below for "The Penitential Observance of Lent").

Eucharistic Fast (CCC #1387.)

Fasting before Communion has been a practice from ancient times. It was prescribed by the Councils of Carthage (254) and Antioch (268) and became universal practice by the fifth century.

Prior to 1953 the faithful fasted from midnight on, including from water and medicine (viaticum being an exception). In 1953 and again in 1957, Pope Pius XII reduced the time to three hours from solid food and alcoholic drink (from before Mass for the priest and from before Communion for the laity); non-alcoholic drink, one hour; water no longer included in the fast. In 1964, Pope Paul VI further reduced the fast to one hour, including all food and drink, allowing water and medicine any time. In 1973 the fast was reduced to fifteen minutes for the elderly and sick, including those attending them if one hour would be too difficult.

The Penitential Observance of Lent

Even by the time of Christ, fasting and abstaining were venerable traditions of piety among the Jews. The practices were not foreign to Christ (Matthew 6:16; Mark 2:20, 9:29) or the apostles (Acts 13:2, 14:23). In the early Church, a two or three day Lenten fast was common. It was not until the fourth century and the Council of Nicaea that a forty-day period was mentioned. In the Middle Ages, the rule relaxed somewhat, with a light second meal and fish allowed. From time to time and place to place, there has been variation in practice, but consistency of spirit: the life of a Christian is a life of penance. The following is an outline of the *Code of Canon Law*, #1249f.

1. The Season of Lent preserves its penitential character.

2. The days of penance are Ash Wednesday and all Fridays in Lent.

3. The manner of fulfilling the precept of penance:
   - Ash Wednesday and Good Friday are days of fast and abstinence.
   - All Fridays in Lent are days of abstinence only.

4. Church Law binds as follows:
   - The law of abstinence (not eating meat) obliges those who have completed their fourteenth year.
   - The law of fast (only one full meal each day, nothing between meals) obliges those who have completed their eighteenth year until the beginning of their sixtieth year.
   - Proportionately grave inconvenience excuses from the laws of fast and abstinence.

5. The substantial observance of these laws is a grave obligation.
   - Anyone who neglects all forms of penance violates divine law and is guilty of grave sin.
   - Anyone who occasionally violates the law of fast and/or abstinence is not guilty of sin.

Almsgiving

Stewardship

The practice of considering and treating all things, the earth and one's own life (time, talent, and treasure) as belonging to God, and oneself as the manager, or "steward" (See 1 Corinthians 4:1–2; 1 Peter 4:10.)

Tithing

Tithing means giving away a portion of one's income, commonly a tenth. In the Old Testament, it involved paying a tenth part of one's property as a tax to one's superior (Genesis 14), and also giving a tenth of the fruit of the land and increase of the flocks and herds to God. (See especially Malachi 3:10, and also Leviticus 27:30–32; Numbers 18:21–32; Deuteronomy 12:5, 6, 11, 17, 18; 14:23, 28; 26:12; 2 Chronicles 31:5f.)

Sacrificial Giving

A voluntary, proportionate, systematic, sacrificial, and liturgical giving of money that is part of the larger self-giving of time, talent, and treasure. ("Church support" is not the same as sacrificial giving, but is a by-product of it.)

1. Voluntary—neither an assessment nor a tax (which the "tithe" became).

2. Proportionate—like the widow Jesus praised, though she gave little (Luke 21:2).

- The Old Testament "tithe" was literally ten percent (of gross income): that may be too much for some, too little for others.
- It includes paychecks, dividends, social security payments, allowances, windfalls, and so on.

3. Systematic (planned)
   - Part of the budget
   - As income is received (not "when somebody needs it")
4. Sacrificial
   - "Making holy" (the literal meaning of "sacrifice") the earnings and efforts of the week
   - If it doesn't hurt (require a sacrifice), it's only a donation, or a contribution, not sacrificial giving, which is a measure of one's trust in God.
5. Liturgical—the bringing forth of the gifts and the offering of money are both part of the same ritual act.
   - Collections at other times and donations in other ways lack this Eucharistic context and don't "consecrate" hours worked and income received
   - Using envelopes gives witness to commitment
6. Giving (usually divided)
   - Half is given weekly by way of the local parish collection.
   - Half is set aside for independent giving (mission appeals, diocesan collections, personal favorite charities, and so forth).

Sin

The Rebellious Angels

There is no one Scripture passage that tells the story of the fallen angels in the way that, for example, Genesis describes the fall of the first humans. The following passages taken together, however, form the foundation of the Church's belief about the origin of evil and the devil.

1. Lucifer's Five "I Wills"

How you are fallen from heaven,
O Day Star, son of the Dawn!
How you are cut down to the ground,
you who laid the nations low!
You said in your heart,
"I will ascend to heaven;
I will raise up my throne
above the stars of God;
I will sit on the mount of assembly . . .
I will ascend to the tops of the clouds,
I will make myself like the Most High."
But you are brought down to the She'ol,
to the depths of the Pit.

—Isaiah 14:12–15

2. The Heavenly Battle

And war broke out in heaven; Michael and his angels fought against the dragon. The dragon and his angels fought back, but they were defeated, and there was no longer any place for them in heaven. The great dragon was thrown down, that ancient serpent, who is called the Devil and Satan, the deceiver of the whole world—was thrown down to earth, and his angels were thrown down with him.

—Revelation 12:7–9

3. The Fallen Angels

For if God did not spare the angels when they sinned, but cast them into hell and committed them to chains . . . to be kept until judgment. . . .

—2 Peter 2:4

. . . I cast you as a profane thing from the mountain of God, and the guardian cherub drove you out from among the stones of fire. Your heart was proud because of your beauty; you corrupted your wisdom for the sake of splendor. . . .

—Ezekiel 28:16–17

And the angels who did not keep their own position, but left their proper dwelling, he has kept in eternal chains in deepest darkness for the judgment of the great Day. . . .

—Jude 6

. . . I watched Satan fall from heaven like a flash of lightning. . . .

—Jesus, Luke 10:18

There is no repentance for angels after their fall, just as there is no repentance for men after death.

—St. John Damascene

> ### *The Four Horsemen of the Apocalypse*
>
> This timeless image of evil is from Revelation 6:1–8; see Zechariah 1:8–10, 6:1–3.
>
> War (white), violence (red), famine (black), and death (green)

Original Sin

The *Catechism of the Catholic Church* speaks of "freedom put to the test" (#396), calling it a sin contracted and not committed, a state and not an act (#404).

1. Original sin (with and in which we are born)

2. Actual sin (which we commit, by omission and commission)

The Triple Concupiscence that Followed the Fall

The *Catechism of the Catholic Church* (#377) cites 1 John 2:16 about this human condition of bondage.

1. Carnal allurements (inordinate desire for sensuality)

2. Enticements for the eye (avarice for material things)

3. The life of empty show (pride and arrogance, independence from God)

The Three Great Preternatural Gifts

This traditional wording refers to the possessions of Adam and Eve before the fall, to which humans now have no title.

1. Infused knowledge   2. Absence of concupiscence   3. Bodily immortality

The Original State of Justice Lost by Original Sin

This is the wording of the *Catechism of the Catholic Church* (#400).

1. The control of the soul's spiritual faculties over the body is shattered.

2. The union of man and woman becomes subject to tensions, their relations now marked by lust and domination.

3. Harmony with creation is broken.

4. Death makes its entrance into human history.

The Effects of Original Sin

1. Human nature corrupted

2. Understanding darkened

3. Will weakened

4. Strong inclination to do evil

Human Nature

According to the *Catechism of the Catholic Church* (#405), human nature isn't totally corrupted: its natural powers are wounded; it is subject to ignorance, suffering, and the power of death; it is inclined to sin—what we call *concupiscence*. Baptism takes away original sin and turns us toward God, but the consequences remain: we are weakened and inclined to evil; as a result we must do spiritual battle.

The Church's teaching on the transmission of original sin became more precise at two points in history, when errors needed to be corrected (see CCC #406):

1. In the fifth century, especially in St. Augustine's reflections against Pelagianism. Pelagius, the champion of human effort, held that a person could lead a morally good life by the natural power of free will and without the help of God's grace, thus reducing the influence of Adam's sin to bad example.

2. In the sixteenth century, in response to the Protestant Reformation. At the opposite extreme of Pelagius, the first reformers held that original sin has radically perverted human nature and destroyed human freedom, and they identified it with the tendency to evil, a tendency which is insurmountable. ("Man is basically evil.") Instead, the Church has consistently taught that humans have a wounded nature inclined to evil.

Some Humanistic Explanations for Sin(s) apart from Revelation

(See CCC #387.)

1. A developmental flaw

2. A psychological weakness

3. A mistake

4. The necessary consequence of an inadequate social structure

Why Did God not Prevent Adam and Eve from Sinning?

These are some reflections on this timeless question cited in the *Catechism of the Catholic Church* (#412).

- St. Augustine: "Almighty God, because he is supremely good, would never allow any evil whatsoever to exist in his works if he were not so all-powerful and good as to cause good to emerge from evil itself."

- St. Leo the Great: "Christ's inexpressible grace gave us blessings better than those the demon's envy had taken away."

- St. Thomas Aquinas: "There is nothing to prevent human nature's being raised up to something greater, even after sin; God permits evil in order to draw forth some greater good."

- St. Paul: "Where sin increased, grace abounded all the more."

- The Church, singing the Exultet at the Easter Vigil: "O happy fault, which gained for us so great a Redeemer!"

Flowers in the Garden of Eden

Flowers must have grown in paradise. Certainly, there have been legends about this. One of them says that there was only one plant salvaged from the Garden of Eden, the lign aloe. Adam took with him one of these Paradise Shoots, from which all lign aloes have descended.

The Rose of Paradise

Before it became a flower of earth, the rose grew thornless in paradise. Only after Adam sinned did it take on thorns to remind humankind of the sin committed and the fall from grace. The fragrance and beauty remain, however, as a reminder of the splendor of paradise. The rose continues to be a classic symbol of Mary, the new Eve, the rose without thorns.

Eve's Tears

Lilies of the Valley sprung up, it is said, wherever Eve's repentant tears fell as she was banished from Eden. In England and France, these same flowers are named after the new Eve: Our Lady's Tears. For centuries, this symbol of humility and purity has been dedicated to Mary.

Actual Sin

"Lead us not into Temptation"

The *Catechism of the Catholic Church* (#2847) explains that this sixth petition of the Lord's Prayer means "Do not allow us to enter into temptation." It makes the following distinction:

1. Trials (necessary for spiritual growth)

2. Temptation (leading to sin and death)

Paul's "Sin Lists"

1 Corinthians 6:9–10, Galatians 5:19–21, Ephesians 5:5, Colossians 3:5, 1 Timothy 1:19–20

Kinds of Actual Sin

1. Venial (Latin: *venia*; grace, pardon) does not forfeit grace (See Matthew 12:31.)

2. Mortal (Latin: *mors, morte*, death) (See 1 John 5:16–17.)

Cooperation in the Sin of Another

Causing	Approving
1. Advice or counsel	5. Praise
2. Command	6. Concealment or silence
3. Provocation	7. Participation
4. Consent	8. Enjoyment of results
	9. Defense

Greater and Lesser Evils

It was the fifteenth-century theologian Thomas à Kempis who advised making the best of a bad situation when he said, "Of two evils, the lesser is always to be chosen" *(De duobus malis, minus est semper eligendum)*. If that's not the way he said it, it's the way we repeat it.

The Effects of Venial Sin

1. Lessening of the love of God in the heart

2. Weakening of the power to resist

The Double Consequence of Sin

In the *Catechism of the Catholic Church* (#1472):

1. Sin damages (or destroys, with grave sin) communion with God and the Church.

2. Sin creates an unhealthy attachment to creatures which must be purified either in this life or after death through a purgation (see "Purgatory") which frees the person from the temporal punishment due to sin.

The Seven Capital Sins (See CCC #1866.)

Christian experience has distinguished these sins as capital, following St. John Cassian and St. Gregory the Great, because they engender other sins and vices.

1. Pride
2. Covetousness
3. Lust
4. Anger
5. Gluttony
6. Envy
7. Sloth

The Seven Christian Virtues

1. Humility
2. Liberality
3. Chastity
4. Gentleness
5. Temperance
6. Brotherly love
7. Diligence

Three Elements of a Mortal Sin

1. Grievous matter
2. Sufficient reflection
3. Full consent of the will

The Six Sins against the Holy Spirit

The *Catechism of the Catholic Church* (#1864) cites Mark 3:29, "Whoever blasphemes against the Holy Spirit never has forgiveness, but is guilty of an eternal sin" (see also Matthew 12:32, Luke 12:10), and then explains that God's mercy has no limits, but that a person who refuses to accept his mercy by repenting rejects forgiveness and the salvation offered by the Holy Spirit. This hardness of heart can lead to a refusal to repent at the time of death and to eternal loss.

1. Despair of one's salvation (of God's mercy)
2. Presumption of saving oneself without merit
3. Resisting the known truth
4. Envy of the graces received by others
5. Obstinacy in one's sins
6. Final impenitence

Sins that Cry to Heaven for Vengeance

These are from the catechetical tradition. (See also CCC #1867.)

1. The blood of Abel (Genesis 4:10) or willful murder
2. The sin of the Sodomites (Genesis 18:20, 19:13) or sins against nature
3. The cry of the people oppressed in Egypt (Exodus 3:7–10) or oppression of those who are poor
4. The cry of the alien, the widow, and the orphan (Exodus 20:20–22) or oppression of aliens, widows, and orphans
5. Injustice to the wage earner (Deuteronomy 24:14–15, James 5:4) or defrauding laborers of their just wages

The End and Eternity

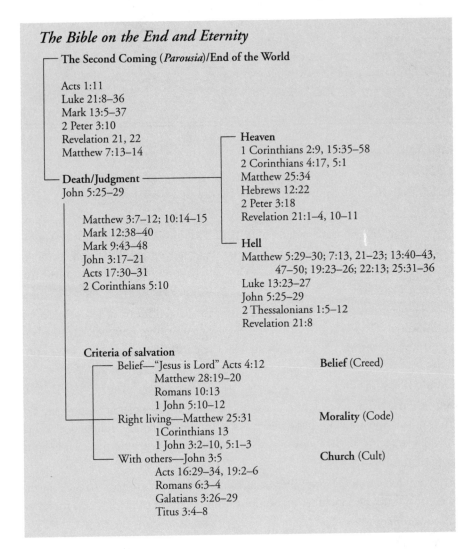

The Bible on the End and Eternity

The Second Coming (*Parousia*)/End of the World

Acts 1:11
Luke 21:8–36
Mark 13:5–37
2 Peter 3:10
Revelation 21, 22
Matthew 7:13–14

Death/Judgment
John 5:25–29

Matthew 3:7–12; 10:14–15
Mark 12:38–40
Mark 9:43–48
John 3:17–21
Acts 17:30–31
2 Corinthians 5:10

Heaven
1 Corinthians 2:9, 15:35–58
2 Corinthians 4:17, 5:1
Matthew 25:34
Hebrews 12:22
2 Peter 3:18
Revelation 21:1–4, 10–11

Hell
Matthew 5:29–30; 7:13, 21–23; 13:40–43,
47–50; 19:23–26; 22:13; 25:31–36
Luke 13:23–27
John 5:25–29
2 Thessalonians 1:5–12
Revelation 21:8

Criteria of salvation
Belief—"Jesus is Lord" Acts 4:12   **Belief (Creed)**
Matthew 28:19–20
Romans 10:13
1 John 5:10–12
Right living—Matthew 25:31   **Morality (Code)**
1 Corinthians 13
1 John 3:2–10, 5:1–3
With others—John 3:5   **Church (Cult)**
Acts 16:29–34, 19:2–6
Romans 6:3–4
Galatians 3:26–29
Titus 3:4–8

The Four Last Things

Death, judgment, heaven, and hell

Death

The Meaning of Death (See CCC #s 1007–1009.)

1. Death is the end of earthly life.

2. Death is a consequence of sin.

3. Death is transformed by Christ.

Redemptive Dolphin

A symbol of the redemption, the dolphin is found on some of the oldest tombs. The dolphin is thought by some to be the most sophisticated and majestic of all marine life. It was said that it carried the souls of the saved "across the sea" to the land of the blessed.

Death Talk

Ars Moriendi

The "art of dying" is acquired, it is said, by the practice of right living.

Ante Mortem

This particular "before death" refers to the period of imminent death. An *ante mortem* or deathbed statement (*novissima verba*, final words), even legally, is well considered, since a person who is dying is presumed to have no reason to tell anything but the truth.

The Great Promise

This is the twelfth of the twelve promises from the Sacred Heart of Jesus to Margaret Mary Alacoque (1647–1690). It promises the grace of final perseverance and a safe refuge in the last moment for the dying (on the condition of the nine First Fridays and the proper dispositions).

The Last Blessing

Given after the last anointing, this apostolic blessing brings a plenary indulgence: "By the power the Apostolic See has given me, I grant you a plenary indulgence and pardon for all your sins, in the name of the Father and of the Son and of the Holy Spirit."

Litany of the Dying

This "Commendation of a Soul Departing" follows the Anointing of the Sick for those in danger of death and includes invocations to the saints to pray for God's mercy.

In articulo mortis

"In the grasp of death" was the expression, more graphic than the simple "in extremis," for the moment of death/before death, especially referring to dying words, a last conscious significant statement.

Passing Bell

In simpler times, a bell was rung when a person was critically ill to hold at bay any evil that was said to lurk about a dying person that would cling to a soul passing from its body. In addition, this bell announced the passing of a soul from this world to the next and invited the escorting prayer by the faithful for its safe passage.

Soul Bell

In some locales the parish church bells would be tolled before a parishioner's funeral. The number of times the bells would be rung would equal the age of the deceased.

The Celebration of Funerals

The Church's Purpose at a Funeral (See CCC #1684.)

1. For the deceased: the expression of an effective communion
2. For the assembly: a participation in that communion
3. For the community: the proclamation of eternal life

Funeral Rites (See CCC #s 1686–1690.)

Vatican II called for a revision to express the Paschal character of Christian death and also a special Mass for the funeral of a child. Our current *Order of Christian Funerals* came into practice in 1989. Its three parts correspond to the three places in which rites are conducted: home, church, and cemetery.

1. Vigil (and related rites and prayers)

- Prayers after death
- Gathering in the presence of the body
- Transfer of the body to the church or place of committal

A "wake," now synonymous with the one or two days before a funeral, was historically simply any watch, or vigil, as before a major holiday. Only later did it become, for some, the watch over a body before burial.

2. Funeral Liturgy

"The Mass of the Resurrection" is an incorrect title for a funeral and is reserved only for the Easter liturgy itself. It was once called the "Requiem Mass" because of the first Latin word *(Requiescat)* of the introit: "Eternal rest grant unto them, O Lord. . . ."

3. Rite of Committal

All who die in the Church have a right to a Church burial in consecrated ground. A Catholic cemetery is blessed by a bishop. A Catholic may choose to be buried in a non-Catholic cemetery, in which case the person's grave can be individually blessed. (*A campo santo* is a consecrated cemetery, especially one whose surface soil is said to have been brought from Jerusalem, the burial place of Christ.)

Funeral Rites Allowed (See the *Code of Canon Law* #1184.)

For baptized members of another Church or ecclesial community:

1. If this would not be contrary to the wishes of the deceased
2. If the minister of the Church in which the deceased was a regular member or communicant is unavailable

Funeral Rites Denied

Assuming there was no sign of repentance before death:

1. Notorious apostates, heretics, and schismatics
2. Those who, for anti-Christian motives, were cremated
3. Manifest sinners for whom a Catholic funeral would scandalize the faithful

Tradition and Terminology

Casket orientation

Some keep the tradition of positioning caskets at funerals with the feet of the deceased to the east (oriented), as they often are in cemeteries. There was a day when a priest's body, however, was placed with his head to the east instead, signifying his relative position at liturgy.

Chapelle Ardente

Chapel for a body to lie in state.

Clothing the dead for burial (traditionally)

1. Bishops and priests: in their liturgical vestments
2. Religious: in their habits
3. Lay: appropriately clothed, preferably holding crucifix or rosary

Dies Irae

The "Day of Wrath" is a medieval hymn about Judgment Day; formerly used as a sequence at funerals and the Mass for the Dead and All Souls' Day; based on Joel 2:31 and probably written by Thomas of Celano (d. 1255).

In Memoriam (Fidelium Defunctorum)

"In memory of the faithful departed." Applied to the means of human assistance to the departed in purgatory; now more commonly referring to the cherished memory of the earthly virtues, achievements of the deceased.

Month's Mind

The special Mass offered for a deceased on or near the thirtieth day after the person's death or burial. (Use of the catafalque has been abolished.)

Pall (Latin: *pallium*, cloak)

A sacred covering; at a funeral, the cloth over a casket, recalling the white garment of the newly baptized; also, at least formerly, a veil placed over a nun at certain orders' profession ceremonies.

Pro Defunctis

Memorial of the dead

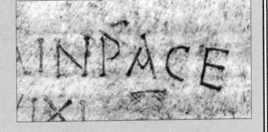
The Resurrection of the Body

Scripture

See 2 Maccabees 7:9, Daniel 12:2, Matthew 27:53, 1 Corinthians 15:35–38, 2 Corinthians 4:14, Philippians 3:21.

Properties of the Glorified Body

"Sown in weakness, raised in power" (1 Corinthians 15:42) describes a body totally submissive to the Spirit.

1. Lucid
2. Agile (movement through space with speed of thought)
3. Immortal
4. Impassible (incapable of suffering, but not insufferable!)
5. Spiritual

The Manner of the Resurrection

1. The redeemed rise in their own body (identity).
2. The redeemed rise in their entire body (entirety).
3. The redeemed rise in their immortal body (immortality).

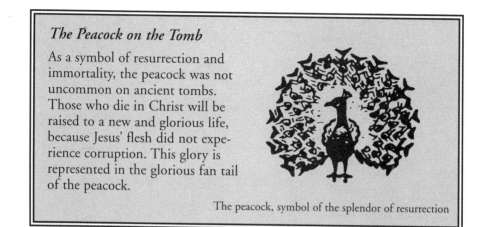

The Peacock on the Tomb

As a symbol of resurrection and immortality, the peacock was not uncommon on ancient tombs. Those who die in Christ will be raised to a new and glorious life, because Jesus' flesh did not experience corruption. This glory is represented in the glorious fan tail of the peacock.

The peacock, symbol of the splendor of resurrection

The Phoenix of the Resurrection

According to one legend, this eagle-like bird lives to an age of 500 years, whereupon it flies to Heliopolis, Egypt, and incinerates itself upon the temple's high altar. The temple priest finds among the ashes a small worm of sweet savor. From this worm evolves a bird, which attains full growth as the phoenix on the fourth day, and then departs with its youth renewed. According to another legend the phoenix, having reached 500 years of age, builds a nest of fragrant twigs and spices. These are set ablaze by the heat of the sun (or by the fanning of the bird's wings) and the phoenix is consumed by the fire. Resurrected and young, it rises from the ashes destined to live another 500 years.

Life Everlasting

In its treatment of this last article of the Christian creed, the *Catechism of the Catholic Church* (#s 1020–1050) teaches about these seven topics.

1. The particular judgment
2. Heaven
3. The final purification (purgatory)
4. Hell
5. The resurrection of all the dead
6. The last judgment
7. The new heaven and the new earth

Terms

Beatific Vision

The "blessed" sight of God, especially as a gift at the moment of death. (See Isaiah 6:1–5, Acts 7:55–56.)

Gabriel's Hounds

Actually, wild geese in flight ("gabble ratchet"). The common sound of these magnificent birds is not unlike the sound of a pack of hounds in full cry. An old fable had it that this sound was the wail of the unbaptized, wandering the air until judgment day.

Heaven

". . . to be with Abraham" (*"Abraham's bosom"* in some translations)

Luke's description (16:22) of the abode of the dead for just persons who died before Christ, before they were admitted to the beatific vision.

Kingdom of God

New Jerusalem

Paradise (Greek: *paradeisos,* park, Garden of Eden, paradise)

Used three times in Scripture as a synonym for heaven:

1. By Jesus, speaking to the good thief—Luke 23:43

2. By Paul, about a Christian "caught up into paradise"—2 Corinthians 12:4

3. In Revelation, referring to "the tree of life in God's paradise"—Revelation 2:7

Limbo

The *limbus* (Latin: edge, fringe) of heaven. A scriptural notion, though the word is not in the Bible; a theological attempt to reconcile the necessity of Baptism (John 3:5) with God's eternal mercy. (See Baptism in Chapter 5.)

St. Dorothea's Roses

St. Dorothea was a victim of the Diocletian persecution of the early fourth century. According to legend, she was scoffed at by Theophilus, the judge's secretary, as she was being led to execution: "Send me some roses and fruit when you get to paradise, Dorothea." Within moments of her execution an angel appeared to him, bearing a basket of apples and roses inscribed, "From Dorothea, in paradise."

Seven heavens

A popular notion, never defined by the Church, that heaven has a seven-tiered hierarchy of beatitude, the highest being seventh heaven.

Angels

Definition

Heavenly beings, genderless, of a fixed population, who neither marry nor are given in marriage (Mark 12:25); distinct from saints (which humans may become); mentioned nearly 300 times in the Bible.

The Three Triads of Celestial Hierarchy

1. Counselors (angels of the Presence)—seraphim (Isaiah 6:2), cherubim (Exodus 10), thrones

2. Governors (angels over forces of nature)—dominations, virtues, powers

3. Messengers (angels ministering directly to humans)—principalities, archangels, angels

The Nine Choirs of Angels

The choirs (classes) are listed in ascending order, named according to their traditionally assigned duties (see Colossians 1:16; Romans 8:38).

1. Angels

Various symbols associated with them: musical instruments, thuribles, shields, scrolls, passion emblems

2. Archangels (named on next page)

Chief angels, mentioned twice in the New Testament (Jude 6, 9; 1 Thessalonians 4:16) as distinct from guardian angels; messengers from God in significant matters

3. Principalities

Depicted as carrying scepters with which they direct God's commands. With archangels and angels they are the heavenly multitude that is in God's ordinary and immediate service in what pertains to the visible world. It was said that countries are assigned to certain principalities.

4. Powers

Shown with swords; given their name because of their special power in restraining the assault of the evil spirit

5. Virtues

Charged with dispensing celestial miracles and accomplishing stupendous works

6. Dominations

Shown in royal robes and crowned for their authority; movers of stars and planets

7. Thrones

Shown in a kneeling posture of adoration; referred to also in Psalm 9:4, ". . . you have maintained my just cause; you have sat on the throne giving righteous judgment."

8. Cherubim (plural of cherub)

Angels of wisdom, guardians and protectors, stationed at Eden (Genesis 3:24), image erected in gold on the ark of the covenant (Exodus 25:18), bore YHWH to the rescue of David (2 Samuel 22:11); pictured as four-eyed, blue-winged, and presenting a book, representative of their great knowledge

9. Seraphim (plural of seraph, "to burn")

Shown with six red wings and eyes; highest choir of angels, named for the seraphim of Isaiah 6:2; distinguished by their burning zeal and love for the Trinity

> ### The Good-Friday Born
> There is an ancient superstition that those born on Good Friday or Christmas Day have the power to see and command spirits.

The Seven Archangels

Three of the names are biblical (the "saints" below); other names and material evolved out of tradition and are gleaned from Jewish apocryphal books (such as Enoch). The "seven" of Tobit (12:15) refers not necessarily to that specific number but symbolically to all those ministers who are entitled to stand before God ready to do his bidding. The meaning of each name is in parentheses.

St. Michael (One who is like God.)

Angel of God's power; leader of the heavenly host (Daniel 10:13, 21; 12:1; Jude 9; Revelation 12:7–17); cast Lucifer and fallen angels from heaven (Revelation 12:7–9; see Ezekiel 28:17); disputed with Satan over Moses' body; Israel's protector; leader of the archangels; considered to be the angel who executes the decision on each person's eternal destiny on judgment day (hence the scales insignia)

St. Gabriel (God is my strength.)

Angel of God's dignity, "Hero of God"; angel of the annunciation (Luke 1:19, 26); explained a vision to Daniel (Daniel 8:16); the "one in rapid flight" (Daniel 9:21); angel of the day of judgment, blowing his horn for the assembling of the nations

St. Raphael (God is my health.)

Has symbolic association with Jesus' priesthood; instructor of Tobit and guardian of Tobias; the angel who moved the waters of the pool when Christ worked a miracle in John 5:1–4; chief of guardian angels

Uriel (God is my light.)

Interpreter of prophecy; guarded Jesus' tomb (see Matthew 28:2); appeared to Ezra in a dream

Jophiel (The beauty of God.)

Has symbolic association with God's splendor; drove Adam and Eve out of Eden (see Genesis 3:24)

Chamael

Angel of God's wrath; wrestled with Jacob; appeared to Jesus in Gethsemane

Zadkiel (The righteousness of God.)

Angel of God's justice; stopped Abraham from sacrificing Isaac

Jophkiel (The purity of God.)

Guided the Jews in the wilderness

The Presence and Ministry of Angels

The *Catechism of the Catholic Church* (#s 332–336) cites many notable instances:

In the Scriptures

Closed the earthly paradise—Genesis 3:24

Defended Lot—Genesis 19

Delivered Hagar and her child—Genesis 21:17

Stayed Abraham's hand—Genesis 22:11

Communicated the law by their ministry—Acts 7:53

Led God's people—Exodus 23:20

Announced vocations and births—Judges 13

Helped the prophets—Isaiah 6:6; 1 Kings 19:5

Announced (Gabriel) the birth of the forerunner and of Jesus himself—
Luke 1:11–20, 26–38

Directed Joseph about Mary—Matthew 1:20

Evangelized the shepherds at Jesus' birth—Luke 2:9–12

Praised God at Jesus' birth—Luke 2:13–14; Hebrews 1:6

Protected Jesus in his infancy—Matthew 2:13, 19–20

Served Jesus in the desert—Matthew 4:11

Constantly ready to deliver Jesus—Matthew 26:53

Strengthened Jesus in his agony in the garden—Luke 22:43

Evangelized Jesus' followers at the resurrection—Mark 16:5–7

In the liturgy

The angels are joined in praising the "holy, holy, holy Lord" God.

The angels' assistance is invoked ("We pray that your angel may take . . .").

The angels' help is sought at a funeral ("May the angels lead you . . . ").

In our lives

The angels surround our life from infancy to death (see, for example, Matthew 18:10; Luke 16:22; Psalms 34:7, 91:10–13; Job 33:23–24; Zechariah 1:12; Tobit 12:11–15).

When Blackberries Turn Tasteless

According to legend, this happens on September 29, after which they are left for the birds. This is Michaelmas Day, honoring the archangel who drove Lucifer out of heaven. In honor of the occasion, the devil spits on the blackberries, leaving them tasteless.

Purgatory

Purgatory is the suffering of the faithful which causes a "purging" of temporal punishment due to sin. It is explained in the *Catechism of the Catholic Church* (#1054) as a process (not a place) a purification after death for those who are saved, so that they may achieve the holiness necessary to enter heaven. It is implied in Scripture (Revelation 6:9–11; 1 Peter 3:18–19), taught by the early fathers, and defined by the Church (especially the Council of Florence, 1439). Pope Paul VI (in his apostolic constitution *Indulgentiarum Doctrina*, 5) reminds us, "A perennial link of charity exists between the faithful who have already reached their heavenly home, those who are expiating their sins in purgatory, and those who are still pilgrims on earth. Between them there is, too, an abundant exchange of all good things."

St. Patrick's Purgatory

There is a cave with this name in Ireland on an islet in Lough Derg, Country Donegal. In the Middle Ages there was a church and a man-made cavern on the island, and it became a great place of pilgrimage. Behind this island's notoriety was an English Cistercian monk, Henry of Saltrey, who wrote of the adventures and punishments of one Owen, or Sir Owain, a knight of King Stephan's court, who descended into "purgatory" on an Irish island.

This popularized the thousand-year-old legend of St. Patrick's Purgatory. The story goes that an earthly purgatory was set up by Patrick, or that God granted him the ability to see and show to others the punishment of sinners, thereby bolstering his teachings with a little demonstration. Patrick would take sinners to this purgatory-on-earth to see the pain and suffering of the souls in purgatory, and thus warn of the evils of sin and the dangers of procrastinating about repentance and reparation. This was a three-day retreat, complete with fasting, sleeping on the ground, and sacramental reconciliation.

Indulgences (See CCC #s 1471–1479.)

"An indulgence is a remission before God of the temporal punishment due to sins whose guilt has already been forgiven, which the faithful Christian who is duly disposed gains under certain prescribed conditions through the action of the Church which, as the minister of redemption, dispenses and applies with authority the treasury of the satisfactions of Christ and the saints." (Pope Paul VI, apostolic constitution *Indulgentiarum Doctrina*, 1).

The *Catechism of the Catholic Church* (#1475) explains this as "a wonderful exchange" in terms of the communion of saints in which the holiness of one benefits others far more than the harm of sin could bring others. The contrite sinner who appeals to the communion of saints is more quickly and efficaciously purified of punishment due to sin.

The Raccolta was a book of the prayers and exercises to which indulgences were attached by the Holy See. It included conditions for gaining the indulgence and their application to the souls in purgatory. Now there is another form of this book; it is called *The Enchiridion of Indulgences*.

Some Means of Gaining a Partial Indulgence

In the Middle Ages the name *pardoner* was used for preachers of indulgences who were "licensed" to solicit alms for church building and crusade sponsoring.

1. Praying the Magnificat or Hail Holy Queen

2. Praying the Acts of Faith, Hope, and Love, and the Creed

3. Making the sign of the cross

4. Visit to the Blessed Sacrament

5. Visit to a cemetery

Conditions for Gaining Plenary (full) Indulgence

1. Sacrament of Reconciliation

2. Reception of Communion

3. Prayer for the Holy Father

Some Means of Gaining Plenary Indulgence

1. Adoration of the Blessed Sacrament for at least one-half hour

2. Scripture reading for at least one-half hour

3. Way of the Cross recited

4. Rosary prayed in a church or with a family group or religious community

---

Trick or Treat

On All Souls' Day, the poor begged for food and, in return, would pray for the dead. "Soul cakes" was the name given to the doughnuts they received. The circle made by the hole cut out of the center represents eternity, with no beginning or end.

Hell

Terms

The following three words are not synonymous, but have at times been loosely translated into English as "hell."

Sheol

This Hebrew word, which occurs sixty-five times in the Old Testament, refers to the gloomy abode of the dead beneath the earth, the destination of the righteous as well as those who are evil. It has been variously translated—nether world, the deep, grave, pit—and is also the personification of death. (See Numbers 16:30–35; 1 Samuel 2:6; 2 Samuel 22:6; Job 11:8; 33:24, 28; Proverbs 9:18; Psalms 9:17–18; 28:1; 30:3, 9; 55:15; 63:9; 88:3–4, 6; Amos 9:2; Isaiah 14:9, 11, 44:23; Ezekiel 31:16–17, 32:21.)

Hades

The Greek version of the underworld is Hades, a word that occurs eleven times in the New Testament. It is left as it is in some translations, but it is rendered "grave" or "hell" in others. According to Greek myth, Hades was ruled by Pluto and Persephone; a place to which the dead (with coin in mouth) were ferried across the River Styx by the avaricious Charon. Judgment followed, with the righteous going to a meadow on the edge of western world (Elysian Fields) and the wicked doomed to eternal suffering in the depths of Hades (Tartarus).

Gehenna

This Hebrew word means "Valley of Hinnom"; it was a deep ravine on the south-west side of Jerusalem, long a dumping ground for human waste, corpses, and rotting matter—hence "incessant fire." Once even the site of human sacrifice, Gehenna became in Jesus' time, a popular symbol for what Christians call "hell." (See Mark 9:43–48; Luke 12:5; Matthew 5:29, 18:9, 23:33.)

"He descended into hell"

In some versions of the Creed, we say Christ descended into hell. We mean Hades or Sheol (the place of the dead), not Gehenna (the place of the damned—the hell of punishment). Jesus Christ experienced death completely, going into the "underworld" and "bursting the bonds of hell (limbo)," thereby showing power and authority over all creation, including death, and releasing the souls of the just who were awaiting salvation through his death and resurrection.

The Devil: Titles, Nicknames, and Euphemisms

The Babylon or Lucifer association and "the five 'I Wills'" are in Isaiah 14:12–15; Michael and the battle between good and bad angels is rooted in Revelation 12:7–9.

Anti-Christ

The unnamed personification of resistance to Christ ("evil," "the devil"). Many interpretations, legends, and bigotries have been spawned by the two classic texts, 2 Thessalonians 2:1–12 and Revelation 13: see "666" (Revelation 13:18) in Chapter 9 particularly. The term is mentioned specifically in 1 John 2:18, 2:22, 4:3 and 2 John 7 (identified with unbelievers who deny the incarnation). It was variously associated with historical figures (for example, Caligula and Nero, as well as more bigoted suggestions) and also heresies (as a personification).

Beelzebub

Correctly *Beelzebul* from *Baalzebal*, *Baal* (possessor, as in lord of a place), a word used for local divinities, a demonic deity or influence common in Canaan, and later the non-Israelite religions denounced by Jewish prophets. Jesus denied that he performed miracles through Beelzebub (Matthew 12:24, Luke 11:19–20). Also the contemptuous "Lord of the Flies."

Beliar

Lawless one, worthless. The term was used as a personification by Paul (2 Corinthians 6:15).

Father of lies

According to Jesus (John 8:44)

Lilith

"Wildcats shall meet with hyenas, goat-demons shall call to one another; there to Lilith shall repose, and find a place to rest" (Isaiah 34:14). In Semitic mythology Lilith is a demon who haunts wildernesses in stormy weather, especially dangerous to children and pregnant women. In Jewish folklore Lilith was the wife that Adam is fabled to have had before Eve was created. She refused to submit to him and left paradise for a region of the air where she still haunts the night.

Lucifer (Latin: light-bearer)

In patristic literature, identified with Satan, leader of the fallen angels, and referring to his status before his fall; see Isaiah 14:12–16.

Old Bendy

Because he can bend to anyone's inclinations

Old Harry

Perhaps from the personal name, similar to the term *Old Nick;* an allusion to "harry" (to harass, lay waste)

Old Nick

May be related to the German nickel, *goblin*; common in the seventeenth century

Old Scratch

From *skratta*, an old Scandinavian term for a monster or goblin

Satan (Hebrew: adversary; to plot against another)

Often applied biblically to a human opposer. The three Old Testament uses of the word to mean an evil spirit: Zechariah 3, Job 1:2, 1 Chronicles 21:1. Tempted Jesus (Matthew 4:1–11), warned about by Paul (1 Corinthians 7:6).

Serpent

From the story of the Fall (Genesis 3). Legend has it that a serpent, remembering his role in the Fall, would flee in terror from a person who quickly disrobes (representing the devil's repulsion for those who have divested themselves of sin).

Good Manners and Self-Defense

In the Middle Ages there were those who taught that the devil entered a person through the mouth, at the time of a yawn. So naturally, when you yawn, you cover your mouth, or make the sign of the cross over it.

The Devil and the Horseshoe

Legend has it that the devil approached Dunstan, known for his horse-shoeing skills, and asked him to shoe his "single hoof." The saint perceived his true identity, so he secured him fast and did the job, but inflicted so much pain in the process that the devil roared for mercy. He was released only on condition that he would never enter a place where a horseshoe was displayed. (Or the idea could be that, ever since, when the devil sees the horseshoe, he is reminded of the episode and flees in fear.)

Ancient Folklore and Christian Analogy

Many symbols and comparisons have found their way into Christian folklore by way of the enthusiastic and imaginative teaching of believers. Not surprisingly, temptation and the devil are often the subject. For example:

How the devil is like the wolf

The ancients believed that the wolf hunts his victims by night, that he frightens his prey by magnifying his voice, that he approaches his prey against the wind, and that he mutes his footsteps with spittle. This image was readily applied to Satan, deceiving and surprising the unsuspecting.

How the devil is like the whale

It is believed that there were whales so enormous that sailors landed on them, believing them to be desert islands, where they built fires. Their fate was sealed when the whale, aroused by the heat, plunged downward and drowned the sailors. Also it was believed that fish would unwittingly swim into the whale's mouth, thinking it a safe harbor. This legend easily lent itself to illustrations of the treachery of Satan, whose designs are not always detected.

St. George and the Dragon

Dragon-slaying is a favorite allegory for the victory of Christ's grace over evil. Versions of St. George's conquest are classic. One story goes that he was summoned to subdue a dragon that inhabited a lake in Silene, Libya, and that fed on folks in the neighborhood. When he arrived, St. George snatched away the princess Saba who was already in the dragon's clutches as its latest victim. Then George dispatched the monster with his sword.

The historical St. George was martyred near Lydda in the early centuries of the Church. Stories of his victory over sin and evil in terms of dragon-slaying are rooted in images from the Book of Revelation and can be compared to similar stories in the lives of Sts. Michael, Martha, Sylvester, and Margaret. Also recall God's original curse of the snake and promise of a victorious redeemer (Genesis 3:15) and the New Testament fulfillment depicted in scenes of Jesus and Mary treading on a snake.

End Times Glossary

Abyss

Revelation 9:1, 20:1

The place of Satan and the fallen angels for the time being (the millennium)

Book of the Living

Revelation 3:5, 13:9, 17:8, 20:12–15, 21:27; Philippians 4:3; Daniel 12:1

The "record" of the names of the redeemed

Day of the Lord

Revelation 6:12–17; Matthew 24:29; Amos 8:8–14; Isaiah 34:3; Joel 2:10, 3:3–21

The occasion of the parousia

Eschatology

A study of the end times, the *eschaton*

Fiery pool of sulphur

Revelation 14:10, 19:20, 20:10

Symbol of hell (distinct from the "abyss")

First resurrection

Revelation 20:4–5

The risen-life experience of those who have died in Christ (the redeemed) while the messianic age on earth continues

Gog and Magog

Revelation 20:8, Ezekiel 38:1–39:20

Symbols of all non-Jewish nations

Harmaged'on (Hebrew; also Armageddon)

"Hill of Megiddo" (Revelation 16:15–16)

Symbol of the final decisive victory over the forces of evil at the end of time (since historically Megiddo was the site of many decisive battles)

Millennium

Revelation 20:1–6

The thousand years, that long period between Christ's resurrection victory and the end of the world. See Romans 6:1–8, Ephesians 2:1–7; and John's "realized eschatology": John 5:24–47, 16:33; 1 John 3:14. Millennialism, which is not an orthodox Catholic position, is a belief in an extended period of prosperity and peace between present temptation or trial and parousia. A millennialist calls the Catholic position "amillennialist"; see 1 Corinthians 10:11.

Parousia

Revelation 1:7; 3:11; 22:7, 10, 12, 20

The second coming, Christ's return in glory at the end of time

Rapture

1 Thessalonians 4:17

The union of Christ with the redeemed who are alive at the time of the parousia

Satan chained

Revelation 20:1–10

As he is now, in the millennium. "Satan unchained for a short time" (Revelation 20:3, 7) and the reference to the "little season" is unclear; it is possibly a scriptural statement against millennialism's theory of pre-parousia prosperity.

Second Death

Revelation 2:11; 20:6, 14–15; 21:8

The time of the bodily resurrection when sinners receive their final punishment; that is, when the dead who did not die in Christ go to hell (said "not to live" between their death and this "second death," Revelation 20:5).

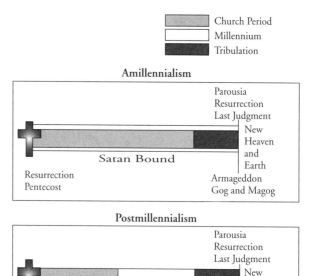

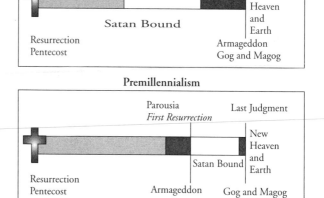

Tribulation

Mark 13:1–37, Matthew 24:1–44, Luke 21:5–36; see 1 Thessalonians 4:13–18.

This word is given to the circumstances of the end times, with vocabulary and images from the apocalyptic (literary style) "eschatological discourse" of Jesus to the disciples. It reflects the prevailing early Church opinion about the imminent second coming. Its literal and historical application is popular with fundamentalists and millennialists. Three versions are: (1) Church period, pre-tribulation, rapture, period of tribulation; (2) Church period including tribulation, with rapture halfway through tribulation and ending with parousia; (3) Church period including tribulation which are ended by post-tribulation rapture and parousia, which are part of the same intervention.

Scripture

Revelation

Definitions of Revelation

1. Revelation (public)

Self-disclosure by God to humanity; revelation that was objectively complete by the death of the last apostle

1. Natural (see Wisdom 13:1; Romans 1:20)—when intermediary is world of space and time

2. Supernatural (see Hebrews 1:1–2)—far exceeding natural; scripturally, "divine speech"
   - Indirectly—through the prophets: including the Old Testament, God's inspired word
   - Directly—through God's Son (the "incarnation"): including the New Testament, God's inspired Word

2. Revelations (private)

Supernatural manifestation, since that brings understanding of revelation to a particular person; not the same as the claims of cults

Sometimes sensory, as Hagar's experience (Genesis 16:7), Moses' at the burning bush (Exodus 3:2), the angel of the Exodus (Exodus 14:19, 24), Balaam's (Numbers 22:22–40), Gideon's (Judges 6:11–27) (See also "Marian apparitions.")

Sometimes merely intellectual (See "Dreams.")

Sometimes approved by the Church; for example, St. Bernadette Soubirous, 1844–1879 (Lourdes), St. Margaret Mary, 1647–1690 (the Sacred Heart)

Never adding to the deposit of faith, or requiring assent

3. Visions and Apparitions

Supernatural experiences wherein objects are seen but not necessarily understood. May or may not be corporeal; called "theophanies" if of God. (See Genesis 16:7, 13; Exodus 3:2; 14:19, 24; Numbers 22:22–35; Judges 6:11–18.)

The Two Senses of Scripture (See CCC #s 115–118.)

There is a medieval verse, "The letter speaks of belief; allegory to faith; the moral how to act; anagogy our destiny."

1. The literal sense—the meaning, interpreted rightly, on which all other senses are based

2. The spiritual sense—the deeper significance of the text
   - The allegorical sense—event's significance recognized in Christ
   - The moral sense—event's role in leading us to act justly
   - The anagogical sense—event's eternal significance

Dreams in the Scriptures

Abimelech: of God, "Return Sarah to Abraham."—Genesis 20:3–7

Jacob (at Bethel): of God, a ladder, and a promise—Genesis 28:10–17

Jacob: of God, "Go back to Canaan."—Genesis 31:10–16

Joseph: of sheaves bowing down—Genesis 37:5–8

Joseph: of the sun, moon, and eleven stars—Genesis 37:9–11

Pharaoh's cupbearer and baker: interpreted by Joseph—Genesis 40:9–23

Pharaoh: of seven fat cows and seven skinny cows—Genesis 41

Gideon: of a loaf of barley bread, a tent, and a victory—Judges 7:13–14

Solomon: of God, and a request for wisdom—1 Kings 3:5–14

Nebuchadnezzar: of a gold, silver, bronze, iron, and clay statue, told and interpreted by Daniel—Daniel 2:1–45

Nebuchadnezzar: of a tree, interpreted by Daniel—Daniel 4:2–27

Daniel: of four beasts, and more—Daniel 7

Joseph: of an angel, "Marry Mary."—Matthew 1:20–21

Astrologers: of a message, "Do not return to Herod."—Matthew 2:12

Joseph: of an angel, "Flee to Egypt."—Matthew 2:13

Joseph (in Egypt): of an angel, "Return to Israel."—Matthew 2:19

Pilate's wife: of Jesus, "Have nothing to do with him."—Matthew 27:19

MAJOR WORLD RELIGIONS

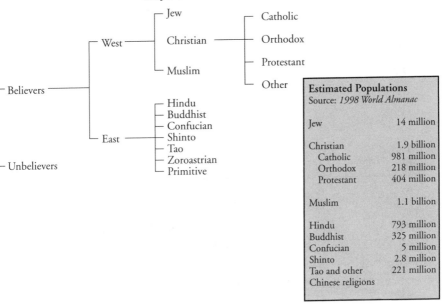

Estimated Populations	
Source: *1998 World Almanac*	
Jew	14 million
Christian	1.9 billion
Catholic	981 million
Orthodox	218 million
Protestant	404 million
Muslim	1.1 billion
Hindu	793 million
Buddhist	325 million
Confucian	5 million
Shinto	2.8 million
Tao and other	221 million
Chinese religions	

RELIGION IN THE WESTERN WORLD

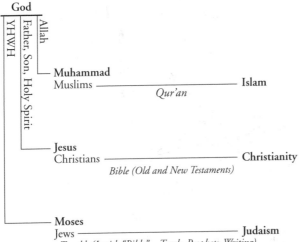

*Muslims do not believe that Jesus is the Son of God, but that he is in the line of prophets that ended with Muhammad, the "Seal of the Prophets," whose revelations are compiled in the Qur'an, or Holy Book. There are notable beliefs that Muslims do share with Christians: (1) There is one God; (2) God created the universe; (3) Abraham, Moses, and Jesus are in the line of prophets; (4) the day of judgment; (5) heaven and hell; and (6) the resurrection of the body.

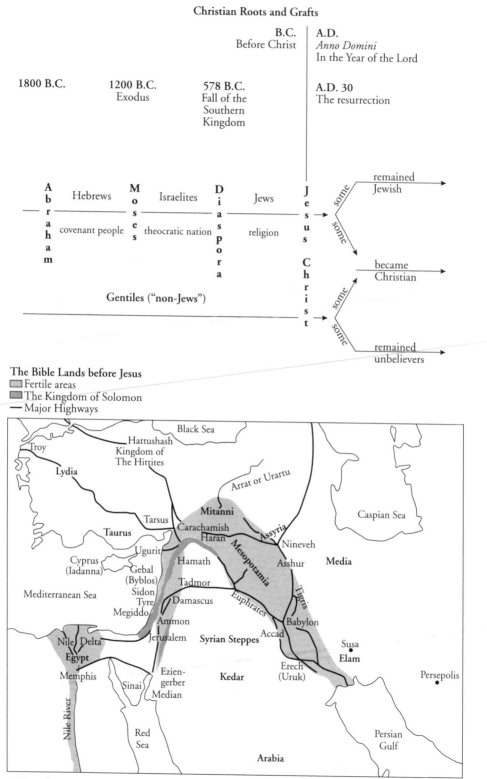

Christian Roots and Grafts

B.C.	A.D.
Before Christ	*Anno Domini* In the Year of the Lord

1800 B.C. 1200 B.C. Exodus 578 B.C. Fall of the Southern Kingdom A.D. 30 The resurrection

A b r a h a m Hebrews **M o s e s** Israelites **D i a s p o r a** Jews **J e s u s   C h r i s t** some → remained Jewish

covenant people theocratic nation religion some → became Christian

Gentiles ("non-Jews") some → remained unbelievers

The Bible Lands before Jesus
- Fertile areas
- The Kingdom of Solomon
- Major Highways

Troy · Black Sea · Hattushash Kingdom of The Hittites · Lydia · Arrat or Urartu · Caspian Sea · Tarsus · **Mitanni** · Carachamish · Haran · Assyria · Nineveh · **Taurus** · Mesopotamia · Media · Cyprus (Iadanna) · Ugurit · Hamath · Asshur · Gebal (Byblos) · Tadmor · Mediterranean Sea · Sidon · Tyre · Damascus · Euphrates · Tigris · Megiddo · Ammon · Babylon · Nile Delta · Jerusalem · **Syrian Steppes** · Accad · Susa · **Elam** · **Egypt** · Memphis · Sinai · Ezien-gerber · Median · **Kedar** · Erech (Uruk) · Persepolis · Nile River · Red Sea · **Arabia** · Persian Gulf

The Book

THE BOOKS OF THE OLD TESTAMENT

Parenthesize words are the former titles/spellings that were used prior to 1970s New American Bible, the first Bible in the Catholic tradition to use proper names derived from the Hebrew instead of the Latin and also name books to agree with the more proper usage of Bibles in the Protestant tradition—"Chronicles" instead of "Paralipomenon" for example.

Pentateuch	Abbrev.	NSRV Abbrev.	Chapters	
Genesis	Gn	Gen	50	
Exodus	Ex	Ex	40	**The Torah** (Law)
Leviticus	Lv	Lev	27	
Numbers	Nm	Num	36	
Deuteronomy	Dt	Deut	34	
The Historical Books				
Joshua (Josue)	Jos	Josh	24	
Judges	Jgs	Judg	21	
Ruth	Ru	Ruth	4	
1 Samuel (1 Kings)	1 Sm	1 Sam	31	Primary Group
2 Samuel (2 Kings)	2 Sm	2 Sam	24	(Former Prophets)
1 Kings (3 Kings)	1Kgs	1 Kings	22	Excluding Ruth
2 Kings (4 Kings)	2 Kgs	2 Kings	25	
1 Chronicles (1 Paralipomenon)	1 Chr	1 Chr	29	
2 Chronicles (2 Paralipomenon)	2 Chr	2 Chr	36	Secondary Group
Ezra (1 Esdras)	Ezr	Ezra	10	
Nehemiah (2 Esdras)	Neh	Neh	13	
*Tobit (Tobias)	Tb	Tob	14	Stories with a historical base
*Judith	Jdt	Jdt	16	Including Ruth
Esther	Est	Esth	10	
*Maccabees	1 Mc	1 Macc	16	Later History
*Maccabees	2 Mc	2 Macc	15	
The Wisdom Books				
Job	Jb	Job	42	
Psalms	Ps(s)	Ps	150	
Proverbs	Prv	Prov	31	**The Writings**
Ecclesiastes (Qoheleth)	Ecc	Eccl	12	Including Daniel, Ezra,
Song of Songs (...of Solomon)	Sg	Song	8	Nehemiah, Chronicles, Ruth,
(Canticle of Canticles)	Wis	Wis	19	Lamentations, and Esther
*Wisdom	Sir	Sir	51	
*Sirach (Ecclesiasticus)				
The Prophetic Books				**Latter Prophets**
Isaiah (Isaias)	Is	Isa	66	
Jeremiah (Jeremias)	Jer	Jer	52	
Lamentations	Lam	Lam	5	Major Prophets
*Baruch	Bar	Bar	6	Excluding Lamentations and
Ezekiel (Ezechiel)	Ez	Ezek	48	Baruch
Daniel	Dn	Dan	14	
Hosea (Osee)	Hos	Hos	14	
Joel	Jl	Joel	4	
Amos	Am	Amos	9	
Obadiah (Abdiah)	Ob	Obad	1	
Jonah (Jonas)	Jon	Jon	4	
Micha (Micheas)	Mi	Mic	7	Minor Prophets
Nahum	Na	Nah	3	Daniel and Jonah being
Habakkuk (Habacuc)	Hb	Hab	3	special cases
Zephaniah (Sophonias)	Zep	Zeph	3	
Haggai (Aggeus)	Hg	Hag	2	
Zechariah (Zacharias)	Zec	Zech	14	
Malachi (Malachias)	Mal	Mal	3	

*Deuterocanonical (Greek: second canon) or **Apocrypha** (Greek: hidden)
Tobit, Judith, 1 and 2 Maccabees, Wisdom, Sirach, Baruch

Called the *Apocrypha* in the Protestant tradition, these books of the Bible found in the Septuagint (ancient Greek translation of the Old Testament), but not the Hebrew canon. Jerome included these books in his Vulgate (Latin translation of the Bible). During the proliferation of published Bibles after the advent of printing, the reformers followed one Jewish tradition of excluding these books. Today in Protestant editions, these books are often included in a section at the end of the Old Testament.

Originally, the word *apocrypha* referred to works claiming a sacred origin but supposedly hidden for generations. Later, a specific body of literature with scriptural or quasi-scriptural pretensions though not canonical or genuine, composed during the two centuries before Christ and the early Christian centuries.

THE BOOKS OF THE NEW TESTAMENT

Gospels

	Abbrev.	NSRV Abbrev.	Chapters	
Matthew	Mt	Mt	28	
Mark	Mk	Mk	16	} Synoptics
Luke	Lk	Lk	24	
John	Jn	Jn	21	

History of the Early Christian Church

Acts of the Apostles	Acts	Acts	28	

Letters ("Epistles")

	Abbrev.	NRSV Abbrev.	Chapters	
Romans	Rom	Rom	16	
Corinthians (2)	(1,2) Cor	1, 2 Cor	16, 13	
Galatians	Gal	Gal	6	
Ephesians	Eph	Eph	6	
Philippians	Phil	Phil	4	> By Paul
Colossians	Col	Col	4	
Thessalonians (2)	(1,2) Thes	1, 2 Thess	5, 3	
Timothy (2)	(1,2) Tim	1, 2 Tim	6, 4	
Titus	Ti	Titus	3	
Philemon	Phlm	Philem	1	
James	Jas	Jas	5	
Peter (2)	(1,2) Pt	1, 2 Pet	5, 3	
John (3)	(1,2,3) Jn	1, 2, 3 Jn	5, 1, 1	} Synoptics
Jude	Jude	Jude	1	
Hebrews	Heb	Heb	13	} Unknown or
Ephesians	Eph	Eph	6	uncertain

Apocalyptic

Revelation or Apocalypse	Rv	Rev	22	

Until the fourth or fifth century of the Christian era, the following books were not universally accepted as part of the New Testament canon: Hebrews, James, 2 Peter, 2 and 3 John, Jude, Revelation, and Mark 16:9–20 (Protestant Bibles today might not include these last twelve verses of Mark).

Fearful Thomas

"Timeo hominea unius libri" "(I fear the man of one book)" is a sentiment attributed to Thomas Aquinas. The traditional interpretation was that a person steeped in a single source made a formidable opponent in debate. More recently another interpretation is suggested: There are those who think that a single source is sufficient, with its knowledge, purpose, and expressions. They cannot then entertain any truth but that contained in the statements of their one book.

Languages of the Bible

The examples below are all translations of John 3.16: "For God so loved the world. . . ."

Hebrew

כִּי־אַהֲבָה רַבָּה אָהַב הָאֱלֹהִים אֶת־הָעוֹלָם עַד־אֲשֶׁר נָתַן אֶת־בְּנוֹ

Old Testament (Exception: a few books of late composition were written in Greek; some parts were written in Aramaic, which became the everyday language of the Jews after the exile, Hebrew being reserved as the language of the Law.)

Greek

Διότι τόσον πολὺ ἀγάπησε ὁ Θεὸς τὸν κόσμον, ὥστε ἔδωκε τὸν Υἱόν του

Original language of the New Testament. Also the language of the third-century B.C. translation of the Old Testament, the Septuagint, given its name because it was said to have been done by 72 scholars in 72 days (Latin: *sept* means seven).

Aramaic

Probably the spoken language of Jesus and still the liturgical language of the Chaldean, Malabar, Malankar, Maronite, Nestorian, and Syrian Rites.

Latin (same alphabet as English)

The *editio vulgata* (common edition or Vulgate) was translated by Jerome about 385–405, but did not appear in print until a thousand years later (1456).

Arabic

أحب الله العالم حتى بذل ابنه الوحيد لكي لآ يهلك كل من يومن

Language of sacred writings of Islam, the Qur'an.

Alphabets

Hebrew				Greek				Arabic		
Letter	Name	Transliteration		Letter	Name	Transliteration		Letter	Name	Transliteration
א	aleph	- or '		A α	alpha	a		ا	alif	-[1]
ב	beth	b,v		B β	beta	b		ب	ba	b
ג	gimel	g		Γ γ	gamma	g		ت	ta	t
ד	daleth	d		Δ δ	delta	d		ث	sa	th
ה	he	h		E ε	epsilon	e		ج	jim	j
ו	vav	v, w		Z ζ	zeta	z		ح	ha	ḥ
ז	zayin	z		H η	eta	e (or ē)		خ	kha	kh
ח	cheth	ḥ		Θ θ	theta	th		د	dal	d
ט	teth	ṭ		I ι	iota	i		ذ	zal	th
י	yod	y, j, i		K κ	kappa	k		ر	ra	r
כ ך[1]	kaph	k, kh		Λ λ	lambda	l		ز	za	z
ל	lamed	l		M μ	mu	m		س	sin	s
מ ם[1]	mem	m		N ν	nu	n		ش	shin	sh
נ ן[1]	nun	n		Ξ ξ	xi	x		ص	sad	ṣ
ס	samekh	s		O ο	omicron	o		ض	dad	d
ע	ayin	'		Π π	pi	p		ط	ta	t
פ ף[1]	pe	p, f		P ρ	rho	r		ظ	za	z
צ ץ[1]	sadi	ṣ		Σ σ, ς[1]	sigma	s		ع	ain	-[2]
ק	koph	ḳ		T τ	tau	t		غ	ghain	gh[3]
ר	resh	r		Υ υ	upsilon	y		ف	fa	f
שׁ	shin	sh, š		Φ φ	phi	ph		ق	qaf	k[4]
שׂ	śin	ś		X χ	chi	ch, kh		ك	kaf	k[5]
ת	tav	t		Ψ ψ	psi	ps		ل	lam	l
				Ω ω	omega	o (or ō)		م	mim	m
								ن	nun	n
								ه	ha	h
								و	waw	w
								ي	ya	y

[1]Functions as the bearer of *hamza* (the glottal stop), or as a lengthener of short *a*. [2]A voiced pharyngeal fricative. [3]A voiced velar fricative. [4]A uvular stop. [5]A voiceless velar stop.

[1]At end of word.

[1]At end of word.

St. Jerome and the Lion

The lion is a common feature of story and legend, especially to illustrate the effect of kindness and the transforming power of gratitude. The following is a Christian version of Androcles and the Lion. The story goes that a lion entered a schoolroom in which Jerome was teaching, and lifted one of its paws. Although the disciples all fled, Jerome noticed that the paw was wounded and proceeded to extract a thorn from it and to dress the wound. The grateful lion "showed a wish to stay with its benefactor." That is why the saint is commonly depicted accompanied by a lion.

It's not surprising that this story's setting is a schoolroom. Jerome spent much time there. St. Augustine said of him, "If Jerome doesn't know, nobody does, or ever did." A prodigious scholar, Jerome's ultimate work was translating the entire Bible into Latin (the Vulgate), the Old Testament from Hebrew and the New from Greek. The Council of Trent, having called for its revision, declared the Vulgate the authentic text for the Church. Jerome mastered not only languages, notably Latin, Greek, Hebrew, and Chaldaic, but also a life of piety. Finally, before the massive undertaking of translating the Bible, he toured the Holy Land, experiencing the very places hallowed by Christ. This pilgrimage culminated in a five-year retreat in the desert of Chalcis for penance, prayer, and more study. Settling in Bethlehem, he lived in a cave that was believed to be the birthplace of Christ.

The Vernacular Bible

Around 400, Jerome translated the Bible into Latin. It was called the *Vulgate*, a word that means "common" in Latin; Latin was the common language until well into the Middle Ages. When vernacular languages began to develop, the Bible was one of the first books to be translated (predating printing by centuries). Translations of the Vulgate Bible into the vernacular were common throughout Europe long before the Protestant Reformation. In the fifty-six years before Luther's German rendition (1522), for example, eighteen translations had been made in Germany. More examples of vernacular translations of the Vulgate include an Italian version in 1471, a Dutch version in 1478, and a French version in 1479.

("OT" and "NT" refer to Old Testament and New Testament in the following pages.)

Catholics Reading the Bible

1. "Easy access to sacred scripture should be provided for all the Christian faithful . . . since the word of God should be available at all times, the Church with maternal concern sees to it that suitable and correct translations are made into different languages, especially from the original texts of the sacred books" (Vatican II, "Dogmatic Constitution on Divine Revelation," 1965, 22. A footnote in Abbott's edition of *The Documents of Vatican II* notes that not since the early centuries of the Church has an official document urged that Scripture be available for all.)

2. The Church "forcefully and specifically exhorts all the Christian faithful . . . to learn 'the surpassing knowledge of Jesus Christ' by frequent reading of the divine Scriptures. 'Ignorance of the Scriptures is ignorance of Christ.'" (Vatican II, "Dogmatic Constitution on Divine Revelation," *Dei Verbum*, 25; referring to Philippians 3:8 and quoting St. Jerome, repeated in CCC #133, on teaching about Scripture, and #2653, on teaching about prayer.)

"Non-Catholic" Bibles

This label is used for translations of the Bible done by Protestants or under the auspices of a Protestant Church or organization. This does not mean that a translation is "theologically slanted." It does mean that seven Old Testament books will not be included or, if included, will be labeled "Apocrypha." It also means that the Catholic Church has not given official approval to that translation or originally did not have anything to do with its development.

Catholics Reading "Non-Catholic" Bibles

The *Catechism of the Catholic Church* (1994) does not mention "Protestant Bibles" in either of its two direct exhortations (paragraphs #s 133 and 2653) to the faithful to read the Bible. The *Jerome Biblical Commentary* (1968) refers to the 1917 *Code of Canon Law* when it says that Catholics may read non-Catholic editions of the Bible under two simple conditions: that the Catholic is involved "in some way" in Scripture study, and if the edition is complete and faithful and without notes that attack or amount to an attack on Catholic faith (a condition most non-Catholic editions of the Bible would meet).

Principles of Translation

A Distinction

The following distinction is a well-known one that explains the differences among Bible translations. St. Jerome himself said, "For I myself not only admit but freely proclaim that in translating from the Greek (except in the case of the holy scriptures where even the order of the words is a mystery) I render sense for sense and not word for word." (In his Vulgate, however, he did not always do this.)

1. Form-centered translation (also known as "formal equivalence")

"Literal," word form for word form (word for word); the word order and sentence structure of the original is preserved as much as possible in translation (a verb is usually translated with a verb and a pronoun with a pronoun, even though there may be a more idiomatic English expression). Expect traditional language and involved sentence structure.

2. Content-centered translation (also known as "dynamic equivalence")

"Idiomatic," thought for thought (idiomatically powerful but still exegetically accurate); also called "functional equivalence," the form of the original is adjusted in translation to English usage, with the translator trying to have the same impact on readers today that the original had on readers then.

A Comparison

In the following translations of Judges 1:35, the first (New Revised Standard Version) is form-centered, the second (Revised English Bible) is content-centered.

1. "The hand of the house of Joseph rested heavily on them."

2. "But the Joseph tribes increased their pressure on them."

Choices of Bibles

Goodspeed observed (see the 1935 "Chicago Bible," page 147), "Any translation of a masterpiece must be a failure." Note the old Latin adage, *Omnis traductor traditor*, "Every translator is a traitor." In other words, there is no perfect translation. Two points:

1. No one translation can become the Bible for all readers.

2. A new translation (or at least a major revision) is needed at least every thirty years. Philip W. Comfort in *The Complete Guide to Bible Versions* suggests the following gradation from literal translation to idiomatic paraphrase.

1. **Strictly literal**—New American Standard Bible

2. **Literal**—New King James Version, Revised Standard Version, The Revised New American Bible (NT)

3. **Literal with freedom to be idiomatic**—New Revised Standard Version, New American Bible

4. **Thought-for-thought**—New International Version, New Jerusalem Bible, Revised English Bible

5. **Dynamic equivalent**—The Complete Bible, Phillips, Today's English Version, New English Bible

6. **Paraphrastic**—The Living Bible

Eras of Translation

In the pages that follow, the history of English Bible translations is divided into six eras.

1. Before 1382: St. Augustine of Canterbury to Wycliffe

Ever since the evangelization of Britain in the sixth century, there were English translations of the Scriptures.

2. 1382–1525: Wycliffe to Tyndale

This era was mainly that of Wycliffe, who first translated the entire Bible into English, plus an associate who revised it.

3. 1525–1611: Tyndale to the King James Version

This era, starting with the first printed English New Testament and, with the Protestant Reformation as a context, was dotted with historic new translations of the Bible. It closed with the Catholic Douay-Rheims in 1609 and the Protestant King James in 1611.

4. 1611–1902: The King James Version to the Twentieth Century NT

Challoner's Bible and the Revised Version were the only two milestones in these three centuries. Challoner's, replacing Douay-Rheims in the mid-1700s, became virtually "the Catholic Bible" until the mid-twentieth century. A century later, the Revised Version was produced as the first serious revision of the King James Version—after 250 years of use. (An American counterpart, the American Standard Version, soon followed.)

5. 1902–1982: Modern Translations

1902's Twentieth Century New Testament, with the discovery of *koine* Greek, departed from the traditional Elizabethan English of the King James Bible, and a whole new era began. During this period, in 1952, the Revised Standard Version came out. The RSV is a modern, much-used rendering of the Bible.

6. Since 1982: New Revisions, not New Versions

Most especially, the Revised Standard Version (NRSV, 1993, Catholic and Protestant editions.)

1. Before 1382: St. Augustine to Wycliffe

In the sixth century, Pope St. Gregory the Great commissioned a party of forty monks under the leadership of Augustine (later known as Augustine of Canterbury) to bring Christianity to Britain. With the faith, these missionaries brought the Bible.

English translations of portions of the Bible followed, notably by St. Augustine (around 600), St. Wilfred (around 670), Caedmon (in song, around 670), the Venerable Bede (St. John's Gospel, the final passages of which he dictated from his death bed, in 735), and King Alfred (901).

Other fragmentary evidence also remains, like the Lindisfarne Gospels (also known as the *Book of Durham*, and *The Gospels of St. Cuthbert*), an inter-linear translation of the gospel by the monks of Lindisfarne, dated around 950. They took a copy of the Gospels and printed Anglo-Saxon equivalents above the lines (like a "crib"). This work, now in the British Museum, is the nearest surviving "Bible" handwritten in Anglo-Saxon. It probably borrowed heavily from a now non-existent work of the Venerable Bede from around 700.

"Old English" or Anglo-Saxon (400s/800s–1150) is the English of this period: the original pre-Norman Germanic stock of English used from the fifth century (or eighth, according to some) to the twelfth century. It is the language of the epic poem *Beowulf* of the early eighth century. The oldest extant Old English translation of the gospel is the tenth-century Wessex Gospels.

Before the flourishing of Middle English (1150–1475) and the age of Chaucer (1340–1400), there is no evidence of English translations of significant portions of the Bible. There was, in the 1300s, a metrical translation of the psalms into English which was done by William of Shoreham and another by Blessed Richard Rolle (first of the great fourteenth-century English mystics).

2. 1382–1525: Wycliffe to Tyndale

These were the years when large portions of the Bible, especially the New Testament, were coming out in translation. In the millennium (more or less) between St. Jerome (331–420) and Wycliffe (c. 1329–1384), Jerome's Latin translation was the Vulgate, and Latin was the dominant language of scholarship. With the Renaissance came a resurgence of interest in the study of the classics, including the Greek and Hebrew languages. Now scholars were reading the New Testament in its original Greek for the first time in nearly one thousand years. By 1500, Greek was being taught at Oxford.

1382, John Wycliffe (NT, 1380)

John Wycliffe (1330–1384), controversial cleric and ex-priest, called the "morningstar of the Reformation," is credited with the first translation of the entire Bible into English from Latin (the Vulgate). It remained unprinted, however, until 1850. The major part of the Old Testament was done by an associate, Nicholas of Hereford. (In the midst of Catholic-Protestant polemics, it was often repeated that it took a Protestant to produce the first English Bible. The much earlier tradition and translations mentioned above, of which we have only fragmentary remains, should not be ignored.)

1388, John Purvey

A close associate of Wycliffe, Purvey produced a revision of Wycliffe's Bible which, in less than a century, replaced it. It's been pointed out that the prologue in Purvey's edition of the Wycliffe Bible "deserved Thomas More's characterization as heretical." It was traditional to construe the hierarchy's opposition to Wycliffe's translation, and others, as a desire to keep the Bible from the people. As a matter of fact, vernacular translations could enjoy Church approval, as stated by the provincial council of Oxford in 1408. (An historic example would be the ninth-century Slavonic translation by SS. Cyril and Methodius.) It should be remembered that there was more to the early Bible translations than the word of God: The circulation of English Bibles, both in England and on the continent, included the circulation of heretical propaganda, most blatantly in the notes that accompanied the translation.

3. 1525–1611: Tyndale to the King James Version

This was the next great era for English translations of the Bible. Although there were translations coming into use in the Mother Church (like Bishop John Fisher's penitential psalms in 1505), it was the Reformation movement that generated the chain of translations that led to the King James Bible of 1611.

1525, Tyndale's Bible

Tyndale's Bible was the first printed English New Testament, to which were later added the Pentateuch (1530) and various Old Testament parts. Its translator was William Tyndale (1490–1536), "The Father of the English Bible," an ex-Augustinian monk, and an Oxford student of the Scriptures in Greek and Hebrew. It was not embraced by the hierarchy in England because of its strident anti-Catholic notes and its theological slant (it was quickly noticed, for example, that the new translation used the terms "congregation," "overseer," and "elder," instead of "church," "bishop," and "priest"). These were finer points, however, compared to what brought the wrath of Henry VIII: the arbitrary omission of 1 Peter 2:13–14 ("Submit yourselves to every human institution for the sake of the Lord, whether to the sovereign as supreme, or to the governor as his deputy . . ."). In 1536, Tyndale was arrested and put to death by the emperor, Charles V, thus becoming a Protestant martyr. (His final revision of the New Testament, published in 1535, gained more acceptance, since by that time Henry VIII had broken with Rome.) It has been estimated that 80 percent of the King James Bible's New Testament is Tyndale's work.

1537, Coverdale's Bible

Miles Coverdale, an associate of Tyndale, published the first complete English Bible, based largely on Tyndale's translation of the New Testament with a makeshift rendering of most of the Old Testament from other secondary sources. It was the first English Bible printed in England.

1537, Matthew's Bible

Thomas Matthew, a pseudonym for a Tyndale assistant (and an ex-priest), John Rogers, collated apparently unpublished Old Testament translations of Tyndale's and parts of Coverdale's work and published the first Bible authorized by the Church of England, beginning an evolution that culminated in the Authorized Version (AV) in 1611 (King James Bible). Many of his "notes" were indecent and objectionable, often abusive of the Catholic Church, its teaching, and clergy. The banning and burning of Bibles (not to mention translators) needs to be understood in the context of the regrettable propaganda ("notes") that became the nasty habit of the day. For a sample: Matthew's "note" on 1 Peter 3:7 suggests that if a "wyfe" be not obedient and helpful to her husband, he should endeavor "to beate the feare of God into her heade, that therby she maye be compelled to learne her dutie, and to do it."

1538, The Great Bible

The Great Bible, so named because of its size (9" X 15") and costliness, was a revision of Matthew's Bible and other earlier translations, including the Vulgate. Printed for distribution in England, it was the first English Bible authorized by the king for public use. (Its Psalter was used in the *Book of Common Prayer*.)

1539, Taverner's Bible

Taverner's Bible was a translation by the Greek scholar Richard Taverner. It was an independent work; that is, it stood apart from the tradition culminating in the Authorized Version ("King James Bible").

1560, The Geneva Bible (NT, 1557)

The Geneva Bible was a translation by English Protestant exiles in Geneva during Mary Tudor's Catholic restoration (1553–1558). It was a revision of Tyndale and the Great Bible, with the influence of the great textual scholar, Theodore Beza. It was very popular and became the Bible of the commoner, in part simply because it was small and moderately priced. Some 200 editions are known. It was also the Bible of Shakespeare, Bunyan, and the Puritans, and the first Bible printed in Roman type instead of black letter, with the verses designated, and with explanatory words and phrases set in italics. Many leaders in the Church of England, while recognizing its superior style and scholarship, were not accepting of it because of its Calvinist preface and notes (which were also predictably anti-Catholic).

A comment on the Geneva Bible by Richard T.A. Murphy OP in Background to the Bible, recognizes a sad part of the story of "the English-ing of the Bible":

It is unfortunate that while the text itself had improved, the notes that accompanied it had not. The notes attacked clerical celibacy, the sacraments, the Roman Catholic Church, and the pope. One can scarcely believe that such abuse was included in the Bible, but this was the mental fare of many sixteenth–and seventeenth–century Bible readers. It explains to some extent the instinctive hostility some have felt toward the Church of Rome and its leader, the pope. Such notes are unthinkable today in the Common Bible which has, since Vatican II, become a happy reality.

1568, The Bishops' Bible

The Bishops' Bible, with contributions by most Anglican bishops, was the answer by the hierarchy of the Church of England to the popular but bitterly sectarian Geneva Bible. (The Geneva Bible had revealed the inadequacy of the Great Bible, and the Bishop's Bible never replaced it in the hearts of the people). This revision of the Great Bible and the second authorized version in English served as the working basis for the King James Bible, which finally superseded it in 1611.

1609, Douay-Rheims (NT, 1582)

This translation from the Vulgate, with careful comparisons to original Hebrew and Greek, was by English Catholic scholars, mainly Gregory Martin (d. 1582) in France. The New Testament was done at Rheims in 1582, the Old Testament at Douay in 1609 (the two towns were the result of the move of the English College where the work was done). It was an effort for accuracy more than literary style. Its "Latinisms," common in the English writing of the day, made it archaic for later generations.

The Vulgate was chosen as a basis of translation instead of Hebrew and Greek for several reasons. Textual criticism as we know it was then non-existent; the collection and collation of manuscripts had only just begun. The Vulgate had also been given primacy of place by the Council of Trent (1545–1563) and therefore had authority. Its antiquity was a genuine asset, and it was closer by far to the originals than some of the manuscripts used by the sixteenth–century reformers. For all its Latinisms, the Douay-Rheims translation was accurate, and no instances of deliberate perversion or twisting of the text can be shown. And it is not as if Latinisms were everywhere; long passages of the work are not at all unusual in diction. It was, in fact, so good that the translators of the King James Version made extensive use of it.

—Richard T.A. Murphy OP, *Background to the Bible.*

1611, Authorized Version (AV or KJV; the so-called King James Bible)

The Authorized Version was commissioned by King James I (hence its common title). It came at the request for a Bible more accurate than previous translations. King James (who had an amateur's interest in Bible translation) approved, knowing that the Bishops' Bible had never enjoyed the success of the Geneva Bible, whose notes he considered seditious. Fifty scholars were instructed to use the Bishops' Bible as their basic version as long as it was faithful to the original text, but to use the translations of Tyndale, Matthew, Coverdale, the Great Bible, and the Geneva Bible, as well as the Catholic translation done at Rheims in 1582. (It was also to be printed without marginal notes!)

As respectfully stated in its preface, "We never thought from the beginning that we should need to make a new translation, nor yet to make of a bad one a good one . . . but to make a good one better, or out of many good ones one principal good one." In the end, it took the best of the rest, and far surpassed them. As is well known, it became the standard and has been through much revision over the years. With its noble simplicity, its turns of phrase, melodious rhythm and cadence, it has been called the noblest monument of English prose. Its Elizabethan English (sixteenth–seventeenth century), gracious in style and majestic in language, is complicated by today's standards.

It included the Apocrypha, with those books placed at the end of the Old Testament and deemed by that fact to be of lesser importance. It also includes the doxology ("for thine is the kingdom . . .") in Matthew 6:13, a verse scholars now recognize to be the addition of a scribe that did not appear in the older and better manuscripts (hence its omission in modern translations like the New International Version, the New Century Version, and the Contemporary English Version). It is written at a twelfth-grade reading level.

4. 1611–1902: The KJV to the Twentieth Century NT

Around 1630, a fifth-century manuscript containing the entire New Testament (called *Codex Alexandrinus*) was brought to England. This was an earlier text than the King James translators had available to them.

1750 and 1763, Challoner's Bible (NT, 1749 and 1752)

This was a revised version, by a Bishop Challoner (1691–1781), of the English translation of the Douay-Rheims (a century ahead of its Protestant counterpart, the King James Bible, which was revised in 1885). It was virtually "the Catholic Bible" for English speakers until the mid-twentieth century.

Among other nineteenth-century finds, a manuscript (*Codex Sinaiticus*) was discovered by German scholar Tischendorf (1815–1874). It offered translators a manuscript from around 350 that was earlier and better than those previously available. In 1850, a manuscript from the Vatican's library (*Codex Vaticanus*) became available. Dated 325, it offered a more accurate and reliable witness of Scripture's original texts than had been available.

1885, Revised Version (RV) (NT, 1881)

The RV was the first serious revision of the Authorized ("King James") Version, after 250 years of its use. It was based on (and required by) the enormous volume of discovery and scholarship of the nineteenth century that had provided far more reliable original-language texts and greater knowledge of the meaning of Hebrew and Greek words. (In the New Testament alone there were about 30,000 changes, 5,000 of them because of better Greek texts.)

The Gideon Bible

The "Gideon Bible" is the Bible (New King James translation) placed in various public places by the Gideons, a non-sectarian evangelical group of Christians who have made it their mission to distribute the Bible and encourage its use. Composed of lay people from various denominations, often business and professional men, their primary goal is "winning people for Christ," with Bible distribution being their principal means. Gideons began when two traveling men, strangers to each other, met in a Wisconsin hotel in the fall of 1898. As they began to share evening devotions, they decided to form an association, taking the name Gideon (from the story in Judges 6 and 7), the leader of a small group of men dedicated to God through whom God accomplished great things. Their Bible distribution program (typically in hotel and motel rooms and to individuals like members of the armed forces) is financed primarily through the support of evangelical Churches.

1901, American Standard Edition of the Revised Version (ASV)

The ASV was a US-published, revised rendition of the RV. It was required for two reasons: Not only was American usage departing significantly from British English, but textual scholarship had already come far enough to provide a much better text base than the 1885 RV had. This revision is commonly called the "American Revised Version" and was generally regarded as superior to the 1885 British version. However, neither the RV nor the ASV replaced the established KJV in Church and private use.

5. 1902–1982: Modern Translations

1902, The Twentieth Century New Testament

This first in a family of new translations departs from the traditional Elizabethan English (as in the King James Bible) in favor of fresh renderings in a more common idiom. This change was prompted by early-twentieth-century discoveries of a *koine* (common) form of Greek, in which most of the New Testament was written. Traditional scholarship had supposed that Bible Greek was the formal, literary language of Greek poetry and tragedy. If "common" was the language in which the Bible was written, so should be the English in which it is translated.

1903, The New Testament in Modern Speech

The English scholar Richard Weymouth translated a modern speech version of the New Testament that was well received and went through several editions and printings.

1924, Moffat (NT, 1913)

The great Scottish scholar, James Moffat, did a new translation of the Bible in modern English ("as one would render any piece of contemporary Hellenistic prose"). This brilliant and independent work was based on what we now know to be a very defective Greek New Testament.

1935, The Complete Bible, An American Translation (NT, 1923)

Edgar Goodspeed, a New Testament professor at the University of Chicago, was critical of modern-style translations and so did his own. The "Chicago Bible" (a New Testament) appeared in 1923 and was the earliest American modern-speech translation. The Complete Bible, produced by others, followed in 1935 and was judged by *The Jerome Biblical Commentary* "both scientifically and stylistically a superior effort and in many ways the best complete Bible available as of early 1968."

1941, Confraternity Revision of the NT (CCD)

Like the Protestant RSV of 1952 and the NEB of 1970, the Catholic CCD Bible answered the call for a contemporary Bible. The Bishops' Committee for the Confraternity of Christian Doctrine (hence "CCD") authorized this revision of the Rheims-Challoner New Testament. Its style was relatively modern, but it still preserved large amounts of Bible English (thou, behold). The Douay-Challoner Old Testament was abandoned with the 1943 publication of *Divino Afflante Spiritu*, Pope Pius XII's encyclical encouraging vernacular translations from the original languages.

1944, Knox

The need for a Douay-Rheims-Challoner update in Great Britain was filled by Fr. Ronald Knox, the eminent convert and classics scholar from Oxford. A rendering from the Latin, it was a complete break from "Bible English" and was more appreciated in literary circles than biblical. Its lively New Testament, especially the Pauline letters, has been called masterful.

A new enthusiasm for modern translations of the Bible came with the end of World War II, a seedtime for translations that were published through the course of the next decades.

1952, Revised Standard Version (RSV) (NT, 1946)

The RSV is a modern American rendering (at a tenth-grade reading level) of the English Bible in the King James tradition. By far the best in its day, the RSV is probably the last Bible in the Tyndale/KJV tradition. Demand for the RSV came for these two reasons: First, the Revised Versions (both British and American) had a reputation for accuracy, but also for being "wooden," translating words with greater care for accuracy than for context, following even the Greek word order regardless of the English result ("unidiomatic"). Second, there had been important manuscript discoveries in the 1930s and 1940s.

As its preface says, "The RSV is not a new translation in the language of today. It is not a paraphrase which aims at striking idioms." Since it preserves the KJV language as much as possible, much Bible English (thou, behold) still remains (although it exchanged "who" for "which" in reference to persons, "know" for "wot" and "knew" for "wist"). It surprisingly changed the KJV's "Lord" to "Jehovah" in the Old Testament. The well-received RSV became a standard for many Protestants—notable exceptions being scandalized fundamentalists and conservative evangelicals who debated over changes like "young woman" for "virgin" in Isaiah 7:14, for example.

1958, New Testament in Modern English (Phillips)

The British vicar J.B. Phillips carried modern idiomatic translation even beyond Goodspeed's. This very readable version is so lively that it becomes almost a paraphrase, making Paul's letters "sound as if they'd just come through the mail."

1961, The New World Translation (NT, 1950)

This translation is only noted here as a warning about reliability. Prepared by the Jehovah's Witnesses (Watchtower Bible & Tract Society), it is probably the only modern translation driven by doctrinal views instead of the text itself. There is no textual reason, for example, for translating the New Testament "Lord" as "Jehovah."

1965, Amplified Bible

Since the RSV had been condemned as unfaithful by a majority of American conservatives, translations like this one were done to provide them with an acceptable updated Bible. (See its descendants, the 1971 New American Standard Bible and the 1978 New International Version, below.)

1966, The Jerusalem Bible (JB)

In 1955, French Dominicans of the *Ecole Biblique* in Jerusalem published in French a new excellent translation from the original languages. It was immediately recognized as one of the greatest achievements of a reborn Catholic biblical scholarship and as a response to the invitation of the 1943 encyclical *Divino Afflante Spiritu*. A free translation, it's been praised for its extensive introductions and footnotes (the most scholarly and comprehensive of any English Bible to that point, and strictly related to the text) that offer help with difficult passages and background information where geography or cultural details need to be clarified. Uniquely, it uses "Yahweh" as God's name in the Old Testament. It was translated (along with its invaluable notes) into English in 1966. In 1985 a revision, the NJB, was produced.

1968, New Confraternity Bible (New CCD)

With the 1943 encyclical calling for recourse to the original languages, the old CCD revision of the Douay-Challoner was abandoned and a new translation of the whole Bible was commissioned by the US Episcopal Committee. The old CCD project, like its Protestant counterpart, the RSV, boldly undertook the revision of a sacrosanct tradition and translation. The New CCD (not unlike the Protestant NEB) used new concepts and tools in both style and scholarship. It avoided Bible English, eliminating all "thou" forms, for example, and using contractions. (Most of its Old Testament came out in three volumes in 1952, 1955, and 1961.)

1970, The New English Bible (NEB) (NT, 1961)

The Church of Scotland (in 1946, the same year the RSV's New Testament was published) proposed a fresh translation in modern idiom (which would be highly British, of course) of the original languages—not a revision of any previous translation and not a literal translation. This was different in theory and practice. A dramatic breakthrough, the NEB was experimental, producing phrasings not seen before. Thus it is praised by some for ingenuity, and criticized by others for the same reason (see for example its rendering of John 1.1: "When all things began, the Word already was"). Its British English includes "cairn" for "heap," "corn" for "wheat," and "thirty pounds" for "300 denarii." Its revision (changing its distinctive nature) was published in 1989.

1970, The New American Bible (NAB)

Published by members of the Catholic Biblical Association as the successor of the Confraternity Bible, which had been translated from the Vulgate, the NAB is the first English Bible from the Catholic Church translated from the original texts. It's a highly regarded work of some fifty scholars, adhering strictly to the rules of biblical criticism. In the functional equivalent category, and at an eleventh-grade reading level, it walks the middle ground between literal fidelity and readability.

One notable change was the use of proper names derived from the Hebrew instead of the Latin ("Isaiah" for "Isaias" and "Elijah" for "Elias," for example). Another change was to name biblical books to agree with the more proper usage employed in the Protestant Bible ("Chronicles" for "Paralipomenon," "Sirach" for "Ecclesiasticus," and "Revelation" for "Apocalypse," for example). It's a respecter of tradition, leaving Isaiah 7:14 as "virgin," for example. Its New Testament was hastened somewhat for use in the new lectionary following Vatican II and the need was soon apparent for its revision (which was done by 1987). Furthermore, the distinctively contemporary sound of the NAB, when read liturgically, revealed the need for a more traditional and formal translation.

1971, The Living Bible (NT, 1966)

Kenneth Taylor's huge success uses the ASV as a working text and rephrases (paraphrases) passages into modern speech so that anyone, including children, can understand it ("expanding where necessary"). "The Way," as it was originally called, along with its earlier New Testament, "Reach Out," is very readable (eighth-grade reading level) of course, but is criticized for being too interpretive. Its theological orientation is conservative and evangelistic. (Taylor originally created The Living Bible for Tyndale House Publishers.)

1971, New American Standard Bible (NAS)

Like the RSV of 1952, the NAS was based on the ASV of 1901. The ASV was a towering and very accurate work of scholarship, but was slipping in popularity. A conservative evangelistic group sought to revive it with the goal of a literal translation in fluent, readable (eleventh-grade reading level), and current English (a literary goal that still suffers for the sake of the literal). This process began with the 1965 Amplified Bible and culminated with the 1978 New International Version (see below). The NAS claims the ASV lineage, but is in fact a different translation to satisfy conservative Protestant congregations. Note, for example, the absence of the Apocrypha and the capitalization of all pronouns referring to God and all Old Testament references thought to be messianic.

1973, The Common Bible

This is an RSV translation of the Bible (including Apocrypha, excluding any polemical notes), published with international Catholic, Orthodox, and Protestant endorsement.

1976, Good News Bible: Today's English Version (TEV) (NT, 1966)

This is an American Protestant counterpart of the 1970 NEB (the completely new British translation in modern English). Very affordable and heavily marketed, it has been embraced by millions as an idiomatic version in modern and simple English, in a style purposely chosen for the elementary age reading level. (Its popular New Testament was called "Good News for Modern Man.") The translation principle, unlike that of RSV a generation before, is dynamic equivalent, standing somewhere between Phillips and the NEB. Often a virtual paraphrase (in "newspaper English"), it is better for private reading than for study. It was revised in the 1980s.

1978, The New International Version (NIV) (NT, 1973)

Since 1987, this reliable and readable Bible has outsold the King James Version, which had been the best-seller for centuries. Now a standard for both private reading and public proclamation in English-speaking countries, it is the fruit of the work of more than a hundred scholars from English-speaking countries around the world with, as they say, "a high view of Scripture."

Designed for conservative evangelical Protestants, it uses a vocabulary common to all English speakers (with a seventh-grade reading level) and strives for a balance between a literal rendering and a paraphrase. It is very successful in fulfilling the goals of major translations since the RSV: contextualizing the meaning of words, modifying sentence structure, and eliminating archaic pronouns and verb forms. (Its goals did not include eliminating unnecessary or unjustified gender-specific language.) It emphasizes the messianic meaning of certain Old Testament texts (for example, still translating Isaiah 7:14 "virgin," contrary to the best scholarly opinion).

6. Since 1982: Revisions of Versions

This era of new revisions more than new translations was prompted by knowledge of still older manuscripts, advances in biblical linguistics, and the continuing evolution of preferred English usage.

1982, The New King James Version (NKJV)

The NKJV is a formal-equivalence translation in the literal tradition of the AV, but with contemporary American English replacing Elizabethan (*thee*s and *thou*s and other archaic words). In its efforts to salvage some of the lyricism of Elizabethan English (at an eighth-grade reading level), this translation satisfies the nostalgia of those familiar with the KJV. Its Old Testament messianic passages are clearly influenced by Christian theology. Its New Testament, depending on the Greek text that it uses, forfeits the best modern text criticism.

1985, The New Jerusalem Bible (NJB)

This revision of the 1966 Jerusalem Bible is based on the 1973 French edition and includes an improved text and updated footnotes (it reflects the new sensitivity to inclusive language).

1986, The Revised New American Bible (RNAB) (NT)

After an original 1970 content-centered translation, this revision reflects (intentionally) a more form-centered approach. Typical of many, many changes, for example, is Matthew 5:18: "of this much I assure you," now is revised to "Amen, I say to you." According to some, this change is "a deliberate step backward," of the worst "formal equivalence." (Likewise, the 1989 REB is less idiomatic than the 1970 NEB it revises.) The revision, with the goal of communicating to "ordinary educated people," also reflects a greater gender inclusivity and "a dignity" more suitable for public reading (liturgical use).

1986, The New Century Bible

This Bible, with a conservative, evangelistic theological orientation, is published in two editions. "The Everyday Bible" is for adults; it is a simple, functional-equivalent translation for those with a limited vocabulary. The "International Children's Version" uses shorter, uncomplicated sentences and vocabulary at a third-grade reading level.

1989, The Revised English Bible (REB)

This extensive revision of the popular British NEB of 1970 was needed to keep the English current and the text up-to-date with modern scholarship. Although something of a disappointment (reverting to more traditional language and exegesis than the NEB), it still remains the foremost dynamic-equivalence

English translation. More inclusive language is used and the *thee*s and *thou*s that had been retained in prayers are now completely abandoned. Some say it is "more restrained" in its paraphrasing tendencies (thinking better, for example, of John 1:1: "When all things began, the Word already was," has become "In the beginning the Word already was").

1990, The New Revised Standard Version (NRSV)

This is the authorized revision of the 1952 RSV, which was a revision of the 1901 ASV which embodied earlier revisions of the 1611 KJV. (It is the text of the Oxford Annotated Study Bible.) It eliminates male-oriented language (where the original text is inclusive—"brothers and sisters" instead of "brethren," for example) and abandons the "thees" and "thous" that had been retained in prayers. Despite attacks on the RSV's translation of Isaiah 7:14, the NRSV keeps "young woman" (that had replaced "virgin"). In 1991 the NRSV was approved by the Catholic bishops for Catholic use in the US. (It was used in the English edition of the *Catechism of the Catholic Church*.)

1992 Today's English Version (second edition)

This new edition of the 1976 TEV eliminates exclusive language. It is the translation used in the Precious Moments Bible.

1993 The Message (NT)

This is a contemporary idiomatic English translation of the New Testament, Psalms, and some other Old Testament books

1994 Contemporary English Version (CEV) (NT, 1991)

This is a youth-oriented, dynamic equivalent translation. The Catholic Edition came later.

1996 The New Living Translation

This revision of the very popular The Living Bible (1967, 1971) is in the dynamic equivalent family.

The evangelization cross (also known as the Jerusalem cross):
Four tau crosses meet at the center, and four Greek crosses
represent the four corners of the world.

Comparing Scripture Translations

These are various versions of the Lord's Prayer (Luke 11:2–4). See previous pages for details about any of these translations.

Lindisfarne Gospels, about 950

This translation is in Old English (or "Anglo-Saxon"), the original pre-Norman Germanic stock of English used from the fifth century (or eighth, according to some) to the twelfth century. It is the language of the epic poem *Beowulf* of the early eighth century.

fader gehalgad sie noma oin tocymaeo ic oin hlaf userne daeghuaemlice sel us eghuelc daege fgef us synna usra gif faestlice aec pe fgefaes eghuelc scyldge us fgef ne usic onlaed ou in costunge

Wycliffe Bible, 1382

This translation is in Middle English, the language of the period from about 1150 to 1475 (which includes Geoffrey Chaucer, 1340–1400).

Fadir, halewid be thi name. Thi kyngdom come to. Zyue to vs to day oure eche dayes breed. And forzyue to vs oure synnes, as and we forzyuen to each owynge to vs. And leed not vs in to temptacioun.

Tyndale New Testament, 1525

This translation is in early Modern English, post-1475 (which includes the works of Shakespeare, 1564–1616).

Oure father which arte in heve, halowed be thy name. Lett thy kyngdom come. Thy will be fulfillet, even in erth as it is in heven. Oure dayly breed geve us this daye. And forgeve vs oure synnes: for even we forgeve every man that traspaseth vs, and ledde vs not into temptacio, Butt delliver vs from evyll. Amen.

Coverdale Bible, 1537

O oure father which art in heauen, halowed be thy name. Thy kyngdome come. Thy wil be fulfilled vpon earth, as it is in heauen. Geue vs this daye oure daylie bred. And forgeue vs oure synnes, for we also forgeue all them that are detters vnto vs. And lede vs not in to temptacion, but delyuer vs from euell.

Matthew's Bible, 1537

O oure father which arte in heauen, halowed be thy name. Thy kyngdome come. Thy will be fulfylled, euen in erth as it is in heauen. Oure dayly breed geue vs euermore. And forgeue vs our synnes: For euen we forgeue euery man yt treaspaseth vs. And leade vs not into temptacion. But delyuer vs from euyll.

The Great Bible, 1538

O oure father which are in heauen, halowed be thy name. Thy kyngdome come. Thy will be fulfylled, eue in erth also as it is in heaue. Oure dayly breed geue vs thys daye. And forgeue vs our synnes; For euen we forgeue euery man that treaspaseth vs. And leade vs not into temptacyon. But delyuer vs from euyll.

Geneva Bible, 1560

Our Father, who art in heaue, halowed by thy Name: Thy kingdome come: Let thy wil be done eue in earth, as it is in heauuen: Our daily bread giue vs for the day: And forgiue vs our sinnes: for euen we forgiue euerie man that is indetted to vs: And lead vs not into temptation: but deliuer vs from euil.

Bishop's Bible, 1568

O our father which art in heauen, halowed be thy name, thy Kyngdome come, thy wyll be fulfylled, euen in earth also, as it is in heaven. Our dayly breade geue vs this day. And forgeue vs our synnes: For euen we forgeue euery man that trespasseth vs. And leade vs not into temptation, but delyuer vs from euyll.

Rheims New Testament, 1582

Father, sanctified be thy name. Thy kingdom come. Our daily bread giue vs this day, and forgiue vs our sinnes, for because our selues also doe forgiue euery one that is in debt to vs. And lead vs not into temptation.

King James Bible, 1611

Our Father which art in heaven, Hallowed be thy name. Thy kingdom come. Thy will be done, as in heaven, so in earth. Give us day by day our daily bread. And forgive us our sins; for we also forgive every one that is indebted to us. And lead us not into temptation; but deliver us from evil.

Revised Version, 1881

Father, Hallowed be thy name. Thy kingdom come. Give us day by day our daily bread. And forgive us our sins; for we ourselves also forgive every one that is indebted to us. And bring us not into temptation.

American Standard Edition of the Revised Version, 1901

Father, Hallowed be thy name. Thy kingdom come. Give us day by day our daily bread. And forgive us our sins; for we ourselves also forgive every one that is indebted to us. And bring us not into temptation.

Revised Standard Version, 1946

Father, hallowed be thy name. Thy kingdom come. Give us each day our daily bread; and forgive us our sins, for we ourselves forgive every one who is indebted to us; and lead us not into temptation.

The New English Bible, 1961

Father, thy name be hallowed; Thy kingdom come. Give us each day our daily bread. And forgive us our sins, for we too forgive all who have done us wrong. And do not bring us to the test.

The Jerusalem Bible, 1966

Father, may your name be held holy, your kingdom come; give us each day our daily bread, and forgive us our sins, for we ourselves forgive each one who is in debt to us. And do not put us to the test.

Today's English Version, 1966

Father, may your name be kept holy, May your Kingdom come. Give us day by day the food we need. Forgive us our sins, for we forgive everyone who has done us wrong. And do not bring us to hard testing.

The New American Bible, 1970

Father, hallowed be your name, your kingdom come. Give us each day our daily bread. Forgive us our sins for we too forgive all who do us wrong; and subject us not to the trial.

The New King James Version, 1982

Our Father in heaven, hallowed be Your name. Your kingdom come. Your will be done on earth as it is in heaven. Give us day by day our daily bread. And forgive us our sins, for we also forgive everyone who is indebted to us. And do not lead us into temptation, but deliver us from the evil one.

The New Century Bible, 1986

Father, may your name always be kept holy. May your kingdom come. Give us the food we need for each day. Forgive us for our sins, because we forgive everyone who has done wrong to us. And do not cause us to be tempted.

Contemporary English Version, 1991

Father, help us to honor your name. Come and set up your kingdom. Give us each day the food we need. Forgive our sins, as we forgive everyone who has done wrong to us. And keep us from being tempted.

The Message, 1993

Father, reveal who you are. Set the world right. Keep us alive with three square meals. Keep us forgiven with you and forgiving others. Keep us safe from ourselves and the Devil.

The Old Testament

Historical Outline

I. Origins of cosmos, earth, humanity

    A. Creation

    B. Paradise   } Pre-history

    C. Original sin

II. Hebrew origins (B.C)

    A. The patriarchs, about 1850–1600

    B. The Hebrews in Egypt, about 1600–1250

The Star of David (formed by superimposing two triangles), also known as the *Magen David* ("Magen" meaning shield) or *Solomon's Seal*, is a symbol of Israel and the Jewish religion.

III. The State of Israel (B.C.)

    A. Origins: Exodus, desert, conquest, about 1250–1200

    B. Period of the judges, about 1200–1000

    C. Monarchy: Saul (1000), David (1000–965), Solomon (965–922)

    D. Divided monarchy; rise of prophecy 922–587

        1. To the fall of the Northern Kingdom (Israel) in 721 (Assyria)

        2. To the fall of the Southern Kingdom (Judah) in 587 (Babylon)

    E. Babylonian Exile (Captivity) 587–538

    F. Early post-Exile period and end of prophecy

        1. Restoration: Ezra and Nehemiah

        2. Persian domination

    G. Greek period 333–363

        1. From Alexander to the Seleucids 333–175

        2. The Maccabean revolt against Syria 175–135

        3. The Hasmonean era: Jewish independence 135 to 63

    H. Roman period

    (From Pompey through New Testament), beginning in 63 (Pompey takes Jerusalem and Israel becomes part of Roman province of Syria.)

How Great Thou Art

Wonders created by the hand of God

According to St. Gregory of Tours, about the year 550

The tides of the ocean	The rebirth of the phoenix
The growth of plants from seeds	The cycle of the sun
The volcano Mount Etna	The cycle of the moon

Note: The rebirth of the phoenix is mythological but was accepted as fact in the Middle Ages. There is a Latin phrase from Psalm 19: *Caeli enarrant gloriam Dei* which means "The heavens declare the glory of God." A simple *Caeli enarrant* alludes to the planets and stars as brilliant evidence of God's power and wisdom.

The wonders of the world

Humans' boasts are many, but can perhaps be represented by the celebrated seven. Interestingly, most are religious monuments, works of piety, except for the lighthouse and the gardens.

1. The Mausoleum at Halicarnassus (Asia Minor)

The tomb erected near the present-day Turkish port of Budrum (about 350? B.C.), by Artemis, widow of the prince of Caria, Mausolus (hence the word mausoleum)

2. The Temple of Artemis (Diana) at Ephesus

An ancient city in west Asia Minor; also the site of an early Christian community

3. The Hanging Gardens of Babylon

Planted on the terraces of the ziggurats (pyramidal temples)

4. The Statue of Zeus at Olympia

Olympia is a plain in ancient Elis, Greece (cite of the Games); by Phidias.

5. The Colossus of Rhodes

A bronze statue of Apollo that stood at the entrance of the harbor of Rhodes, a Greek island in the southeast Aegean Sea, between the southwest coast of Turkey and Crete

6. The Lighthouse at Alexandria

The "Pharos" was built by Ptolemy. (Alexandria is in Egypt.)

7. The Pyramids of Egypt (the only extant Ancient Wonder)

Near El Giza, which is near Cairo; especially the one built by Cheops (Khufu), king of Egypt about 2650–2630 B.C.

The modern world may not match the mystique of those ancient wonders, but may rival their grandeur with a list of its own:

1. The Coliseum of Rome	5. The Leaning Tower of Pisa
2. The Catacombs of Alexandria	6. The Porcelain Tower of Nankin
3. The Great Wall of China	7. The Mosque of St. Sophia at
4. Stonehenge	Constantinople

Divine Choice

In the garden, after the Fall, the God who had created all things promised to restore all things, "I will put enmity between you and the woman, and between your offspring and hers; he will strike at your head, and you will strike at his heel" (Genesis 3:15). At the heart of this saving will is divine vocation (call, or election), typically:

1. From before birth (Isaac, Samson, Samuel)
2. Of sterile or aged (or virginal) parentage (Isaac, Jesus)
3. From unpromising stock/circumstances (Gideon, Mary)
4. Initially causing question/disbelief/self-doubt (Jeremiah)
5. With promise of divine assistance (Moses, Gideon)
6. Necessitating an exodus/conversion (Abraham, Paul)

Abraham—Genesis 12:1–5a

Isaac—Genesis 18:9–15, 21:1–8

Moses—Exodus 3:1–12

Gideon—Judges 6:11–24

Samson—Judges 13:2–24

Samuel—1 Samuel 1, 3:1–20

David—1 Samuel 16:1–13

Elisha—1 Kings 19:19–21

Suffering Servant—Isaiah 49:1–7

Amos—Amos 7–9

Isaiah—Isaiah 6, 40:6–9

Jeremiah—Jeremiah 1:1–19

Ezekiel—Ezekiel 1–3

Zechariah—Zechariah 1:7–6:8

John the Baptist—Luke 1:5–25

Mary—Luke 1:26–38

Joseph—Matthew 1:18–24

Jesus—Luke 1:26–38

The Twelve—Matthew 4:18–22, 9:9; Mark 1:16–20, 2:14; Luke 5:1–11, 27–28; John 1:35–51

Paul—Acts 9:1–19; Galatians 1:11–24

Old Testament Table of Contents

I. Human Origins: Genesis 1–11

  A. Creation

    1. 1:1–2:4

    2. 2:4–25

  B. Paradise

  C. Original sin

    1. The Fall—3   **Genesis 1–11**

    2. Cain and Abel—4:1–16

    3. Adam–Noah generations—4:17–6:4

    4. The Flood—6:5–8:22

    5. God's covenant with Noah—9:1–17

    6. Tower of Babel—11:1–9

  D. Restoration ("The fourth theme" of Genesis 1–11, alluded to in the divine promises after the Fall, is a unifying theme of the rest of the Bible and the goal of revelation.)

II. Hebrew Origins: Genesis 12–50

  A. Patriarchal period—Genesis 12–36

    1. Migration—11:27–12:9

    2. Melchizedek—14:18–20 (See Psalm 110:4; Hebrews 7.)

    3. Covenant—15:1–21

    4. Sodom and Gomorrah—18:16–19:29   **Genesis 12–50**

    5. Sacrifice of Isaac—22:1–19

    6. Betrothal of Rebekah—24

    7. Jacob-Esau conflict—25:19–28:9

    8. Jacob's dream at Bethel—28:10–22

    9. The winning of Rachel—29:1–30

    10. Jacob-Esau reconciliation—32–33

    11. Rape of Dinah—34

  B. Joseph Stories—Genesis 37–50

    1. The brothers—37:2–36

    2. Joseph's temptation (Potiphar's wife)—39:1–23

    3. Dreams—40–41

    4. Reunion—42–44

    5. Judah's speech ("Paragon of Hebrew eloquence")—44:18–34

    6. Disclosure—45

    7. Central theme—45:7–9

    8. Jacob in Egypt—46–47

    9. Deaths—49:28–50:26

   10. Patriarchal burials—Genesis 23:1–20, 25:9, 49:31, 50:13 (Sarah, Abraham, Isaac, Rebekah, Leah, Jacob: all at Cave of Machpelah in Hebron)

III. The State of Israel—Exodus

  A. National origins

    1. In Egypt

     Bondage in Egypt—Exodus 1–5   **Exodus**

     The plagues—Exodus 7:8–12:32

     Deliverance—Exodus 13:17–15:21

     Exodus—Exodus 14:21–31 (prose), 15:1–18 (poetry)

     Miriam, prophetess—Exodus 2:4–9, 15:20–21; Numbers 12:1–16, 20:1

    2. In the desert

     Journey from Red Sea to Sinai—Exodus 15:22–19:2

     The quail and manna—Exodus 16; Numbers 11:1–15, 31–34

     Water from the rock—Exodus 17:1–7; Numbers 20:2–13

     Sinai covenant—Exodus 19:1–24:11

     The Decalogue—Exodus 20:1–17 (See Deuteronomy 5:6–21.)

     The sanctuary and its furnishings—Exodus 25–30

     The golden calf—Exodus 32

     Israelite sacrificial and other ritual legislation—Leviticus 1–27

     Social laws—Leviticus 19   **Leviticus**

     The sabbatical and jubilee year—Leviticus 25

     The reward of obedience—Leviticus 26

     The first census—Numbers 1–3

A Horned Moses

Michelangelo's statue of Moses, following earlier paintings, includes horns because of a mistranslation of the Hebrew word for "radiant" in Exodus 34:29—"As he came down from the mountain, he did not know that the skin of his face had become radiant" (formerly "horned").

Further legal observances—Numbers 3–10:10

Aaron's blessing—Numbers 6:22–27

Journey from Sinai to Moab (thirty-eight years)—Numbers 10:11–22:1

Jealousy of Aaron and Miriam—Numbers 12

3. Toward Canaan

Reconnoitering Canaan—Numbers 13–14   **Numbers**

Korah's sedition—Numbers 16

The sin of Moses and Aaron—Numbers 20:2–13

Aaron's death—Numbers 20:22–29

The bronze serpent—Numbers 21:4–9

Baalam, religious compromiser—Numbers 22:2–41, 31:16
(See 2 Peter 2:15; Jude 11; Revelation 2:14–17.)

The second census—Numbers 26

The succession of Joshua—Numbers 27:12–23

4. Moses' testament: Deuteronomy   **Deuteronomy**

Historical review—Deuteronomy 1:1–4:43

Exhortation to covenant fidelity—Deuteronomy 5–11

Keynote of Mosaic Law (see Jewish "Shema")—Deuteronomy 6:4–5

Recapitulation/completion of Exodus 20–23 (Second Law)—
Deuteronomy 12–26

Synopsis of sacred story—Deuteronomy 26:5–9

Moses' final words—Deuteronomy 27–33

The two ways—Deuteronomy 30:15–20

5. Into Canaan

The Jordan crossing—Joshua 3

Joshua, military strategists—Joshua 3, 6, 8   **Joshua**

The fall of Jericho—Joshua 6

Rahab and the red rope—Joshua 2, 6:22–23 (See Matthew 1:15.)

The day the sun stopped—Joshua 10 (10:13)

Joshua's farewell and death—Joshua 23–24

B. The Period of the Judges

1. The Book of Judges

Thesis and interpretation for the Book of Judges—Judges 2:1–3:6

Deborah, prophetess and judge—Judges 4–5

Jael, deceitful hostess, and the defeat of Sisera—Judges 4:17–22,
5:24–27

Gideon the conqueror—Judges 6:1–8:33

Abimelech the usurper—Judges 9 **Judges**

The parable of Jotham—Judges 9:7–21

Jephthah and the fateful vow—Judges 11:1–12:7

The "Shibboleth"—Judges 12:1–6

Samson—Judges 13:2–16:31

Micah and the stolen silver—Judges 17–18

2. Ruth, Moabite become Israelite—The Book of Ruth

"Wherever you go. . . ."—Ruth 1:16–17 **Ruth**

Ruth-David lineage—Ruth 4:18–22 (See Matthew 1:5.)

C. The Monarchy (united: about 1000–922 B.C.)

1. Eli and Samuel

Birth of Samuel—1 Samuel 1

Eli's sons—1 Samuel 2:11–26

Samuel's call—1 Samuel 3:1–4:1a

The beginning of prophetic ministry—1 Samuel 3, 9, 10, 12

Eli's death—1 Samuel 4:12–18

The demand for a king—1 Samuel 8

2. Samuel and Saul

The anointing—1 Samuel 9:1–10:16, 11:12–15

Saul's disobedience—1 Samuel 13–15

3. Saul and David

David's anointing—1 Samuel 16 **1 Samuel**

Goliath—1 Samuel 17:1–18:16

Jonathan friendship—1 Samuel 18, 20; 2 Samuel 1

Mephibosheth (or Meribbaal), lame prince—2 Samuel 4:4, 9:6–13, 16:1–4, 19:24–30, 21:7; 1 Chronicles 8:34, 9:40

The widow Abigail—1 Samuel 25, 30; 2 Samuel 2:2, 3:3; 1 Chronicles 3:1

Saul pursues David—1 Samuel 26

Saul, Samuel, and the Witch of Endor—1 Samuel 28:3–25

Saul's death—1 Samuel 31

4. King David

Mourning for Saul and Jonathan—2 Samuel 1

The oracle of Nathan ("*Magna Charta* of Royal Messianism")—2
Samuel 7:8–16 (See 1 Chronicles 17; Psalm 89:20–38, 132:11–18;
Acts 2:30; Hebrews 1:5.)

David's prayers—1 Chronicles 17:16–27, 29:10–19

Bathsheba—2 Samuel 11

Nathan—2 Samuel 12

2 Samuel

Absalom—2 Samuel 13–18

Rizpah and the longest wake—2 Samuel 21:1–10

5. King Solomon

Reign—1 Kings 1–5, 9–11

Solomon's judgment—1 Kings 3:16–28

1 Kings

Temple dedication—1 Kings 8; 2 Chronicles 5–7

The visit of the Queen of Sheba—1 Kings 10:1–13

Solomon's Cedar

The cross of the crucifixion has always excited and mystified the
imagination. There is a legend that Solomon cut down a cedar tree
and buried it. Years later, the pool of Bethesda was built on the very
site of this cedar's grave. Still later, when Jesus entered Jerusalem on the
Sunday before his death, the ancient cedar, rising to the surface of the
pool, was retrieved. The upright beam of Christ's cross was said to be
made from that cedar tree.

D. The Divided Monarchy and the rise of prophecy

1. From the death of Solomon (922) to the fall of the North (721)

Division of the Kingdom—1 Kings 11–16

a. **The Elijah Cycle**—1 Kings 17–19, 21—2 Kings 1

The widow of Zarapheth—1 Kings 17:8–24

The Baal prophets—1 Kings 18

Jezebel's wrath—1 Kings 19:1–18

Ahaziah and the captains' fate—2 Kings 1

Elijah's ascension—2 Kings 2:9–14 (see Matthew 17:9–13)

Ahab's reign—1 Kings 16:29–22:40

Naboth's vineyard—1 Kings 21

Jezebel, paragon of the non-Jew—1 Kings 16:31–32; 18:1–19:3, 21;
2 Kings 9:7–37 (See Revelation 2:20.)

b. **The Elisha Cycle**—2 Kings 2–9

    Call—1 Kings 19:19–21

    The Curse, or "Elisha's sense of humor"—2 Kings 2:23–25

    Miracles of Elisha (2 Kings)

      — The poor widow—2 Kings 4:1–7

      — The rich woman of Shunem—2 Kings 4:8–37

      — The poisoned stew—2 Kings 4:38–41

      — Multiplication of the loaves—2 Kings 4:42–44

      — Naaman the leper and Gehazi—2 Kings 5:1–27

      — The lost ax—2 Kings 6:1–7

      — The foiled ambush—2 Kings 6:8–23

      — Ben-hadad's siege of Samaria—2 Kings 6:24–7:20

      — The prediction of famine—2 Kings 8:1–6

      — Hazael and the death of Ben-hadad—2 Kings 8:7–15

    Elisha's death and corpse—2 Kings 13:14–21

    Jehu's purge—2 Kings 9:1–10:27   **2 Kings**

    Jezebel's "demise"—2 Kings 9:30–37

    Athaliah, Israel's only queen—2 Kings 11

    Origin of the Samaritans—2 Kings 17

    Assyrian invasion—2 Kings 18–20

c. **Isaiah prophecies**, 742—about 690 (Judea addressed)

    Call—Isaiah 6   **Isaiah**

    Arraignment of Jerusalem—1–5

    The sin of Judah—1:1–20, 5:7

    Messianic oracles—2:2–4 (See Micah 4, 9:1–6, 11:1–9.)

    Emmanuel oracle—7:14

    Israel and Judah's foreign policy—7:1–17

    Lucifer myth—14:12–23

    Song of redemptive joy—26

    Messianic bliss—35

d. **Micah prophecies**, contemporary of Isaiah (Judea addressed)

    The glory of the remnant—Micah 4–5 (See Isaiah 2:2–4.)

    The case against Israel—6:1–7:20   **Micah**

    On religion—6:1–8 (See Isaiah 1:1–20; Matthew 7:21; John 4:21–24.)

e. **Jonah** (Nineveh addressed)   **Jonah**

   Jonah, a prophet in a separate category, is the name of the central
   figure in this story that was written much later, in the fifth century.

   Jonah's prayer from fish's belly—Jonah 2:3–10

The Fast of the Ninevites

Syrian and Chaldean Christians (the faithful using the East Syrian Rite,
mostly in Syria, Iraq, and Iran) and Copts (Eastern Rite faithful in Egypt)
observe three days of fast and penance before Lent, using a name that
recalls the fasting of the Ninevites by which they avoided the wrath of
God (Jonah 3:5–10).

---

2. The Fall of the North

   a. **Amos prophecies**, during Jeroboam II's reign, 786–746 (Israel
      addressed)

      Judgment of the nations (woes)—Amos 1–2   **Amos**

      On religion—5:21–27

      Against luxury and complacency—6

      Visions: threats and promises—7–9

      Messianic restoration ("fallen hut . . .")—9:8–15

   b. **Hosea prophecies**, during Jeroboam II's reign, 786–746 (Israel
      addressed)

      Hosea's marriage—Hosea 1–3   **Hosea**

      On religion (insincere conversion)—5:15–6.6

      "Out of Egypt I called my son . . ."—11:1–11

      Israel's corporate personality—12:3–7

3. Pre-Exilic Judah

   Judah after 721—2 Kings 18–25

   Discovery of Deuteronomy (622) and Josiah's reform—2 Kings 22–23

   a. **Jeremiah prophecies**, about 650–585   **2 Kings**

      Call—Jeremiah 1:1–10 (See 15:16, 20:9.)

      Early prophecy—2:1–3:5   **Jeremiah**

      Against infidelity—2–3, 5–7

      The temple sermon—7:1–15

      Indictment of Jerusalem for idolatry—10

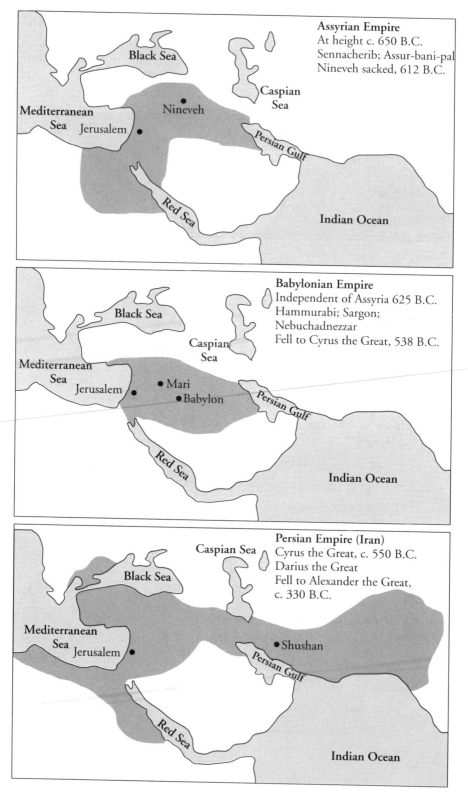

Assyrian Empire
At height c. 650 B.C.
Sennacherib; Assur-bani-pal
Nineveh sacked, 612 B.C.

Black Sea

Caspian
Sea

Mediterranean
Sea Jerusalem

Nineveh

Persian Gulf

Red Sea

Indian Ocean

Babylonian Empire
Independent of Assyria 625 B.C.
Hammurabi; Sargon;
Nebuchadnezzar
Fell to Cyrus the Great, 538 B.C.

Black Sea

Caspian
Sea

Mediterranean
Sea Jerusalem

Mari
Babylon

Persian Gulf

Red Sea

Indian Ocean

Persian Empire (Iran)
Cyrus the Great, c. 550 B.C.
Darius the Great
Fell to Alexander the Great,
c. 330 B.C.

Caspian Sea

Black Sea

Mediterranean
Sea Jerusalem

Shushan

Persian Gulf

Red Sea

Indian Ocean

Jeremiah's complaints ("jeremiads")—15:10–21, 18:18–23, 20:7–18
(See Job 3.)

Potter symbol—18:1–6

Potter's flask symbol—19

The two baskets of figs—24

Promises of Israel's restoration—30–32

The new covenant prophecy ("gospel before the gospel")—31:31–34

Jeremiah's place in Jerusalem's last days—36:1–40:6

b. **Zephaniah prophecies**, Josiah's reign 640–609

The Day of the Lord 1 (classic description, see *Dies Irae*)

The remnant—3 (Remnant's Hymn 3:14–20)

c. **Nahum prophecies**, about 615 (against Nineveh)

The fall of Jerusalem—2 Kings 24–25

E. The Babylonian Exile

1. Lamentations

2. Baruch

3. **Habakkuk prophecies**

A person questions God
(first Jewish example?)—1

Habakkuk's prayer, a religious lyric—3

4. **Ezekiel prophecies**

Call—Ezekiel 1–4

Revelation of his mission—1–3; 5; 10

First vision—1:4–3:15

Vision of temple abominations—8:1–18

Glory of God departs—10

Individual accountability—14:12–23, 18; 33:10–20 (See Jeremiah 31:29–30.)

Marriage-adultery image—16, 20, 23

The prophet as watchman—33:1–9

The prophet's false popularity—33:30–33

Parable of the shepherds—34

Visions of restored community— 36:16–37:14

Dry bones—37:1–14

Vision of temple restoration—40–43

Zephaniah

Nahum

Nahum
Lamentations
Baruch
Habakkuk

Ezekiel

F. Early Post-Exilic Period

   1. Liberation and return

      a. **Second Isaiah prophecies**—Isaiah 40–55

         Suffering servant oracles—42:1–4, 49:1–7, 50:4–11, 52:13–53:12

         Message of deliverance—40   **"Second Isaiah"**

         Gift of the restoration—43–44

         Effectiveness of God's word—55:10–11

      b. **Third Isaiah prophecies**—Isaiah 56–66

         True fasting—58

         Confessions—59

         Glory of the New Jerusalem—60   **"Third Isaiah"**

         The good news—61

         Supplication—62–64

   2. Restoration

      a. Ezra, religious and cultic reformer

         The decree of Cyrus (538–529 B.C.)—Ezra 1

         Samaritan interference—4:1–5   **Ezra**

         Temple rebuilding—5–6

         The "Ezra Memoirs"—7–10 (and Nehemiah 8–9)

      b. Nehemiah, builder and administrator

         Prayer—Nehemiah 1:5–11

         Return to Jerusalem—2   **Nehemiah**

         Temple rebuilding—4–6

         Ezra reads the Law—8:1–12

         Confession prayer—9–10

      c. **Haggai prophecies**, 520f

         Exhortation to rebuild the temple—Haggai 1   **Haggai**

      d. **Zechariah prophecies**, 520f

         Promoting temple rebuilding—Zechariah 6:9–15

         Entry of the messiah (See Palm Sunday.)—9:9–17   **Zechariah**

         The Day of the Lord (apocalyptic)—14

      e. **Malachi prophecies**, about 450   **Malachi**

         The messenger of the covenant (See John the
           Baptist.)—Malachi 3:1–3

      f. **Obadiah prophecies**, fifth century   **Obadiah**

g. **Joel prophecies**, about 400

>The Day of the Lord—Joel 2–3
>
>Call to repentance—2:12–17 (Ash Wednesday)
>
>Spirit poured out—2:28–29
>
>Last judgment—3:1–21

Joel

G. Post-Exilic Jewish Literature

"Short story" style: How should Jews relate to their Gentile neighbors? (nationalistic)

1. **Esther**, late fourth-century Jewess become queen of Persia

>Queen Vashti, rebellious beauty—Esther 1
>
>Esther intercedes with Ahasuerus—5; 7
>
>Prayers of Mordecai and Esther—13:9–17, 14:3–19 (Addition C)

Esther

2. **Tobit**, early second century

>Tobit's prayers—3:2–6; 8:5–7, 15–17; 13
>
>Raphael reveals his identity—12:11–22

Tobit

3. **Daniel**, about 165 (Antiochus IV Epiphanes' reign)

>a. Six folk tales about Daniel—Daniel 1–6
>
>>(1) Daniel and his friends in king's palace—1
>>
>>(2) Daniel's interpretation of an unrevealed dream—2
>>
>>(3) Shadrach, Meshack, Abednego in the furnace—3
>>
>>(4) Nebuchadnezzar's dream—4
>>
>>(5) Belshazzar's party and the writing on the wall—5
>>
>>(6) Daniel in the lion's den—6
>
>b. Four visions—7–12
>
>>(1) The four beasts (See Daniel 2:36–45.)—7
>>
>>(2) The ram and the he-goat—8
>>
>>(3) The "seventy weeks" (see Jeremiah 25:11, 29:10)—9
>>
>>(4) A history of the world's kingdoms, Cyrus to Antiochus—10–12
>
>c. Appendix: two didactic short stories
>
>>(1) Susanna's virtue—13
>>
>>(2) Bel and the dragon—14

Daniel

4. **Judith**, about 100

>Achior's speech before Bethulia—Judith 5:5–21
>
>Prayer of Judith—9
>
>Judith and Holoferenes—10:20f
>
>Hymn of praise of Judith—16

Judith

H. Wisdom Literature
1. Job (seventh to fifth century B.C.)
    Core story—Job 1–2; 42:7–17 (prologue and epilogue)

    Dialogues with comforters (Eliphaz, Bildad, Zophar)—3–31

    Elihu speeches—32–37

    YHWH speeches—38:1–40:26

2. Ecclesiastes (about 300 B.C.)
    Vanity of vanities—Ecclesiastes 1:2–11

    A time to be born, a time to die—3:1–15

    Cast your bread upon the water—11

3. Psalms (to fourth century B.C.)
4. Proverbs (edited early fifth century B.C.)
    Exhortations of the wise man to his son—1–6

    Religious-pedantic—10–22:16

    Secular-pedantic—22:17–24

    Secular-shrewd—25–29

    The numbered maxims—30:7–33

    Poem of the valiant woman—31:10–31

5. Song of Solomon (late sixth century B.C.)
    "A tryst in spring"— Song of Solomon 2:8–17

6. Sirach (Ecclesiasticus, early second century B.C.)
    Duties toward God—Sirach 2

    True friendship—6:5–17, 9:10–16

    A really good wife—26:1–18

    A prayer for God's people—36

    Hymn of the Ancestors—44–51

7. Wisdom (about 100 B.C.)
    On suffering ("The souls of the just are in the hand of God")—Wisdom 3:1–12

    Solomon's prayer—9

I. Rebellion and Jewish independence

1. 1 Maccabees (about 100 B.C.)

    Portrait of Judas Maccabeus—3

    Four laments—1:25–28, 36–40; 2:7–13; 3:45

Three hymns of praise—2:51–64 ("our fathers"), 3:3–9 (Judas), 14:4–15 (Simon)

The death of Antiochus Epiphanes and the battle of Bethzacharam—6

Roman alliance—8

Death of Judas Maccabeus—9:1–22

Simon's rule and death—13–14

2. 2 Maccabees (about 100 B.C.)

Preface—2:19–32

Heliodorus—3

The martyrdom of Eleazar and the seven brothers—6–7

Ms. Wisdom

It is not uncommon for wisdom to be portrayed as a person. In the Hebrew Bible, "she" is portrayed not as abstract virtue but as a concrete person, divine even (see Proverbs 1, 8; Sirach 1, 24; Wisdom 6, 9). It was a familiar device for Israel's neighbors too. The name *Sophia* is derived from the Greek word for wisdom. Legend tells of a Roman widow named Sophia who had three daughters named Faith, Hope, and Charity. The whole family was martyred, as the story goes—the three daughters first and then "Wisdom" herself, slain as she prayed for her daughters. Her feast day was September 30. Christians see Wisdom personified in Jesus.

Divine Names and Titles

Out of respect for God's holiness, the people of Israel do not pronounce the name of God. In reading Scripture, the revealed name of YHWH is replaced by the divine title "Lord" (*Adonai* in Hebrew, *Kyrios* in Greek). This is the same title by which the divinity of Jesus is acclaimed ("Jesus is Lord").

The Seven Names of God

Below are the traditional Seven Names of God. Over these the scribes exercised special care, especially mindful of the Decalogue mandate (Exodus 20:7). Hence, in the Middle Ages, God is sometimes referred to as *The Seven*.

1. *El*

Hebrew: common stem word used for a deity in Semitic languages; the earliest Hebrews used it in forming words about God. Etymologically uncertain: Power? Wholly other? Highest? See *el* root in Michael (Who is like God?), Samuel (The name of God), Gabriel (Man of God), Israel (One who has striven with God).

2. *Elohim*

Common, appearing several thousand times in the Old Testament; Hebrew plural of *El* (singular understood); used (or meant) in the plural for the gods of the other nations or groups (Genesis 35:2, Exodus 18:11); Jesus' cry from the cross, "Eli, Eli . . ." (Matthew 27:46) is a form of this.

3. *Adonai*

Hebrew (Greek: *Kyrios*; Latin: *Dominus*; English: *Lord*); for late pre-Christian Jews the Hebrew substitute for the unspeakable YHWH. This title is used about Jesus in order to proclaim his divinity.

4. *Yahweh* (or mistakenly *Jehovah*)

English rendering of the enigmatic sacred tetragrammaton, YHWH, with vowels from Adonai (sometime in the late pre-Christian era Jews stopped pronouncing it out of reverence and substituted *Adonai*). God's self-revelation to Moses (Exodus 3:14); maybe "I Am Who Am" or "I will be with you" (absolute being). Occurs over 6,700 times in Old Testament, more often than all other designations combined. Frequent component for personal names: See prefixes Je, Jehu, Jeho and suffixes iah, jah.

5. *Ehyeh-asher-Ehyeh*

6. *(El) Shaddai*

"Pantocrator" (almighty) in Greek; according to Genesis 17:1, 35:11; and Exodus 6:3, God used this in speaking to Abraham and Jacob; appears in the celebrated YHWH text; in English it means "Lord of the Mountain."

7. *Zebaot*

Other Names of God

Ancient of Days

Daniel 7, 9, 13, 22; emphasizing his eternity compared to the frailty of earthly empires

Father

Jesus' revelation of God; see John 14:6–31, 16:12–15

God

English (Latin: *Deus*; Greek: *Theos*).

Jehovah

A non-word; a linguistic mistake. Appeared for the first time in 1530. Since written Hebrew did not use vowels until quite late, the ancient manuscripts read simply YHWH (as this would be expressed in English) for "God." Through the centuries, the name of God came to be considered so sacred that it was not to be pronounced. So wherever YHWH appeared in the ancient text, the scribes added vowel marks signaling the reader to say *Adonai* instead of Yahweh. These marks, "vowel pointings," were not separate letters, but smaller symbols usually below a consonant to indicate its vowel sound. When one adds the vowels of *Adonai* to the consonants of *Yahweh* (YHWH), the result, if you're not aware that *Adonai* is to be read, comes out sounding like *Yahowah* (Jehovah).

Malek

King; used frequently for Yahweh

Trinity

God revealed in three Persons: the Father (who is God, but is not the Son or the Holy Spirit), the Son (Jesus, who is God, but is not the Father or the Holy Spirit), and the Holy Spirit (who is God, but is not the Father or the Son). See Matthew 28:18–20; John 14:6–31.

The three interwoven circles of the Trinity.

YHWH Sebaoth

YHWH (God) of Hosts; not found in the first seven books of the Bible; the meaning here of "Hosts" is uncertain: armies of heaven? armies of Israel?

Principal Deities of Old Testament Neighbors

Mesopotamia: A triad of Anu, Bel, and Ea

Canaan: A pantheon headed by El, son Baal and goddesses (of sex and war) Anath, Astarte, and Asherah (Ashtaroth)

Egypt: Isis, wife of Osiris and mother of Horus; also Aton Re

Philistia: Dagon ("little fish"); also Ashtaroth

Moab: Chemosh

Ammonites: Molech (or Milcom)

Phoenicia: Astarte, Melkart (Baal)

Amorites: Annurru, Asherah

Babylon: Ishtar, Marduk (with which Bel would be identified)

The Covenant in the Old Testament

Jeremiah 31:31–34 is the one passage in the Old Testament where the idea of a *new* testament is expressly mentioned.

1. Yahweh and Noah (God and earth)—Genesis 6:18, 9:8–17

2. Yahweh and Abraham (God and individual)

Repeated to Isaac—Genesis 26:24, Jacob—Genesis 28:13–15, and Moses—
Exodus 6:2–4

a. Promise of numerous descendants—Genesis 12:2–3

b. Promise of descendants, land; (renamed)—Genesis 15:18–21; 17:2–8,
   15–16

c. Sign: circumcision—Genesis 17:10–14

3. Yahweh and Moses (God and community)

a. Agreements and negotiations—Exodus 19

b. Reception of the Law—Exodus 20–23

c. Ratification of the covenant—Exodus 24

Old Testament Terms

Names for the Chosen People

Hebrew

Abraham (Hebrew)

Semitic language (of the Hebrews), called the "language of the Canaanites"
   in the Bible

Israel

Jacob (after the angel renamed him); see Genesis 35:10.

The nation of the twelve Hebrew tribes following liberation (Exodus) from
   Egypt under Moses (Father of his Country)

The Northern Kingdom after the division (922 B.C., end of Solomon's reign)

Judah

Fourth son of Jacob (Israel)

The tribe (descendants) of Judah

The Southern Kingdom after the division

All Hebrews left in the Promised Land after the fall of Israel (the Northern
   Kingdom), 721 B.C.

Jew

From "Judah"; linguistically Latin and Greek

All Hebrews after the Babylonian captivity (587–538 B.C.)

The Seven Patriarchs

Adam, Noah, Shem, Abraham, Isaac, Jacob, and Joseph

Some of Israel's holy women

The wedding blessing of a bride refers to the women "whose praises are sung in the Scriptures": Sarah, Rebecca, Rachel, Miriam, Deborah, Hannah, Judith, and Esther

Names for the Promised Land

The Promised Land

Chosen by God (Genesis 15:18), for the chosen people led by Moses from Egypt

Land of Milk and Honey

God's utopian description (Exodus) of the Promised Land

Canaan

Land in the middle of the fertile crescent, between the Jordan River and the Mediterranean Sea, occupied by Canaanites whom Israel gradually displaced/absorbed

Israel

The kingdom established by Moses and Joshua in Canaan, with intermittent independent political rule until 587 B.C., and never since; also the "Northern Kingdom" after Israel's split following Solomon's reign

Palestine

From "Philistine," the name of the area's southern inhabitants

Judah

The Southern Kingdom after the split following Solomon's reign

The Holy Land

For Jews, Christians, and Moslems

Zion

Jebusite city that became Jerusalem. When it was captured by David it was named the *Citadel of David* (2 Samuel 5:7). It assumed a sacred character when he brought to it the ark of the covenant. After the temple was built on the northeastern hill ("Mt. Moriah"), the term *Zion* (or *Sion*) was applied to the hill too. Gradually the name came to be applied to all of Jerusalem (2 Kings 19:21; Psalm 125, 126), ultimately even to the Holy Land generally, indeed to the Jewish faith itself—hence the modern movement to make Palestine the Jewish homeland is called *Zionism*. In particular, Mt. Moriah is the site, according to legend, of King David's tomb and Jesus' Last Supper. It is also where Abraham intended to sacrifice Isaac, the locale of Jesus' trial, the location of the Dome of the Rock mosque, the place where the Western Wall is found, and the site revered by Muslims as the place from which Muhammad rode a steed to heaven.

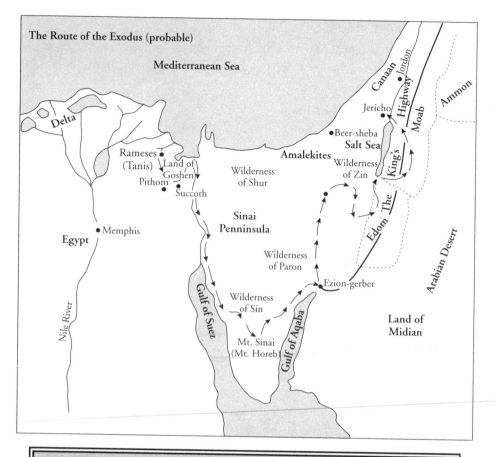

The Route of the Exodus (probable)

Cities of Refuge

These were asylums for "accidental" murderers (see Numbers 35; Deuteronomy 19; Joshua 20). Moses set the first three apart east of the Jordan (Deuteronomy 4:43); the Israelites under Joshua set the other three apart west of the Jordan (Joshua 21).

1. Bezer (Moab desert)   4. Kedesh (Galilee, by Naphtali)

2. Ramoth-Gilead   5. Shechem (mountain region of Ephraim)

3. Golan (Bashan)   6. Hebron (mountain region of south Judah)

In medieval Europe, churches provided such sanctuary for hunted persons, the altar guaranteeing immunity from arrest. Later these names were applied to Jesus, the "refuge of the repentant."

1. "Fortress"   Jesus' strength

2. "High"   Jesus' dignity

3. "Joy"   Jesus' gift

4. "Holy"   Jesus' sanctity

5. "Shoulder"   Jesus' responsibility

6. "Brotherhood" Jesus' following

Old Testament Places and Things of Worship

Patriarchal Sanctuaries

1. Shechem (Genesis 12:6–7, 33:18–20), Abraham's first stop in Canaan

2. Bethel (Genesis 12:8, 28:10–22), site of Jacob's ladder/stairway vision

3. Mamre (Genesis 13:18), point of reference for patriarchs' graves

4. Beersheba (Genesis 26:23–25), God's promises to Isaac (repetition of the promises to Abraham)

The Tent ("Tabernacle") of the Exodus (to house the ark)

1. Description—Exodus 26, 36:8–38

2. Divine presence—Exodus 40:34–38; Numbers 9:15–23; Exodus 33:7–11; Numbers 12:8

The Ark of the Covenant (housing the tablets of the Decalogue)

1. Descriptions—Exodus 25:10–22, 26:33, 37:1–9, 40:21

2. Religious Significance

   a. A place of divine presence—see 1 Samuel 4:7, 22; Numbers 10:35; 1 Samuel 5:1–7:1; 2 Samuel 6:6–7

   b. An archive for the Law—see Deuteronomy 10:1–5; Exodus 25:16, 40:20

3. Ark brought by David—2 Samuel 6

4. Altar built on site of future temple—2 Samuel 24:16–25

Sanctuaries in Israel before the temple

1. Gilgal—Joshua 4:19, 5

2. Shiloh—Joshua 18:1; 21:2; 22:9, 12; 1 Samuel 3; Judges 21:19–21

3. Mizpah—Judges 20:1, 3; 21:1, 5, 8

4. Ophrah—Judges 6:11–24

5. Dan—Judges 17–18

6. Jerusalem

Temple of Jerusalem

1. The temples:

   a. Built by Solomon on Mt. Moriah about 1000 B.C. Destroyed in 587 B.C. in the siege of Jerusalem by Nebuchadnezzar—1 Kings 5–8; 2 Chronicles 3, 5; Exodus 40.

   b. The temple of Zerubbabel (Post-Exilic). Completed about 515 on the same site—Ezra 3–5.

c. Third—Begun in 20 B.C. by Herod the Great and destroyed in A.D. 70 in the siege of Jerusalem by Vespacian and Titus. This was the conquest commemorated in the Roman Arch of Titus, which includes relief depictions of the spoils taken from the temple. It was in the temple area that Muslims built a splendid mosque, the Dome of the Rock, in the seventh century, commemorating their belief in Muhammad's ascent into heaven on this spot. Nearby stands Judaism's revered Western (Wailing) Wall, believed to be the remains of the western wall of Herod's temple.

2. Religious Significance

a. Divine presence—1 Kings 8:10f; 2 Kings 19:14f; 2 Chronicles 5:14; Ezekiel 10:4, 43:5; Psalms 27:4, 84; Amos 1:2; Isaiah 2:2–3, 6:1–4; Jeremiah 14:21

b. Warnings about divine gratuity—Jeremiah 7:1–15 (See Exodus 20:10.)

c. Sign of divine choice—2 Samuel 24:16; 2 Chronicles 3:1; Psalms 68:17, 78:68

Shekinah

Shekinah is a Hebrew word that can mean the presence of God on earth, or a manifestation or symbol of God's presence, or God's dwelling place. Although not found in the Bible, it was used by Jews in the late Old Testament period in reference to the visible majesty of the divine presence (see Exodus 19:16–19, 40:34–38; 2 Chronicles 5:13–14 for allusions). Corresponds to the glory of God (Isaiah 60:2; Romans 9:4) and the cloud of the Israelite's journey (Exodus 14:19). The ultimate *shekinah* is the incarnation of the Son of God, Jesus Christ.

Altars

1. Patriarchal altars—Genesis 22:9, for example

2. Tabernacle altars (Holocaust; incense)—Exodus 27:1–8, 30:1–5, 37:25–28, 38:1–7

3. Temple altars

a. Solomon's—1 Kings 6–7

b. Ahaz's (Damascus style; Ezekiel's)—2 Kings 16:10–16

4. Religious significance

a. Divine hearth—Leviticus 6:5–6

b. Divine presence—Genesis 12:7, 26:24–25

Menorah

Seven-branched candelabrum—Exodus 25:31–40,
1 Kings 7:49, for example

Shofar

Ram's horn trumpet—Exodus 19:13, for example

Ephod

Article of priestly clothing. See 1 Samuel 2:18, 2 Samuel 6:14, Exodus 29:5,
Leviticus 8:7.

Urim and Thummin

Lots used in determining the divine will (sticks, stones, dice?). See 1 Samuel
14:41–42, Exodus 28:6–30.

The Twelve Tribes of Israel

Founded by ten sons and two grandsons of Jacob ("Israel"); mothers' names are
in parentheses. See Genesis 35:23–26.

1. Reuben (Leah)

2. Simeon (Leah)

3. Levi (Leah)

4. Judah (Leah)

5. Issachar (Leah)

6. Zebulun (Leah)

7. Joseph (Rachel)

8. Benjamin (Rachel)

9. Dan (Bilhah, Rachel's maid)

10. Naphtali (Bilhah, Rachel's maid))

11. Gad (Zilpah, Leah's maid)

12. Asher (Zilpah, Leah's maid)

Often Levi is not included because Levites were
priestly and were not given land, but were dispersed
among other tribes and were supported by them. In
this case, two of Jacob's grandsons (children of Joseph
adopted by Jacob), Ephraim and Manasseh, are considered one tribe, thus keeping the number twelve.
When Levi is counted, these two tribes are included
with Joseph.

The twelve-pointed star of the
twelve tribes of Israel

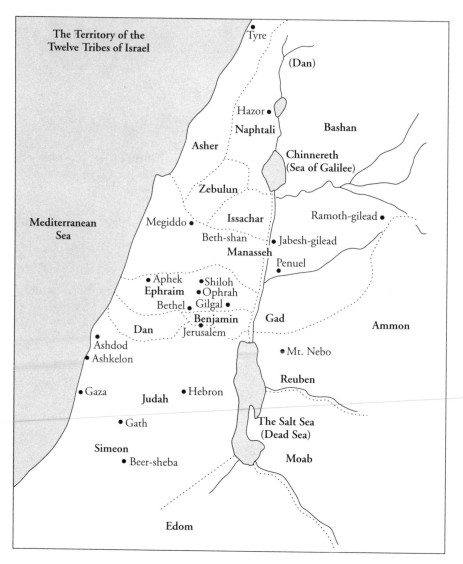

The Territory of the
Twelve Tribes of Israel

Tyre

(Dan)

Hazor

Naphtali

Bashan

Asher

Chinnereth
(Sea of Galilee)

Zebulun

Mediterranean
Sea

Megiddo

Issachar

Ramoth-gilead

Beth-shan

Jabesh-gilead

Manasseh

Penuel

Aphek

Shiloh

Ephraim

Ophrah

Bethel

Gilgal

Benjamin

Gad

Ammon

Dan

Jerusalem

Ashdod

Ashkelon

Mt. Nebo

Reuben

Gaza

Hebron

Judah

Gath

The Salt Sea
(Dead Sea)

Simeon

Beer-sheba

Moab

Edom

The Divided Kingdom

The monarchy endured under three kings—Saul, David, and Solomon.
After the death of Solomon in 922 B.C., it was divided.

Northern Kingdom ("Israel")

Formed by ten of the twelve tribes in 922 B.C.

Included nine dynasties (royal family lines)

Conquered by Assyria in 721 B.C.

Southern Kingdom ("Judah")

Formed by the tribes of Judah and Benjamin in 922 B.C.

Ruled by one dynasty—the royal line of David

Conquered by Babylon in 587 B.C.

The Prophets

Prophet and King: A Thorn in the Flesh

Some classic examples:

1. Samuel and Saul—1 Samuel 9:1–10:8 (28:3–25: postmortem?)

2. Gad and David—1 Samuel 22:5, 1 Chronicles 21, 2 Samuel 24:18–25

3. Nathan and David—2 Samuel 7:1–17 (12:1–12: "The man should die!")

4. Ahijah and Jeroboam—1 Kings 11:31–40, 14:5–16

5. Elijah and Ahab—1 Kings 17–19 (1 Kings 21—Jezebel; Naboth's vineyard)

6. Micaiah and Ahab—1 Kings 22:8–28

Daniel's Vision of the Four Beasts—Daniel 7; see Daniel 2 and 8

They represent the four succeeding world kingdoms opposed to the messianic kingdom and they have the same significance as Nebuchadnezzar's dream about a statue (Daniel 2). In the Book of Revelation this image is applied to the Roman Empire and its persecution of the Church.

1. **Babylonian:** Winged lion (gold part of statue)

2. **Median:** Bear (silver part of statue)

3. **Persian:** Winged leopard (bronze part of statue)

4. **Greek:** Horned beast (iron part of statue)

Oral Prophets

The oral prophets are distinct from the literary prophets whose books are contained in the prophetic books of the Bible. There are five major oral prophets.

1. Samuel (enthroned David)

2. Nathan (advisor to David)

3. Ahijah (advisor to Jeroboam)

4. Elijah (led resistance against Baal cult)

5. Elisha (led resistance against Baal cult)

Literary Prophets (Latter Prophets)

1. Early, about 721, the fall of the North:
   Amos, Hosea (Israel addressed)

   Isaiah, Micah (Judah addressed)

   Jonah (Nineveh addressed)

2. Pre-Exilic (587) Judah
   Jeremiah, Habakkuk, Zephaniah

   Nahum (Nineveh addressed)

3. Babylonian Captivity (from 587)
   Ezekiel, Daniel

4. Post-Exilic Jewish Community
   Haggai, Zechariah, Malachi

   Obadiah (against Edom); Joel (the Day of the Lord)

The Seven Women Prophets

Sarah, Miriam, Deborah, Hannah, Abigail, Hulda, and Esther. These are traditionally recognized in the Old Testament. Anna is the only New Testament prophetess named (Luke 2:36–38).

The Relationship Between the Old Testament and the New Testament

There is an old saying, "The New Testament lies hidden in the Old and the Old Testament is unveiled in the New." Jesus of Nazareth said that he came to fulfill the Law, not destroy it. The Paschal mystery (his life, death, and resurrection) is a study in fulfillment according to the divine plan and difficult to appreciate apart from its Old Testament background and circumstances. Note well:

1. Many Old Testament quotations and references by Jesus

2. Old Testament allusions by Jesus, evangelists, and others

3. Old Testament foreshadowings

4. Prophecy fulfillment

Nativity Scenes

It is because of the Isaian prophecy, "The ox knows his owner and the ass his master's crib," that contemporary art so often includes those particular animals at the crèche.

Prophecy Fulfillment in Jesus Christ

The asterisks (*) below indicate the evangelists' explicit reference to the fulfillment of prophecy. This is not an exhaustive listing. Not surprisingly, Matthew, with his Jewish audience, provides the most. Many of these are unique to him (where there are parallels in the other evangelists, reference is usually not made).

Jesus would . . .

Be God's son—Mark 1:1, 11; Psalm 2:7

Be God's glory filling the temple of Mary, Church—Luke 1:35; Haggai 2:7

Be born of a woman—Luke 2:12; Isaiah 9:5

* Be born Emmanuel, of a virgin—Matthew 1:23, Luke 1:35; Isaiah 7:14

Descend from Abraham—Matthew 1:2, 16, 18–25; Genesis 12:2, 15:5, 17:2

Descend from David in the tribe of Judah—Matthew 1:6, 16, 18–25; Mark 11:9–10; Luke 1:32; 2 Samuel 7:8–16; Psalm 89:20–38, 132; Jeremiah 23:5–6; Genesis 49:10; Isaiah 9:6; Matthew 4:7

* Be born in Bethlehem—Matthew 2:1, 5–6; Micah 5:1, 2 Samuel 5:2

Be announced by a star—Matthew 2:2; Numbers 24:17

Be given homage by Gentiles—Matthew 2:11; Psalm 72:10–11, Isaiah 60:5–16, Numbers 24:17, Isaiah 49:23

* Come out of Egypt—Matthew 2:15; Hosea 11:1

* Be called a *Nazorean* (hence: messianic mission to Gentiles?)—Matthew 2:23; see Isaiah 66:19

* Be a Galilean, making Capernaum the center of his ministry—Matthew 4:12–17, see John 7:40–42; Isaiah 8:11

* Be announced by a herald's voice in the desert—Matthew 3:3; Isaiah 40:3

* Be prepared for by a messenger—Matthew 11:10; Malachi 3:1

* Be prepared for by the second coming of Elijah—Matthew 11:14, 17:10–13; Mark 9:11–13; Malachi 4:5–6

Experience the spirit of the Lord come to rest on him—Matthew 3:16, 17; Isaiah 11:2

Inaugurate the judgment of the reign of God—Matthew 3:12, 13:42, 50; Isaiah 1:25; Zechariah 13:9; Malachi 3:2; Isaiah 41:16; Jeremiah 7:20, 15:7

Universalize the covenant—Matthew 2:1–12; Isaiah 60:1–6, 9, 11; see Epiphany

* Bear our infirmities as the Suffering Servant—Matthew 8:17, Mark 9:12; Isaiah 53:4

* Be resisted in certain key cities in Galilee—Matthew 11:23; Isaiah 14:13–21

* Be meek—Matthew 12:17–21; Isaiah 42:1–4

* Teach a message that would be rejected—Matthew 13:14–15, Mark 4:11–12, John 12:40; Isaiah 6:9–13, 53:1

* Teach by means of parables—Matthew 13:10–11; Psalm 78:2

* Contend with hypocrisy in his hearers—Matthew 15:7–9, Mark 7:6–7; Psalm 78:36–72, Isaiah 29:13

Administer the key of the house of David—Matthew 16:19; Isaiah 22:22

Be a good shepherd—Matthew 18:12–14, John 10:1–18; Ezekiel 34:11–31, Micah 2:12, 7:14, Zechariah 11:17

Reconcile parents and children, rebellious and wise—Luke 1:17; Sirach 48:10

Bring grace ("living water")—John 4:10–14; Isaiah 55:1–2

* Teach all for God—John 6:45; Isaiah 54:13

Free people with the truth—John 8:32; Isaiah 42:7

Open the eyes of the blind—John 9; Isaiah 42:7

* Enter Jerusalem meek, astride an ass—Matthew 21:5; Isaiah 62:11, Zechariah 9:9

* Preach the kingdom of God as a vineyard taken away from Israel—Matthew 21:33–46, John 15:1–7; Isaiah 5:1–2:7

* Be rejected as a stone by builders—Matthew 21:42; Daniel 2:45, Psalm 118:22–23, Isaiah 28:16

* Be betrayed by a companion—John 13:18; Psalm 41:10

* Be betrayed for thirty pieces of silver—Matthew 26:15, 27:9; Zechariah 11:12–13

* Be a shepherd struck down while sheep scatter—Matthew 26:31; Zechariah 13:7

Be silent before his accusers—Matthew 26:63; Isaiah 53:7

* Occasion divine judgment to be worked on his betrayer—Matthew 27:3–10; Jeremiah 19, 32:6–15

Be beaten and spat upon as the Suffering Servant—Matthew 27:30; Isaiah 50:6

Be stripped of his garments, which would be divided—Matthew 27:35; Psalm 22:19

Endure public humiliation—John 19:5; Isaiah 52:14

Be insulted—Matthew 27:39; Psalm 22:8

Be taunted for his reliance on God—Matthew 27:43; Psalm 22:8

Feel forsaken—Matthew 27:46; Psalm 22:2

Be abandoned—Matthew 27:49; Psalm 69:21

Thirst on the cross—John 19:28–30; Psalm 69:22, 22:16

* Be pierced by a sword—John 19:34; Psalm 22:20

* Be killed without his bones being broken—John 19:36; Exodus 12:46, Numbers 9:12, Psalm 34:19–20

Be buried in someone else's tomb—Matthew 27:59–60; Isaiah 53:9

Bear much fruit by dying ("grain of wheat")—John 12:24; Isaiah 53:10–12

Typology

The mystery of Christ, hidden under the letter of the Old Testament, is revealed in a Christian understanding of the relationship between the Old Testament and the New. This understanding is called "typology" because Christ is revealed on the basis of figures (types)—historical persons and events foreshadowing or pre-figuring a future person or event—which are thereby explained in their richness and significance by the type. They are distinct from symbols. Symbols represent ("symbolize"). (See CCC #s 1094, 128–130; Luke 24:13–35, the Emmaus event, and 2 Corinthians 3:14–16.)

The Annunciation

God announcing to Moses from the burning bush the delivery of Israel

Announcement of birth of Isaac, of Samson, of Samuel

Incarnation

The fleece of Gideon; Jacob's ladder

Divine presence in a dwelling (Exodus 40:34; Luke 1:35), in the temple (1 Kings 8:10)

Nativity

Flowering of Aaron's rod; birth of Eve; Moses in the bulrushes

---

Straw Under the Tablecloth

It may not seem very sanitary, but the Slavic custom of putting straw under the tablecloth, and of bedding down the small children on straw or hay, was a vivid memorial to Jesus' first night's sleep in this world.

Presentation

Presentation in the temple of Israelite firstborn, of Samuel

Joy of Jacob at the sight of his long lost son Joseph (compare Simeon and Messiah)

Epiphany

Queen of Sheba visiting Solomon

Abner's visit to David at Hebron

Joseph's brothers bowing before him

Three strong men bringing David water

The star of the Epiphany

Multiculturalism at the Crèche

Of the mysterious magi, there is little more than mention in the gospel. The Venerable Bede is the one who gives the colorful details: "The first was called Melchior; he was an old man, with white hair and long beard; he offered gold to the Lord as to his king. The second, Gaspar by name, young, beardless, of ruddy hue, offered to Jesus his gift of incense, the homage due divinity. The third, of black complexion, with heavy beard, was called Baltasar; the myrrh he held in his hands prefigured the death of the Son of Man."

About their lives after leaving that day, the Scriptures say nothing. Never at a loss, legend has filled the vacuum: Many years after Christmas, St. Thomas the apostle visited the magi and, after catechizing them, initiated them into the Christian faith. They were then ordained priests, and later bishops. Toward the end of their lives, the Christmas star revisited them, this time leading them to one another for a reunion. The city of Sewa in the Orient is said to be the place of their burial. It was in the sixth century that their legendary relics were brought from Constantinople to Milan, and from there in 1164, by Emperor Frederick Barbarossa, to Cologne where pilgrimage has honored them for centuries.

Flight into Egypt

Flight of Jacob to Laban; Jacob's flight into Egypt to escape famine

Moses concealed from Pharaoh's soldiers

Two spies' flight from Rahab's house

David's flight through the window

Holy Innocents

Rachel bewailing Israel's exile (Matthew 2:18; Jeremiah 31:15)

Pharaoh's slaughter of Israelite children

Saul's slaughter of the priests; Athaliah's slaughter of the king's sons

Holy Family in Egypt
  The Egyptian migration of Jacob's family

Return from Egypt
  Jacob's return to Israel; David's return to Hebron; Moses' return to Egypt

John the Baptist
  Isaac/Samuel (faith, parentage, consecration)

  Elijah (attire, locale, message, way of life)

Temptation
  Esau (birthright); Adam and Eve; Joseph (Potiphar's wife)

  Moses overcoming the Egyptians; Moses on the mountain forty days and nights

  Samson (the lion); David (the lion; Goliath)

Sermon on the Mount
  Moses on Mt. Sinai

Raising of Lazarus
  Elijah's raising of the son of the widow of Sarepta

  Elisha's raising of the Shunammite's son

Transfiguration
  Angel's appearing to Abraham (see Moses and Elijah)

  Moses' transfiguration

  Nebuchadnezzar seeing the three youths in furnace

Messianic entry into Jerusalem
  Elisha met at Bethel by prophets' sons

  David's entry in triumph with Goliath's head

Jesus weeping over Jerusalem
  Jeremiah weeping over Jerusalem

Cleansing the Temple
  King Darius's mandating Ezra to cleanse the temple

  Judas Maccabeus purging the profaned temple

Last Supper
  Melchizedek's bread offering to Abraham; desert manna

  The farewell conversation between Moses and Joshua (Jesus and his disciples)

Prediction of the Passion
Predicted death of Ahab (by Micaiah), of king's servant (by Elisha), and of Belshazzar (by Daniel)

Agony in the Garden
Abraham escorting Isaac up the mountain

Angel wrestling with Jacob, comforting Elijah

Betrayal
Joseph sold to Ishmaelites/to Potiphar

Saul jeopardizing David; Absalom plotting against David

Tryphon betraying Jonathan; Joab murdering Abner

Jesus Before Pilate
Daniel/Babylonians; Elijah/Jezebel; Job/the devil; Susanna/corrupt judges; Joseph/Potiphar's wife

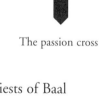

The passion cross

Crowning with thorns
Mutilation of David's messengers by the king of Ammon; Elisha mocked at Bethel

Jesus mocked by soldiers
Noah/Ham; Samson/Philistines; Elisha/children; Elisha/priests of Baal

Scourging at the pillar
Lamech tortured by wives; Job by the devil; Achor tied to a tree

Way of the cross
Isaac with the wood for his own sacrifice

Sarepta women with two cruciform bundles of wood

Crucifixion
Abel's murder; Isaac on Mt. Moriah

Sacrifice of Moabite king's son

Joseph's imprisonment with two thieves

Moses' lifting brazen serpent in the desert

Martyrdom of Isaiah/of Jeremiah (traditional)

The graded (or Calvary) cross

Seamless garment
Joseph's coat

Pierced side
Eve from Adam's side; Moses evoking water from the rock

New covenant in Christ's blood
The Old Testament covenant sealed with the blood of the lamb

Mary's sorrow
Adam and Eve/Abel; Naomi/sons; Jacob/Joseph (coat)

Descent from the cross
Rizpah and her sons who were hanged

Burial
Joseph/pit; Jonah/sea; burial of Jacob/of Abner/of Moses

Descent into hell or to the dead
Moses/Egypt; Samson/lion; Elijah/priests of Baal; David/Goliath; Joshua/walls of Jericho

Resurrection
Samson carrying off the gates of Gaza; Jonah/whale; Daniel/lion's den; three youths/furnace

Women at the tomb
Reuben looking for Joseph

Daughter of Sion (Song of Solomon) searching for her missing spouse

Appearance to Mary
"Resurrection" appearances of Daniel/of Jonah/of three youths

Appearance to the disciples
Joseph revealing himself to his brothers

Prodigal Son, forgiven by his father (as disciples were for their cowardice)

The Russian Orthodox cross, upper cross member: INRI; lower: footrest

The Easter cross, white, with lilies

Polish Emmaus Walks

The ritual of an Easter Monday Emmaus walk was inspired by the resurrection appearance of Christ that first Easter to the two who were making their way to Emmaus (Luke 24:13–35). With simple variations, this tradition of a outing or long walk into the fields, forests, and mountains has been kept among many peoples of the Christian world. In particular, Poles made these into gatherings of larger groups, the residents of a whole community often coming together in some rural "Emmaus grove" for picnicking, playing games, dancing, and singing.

Thomas
Angel's appearance to Gideon/to Jacob

Ascension
Elijah's fiery chariot; the translation of Enoch

Pentecost
Stone tablets given to Moses; descent of fire upon Elijah's altar

A seven-pointed star representing the seven-fold gift of the Spirit

Damnation
Expulsion of Hagar and her son

Judgment, destruction of Korah, Dathan, and Abiram/of Sodom/of Jericho

The writing on the wall at Belshazzar's feast

Salvation
Jacob's ladder

Joseph's brothers/famine; feast of Job's sons

Blood on the doorposts

Daniel/lion's den; three youths/furnace; Israel/Red Sea

The eight-pointed star, eight being a symbol of regeneration

Church
Eight people in Noah's ark

Isaac meeting Rebecca (Church, the bride of Christ)

Solomon building his temple (Christ building his Church)

Laying the cornerstone of the temple (Christ)

Bridegroom meeting bride in Song of Solomon

Baptism
The flood; Red Sea; washing of Naaman the Syrian; water in the desert

Eucharist
Melchizedek bringing bread and wine to Abraham; Elijah fed by angels; manna

Principal Christological Titles

With representative Scripture references for some; a glossary follows.

Jesus
Given name *Yeshuah*: "YHWH is salvation"; common Jewish name—Matthew 1:21

Identifying his mission—Matthew 1:21; Acts 4:12, 10:43; 1 Corinthians 3:11

Jesus the Nazorean
A "last name," which developed later in history to distinguish among those with the same name. (Surnames usually originated with occupation, parentage, appearance, or place of origin, as in this case.)

Christ (over one hundred uses)

Greek *Christos,* translating Hebrew *Masi ah* ("anointed one"). The Messiah, the fulfillment of Jewish hope. See John 1:41, 4:25, 10:22–39.

Jesus Christ

From Jesus the Christ, evolving into a kind of proper name

Rabbi

Teacher—Luke 10:25

Savior

English expression from Latin word used for Jesus' given name—John 3:16–17

Lord

Common expression used in Middle East, with the connotations it still has today.

Reserved for YHWH in the Old Testament.

Used as an act of faith in Jesus as Son of God (our Lord and God). See John 20:28, Philippians 2:6–11.

Judge

Old Testament forger and leader of the people

Later refers to Jesus' role in the judgment—John 5:22–23

Priest, Prophet, King

Related terms referring to the fullness of Jesus' role as the Christ

Lamb of God

Jesus' sacrificial role as the authentic and final Passover lamb of Old Testament—John 1:29, 35; Revelation 5:12, 14:1–5; 1 Peter 1:19; Acts 8:32 See Exodus 12; Isaiah 53:7.

Son of David

Jesus as legal claimant to the throne of David and as the one establishing the kingdom of God, which David established in a political sense—John 18:36

Son of Man

A favorite of Jesus and used of or by him some eighty-two times, making it the most frequently used title in the New Testament (eighty-one times in the Gospel, once in Acts 7:56). It is messianic (Daniel 7:2–14) and a key to Jesus' self-understanding (see Hebrew *bar nas*: the man) as the first of a new race who possesses the life of God. Emphasizes:

1. Jesus' humanity—Matthew 8:20, 11:19, 12:32

2. Jesus' role—Matthew 9:6, 12:8, 13:37, 16:13, 20:28; Luke 6:22, 19:10; John 9:35

3. Jesus' destiny—Daniel 7:13; Matthew 24:37

The Word

Jesus as God's definite self-communication—John 1:1, 14

Alpha and Omega

Jesus as the beginning and the end of human history; from the first and last letters of the Greek alphabet—Revelation 1:8; 22:13

Suffering Servant

Applying Old Testament prophecy—Isaiah 42:1–4; 49:1–7; 50:4–11; 52:13–53:12

Son of God

Ichthys means fish; its letters were made to stand for "Jesus Christ, Son of God, Savior" by the early Christians.

1. Post-resurrection term, used especially by those with Jewish background. *The*, not *a*, Son of God, explaining Jesus' nature and role in God's plan for the world (John 17:5; Romans 8:3).

2. Used in all four Gospel accounts:
   Matthew—3:17; 4:3, 6; 8:29; 14:33; 16:16; 17:5; 26:63; 27:54
   Mark—1:1, 11; 3:11; 5:7; 9:7; 14:61, 62
   Luke—1:32, 35; 3:22; 4:41; 22:70
   John—1:34, 49; 3:16, 18; 5:25; 9:35; 10:36; 19:7; 20:31

3. Jesus called himself Son of God: Mark 14:61–62; John 8:35–37, 10:36.

4. The Father called Jesus his beloved Son: Matthew 3:17, 17:5; Mark 1:11, 9:7; Luke 3:22; 9:35.

5. Others called Jesus son of God:
   John the Baptist—John 1:34
   Nathanael—John 1:49
   Martha—John 11:27
   Roman guard—Matthew 27:54
   Peter—Matthew 16:16
   Disciples—Matthew 14:33
   Gabriel—Luke 1:32, 35
   The devil—Matthew 4:3, 6
   Evil spirits—Matthew 8:29; Mark 3:11, 5:7; Luke 4:41, 8:28

The New Testament

A Glossary of Titles of Christ

Advocate—1 John 2:1

Alpha and Omega—Revelation 1:8, 22:13

Amen—Revelation 3:14

Apostle and high priest of our confession—Hebrews 3:1

Author and finisher of our faith—Hebrews 12:2

Beloved—Matthew 12:18

Beloved son—Colossians 1:13

Bread of God—John 6:33, 50

Bread of life—John 6:35

Bread, living—John 6:51

Bridegroom—John 3:29

Brother—Matthew 12:50

Captain of our salvation—Hebrews 2:10

Carpenter—Mark 6:3

Carpenter's son—Matthew 13:55

Chief shepherd—1 Peter 5:4

Chosen one—Luke 23:35

Christ—Matthew 16:20

Christ Jesus—1 Timothy 1:15; Colossians 1:1

Christ of God—Luke 9:20

Christ the Lord—Luke 2:12

Christ who is above all—Romans 9:5

Consolation of Israel—Luke 2:25

Cornerstone, chief—Ephesians 2:19–20; 1 Peter 2:6

Dayspring—Luke 1:78

Deliverer—Romans 8:29

Eldest of many brothers—Romans 8:29

Emmanuel—Matthew 1:23

Faithful witness—Revelation 1:5, 3:14

First and the Last—Revelation 1:17, 2:8

Firstborn among many brothers—Romans 8:29

Firstborn from the dead—Revelation 1:5

Firstborn of all creation—Colossians 1:15

First fruits—1 Corinthians 15:20

Friend of tax collectors and sinners—Matthew 11:19

Gate of the sheepfold—John 10:7

Glory—John 12:41; Luke 2:32

Good shepherd—John 10:11, 14

Grain of wheat—John 12:24

Great shepherd of the sheep—Hebrews 13:20

Head—Ephesians 4:16; 1 Corinthians 11:3; Colossians 2:10

Head of the Church—Colossians 1:18; Ephesians 1:22

Hidden manna—Revelation 2:17

High priest—Hebrews 3:1, 4:14, 7:26

Holy one—Acts 2:27

Holy one of God—Mark 1:24

Holy servant Jesus—Acts 4:27

Hope—1 Timothy 1:2

Horn of salvation—Luke 1:69

I Am—John 8:58

Image of God—2 Corinthians 4:5; Colossians 1:15

Indescribable gift—2 Corinthians 9:15

Intercessor—1 John 2:1

Jesus—Matthew 1:21

Jesus the Nazarene—John 18:5

Just one—Acts 7:52

Just judge—2 Timothy 4:8

King—Matthew 21:5

King of Israel—John 1:50

King of kings—Revelation 17:14, 19:16; 1 Timothy 6:15

King of nations—Revelation 15:3

King of the Jews—Matthew 2:2

Lamb of God—John 1:29, 37; 1 Peter 1:20; Revelation 5:12

Last Adam—1 Corinthians 15:45

Leader—Matthew 2:6; Hebrews 2:10

Leader and perfecter of faith—Hebrews 12:2

Leader and savior—Acts 5:31

Life—John 14:6; Colossians 3:4

Light—John 1:9, 12:35

Light of all—Luke 2:32; John 1:4

Light of the world—John 8:12

Lion of the tribe of Judah—Revelation 5:5 (see Genesis 49:9)

Lord—Luke 1:25

Lord, one—Ephesians 4:5

Lord and my God, my—John 20:28

Lord both of the dead and of the living—Romans 14:9

Lord God almighty—Revelation 15:3

Lord Jesus (Jesus is Lord)—Acts 7:59; 1 Corinthians 12:3

Lord Jesus Christ—Acts 15:11

Lord of all—Acts 10:36

Lord of glory—1 Corinthians 2:9

Lord of lords—1 Timothy 6:15

Lord of peace—2 Thessalonians 3:16

Man, the—John 19:5

Master—Matthew 17:24

Mediator—1 Timothy 2:5

Messiah—John 1:41, 4:25

Mighty God—Isaiah 9:6

Morning star—2 Peter 1:20; Revelation 2:29, 22:16

Nazarene—Matthew 2:23

Passover—1 Corinthians 5:8

Power and the wisdom of God—1 Corinthians 1:25

Power for salvation—Luke 1:69

Priest for ever—Hebrews 5:6

Prince (of life)—Acts 3:15, 5:31

Prince of peace—Isaiah 9:6

Prophet of the Most High—Luke 1:76

Ransom—1 Timothy 2:6

Reconciliation—Romans 3:25

Redeemer—Isaiah 59:20

Refulgence of God's glory—Hebrews 1:3

Resurrection (and the life)—John 11:25

Rising sun—Luke 1:78

Root of David—Revelation 12:16, 22:16

Root of David's line—Revelation 22:16

Root of Jesse—Isaiah 11:10

Ruler—Matthew 2:6

Ruler of the kings of the earth—Revelation 1:5

Ruler and savior—Acts 5:31

Savior—2 Peter 2:20, 3:18

Savior of the world—1 John 4:14; John 4:42

Second Adam—Romans 5:12–19

Servant of circumcised Jews—Romans 15:8

Shepherd and guardian of your souls—1 Peter 2:24

Slave—Philippians 2:7

Son—Galatians 4:5

Son, beloved—Colossians 1:13

Son, firstborn—Luke 2:7

Son of Abraham—Matthew 1:1

Son of David—Matthew 1:1

Son of God—Luke 1:36

Son of Joseph—John 1:45

Son of man—John 5:27

Son of Mary—Mark 6:3

Son of the Blessed One—Mark 14:61, 62

Son of the Father—2 John 3

Son of the living God—Matthew 16:17

Son of the Most High—Luke 1:32

Son of the Most High God—Mark 5:7

Son, only Son of the Father—John 1:14

Son, the beloved—Matthew 17:5

Source of God's creation—Revelation 3:14

Spiritual rock—1 Corinthians 10:4

Stone, living—1 Peter 2:4

Stone rejected—Matthew 21:42; 1 Peter 2:8

Stone to stumble over—1 Peter 2:8

Teacher—Matthew 8:19, 23:11

Testator—Hebrews 9:16

True God—1 John 5:20

True vine—John 15:1

Truth (the way and the life)—John 14:6

Way (the truth and the life)—John 14:6

Wisdom of God—1 Corinthians 1:25

Wonderful counselor—Isaiah 9:6

Word—John 1:1; 1:14

Word of God—Revelation 19:14

Word of life—1 John 1:1

The Three Stages in the Formation of the Gospels (See CCC #126.)

1. **The life and teaching of Jesus**—Jesus' actual words and deeds

2. **The oral tradition**—After the ascension, the apostles with fuller understanding handed it on.

3. **The written Gospels**—The sacred authors took certain of the many elements which had been handed on, at times explaining or synthesizing in light of the situation of the churches.

The Four Evangelists

Their traditional symbols, the four living creatures, are taken from (anticipated in?) the prophecy of Ezekiel (1:5–21, 10:20). Of these same living creatures, borrowed by the Book of Revelation (4:6–8), St. Irenaeus says, "The lion signifies the royalty of Christ, the calf his priestly office, the man his incarnation, and the eagle the grace of the Holy Spirit."

Matthew, Apostle and Martyr

Matthew is called the divine man, since he teaches about the human nature of Christ and since his version of the Gospel begins with Jesus' paternal genealogy.

Mark, Martyr

Mark is called the winged lion, since he informs us of the royal dignity of Christ and since his version of the Gospel begins: "The voice of one crying in the wilderness," suggesting the roar of the lion.

Luke, Martyr

Luke is called the winged ox, since he deals with the sacrificial aspects of Christ's life and since his version of the Gospel begins with a temple scene.

John, Apostle

John is called the rising eagle, since his gaze pierces so far into the mysteries of heaven and since his version of the Gospel begins with a lofty prologue that is a poem of the Word become flesh.

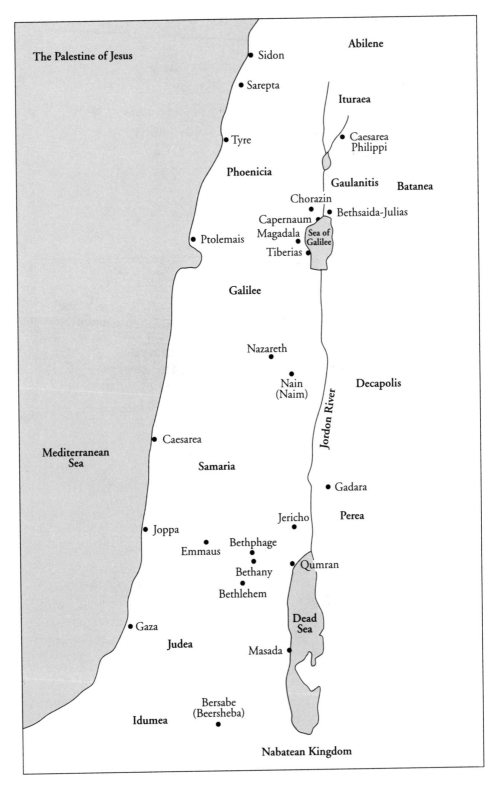

The Palestine of Jesus

Abilene

Sidon

Sarepta

Ituraea

Caesarea
Philippi

Tyre

Phoenicia

Gaulanitis   Batanea

Chorazin

Capernaum   Bethsaida-Julias

Magadala   Sea of
Galilee

Ptolemais

Tiberias

Galilee

Nazareth

Nain
(Naim)   Decapolis

Jordon River

Caesarea

Mediterranean
Sea

Samaria

Gadara

Jericho   Perea

Joppa

Bethphage

Emmaus

Bethany   Qumran

Bethlehem

Gaza

Dead
Sea

Judea

Masada

Bersabe
(Beersheba)

Idumea

Nabatean Kingdom

A New Testament Table of Contents

I. John the Baptist

    A. His ministry—Matthew 3:1–12; Mark 1:1–8; Luke 3:1–20; John 1:19–28

    B. His messengers to Jesus, Jesus' testimony to him—Luke 7:18–35

    C. His execution by Herod—Matthew 14:1–12; Mark 6:14–29

II. The Life of Jesus

    A. The Hidden Life

        1. Nativity—Matthew 1:18–2:15; Luke 1:5–2:40

        2. Early years—Luke 2:41–52

"For My Yoke Is Easy . . ."

There is an ancient story which says that in the carpenter's shop at Nazareth Jesus made yokes, and made them to fit the animals better than any other carpenter in Galilee. When he said, "Take my yoke upon your shoulder and learn from me, for my yoke is easy. . . ," he knew what he was talking about. That metaphor was born in his shop. He was speaking as Lord. He was also speaking as a carpenter. ("Easy" can be translated "well fitting.")

    B. The Public Ministry

        1. Baptism—Matthew 3:13–17, Mark 1:9–11, Luke 3:21–22, John 1:31–34

        2. Call of the apostles—Matthew 4:18–22, 9:9, 10:1–4; Mark 1:16–20, 3:13–19; Luke 5:1–11; 6:12–16; John 1:35–51

        3. Temptation—Matthew 4:1–11, Mark 1:12–13, Luke 4:1–13

        4. Sermon on the mount/plain—Matthew 5:1–7:29, Luke 6:20–49

        5. Transfiguration—Matthew 17:1–8, Mark 9:2–8, Luke 9:28–36
        According to tradition, the transfiguration took place on Mt. Tabor, making it the counterpoint to Gethsemane, the place of Jesus' agony on the eve of Good Friday.

        6. Messianic entry into Jerusalem—Matthew 21:1–11, Mark 11:1–11, Luke 19:28–38, John 12:12–15

        7. Last Supper—Matthew 26:17–35, Mark 14:12–26, Luke 22:1–38

        8. Agony in Gethsemane—Matthew 26:36–46, Mark 14:32–42, Luke 22:39–46

        9. Passion—Matthew 26:47–27:66, Mark 14:43–15:47, Luke 22:47–23:56, John 18:1–19:42

Jesus and the Jews

Opposition to Jesus in Israel (See CCC #s 574–582, 587–590.)

1. He offended some of the teachers of the Law.
   He was not content to give his interpretation alongside others.—Matthew 7:28–29

2. He alienated some of the Pharisees by
   - Interpreting the Law in an ultimate/divine way—Matthew 5:1, 33–34; Mark 7:13
   - Perfecting the dietary law—Mark 7:18–21
   - Violating the Sabbath law in favor of service—Matthew 12:5

3. He encountered suspicion of demonic possession by
   - Expelling demons, forgiving sins, healing
   - New interpretation of ritual purity laws
   - Familiarity with tax collectors and public sinners

4. He seemed to act contrary to Jewish practices:
   - Healing on the Sabbath
   - Gathering food to eat on the Sabbath
   - Speaking with non-Jews and public sinnerss

5. He scandalized the Jewish authorities when he revealed:
   - His role in the redemption of sins, his divine work—Luke 2:34, 20:17–18
   - The place for sinners in God's messianic banquet—Luke 15:1–2, 22–32

Jesus not in conflict with Pharisees (See CCC #575.)

1. He is warned by some of the danger he was risking.—Luke 13:31

2. He praises some of them (Mark 12:34) and dines with them.

3. He confirmed some of their teachings:
   - Resurrection of the dead—Matthew 22:23–34
   - Certain forms of piety, like almsgiving, fasting, prayer—Matthew 6:18
   - Custom of addressing God as Father
   - Centrality of commandment to love God and neighbor—Mark 12:28

The Work of Jesus

His Discourses

Vindication of his authority—John 2:18–22

To Nicodemus—John 3:1–21

To a Samaritan woman—John 4:7–26

Defense of his disciples (not fasting, corn on the Sabbath)—Matthew 9:14–17, 12:1–8; Mark 2:18–28; Luke 5:33–39, 6:1–5

Defense of himself (Sabbath healing of withered hand)—Matthew 12:9–13; Mark 3:1–5; Luke 6:6–10

Sermon on the Mount/Plain—Matthew 5:1–7:29; Luke 6:20–49

Testimony concerning John the Baptist—Matthew 11:7–19; Luke 7:24–35, 16:16

Instructions for the apostolate—Matthew 10:5–42; Mark 6:7–13; Luke 9:1–6, 10:1–12

Defense of his claim to divinity—John 5:19–47

Bread of life—John 6:22–71

Defense of his disciples (Jewish tradition)—Matthew 15:1–20; Mark 7:1–23

Promise of primacy to Peter—Matthew 16:13–20

Predictions of the passion and resurrection—Matthew 16:21–23, 17:22–23, 20:17–19; Mark 8:31–9:1, 9:30–31, 10:32–34; Luke 9:22–27, 9:44–45, 18:31–34

Doctrine of the cross—Matthew 16:24–28; Mark 8:34–38; Luke 9:23–27

Scandal—Matthew 18:6–9; Mark 9:42–48; Luke 17:1–2

Fraternal correction—Matthew 18:15–17; Luke 17:3–4

Conversation with Martha and Mary—Luke 10:38–42

Conversation with an adulteress—John 8:3–11

Fruitfulness of prayer—Matthew 7:7–11; Mark 11:24; Luke 11:9–13

Defense of his authority—Matthew 21:23–27; Mark 11:27–33; Luke 20:1–8

Tribute to Caesar—Matthew 22:15–22; Mark 12:13–17; Luke 20:20–26

Great commandment—Matthew 22:34–40; Mark 12:28–34; Luke 10:25–28

End times—Matthew 23:37–25:46; Mark 13:1–37 (the Little Apocalypse); Luke 21:5–36

Last judgment—Matthew 25:31–46

At the Last Supper—Matthew 26:20–29; Mark 14:17–25; Luke 22:14–38; John 13:2–17:26

Peter the chief shepherd—John 21:15–19

Apostolic mandate—Matthew 28:16–20; Mark 16:15–18; Luke 24:36–49; John 20:19–23

His Parables

The House Built on Rock—Matthew 7:24–27; Luke 6:47–49

The Sower—Matthew 13:1–23; Mark 4:1–12; Luke 8:4–10

The Seed Grows of Itself—Mark 4:26–29

The Weeds—Matthew 13:24–30, 36–43

The Mustard Seed—Matthew 13:31–32; Mark 4:30–32; Luke 13:18–19

The Leaven—Matthew 13:33; Luke 13:20–21

The Found Treasure—Matthew 13:44

The Precious Pearl—Matthew 13:45–46

The Net—Matthew 13:47–50

The Unmerciful Servant—Matthew 18:23–35

The Laborers in the Vineyard—Matthew 20:1–16

The Two Sons—Matthew 21:28–32

The Tenants—Matthew 21:33–46; Mark 12:1–12; Luke 20:9–19

The Marriage Feast—Matthew 22:1–14; Luke 14:15–24

The Wedding Garment—Matthew 22:11–14

The Ten Virgins—Matthew 25:1–13

The Talents—Matthew 25:14–30; Luke 19:12–27

The Sheep and the Goats—Matthew 25:31–46

The Two Debtors—Luke 7:36–50

The Good Samaritan—Luke 10:29–37

The Importunate Friend—Luke 11:5–8

The Rich Fool—Luke 12:16–21

The Servants Who Waited—Luke 12:35–48

The Barren Fig Tree—Luke 13:6–9

The Last Seat—Luke 14:7–11

The Great Supper—Luke 14:15–24

The Lost Sheep—Luke 15:3–7 ⎤

The Lost Coin—Luke 15:8–10 ⎬— Luke's Three Parables of Mercy:

The Prodigal Son—Luke 15:11–32 ⎦ "The gospel within the Gospel"

The Dishonest Steward—Luke 16:1–13

The Rich Man and Lazarus—Luke 16:19–31

The Persistent Widow—Luke 18:1–8

The Pharisee and the Tax Collector—Luke 18:9–14

The Gold Pieces—Luke 19:11–27

Similitudes and Allegories Jesus Used

"Physician, cure yourself"—Luke 4:23

The flavor of salt—Matthew 5:13; Mark 9:50; Luke 14:34–35

The lamp under a basket—Matthew 5:14–15; Mark 4:21; Luke 8:16, 11:33

The city on a mountain—Matthew 5:14

The opponent—Matthew 5:25–26; Luke 12:58–59

The lamp of the body—Matthew 6:22–23; Luke 11:34–36

The two masters—Matthew 6:24; Luke 16:13

A son's request—Matthew 7:9–11; Luke 11:11–13

The tree and its fruit—Matthew 7:15–20, 12:33; Luke 6:43–44

The physician and the sick—Mark 2:17; Luke 5:31–32

The bridegroom and the guests—Matthew 9:14–15; Mark 2:18–20; Luke 5:33–39

A patch of new cloth on an old garment—Matthew 9:16; Mark 2:21; Luke 5:36

New wine in old wine-skins—Matthew 9:17; Mark 2:22; Luke 5:37–38

The servant not above the master—Matthew 10:24–25; Luke 6:40; John 13:16, 15:20

Secrets to be revealed—Matthew 10:26–27; Mark 4:22; Luke 8:17, 12:2–9

The wayward children—Matthew 11:16–19; Luke 7:31–35

The divided kingdom—Matthew 12:25–26; Mark 3:23–27; Luke 11:17–22

The unclean spirit—Matthew 12:43–45; Luke 11:24–26

The wise scribe—Matthew 13:52

A person's defilement—Matthew 15:10–20; Mark 7:14–23

Blind guides of the blind—Matthew 15:14; Luke 6:39; John 9:40–41

The children's bread—Matthew 15:26–27; Mark 7:27–28

The watchful servants—Mark 13:34; Luke 12:35–38 (also Matthew 25:14–30; Luke 19:12–27)

Faithful and unfaithful servants—Matthew 24:45–51; Luke 12:42–48

Building a tower—Luke 14:28–30

Preparation for war—Luke 14:31–33

The servant doing his duty—Luke 17:7–10

The body and the vultures—Matthew 24:28; Luke 17:37

The thief—Matthew 24:43–44; Luke 12:39–40

The fig tree and the branches—Matthew 24:32–33; Mark 13:28–29; Luke 21:29–31

The good shepherd—John 10:1–18

The vine and the branches—John 15:1–17

His Miracles

1. Nature miracles

The only miracle recorded by all four evangelists is the multiplication of the loaves.

Changing water into wine at Cana—John 2:1–11

First miraculous catch of fish—Luke 5:1–11

Calming of the storm—Matthew 8:23–27; Mark 4:35–41; Luke 8:22–25

Multiplication of loaves—Matthew 14:13–21; Mark 6:32–44; Luke 9:12–17; John 6:1–13

Walking on water—Matthew 14:22–33; Mark 6:45–52; John 6:16–21

Second multiplication of loaves—Matthew 15:32–38; Mark 8:1–9

Coin in the fish's mouth—Matthew 17:24–27

Cursing the fig tree—Matthew 21:18–19; Mark 11:12–14

Second miraculous catch of fish—John 21:1–14

2. Healings

Very numerous in Jesus' ministry, and often only referred to scripturally (Matthew 4:23–25; Luke 4:16–30; Mark 6:1–6). Many are mentioned specifically:

Healing of the royal official's son—John 4:46–54

Cleansing a leper—Matthew 8:2–4; Mark 1:40–45; Luke 5:12–14

Cure of the mother-in-law of Peter—Matthew 8:14–15; Mark 1:29–31; Luke 4:38–41

Healing a paralytic—Matthew 9:1–8; Mark 2:3–12; Luke 5:18–26

Healing a sick man at Bethesda—John 5:1–9

Restoring a man with a withered hand—Matthew 12:9–13; Mark 3:16; Luke 6:6–11

Healing a centurion's servant—Matthew 8:5–13; Luke 7:1–10

Healing of a blind and mute person—Matthew 12:22

Healing a woman with a hemorrhage—Matthew 9:20–22; Mark 5:25–34; Luke 8:43–48

Opening the eyes of two blind men—Matthew 9:27–31

Cure of a mute man—Matthew 9:32–34

Healing a deaf and mute man—Mark 7:31–37

Opening the eyes of a blind person at Bethsaida—Mark 8:22–26

Opening the eyes of a person born blind—John 9:1–41

Restoring an infirm woman—Luke 13:10–17

Healing of a man with dropsy—Luke 14:1–6

Cleansing the lepers—Luke 17:12–19

Opening the eyes of the blind man—Matthew 20:29–34; Mark 10:46–52; Luke 18:35–43

Healing Malchus's ear—Matthew 26:51–52; Mark 14:47; Luke 22:49–51; John 18:10–11

3. Deliverances

Evidently very numerous in his ministry, given the scriptural formulas (see Mark 1) that recur. Seven are mentioned specifically:

Demoniac at Capernaum—Mark 1:23–28; Luke 4:33–37

Blind and mute demoniac—Matthew 12:22–29; Luke 11:14–15

Gadarene demoniacs—Matthew 8:28–34; Mark 5:1–15; Luke 8:26–39

Mute demoniac—Matthew 9:32–34

Daughter of Syro-Phoenician woman—Matthew 15:21–28; Mark 7:24–30

Child with a demon—Matthew 17:14–21; Mark 9:14–29; Luke 9:37–43

Infirm woman—Luke 13:10–17

4. Victories over hostile wills

It is difficult to distinguish in many instances between a miraculous action of Christ and a merely natural and effective act or influence. (See, for example, John 7:30, 44; 8:20, 59, where Jesus disallows his enemies from arresting him.)

Cleansing of the temple—Matthew 21:12; Mark 11:15–16; Luke 19:45–46; John 2:13–16

Escape from the hostile crowd at Nazareth—Luke 4:28–30

5. Resuscitations

Not truly resurrections, like Jesus' own; that is, these people were brought back to life; they still had to die eventually.

The daughter of Jairus—Matthew 9:18–26; Mark 5:21–43; Luke 8:41–56

The son of the widow of Naim—Luke 7:11–17

Lazarus—John 11:1–44

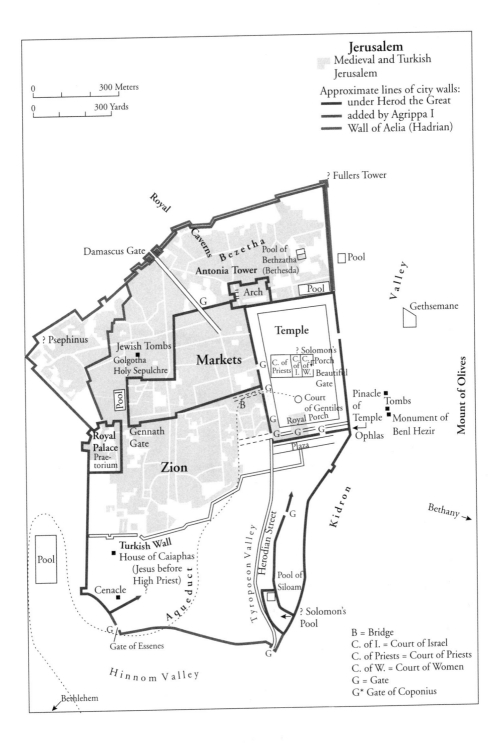

Jerusalem

Medieval and Turkish Jerusalem

Approximate lines of city walls:
— under Herod the Great
— added by Agrippa I
— Wall of Aelia (Hadrian)

0 — 300 Meters

0 — 300 Yards

? Fullers Tower

Royal
Caverns

Damascus Gate

Bezetha

Pool of Bethzatha (Bethesda)

Antonia Tower

Arch

Pool

Pool

Valley

Gethsemane

Temple

? Psephinus

Jewish Tombs

Golgotha
Holy Sepulchre

Markets

? Solomon's Porch

C. of Priests | C. of I. | C. of W. | Beautiful Gate

Pool

Court of Gentiles

Royal Porch

Pinacle of Temple

Tombs

Monument of Benl Hezir

Ophlas

Mount of Olives

B

G G G

Plaza

Royal Palace
Prae-torium

Gennath Gate

Zion

Bethany →

Kidron

Turkish Wall

House of Caiaphas
(Jesus before High Priest)

Pool

Cenacle

Aqueduct

Tyropoeon Valley

Herodian Street

G

Pool of Siloam

? Solomon's Pool

G

Gate of Essenes

G

Hinnom Valley

B = Bridge
C. of I. = Court of Israel
C. of Priests = Court of Priests
C. of W. = Court of Women
G = Gate
G* Gate of Coponius

Bethlehem →

The Seven Signs from St. John's "Book of Signs"

1. Changing water to wine at Cana	John 2:1–11
2. Cure of royal official's son	John 4:46–54
3. Cure on a Sabbath feast	John 5:1–15
4. Multiplication of loaves at Passover	John 6:1–15
5. Walking on the sea	John 6:16–21
6. Cure of man blind from birth	John 9:1–34
7. Raising of Lazarus	John 11:1–44

The Last Supper

Luke's Banqueting Scenes

Jesus' table ministry, leading up to the Last Supper, is a pattern and a study.

1. Levi's reception for Jesus—Luke 5:29–32
   "Eating and drinking with sinners"

2. Simon the Pharisee's dinner—Luke 7:36–50
   A woman bathes Jesus' feet.

3. At Martha and Mary's house—Luke 10:38–42
   Mary chooses the better part.

4. A Pharisee's dinner—Luke 11:37–54
   "Woe to you, Pharisees."

5. A leading Pharisee's Sabbath meal—Luke 14:1–24
   "Is it lawful to cure on the Sabbath?"

6. Parable told at a Pharisee's meal: The Marriage Feast—Luke 14:7–14
   Highest place and lowest place

7. Parable told at a Pharisee's meal: The Great Supper—Luke 14:15–24
   "Bring in the poor and the crippled."

8. Parable of the Prodigal Son—Luke 15:11–32
   Celebration: "Kill the fatted calf."

9. At Zacchaeus's house—Luke 19:1–10
   "I must stay at your house today."

10. The Last Supper—Luke 22:14–38
    "Do this in memory of me."

11. The Emmaus meal—Luke 24:13–32
    "Then their eyes were opened."

The Passion of Jesus

The Passion Foretold

Following the confession by Peter that Jesus is the Messiah, at the high point of Mark's Gospel (8:29), there are three teachings on the passion (each following by an instance of resistance to the cross and humility):

1. 8:31–33—followed by Peter protesting to Jesus
2. 9:30–32—followed by the apostles arguing about their own importance
3. 10:32–34—followed by James and John jockeying for position

There are, in all, five occasions recorded when Jesus spoke of his death and resurrection:

1. After Peter's confession—Matthew 16:21; Mark 8:31; Luke 9:22
2. After the transfiguration—Matthew 17:9, 12; Mark 9:9, 12
3. After healing the epileptic—Luke 9:44
4. While passing through Galilee—Matthew 17:22–23; Mark 9:31
5. Near Jerusalem—Matthew 20:17–19; Mark 10:32–34; Luke 18:31–33

I.N.R.I.

The inscription on the cross in "the three tongues" means *Iesus Nazarenus Rex Iudaeorum* (Jesus of Nazareth, King of the Jews). In the Middle Ages, a thorough knowledge of Hebrew, Greek, and Latin was the prerequisite for theological training and a mark of such an education.

> **"They Have Pierced My Hands and My Feet"**
>
> Although crucifixion was a common form of execution in Jesus' day, later generations were left with only scant scriptural evidence and their own imagination to determine details of how, for example, his feet were affixed. Michelangelo's *Crucifixion*, showing the feet of the crucified Jesus separated, with a nail through each, has influenced more images than has contemporary archeological and literary evidence.

The Seven Last Words

1. Father, forgive them; for they do not know what they do.—Luke 23:34

2. Woman here is your son . . . Here is your mother.—John 19:26–27

3. I am thirsty.—John 19:28

4. Today you will be with me in paradise.—Luke 23:43

5. My God, my God, why have you forsaken me?—Matthew 27:46; Mark 15:34

6. It is finished.—John 19:30

7. Father, into your hands I commend my spirit.—Luke 23:46

No Rest for the Wicked

Isaiah has been quoted in Latin, *Nemo malus felix* (No bad person is happy), and we have said, "No rest for the wicked." If this is true, there is abundant illustration in stories of Pilate's life after Good Friday. They are suitably dramatic. One tradition relates that his life became so unfortunate that he committed suicide in Rome in the days of Caligula. Thereupon his body was disposed of in the Tiber, whose waters became so troubled by evil spirits that his corpse was retrieved and transported to Vienna. A similar disposal was attempted, this time into the Rhine, which washed Pilate's remains into the recesses of a lake on Mount Pilatus, between the cantons of Lucerne and Unterwalden. This is too coincidental to ignore: It is more likely that it was the name of the lake that brought the story, not the river that brought the body. Pilatus earned its name from the westerly winds that cover it with a white cloud cap (Latin: *pileatus*; *pileus*, felt cap).

The mount named Pilatus has spawned another legend: After being banished by Tiberius to Gaul, Pilate wandered to Mount Pilatus and threw himself into a black lake on its summit. Ever since, the ghost of Pilate reappears on the mountain annually; anyone cursed with a glimpse of the ghost is destined to die before another year is over. (A sixteenth-century law prohibited the throwing of stones in the lake for fear of bringing a tempest on the country.)

Flowers on Calvary

It is not uncommon for a plant to have a Christian fable associated with it, as with the aspen and the passion flower. The red anemone, the purple orchis (orchid), the arum, and the spotted persicaria were all stained red, it is said, by blood falling from the crucified Christ. There is more elaborate symbolism to come: The Calvary flower (common trefoil, *medicago echinus*) is said to have sprung up in the footsteps taken by Pilate when he walked to the crucifixion "to see his title affixed" (INRI). There are resemblances in the flower to crucifixion symbols; that is, in the center of each of its three leaves is a carmine spot, which takes on a cross form in the daylight hours. Moreover, the plant sports a little yellow flower that resembles a crown of thorns.

St. Peter's Cross   St. Andrew's Cross   St. Anthony's Cross (Egyptian, or tau; his origin and monastic locale)   St. Chad's Cross (four tau crosses joined in quadrate)   St. Julian's Cross (four Latin crosses joined saltirewise)

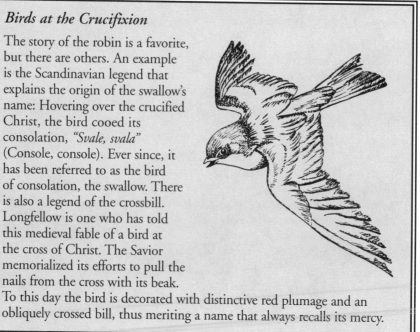
The Resurrection of Jesus

1. According to Matthew

Mary Magdalene and the other Mary visit tomb.

Jesus appears to the women.

Chief priests bribe guards.

Jesus appears to the eleven in Galilee.

2. According to Mark

Mary Magdalene, Mary mother of James, and Salome visit tomb.

Jesus appears to Mary Magdalene.

Jesus appears to three disciples going to the country.

Jesus appears to the eleven at table.

3. According to Luke

Mary Magdalene, Mary mother of James, and Joanna visit tomb.

Peter runs to tomb.

Jesus appears to two on way to Emmaus, and to Peter.

Jesus appears to the eleven in Jerusalem.

The ascension

4. According to John

Mary Magdalene visits tomb.

Peter and John run to tomb.

Jesus appears to Mary Magdalene.

Jesus appears to the eleven, minus Thomas, Sunday evening.

Jesus appears to the eleven, including Thomas, one week later.

Jesus appears to two apostles by Sea of Galilee later.

The Glory of Jesus (See CCC #s 659–660.)

These experiences are apart from the exceptional and unique post-ascension appearance to Paul.

1. Revealed—in the resurrection

2. Veiled—in the post-resurrection appearances

3. Exalted—in the ascension to the Father's right hand

Noli me tangere

In John's Gospel, Jesus says to Mary Magdalene after his resurrection, "Do not touch me." Hence these words, in Latin, are the name given to a painting representing Mary Magdalene meeting Christ after his resurrection. (The impatiens plant uses this title, the "Touch-me-not.")

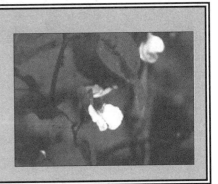

The Post-Resurrection Appearances of Jesus

According to Paul (1 Corinthians 15:5–8)

> . . . *he was seen by Cephas, then by the twelve. After that he was seen by five hundred brothers at once . . . Next he was seen by James; then by all the apostles. Last of all he was seen by me, as one born out of the normal course.*

According to Luke (Acts 1:3 and 13:30–31)

> *After his suffering he presented himself alive to them by many convincing proofs, appearing to them during forty days and speaking about the kingdom of God . . . God raised him from the dead; and for many days he appeared to those who came up with him from Galilee to Jerusalem.*

The "Gospel of the Holy Spirit" (see next chapter)

Acts of the Apostles (See for example 13:4, 16:7, 20:22.)

Ascension window

Church

The Nature of the Church

The Word Church (See CCC #752.)

1. The liturgical assembly (1 Corinthians 11:18; 14:19, 28)
   "A parish is a definite community of the Christian faithful established on a stable basis within a particular Church (diocese); the pastoral care of the parish is entrusted to a pastor as its own shepherd under the authority of the diocesan bishop" (*Code of Canon Law*, 515.1).

2. The local community (otherwise known as):
   • The particular Church
   • The diocese
   • The assembly of many assemblies

3. The universal community of believers (known in the New Testament as):
   • The People of God (See CCC #s 781–782.)
   • The Body of Christ (See CCC #s 787–795.)
   • The Temple of the Spirit (See CCC #s 797–801.)

Characteristics of the Church (Acts 2:42–47)

1. The teaching of the apostles (Greek: *Didache*)

2. The communal life (Greek: *Koinonia*)

3. The breaking of the bread

4. The prayers

The Mission of the Church (See CCC #s 849–856.)

1. Message (Greek: *kerygma*). The proclamation of the good news, the core of which is that Jesus who died is risen and now lives among us (see Romans 16:25–26). Distinct from the teaching mission (Greek: *didache*).

2. Fellowship (Greek: *koinonia*). The responsibility of Jesus' followers for a visible demonstration of what they are proclaiming in the message. The building of Christian community in the bond of faith, hope, and love (see Acts 2:42–47).

3. Service (Greek: *diakonia*). The act of healing and reconciling, of binding up wounds and restoring health, with the example and power of Jesus.

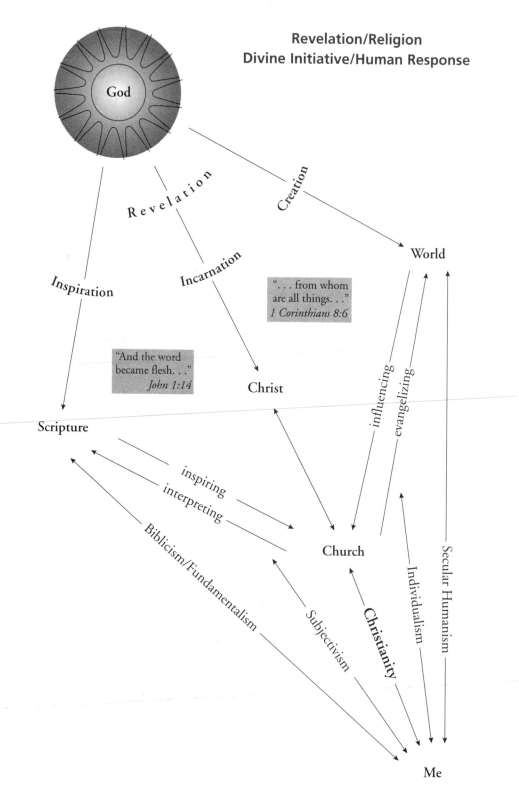

Revelation/Religion
Divine Initiative/Human Response

God

Creation

Revelation

Inspiration

Incarnation

". . . from whom
are all things. . ."
1 Corinthians 8:6

World

"And the word
became flesh. . ."
John 1:14

Christ

influencing

evangelizing

Scripture

inspiring

interpreting

Church

Biblicism/Fundamentalism

Subjectivism

Christianity

Individualism

Secular Humanism

Me

New Testament Symbols of the Church (See CCC #s 753–757.)

1. From the life of the shepherd: sheepfold

2. From the cultivation of the land: cultivated field

3. From the construction trade: building of God

4. From marriage and family life: bride of Christ, mother

The Four Marks of the Church (See CCC #s 811–812.)

1. One

2. Holy

3. Catholic

4. Apostolic

The Fifteen Marks of the Church

This expansion of the four marks of the Church is by St. Robert Bellarmine who lived in the wake of the principal Protestant reformers (1542–1621) and was a cardinal, archbishop of Capua, and doctor of the Church.

1. Catholicity, being worldwide and not confined to a particular nation

2. Antiquity, tracing ancestry directly to Christ

3. Duration, lasting substantially unchanged for centuries

4. Extensiveness, in the number of members

5. Episcopal succession, from the twelve apostles to the current hierarchy

6. Doctrinal agreement between current teaching and apostolic Church

7. Unity among members, and between members and visible head (pope)

8. Holiness of doctrine, reflecting the holiness of God

9. Efficacy of doctrine, powerful in sanctifying and inspiring believers

10. Holiness of life of representative writers and defenders

11. Miracles worked in the Church and under its auspices

12. Gift of prophecy among its saints and spokespersons

13. Opposition aroused on same ground as Christ was opposed

14. Unhappy end of its enemies

15. Temporal peace and earthly happiness of those who are faithful to its teaching and who defend its interests

---

The Catholic Church Is Apostolic (See CCC #857.)

1. Because the apostles founded it

2. Because the apostles' teaching is handed on by it

3. Because the apostles' successors, the bishops, lead it

The Three States of the Church (the communion of saints) (See CCC #962.)

Traditional	Contemporary
1. The Church militant on earth	1. Faithful pilgrims on earth
2. The Church suffering in purgatory	2. Souls being purged
3. The Church triumphant in heaven	3. Blessed in heaven

Catholic

1. **Literally** the word catholic means *"universal."* Greek: *katholikos*, from *kata*, "concerning," and *holou*, "whole"; that is, "concerning the whole." Latin: *catholicus*.

2. **Originally**, in reference to the Christian Church, the title *Catholic* was used by St. Ignatius of Antioch (35–107) in his letter to the Smyrneans (8, 2).

3. **Specifically** the name *Catholic* has at least four common meanings:
   - The Catholic Church—as distinct from Christian Church bodies that do not recognize papal primacy
   - The Catholic faith as the belief of Catholics ("everywhere, always, and by all")
   - The orthodox Catholic faith—as distinguished from heresy and schism
   - The undivided (Catholic) Church before the Eastern Schism (1054), after which the Eastern Church called itself *Orthodox,* distinguishing itself from Christian bodies which rejected the definitions of (the Councils of) Ephesus (431) and Chalcedon (451) on Christ's divinity.

4. **Commonly** the name *Catholic* refers to those Christians who live a continued tradition of faith and worship, and who hold to the apostolic succession of bishops and priests since Christ:

   Catholic because:
   - It is intended for all people.
   - It is intended for all time.
   - It is appropriate in every circumstance of human life.

5. In the *Catechism of the Catholic Church*:
   - The Church is catholic (universal) (see CCC #s 830–831) because of:
     - (1) The presence of Jesus Christ in the Church
     - (2) The mission from Christ to the whole human race
   - Who belongs to the Catholic Church?
     - (1) The Body of Christ—those who are called to unity (with different degrees of communion) (see CCC #836):

— The Catholic faithful (those who are fully incorporated into the Catholic Church) (see CCC #837)

— Others who believe in Christ; first among them, the Orthodox Church (see CCC #838)

(2) Those related to the Body of Christ (see CCC #s 839–845):

— Jewish people

— Muslims

— Other non-Christian religions

(3) All humankind, called by God's grace to salvation

The Apostolic Church

Ascension—Acts 1:1–12

Pentecost—Acts 2

The ministry of deacons—Acts 6:1–7

Stephen, the first martyr—Acts 6:5–15, 7

Philip and the Ethiopian—Acts 8:26–39

Saul of Tarsus—Acts 9:1–30

Peter and Cornelius—Acts 10

Peter in prison—Acts 12:1–19

Paul's first missionary journey—Acts 13:4–14:27

The first council—Acts 15:1–35

Paul's second missionary journey—Acts 15:36–18:22

Paul in prison—Acts 16:16–40

Paul's third missionary journey—Acts 18:23–21:16

The riot of the Ephesus silversmiths—Acts 19:23–41

Paul's voyage to Rome—Acts 27, 28

One Greeting in a Diversity of Tongues

The faithful of the early centuries embraced each other with the Easter greeting, *Surrexit Dominus vere* (Christ is truly risen), to which the response was made, *Deo gratias* (Thanks be to God). As Christian faith passed from one generation to the next, the same greeting was exchanged in a diversity of tongues: *Christos aneste/Alethos aneste* (Christ is risen/Christ is truly risen) in the Greek Church, *Christos voskres/Vo istinu voskres* by the Russians and Ukrainians, and *Wesolego Alleluja* (A joyful alleluia to you) by the Poles and western Slavs.

The Eight Kerygmatic Sermons in Acts

In 1 Corinthians 15:1–11, Paul writes of Christ's resurrection as the core of the message (that which has been handed on), and as the foundation of Christian faith. Salvation and resurrection are the message, "the proclamation" (Greek: *kerygma*). There are eight of these kerygmatic sermons in the Book of Acts, six to Jews, two to Gentiles.

Six Sermons to Jews   (five by Peter, the sixth by Paul)

1. On the day of Pentecost—Acts 2:14–36

2. After the cure of a cripple, with John—Acts 3:12–26

3. The next day before the Sanhedrin after Peter and John spend a night in jail—Acts 4:8–12

4. At a second trial after another night in jail—Acts 5:29–32

5. In Caesarea, after a vision, leading to Cornelius's baptism—Acts 10:34–43

6. On a mission of Barnabas and Paul, at an Antioch synagogue—Acts 13:16–41

Two to Gentiles   (by Paul)

1. After a cure, acclamation in Lystra, "The gods have come down to us in human form" (Acts 14:11)—Acts 14:15–17

2. In the Athens Areopagus, referring to "an unknown god"—Acts 17:22–31

Historical Development of the Church

An Chronological Outline of the Early Church

These are all first-century dates and approximate in most cases (relying on the scholarship and estimations of the *New Jerome Biblical Commentary*). At least three dates from secular history, however, are established ones and helpful in determining dates in early Church history:

1. Herod Agrippa's reign in Judea (41–44; see Acts 12)

2. Festus's appointment as governor at Caesarea (60; see Acts 24:27)

3. Nero's reign as Roman emperor (54–68)

By putting 19 ahead of each year and "contemporizing" the events, one gets a better sense of the lapse of time between these events and of their relationship to each other. By considering first-century events as if they were twentieth-century ones chronologically, one can better see the written word (the Bible) as the Church's inspired reflection on the interpretation of its experience of the incarnate Word (Jesus Christ).

Numbers in parentheses are Acts of the Apostles references. **Boldface** indicates a different New Testament book.

1930	Formation of the Church in Jerusalem (2)
1931–1932	Ministry of Stephen, first martyr (7, 8)
1931–1932	Saul's conversion (9)
1934–1935	Paul's first visit to Jerusalem (as a Christian, 9:23–30)
1944	Paul's second visit to Jerusalem (11:27–30)
1945–1948	Paul's first missionary journey: Galatia (13–14)
1950	The Council in Jerusalem (15)
1950–1953	Paul's second missionary journey: Greece (16–18)
1950	**1 Thessalonians** (from Corinth)
1952+	**2 Thessalonians** (from Corinth)
1954–1957	Paul's third missionary journey: Ephesus (18–21)
1954–1957	**1 Corinthians** (from Ephesus)
1954–1957	**Galatians** (from Philippi)
1955–1957	**2 Corinthians** (from Philippi)
1954–1958	**Philippians**
1957–1958	**Romans** (from Corinth)
1958	Paul in Jerusalem (20:16)
1958–1960	Paul in Caesarea
1960–1961	Paul's journey to Rome (27, 28)
1961–1963	Paul's first Roman captivity (28:16)
1961–1963	**Philemon**
1961–1963 or 1970–1980	**Colossians**
1961–1963 or 1980–2000	**Ephesians** (to Churches in Asia Minor)
1964	**1 Peter**
1964	Peter's death in Rome
1963–1967	**1 Timothy** (between first and second captivities)
1963–1967	**Titus** (between first and second captivities)
1963–1970	**James**
1967	Paul's second captivity
1965 or 1980–1990	**Hebrews** (in Italy, authorship?)
1967	**2 Timothy**
1967	Paul executed (during Nero's reign, 54–68)
1965–1970	**The Gospel according to Mark**
1970	**The Gospel according to Matthew**
1970–1985	**The Gospel according to Luke**
1970–1985	**Acts of the Apostles**
1990s	**Jude**
1990s	**The Gospel according to John**
1995–1996	**The Book of Revelation**
2000	**2 Peter**
2000	**1, 2, 3 John**

Paul's Missionary Journeys

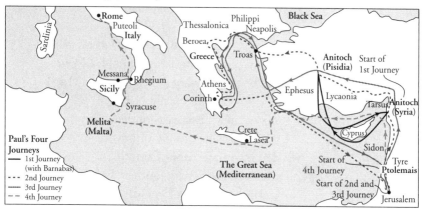

The Church of the Acts of the Apostles

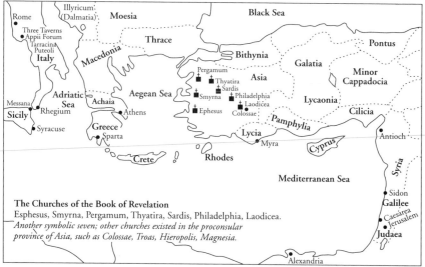

The Twelve Apostles Teach All Nations *(according to tradition)*

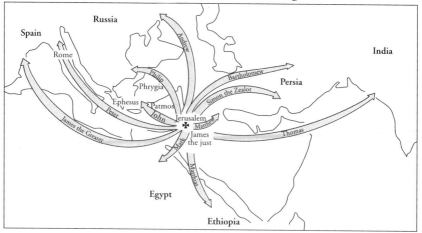

The Ten Great Persecutions

1. **Nero** (54–68) accused Christians of being enemies of mankind.

2. **Domitian** (81–96) victimized mainly nobility.

3. **Trajan** (98–117) considered Christians state enemies.

4. **Marcus Aurelius** (161–180) confiscated Christians' property and tortured his victims.

5. **Septimius Severus** (193–211) outlawed conversion to Christianity.

6. **Maximinus Thrax** (235–238) persecuted clergy.

7. **Decius** (249–251) ordered death for any citizen refusing sacrifice to the state gods.

8. **Valerian** (253–260) outlawed Christian assembly, persecuting mainly clergy and nobility.

9. **Aurelian** (270–275) allowed the anti-Christian laws, without seriously enforcing them.

10. **Diocletian** (284–305) reversing Aurelian's policy, engineered the bloodiest persecution.

The Edict of Milan (313) promoted tolerance, thus giving Christianity legal status, ending the age of Roman persecution.

> ### *The Wheat of St. Ignatius*
>
> St. Ignatius of Antioch, said to be a convert of St. John, was said to be consecrated bishop of Antioch by St. Peter, and was martyred by Trajan in the Roman amphitheater. "Let me be food for the wild beasts . . . I am God's wheat and shall be ground by their teeth so that I may become Christ's pure bread." Legend has it that Ignatius was the child that Jesus set in the midst of his disciples as an example: ". . . unless you change and become like children . . ." (Matthew 18:2–3)

The Episcopacy
(See CCC #s 861–862, 871–896.)

Terms

Bishop

The "ordinary" of a diocese with personal jurisdiction as a successor of the apostles over people within his diocese or "see."

Pope

The bishop of Rome, successor of St. Peter, first among equals (bishops) and visible head of the Catholic Church.

The universal hierarchy

Entered through episcopal (bishop) ordination, the fullness of Holy Orders.

The Holy See

The office of the papacy in terms of its jurisdiction and court.

> ### *Ad Limina*
>
> It is canonically required of bishops to make an *ad limina* visit every three to ten years. It is a pilgrimage to Rome *ad limina apostolorum* (to the threshold of the apostles), during which the bishops render to the pope an account of their diocese.

Species of Bishops and Related Terms

Patriarch

There are seven bishops and the pope who are called *patriarchs*. Historically, the patriarchates (jurisdictions) were Rome, Antioch, and Alexandria, expanded to include Constantinople in 381 and Jerusalem in 451. The Eastern Rite Catholic patriarchs have jurisdiction over the faithful in their Churches throughout the world and are subject only to the pope. Currently, there is an Eastern patriarch in Alexandria for the Coptic Catholics; three in Antioch—for the Syrian Catholics, the Greek Melkite Catholics, and the Maronite Catholics; one in Babylon for the Chaldean Catholics; and one in Cilicia for the Armenian Catholics. Finally, there is a Latin Rite patriarch in Jerusalem. All the faithful in these jurisdictions are fully Catholic, sharing the doctrines and sacraments of the universal Church, although their liturgical rites are very different.

Archbishop

The leader of the principal see within a particular province (region or jurisdictional unit) is called an archbishop. Bishops of the other dioceses of the province are said to be suffragan to him. His immediate jurisdiction, however, pertains only to his own diocese. He is often called a *metropolitan* if he is an ordinary (and not merely titular or auxiliary) because of the importance of his see city.

Cardinal

A cardinal is a(n) (arch)bishop of a higher rank, with special responsibility and prominence in the universal Church but with no increase in regional jurisdiction. They are also the papal electors (their eligibility ceasing at age eighty). The word *cardinal* comes from *cardo*, the Latin word for hinge, "that on which another thing depends." So cardinal archbishops are the principal ones, like cardinal virtues or cardinal rules are. These cardinals have, instead of a diagnostic red crest, a red hat, which became customary after Innocent IV (1245), as they were ". . . ready to lay down their life for the gospel." A cardinal is sometimes called a "prince of the Church," because of his ecclesiastical equivalency to a prince in a monarchy. Cardinals in the privileged confidence of the pope are called a *latere* cardinals. It means "from the side." The designation of a cardinal *in pectore* (in the breast) means the cardinalship is still secret and not yet publicly announced.

The Sacred College

The College of Cardinals has existed since the early Church, though its exact origins are unclear. By the eleventh century, it had become a body with great influence, being composed of the pope's principal advisors on both governance and doctrine. It included bishops, priests, and some deacons of Rome and surrounding dioceses. In the time of Pope Nicholas II (1509), cardinals became papal electors. Today the college still functions in an advisory capacity to the pope, and can have not more than 120 cardinals who are under the age of eighty, and thus eligible to elect a pope. (The consistory is a Church court, commonly referring to the assemblage of cardinals presided over by the pope for deliberation; either secret, if only cardinals are present; semipublic, if bishops participate; or public, if other prelates are invited.)

Metropolitan (see Archbishop)

The metropolitan is an archbishop with suffragan bishops under him; the metropolis is the mother Church of an area that includes other see Churches. In the Greek Church, the ranking of the hierarchy is the patriarch, then metropolitan, then archbishop.

Primate

Formerly (though never according to canon law), a primate was a bishop with authority over a national territory, and not merely over his own diocese/province; he had authority for convoking and presiding over national councils and hearing appeals. Today, *primate* is simply an honorific title.

Suffragan bishop

Suffragan bishops are not metropolitans or archbishops, but they are related to one. They are so designated because they can be convened to give their "suffrage" (vote, consent, approval). The term is also a generic designation for a bishop without his own see (such as an auxiliary, a coadjutor, or a titular bishop).

Titular bishop

A titular bishop has no regional jurisdiction. Such a bishop may be entitled *in partibus infidelium* (in the lands of the infidels) or simply *in partibus*, designating a bishop with the title but not the jurisdiction of a particular area.

Vicar apostolic

This is a bishop appointed to act as the representative of the pope in an area not yet designated a diocese. (Originally the terms referred to a bishop to whom the pope delegated some of his jurisdiction.)

Auxiliary bishop

An auxiliary bishop aids a bishop; he is without personal jurisdiction (that is, not an ordinary).

Coadjutor bishop (Latin: *ad, juvare,* to help)

This is an auxiliary with right to succession.

The Five Patriarchates

Christianity was first established in the Eastern (Greek) part of the Roman Empire. (Note the Greek language of the Christian Scriptures and other early Christian writings.)

Peter and Paul took Christianity to Rome. In the year 330 Constantine made Constantinople the capital of the Roman Empire, raising its position as a see city. By the end of the fourth century, Christendom was dominated by these five great centers and their bishops (patriarchs):

1. Alexandria
2. Antioch
3. Constantinople
4. Jerusalem
5. Rome

In 395 the Empire was divided into East (with the ecclesiastical seat in Constantinople) and West (with the seat in Rome). Thereafter, the patriarchates of Antioch, Jerusalem, and Alexandria gradually came to acknowledge the leadership of Constantinople. Their loss of universal Christian prominence was complete when they were absorbed by Islam (632–638).

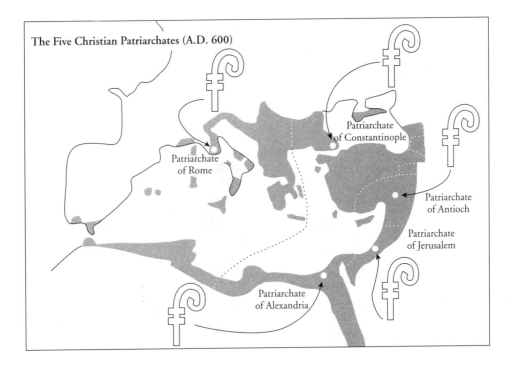

The Five Christian Patriarchates (A.D. 600)

Patriarchate of Rome

Patriarchate of Constantinople

Patriarchate of Antioch

Patriarchate of Jerusalem

Patriarchate of Alexandria

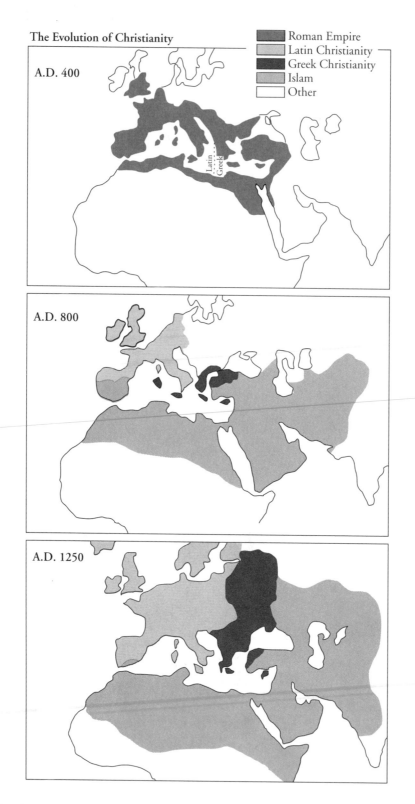

The Evolution of Christianity

Roman Empire
Latin Christianity
Greek Christianity
Islam
Other

A.D. 400

Latin
Greek

A.D. 800

A.D. 1250

The Papacy

Papal Election

Since 1274, a **conclave** is the enclosure of cardinals to elect a pope. By tradition, if a pope was not elected in five days, cardinals in conclave were reduced to bread and water rations. In 1271, the deadlocked cardinal electors were finally locked in with no supplies! Changes by Pope Paul VI (1963–1978) included limiting the number of electors to 120 and, if no one is elected in three days, there is a required day of prayer, allowing for conversation among electors.

Tiara and crossed keys, symbols of the papal office

The **chamberlain** becomes head of the college and directs the conclave *januis clausis* (behind closed doors) at the death of a pope.

A **papabile** is one who has some probability of becoming pope.

The **Sistine Chapel** is the location of the conclave.

When all the **canopies** except the one of the newly elected are lowered over the cardinals' chairs, a cardinal knows he is elected pope.

Black smoke emerging from the Vatican indicates no decision; white smoke, *Habemus papam* ("We have a pope").

The **pontificate**, or patriarchate, of a pope begins when he accepts election.

Resignation of a pope would be given to the college of cardinals.

An **interregnum** (*sede vacante*) is the period between the death of a pope and the election of a successor.

Sic transit gloria mundi

Thomas à Kempis spoke thus, in commenting on the vanity, the fleeting nature, of human life. "Thus passes the glories of the world." This truth is echoed in the papal coronation: A rope bundle is burned and, as the flame dies, the words are spoken, *"Pater Sancte (Holy Father), sic transit gloria mundi."*

Apostolic Succession (See CCC #s 77, 830, 833, 860–862.)

The continuity of shepherding responsibility given by Christ to the Church leadership (John 20:23; Matthew 28:19) is realized in the line of authority passing from the apostle Peter to each of his legitimate successors. This empowers ("legitimizes") the sacramental ministry of a parish priest since he is ordained by a bishop who is consecrated by a successor of St. Peter.

Popes of the First Century

1. St. Peter (Simon bar-Jonah); Capernaum, Galilee; died in about 64

2. St. Linus; Tuscia; 67–76

3. St. Anacletus (Cletus); Rome; 76–88

4. St. Clement; Rome; 88–97

5. St. Evaristus; Greece; 97–105

Popes of the Twentieth Century

Leo XIII (Gioacchino Pecci); Carpineto, Anagni, Italy; 1878–1903

St. Pius X (Giuseppe Sarto); Riese, Treviso, Italy; 1903–1914

Benedict XV (Giacomo delta Chiesa); Genoa, Italy; 1914–1922

Pius XI (Achille Ratti); Desio, Milan, Italy; 1922–1939

Pius XII (Eugenio Pacelli); Rome, Italy; 1939–1958

John XXIII (Angelo Roncalli); Sotto il Monte, Bergamo, Italy; 1958–1963

Paul VI (Giovanni Montini); Concessio, Brescia, Italy; 1963–1978

John Paul I (Albino Luciani); Forno di Canale, Italy; 1978

John Paul II (Karol Wojtyla); Wadowice, Poland; 1978–

A Distinctive Pope

John Paul II, at age 58, was the youngest pope chosen since 1846, the only pope elected from a Communist country, the only Polish pope, the first pope since Pius II in the fifteenth century to be a man of letters, and the first non-Italian pope since the Dutch Adrian VI who died in 1523 (58 popes have been non-Italian, including fifteen Greeks, fifteen Frenchmen, six Germans, and an Englishman).

A Resigning Pope

In 1294 Pope St. Celestine V (Peter di Morone), without precedent, voluntarily resigned after five months in office. He was an 84-year-old hermit when elected pope to follow Nicholas IV. Very soon he realized that he lacked the competence and experience for such a leadership task and was unable to cope with the pressure from secular rulers. He therefore issued a constitution declaring a pope's right to resign, which was accepted by the cardinals. Two years later he died and in 1313 was canonized.

First, Last, and Only Popes

John II, in 533: first pope to change his name (his given name was *Mercury*, the name of a pagan deity)

Adrian IV, 1154–1159: only English pope (Nicholas Breakspear)

Gregory XII, in 1415: last pope to resign

Felix V, in 1440: the last anti-pope or false claimant to be pope

Adrian VI, 1522–1523: the last non-Italian pope (from Utrecht, Holland) until John Paul II

Marcellus II, in 1555: last pope to keep his own name (Marcello Cervini)

Pius X, 1903–1914: last pope to be canonized (beatified in 1951)

John XXIII, 1958–1963: was a World War I corpsman and an army chaplain

Paul VI, in 1963: first pope to address a United Nations General Assembly

John Paul II, 1978– : only Polish pope and first non-Italian in 450 years

Papal Titles

Pope (Greek: *pappas*; Italian: *papa*, father)

Not uncommon designation in the early Church, Leo the Great (440–461) first using it officially, Gregory VII (1073–1085) first reserving it to the bishop of Rome; paternal authority, after the example of Christ

Bishop of Rome

First among equals *(primus inter pares)*, the pope is a bishop, the fullest office of Holy Orders. Vatican I defined that the successors of Peter in primacy are the bishops of Rome.

Vicar of Christ

As representative of Christ, the head of the Church; the title was adopted by Innocent III (1198)

Supreme Pontiff of the Universal Church

Pontiff is from the Latin *pons, pontis* (bridge); *facio, fecit* (to do, make); so a *pontifex* (pontiff) is a bridge-builder. Originally any bishop, "one in charge of the bridges" (high priest), later reserved for the supreme or sovereign (first) pontiff (the bishop of Rome). The pontiff has antecedents in the Roman religious office of *pontifex maximus*, the bridge-builder between gods and mortals.

Patriarch of the West (see "Patriarch")

Primate of Italy (see "Primate")

Archbishop and Metropolitan of the Roman Province

Successor of St. Peter, Prince of the Apostles

Servus servorum Dei (Latin: servant of the servants of God)

First used by Pope St. Gregory the Great (590–604), after Mark 10:44; in common use after Pope Gregory VII (1073–1085)

Sovereign of Vatican City

Slave of the Slaves

"Servant of the Servants of God" was the preferred papal title of Pope Gregory. Peter Claver preferred for his own title "slave of the slaves of the people." Slaves, not servants, were his mission. A Spanish Jesuit (1581–1654), Peter came to Cartagena, the great port of entry for Africans in South America (contemporary Colombia). Each year 10,000 Africans were imported for work in the mines. The conditions of their Atlantic passage were unspeakable. One-third did not survive. To the pitiable ones who did, St. Peter Claver dedicated his life. Making his way through the "cargo" of ship after ship, Peter carried to them medicine, food, respect, and good news—a ministry made more daunting by the fact that "Christianity" was the religion of the slave masters. By preaching to the Blacks a sense of their dignity and their preciousness in the eyes of God, Peter made himself a subversive in a slave-based society and economy.

Dear Pope

Pope John Paul II set the record for the amount of correspondence received, more than any of his predecessors, and from a whole range of correspondents. Some, such as heads of state, send communication by way of diplomatic pouch; others deliver it themselves, by way of the Swiss guards at the bronze door, the main entrance to the apostolic palace where the pope lives; most however simply mail their letters to the pope like any other letter.

It is the Vatican Secretariat of State who first receives the letters. Here they are sorted, divided mainly into eight language categories: Italian, English, French, Spanish, Portuguese, German, Polish, and Latin. Letters in other languages go to translators. Ultimately, almost all letters addressed to the pope go to him. The Secretariat staff, prior to delivering the pope's mail, sorts the letters into envelopes according to subject matter, and summarizes the contents on a paper attached to the envelope. It takes nine priests working full time to read, summarize, and often respond to just the English-language letters. Only the Italian-language correspondence, with its greater volume, requires a larger staff. Even letters destined for a specific office, for example, the Office of the Doctrine of the Faith, go to the pope if they are addressed to him. In most cases, letters are answered by the Secretariat of State, or by the Congregation which handles the topic of the letter. Personal responses from the pope are rare, usually written only to heads of state.

Papal Statements

Anathema

This solemn condemnation is found in Scripture, for example, when Paul writes, "If anyone preaches to you a gospel besides what you have received, let him be anathema" (Galatians 1:9). Historically in the Church, the condemnation declares that some teaching or position contradicts Catholic faith and doctrine. The form *anathema sit* ("Let the person be anathema," excommunicated) was probably first used in the fourth century.

Apostolic brief

Less formal than a bull and regarding less serious matters, an apostolic brief is sealed with a representation of St. Peter landing his fisherman's net.

Apostolic bull

This is a solemn, formal document regarding serious matters. It opens with the current pope's name, then *servus servorum Dei* (Latin: servant of the servants of God), and *ad perpetuam rei memoriam* (Latin: for the perpetual remembrance of the thing). The apostolic bull closes with its place of origin, date of issue, and the year of the current pontificate. It gets its name from the leaden seal (Latin: *bulla*) on the document.

Encyclical

This is a letter, usually doctrinal, to the universal Church.

Ex cathedra (Latin: from the chair)

The Church's visible seat of authority is the chair of St. Peter; this visible symbol is occupied day by day by his successor, the bishop of Rome, exercising universal authority with the college of his brother bishops.

Indult

This is the Holy See's temporary favor allowing a bishop to do something not otherwise allowed.

In petto (Italian; Latin: in pectore, in the breast)

This designation is for something done privately, or held in reserve, as the names of cardinals chosen but not yet announced.

Motu proprio (Latin: by one's own accord)

This is a letter which the pope himself writes, signs, and issues on his own initiative.

Pontifical letter

This is a papal letter; it might be an explanation of a certain doctrinal point, an instruction, or a congratulatory message.

Urbi et orbi (Latin: to the city—Rome—and to the world)

This solemn papal blessing is given from St. Peter's balcony on special occasions.

Non possumus

Just as Peter and John responded "We cannot" (Acts 4:20) when they were asked to stop preaching, so does the pope speak in response to a suggested false innovation in doctrine.

Defender of the Faith

This title, *Fidei Defensor* (abbreviated *F.D.*), is not one the pope takes; it's one the pope gives; or gave. It is one of the many titles of the English monarchs, first applied in 1521 by Pope Leo X to Henry VIII for his treatise *Assertio Septem Sacramentorum*. That was then. In 1534, after continued conflict with papal power, Henry VIII obtained the Act of Supremacy from parliament creating a national Church (Anglican), apart from the Catholic Church and he appointed the king protector and sole supreme head of the Church and the clergy of England. Thomas More, his chancellor, was executed for refusing to acknowledge this. Henry's suppression of monasteries, confiscation of monastic properties, and beheading of two wives are other stories of the first Defender of the Faith. Present-day Prince Charles prefers "Defender of Faith."

The Order of St. Gregory the Great

An order originally established by Pope Gregory XVI in 1831 to honor citizens of the Papal States. In modern times the pope confers this order on those who are distinguished for personal character and reputation or for some significant accomplishment. It has civil and military divisions and three classes of knights.

Papal Places

Vatican City

The geopolitical area, recognized by the Treaty of the Lateran (1929), including the buildings of the Holy See (109 acres, slightly less than a square mile). Napoleon had annexed the Papal States and made a prisoner of Pope Pius VII, who excommunicated Napoleon. St. Ann's is the parish church of Vatican City.

Vatican (Latin: *Vaticanus*, name of a hill in Rome)

The papal palace and the popes' residence since the Avignon Papacy in the fourteenth century, before which the residency was at the Lateran. It has 10,000 rooms and hallways and 997 stairways, thirty of them hidden.

Lateran Palace

An edifice in Rome, used as the papal residence from the fourth century (when it was given to Pope Miltiades by Constantine) until the fourteenth century (when Pope Gregory XI returned from Avignon and took up residence at the Vatican). The Church of St. John Lateran adjoins it.

The seven hills of Rome

Vaticanus and Quirinal are two of the seven hills on which ancient Rome was built. "The Vatican" refers to papal authority and government whereas "the Quirinal" refers to Italian civil authority and government. There is also the Esquiline (of the miraculous fall of snow) and the Capitoline (on which the ancient Temple of Jupiter was built).

The *Scala Sancta*

The twenty-eight marble steps (now covered with wood) in the Lateran that lead to the papal chapel. Believed to be the steps of Pilate's praetorium, sanctified by Jesus' use during the passion. Brought to Rome by St. Helena, they are often climbed by pilgrims on their knees.

The Sistine Chapel (from Pope Sixtus IV under whom it was designed)

Main chapel of the Vatican palace and the private chapel of the pope; only the pope uses its altar (made of mother of pearl). Locale for papal election conclaves. Designed by Giovanni de Dolci; painted by Michelangelo, 1475–1483; dedicated to Our Lady of the Assumption.

Castel Gandolfo

The papal summer residence, established by Pope Urban VIII in the seventeenth century and named after the town in which it is located; it is some fourteen miles southeast of Rome

---

Swiss Guards and Designer Clothes

Since the fourteenth century, the Swiss Guards are the official Vatican police officers and the pope's bodyguards. Their red, yellow, and blue uniforms were designed by Michelangelo. They number 110, plus six officers, and their main responsibility is guarding the apostolic palaces. These soldiers are veterans of the Swiss military and are diplomatic enough to handle the occasional charlatans who arrive in clerical clothing, insisting they are expected for dinner with the pope!

Papal Things

Flag

White and gold, with the Vatican seal on the white half

Radio station

HVJ (originally designed and supervised by Guglielmo Marconi, the inventor of radio)

Printing press

Vatican Polyglot Press

Newspaper

A daily, *L'Osservatore Romano*. The first copy of the original edition was received by the pope.

Harbor

The Civita Vecchia, northwest of Rome

Phone

6982

The seal of Vatican City

Address

Palazzo Apostolico Vaticano, Vatican City, Europe 00121

Appearances

The Holy Father addresses visitors in St. Peter's Square on Sunday, at noon, with a general audience on Wednesdays.

Theologian

The "master of the sacred palace" is always a Dominican.

Representatives

Apostolic delegate (papal liaison to the Church in a given country) or nuncio (papal ambassador, diplomatic representative to a civil government)

Papal coffin

According to the Vatican protocol, when a pope dies, his body, along with medals struck during his pontificate, are placed in a cypress coffin. This coffin is then placed in one of lead which bears the pope's coat of arms and death certificate. These coffins are then housed in an oak casket. This is not to symbolize anything, but simply to conserve and preserve, and (ceremoniously) provide identification.

The Ecumenical (General) Councils (See CCC #884.)

An ecumenical council is a gathering of the bishops of the world called together by the pope to share the responsibility of teaching and guiding the Church. There have been twenty-one such worldwide councils.

1. Nicaea I, 325
2. Constantinople, 381
3. Ephesus, 431
4. Chalcedon, 451
5. Constantinople II, 553
6. Constantinople III, 680–681
7. Nicaea II, 787

These first seven, "The Seven Great Councils of the Early Church," are the only ones on which the Eastern and Western Churches agree; they are the only test of orthodoxy among the Eastern Churches separated from Rome.

8. Constantinople IV, 869–870
9. Lateran I, 1123
10. Lateran II, 1139
11. Lateran III, 1179
12. Lateran IV, 1215
13. Lyons I, 1245
14. Lyons II, 1274
15. Vienne, 1311–1312
16. Constance, 1414–1418
17. Basel-Ferrara-Florence-Rome, 1431–1445
18. Lateran V, 1512–1517
19. Trent, 1545–1547, 1551–1552, 1562–1563
20. Vatican I, 1869–1870
21. Vatican II, 1962–1965

Documents of Vatican II

The Second Vatican Council was called by Pope John XXIII, who died before it ended. It was then presided over by Pope Paul VI, who called its documents "the greatest catechism of our times." The council lasted from 1962 until 1965, and about 2,500 bishops attended. Also present were leading Catholic theologians and teachers, religious, and lay people—all contributing to the discussions. Non-Catholic observers and delegates were also present and made informed contributions to related discussions.

Constitutions

"The Church" (*Lumen Gentium*), "The Church in the Modern World" (*Gaudium et Spes*), "Divine Revelation" (*Dei Verbum*), and "Liturgy" (*Sacrosanctum Concilium*)

Decrees

"Communications," "Ecumenism," "Eastern Churches," "Bishops," "Priestly Formation," "Religious Formation," "Laity," "Priests," and "Missions"

Declarations

"Education," "Non-Christians," and "Religious Freedom"

Coats of Arms

Emblems of nobility, these "achievements" are of military origin and a by-product of medieval feudalism. Consisting of certain tinctures (metals and colors) and figures, they were later adopted by ecclesiastical dignitaries and religious communities to symbolize special characteristics of the person or community. The arms of the (arch)diocese occupy the left side of the shield; personal arms, the right.

Papal

(Illustration at left): Tiara (triple crown, *tri-regnum*); crossed keys, one gold, one silver, in saltire (crossed); no motto; first used officially in the thirteenth century.

Cardinal

(Second illustration at left): Red pontifical hat and fifteen red tassels in five rows on each side.

Archbishop

(Third illustration at left): Green hat and ten green tassels in four rows on each side; gold cross with double crossbeam, sometimes flanked by miter and crosier (curved outward).

Bishop

(Fourth illustration at left): Green hat and six green tassels in three rows on each side, gold cross with single crossbeam, sometimes flanked by miter and crosier (curved outward).

Bishop (auxiliary or coadjutor)

Same as bishop/archbishop but no diocesan arms (personal arms displayed on whole shield).

Bishop (Archbishop), Eastern Rite

(Third illustration): Same except tassels are purple, and miter and crosier are in the Eastern style.

Abbot

Same as bishop (minus cross) except tassels are black (Benedictine) or white (Cistercian or Premonstratensian) and crosier is curved inward (with veil attached to knob).

Archdiocese, diocese, or abbey

(Illustration at left): These arms appear as part of the individual's coat of arms (see above), or alone: miter surmounting shield, with no personal arms attached.

The "M" of the Archbishop

As a young Polish priest he had consecrated himself to the Blessed Mother—as he would one day teach the world: "spiritually taking her into his home," as the apostle John had done. So it was not surprising when he became an archbishop that he would choose to recognize her with a large M on his coat of arms. But when Archbishop Karol Wojtyla was elected pope, the designers of the papal coat of arms objected. They insisted that a star or a crown would be more appropriate. In the argument that ensued, Pope John Paul II remained adamant. His coat of arms would still have the M of the houseguest of his soul.

Mottoes

Catholic Mottoes

Integral part of Catholic history, motivating the faithful. In the sampling that follows, the more common Latin original of some is noted.

Always go forward and never go back.

Fr. Junipero Serra

For the greater glory of God

(*Ad Majorem Dei Gloriam*, AMDG) The motto of St. Ignatius and the Jesuits

God willing

DV *(Deo Volente)*

God wills it.

The faithful who gathered to hear Pope Urban II in 1095 at the Council of Clermont responded *"Deus vult!"* which became the battle cry of the First Crusade at the end of the eleventh century. It resulted in the recovery of the Holy Land from the Muslims.

Heraldic cross pattée, fitched at the bottom, representing the crusaders, and the cross they would implant in the ground.

It is better to light one candle than to curse the darkness.

The Christophers

Lift up your hearts.

(*Sursum corda.*) This liturgical phrase was common in Christian heraldry.

Praise God always.

(*Laus Deo semper.*) This motto was common for saints, especially monastics.

Pray and work.

(*Ora et labora.*) The motto of St. Benedict

Thanks be to God.

(*Deo gratias.*) We end the liturgy with this statement, as we could many undertakings.

There is nothing without God.

(*Nihil sine Deo.*) A once-familiar motto

To God who is the best and the greatest

(*Deo optimo maximo*, DOM) A motto of the Benedictines

To restore all things in Christ

Pope St. Pius X

Totally Yours

(*Totus Tuus*) The motto of Pope John Paul II

With God's favor

(*Deo Favente*) A motto invoking or citing God's cooperation

With God's help

(*Deo Iuvante [Juvante]*)

Secular Mottoes

Annuit Coeptis

"(God) has favored our undertaking" is from Virgil's *Aeneid*, and appears on the reserve of the United States' Great Seal, which appears on the dollar bill. With such an application of the phrase, this country joins many others in believing that God takes special interest in particular societies.

The Lord is my light.

(*Dominus illuminatio mea.*) The motto of Oxford University

The truth shall make you free.

(*Veritas vos liberabit.*) The motto of Johns Hopkins University

To consecrate life to truth

(*Vitam impendere vero*, Juvenal, *Satires IV*, 91) The motto of J.J. Rousseau

Insignia

These are some of the paraphernalia of traditional ceremonial.

Episcopal

The crosier (late Latin: *crocia*, crook)

The pastoral staff; turned outward when carried by the bishop within his diocese, inward when outside his diocese. Since the eleventh century the pope has not carried one.

The miter (Greek: headband, turban)

The ceremonial headgear (for abbots as well as bishops): folding, two-piece stiffened hat of silk or linen, joined with soft material allowing it to be open or folded flat; usually with two fringed tappets (*infulae*) hanging on the back. According to the occasion or liturgical season it is either: (1) golden, (2) decorated with precious stones, or (3) simple (white, formerly for use on Good Friday or funerals). It is removed during prayers.

A pectoral cross

A necklace cross (in common use since the seventeenth century)

A ring

In gold (with an amethyst stone at one time), worn on the third finger of the right hand; formerly kissed respectfully by one on bended knee.

Other episcopal ceremonial

Includes buskins (decorative stockings), *cappa magna* (a cape with trim and silk or fur-lined hood), dalmatic (squarish, chasuble-like garment worn over the alb; proper to a deacon), gloves, gremial veil (a lap cloth used during ordinations), mantelletta (a knee-length, sleeveless vestment of silk or wool), morse (an ornamental clasp for a cope), mozzetta (a short, front-buttoning cape), rochet (a surplice-like vestment of linen or a sheer material), sandals, skullcap (the bishop's zucchetto is purple, the cardinal's red, the pope's white), and tunicle (a chasuble-like vestment, formerly proper to a subdeacon)

Bishop in violet mozzetta over rochet and violet cassock; zucchetto on head.

Bishop in violet mantelletta (faced in red) over rochet and violet cassock, violet biretta on head.

Archbishop in full pontificals with miter on head and crosier in hand. Pallium is over chasuble, under it is dalmatic and tunic.

The pallium of the archbishop

Along with a cross with an additional and shorter cross member, the pallium distinguishes the archbishops among bishops. The *pallium* (Latin: covering) is a liturgical vestment symbolizing the fullness of episcopal (bishop's) office; thus worn not only by the pope, but also by metropolitan archbishops (archbishops with suffragan dioceses related to them) and patriarchs. The pallium is also symbolic of personal loyalty to the pope and thereby the sign of unity between a local Church and the universal Church.

The pallium is a white, woolen, circular, two-inch band worn loosely around the neck, breast, and shoulders. It has a weighted pendant front and back, each ornamented with six black silken crosses, extending nearly to the waist. When an archbishop receives a pallium from the pope, he may exercise metropolitan jurisdiction. Should he transfer to another archdiocese, he is vested in a new pallium. (It is worn for such liturgical ceremonies as priest ordinations, bishop consecrations, and church dedications.)

The pallium is made from the wool of two lambs, representing Christ, the Lamb of God and the Good Shepherd. These animals are furnished from the lambs raised by the convent of St. Agnes in Rome and chosen and blessed each year on the feast day of St. Agnes (January 21) for their quality and whiteness. The lambs are sent to the Benedictine Sisters of St. Cecilia in Trastevere where they are cared for and shorn of their wool from which the pallia are woven.

On the eve of Saints Peter and Paul (June 29), the pallia are laid upon the tomb of St. Peter in the basilica, to rest above his body for the night, "contracting a share of apostolic authority," as it were. Following vespers on the feast day itself, the pallia are placed on the high altar to be blessed by the pope and placed on his own shoulders. After the ceremonies, the pallia are placed in a silver urn and enclosed in a cabinet under the altar of crucifixion, over the traditional tomb of St. Peter. Here they await delivery by papal embassy to the metropolitans or patriarchs who will wear them. The pallium is buried with the churchman when he dies.

Papal

The most well-known insignia of the pope are:

The papal ring of the fisherman

Bestowed at election, it is inscribed with a figure of St. Peter fishing. Used for sealing documents, it is ceremonially broken at the pope's death.

The tiara

A beehive-shaped triple crown of richly ornamented gold cloth, topped by a gold globe and cross. The papal crown was a development of the medieval papacy, above and beyond the miter of other bishops (and popes of the first five centuries). Symbolic interpretations of its significance abound, but primarily it represents his triple authority as pontiff, serving the Church militant, suffering, and triumphant. According to another interpretation, the first circlet symbolizes the pope's universal episcopate; the second, his primacy of jurisdiction; the third, his temporal influence. Formerly, the crowning marked the beginning of a pontificate, a tradition changed by Pope John Paul I (1978) and Pope John Paul II (1978–) when they were invested with the pallium instead. The tiara does remain part of the papal coat of arms and Vatican flag.

Other papal ceremonials

These include the *epigonation* (a Eucharistic vestment, representing the spiritual sword of justice; an embroidered, stiff garment hanging diamond-shaped from the waist to below the right knee; actually belonging to the Greek and Armenian Rites, it's worn also—and in the West, only—by the pope), the falda (a white silk vestment from the waist to ground, over the cassock), the fanon (a scarf-like vestment), the *sedia gestatoria* (the portable throne), and the subcinctorium (a broad, embroidered silk maniple).

Religious Life
(See CCC #s 914–933.)

A Glossary

Religious Order

Generally, a community of men or women (usually under solemn vows as priests, brothers, or nuns) living a stable manner of life in which they observe the evangelical counsels by means of the vows of poverty, chastity, and obedience. Usually not attached to a diocese (as a "secular" or diocesan priest is), they usually live a communal life with a specific apostolate and a particular charism and spirituality. Traditionally, they have been either active or contemplative, and have worn a distinctive habit. Exclaustration is permission for religious to live outside the community for a specified time (with vows still binding). A religious order is technically distinct from a religious institute, though they are basically equivalent, distinguished only by certain points of canon law.

Second Order

Feminine counterpart of a religious order whose founder first established an order of men (notably Franciscans and Dominicans).

Third Order

Association established by a religious order; originated by Franciscans and Dominicans in the thirteenth century. Today there are many such groups. They are either regular (TOR, Third Order Regular) (these are religious in community and under vows) or they are secular (called *tertiaries*) and lay.

Brother or Nun (Sister)

Member of a religious order or community who has taken solemn vows. Technically, one bound only by simple vows is called a "Sister."

Religious Rule

The plan of life and discipline by which religious strive to Christian perfection and accomplish the mission proper to their order.

Vows

Solemn vows include those taken by members of religious orders after a period of temporary, simple vows. Solemn vows are absolute, irrevocable vows under which ownership of property is prohibited and marriage is invalid. Simple vows, whether temporary or perpetual, allow ownership of personal property. Nuns either live cloistered lives or have limited ministries outside the convent, while sisters usually pursue ministries outside the convent.

Canons

Certain orders of religious men are distinct from monks because of certain duties, often connected with a particular church (usually a cathedral), shrine, or ecclesiastical function. They are either "regular," priests under public religious vows, living in a religious order community (any cathedral to which they were attached was "monastic"); or they are "secular," priests in community, but not under public vows or of a religious order (any cathedral to which they were attached was "diocesan").

The Scapular

History

Primarily and originally a garment, the frock-like working habit of the Benedictines; a long, shoulder-width piece of material, put on over the head, covering front and back, like a durable apron. With the rise of the third orders in the thirteenth century, it evolved into a more symbolic garment ("the yoke of Christ"), a monastic overtone in many religious habits. It was modified, becoming part of the habit, then worn under clothing (two small double squares of cloth suspended on strings). Finally, a lay scapular evolved, a devotional article worn by anyone, but especially as a sign of membership in a confraternity.

The lay scapular

Here are five special devotions that are Church approved related to five of the eighteen most familiar scapulars:

1. The brown scapular of Our Lady of Mt. Carmel is the one most celebrated and is worn by members of the Confraternity of Our Lady of Mt. Carmel. The brown scapular is associated with the Sabbatine (Saturday) Privilege which promises that the qualified wearer will be delivered from purgatory on the Saturday after death. This pious belief originated in a vision of Pope John XXII in 1322 (the documentation of which now has been judged to be doubtful).

2. The red scapular of Christ's passion

3. The black scapular of the seven sorrows of Mary

4. The blue scapular of the Immaculate Conception

5. The white scapular of the Holy Trinity

The green scapular is not a scapular in the strict sense, but more a "cloth medal." It has an image of the Immaculate Heart of Mary on one side and a prayer on the other. Traditionally, it had the special efficacy of healing and of bringing the lapsed back to the practice of the faith. The scapular medal was authorized in 1910 by the Holy See as a substitute for a scapular (that is, with the same privileges attached). It has images of the Sacred Heart on one side and Mary on the other.

Our Lady of Mount Carmel

This is the patronal feast of the Carmelite order. Pious legend tells how in the thirteenth century (the "Age of Faith") the Carmelite St. Simon Stock asked Mary to grant a special privilege to his order. And so it happened that on a certain day the Blessed Virgin appeared to him with a brown scapular in her hand saying, "Here is the privilege I grant to you and to all children of Carmel. Whoever dies clothed in this habit shall be saved."

This is the traditional prayer of Our Lady of Mount Carmel:

O beautiful Flower of Carmel, most fruitful vine and splendor of heaven, O holy and singular one who brought forth the only Son of God while remaining still a pure virgin, watch over us this night. O Star of the Sea, O Mother of Christ, show us you are our mother, too.

The feast of Our Lady of Mt. Carmel is July 16, and it commemorates eighteen various scapular devotions, including the brown scapular.

> ### *The Ascetic St. Giles*
>
> The story goes that Giles, a hermit, was accidentally wounded in the knee by Childeric, the King of France, who was out hunting. Giles remained crippled for life because he refused treatment for the injury "that he might better mortify the flesh."
>
> He is pictured with a hind or deer, alluding to the form which providence took for him in his asceticism: To his cave by the mouth of the Rhone a "heaven-sent hind" would come daily to give him milk.
>
> Historically, churches dedicated to him were often the ones on a city's outskirts, even outside its walls, thus the only churches accessible for cripples and beggars, who were not allowed in the city.

Anchorites (Contemplatives)

Anchorites (from the Greek word for recluse) retire from worldly activity to spend their days in contemplation. They are the original "monks" (Greek: *monachos*, living alone, solitary).

1. Hermits

Withdrawing to desert places, living in essential simplicity, subsisting on manual labor; for example, the Augustinian Recollects (Discalced hermits); see St. Anthony, first famous hermit.

2. Anchorites

Most radical, solitary, with only the essentials of food and cover.

> ### *Stylites or Pillar Ascetics*
>
> Ascetical zealots of the early and medieval Church (chiefly in Syria) who confined themselves to the top of pillars. The first and most widely known stylite (Greek: *stylos*, pillar) was Simeon Stylites of Syria (390–459) who reputedly spent forty years on pillars, each higher and narrower, the last being sixty-six feet high. He preached from this perch, bringing many to conversion and influenced many through his disciples. Another pillar ascetic was Daniel the Stylite of Constantinople (died in 494) who lived thirty-three years on a pillar, often nearly blown off by the storms of Thrace.

Cenobites (Monastics)

(Latin: *coenobium*, monastery; Greek: *koinos*, common; *bios*, life.) A monk or nun living in a religious community. Most are called monks, even though historically (and etymologically) this meant a solitary religious; now monks live in common in monasteries, taking the three vows according to a specific rule. St. Pachomius (290–346), an Egyptian, is the founder of cenobitic life in the East, having drawn up the first systematic rule of life for a religious community. St. Basil (329–379) modified it. St. Benedict, whose rule developed it, fitted it to the West. Generally, cenobites are members of the following orders, three larger and four smaller.

1. Benedictines (Black Monks)

This community was founded by St. Benedict at Subiaco and Monte Cassino around 530, to sanctify the Church's day (pray the Liturgy of the Hours), study, teach, and labor. Uniquely, there is a vow of stability taken under the Rule of St. Benedict to stay attached to the monastery of one's profession, thus fostering, in the spirit of St. Benedict, unity around one abbot and continuity of each monastery as a family. As early as the mid-fourteenth century, Benedictines had furnished the Church with 24 popes (a number now increased to 50, beginning with Gregory the Great), 200 cardinals, 7,000 archbishops, 15,000 bishops, 1,560 canonized saints, and 5,000 holy persons worthy of canonization.

2. Carthusians

This community was founded by St. Bruno of Cologne, about 1086, when he retired with six companions to the solitude of LaGrande Chartreuse, northeast of Grenoble.

3. Cistercians

This reform of the Benedictines was established in Burgundy in 1098 by St. Robert, Benedictine abbot of Molesme, at Citeaux (Latin: *Cistercium*). In 1115 St. Bernard joined the Citeaux monastery as a novice. Two years later he became the founding abbot of Clairvaux, and in time, the most influential spiritual leader of the day. He was largely responsible for the rapid expansion of the order (whose members for that reason were sometimes called Bernardines). Cistercians made a substantial contribution to economic life in the Middle Ages, especially because of the techniques they developed for reclaiming wasteland and the production and marketing methods they introduced in the grain and wool trade. They influenced the spread of Gothic architecture across Europe and preserved culture by their dedication to collecting and copying manuscripts for their libraries.

4. Trappists (Cistercians of the Strict Observance)

A reformed branch of the Cistercians that originated in France in 1098 under the leadership of St. Robert Molesme and St. Stephen Harding. After 1664 the name *Trappist* became common, with the reforms instituted by Armand Jean le Bouthillier de Rance (1626–1700) at the order's monastery of La Trappe in Normandy. Rance, imposing a strict rule of fasting, prayer, meditation, and manual labor, believed monasticism should be basically penitential.

5. Basilians

This is a general name for various religious institutes who have inherited the spirit of St. Basil (329–379), though with no uniform rule. There are five distinct Basilian orders of men and four congregations of women. Together, the "Basilian" institutes have been called an order from which have come fourteen popes, 1,800 bishops, 3,000 abbots, and 11,000 martyrs.

6. Premonstratensians (Norbertine Fathers)

This cloistered order of Augustinian canons was founded by St. Norbert (1120) in the diocese of Laon, France. So called because in a vision "a place (meadow) was pointed out" (*pre montre; pratum monstratum*). The order was inspired by and imitates the Cistercian ideal but takes the more flexible Augustinian Rule instead of the Benedictine. Canons are clergy living in community, but not monks.

7. Augustinian Canons

This order of men was founded by Ivo, Chartres bishop in the eleventh century, and follows the traditional Rule of Augustine.

The California Missions

There were many parish centers established among the Native American nations along the west coast of the present-day United States by Catholic missionaries from Spain. Between 1769 and 1845, it was followers of Francis who founded the missions in Upper California along the El Camino Real (The Royal Road). Although generally established later than those of the Jesuits and Dominicans in Lower California (Mexico), these twenty-one of the Franciscan Missions are the ones that are best known. From south to north and, at the time of their building, about a day's journey apart, they are:

San Diego	Santa Inez	Santa Cruz
San Luis Rey	Purisima Concepcion	San Juan Bautista
San Juan Capistrano	San Luis Obispo	Santa Clara
San Gabriel	San Miguel	San Jose
San Fernando	San Antonio de Padua	San Francisco
San Buenaventura	Soledad	San Rafael
Santa Barbara	San Carlos or Carmelo	San Francisco Solano

Mendicants (Latin: *mendicus,* beggar; an infirm, wretched person)

Members of a mendicant order are required to work or beg for their living; they are also not bound to one monastery by a vow of stability. Originally the name applied only to Franciscans and Dominicans. In time, the name and privileges were extended to Carmelites (1245), Hermits of St. Augustine (1256), and Servites (1424). Later, other orders were also accorded the title. Members of mendicant orders are called friars from the Latin *frater,* brother.

1. Franciscans (OFM: Order of Friars Minor)

Founded by St. Francis of Assisi in 1209; "Gray Friars" because of the indeterminate color of their habit (which is now brown)

Friars Minor (OFM)—Keeping the radical rule of St. Francis including poverty, abstinence, and preaching

Friars Minor Conventual (OFM Conv)—Modified rule; relaxed rule about holding property; habit: black tunic, white cord

Friars Minor Capuchin (OFM Cap; Latin: *capuce*, pointed cowl)—Most radical, established in 1525; relying on begging by lay brothers

Franciscan Nuns—Instituted by St. Francis in 1212; named after the first abbess, Clare of Assisi, (hence, Poor Clares, or Clares); through reforms: Colettines, Gray Sisters, Capuchin Nuns, Sisters of the Annunciation, Conceptionists, Urbanists

The symbol of St. Clare

2. Dominicans (OP: Order of Preachers)

The "Friars Major" were founded by St. Dominic in 1215. Called *Black Friars* from their black cloaks, they are one of the Church's intellectual pillars, personified in the renowned Dominican Thomas Aquinas. The order took the name of the founder, Dominic.

Hounds of the Lord

There is a story that Dominic's mother, while pregnant with him, dreamed she bore a black and white spotted dog. This canine offspring carried in his mouth a burning torch which illumined the world. Hence Dominic is often depicted with a dog at his side, because he fulfilled in life the prophecy in his mother's dream, especially in his forceful preaching against the Albigensian heresy. The light he gave the world was also accomplished through the order of preaching friars he established in 1215, the Dominicans (*domini canes* means hounds of the lord of the manor; Dominicans are "hounds of the Lord" —God!) This intellectual pillar of the Church boasts St. Thomas Aquinas as one of its most distinguished members.

---

3. Carmelites

Organized as mendicant friars by St. Simon Stock (died in 1265); "White Friars," because of the color of their habit.

The **Order of Our Lady of Mt. Carmel** was founded by St. Berthold about 1154 in Palestine. Their rule was set down in 1209, claiming continuity with a rule given by John, patriarch of Jerusalem (about 400), and the record of Elijah's life on Mt. Carmel. Their ancestors include hermits on Mt. Carmel from ancient times.

Discalced Carmelites (Latin: *calceos*, shoe; hence, discalced means barefooted). Carmelite nuns followed the reforms in the order by St. Teresa of Avila (1515–1582), and men followed St. John of the Cross (1542–1591). There was an independent Calced branch also.

The Little Flower

Thérèse Martin entered a Carmelite convent at age fifteen. As Sister Thérèse of the Child Jesus, she lived a hidden life. She was just twenty-four when she died of TB. The world came to know her through her autobiography, *The Story of a Soul.* She described her life as "a little way of spiritual childhood." She lived each day with unshakable confidence in God's love. What matters in life is "not great deeds, but great love." "My mission—to make God loved—will begin after my death," she said. "I will spend my heaven doing good on earth. I will let fall a shower of roses." This is the reason St. Thérèse's emblem is a crucifix covered with a profusion of roses.

---

4. Augustinians

This is a generic name for many institutes (orders) whose religious life is based on the Rule of St. Augustine (died in 430). There are fourteen distinct Augustinian communities, including hermits (or friars). Martin Luther belonged to one.

5. Servites ("Order of the Servants of the Blessed Virgin Mary")

This order was founded in Florence in 1233 by seven city councilors (canonized as "The Seven Holy Founders").

Jesuits (Latin: *Jesus* plus-*ite* suffix meaning "associated with")

The Society of Jesus (SJ) was founded by St. Ignatius Loyola in 1513 ("We are a little battalion of Jesus"). First purposes were defending the faith in the wake of the break-up of the Church and evangelization among the unchurched. Their leader has been referred to as the "black pope," very influential in the Church, wearing black in contrast to the white worn by the pope.

This "clarification" was required, by declaration of Pope Paul III in 1537, in the face of the Spanish conquistadors' work in the New World. Some of the early Spanish invaders came to Latin America with selfish intentions. In a classic conflict of interest, the kings of Spain desired to add the Americas to the kingdom of God and also to their own. On this remote frontier of European civilization, the conquistadors in their greed for gold enslaved the Indian, declaring them mere animals, incapable of understanding and embracing the Christian faith.

When this came to the attention of Pope Paul III, he recognized an enormous obstacle in the European mind to Christ's command, "Teach all nations." On June 2, 1537, he published *Sublimis Deus*, an official declaration contradicting the heresy of the conquerors: "It is Satan and his satellites who are encouraging the view that American natives are 'dumb brutes' created for our service . . . incapable of receiving the Catholic faith. The Indians are truly human, and they are not only capable of understanding the Catholic faith, but according to our information they desire exceedingly to receive it." The future experience of missionaries in the Americas would show the truth of his word. Pope Paul's pioneer denunciation of racism included the command that no Native American be deprived of property or liberty.

Rites of the Catholic Church

In an article called "Liturgical Diversity and the Unity of the Mystery" (#s 1200–1206), the *Catechism of the Catholic Church* says, "The mystery of Christ is so unfathomably rich that it cannot be exhausted by its expression in any single liturgical tradition. The history of the blossoming and development of these rites witnesses to a remarkable complementarity" (#1201).

The Diversity in the Catholicity of the Church

"Churches of the same geographical and cultural area came to celebrate the mystery of Christ through particular expressions characterized by the culture" (#1202):

1. In the tradition of the "deposit of faith"

2. In liturgical symbolism

3. In the organization of fraternal communion

4. In the theological understanding of the mysteries

5. In various forms of holiness

The Unity in the Catholicity of the Church (See CCC #1399.)

1. One profession of faith
2. One celebration of the seven sacraments ("mysteries")
3. One hierarchical unity

Rites (liturgical traditions) of the Catholic Church

Rites evolved throughout Church history, based on the culture of a particular time, place, and people. Since all these Rites are Catholic (in union with Rome), Catholics may fulfill worship obligations in any Rite, with no restrictions. The distinction *Eastern* or *Western* depends on the Rite's area of origin within the Roman Empire. The Latin Rite is most common in the Western Church (hence the popularized "Roman Catholic," Latin being Roman).

Western

Mainly the Latin Rite, but also the rites of certain local Churches (such as the Ambrosian rite in Milan, Italy, and the Mozarabic Rite in Toledo, Spain) and those of certain religious orders (such as Dominican, Carmelite, and Carthusian)

Eastern

All have non-Catholic or Orthodox counterparts except Maronites. All are practiced in the United States except Alexandrian. There are more than three million in the United States and over fifteen million throughout the world. (The following figures are low estimates, since it has not been possible to count many groups accurately.)

Byzantine (8,050,000)

Used by fourteen major groups: Albanian, Bulgarian, Byelorussian, Georgian, Greek, Italo-Albanian, Melkite, Hungarian, Russian, Ruthenian, Romanian, Ukrainian, Yugoslav, Slovak

Alexandrian (330,000)

Coptic (Egypt) and Ethiopian (Abyssinian)

Antiochene (2,700,000?)

East Syrian: Chaldean (Middle East, Europe, Africa, the Americas) and Syro-Malabarese (India)

West Syrian: Malankarese (India), Maronite worldwide (mainly Lebanon), Syrian (Syria, Lebanon, Iran, Egypt, Turkey)

Armenian (150,000)

Near East, Middle East, Europe, Africa, Americas, Australia

The Legacy of St. Maron

Maronite history goes back approximately 1,600 years. In the late fourth century, a community of disciples gathered around the hermit St. Maron. This Syrian priest had retired to a mountain of Taurus near Antioch, converting a pre-Christian temple into a shrine. This community of St. Maron dedicated itself to prayer, sacrifice, the healing ministry, and teaching the Catholic faith in the face of heresies. These "Maronites" grew in numbers and expanded into central and northern Syria; many were martyred because of their beliefs. By the seventh and eighth centuries, the hostilities and pressure of persecution drove them to Lebanon. The Maronite liturgy is in the family of the Syriac liturgy of St. James the Less, first bishop of Jerusalem, but is similar to other Eastern-Rite liturgies. To this day, most Maronites live in Lebanon, with the United States and Australia having the next largest populations.

European Co-Patrons

Pope John Paul II named Saints Cyril and Methodius co-patrons of Europe, along with beloved Benedict. Until recently, all the nations where these two evangelists and pastors brought the gospel and ministered were behind the Iron Curtain. They are the apostles of the southern Slavs, fathers of the Slavonic liturgy, and patrons of Christian unity. From the capitals of the Greek alphabet, they invented the Cyrillic-glagolithic alphabet as a conveyor of the Byzantine liturgy and the Bible to the Serbs, Bulgarians, Ukrainians, and Russians.

Genealogy of Christian Churches/Nationalities/Liturgies

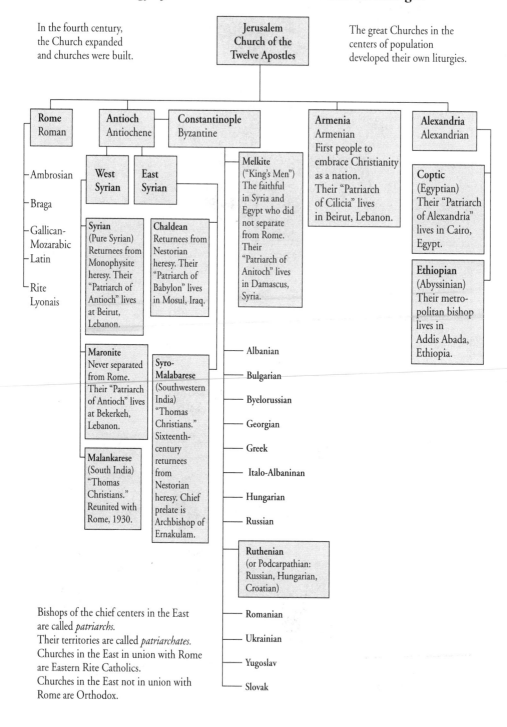

In the fourth century, the Church expanded and churches were built.

Jerusalem Church of the Twelve Apostles

The great Churches in the centers of population developed their own liturgies.

Rome
Roman

Antioch
Antiochene

Constantinople
Byzantine

Armenia
Armenian
First people to embrace Christianity as a nation. Their "Patriarch of Cilicia" lives in Beirut, Lebanon.

Alexandria
Alexandrian

– Ambrosian

– Braga

– Gallican-
Mozarabic
– Latin

– Rite
Lyonais

West Syrian

East Syrian

Melkite
("King's Men")
The faithful in Syria and Egypt who did not separate from Rome. Their "Patriarch of Anitoch" lives in Damascus, Syria.

Coptic
(Egyptian)
Their "Patriarch of Alexandria" lives in Cairo, Egypt.

Syrian
(Pure Syrian)
Returnees from Monophysite heresy. Their "Patriarch of Antioch" lives at Beirut, Lebanon.

Chaldean
Returnees from Nestorian heresy. Their "Patriarch of Babylon" lives in Mosul, Iraq.

Ethiopian
(Abyssinian)
Their metropolitan bishop lives in Addis Abada, Ethiopia.

Maronite
Never separated from Rome. Their "Patriarch of Antioch" lives at Bekerkeh, Lebanon.

Syro-Malabarese
(Southwestern India)
"Thomas Christians."
Sixteenth-century returnees from Nestorian heresy. Chief prelate is Archbishop of Ernakulam.

— Albanian

— Bulgarian

— Byelorussian

— Georgian

— Greek

— Italo-Albaninan

— Hungarian

— Russian

Malankarese
(South India)
"Thomas Christians."
Reunited with Rome, 1930.

Ruthenian
(or Podcarpathian: Russian, Hungarian, Croatian)

Bishops of the chief centers in the East are called *patriarchs.*
Their territories are called *patriarchates.*
Churches in the East in union with Rome are Eastern Rite Catholics.
Churches in the East not in union with Rome are Orthodox.

— Romanian

— Ukrainian

— Yugoslav

— Slovak

Patriarch ("Prince of the Fathers")

Patriarchs are the highest rulers in their Churches, with only the pope having authority over them. Since the Eastern Schism, their importance, except for that of the pope, has diminished. They are without jurisdiction except in virtue of some particular law.

In the order of precedence: patriarch, then primate, then metropolitan, then bishop

In order of dignity, the patriarch of Rome precedes those of the Armenian, Maronite, Melkite, and Chaldean Rites.

The minor patriarchs include Venice, Lisbon, West Indies, and East Indies

The rights and role of the patriarchs:

1. Ordain all bishops of their patriarchate.

2. Consecrate the holy chrism.

3. Summon synods.

4. Send the omophorion (pallium) to their metropolitans.

5. Hear appeals from lower courts.

Orthodox or "Eastern Orthodox" (See CCC #1399.)

Orthodox Churches are Eastern Rite Churches that are not Catholic. They were called *Orthodox* after the Great Schism (division, "cutting") of 1054, though a natural division of a sort existed long before the ecclesial division. A milestone was the division of the Roman Empire into East and West by Theodosius in 395. Principally:

1. Greek Patriarchates (Jurisdictions): Constantinople, Alexandria, Antioch, Jerusalem

2. Russian Patriarchate (Jurisdiction): Moscow

The Patriarchal cross, the shorter cross member representing the inscription INRI

Greek cross

Russian Orthodox cross, the lower cross member representing the footrest

Protestantism

(See CCC #s 817–822, 836–838, 1400.)

The Reformation (Latin: *reformare*, to renew)

The Reformation as we know it was a sixteenth-century movement within Western Christendom aimed at Church reform. The reform movement led eventually to the emergence of several Protestant Churches, though the intent of the leading reformers was at first reform, not separation.

The Reformation originated in a controversy over indulgences (remissions for sins), precipitated by Martin Luther's Ninety-five Theses of October 1517. Luther, an Augustinian priest, had inadvertently gotten into a politically sensitive area between the Holy Roman Empire of the Middle Ages, closely aligned with the Church, and the fledging nationalistic movement in the German states. Among oher things, Luther objected to the sale of indulgences, a practice in the Church at the time for the financing of new churches.

By early 1518 Luther was cited as a suspected heretic, and in 1521 he was excommunicated and declared a political outlaw. His call for reform and a deepened spirituality led to a movement that spread rapidly.

Attempts at reconciliation between Luther and the Church resulted in the Peace of Augsburg in 1555. With this ruling territorial rulers were left free to choose Lutheranism or Catholicism as the official religion of their territories.

In time Swiss reformer Ulrich Zwingli pressed for local autonomy. Out of his followers came the breakaway Anabaptists (rebaptizers, that is, baptism of adults) who emphasized the personal commitment to follow Christ.

Then came John Calvin, based in Geneva, Switzerland, who published his Reformation theology. Calvinism became the force of the Reformation in the second half of the sixteenth century. Calvinism opposed Catholicism and demanded a strict adherence to the authority of Scripture.

The reform moved to England with Henry VIII, Anglicanism, and a new order of worship, published in *The Book of Common Prayer* (1549). Then some in England felt that Anglicanism was too Catholic and wanted a "pure" Church; they became known as *Puritans*. While Reformation controversies died down on the mainland by the end of the sixteenth century, they continued in England, giving rise to Congregationalists, Baptists, and Quakers, among others.

For Protestants, the Reformation was seen as the restoration of biblical Christianity against a worldly Church. Catholics saw the Reformation as a rebellion against truth and a triumph of subjectivism. The theological differences seem now to have been around authority and salvation—authority of Scripture and the Church or of Scripture only; salvation by grace and works or by grace alone.

PROTESTANTISM/DENOMINATIONALISM

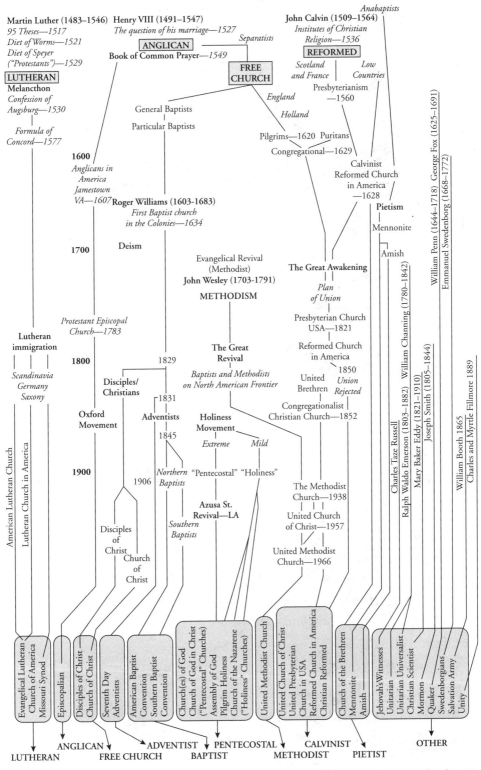

Martin Luther (1483–1546) Henry VIII (1491–1547)
95 Theses—1517   *The question of his marriage—1527*
Diet of Worms—1521   *Separatists*
Diet of Speyer   **ANGLICAN**
("Protestants")—1529   **Book of Common Prayer—1549**

LUTHERAN   **FREE**
Melancthon   **CHURCH**
Confession of
Augsburg—1530
                              General Baptists
Formula of
Concord—1577   Particular Baptists

1600
Anglicans in
America
Jamestown
VA—1607 Roger Williams (1603-1683)
           First Baptist church
           in the Colonies—1634

1700   Deism

                    Evangelical Revival
                    (Methodist)
                    John Wesley (1703-1791)

                    METHODISM

Protestant Episcopal
Church—1783

Lutheran
immigration

1800   1829

Scandinavia
Germany   **Disciples/**
Saxony   **Christians**
                    1831   **The Great**
Oxford   **Adventists** **Revival**
Movement
                    1845   *Baptists and Methodists*
                                on North American Frontier
1900
           1906 *Northern* Holiness
                Baptists Movement
                             Extreme   *Mild*

                    Disciples   "Pentecostal" "Holiness"
                    of
                    Christ   Azusa St.
                    Church   Revival—LA
                    of
                    Christ   *Southern*
                                Baptists

John Calvin (1509–1564)   *Anabaptists*
Institutes of Christian
Religion—1536
                    REFORMED
Scotland   *Low*
and France   *Countries*
                Presbyterianism
                    —1560
England
                Calvinist
Holland   Reformed Church
                in America
Pilgrims—1620 Puritans   —1628
Congregational—1629   **Pietism**
                                Mennonite

The Great Awakening   Amish
                Plan
                of Union
           Presbyterian Church
                USA—1821
           Reformed Church
                in America
           United   1850
           Brethren   *Union*
                       Rejected
           Congregationalist
           Christian Church—1852

           The Methodist
           Church—1938
           United Church
           of Christ—1957

           United Methodist
           Church—1966

William Penn (1644–1718) George Fox (1625–1691)
Emmanuel Swedenborg (1668–1772)

Charles Taze Russell
Ralph Waldo Emerson (1803–1882) William Channing (1780–1842)
Mary Baker Eddy (1821–1910)
           Joseph Smith (1805–1844)

William Booth 1865
Charles and Myrtle Fillmore 1889

American Lutheran Church
Lutheran Church in America

Evangelical Lutheran
Church of America
Missouri Synod

Episcopalian

Disciples of Christ
Church of Christ

Seventh Day
Adventists

American Baptist
Convention
Southern Baptist
Convention

Church(es) of God
Church of God in Christ
("Pentecostal" Churches)
Assembly of God
Pilgrim Holiness
Church of the Nazarene
("Holiness" Churches)

United Methodist Church

United Church of Christ
United Presbyterian
Church in USA
Reformed Church in America
Christian Reformed

Church of the Brethren
Mennonite
Amish

Jehovah's Witnesses
Unitarian
Unitarian Universalist
Christian Scientist
Mormon
Quaker
Swedenborgians
Salvation Army
Unity

LUTHERAN   ANGLICAN   ADVENTIST PENTECOSTAL CALVINIST   OTHER
              FREE CHURCH   BAPTIST   METHODIST PIETIST

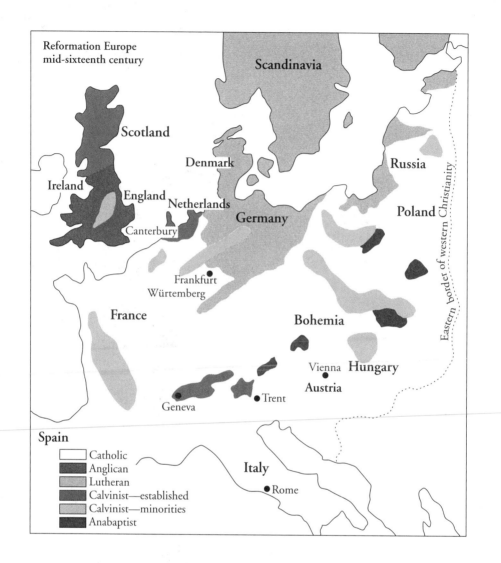

Reformation Europe
mid-sixteenth century

Scandinavia

Scotland

Denmark

Russia

Ireland

England Netherlands

Germany

Poland

Canterbury

Frankfurt
Würtemberg

France

Bohemia

Vienna Hungary

Austria

Geneva · Trent

Eastern border of western Christianity

Spain

	Catholic
	Anglican
	Lutheran
	Calvinist—established
	Calvinist—minorities
	Anabaptist

Italy

· Rome

Cuius regio eius religio

"Whose the region, his the religion" meant that territorial rulers were free to choose Lutheranism or Catholicism as the official religion in their territory.

Protestant Confessions of Faith (principal)

Lutheran Augsburg Confession (1530)

Calvinist Catechism of Geneva (1542–1545)

Reformed Belgic Confession (1561)

Reformed Heidelberg Catechism (1563)

Anglican Thirty-nine Articles (1563)

Presbyterian Westminster Confession (1648)

Canterbury cross

Ecumenical Movement and Topics of Discussion

Dialogue between Christian denominations is ongoing. This chart shows some of the topics being discussed as gorups move closer to reunion.

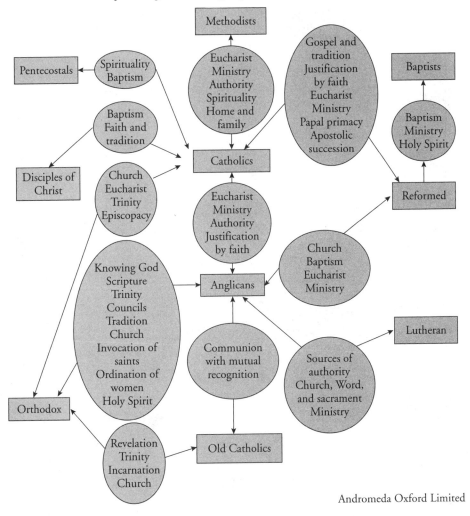

Andromeda Oxford Limited

Requirements of the Gift of and Call to Christian Unity (See CCC #821.)

1. An ongoing renewal of the Church

2. Conversion of heart among Catholics

3. Prayer in common

4. Accurate and caring knowledge of each other

5. Ecumenical formation of the faithful, especially of priests

6. Dialogue among theologians and meetings among Christians

7. Collaboration among Christians in various areas of human service

> ### Catholicism in Mary's Land
>
> In 1607, Lord Baltimore of England sent ships, *The Ark* and *The Dove*, to the New World, in particular, to Maryland, to establish an English Catholic plantation. But in 1620, when *The Mayflower* left Southampton, there were no Catholics aboard. And in 1776, when the Declaration of Independence was signed, only one signer was Catholic: Charles Carroll of Maryland. (In spite of the prejudice against Catholics at the time—"nativism"—Carroll served a career as a public servant. Called by some the most distinguished Catholic layman in American history, Carroll was a dedicated patriot.)
>
> In the Revolutionary War, a Catholic, Casimir Pulaski, was an American general. It was not until 1831, during the presidency of Andrew Jackson, that a Catholic, Attorney General Roger B. Taney, served in the president's cabinet. It was not until 1928 that a Catholic, Al Smith, ran for president, and it was 1960 before a Catholic, John Kennedy, was elected president. In 1963 Pope John XXIII was posthumously awarded the US Presidential Medal of Freedom. In the 106st Congress (1999) there were 153 Catholics, 25 in the Senate and 128 in the House. Thirteen Catholics, including Fr. Junipero Serra, are honored in Statuary Hall.

> ### Missionaries in Statuary Hall
>
> Here is secular testimony of the impact missionaries have on a nation as well as a Church: Catholic missionaries were chosen by five different states to represent them in the US Capitol's famed National Statuary Hall. They are, with the state who chose them, Fr. Eusebio Kino (Arizona), Blessed Junipero Serra (California), Blessed Fr. Damien de Veuster (Hawaii), Fr. Jacques Marquette (Michigan), and Mother Joseph (Washington), who just beat out another Catholic, Bing Crosby, for the coveted spot.

Places and Practices

Sacred Places

The Church as a House of Prayer (See CCC #s 1179–1185.)

The word *church* comes originally from Greek *kuriakos* (of the Lord). *The Catechism of the Catholic Church* teaches (#1180), "These visible churches are not simply gathering places but signify and make visible the Church living in this place, the dwelling of God with men reconciled and united in Christ." It goes on to quote paragraph 5 of Vatican II's "Decree on the Ministry and Life of Priests" (see also the "Constitution of the Sacred Liturgy," #s 122–127, Vatican II):

1. A church is a house of prayer
2. where the Eucharist is celebrated and reserved,
3. where the faithful assemble, and
4. where the presence of the Son of God our Savior is worshiped.

The Church as House of God

The Catechism of the Catholic Church also teaches (#1186), "Finally, the church has an eschatological significance. To enter into the house of God, we must cross a threshold, which symbolizes passing from the world wounded by sin to the world of the new Life to which men are called. The visible church is a symbol of the Father's house toward which the People of God is journeying and where the Father 'will wipe every tear from their eyes.'"

Cathedral

The church of the diocesan Church; bishop's "chair" (Latin: *cathedra*). It is traditionally located in the see city from which the diocese takes its name. The pastor of the cathedral is the ordinary (bishop or archbishop); hence, the priest who actually conducts the cathedral parish and its affairs has the title *rector*, not *pastor* or *parish priest*. (A pro-cathedral is a church used by a bishop as a cathedral (for his *cathedra*) until a permanent, suitable church is built; it has the same rights and privileges as a cathedral.)

Basilicas

Originally, a basilica was one of the seven main churches of Rome and/or an ancient pilgrimage church:

1. St. Peter (at one time the Basilica in Rome for the Patriarch of Constantinople). The largest church building in Christendom (covering about four acres), it was completed in 1626 and is maintained by the *sampietrini*, a permanent group of skilled workers and artisans representing every trade. It is fronted by "St. Peter's Square" which is encircled by the Bernini colonnade (after its designer). The basilica's bell, weighing about ten tons, is rung on special occasions.

2. St. John Lateran—the Mother Church; archbasilica for the patriarch of the West (the pope)

3. St. Mary Major Basilica—for the patriarch of Antioch

4. Holy Cross in Jerusalem (within Rome proper)

5. St. Paul's Outside the Walls—for the patriarch of Alexandria

6. St. Lawrence Outside the Walls—for the patriarch of Jerusalem

7. St. Sebastian Outside the Walls

Through the years, churches throughout the world have been given basilica status and ceremonial rights according to certain criteria. In the fourth century it became customary to position a basilica so that its altar would be over the grave of a martyr.

The "pavilion" and bell are the two public indications of basilica status in a church's sanctuary. The pavilion, or umbrella, originates in the oriental courtesy and honor accorded a visiting potentate when he or she appears in public ceremony. It shields him or her from the sun. In deference to the pope on his occasional visits, Rome eventually adopted the device and practice for its basilicas; later, it spread to minor basilicas.

The bell also probably has origins in the papal visit, for the purpose of announcing his presence at the church door. It represents the building's belfry, being in effect a portable and elaborately mounted version, and it is carried, along with the pavilion, in all processions. By virtue of its rank, a basilica also has the distinction of its own coat of arms (armorial shield).

Chapel

Place of liturgical worship for a community other than a parish (school, hospital, convent, seminary, and so forth); a room within a building, or a separate building. The word *chapel*, interestingly, comes from the famous story of St. Martin and the cloak he gave to a beggar. Cloak in Latin is *cappa*, and *cappella* is the diminutive. In Old French the same word is *chapele*, and that was the name given to the oratory in which the alleged *chapele* of St. Martin was preserved. And so it is that a chaplain originally was a keeper of St. Martin's cloak.

Oratory

Place of prayer other than a parish church, designated by ecclesiastical authority for Mass and devotions; public, semipublic, or private (which is a private family chapel)

Shrine

Designated devotional place, significant historically or because of an approved miraculous phenomenon, especially those that have become pilgrimage destinations, like Lourdes and Guadalupe

---

Consecration of a Church

Only certain churches have the distinction of being a consecrated church, provided they are debt free, and have an altar based on a solid foundation resting on the ground. Twelve eye-level candle sconces and crosses, representing the teaching of the twelve apostles, encircling its inside walls, signal this particular dignity. Ceremonies of consecration include blessing the cornerstone, washing the altar (using wine), and using holy water (including salt, wine, and ashes). "Brands" on a church that has been consecrated are small crosses in circles. A church is desecrated by a notorious crime within its walls or the use of holy things for unholy purposes. It must then be reconsecrated before it may be used for divine services.

Temple
The Jewish holy place; destroyed (as a specific place) in 70

Synagogue
Gathering place of Jews for worship

Mosque
Gathering place of Moslems for worship

Pilgrimage
The sign of a pilgrim Church in search of a future and permanent city; pilgrimages were popular in the eleventh and twelfth centuries, then interst slackened during the Renaissance and Reformation, and they declined by the eighteenth century

A journey to a holy place
1. as a form of religious devotion,
2. as an act of penance (even barefooted), or
3. to seek the intercession of a saint.

The Three Primary Pilgrimage Routes of the Middle Ages
1. To Jerusalem and the Holy Land
   See "The Pilgrimage of the Way of the Cross," page 263.

2. To Rome
   Seat of the universal Church, rich in the history of the martyrs.

3. To Santiago de Compostella (Spain)
   Tomb of the apostle James, first of the apostles martyred. The Santiago Trail is an historically popular pilgrimage, "the pathway to conversion and extraordinary witness to faith," in the words of Pope John Paul II. It is actually a network of pilgrimage roads, five major routes with spacious and spectacular churches (like Vezelay, Poitiers, Aulnay, Le Puy, St. Sernin at Toulouse) and hospices all along its way.

El Camino de Santiago
"The Way of St. James" is what the Spanish call the Milky Way, so much is it like the path of countless pilgrim candles to Compostela, Spain. St. James in Spain? It has been long believed by some that after his death in Palestine, the body of St. James the apostle was put in a boat with sails set. The next day it reached the Spanish coast, near the modern city of Compostela. St. James (*Santiago* in Spanish) of Compostela has been made a holy place by the prayers of millions and millions of pilgrims. During the Middle Ages his shrine there rivaled Rome and Jerusalem as a pilgrimage destination. Such honor, and the Milky Way besides, was probably not what James had in mind when he and his brother asked for seats of honor in the kingdom (Mark 10:35–40), but it's pretty glorious.

Some European Pilgrimage Shrines

From a list that is endless, the following sample includes references to persons or events or artifacts that have made them significant.

England

Canterbury (seat of Catholic Church in England; St. Thomas Becket, famous archbishop, martyred); Glastonbury (Joseph of Arimathea and the Holy Grail); Walsingham (dream-inspired replica of Mary's house); York (St. Paulinus); and Winchester (St. Swithin)

France

Chartres (Mary's tunic), LaSalette (Mary apparition in 1846), Lourdes (Mary apparition in 1858), Mont-St-Michael (the archangel Michael), Poitiers (St. Hilary), and Tours (St. Martin)

Germany

Aachen (relics) and Cologne (magi relics)

Ireland

Knock ("the Lourdes of Ireland," 1879 Marian apparition) and Lough Derg ("St. Patrick's Purgatory")

Italy

Assisi (St. Francis), Bari (St. Nicholas), Bologna (St. Dominic), Loreto (house of Mary), Monte Cassino (St. Benedict), Padua (St. Anthony), and Turin (Holy Shroud)

Poland

Czestochowa (The Black Madonna)

Portugal

Fatima (Mary apparition in 1917)

Some Shrines in the Western Hemisphere

Canada

Quebec (Sainte Anne-de-Beaupre); Montreal (St. Joseph's Oratory); Midland, Ontario (Martyrs' Shrine)

Mexico

Mexico City (Our Lady of Guadalupe)

United States

District of Columbia (Basilica of the National Shrine of the Immaculate Conception); Belleville, IL (Our Lady of the Snows); North Jackson, OH (Our Lady of Lebanon); New York City (St. Frances Cabrini); New Orleans (St. Jude); Juneau, AK (St. Thérèse); San Francisco (La Mision de San Francisco de Asis); Chimayo, NM (El Santuario de Chimayo)

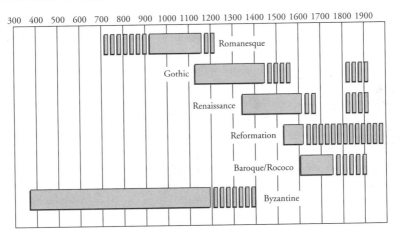

The Pilgrimage of the Way of the Cross (See CCC #2669.)

By your holy cross

A Christian's faith never required pilgrimage to Jerusalem as a Muslim's faith required pilgrimage to Mecca (commemorating Muhammad's *hegira*, or flight). However, the Christian holy places have been transported, as it were, to churches throughout the Catholic world in the form of the stations of the cross. Although the *Stabat Mater* and Good Friday's "We adore you, O Christ . . ." have become traditional, the devotion itself—that is, "making the stations"—requires only the movement from one station to the next. The stations themselves, despite the elaborate depictions that have evolved, are mere wooden crosses.

The Middle Ages' passion for the Passion

Tradition says Mary daily retraced the *via dolorosa* (the way of sorrow, the way of the cross); however, it was only in the Middle Ages that devotion to Christ's passion flourished. The early Christians' focus was on the risen Christ. The medieval mind, however, captivated by Christ's suffering humanity, sought to tread his very steps. Those with time and money could; others had the Holy Land brought to them in the form of "stations," reproductions in their own place of the holy places of Jerusalem.

A Franciscan mission

The Franciscans, receiving custody of the holy places of Jerusalem in 1343, stirred an interest among the faithful, in the passion of Christ. The Franciscan St. Leonard of Port Maurice, the "preacher of the way of the cross," spread the devotion in the eighteenth century, making it possible even for non-Franciscan churches to have the stations (previously not allowed). From the beginning, there have been more and less than fourteen. In 1975, Pope Paul VI approved a new set of stations which includes a fifteenth, the resurrection.

The Church Building

Main Periods of Church Architecture

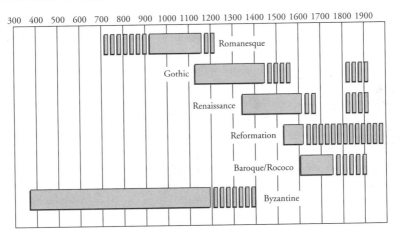

Romanesque or Gothic?

In these periods, the evolution of the window provides a way to date and name an architectural style.

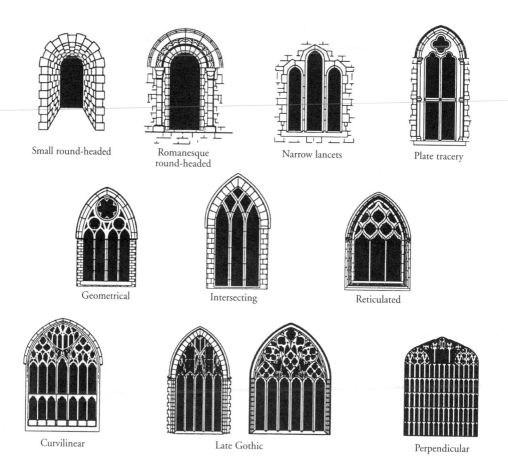

Small round-headed

Romanesque round-headed

Narrow lancets

Plate tracery

Geometrical

Intersecting

Reticulated

Curvilinear

Late Gothic

Perpendicular

Roman or Byzantine?

The Latin cross and the steeple

In the West, church buildings followed a Roman style and the basilica plan, typically in the shape of a Latin cross (hence no natural center), with its nave, transept, and apse.

The Greek cross and the dome

In the East, the Greek cross allowed for a central design for the building, which was typically topped with a massive dome. This gilded dome's radiance lent an aura of mysticism, so typical of Eastern Christianity, whose very architecture suggested heaven on earth. Its next most distinguishing characteristic is the use of mosaics.

The Exterior

Orientation

The great churches of Europe were commonly positioned with the axis of their nave pointing due east (Latin: *orient*), thus oriented so that:

1. The rising sun would shine on the altar.

2. The faithful would face the rising sun while praying, ready to greet the glorious risen Christ who will put darkness to flight and inaugurate a new day.

3. The church would face Jerusalem, so honoring the city of David which many medieval maps showed as the center of the world, with east rather than north appearing at the top.

This was mandated since the tenth century and had been observed as a custom long before (except by Emperor Constantine, so that St. John Lateran, St. Peter's, and San Lorenzo's are exceptions). Because construction normally began with the east end, its style often predates the west end, which was often completed many years later. In modern times the orientation of a church is secondary to more pressing practical issues concerning the available space. Those with a symbolic orientation, however, still refer to a church's altar end as the east end. Liturgically, a custom arose of facing east during the creed to demonstrate faith in the Dayspring and Sun of Righteousness.

St. Thomas the Builder

Legends of Thomas in India abound. In one, the King of the Indies, Gondoforus, gave a small fortune to Thomas to build a palace. Thomas turned around and spent it on the poor, thus "building a superb palace in heaven." Hence he is called by some the patron of architects and masons, and his symbol is the builder's square. In another legend, Thomas saw the king trying in vain to haul ashore a huge beam of timber. Even with men and elephants, he failed. So Thomas asked to have the beam, intending to use it in building a church. His request being granted, he hauled the beam ashore with a string.

Belfry

A tower on a church, with or without bells

Buttress

An external reinforcement, strengthening the walls and supporting the roof of a Gothic church

Campanile

A bell tower (separate from a church building)

Carillon

A set of bells developed in the seventeenth century for playing songs mechanically. They number about twenty-two, technically; a lesser number being "chimes." (In England, the "change ringing" of six or more bells in intricately varying sequences is more popular.)

Devil's door

A small door of some old churches' north wall, or baptistery wall, to "let out the devil" during a Baptism or Communion service. It was common among the superstitious to consider the north side of a church "Satan's side," where the devils lurked to prey on the unwary.

Door

Symbolic of the gates of heaven (often red, for the blood of Christ)

Gargoyle

Water spouts built as decorations in the form of often unsightly human/beast heads on Gothic churches; symbolic of evil exorcised by the gospel

Leper window

A low window in the sanctuary wall of medieval churches in some locales, often shuttered or iron-barred, enabling lepers to attend Mass while remaining outside

Spire

The point of a steeple or tower, symbol of humanity's aspiration to be united with the Creator

Squint

A small opening in the sanctuary wall giving visual access to ceremonies within; this enabled the ancient anchorites to assist at Mass

Steeple (tower)

Functioned to support a spire, a symbol of local pride, making the building more visible; also to support bells. Medieval cathedrals have as many as nine, but most commonly have either a single tower or twin towers at the west front, one at either side with a third large tower at the crossing (of cruciform-style building).

West front

Most deliberated feature of the classic cathedrals and larger churches. This large facade, incorporating the entrance to the building, was thought to represent the gates of heaven. Large windows are typical on its upper face, with twin towers becoming the norm in the eleventh century.

The Interior

This list includes more permanent, stationary features of a church, some liturgical, some architectural. For liturgical vessels and other more portable objects used in liturgy, see the next chapter on liturgy.

Directions

The traditional orientation symbolism of the church's exterior carries through on the inside: The east is God's side, with his throne; the west is the human side; the south is the saints' and angels' side (where the sun shines most); and the north is the devil's side. This north side was once called "the bachelor's porch" where there were benches down the aisle. This was the place for male servants and the poor (correspondingly, females were seated on the south side). Further, there was a superstition about only evildoers being buried on the north side of a graveyard, symbolized by the want of sun.

Altar

The altar is a table of solid or suitable material for the meal of sacrifice, the Eucharist; a symbol of Christ. Traditionally it was made of stone or at least contained a consecrated stone, which in turn contained relics of a martyr (and sometimes incense grains) which were enclosed in it by the bishop at its consecration. The relics and incense recalled Masses thought to have been offered in catacombs, and they recognized Christ's union with the faithful in the Eucharist. Rests on the sanctuary level were called the *predella*, representing, according to the early Church fathers, the mediating power of the word of the gospel and the grace of the sacraments.

Altar cloth

A (usually) white linen to cover the altar; formerly three were required.

Altar, Privileged (traditionally)

An altar with certain indulgences attached when used in liturgies for the deceased

Altar rail

A low, gated demarcation between sanctuary and church body over which Communion was formerly distributed

Altar stone (portable altar)

This stone is in the altar and is technically identified as the altar itself, usually being only large enough to hold the chalice and paten; it is seated in a receptacle that leaves its top flush with the altar. Its upper surface bears five crosses, for Christ's wounds, where anointings were made in its consecration; it contains sealed relics of two martyr saints. Formerly required; since Vatican II "commended," with an emphasis on the importance of verifying authenticity.

Ambry (Latin: *armaria*, cupboard)

The container, often in or on the sanctuary wall and labeled O.S. (Latin: *olea sancta*, holy oils), for the stocks of consecrated oils. Formerly used more generally as a storage area for liturgical items.

Antependium

A banner-like cloth "hung before," for example, the altar or the pulpit

Apse

A semicircular, often domed projection of traditional churches which houses the sanctuary (historically, the east end)

Baldacchino

This word is Italian for Baghdad, whence came precious building materials, and it refers to the canopy or dome over the altar or bishop's chair. The most famous is the one in St. Peter's in Rome, which was designed by Bernini.

Baptistry

The baptismal font and area

The Womb of the Baptistry

The baptistry is the womb of Mary, Mother of the Church, and also the womb of Holy Mother Church whose pattern and promise is Mary. She is expectant in a kingdom yet-to-be, and fruitful in a kingdom here-and-now. At the womb of the baptistry, we encounter her, pregnant with Christ.

Bier

The structure on which a coffin is placed

Brass

A church brass is a latten funeral effigy affixed to a tombstone on the floor of a church; popular in the fourteenth and fifteenth centuries. (Latten is an alloy made of brass, or to resemble it, hammered thin and used in church vessels.)

Cathedra

The bishop's chair in a cathedral church

Ceiling with open dome

According to the early fathers, a symbol of the firmament, often including a figure of Christ the Pantocrator (Ruler of All), who is the omnipresence and is over the assembly

Cerecloth

A moisture-resistant altar cloth under the fair linen

Chair

A seat for the presiding minister of the assembly

Chancel

The area around the altar for clergy choir, from the Roman custom of separating lawyers from the public in court by a lattice screen (Latin: *cancellus*, screen). See the more liturgical word "Sanctuary."

Credence table (Italian: *credenza*; shelf, buffet)

A side table for articles used at Mass, especially bread and wine

Crucifix

A cross bearing the figure of the crucified Christ (*corpus*). The sacrificial aspect of the Eucharist, "the unbloody sacrifice of Calvary," is emphasized where the crucifix is prominent above the altar. See "Reredos."

The Nine Crosses

Ancient architects often used "the nine crosses," nine being the trinity of trinities, the perfect plural (thrice three, the perfect unity), thus building an added mystique into the church.

1. Altar cross
2. Processional cross
3. Rood cross (on loft)
4. Reliquary cross
5. Consecration cross
6. Pectoral cross
7. Spire cross
8. Marking cross
9. Cross pendant over altar

Crypt

A vault under a church

Dossal

Large ornamented wall tapestries; formerly often hung behind an altar in the absence of a reredos

Fair linen

A fine linen cloth covering the altar, traditionally with a cross in each corner and one in the center representing the five wounds of Christ

Fald stool

A portable, folding chair for the bishop's use at formal liturgical ceremonies

Floor

Symbolic of the world, and the way of the pilgrim people, according to early Church fathers

Font

A holy water dispensary; also the baptistry itself

Frontal (full altar frontal)

A hanging, covering the entire front of an altar from top to floor

Frontlet

A cloth pendant, narrower than an antependium, over an altar and hanging down the front

Icon (Greek: image, representation)

A religious image, primarily of Christ, but also of Mary and the saints, painted according to a conventional model or symbolism, part of a place and act of worship. Iconography grew out of Eastern (Byzantine) Christianity and reached its highest point, some say, in the Russian Orthodox Church. In the Eastern Church iconography has sacramental overtones and has developed with the divine liturgy of which it is an organic part. As a visual expression of revelation, the icon pairs up with the Bible, the word of God, which is the written expression.

Lectern

The place for song-leading and all nonscriptural speaking

Mensa

The top of a consecrated altar

Narthex

A pre-nave entrance, or lobby, or portico area

Nave (Latin: *navis*, ship)

The church's central and primary structural feature, extending from the entry to the sanctuary, so called because of its resemblance to ships of the era. Symbol of the sensory world and humanity, according to the early Church fathers.

Ombrellino

A canopy for the Blessed Sacrament in procession

Parament (Latin: ornament)

A decoration, usually of cloth, especially in a tapestry form, but including even chasubles and chalice veils; often appliquéd. See antependium, frontal, dossal.

Predella

Benches in a place of worship; also, the base of a reredos (altarpiece), often embellished with small reliefs or paintings

Prie-dieu (French: pray to God)

A kneeler

Pulpit or ambo

A place for Scripture proclaiming and preaching; common only in the later Middle Ages; prior to this a bishop preached from the chair (cathedra).

Reconciliation room or confessional

The place for celebrating the Sacrament of Reconciliation, either a booth with a screen between priest/confessor and penitent, or a room with option to pray with the priest face to face

Reliquary

A place in which a relic is sealed and kept; of varying size, from portable objects to actual caskets.

Repository

A shrine ("side altar") or secondary chapel where, for instance, the Blessed Sacrament that was consecrated on Holy Thursday is reposed until the Easter Vigil.

Reredos (or retable or altarpiece)

A richly carved or painted or decorated structure forming the back of the altar, usually of wood or stone, sometimes including an overhanging shelf, frame, niches for statues, and so forth.

Rood screen

An ornamented altar screen, usually surmounted with a crucifix, separating the sanctuary from the body of the church. Properly, "rood" (rod) is the crucifixion cross (crucifix) which was originally enshrined on the stone or wooden screen. This came to be ornamented with saintly statuary and symbols.

Rood screen

Rose window

A circular window embellished with tracery that is symmetrical around its center

Sacrarium or ***piscina*** (Latin for reservoir)

A sacristy sink with a drain directly into the earth for the fitting disposal of blessed ashes, oils, or holy water. Also used for the cleaning of Mass vessels and Eucharistic vessels.

Sacristy or vestry

A room for sacred vessels and vestments

Sanctuary

Traditionally, the altar, pulpit, and chair area, usually set apart structurally; it is symbolic of the spiritual world and of humanity's spirituality, according to early Church fathers. As the place of holiness and nearness of God, the word is now used more broadly by some, especially Protestants, for the whole worship space, created by the gathered faith community, and not limited to the part of the church for the activity of ordered and specific ministries.

Sanctuary lamp

A light indicating the presence of the reserved Sacrament, the real presence of Christ (formerly, like altar candles, made of beeswax, or at least 51 percent beeswax)

Sanctuary screen or iconostasis

A part of Eastern Rite tradition. Symbolic of the unity of the divine world and the human world, the reconciliation achieved between God and creation, according to early Church fathers.

Sedilia

A series of usually three seats for officiating clergy. Historically often positioned on the south side of the sanctuary.

The Simple Harmonic Motion of a Sanctuary Lamp

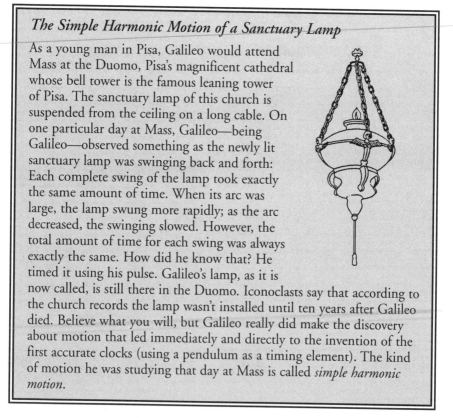

As a young man in Pisa, Galileo would attend Mass at the Duomo, Pisa's magnificent cathedral whose bell tower is the famous leaning tower of Pisa. The sanctuary lamp of this church is suspended from the ceiling on a long cable. On one particular day at Mass, Galileo—being Galileo—observed something as the newly lit sanctuary lamp was swinging back and forth: Each complete swing of the lamp took exactly the same amount of time. When its arc was large, the lamp swung more rapidly; as the arc decreased, the swinging slowed. However, the total amount of time for each swing was always exactly the same. How did he know that? He timed it using his pulse. Galileo's lamp, as it is now called, is still there in the Duomo. Iconoclasts say that according to the church records the lamp wasn't installed until ten years after Galileo died. Believe what you will, but Galileo really did make the discovery about motion that led immediately and directly to the invention of the first accurate clocks (using a pendulum as a timing element). The kind of motion he was studying that day at Mass is called *simple harmonic motion*.

Steps (to the altar)

Symbolic of spiritual ascent to Christ, according to early Church fathers. Their Latin name, *graduales*, gave their name to the antiphon formerly sung between the epistle and the gospel at high Mass as the proclaimer climbed the steps of the altar. (See "Gradual" psalms of the Old Testament.) Also, by association, the book of the Mass music (Graduals, Introits, Kyries, Gloria, Credo, and so on).

Superfrontal

The covering for the front of the altar proper (the depth of the altar top), often attached, or extended only partly over the front edge

Tabernacle

A safe-like, secure place of reservation for and worship of the Blessed Sacrament, the consecrated hosts to be used as Communion for those who are homebound, sick, and dying, and sometimes for those at Mass. (The watch-shaped container for transporting the host is called a *pyx*.) Sometimes a veil (*canopaeum*) covers it; the veil is white, gold, or the color of the feast or season.

Vestibule

The lobby or small antechamber between the outer and inner doors of a church

Residences

Abbey

An independent monastery with a required minimum of religious, led by an abbot or abbess. Traditionally, most are quadrangular, except for the Carthusian order whose members have cottages for individual monks. Most abbeys are either Benedictine or Carthusian.

Cloister

The covered walk of a monastery; hence, *cloistered* means "belonging to a monastery"

Convent (Latin: *convenire*, to convene)

The residence of religious, commonly women, under a superior. Traditionally, six solemnly professed women must occupy the residence together before it qualifies as a religious community house.

Friary

A brotherhood of (or monastery for) friars

Manse (a farm, from Latin: *manere*, to dwell)

The residence (and land) occupied by a minister; formerly, the dwelling of a landlord; a mansion. "Mensa" in the Catholic tradition is the portion of the Church property for supporting the clergyman.

Monastery (Greek: *monazein*, to live alone)

The place where religious dwell in seclusion; historically referring to the cloistered, contemplative life where the entire Liturgy of the Hours is celebrated in common. Usually quadrangular in structure.

Motherhouse

Originally the autonomous monastic institution with jurisdiction over daughter houses (monasteries) that derive from it

Parsonage

The residence of a parson. Different Churches use different terms. *Manse* is usually Episcopalian and Presbyterian, *parsonage* is common with Baptists and Methodists. *Parson* is archaic, *Pastor* common. Some church homes are called *pastoriums.*

Priory

A monastery governed by a prior(ess); either autonomous (conventual) or dependent upon an abbey or motherhouse (obedientiary). A cathedral priory (in England) is a monastery attached to a cathedral church.

Rectory

The residence of a rector (see Rector)

Monastery at New Melleray, Iowa

Liturgy

Background Information

Liturgical Prayer

1. Trinitarian (centered on Christ)

2. Ecclesial (rooted in the Church)

3. Scriptural (nourished by the Bible)

4. Sacramental (celebrated in the Eucharist/Sacraments/Hours)

5. Liturgical (ordered through the calendar of feasts/seasons)

Definitions of Sacrament (Latin: *sacramentum*; Greek: *mysterion*)

1. Jesus is the Sacrament
   - In whom life is found
   - In whom the Father is encountered

2. The Church is a kind of sacrament . . .
   - The "body" of Christ (1 Corinthians 12:12–27)
   - In which Jesus' Person and saving action is incarnate

3. The seven-fold ministry is sacramental . . .
   - Outward signs instituted by Christ to give grace
   - Signs of worship communicating the grace of Jesus' dying and rising
   - Tangible expressions of intangible grace, accomplishing what they signify

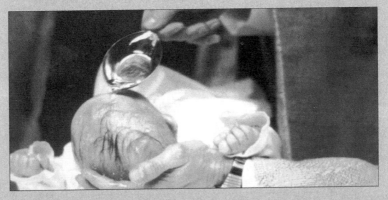

The Sacraments

Signs	Words	Scriptures
Baptism Pouring of water (Baptism, Chrismation, and Eucharist are celebrated together in the Eastern Rites.)	*"N., I baptize you in the name of the Father, and of the Son, and of the Holy Spirit."*	Necessity of rebirth—John 3:5 Institution by Christ—Matthew 28:18–20 In the early Christian community: • Acts 8:26–39 (the Ethiopian eunuch) • Acts 16:16f (the jailer of Paul and Silas) • Acts 19:1–7 (the disciples in Ephesus) Paul's theology of baptism: • Romans 6:3–11 • Meaning and effect: Galatians 2:19–20; 3:14, 26–29; Ephesians 1:3–5, 2:4–10; Colossians 1:14, 2:9–13, 3:1–3; 1 Peter 1:3–5
Confirmation Laying on of hands, anointing with oil	*"N., be sealed with the Gift of the Holy Spirit."*	Acts 8:14–17, 9:17–19, 10:5, 19:5; Titus 3:4–8
Eucharist Bread and wine	*The Eucharistic Prayer within the liturgy, with its institution narrative: "This is my body . . . this is my blood. . . ."*	Roots in Jewish Passover—Exodus 12:1–28 Melchizedek's offering—Genesis 14:18 The priesthood of David—Psalm 110 The priesthood of Jesus—Hebrews 8–10 Multiplication of loaves—John 6:1–15 The Bread of Life—John 6:25–71 The Last Supper—Matthew 26:26–28; Mark 14:22–25; Luke 22:7–20 The Emmaus event—Luke 24:13–53 Apostolic Church—Acts 2:42–47, 20:7 The meaning and effect of the Eucharist—1 Corinthians 10:16–17
Reconciliation Contrition, confession, and satisfaction	*"God, the Father of mercies, through the death and resurrection of his Son, has reconciled the world to himself and sent the Holy Spirit among us for the forgiveness of sins; through the ministry of the Church, may God give you pardon and peace; and I absolve you from your sins in the name of the Father, and of the Son, ✠ and of the Holy Spirit."*	Sin lists: 1 Corinthians 5:3–5, 6:9–10; Galatians 5:19–20; Ephesians 5:5; 1 Timothy 1:19–21 Jesus' mission • Mark 2:16–17 ("I have come to call sinners . . .") • Luke 7:47–50 (Mary Magdalene) • Luke 19:7–10 (Zacchaeus) Christ's continued ministry in the Church • John 16:1–8 (coming of the Paraclete) • Matthew 16:13–19 (keys of the kingdom) • John 20:19–23 (commissioning the Church) • Acts 9:1–5 (Saul's conversion) Early Church ministry regarding post-baptismal sin • Matthew 18:15–18 (fraternal correction, Church authority) • 2 Thessalonians 2:6, 14–15 (excommunication) • 1 Timothy 1:19–20 (ostracization) Reconciliation before Communion • Mark 11:25 ("When you pray, forgive . . .") • Mark 5:23–24 ("If you bring your gift . . .") Scandal: Matthew 18:5–7
Anointing of the Sick Anointing with oil and laying on of hands	*"Through this holy anointing may the Lord in his love and mercy help you with the grace of the Holy Spirit."* *"Amen."* *"May the Lord who frees you from sin save you and raise you up."* *"Amen."*	Institution—James 5:13–16 The ministry of the community to the sick—Isaiah 52:13–53:12; 1 Corinthians 12:12–22, 24b–27; Matthew 25:31–40 Suffering—2 Corinthians 12:9–10 Anointing the sick—Isaiah 61:1–3a; John 9:1–7 Healing—1 Kings 19:1–8; Acts 4:8–12 (3:1–10); Matthew 8:1–4 (5–17) Healing and forgiveness—Job 7:12–21; Mark 2:1–12 Faith—Job 3:1–3, 11–17, 20–23; Isaiah 35:1–10 Hope and confidence—Job 19:23–27a (7:1–4, 6–11); Romans 8:18–27; 1 Corinthians 1:18–25; Matthew 8:1–4, 25:31–40 The power of prayer—Job 7:12–21; James 5:13–18; Luke 11:5–13
Marriage Mutual consent to live together as husband and wife (In Eastern Rites, priest is the minister.)	*In the West, the external expression of this is through the interchange of the couple with the Church witness (priest, deacon), as he elicits their intention (questions preceding the vows) and their consent (wedding vows).*	The question of divorce—Matthew 19:3–12 (Mark 10:2–12) Christian wives and husbands—Ephesians 5:25–32 A believing spouse consecrates a partner—1 Corinthians 7:12–16
Holy Orders Laying on of hands	*The Prayer of Consecration that follows the laying on of hands.*	Presbyters installed in the early Church—Acts 14:22–23 The priestly role—Hebrews 5:1–10 Counsel to Timothy—1 Timothy 4:12–16 Exhortation to faithfulness—2 Timothy 1:6–8 Apostolic charge—2 Timothy 4:2, 5:7–8 Qualities of a presbyter—Titus 1:5–9

The Seven Sacraments

A List (See CCC #s 1210–1211.)

There is "a certain resemblance between the stages of natural life and the stages of the spiritual," the *Catechism of the Catholic Church* (#1210) says before treating the seven sacraments in the following order, noting that they could be listed other ways, but this way shows how they form an "organic whole," each sacrament in its own vital place.

Sacraments of Christian Initiation ("birth and increase")

1. Baptism
2. Confirmation
3. Eucharist

Sacraments of Healing

4. Penance (Reconciliation)
5. Anointing of the Sick

Sacraments of Mission (service of community/mission of the faithful)

6. Holy Orders
7. Matrimony

Other Categories

This language was more common in the catechesis of the past.

Sacraments of the Dead

These sacraments confer or restore sanctifying as well as actual grace; they can be and often are celebrated validly and fruitfully by those not in the state of grace.

1. Baptism
2. Reconciliation
3. Anointing of the Sick

Sacraments of the Living

These sacraments require the state of grace for their fruitfulness, but the absence of the state of grace would not thereby render the sacrament invalid (except for Eucharist in the case of sacrilege by the priest "presiding").

1. Confirmation
2. Eucharist
3. Matrimony
4. Holy Orders

The Last Rites or Last Sacraments

These sacraments are now considered part of the pastoral care of the sick and are not reserved for the dying. The *Catechism of the Catholic Church* suggests (#1525) that a comparison can be drawn between the unity of the Sacraments of Initiation (Baptism, Confirmation, and Eucharist) and a unity that can be seen in these three sacraments for the end of Christian life, the sacraments that "prepare for our heavenly homeland" or the sacraments that complete the earthly pilgrimage.

1. Penance
2. Anointing of the Sick
3. Eucharist (*viaticum*)

Sacraments Imparting Sacramental Character

These sacraments impart an indelible spiritual mark and therefore cannot be repeated.

1. Baptism
2. Confirmation
3. Holy Orders

The Sacraments of Initiation

These three sacraments immerse a person in the Church, the risen body of Christ.

1. Baptism (in his identity)
2. Confirmation (in his mission)
3. Eucharist (in his destiny)

The Two Principal Effects of Baptism (See CCC #1262.)

Baptism makes one a member of the Body of Christ and incorporates one into the Church, sharing in its mission (CCC #s 1267–1270). The principal effects of Baptism are:

1. Purification from sins
2. Regeneration (new birth) in the Holy Spirit

Some Old Testament Prefigurations of Baptism

Creation, the Flood, the Red Sea, and the Jordan River

The Necessity of Baptism for Salvation

"The Church does not know of any means other than Baptism that assures entry into eternal beatitude ..." (CCC #1257).

1. John 3:5 ("Unless one is born again ...")
2. Matthew 28:19–20 (The command to proclaim the gospel and baptize)

"God has bound salvation to the sacrament of Baptism, but God is not bound by his sacraments" (CCC #1257).

1. Baptism of blood (see CCC #1258). Those who die for the faith without being baptized are baptized by their death for and with Christ (it bring the fruits without the sacrament).

2. Desire for Baptism (see CCC #1259). The explicit desire of catechumens to be baptized, along with repentance for their sins and charity, brings the assurance of salvation they were not able to receive in Baptism (having died before their Baptism).

3. Christ's redemption (see CCC #1260). "Since Christ died for all . . . and since all are in fact called to one and the same destiny, which is divine, we must hold that the Holy Spirit offers to all the possibility of being made partakers, in a way known to God, of the Paschal mystery" (*Documents of Vatican II*, "Pastoral Constitution on the Church in the Modern World," 22.5).

4. God's mercy. "As regards children who have died without Baptism, the Church can only entrust them to the mercy of God, as she does in her funeral rites for them. Indeed, the great mercy of God who desires that all . . . should be saved, and Jesus' tenderness toward children . . . allow us to hope that there is a way of salvation for children who have died without Baptism" (CCC #1261).

The Rite of Christian Initiation of Adults (RCIA)

The Steps

First step: Acceptance into the Order of Catechumens

A catechumen (Greek: *katecheein*, to put in the ear) is one preparing and being catechized for initiation. The term *candidate*, also used, is appropriate because of the white (*candidus*) garment used in Baptism. In about 1600 the word *candidate* came into the English language for one seeking public office (whether candid or not), echoing the candidacy of the catechumen as well as the candidacy of politicians in ancient Rome who wore white togas as a symbol of purity. The presentation of the Gospels takes place during the catechumenate.

Second step: Election, or Enrollment of Names

Followed by the scrutinies on the:

Third Sunday of Lent (with the presentation of the Creed)

Fourth Sunday of Lent

Fifth Sunday of Lent (with the presentation of the Lord's Prayer)

Third step: Celebration of the Sacraments of Initiation

Baptism, Confirmation, and Eucharist are traditionally celebrated at the Easter Vigil. A neophyte (Greek: *neophytos*, newly planted) is a newly baptized. They were also called *illuminati* because they were illuminated by the Holy Spirit, as the lighted candle signifies. The alb-like white garment (*chrisom*) of the newly baptized signifies cleansing and putting on Christ. Formerly, if a baptized child died within a month, the garment was used as a shroud and the infant was called a *chrisom child*.

Sponsor (See CCC #1311.)

Candidates for Confirmation, as for Baptism, need the spiritual help of a sponsor. This person must be an active, fully initiated member of the Church. In light of the unity of the two sacraments, one of the baptismal godparents is appropriate as a Confirmation sponsor.

Naming

Scripturally, a name is not only what the person is a called but also who the person is—the special meaning of that person. In Semitic thought, the name conveyed the truth of the person. God was YHWH ("I AM"; "I AM HERE"); Jesus was *Yeshua, Joshua* ("One who saves").

The first name (chosen by one's parents)

The Christian and personal name. In Genesis God gave Adam the responsibility to name those things over which he was given authority.

The Confirmation name (chosen by oneself; not required)

Reflects the individual's choice of a saintly patron, which sometimes means claiming one's baptismal name.

The last name (chosen before one was born)

The family name (surname) is over and above the Christian name. The use of a surname originated in the late tenth century, though it became common practice only much later. Its purpose was to specify an individual, usually according to parentage (patronymic) (Johnson, Ivanovich, MacCallum, McDonald, Novinski), trade/occupation (Baker, Taylor, Schumacher or Shoemaker, Smith), personal/physical characteristics (Short, Strong, Klein [small]), or place of residence (York, Westerfield, Berg [mountain]).

"What name do you give your child?"

The sixteenth-century *Catechism of the Council of Trent* directed that the baptismal name should be taken from some person whose eminent sanctity had been recognized. Actually, naming after saints was a common practice centuries before this in France and Germany, and by the thirteenth century, throughout Europe. This was a major change in Ireland, where Gaelic Christians had been reluctant to use hallowed names, like Mary. Those named after the Blessed Mother, *Muire* in original Gaelic, were called "Maire," or a similar variation. Today, the *Code of Canon Law* simply says, "Parents, sponsors, and the pastor are to see to it that a name alien to a Christian sense is not given."

Renaming

Changing the name in the Scriptures and Christian history signaled the change of one's vocation and even identity. A name change is a scriptural expression for a new life: "You shall be called by a new name . . ." (Isaiah 62:2; see also Isaiah 65:15; Revelation 2:17, 3:12, 19:12).

Abram (Genesis 11:27)	became Abraham (Genesis 17:5)
Sarai (Genesis 11:29)	became Sarah (Genesis 17:15)
Jacob (Genesis 25:26)	became Israel (Genesis 35:10)
Simon (Matthew 4:18)	became Peter (Matthew 16:18)

Saul (Acts 7:58) and Paul (Acts 13:9), however, are both names used by this individual; Saul was his Jewish name and Paul his Roman name.

The Juniper

One of Miguel Serra's favorite books was the *Little Flowers of St. Francis*, and his favorite character was the playful monk, Brother Juniper. Of him Miguel exclaimed, "Would to God that I had a whole forest of such Junipers!" It was the brother's humor that Miguel admired, but more, it was his total selflessness and deep concern for the needs of his companions. On September 15, 1731, Miguel knelt before the provincial and made his vows as a Franciscan. His name? . . . the jolly, holy jester of St. Francis, Juniper (in Spanish, *Junipero*).

The Three Valid Methods of Baptism

1. Aspersion (sprinkling): Used only in exceptional circumstances.

2. Infusion (pouring): A practice already in the first century, according to *The Didache*. Paul was baptized in a private house (Acts 9:17–18), and Peter baptized his jailer's family presumably still in the prison area (Acts 16:33). Many have concluded that these Baptisms and others were done either by sprinkling or pouring, since no river or stream is mentioned, and since pools/tubs were rare among those who were poor.

3. Immersion (dipping or plunging): Generally used in the early Church, common in the Eastern Church and certain Protestant traditions; since Vatican II, permissible in the Latin Rite.

Shell and water (Baptism)

The Sacrament of Confirmation (See CCC #s 1299–1300.)

1. The bishop (the ordinary ministry) extends hands over the confirmands, signifying the gift of the Spirit, and prays a prayer invoking the Spirit.

2. The essential rite follows, that is, the anointing with chrism on the forehead, which is done by the laying on of the hand and the words: "N., be sealed with the Gift of the Holy Spirit."

The Effects of Confirmation (See CCC #s 1302–1303.)

The full outpouring of the Holy Spirit, given to the apostles on Pentecost; it increases and deepens baptismal grace.

1. Roots us more deeply as a child of God

2. Unites us more closely to Christ

3. Increases in us the gifts of the Holy Spirit

4. Perfects our bond with the Church

5. Gives us a special strength of the Holy Spirit to spread and defend the faith by word and action as true witnesses of Christ, to boldly confess the name of Christ, never to be ashamed of the cross

Becoming a Catholic

1. From non-Christian adulthood:
Baptism→Confirmation→Eucharist

2. From non-Catholic, Christian adulthood:
Reconciliation→reception into the Catholic Church→Confirmation→ Eucharist

3. Frequently, from infancy:
Baptism→Eucharist→Confirmation

Apologia Pro Vita Sua

After John Henry Cardinal Newman, the well-known Anglican theologian, became a Catholic in 1845, he wrote a religious auto-biography (1864), *A Defense of His Life*, as a defense of the things he did in his life by explaining the basis for his faith. He was made a cardinal in 1879. Although it could refer to anyone's "apologia" (explanation), that phrase has become synonymous with Newman's masterpiece.

Rite of Reception of Baptized Christians into Full Communion

Reception takes place, ideally, within Mass, after the homily.

1. Profession of faith by the assembly and the one being received

2. Declaration of reception by the bishop (or priest taking his place)

3. Sacrament of Confirmation

4. General intercessions

5. Sign of peace

6. Liturgy of the Eucharist, in which the person receives Communion for the first time with the members of the Catholic community

---

A Covenant of Salt

There was an ancient practice of partaking of the same salt by the parties entering a covenant. This signaled its permanence, given the natural properties of the preservative salt (hence the proverbial "covenant of salt"). The tasting of salt by those sharing a table is a venerable symbol of alliance and friendship. God used the symbol with Aaron and his family, ". . . it is a covenant of salt [inviolable covenant] forever before the Lord, for you and your descendants as well" (Numbers 18:19b).

In directives to Moses on the ritual of sacrifices, God said: "You shall not omit from your grain offerings the salt of the covenant with your God; with all your offerings you shall offer salt" (Leviticus 2:13). King Abijah declared that when the Lord God gave the kingdom of Israel to David, it was by a covenant of salt (2 Chronicles 13:5).

Because salt is a symbol of immortality (being by nature a preservative), it was part of the baptismal ceremony (until the 1969 revision) to put salt on the child's tongue: "Receive the salt of wisdom. May it be for you a propitiation into eternal life." And just as the baptismal candle and white garment have found their way into the funeral liturgy, so, in another era, did salt. It was not an uncommon practice among Christians to put salt into a coffin when burying a believer so that, at this ultimate birth, the devil was given another taste of grace, for which he has a hatred.

Eucharist

Names for the Eucharist

This vocabulary list is from the *Catechism of the Catholic Church* (#s 1328–1332), in the order used here, and refers (with the exception of #8 and #9) to the Eucharist celebrated, not the Eucharistic species. ("High Mass," historically, was the *missa solemnis*, solemn Mass, a phrase translated and often spoken before the renewal of the liturgy.)

1. The Lord's Supper

2. The breaking of the Bread

3. The Eucharistic assembly

4. The memorial of the Lord's passion and resurrection

5. The holy sacrifice (of the Mass), sacrifice of praise, spiritual sacrifice

6. The holy and divine liturgy

7. The celebration of the sacred mysteries

8. The Blessed Sacrament (as the Sacrament of sacraments)

9. Holy Communion

10. Holy Mass

Names for Communion

Starting with the two terms from the list above that refer to the Eucharist when it is received (not celebrated), the following list includes names for "the Eucharistic species." (See CCC #s 1330–1331; 1384–1390.)

1. The Blessed Sacrament

2. Holy Communion (which is also the result)

3. The holy things

4. The bread of angels

5. Bread from heaven

6. Medicine of immortality

7. *Viaticum* (Latin: *via*, way + *ticum*, with you; take with you on the way; supplies); Communion received by the dying is called *Viaticum*.

8. The Body of Christ (which is also the Church)

9. The host (Latin: *hostia*, a sacrificial lamb—a larger animal is a *victima*)

The Real Presence

This phrase traditionally refers to the Body and Blood of Christ present in the Eucharist. Open to grace, we experience Christ in all creation, within ourselves, and within all people (John 14:18–20; 17:23, 26; Colossians 1:27)—in a special way, in those who are poor and suffering (Matthew 25:30). We experience Christ in the Church (Matthew 18:20) and in the liturgical celebrations of the Church. At Mass we experience the presence of Christ in:

1. The priest   3. The assembly
2. The Scriptures   4. The consecrated Bread and Wine

> ### *Oplatki*
>
> Another enrichment and morsel from Eastern Europe is this wafer (*oplatki*), and the meatless Christmas Eve dinner of the Slavic people. Resembling the *agape* (love) meals of the apostolic Church, this touching ritual calls for the family's father to solemnly break and distribute wafers (sometimes blessed beforehand by the priest), and to offer a holy kiss and wish for a joyful feast.

Three Meanings of the Sacramental Sacrifice (See CCC #s 1356–1381.)

1. Thanksgiving and praise   to the Father

2. Sacrificial memorial   of the Son

3. Presence of Christ   by the power of his Word and the Holy Spirit

The Significance of Sacrifice (Latin: *sacrum*, holy; *facere*, to make)

The fire of the Old Testament sacrifice takes on a new significance.

1. Purifying ("In his sacrifice to purify us . . .)

2. Consuming (. . . Christ was consumed . . .)

3. Illuminating (. . . revealing the light of truth . . .)

4. Warming (. . . and the warmth of love.")

The Three Tenses of the Memorial Acclamation

1. Past (commemorative): "Christ has died."—the memorial of Christ's sacrifice

2. Present (affective): "Christ is risen."—the celebration of saving grace

3. Future (prognostic): "Christ will come again."—the sign of hope and pledge of glory

Both forms

The *Catechism of the Catholic Church* gives the assurance (#1390) that Christ is present in a sacramental way under each form—the bread and the wine—and that receiving only the bread (the host) brings all the grace of the Eucharist. At the same time, "the sign of communion is more complete when given under both kinds, since in that form the sign of the Eucharistic meal appears more clearly." (Receiving both forms is common practice in the Eastern Rites.) "Intinction" is receiving Communion under both forms by dipping the host in the chalice; this practice is discouraged in many dioceses because the sign value of dunking is weaker than drinking in response to the mandate "Take and drink. . . ." *Utraquists* (Latin: *utraque specie*, both species), or *calixtines* (Latin: *calix*, chalice), were an unorthodox group of fifteenth-century Bohemian Christians who believed Communion was valid only if both bread and wine were received.

The Legend of St. Gertrude

The German St. Gertrude the Great, famed for supernatural visions, is the patron of travelers, since in her life she established hospices for pilgrims. This gave rise to the legend that St. Gertrude harbored souls on the first night of their three-day journey to heaven. Historically, she was an abbess and the aunt of Pepin, who was the father of Charles Martel, who was in turn the grandfather of Charlemagne who became king of the Franks (768–814) and emperor of the West (800–814). Charlemagne was crowned "Emperor of the Romans" on Christmas Day, 800, by none other than the pope, Leo III. Now those were the days.

Christmas Tree, Fruit Tree

Medieval mystery plays employed fir trees decorated with apples to symbolize the Garden of Eden with its tree of life and forbidden fruit. Long after the mystery plays, the Germans remembered the tree, modifying its decoration by adding sacramental wafers along with the apples, to contrast the eating that brought death with the eating that brings life. As the decorations became more elaborate, the symbolism of the fall and redemption faded. Apples were joined by oranges and then brightly colored balls, while wafers became cookies cut in the shape of angels, stars, animals, and flowers.

The Mass in the Year 150

This description by the apologist and martyr St. Justin is a passage from his *First Apology*, 67, which was rediscovered in the sixteenth century.

On the day called Sunday there is a meeting in one place of those who live in cities or the country, and the memoirs of the apostles or the writings of the prophets are read as long as time permits. When the reader has finished, the president in a discourse urges and invites us to the imitation of these noble things. Then we all stand up together and offer prayers. And, as said before, when we have finished the prayer, bread is brought, and wine and water, and the president similarly sends up prayers and thanksgiving to the best of his ability, and the congregation assents, saying the Amen; the distribution, and reception of the consecrated elements by each one, takes place and they are sent to the absent by the deacons. Those who prosper, and who so wish, contribute, each one as much as he chooses to. What is collected is deposited with the president, and he takes care of orphans and widows, and those who are in want on account of sickness or any other cause, and those who are in bonds, and the strangers who are sojourners among us, and, briefly, he is the protector of all those in need.

A Selected Chronology of Changes in the Mass

1922: Assembly permitted to make responses

1953: Modification of the Eucharistic fast

1953: Permission for afternoon and evening Mass

1956: Revision of the rites of Holy Week

1964: Use of the common spoken language approved

1965: Last gospel and "Leonine" prayers after Mass eliminated

1967: Purple allowed instead of black in Masses for the dead

1968: Three additional Eucharistic prayers authorized

1969: Instruction on Masses in the home

1970: New Order of Mass replacing sixteenth-century Tridentine Mass and including:
  — Clear structure of Word and Sacrament
  — New Lectionary
  — Reinstated prayers of the faithful

1970: New Lectionary introduced, including:
  — Mark and Luke added to Matthew for gospel readings
  — Three-year Sunday and two-year daily cycles of readings
  — Three readings instead of two on Sunday
  — Responsorial psalms

1970: Sunday Mass on Saturday approved, where necessary

1973: Special guidelines for Masses with children

1974: New Roman Missal (Sacramentary); the first in 400 years

1977: Communion in the hand allowed

1978: Permission given for lay Eucharistic ministers

1991: Lectionary for Masses with Children approved

1998: Use of a revised English Lectionary begun in Advent

The Parts of the Mass

1. Introductory Rites

2. The Liturgy of the Word ⎤

⎟ The Two Great Parts (See CCC #s 1346–1347.)

3. The Liturgy of the Eucharist ⎦

4. Concluding Rite

"The Eucharistic table set for us is the table both of the Word of God and of the Body of the Lord" (*Documents of Vatican II*, "Divine Constitution of Divine Revelation," 21). Formerly, the first part of the Mass, known as the *Mass of the catechumens*, was seen only as preparatory for the *Mass of the faithful* with its principal parts of offertory, consecration, and Communion.

The Movement of the Celebration (See CCC #s 1348–1355.)

One analogy drawn from this "movement" is from the domestic Church in which the family sets the table (the preparation), says grace (the Eucharistic Prayer), and shares the food (Communion).

1. The Introductory Rites (the gathering)
   Greeting
   Penitential rite
   Kyrie ("Lord, have mercy")
   Gloria (in season)
   Opening prayer (the "Amen" of which closes the gathering rite)

2. The Liturgy of the Word
   First reading
   Responsorial psalm
   Second reading
   Alleluia
   Gospel
   Homily
   Creed
   General intercessions (the "Amen" of which ends the Liturgy of the Word)

3. The Liturgy of the Eucharist
   Preparation of the gifts
   - The presentation of the gifts
   - Preparation of the bread and wine

   Prayer over the gifts
   The Eucharistic Prayer
   - Preface
   - Acclamation (Holy, holy, holy Lord)
   - Eucharistic Prayer (ended by the "Great Amen")

   Communion Rite
   - The Lord's Prayer
   - The breaking of the Bread
   - Holy Communion
   - The prayer after Communion (the "Amen" of which ends the Liturgy of the Eucharist)

4. The Concluding Rite (dismissal)
   (from which the word "mass" came: *Ite, missa est*: Go, the Mass is ended.)
   Greeting
   Blessing
   Dismissal

The Sacramentary

The presider's book; the part of the Roman Missal containing mainly the Mass prayers and rubrics, excluding the readings (which make up the Lectionary).

Ordinary Time Readings: Outline

Sundays

	Second reading				Gospel		
Sun.	Year A	Year B	Year C	Sun.	Year A	Year B	Year C
2	1 Cor 1	1 Cor 6	1 Cor 12	2	John 1	John 1	John 2
3	1 Cor 1	1 Cor 7	1 Cor 12	3	Mt 4	Mk 1	Lk 1, 4
4	1 Cor 1	1 Cor 7	1 Cor 12–13	4	Mt 5	Mk 1	Lk 4
5	1 Cor 2	1 Cor 9	1 Cor 15	5	Mt 5	Mk 1	Lk 5
6	1 Cor 2	1 Cor 10–11	1 Cor 15	6	Mt 5	Mk 1	Lk 6
7	1 Cor 3	2 Cor 1	1 Cor 15	7	Mt 5	Mk 2	Lk 6
8	1 Cor 4	2 Cor 3	1 Cor 15	8	Mt 6	Mk 2	Lk 6
9	Rom 3	2 Cor 4	Gal 1	9	Mt 7	Mk 2–3	Lk 7
10	Rom 4	2 Cor 4–5	Gal 1	10	Mt 9	Mk 3	Lk 7
11	Rom 5	2 Cor 5	Gal 2	11	Mt 9–10	Mk 4	Lk 7
12	Rom 5	2 Cor 5	Gal 3	12	Mt 10	Mk 4	Lk 9
13	Rom 6	2 Cor 8	Gal 5	13	Mt 10	Mk 5	Lk 9
14	Rom 8	2 Cor 12	Gal 6	14	Mt 11	Mk 6	Lk 10
15	Rom 8	Eph 1	Col 1	15	Mt 13	Mk 6	Lk 10
16	Rom 8	Eph 2	Col 1	16	Mt 13	Mk 6	Lk 10
17	Rom 8	Eph 4	Col 2	17	Mt 13	John 6	Lk 11
18	Rom 8	Eph 4	Col 3	18	Mt 14	John 6	Lk 12
19	Rom 9	Eph 4–5	Heb 11	19	Mt 14	John 6	Lk 12
20	Rom 11	Eph 5	Heb 12	20	Mt 15	John 6	Lk 12
21	Rom 11	Eph 5	Heb 12	21	Mt 16	John 6	Lk 13
22	Rom 12	Jas 1	Heb 12	22	Mt 16	Mk 7	Lk 14
23	Rom 13	Jas 2	Philemon	23	Mt 18	Mk 7	Lk 14
24	Rom 14	Jas 2	1 Tim 1	24	Mt 18	Mk 8	Lk 15
25	Phil 1	Jas 3	1 Tim 2	25	Mt 20	Mk 9	Lk 16
26	Phil 2	Jas 5	1 Tim 6	26	Mt 21	Mk 9	Lk 16
27	Phil 4	Heb 2	2 Tim 1	27	Mt 21	Mk 10	Lk 17
28	Phil 4	Heb 4	2 Tim 2	28	Mt 22	Mk 10	Lk 17
29	1 Thes 1	Heb 4	2 Tim 3–4	29	Mt 22	Mk 10	Lk 18
30	1 Thes 1	Heb 5	2 Tim 4	30	Mt 22	Mk 10	Lk 18
31	1 Thes 2	Heb 7	2 Thes 1–2	31	Mt 23	Mk 12	Lk 19
32	1 Thes 4	Heb 9	2 Thes 2–3	32	Mt 25	Mk 12	Lk 20
33	1 Thes 5	Heb 10	2 Thes 3	33	Mt 25	Mk 13	Lk 21
34	1 Cor 15	Rev 1	Col 1	34	Mt 25	John 18	Lk 23

Ordinary Time Readings: Outline (continued)

Weekdays

First reading			Gospel	
Week	Year 1	Year 2	Week	
1	Heb	1 Sm	1	
2	Heb	1 Sm	2	
3	Heb	1 Sm	3	
4	Heb	2 Sm; 1 Kgs 1–16	4	
5	Gn 1–11	1 Kgs 1–16	5	Mark
6	Gn 1–11	Jas	6	
7	Sir	Jas	7	
8	Sir	1 Pt; Jude	8	
9	Tb	2 Pt; 2 Tim	9	
10	2 Cor	1 Kgs 17–22	10	
11	2 Cor	1 Kgs 17–22; 2 Kgs	11	
12	Gn 12–50	2 Kgs; Lam	12	
13	Gn 12–50	Am	13	
14	Gn 12–50	Hos; Is	14	
15	Ex	Is; Mi	15	
16	Ex	Mi; Jer	16	Matthew
17	Ex; Lv	Jer	17	
18	Nm; Dt	Jer; Na; Hb	18	
19	Dt; Jos	Ez	19	
20	Jgs; Ru	Ez	20	
21	1 Thes	2 Thes; 1 Cor	21	
22	1 Thes; Col	1 Cor	22	
23	Col; 1 Tim	1 Cor	23	
24	1 Tim	1 Cor	24	
25	Ezr; Hg; Zec	Prv; Eccl	25	
26	Zec; Neh; Bar	Jb	26	Luke
27	Jon; Mal; Jl	Gal	27	
28	Rom	Gal; Eph	28	
29	Rom	Eph	29	
30	Rom	Eph; Phil	30	
31	Rom	Phil	31	
32	Wis	Ti; Phlm; 2, 3 Jn	32	
33	1, 2 Mc	Rv	33	
34	Dn	Rv	34	

Lectionary

The "collection of readings" (Scripture), assigned by the Church for liturgical proclamation. The present one was introduced March 22, 1970, and revised in 1998. It consists of:

1. A three-year cycle of Sunday readings
2. A two-year weekday cycle
3. A one-year sanctoral cycle
4. A variety of other readings for various occasions
5. Responsorial psalms and alleluia verses

General Principles of the New Lectionary

Gospel (both Sundays and weekdays)

During Ordinary Time: Readings are *organic,* which is the term for a continuous or semi-continuous reading of a text (beginning one week where the previous week ended). A particular book or letter is treated as a whole and not "as related to something else." Notice this in the tables, for example: Matthew, one year; Mark, the next; and then Luke. For special feasts and seasons, readings are *thematic,* which is the term used when a passage is chosen because of its relationship to a theme chosen beforehand or suggested by another reading or by a feast (Christmas and Easter readings, for example).

First reading (Sundays)

Old Testament readings are chosen thematically. (There is no table of these readings provided here, since there is no pattern from week to week regarding the source of these readings. The selections are not organic in the sense used here.) The choices according to themes show clearly the unity and relationship between the Old and New Testaments.

Second reading (Sundays)

The choices are organic, as the tables illustrate, providing a semi-continuous reading of Paul and James. (Peter and John are read during the Easter and Christmas Seasons.)

First reading (weekdays)

Like the second reading on Sunday, the first reading of weekend liturgies is organic, although more selective than on Sundays, since both Testaments are used (Old Testament, organic in a limited way; New, organic in an extensive way). Sometimes Scripture reading is both organic and thematic, as when Daniel and Revelation are read at the end of the liturgical year because of their eschatological (end times) themes.

The Last Gospel

Before the reform of the liturgy, John 1:1–14 was proclaimed at the end of Mass (except on days in Lent and various other occasions).

Sequence (Latin: *sequentia,* a following, sequence)

The sequence is a hymn of joy, of varying length and meter, sung or recited before the gospel on certain feasts. The *Dies Irae,* formerly common in requiem Masses, is not a liturgical sequence, strictly speaking. Three remain in the revised liturgy:

1. Easter's *Victima Paschali* ("Paschal Victim"), by Wipo of Burgundy (d. 1050)

2. Pentecost's *Veni, Sancte Spiritus* ("Come, Holy Spirit"), probably by Stephen Langston (d. 1228), archbishop of Canterbury; called the *Golden Sequence*

3. *Lauda Sion* ("Praise, O Zion") for the Solemnity of the Body and Blood of the Lord (Corpus Christi), by St. Thomas Aquinas in 1274

Preaching

A "sermon" is a talk on a religious topic, usually at a worship service. *Dabitur vobis* is an old piety that a preacher need not prepare because "it will be given to you" in the pulpit.

1. Pre-evangelization, addressing the human situation. **Object:** readiness.

2. Evangelization, proclaiming who Jesus is. **Object:** conversion.

3. Catechesis, teaching about religion, God, Jesus, or faith, for example. **Object:** understanding.

4. Homily, demonstrating what the Lord is doing. **Object:** Eucharist, to bring worshiper to say from the heart: "It is right to give him thanks and praise." (Preface)
   • Presents the mystery of Christ, based on readings and Mass texts
   • Applies Scripture to daily Christian life
   • Unites Liturgy of the Word with Liturgy of the Eucharist

General intercessions

The baptized exercise their priesthood when they intercede for all humankind.

1. Introduction (by the presider)

2. Intercessions (with assembly responses to each)
   • For the needs of the Church
   • For public authorities and the salvation of the world
   • For those oppressed by specific need
   • For the local community

3. Conclusion (by the presider)

The Eucharistic Prayer

The Roman canon, the first of the Eucharistic Prayers, is from the sixth century and is based on the *Gelasian Sacramentary* (Pope Gelasius I, 492–496). The Roman canon was called by some the *Te igitur* (You, therefore . . .) after its first words in Latin. This central proclamation of the Liturgy of the Eucharist is a prayer of thanksgiving and sanctification, and it consists of these parts:

1. Thanksgiving, expressed especially in the preface, for salvation or some specific aspect of it

2. An acclamation, in the "Holy, holy, holy Lord" (*sanctus* in Latin, or the *tersanctus*, or "the Seraphic Hymn," because it was sung by the seraphim, as Isaiah 6:3 relates); all proclaim, united with the angels, the holiness of God; concludes with Matthew 21:9, the Palm Sunday acclamation (which quotes Psalm 118:26)

3. An *epiclesis*, invoking the Holy Spirit, asking that the gifts be consecrated and become a source of salvation; in the Orthodox Church, considered essential for the validity of the Eucharist; since Vatican II, all Eucharistic Prayers include it

4. The institution and consecration narrative, in the words and actions of Christ at the Last Supper

5. An *anamnesis*, acclaiming, at Christ's command, Christ's presence: passion and death, resurrection, and return at the end of time

6. The offering, of the victim in memorial, whom the Church becomes in Eucharist, to the Father in the Spirit

7. Intercessions, expressive of the Eucharist as the assembly's celebration with the whole Church of heaven and earth and for the Church and all her members living and dead

8. A doxology, expressing praise of God, confirmed and concluded by the acclamation of the people

---

Fruits of the Mass

According to Christian tradition and a human understanding of what God does in his wisdom and love, the spiritual benefits are three-fold:

1. The universal Church is graced.
2. The person/intention for whom the Mass is offered is graced.
3. The priest who offers it is graced.

The Fruits of Holy Communion (See CCC #s 1391–1397.)

1. Causes an intimate union with Christ
2. Preserves, increases, and renews the life of grace received at Baptism
3. Cleanses past sins and preserves from future sins
4. Strengthens the unity among members of the Church
5. Fosters a commitment to those who are poor

Languages of a Catholic Tradition

Even in this age of the vernacular, there are still phrases in our prayer life that remain in beloved use in their original form, exactly as our ancestors spoke them.

Hebrew

Alleluia, "Praise the Lord."
Catholics fast from this acclamation during Lent.

Amen, "It is true" or "So be it."
First and foremost a word of commitment to what has been spoken; also a title for Christ (Revelation 3:14)

Hosanna
Originally an acclamation for safety and salvation; still used in the "Holy, holy, holy Lord" of our English liturgy

Greek

Kyrie, eleison, "Lord, have mercy."
A Greek prayer kept even when Latin became the liturgy's vernacular

Aramaic

Marana tha, "Our Lord has come" or "Come, our Lord."
See 1 Corinthians 16:22; in Revelation 22:20 is the similar "Come, Lord Jesus."

Latin

Adoramus te, Christe, "We adore you, Christ."
A translation is still commonly used fourteen times during the stations of the cross (". . . because by your holy cross you have redeemed the world")

Deo gratias, "Thanks be to God."
A response to Scripture in the liturgy

Dominus vobiscum, "The Lord be with you."
A common Christian greeting, used liturgically at Mass

Fiat voluntas tua, "Let your will be done."
The familiar phrase from the Lord's Prayer. The same *fiat* is spoken by Mary in her celebrated response in the annunciation, "Let it be with me according to your word" (Luke 1:38).

Gloria in excelsis Deo, "Glory to God in the highest."
See "Angelic Hymn" and the "Greater Doxology."

Mea culpa, "Through my fault"
The prayer of a Confiteor ("I confess . . .")

Sanctus, "Holy"
A translation of the Greek *Hagios*; used regularly in the acclamation of the preface of the Eucharistic Prayer

Veni, Sancte Spiritus, "Come, Holy Spirit."
The first words of the "Golden Sequence" (q.v.)

Navajo and Choctaw

In 1986 the Vatican approved a translation of most parts of the Mass into Navajo, the first Native American language to be so approved. It had been given liturgical language status in 1983, which enabled the translation to proceed. Following Navajo, Choctaw became a liturgical language in 1984, with a translation approved in 1987.

Liturgical Objects and Vessels

A *sacristan* is one in charge of sacred articles/vestments; the *sacristy* is the room near the altar, for storage of liturgical things (and for vesting, for some). Both words come from the Latin word for holy (*sancte; sanctus*), as does the word *sexton* (church custodian; grave digger). Sacred vessels, properly, are those receptacles and utensils which come in direct contact with the Blessed Sacrament (chalice, paten, ciborium, pyx, capsula, lunette, and monstrance). Other vessels traditionally include cruets, lavabo dish, thurible, boat, and aspergillum.

Amphora (Greek: *amphi,* both sides; *phero,* to carry)
A wine vessel for Mass; tall, two-handled, often pottery (Symbolically inscribed ones were found in catacombs.)

Ampullae
Two-handed vessels for holding oils or burial ointments

Aspergillum (sprinkler)
An instrument (brush or branch or perforated container) for sprinkling holy water; the pail for holy water is an aspersory

Candles
See sacramentals.

Capsula
The container for reserving the consecrated host for exposition in the monstrance

Censer
A vessel for burning incense (mixture of aromatic gums) at solemn ceremonies. Its rising smoke symbolizes prayer. It's also called a *thurible,* a thurifer being its user. The supply container for the incense is called a *boat.*

Chalice
A cup that holds the wine (grape, "fruit of the vine"). Formerly of precious metals (if not gold, gold plated inside). Since Vatican II it must at least be a non-porous material of suitable dignity. Consecrated with holy chrism by a bishop; also "consecrated by use" (contact with Christ's blood). Eight inches was the traditional and common height. Christ's Last Supper chalice is the centerpiece of the medieval Holy Grail legends.

> ## The Holy Grail
>
> This is the legendary cup identified with the chalice of the Last Supper. Popular folk etymology explained the word as meaning "real blood" (hence *sangrail* or *sangreal*). Actually, it is from an old word meaning platter and is a symbol of Christian purity, or its reward. The quest for the Holy Grail has formed the basis for many a popular story, the most well known (from Arthurian romances) being the legend that Joseph of Arimathea preserved the Grail, receiving into it some of Christ's blood at the crucifixion. This Joseph is the one in whose own tomb Christ was buried (Matthew 27:57–60; Mark 15:42); this wealthy man had appeared earlier in the Gospels as a secret believer.
>
> During his subsequent forty-two-year imprisonment, legend relates, Jospeh of Arimathea was miraculously kept alive by the Holy Grail. Upon his release he bore the relic, along with the spear with which Longinus pierced Christ's side, to England, Glastonbury County, Somerset, where it disappeared. In this famed place, designated as King Arthur's burial place (Avalon), Joseph of Arimathea rested his staff, which took root as the legendary Glastonbury thorn which leafs out every Christmas Eve. (There is a variety of hawthorn still claiming this fabled lineage.) It was also in this place that, according to legend, this same Joseph founded the famed abbey, the first Christian church there, and proceeded with the conversion of the Britons.
>
> There are many other legends involving the Grail, like the one that says it was delivered from heaven by angels and entrusted to a body of knights who guard it on a mountain top. When the Grail is approached by anyone whose purity is imperfect, it disappears. Its quest became the principal source of adventures of the Knights of the Round Table. Malory's *Le Morte d'Arthur* and Tennyson's *Idylls of the King* are favorite English versions of the quest for the Holy Grail.

Chalice veil (no longer in common use)

Covers the chalice and paten from the beginning of Mass until the offertory and after the ablutions

Ciborium

Container for the communion hosts; similar to a paten and traditionally resembling the chalice except for its cover

Corporal

A square of linen cloth placed upon the altar and upon which the chalice and paten are placed (Its container, when the corporal is not in use, is called the *burse*. Like the chalice veil, the burse is no longer in common use.)

Crescelle

The knocker formerly used in place of the bell (at the consecration, for example) during Holy Week

Cruets

Water and wine containers; an A and V indicating *aqua* (water) and *vinum* (wine)

Finger bowl and towel

Used for the rite before the Eucharistic Prayer. The linen for drying was called a *manuterge*.

Lavabo dish

The saucer for the presider's ceremonial washing of fingers, called this because the first words of the prayer formerly used by the priest, "I wash (Latin: *lavabo*) my hands in innocence" (Psalm 26:6; see also Matthew 27:24–26).

Liber Usualis (no longer commonly in use)

A book containing most of the Gregorian chants and readings for the Mass and the Divine Office

Luna (lunette)

See monstrance.

Monstrance (*ostentorium*)

Container for the host in exposition of the Blessed Sacrament, commonly surmounted by a cross. The glass-sided, removable receptacle at its center, the *luna* (or *lunette*), actually holds the host.

Ordo

Mainly, an annual calendar of directions for each day's Mass and Liturgy of the Hours

Pall

A stiff square of cardboard covered by linen and used to cover the top of the chalice

Paten

A flat saucer of the same material as the chalice; it is for the host (which is made of unleavened wheat bread)

Processional cross

A mobile cross or crucifix that leads the procession and recession of liturgical ministers, placed in the sanctuary to signal the presence of the assembled praying community

Purificator

A band of linen used to cleanse the chalice

Pyx

The container for the communion host outside of church and Mass

Roman Missal (Latin: *missalis,* pertaining to Mass)

The liturgical book, combining mainly the Sacramentary and the Lectionary, which became the norm in the ninth century. The liturgical restorations of Vatican II involved separating these two books.

Thurible

See "Censer."

Liturgical Vesture

Alb

A long, loose-fitting tunic worn under other vestments, common to all ministers in worship. Adaptation of fourth-century Greek and Roman undertunic. Symbolizes the garment of the newly baptized, also the purity of soul required for Mass, also the garment in which Pilate clothed Christ.

Amice

A white linen square worn over the neck and shoulders under the alb; formerly used as a cape to cover the priest's head

Biretta (no longer in common use)

A square hat with three ridges or peaks worn mainly by principal ministers on the way to and from the altar. In its place, religious cover their heads with an amice and a hood.

Cassock

A full length, fitted robe for ordinary use, either black (priest), purple (bishop), red (cardinal), or white (pope)

Chasuble

The external garment worn by the presider at the Eucharist, with a stole worn over it (or, depending on style, under it); sometimes designed so that the chasuble serves the purpose of both vestments

Cincture

A cord used to belt the alb

Cope

A long cloak with a fastening in front, worn on solemn occasions and for specified ceremonies (for example, Eucharistic benediction) outside of Mass

Dalmatic

A sleeved outer garment, fashioned after the chasuble, worn by a deacon in place of a chasuble; patterned on the royal vest of Dalmatia, once worn by kings at solemnities like coronations

Humeral veil (Latin: *humerus,* shoulder)
A wide scarf worn over the shoulders for carrying the sacred vessels or the Blessed Sacrament

Maniple (no longer in common use)
An ornamental strip of cloth pinned or tied to the left forearm signifying authority; formerly a handkerchief worn on or carried in the left hand

Orphrey (Latin: *aurum,* gold; from the ancient country of Phrygian)
The painted or embroidered images or symbols on a chasuble, front and back, and around a cope's opening

Pallium
This is a vestment signifying the fullness of the bishop's office, so is worn only by the pope and metropolitan archbishops. (See "Insignia" in Chapter 4.)

Stole
A sign of priestly office, worn in the celebration of sacraments; a narrow strip of cloth of a liturgical color worn over the shoulders; on a deacon, worn over the right shoulder and crossing to the left side of the body

Surplice
A vestment of white linen with wide sleeves worn over a cassock, often used by ministers other than the presider; sometimes worn by a priest for the administration of the sacraments

Liturgical colors

Black: death, mourning, despair. May be used for Masses for the dead (as well as violet and white).

Blue: not an approved liturgical color (See *Violet* below.)

Green: hope, growth, increase, life, immortality, fidelity. Used on Sundays in Ordinary Time.

Red: sacrifice (blood, life itself), charity, zeal, Holy Spirit. Used on commemorations of our Lord's passion (Passion Sunday, Good Friday), the apostles, evangelists, and martyrs for the faith; Pentecost.

Rose: subdued joy, relieved repentance. May be used on Gaudete Sunday (Third Sunday of Advent) and Laetare Sunday (Fourth Sunday of Lent).

Violet: sorrow, penitence, preparation. Used during the Seasons of Advent and Lent. Often called purple, it has a variety of shades ranging from blue-violet to red-violet. Whereas the traditional "Roman purple" is actually a red-purple, a more blue-purple has prevailed in other parts of Europe. Some have taken advantage of this hue variation to differentiate between Lent (red-purple shades) and Advent (blue-violet).

White: innocence, purity, virginity, victory, joy. Used on all occasions of the joyful and glorious mysteries of our Lord (like Christmas and Easter), of Mary (like the Assumption), of angels, and of saints who were not martyrs; traditionally worn on celebrations honoring John the Baptist, the Chair of Peter, and the Conversion of St. Paul. It may be used for funerals.

Liturgical Gestures and Postures

Sign of the Cross

Externalizing the faith of anything done in the name of the Lord; blessing oneself or marking another in Baptism, Confirmation, or Anointing, for example

Benediction

- The Latin form: Thumb and first two fingers extended, last two fingers closed; representing the Trinity: the strong thumb, the Father; the long middle finger, the Son; and the first finger, the Holy Spirit, proceeding from the Father and the Son

- The Greek form: First finger extended, second finger curved, thumb and third finger crossed, fourth finger curved, thus forming Greek letters ICXC, the first and last letters in Greek of Jesus and Christ

Bowing

Profound (from the waist) or simple (a reverent nod)

Folded hands

Traditional prayer posture (Arms folded, palms inward, is a fuller sign of prayerfulness, attentiveness to the divine presence, and of humility.)

Pretzels

This snack food, some say, originated as a Lenten snack; it is shaped like arms crossed in prayer. According to one derivation, that is where the word *pretzel* comes from: a Latin word meaning branched, with little arms. That makes the shape as well as the food itself right for Lent, a time of fasting and spiritual renewal.

Another explanation says the word comes from a Latin word for "little reward." That's what the snack was called because of the legend of a seventh-century monk who made them and gave them as little rewards to children for learning their prayers. The monk took a strip of bread dough that was left over, twisted it into the shape of arms folded in prayer, and baked it. As a nice *pretzel*.

Genuflection

Bending the right knee to touch the floor as an act of worship. Since a 1973 instruction, this "single" genuflection before the Blessed Sacrament, whether reserved or exposed, is called for, and not a double (both knees) that formerly was used formerly when the Blessed Sacrament was enthroned in the monstrance.

Invocation

The extended arms, with palms down, signify blessing, invoking the Spirit

Kneeling

In the strict sense, the posture of repentance and private adoration

Orans

Open hands, palms up. In Exodus 17:8–16 there is a classic illustration of the orans of Moses, during the battle with Amalek at Rephidim: "Whenever Moses held up his hand, Israel prevailed. . . . But Moses' hands grew weary; so . . . Aaron and Hur held up his hands. . . ."

Prostration

To lie face down (not supine). Its two most common uses are on Good Friday (by the presider) and at ordinations (by candidates for orders). Kneeling on both knees with head bowed is a form of prostration.

Sitting

Passive posture of reflection and receptivity

Standing

Active posture of receptivity, respect, witness, and readiness for mission

The Sacraments of Healing

The Sacrament of Penance

Names for the Sacrament of Penance and Reconciliation

In its article on this sacrament (#1422f), the *Catechism of the Catholic Church* uses both of these terms and then mentions and explains a few more (#s 1423–1424).

1. Sacrament of conversion

2. Sacrament of penance

3. Sacrament of confession

4. Sacrament of forgiveness

5. Sacrament of reconciliation

Reconciliation and Healing

Forli, Italy, was once part of the Papal States and governed by the pope. A man named Peregrine, born around 1265, grew up there and was active in an anti-papal, opposition party. The prior general of the Servants of Mary, Philip Benizi (now canonized), was sent to preach reconciliation in Forli. Peregrine obstructed him, heckled him. His political fervor even brought him to strike Philip—an action that became a turning point.

Peregrine changed. His dynamic energies began to be channeled in another direction. Philip's preaching had provoked attraction as well as reaction: Peregrine himself eventually entered the Servants of Mary at about the age of thirty, pronouncing his vows in the Servite priory in Siena, Italy. Peregrine's transformed zeal took him back to Forli where he was to live out his life. His fervor that had been so intense politically was no less so spiritually. He became a special advocate of those who were sick, poor, and on the edge of society. He assumed special penances, one of them—standing whenever it was not necessary to sit—led to varicose veins.

His condition worsened, becoming an open, running sore, which was diagnosed as cancer. The wound became so extreme, odorous, and painful as to require amputation. This was another turning point for Peregrine. He was sixty. The one who had seen ugliness and suffering and had served and supported others now faced the ugliness and suffering in himself. The healer was wounded, and the servant needed to be served. He went to the faith he had preached to others, and the goodness of God he had administered so long. The night before the surgery, in the priory chapel room, he prayed before the image of the Crucified. In the prayer-filled sleep that followed, he envisioned his crucified Lord descending the cross and touching his cancerous leg. Upon awakening, he discovered his wound healed.

The reputation of this beloved holy man grew as the years passed. Twenty years later, on May 1, 1345, he died at age eighty. He was canonized in 1726 and is universally invoked as the patron of cancer victims. (The National Shrine of St. Peregrine is in Chicago at Our Lady of Sorrows Basilica.)

The Four Traditional Parts of Reconciliation

The *Catechism of the Catholic Church* teaches that the sacrament's two essential elements are the human part (through the action of the Holy Spirit; numbers one, two, and four below) and God's action (through the intervention of the Church; number three below).

1. Contrition: internal attitude of sorrow and repentance.
2. Confession: clear telling of sin for which absolution is requested.
3. Absolution: emphasizing the healing power of Jesus.
4. Satisfaction: penance, reform of life, amends.

> ## Going to the Table, Not Confession
> The penitential rite of the Mass is not to be confused with the Sacrament of Reconciliation. Lacking sacramental absolution, it is an understated, preparatory, and optional rite, to help the assembly reflect on its spiritual condition and praise God for his mercy. At times, a sprinkling rite may replace it, recalling the waters of Baptism as well as the tears of repentance.

The Movement of Return to God (See CCC #s 1430–1432.)

Called *interior conversion* and *repentance,* it comes with a beneficial pain and sadness traditionally called *affliction of spirit* and *compunction* (repentance of heart). Repentance (also called *contrition*) is "perfect" when it arises from love for God, "imperfect" if it is founded on other motives. Repentance is:

1. A work of God's grace
2. A discovery of the great love of God
3. Sorrow for sins
4. A fear of offending and being separated from God

Major Forms of Penance in Christian Life

The *Catechism of the Catholic Church* mentions many (#s 1434–1439), emphasizing the first.

1. Fasting, prayer, and almsgiving, first of all
2. Efforts at reconciliation with one's neighbor
3. Tears of repentance
4. Concern for the salvation of one's neighbor
5. The intercession of the saints
6. Practicing charity "which covers a multitude of sins"
7. Concern for those who are poor
8. Exercising and defending justice and right
9. Admitting faults to others
10. Loving correction
11. Amendment of life
12. Examination of conscience
13. Spiritual direction
14. Acceptance of suffering
15. Endurance of persecution for holiness sake
16. Taking up one's cross daily and following Jesus
17. The Eucharist

18. Reading Sacred Scripture

19. Praying the Liturgy of the Hours and the Lord's Prayer

20. Every sincere act of worship or devotion

21. Using the season and days of penance in the course of the liturgical year

22. Pilgrimages

The Effects of the Sacrament of Penance (See CCC #1496.)

1. Reconciliation with God by which grace is recovered

2. Reconciliation with the Church

3. Remission of the eternal punishment that comes with mortal sin

4. Remission, at least partially, of sins' temporal punishment

5. Peace and serenity of conscience, and spiritual consolation

6. Strength of spirit for the Christian battle

The Three Elements of Contrition

1. In the mind: hatred of the sin

2. In the heart: grief

3. In the will: firm purpose of amendment

The Four Qualities of Genuine Contrition

1. Internal

2. Supernatural

3. Universal (extending to all sins)

4. Sovereign (recognition of sin as the greatest evil)

Sacramental Seal

The obligation of secrecy enjoined on the minister of reconciliation; sometimes called the *seal of confession*

Under the Rose

Sub rosa, some would say. In any language it means "in strictest confidence." Beginning in the sixteenth century, the rose was occasionally enshrined over a confessional to symbolize the sacramental seal. Its origin is obscure. It may refer to the myth of Cupid bribing Harpocrates (the god of silence) with a rose so that he would not reveal the amorous activities of Venus, the goddess of sensual love (and well known for practicing what she preached). Likewise, a rose over a dining room table means that anything spoken around the table is to remain in the room.

Outline of the Rite of Penance

Form 1	Form 2	Form 3
Reconciliation of Individual Penitents	*Reconciliation of Several Penitents with Individual Confession and Absolution*	*Reconciliation of Several Penitents with General Confession and Absolution*
Introductory Rite	**Introductory Rite**	**Introductory Rite**
1. Greeting	1. Hymn/antiphon/psalm	1. Hymn/antiphon/psalm
2. Sign of the Cross	2. Dialogue salutation— priest/assembly	2. Dialogue salutation— priest/assembly
3. Priest draws penitent to faith and trust in God's healing mercy and welcomes the penitent.	3. Oration by priest: exhortation, statement of purpose	3. Opening prayer: exhortation, invitation, silence, prayer
	4. Opening prayer: invitation to pray, silent moments, prayer	
Celebration of the Word	**Celebration of the Word**	**Celebration of the Word**
4. Recommended: Priest offers text with announcement of God's mercy and call to conversion.	5. One text (gospel— obligatory) or several (first reading, responsorial psalm, possibly a second reading, gospel acclamation, gospel)	4. One text (gospel— obligatory) or several, response, and/or silence
	6. Homily	5. *Monitio* (homily and examen) drawing out confession of sinfulness
Reconciliation Rite	**Reconciliation Rite**	**Reconciliation Rite**
5. Confession and possible advice from priest; suggested penance	7. Examination of conscience	6. Sign of penance
6. Prayer of penitent in which sorrow is expressed	8. General confession of sin	7. General confession (some sign by those desiring to receive, Confiteor)
7. Absolution, with gesture of imposed hands	9. Litany or hymn	8. Litany or song
	10. Lord's Prayer	9. Lord's Prayer
	11. Individual confession	10. General absolution*
	12. Individual penance assigned	
	13. Individual absolution	
Concluding Rite	**Concluding Rite**	**Concluding Rite**
8. Praise of God in dialogue with priest	14. Proclamation praising God's mercy (hymn, antiphon, psalm, or prayer by priest)	11. Song or hymn: proclamation of God's mercy
9. Dismissal of penitent: prayer of proclamation	15. Concluding prayer of thanksgiving	12. Blessing of all
	16. Blessing	13. Dismissal
	17. Dismissal dialogue, priest/assembly	

* General absolution may be given only in restricted circumstances as described in the Rite of Penance and determined by the National Conference of Bishops: (1) Danger of death. (2) Number of penitents: insufficient number of confessors to hear individual confessions properly within a suitable period of time, requiring penitents (through no fault of their own) to go without sacramental grace or Holy Communion for a long time.

Censures

Each is surrounded by technicality and can take many forms.

Interdict (on a place or its inhabitants)

Withholds certain privileges from the faithful who remain, nevertheless, in communion with the Church. Examples of privileges withheld by interdict are attendance at liturgical services, Christian burial, some of the sacraments. The bishop of LaCrosse, Wisconsin, imposed an interdict in 1975 on those who followed the false apparitions at Necedah.

Excommunication (*anathema*, if formal)

Affects generally one's ability to receive the sacraments, notably Eucharist; it pertains to one's relationship to the communion of the faithful and depends on such factors as public obstinacy. It may be remitted by the pope, bishop, or in certain cases, even by a priest confessor.

Vitandus

The most severe form of excommunication: public, by name, by the Holy See; literally, "to be avoided"—shunned ("except in the case of husband and wife, parents, children . . ."). A remedial measure reflecting Paul's mandates to the early Christian community (2 Thessalonians 3:6, 14–15).

Abortion and excommunication

"A person who actually procures an abortion incurs an automatic (*latae sententiae*) excommunication." So says the *Code of Canon Law*, practically repeating the former (1917) code. This excommunication can be remitted by the local bishop. (Confessors have been delegated by many bishops to absolve from this penalty—at least in the case of a first abortion.) This penalty:

1. Includes accomplices without whom abortion would not have happened.
2. Presumes other requirements of the law are present:
   - The abortion was intended and successful.
   - There is knowledge of this penalty attached to the law.
   - The individual is of majority age (at least eighteen).
   - The person has the full use of reason.
   - There is full consent (one is not acting out of serious fear).

The Anointing of the Sick

The Elements of the Anointing of the Sick (See James 5:14, CCC #1519.)

1. The priest of the Church
2. The laying on of hands in silence
3. The prayer in faith of the Church
4. The anointing with oil (blessed by the bishop)

The Effects of the Anointing of the Sick (See James 5:14, CCC #1532.)

1. Joins the sick person to the passion of Christ

2. Gives power, peace, and the courage to endure suffering

3. Forgives sins

4. Restores health (if conducive to the soul's salvation)

5. Prepares for the passage to eternal life

The Recipient of the Anointing of the Sick

1. Those whose health is seriously impaired by sickness or old age

2. Those about to undergo surgery because of a serious illness

3. Those who are elderly and weakened by age, even if there is no serious illness

4. Sick children who are mature enough to be comforted by it

Snakes and Healing

A single snake wound about a staff is the symbol of Asclepias, the ancient Greek god of medicine (the Roman version being Aesculapius). Serpents were sacred to Asclepias, maybe because of the superstition that they are able to renew their youth by a change of their skin. Since 291 B.C. there was a temple dedicated to Asclepias on the Tiber Island in Rome. In the Christian era, there was a church built on the same island, in honor of St. Bartholomew, to which healing hostelries were annexed, thus illustrating the mutual relationship of the ministry and the profession.

The caduceus, often confused with the medical symbol, is another symbol, similar but definitely distinct. Twin snakes intertwined on a winged staff, it is the symbol of Mercury, messenger of the gods and god of merchants. (He got it from Apollo in exchange for the famous lyre Apollo made out of a shell.)

Others, putting all this serpentine mythology aside, prefer to believe that the snake-on-a-stick symbol derives from the biblical story in Numbers 21. The Lord directed Moses to make a poisonous snake and mount it on a pole. Moses made a bronze snake and raised it up. The repentant Israelites, dying from snakebites, were healed with just one look. Either way, the snake-encircled-staff is one thing, and the caduceus is something else again.

The Sacraments of Mission

The Sacrament of Marriage

The Elements of a Marriage Bond (See CCC #s 1621–1632.)

1. A baptized man and woman

2. The freedom to enter marriage
   • Not being under constraint
   • Not impeded by any natural or Church law

3. Public ratification (expression of consent). The presiding priest or deacon, in the name of the Church, receives the consent and gives the blessing. The Church requires that the faithful marry according to the ecclesiastical form because the ecclesial dimension of marriage is visibly expressed by the presence of the Church's minister (and the witnesses). The consent includes these essential intentions:
   • Unity (the intention of an exclusive love)
   • Indissolubility (the intention of a permanent love)
   • Openness to fertility (the intention of a love open to children)

4. Sexual consummation

The Exchange of Rings

1. Symbolizes fidelity and permanence

2. Follows the declaration of marriage and does not precede it

The Grace of Marriage (See CCC #1641.)

1. Perfects the spouses love for one another

2. Strengthens the spouses unbreakable unity

3. Sanctifies the spouses on their way to eternal life

Banns (Anglo-Saxon: *bannan,* to summon; later: to proclaim)

It is an ancient custom to publicize a marriage in the parishes of the marrying party for the purpose of discovering any impediments to the marriage. Anyone with such knowledge is conscience bound to reveal it to the pastor. Originally it was done after the second reading.

Marriage as Metaphor (Revelation 19:7, 21:1–22:5; Hosea 1–3; Jeremiah 2:2)

The Covenant is a marriage (Hosea 2:16–22; Isaiah 54:4–10, 62:5).

Idolatry (sinning) is adultery (Hosea 2:4–15; Ezekiel 16:15–63, 23:1–21).

Christ is the bridegroom (Matthew 9:15, 25:1–13; John 3:29).

The Church is the bride (2 Corinthians 11:2; Ephesians 5:22–33).

Mothers' Patrons

St. Monica is the celebrated patron of mothers, given her experience with the wayward-son-become-saint, Augustine. Anne, mother of the mother of the Savior, is another natural as a mother's patron, as is Elizabeth, mother of John the Baptist. There are other saints who are also mothers of saints, though less well known: Blanche, mother of Louis; Bridget, mother of Catherine of Sweden; Emilia, mother of Basil the Great; Margaret of Scotland, mother of David; Philippa, mother of Theodore; and Sylvia, mother of Gregory the Great. Finally, Sophia (Wisdom) is the mother of Charity, Faith, and Hope.

Recognizing an Unsacramental Marriage

Death ends a sacramental marriage. Divorce ends a marriage legally or civilly. The following are three ways the Church recognizes that a marriage is unsacramental (some of which, in the case of declarations of nullity, for example, had been presumed at the time of celebration to be sacramental).

1. By dissolution (a privilege of the faith)
   - Pauline (unbaptized parties; see 1 Corinthians 7:12–16)
   - Petrine ("privilege of the faith" of the one baptized party)

2. By declaration of nullity (annulment), a process of the Church
   - Lack of freedom
   - Intention against permanence or fidelity or children
   - Inadequate mental competence

3. By decree (a declaration of lack of form)
   - A civil marriage of a Catholic without dispensation
   - A non-Catholic wedding of a Catholic without dispensation

The Sacrament of Holy Orders

Priesthood

1. The one priesthood of Christ
2. The two participations
   - Baptismal priesthood
   - Ministerial priesthood (bishops, priests, and deacons)

The Three Degrees of Ministerial Priesthood

1. Bishops (the episcopate, the fullness of holy orders). See chapter 4 on the episcopacy and the kinds of bishops.

2. Priests (the presbyterate, co-workers of the bishops). In most cases, only deacons who are unmarried may be ordained priests. Traditionally, a distinction is made between (1) secular priests, that is, those living in daily contact with the world, notably diocesan priests, sharing/assisting the bishop's pastoring of a diocese, promising celibacy (single for the Lord) and obedience to the bishop, and (2) religious (order) priests, those living out the three vows in monastic and/or community life.

3. Deacons (the diaconate, in order to serve). A candidate for the diaconate must be thirty-five years old and may be married (however, once ordained he may not remarry if his wife dies).

The Essential Rite of the Sacrament of Holy Orders

These two elements are preceded by the calling and presentation of the candidate, the election by the bishop and consent of the people, the instruction and examination of the candidate, the promise of obedience, the invitation to prayer, and the Litany of the Saints (candidate is prostrate). They are followed by the investiture with stole and chasuble, the anointing of hands, the presentation of gifts, and the sign of peace.

1. The bishop's imposition of hands on the head of the ordinand

2. The prayer of consecration asking for and conferring the outpouring of the Holy Spirit

The ways ordained priests exercise their service (See CCC #1592.)

1. By teaching

2. By divine worship

3. By pastoral governance

Minor Orders (formerly)

These were stages of preparation for priestly ministry following upon tonsure (initiation into clerical state). Suppressed in 1972, they are today largely unused or integrated and exercised within normal Church life and ministry in the broad sense. (The subdeacon functioned liturgically, in part, the way a lector does today; it was considered a major order in the West.)

1. Porter (doorkeeper): A symbolic office, though functional in the early Church

2. Lector: Now the liturgical ministry of proclaiming the word of God, except the gospel, during Mass; a distinction is made regarding those men who officially receive this ministry as they prepare for the diaconate or priesthood.

3. Exorcist: An exorcism is the expulsion of evil spirits; this power, never confined to any particular order, originally included the right to lay hands on a possessed person and to exorcize catechumens

4. Acolyte: The liturgical ministry of the altar server at Mass, but distinguished when it is received as a ministry that leads eventually to the diaconate or priesthood.

A Clerical Haircut

In the fifth–sixth century when it originated, there was a priestly practice called *tonsure* that involved a shaving of the head, or part of it, symbolic of the crown of thorns. More recently and with secular clergy, only a token clip has been retained, with no literal tonsure worn after the ordination. Historically among "regular clergy" (religious), this took as many forms and symbolisms as religious garb took. A classic example is the former Dominican practice of shaving the whole crown above the top of the ears. In 1972, tonsure was discontinued and, instead, "entrance into the clerical state" has been joined with the diaconate.

Garb

1. Clerical dress (uniforms): worn for work
2. Liturgical dress (vestments): worn during liturgy
3. Religious dress (habits): worn after postulancy (upon entrance into the novitiate)

The Roman collar

In the early Church, priests wore contemporary dress, just as did the Lord, who dressed in a common way, not a distinctive way. In the year 313, the Edict of Milan put the Church and priests in a different posture in society. Marks of distinction and signs of respect began to arise, although most changes were more liturgical than public. It was in the Middle Ages, and among religious, not secular clerics, that distinctive dress definitively evolved. Over time, the full-length work apron of the Benedictines, for example, became the black "scapular" that distinguished this religious community. Mendicant orders too, like the Franciscans and Dominicans, adopted a comparable habit.

Some form of clerical dress among some secular priests probably arose in the eighth century with a directive to them suggesting a distinctly religious mode of dress. Some say that the Roman collar evolved from this. Others say it has a military origin. Still others explain that diocesan clergy, unlike religious, had no uniform habit but only street clothes. It was the common cloak that evolved into a cassock, and the Roman collar from this (or under it): When high, detachable collars on shirts became the fashion for men, secular priests followed suit, except that they reversed the collar so the opening ended up in back and a white band in front. Under the upturned collar of the cloak-become-cassock, this white band became a Roman collar. There is mention of a collar by the Second Council of Nicaea (787), which explains its symbolism in terms of poverty. To this, the Council of Trent (1545) added the symbolism of dignity. In 1931 the symbolic meaning of protection was added in the decrees of one of the sacred congregations.

Titles

For those in the universal hierarchy (pope, cardinal, archbishop, patriarch, primate). The phrase *Dei gratia* (Latin: by the grace of God), sometimes following a title, expresses the divine vocation.

Abbot/abbess (Aramaic: *abba,* father; Latin: *abbat/abbas,* father/mother)

A monastic superior, fixed as a title by St. Benedict; elected, usually for life, by the secret ballot of the community; has paternal/maternal authority within the monastery, and also in case of an abbot quasi-episcopal authority in the Church because of the territorial jurisdiction. Insignia are pectoral cross and ring; as a bishop, has priority over a prior, whose priory is within the jurisdiction (the territory) of the abbey.

Bishop (Greek: *episkopos,* overseer)

An ordained man exercising the fullest degree of ministerial priesthood (see "Bishop" in Chapter 4).

Celebrant

An ordained minister officiating (although the word *presider* is used by some today, since the whole assembly, not only the presider, is celebrating).

Chaplain (Latin: *cappella,* cloak)

A minister with the pastoral care of a group other than a parish. The cloak that is at the root of this word refers to the cloak of St. Martin, and its guardian. (See the story in Chapter 4.)

Cleric (clergyman) (Greek: *kleros,* portion; see Deuteronomy 18:2; Acts 1:17.)

An ordained minister: In 1 Peter 5:2, the elders are told to "tend the flock . . . as God would have you do. . . ."

Curate (Latin: *cura,* care; French: *cure,* curator, overseer)

One with the care (*cura*) of souls, especially a parish priest (as St. John Vianney, "The Curé of Ars"). Often used for a pastor's assistant or associate.

Deacon (Greek: *diakonos,* servant)

An ordained man in the partial exercise of Holy Orders.

Dom (Latin: *dominus,* master, lord)

A title used by religious of Benedictine, Carthusian, and Cistercian Orders; originally applied to popes, later to bishops, then to monks.

Father (Spanish: *padre*)

A title given to priests that emphasizes both the life-giving power of the gospel as well as faith-family relationships. Paul was "like a father" to the Christian communities: "For though you might have ten thousand guardians in Christ, you do not have many fathers. Indeed, in Christ Jesus I became your father through the gospel" (1 Corinthians 4:15); "I am appealing to you for my child, Onesimus, whose father I have become during my imprisonment" (Philemon 10, an appeal for Onesimus, Philemon's runaway slave whom Paul converted to the Christian faith).

Man of the cloth

Cloth refers to vestments, the distinctive dress expressive of the office; formerly, "the cloth" designated the distinctive garb of any trade, then more specifically, around the seventeenth century, the clergy's cloth.

Minister (Latin: *mini,* little)

A person in the service of Christ and the Church with a title that emphasizes service ("doer of little things") and not status, like a magister (Latin: *magi*) which suggests triumphalism ("doer of great things").

Monsignor

A title of honor, derived from the Italian word for "my lord." The title originated in feudal Europe when clergy designated with this courtly title of distinction were considered to be connected in some way with the papal household. It is still a practice in some dioceses for a bishop to recommend and the pope to approve this designation for certain diocesan clergy. (Technically, either prothonotary apostolic, domestic prelate, or papal chamberlain.)

Parson (Middle English: *persone,* person; Latin: *persona,* mask)

Today referring mainly to Anglican ministers, the word's roots emphasize identity (*alter Christus,* other Christ); pre-Reformation meaning is "person of the Church" (*persona Ecclesiae*), a priest in charge of a parish.

Parochial vicar

Associate pastor, assistant pastor, and curate are the equivalent terms used in English-speaking countries for this term now used in the *Code of Canon Law,* which no longer distinguishes between various types of "vicars" as it did in the past (see canons 545–552).

Pastor (Latin: shepherd)

An ordained servant-leader of a parish; a favorite term in the early Church.

Preacher (Latin: *praedicare,* to speak before)

A minister of the word of God.

Prelate (Latin: *praelatus,* carried before)

A term technically designating "one promoted" or ranking above, in an office with jurisdiction over other clergy, which would include especially cardinals and bishops; by association, other more historically ephemeral positions of honor (monsignors).

Presbyter (Greek: *presbyteros,* elder)

An ordained priest.

Priest (English: corruption of the word *presbyter*)

An ordained minister of word and sacrament, and a common term among Catholics, the Orthodox, and Episcopalians.

Prior (Latin: *prior,* former, first, superior)

A superior in a monastery that, usually, is a dependency of an abbey, hence "prior simplex."

Provincial

A superior of an order's monastic houses in a province.

Rector

Popularly, a pastor: the chief clergyman of a parish (hence, "rectory" as a parish's office building/pastor's residence); common with the Episcopal Church. Technically, the head of a religious community of men or of an educational institution. Canonically, the priest in charge of a church that is not (only) parochial (for example, a cathedral).

Reverend (Latin: *reverentia,* respect)

A term of respect, having the same root as reverent, revered, and reverence (the virtue that honors those with dignity); a title for clergy.

Right Reverend/Very Reverend

This use of the adjective "right" has the archaic meaning of "in great degree" or "extremely"; it is sometimes used in reference to bishops and monsignors; Very Reverend often designates abbots.

Superior

A generic term, often synonymous with abbot or prior; one in authority in a religious order.

Vicar (Latin: in place of)

A clergyman who serves in the place of or as a representative of another.

The Four Forms of Reverence
(corresponding to the four forms of dignity)

1. Familial reverence (toward parents or those taking their place)
2. Civil reverence (toward civil authorities)
3. Ecclesiastical reverence (toward those in the service of the Church)
4. Religious reverence (toward any person, place, or thing related to God)

A Clerical Glossary

Celebret (Latin: Let him celebrate.)

A document stating that a person is a priest in good standing and requesting that he be permitted to celebrate the Eucharist; requiring the signature of his bishop (or superior).

Excardination

Release of a priest from the jurisdiction of one bishop to another (who would "incardinate" him).

Exeat (Latin: Let him go forth.)

Official permission for a priest to leave his diocese or a monk his monastery.

Faculties

Practically, the right granted by an ordinary (bishop) to a priest for administering the Sacrament of Reconciliation; technically, the rights granted by the pope to ordinaries, and ordinaries to priests, enabling the exercise of the ministry for the sake of the faithful in their care.

Sinecure (Latin: *sine cura*, without cure/care)

A position (and salary), a benefice, without pastoral responsibility (the care for souls).

The Liturgy of the Hours

The Church's full cycle of daily prayer, opened with the *Venite Exsultemus* (Psalm 95). The fulfillment of the obligation to pray at stated times: in the morning, in the evening, and before retiring. Called the *Divine Office* (sacred duty), it was updated by Vatican II and published as *The Liturgy of the Hours* in 1971. The book used for its celebration was called the *Breviary*. It is referred to as the *opus Dei* (Latin: work of God) by the Benedictines.

The *Catechism of the Catholic Church* teaches (#1175) that the Liturgy of the Hours is intended to become the prayer of the whole people of God and encourages the common celebration of the principal hours, like vespers (evening prayer), in common on Sundays and the more solemn feasts. This prayer ministry is to include all the baptized, either with priests, among themselves, or even individually.

Obligation

Although the ordained as well as certain religious communities have been obliged, historically, to celebrate this liturgy, the exhortation to pray the Liturgy of the Hours belongs to the whole Church (CCC #1175). (The Little Office of the Blessed Virgin Mary, introduced by St. Peter Damian in the eleventh century, is a version of the hours traditionally used by many religious communities and members of sodalities.)

Formerly

Traditionally, there were seven canonical hours ("Seven times a day I praise you," Psalm 119:164), chanted in monastic communities. With much variation, the pattern was seven daytime offices and the night office:

1. Lauds (Latin: praise, from Psalms 148–150)
2. Prime ("first" hour: 6 A.M.)
3. Terce ("third" hour: 9 A.M.)
4. Sext ("sixth" hour: noon)
5. None ("ninth" hour: 3 P.M.)
6. Vespers ("evening," hence the medieval English term *evensong*)
7. Compline (from *completorium*, "completing" day's services)
8. Matins (French: morning; for the early hours, after midnight)

Currently

Morning and Evening Prayer are restored as the most important "hinges" of each day's office. The Office of Readings is not an hour (time) in the sense the other hours are, but two readings: one biblical and one patristic (from the fathers) or hagiographical (of the saints). Daytime Prayer consolidates the little hours of Prime, Terce, Sext, and None for those not saying the Office in choir (depending on the time one has, the choice is of midmorning, midday, or mid-afternoon).

First hour: Office of Readings (corresponding to ancient Matins)

Second Hour: Morning Prayer (Lauds)

Third Hour: Daytime Prayer (Middle Hour)

Fourth Hour: Evening Prayer (Vespers)

Fifth Hour: Night Prayer

Elements of the Liturgy of the Hours

Morning Prayer	Daytime Prayer	Evening Prayer	Night Prayer
Introduction (Invitatory)	Introduction	Introduction	Introduction
Verse	Verse	Verse	Verse
Antiphon	Doxology	Doxology	Doxology
Psalm 95	Alleluia	Alleluia	Alleluia
			Examination of Conscience — Penitential Prayer
Hymn	Hymn	Hymn	Hymn
Psalmody	Psalmody	Psalmody	Psalmody
Psalm	Psalm	Psalm	
Old Testament Canticle	Psalm	Psalm	
Psalm	Psalm	New Testament Canticle	
Reading	Reading	Reading	Reading
— pause for reflection	— pause for reflection	— pause for reflection	— pause for reflection
Responsory	Responsory	Responsory	Responsory
Gospel Canticle		Gospel Canticle	Gospel Canticle
— of Zechariah		— of Mary	— of Simeon
Intercessions		Intercessions	
Lord's Prayer		Lord's Prayer	
Final Prayer	Final Prayer	Final Prayer	Final Prayer
— Trinitarian ending	— simple ending	— Trinitarian ending	— simple ending
Conclusion	Conclusion	Conclusion	Conclusion
			Marian Antiphon

Sacramentals

Sacred signs that "extend and radiate the sacraments," signifying the mostly spiritual effects obtained through the Church's intercession and disposing a person to the grace of the sacraments.

The Purpose of Sacramentals

The sanctification of:

1. Certain ministries of the Church
2. Certain states of life
3. A great variety of circumstances of Christian life
4. The use of many helpful things

The Elements of a Sacramental

1. There is always a prayer (see CCC #1672).
   - Blessings (of persons, meals, objects, and places) first of all: Some with a lasting importance, like consecrations of persons (like abbots/abbesses, professed religious, and liturgical ministers), places (like churches and shrines), and things (like altars, oils, vessels, and vestments).
   - Exorcisms (see CCC #1673): Public, authoritative requests in Jesus' name that a person or object be protected against and/or withdrawn from the dominion of the power of the evil one.
2. There is often a specific sign like
   - Laying on of hands
   - Sign of the cross
   - Sprinkling of holy water

Expressions of Piety

In its article on sacramentals, the *Catechism of the Catholic Church* recognizes what it calls "expressions of piety" that surround the Church's sacramental life in which "the religious sense of the Christian people" has found expression (#s 1674–1676).

The Catechism mentions veneration of relics, visits to sanctuaries, pilgrimages, processions, the stations of the cross, religious dances, the rosary, and medals. There is something about most of these elsewhere in this book. To that list we add the following sacramentals.

Holy Oils (O.S., *Olea Sancta*)

Used in the sacraments which impart a sacramental character (Baptism, Confirmation, and Holy Orders), in the Sacrament of Healing (Anointing of the Sick), and in the blessing of various objects. In 1970 it was allowed that, if necessary, holy oils may be from any plant, not only from olives. The blessing of oils has traditionally been done on Holy Thursday by a bishop at a cathedral. The supply distributed to local churches is kept in the ambry, and the unused portion, a year later, burned in the sanctuary lamp.

Chrism (S.C., *Sacrum Chrisma*)

Used in Baptism, Confirmation, and Holy Orders, as well as blessing tower bells and baptismal water and for consecrating churches, altars, chalices, and patens. Only chrism among the holy oils includes balsam, or balm, giving it an unmistakable fragrance, alluding to Paul's "odor of life" or "aroma of holiness" metaphor in 2 Corinthians 2:15–16.

Oil of Catechumens (O.C., *Oleum Catechumenorum*)

Also known as the oil of the saints (O.S., *Oleum Sanctorum*), it's used during the prayer of exorcism and anointing when a catechumen is initiated, whence the name.

Oil of the Sick (O.I., *Oleum Infirmorum*)

Used in the Anointing of the Sick.

St. Aidan's Cruse of Oil

In his eighth-century *Ecclesiastical History*, the Venerable Bede relates that St. Aidan entrusted a cruse of oil to a young priest who was to escort a maiden to King Oswin for his wedding. In case of troubled waters, the oil was to be used for calm. A storm did arise, and Aidan's oil reduced the trauma.

Bells

In addition to a simple blessing, there is a solemn ceremony done by a bishop in which church bells are washed with holy water, anointed with holy oils inside and out, and prayed over, so that at the sound of these bells, evil spirits may be put to flight and God's people summoned to prayer.

A single swinging bell

Traditionally called people to church. Pulled by a bell rope, the pivoted bell swings, causing the clapper inside to strike. As the bell swings toward and then away, tone and volume change, creating the familiar ding–dong. The church bell has been traditionally rung at dawn, noon, and evening. In some places it was more than a "church-going bell"; it originally rang as an "*Ave* bell," inviting worshipers to prepare to pray with a Marian prayer. In another era, there were also local customs like ringing the church bell during the elevation at Mass, inviting people through the countryside to join the prayer.

Pealing bells

Two or more swinging bells, synonymous with celebration, produce a random, beautiful sound, given the difference in speed and sound between lighter and heavier bells (as in the famous and beautiful St. Anne de Beaupre three-bell Angelus).

A tolling bell

A stationary bell struck by a heavy clapper produces a stately, solemn sound, as for funerals. The *De Profundis*, the methodical, solemn toll of the bourdon bell (the bell of lowest pitch in a carillon) marked the end of the day at 9:00 P.M., the traditional occasion of the common community night prayer for the faithful departed. (See "Passing bell" and "Soul bell.") The Angelus bell consists of three strokes, each followed by a pause, then nine peals while the Angelus prayer is being finished.

A hand bell

The "Sanctus bell" (also known as a *sance*, or *sacring bell*), traditionally rung during the Mass in some places, is a practice which began in the sixth century. It was rung at the *Sanctus*, before the consecration (at the *hanc igitur*), at the institution (three times each at the elevation of the consecrated Bread and Wine), three times before the priest's Communion (*Domine, non sum dignus*), and in some places again three times before the assembly's Communion. This bell was silenced from the Gloria of Holy Thursday until the Gloria of the Easter Vigil, and a wooden clapper was used instead. (A "sick–call bell" rung in the home announces the presence of the Eucharist and the service of a priest.)

Slavic Bells

There is an ancient custom in Slavic countries like Russia, the Ukraine, and Poland to ring the church bells, with short respites, throughout the day on Easter Sunday, in order to celebrate the highest feast of the year.

Incense

Origin

Frankincense, *boswellia carterii*, is the main ingredient in the incense used in today's liturgies. A resin produced by a family of desert trees that grow in southern Arabia, it is derived from a sap that dries, forming crystalline lumps of an amber/gold color. For Christians, it has a rich prayer and purification symbolism. From earliest Christian days, it has been associated with Christ, beginning with the magi gift (Matthew 2:10–11). Even before that, the Jews regarded its rich spicy scent as a pure offering, pleasing to God. Even beyond Judeo-Christian circles, frankincense was prized for centuries in Palestine, Egypt, Greece, and Rome not only as a way to honor gods, but as a medicine and as a base for perfume.

Purpose

Veneration is shown by incensing, as in the incensation of the altar, the Book of the Gospels, the gifts of bread and wine, the assembly, and the body of the deceased during a funeral. Five grains of it can be deposited in the Paschal candle at the Easter Vigil, representing Christ's five wounds. The old blessing of incense included the prayer, "Be blessed by him in whose honor you will burn."

Symbolism

1. Its burning represents zeal and fervor.

2. Its fragrance represents virtue.

3. Its rising smoke represents acceptable prayer, as noted in Psalm 141:2.

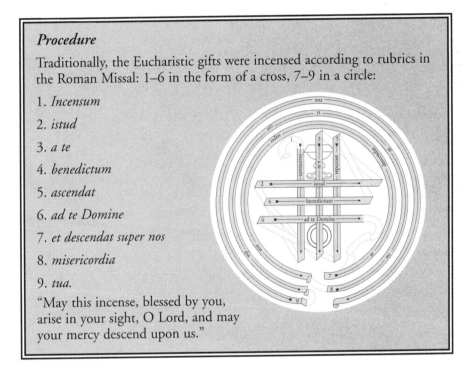

Procedure

Traditionally, the Eucharistic gifts were incensed according to rubrics in the Roman Missal: 1–6 in the form of a cross, 7–9 in a circle:

1. *Incensum*

2. *istud*

3. *a te*

4. *benedictum*

5. *ascendat*

6. *ad te Domine*

7. *et descendat super nos*

8. *misericordia*

9. *tua.*

"May this incense, blessed by you, arise in your sight, O Lord, and may your mercy descend upon us."

Candles

The Christ (Paschal) candle

A prime Christ/Easter symbol, it remains lit from its enthronement during the Easter Vigil, throughout the Great Feast (the fifty days of Easter), until it is extinguished and transferred to the baptistry on Pentecost. Thereafter, it is used for its resurrection symbolism at Baptisms and funerals. Formerly, there was a "triple candle" used at the Easter Vigil, lit by the deacon chanting *Lumen Christi* (Latin: Light of Christ) while the choir answered *Deo gratias* (Thanks be to God). From this the Paschal candle was then lit.

Today the Paschal candle is lit directly from the new fire. It is still an optional part of the Easter Vigil to stress the Christ candle's dignity and significance by decorating it with a cross ("Christ yesterday and today / the beginning and the end"), the Greek *alpha* and *omega,* and the numerals of the current year ("All time belongs to him / and all the ages / to him be glory and power / through every age for ever. Amen"), and then inserting five grains of incense in the cross ("By his holy / and glorious wounds / may Christ our Lord / guard us / and keep us. Amen").

Baptism candles

Their lighting (from the Christ candle) and presentation are part of Christian initiation, with the exhortation to keep the flame of faith burning brightly. One custom is to light one's baptismal candle each year on the anniversary of one's baptism.

Sanctuary candle

This sanctuary lamp or light signals the presence of the Blessed Sacrament.

Altar candles

Express "devotion or the degree of festivity" according to the General Instruction of the Roman Missal, on or around the altar (formerly, at least 51 percent beeswax).

Vigil lights

Candles are common in church; associated with a donation. Representing the prayerful vigilance of expectant faith, they are often either the large, six-day bottle candle or a smaller version in an often red, blue, or amber votive cup.

Unity candle

A recent folk innovation for weddings, doing the wedding ring one better, the unity candle is a single candle flanked by two others representing the couple (and their Baptism).

Blessed candles

Often blessed on Candlemas Day, candles for home use borrow symbolism from all the candles used in church and liturgy and bring it into the domestic Church of the home. Faith in things unseen can be bolstered by things seen—like a burning candle. Especially during a storm (including those within), forgetfulness of the Guardian threatens heart and home. And so popular piety would light a candle—blessed at Candlemas, of course—for protection, if not from the storm, then at least from the thunder and lightning of fear itself.

Several centuries ago in Ireland, during the suppression of Catholicism by the English persecution, priests were driven to visiting homes in secret, where the Eucharist could be celebrated at night. At Christmas time, the Catholic families would leave their doors unlocked and put candles in the windows to guide priests to their homes. Any soldiers noticing the open doors and lit candles were simply told that it was to welcome Mary and Joseph on Christmas Eve. The signal remained, as the soldiers dismissed the story as harmless superstition.

The Christmas Candle

In the Slavic nations, Poles, Ukrainians, and Russians make a large Christmas candle, often blessed at church, to serve as the table centerpiece at home. Sometimes with a loaf of bread as the candlestick, it represents the birth of Christ, the light of the world.

Candlemas Day

Old Simeon said, "Master, now you are dismissing your servant in peace, according to your word, for mine eyes have seen your salvation . . ." (Luke 2:29–30)—and if that sounds familiar ("mine eyes have seen the glory of the coming of the Lord"), it's because this is where Julia Ward Howe got her idea for "The Battle Hymn of the Republic."

The occasion of Simeon's song, the *Nunc Dimittis* (Latin: Now you may dismiss), was the presentation of Jesus in the temple, and it is all in Luke 2. In the East and in the early Middle Ages, it was called the *Hypapante,* or The Meeting (between Jesus, Simeon, and Anna). It's an epiphany too, part of the Lord's whole pattern of manifestation: nativity, magi visit, baptism, first miracle at Cana. It was also known as the Feast of Simeon, the Old Man.

When the feast was later adopted in the Western Church, the increasing devotion to the Blessed Mother made it a day to honor her: the Purification, which was the reason for the presentation. In common with all Jewish mothers, Mary took her child to the temple after forty days, the period during which she was excluded from public worship according to the Law of Moses (Leviticus 12:2–8). To this day, the feast is kept forty days after Christmas, not as a Marian feast but as the Presentation of the Lord.

The English name *Candlemas,* "Candle Mass," was common because the Mass has often been preceded by the blessing and distribution of candles (at least since the seventh century) probably to symbolize Christ's role as light of the world. What better way to give one last hurrah to the victory of the season of light over darkness? Some suggest that the candle association grew out of the light processions in honor of Mary in Rome on the occasion. They were a Christian substitute for the ancient torch parades.

Though the revised calendar has overshadowed this lightsome feast, we may still like to keep till Candlemas at least a remnant of the greenery and lights of the Christmas Season. But not a day longer! There's an old legend that houses will be haunted by goblins that are still decorated for Christmas after Candlemas eve.

Holy water

Used for baptizing, and to recall it; symbolizing exterior and interior purity; some is blessed in solemn ritual during the Easter Vigil; in fonts (like miniature baptistries) at church doorways and in homes, for use coming and going; sometimes sprinkled on individuals/assemblies/objects as part of a blessing; part of the revised penitential rite. (The *asperges* is the old Latin name used for the ceremony of sprinkling with holy water at Mass, from the first words of the psalm used in the rite, "You will sprinkle me with hyssop. . . ." The *asperges* is replaced in the Easter Season by the hymn "*Vidi Aquam*," "I Beheld Water," from Ezekiel 47:1–12.)

African Epiphany Water Blessing

The blessing of baptismal water has long been part of the Church's commemoration of the Lord's baptism, one of the manifestations or epiphanies of the Lord. In addition to the blessing of water in Church, there was also in the eastern reaches of the Church the blessing of any nearby fountain or river. In the Holy Land itself, of course, it was the Jordan River. In Africa it was the mighty Nile. After the colorful rite of blessing, throngs of the Christian population, and even many Muslims, would then submerge themselves three times, for the benefits of the blessings. Animals too would be driven in, and pictures, statues, and crosses would be submerged for the Epiphany blessing.

Crucifixes

See Chapter 9 and symbols.

Images

See Chapter 7 and devotions to Christ.

Medals

To commemorate, memorialize, and inspire; typically of or about the Lord, the Blessed Mother, or other saints.

Scapulars

Originally, part of the habit of a religious (See "Scapular.")

Palms

Received and used on Palm Sunday as a prayerful reminder of Christ's triumphant entry into Jerusalem and his death and resurrection. After Palm Sunday, it has become tradition to display the palms, often in some artistic form (braided, woven, crosswise), often with a crucifix or sacred picture. For the following Ash Wednesday they may be burned, with the ashes then used for the beginning of Lent.

Ashes

Used principally for Ash Wednesday markings, the consecration of an altar, and the dedication of a church

The Liturgical Year

Time (See CCC #1165.)

Two Kinds of Time

1. *Chronos*
   - Quantity ("What *chronos* is it?")
   - It's the time something happens.

2. *Kairos*
   - Quality ("Is it *kairos*?"). *Kairos* is sacred time.
   - It's the moment of something significant, and it is opportunity:
     — "Conduct yourselves wisely . . . making the most of the time."—Colossians 4:5; Ephesians 5:16
     — "Be aware, keep alert; for you do not know when the time will come."—Mark 13:33

The Calendar

The liturgical year emerges from the civil calendar. Our current calendar is the Gregorian (or Reformed, or New Style), which is the civil year according to the correction made in the Julian calendar by Pope Gregory XII in 1582.

The Julian (Old Style) Calendar

In 46 B.C., Julius Caesar attempted to adapt the calendar year to the time required by the earth to make one complete revolution around the sun (a "solar year"). He established the current number of days per month and, incidentally, gave his name to the fifth month, July. He allotted $365\frac{1}{4}$ days per year, the "common year," with the quarter day included by adding one day every four years, "leap year."

The Gregorian (New Style, or Reformed) Calendar

By 1582 the calendar was reading March 11 at the time of the vernal equinox (which had occurred on "March 25" in Caesar's day). On a solar calendar, such annual and predictable solar phenomena (seasons) should have been "immovable feasts," falling on the same date every year. This should be as true as the fact that lunar phenomena (full moons) are to be "immovable feasts" on a lunar calendar (see fourteenth Nisan and the Jewish lunar calendar). But even with Caesar's system, the calendar and Mother Nature were not keeping in step. This was because Caesar's allotment of 365 days per year was 11 minutes and 10 seconds too much. The sun was faster than Julius calculated, and by 1582 his calendar was two weeks behind.

Two astronomers, Lilius and Clavius, calculated the astronomical year to be 365.2422 days rather than 365.25. In his calendar reform, Gregory therefore decreed that an exception to leap year would be made: the intercalary day would not be added in centenary years not divisible by 400 (hence, 1600 and 2000 would be leap years and 1700, 1800, and 1900 would not be. Gregory then selected March 21 as the equinox date because that was the equinox date in the year of the Council of Nicaea (which fixed the dating of Easter). Then, on October 4, 1582, Gregory suppressed ten days, making 1582 the year that October 15 followed October 4, immediately! By using the simple new formula, people were able to prevent the original "calendar error" from recurring (except for the one day every thirty-five centuries).

It took some time for Protestant and Orthodox countries to agree to the Reformed Calendar. England finally adopted it in 1752 and Russia in 1918.

The Year

Christian: A.D. and B.C.

A.D. (Latin: *Anno Domini*, In the year of the Lord); B.C. (Before Christ)

It was not until the sixth century that each *annus* would be called *Domini,* "of the Lord." It was the idea of the sixth-century monk, Dionysius Exiguus, to make the incarnation—the birth of Christ—the centerpiece of history for Christian Europe. The time before Christ's birth would be a countdown to Christmas; the time after, a count-up. The change from A.M. (*Anno Mundi*) to A.D. did not come overnight. It took the promotional efforts of the Venerable Bede, a century and a half later, to bring Dionysius's idea into common usage. The precise *annus Domini* in which we now live is based on the supposed year Jesus Christ was born (according to Dionysius). The consensus of modern scholarship is that the actual birth was several years earlier, either between 7 B.C. and 4 B.C. (based on the death of Herod the Great—Matthew 2:19—in 4 B.C.) or in A.D. 6 (based on the great taxation of Quirinius—Luke 2:1–2).

Hebrew: A.M.

Latin: *Anno Mundi*, In the Year of the World

In the Hebrew tradition, the year of creation corresponds to 3761 B.C.

Muslim: A.H.

Latin: *Anno Hegira*, In the Year of the Hegira

In the Islamic tradition, Muhammad's flight from Mecca to Medina corresponds to A.D. 622 (beginning the Muslim era).

Roman: A.U.C.

Latin: *Ab Urbe Condita*, From the Founding of the City

The city is Rome, and the year corresponds to 753 B.C.

Civil

C.E. (Common Era) and B.C.E. (Before the Common Era)

These are more inclusive terms frequently used in place of A.D. and B.C.

Good Luck and Amazing Grace

In more superstitious times, while grace may have been amazing enough, luck was too good not to want it. In Highland Scotland, for example, it was believed that June 9 was the luckiest day of the whole year, especially those years when it fell on a Thursday. Why June 9? That was the day St. Columba died, in 597, and so is his feast day. More edifying than superstition is the amazing grace at work in evangelists like Columba. He was a priest who determined to convert the Picts to the Lord, relying not on good luck, but on grace. He embarked with twelve disciples around 563 to build a church and a monastery on the island of Iona, near Scotland.

Seasons, Months, and Days

Ember Days

Originally nature feasts at the changes of the seasons (Anglo-Saxon: *ymbren*, running about, revolution), Ember Days are three days of prayer, fasting for spiritual renewal, and blessings on the seasons and especially on the crops and the harvest. Ember days come four times a year: the Wednesday, Friday, and Saturday of the weeks which include St. Lucia's Day, December 13 (the Third Sunday of Advent); the First Sunday in Lent; Pentecost; and Holy Cross Day, September 14. Ember Days and Ember Weeks were fixed by the Council of Placentia in 1095.

Tide

Through the ages people have thought of time as a vast, flowing sea, with its rising and falling. Just as the tide has its ebb and flow, so an event—an occasion—has a build-up and a denouement. So naturally it became traditional for a feast, a festive moment, to have a season: not just time, but a tide. So Christmas time becomes Yuletide, and so on with Shrovetide, Eastertide, Whitsuntide, time flowing through the seasons, even as it does through the day—noontide, eventide—with its glad or sad tidings.

Months' Names

January (Janus, god of doors)

With two faces, looks forward to the current year as well as back at the former year

February (Latin: *Februa*)

Roman festival of expiation celebrated on the fifteenth of the month (*februare*, to expiate); hence, the month of expiation

March (Mars, god of war)

April (Latin: *aperier*, to open)

In the midst of spring, the buds open. Another suggestion is the Greek word *Aphro*, short for Aphrodite, the goddess of love, because in spring human fancy turns to love.

May (ancient Italic goddess Maia)

"The greater goddess, the increaser," hence month of growth

June (Roman clan Junius)

July (Julius Caesar)

August (Caesar Augustus)

The Latin root is *augurs,* so August is "consecrated by or undertaken under favorable signs."

September (Latin: *septem,* seven)

Seventh month in the Roman calendar (*ber* probably meaning "month of"). For the Romans, September through December were the seventh through the tenth months, since March was the first month of the year.

October (Latin: *octem,* eight)

November (Latin: *novem,* nine)

December (Latin: *decem,* ten)

"Beware the Ides of March"

There is no religious significance to the *ides* (the middle) of a month, as in the "*ides* of March" popularized by Shakespeare's play *Julius Caesar,* in which the *ides* was the day of the Emperor's assassination. The *ides,* the *calends* (first day of the month), and the *nones* (ninth day before the *ides*) are simply the three specific days each month that the Romans used to compute the divisions when they divided the year into twelve months. The *ides* are always either the thirteenth or the fifteenth.

Months' Dedication

January	Holy Childhood
February	Holy Family
March	St. Joseph
April	Holy Spirit/Holy Eucharist
May	Mary
June	Sacred Heart
July	Precious Blood
August	Blessed Sacrament
September	The Seven Sorrows
October	The Holy Rosary
November	Souls in Purgatory
December	Immaculate Conception

Names of Weekdays

Christians call the first day of the week the Lord's Day (Revelation 1:10) after Jesus' resurrection. Otherwise, the days of the week take their names from non-Christian sources, according to the belief in the influence of the planets (which included for the ancients the sun and the moon) on certain days. Planetary names are derived from names of Roman gods which gave their names, or their Germanic equivalent, to our weekdays. While the names of the months have a Roman origin, the days are of Anglo-Saxon origin.

Sunday	Sun's Day
Monday	Moon's Day
Tuesday	Tiu's (Mars's) Day (god of war)
Wednesday	Woden's Day (god of storms)
Thursday	Thor's (Jove's/Jupiter's) Day (god of thunder)
Friday	Frigg's (Venus's) Day (goddess of marriage)
Saturday	Saturn's Day (god of time)

> ### Why Seven?
> A solar year, a lunar month, and a twenty-four-hour day are naturals, but a seven-day week is supernatural. Seven is holy. Seven is magic. Seven days make a week. This was determined even by the author of Genesis—or God himself—who, in seven days or one "week," according to the story, created the world, and rested from it. So this seven-day cycle from the beginning was religious. The Romans' week was also seven days, named after the heavenly bodies of the sun, the moon, and the planets (five of which the Romans knew). Seven . . . one week's worth of days.

Weekdays' Dedication

Sunday	Holy Trinity
Monday	Souls in Purgatory/Holy Spirit
Tuesday	Guardian Angels
Wednesday	St. Joseph
Thursday	Blessed Sacrament
Friday	Precious Blood
Saturday	Mary

The *fleur-de-lis*, a stylized lily, is a classic Marian symbol.

Poor Friday

Some say Friday is a good day for bad things. Some say that the first humans fell from grace on a Friday, that the Great Flood started on a Friday, and that Solomon's temple fell on a Friday. Jesus was crucified on a Friday. Paradoxically, we call Adam's fault "happy" and Christ's crucifixion day "Good Friday."

By the Dark of the Moon

There is a folk custom of planting potatoes on Good Friday, partly because of a rule by those who plant by the moon: Vegetables that produce above ground should be planted by the light of the moon (from the day of the new moon to the day of the full moon), whereas underground vegetables should be planted by the dark of the moon (from the day of the full moon to the day of the new moon). Remember that in the West, Easter traditionally came on the first Sunday after spring's first full moon, add the mystique of that day, and there is the tradition of planting potatoes on Good Friday, at least in some climes.

The Life of a Day

Our Jewish ancestors conceived of the day this way: Each day ends with the dying of the light—nightfall. Each new day is born with the rising sun, beginning its life in the womb of the night. Vigils and eves then are pregnant with meaning. From time immemorial—almost— we began celebrating Christ's resurrection at Easter with a vigil (the "mother of all vigils"), Christ's birth with a Mass ("Christmas") on the night before ("Christmas Eve"), and we celebrate All Saints' (hallows) on its eve (Hallows' Eve, or Halloween).

The Church Year
(See CCC #s 1163–1173.)

Through the course of a year, the Church experiences and celebrates redemption in Christ. We are shaped anew through the various festivals and seasons.

Easter

The resurrection of Jesus from the dead is the sun around which revolves the solar system of Sundays, seasons, and saints' days. The traditional date of Easter in the West is based on the resurrection of Jesus, three days after his crucifixion, which occurred on Passover, the fourteenth of the month of Nisan, according to the Jewish calendar.

The date of Easter (See CCC #1170.)

Much debate and conflict has been spawned by efforts to determine the date this feast should be celebrated annually. The difficulty comes in translating an "immovable feast" from a lunar to the Christian solar calendar (Julian, and now Gregorian), on which it becomes a movable feast (one that moves to a certain day of the week, the way Thanksgiving moves to a Thursday, instead of one that is always celebrated on a particular date, immovably, like a birthday). The Council of Nicaea in 325 placed Easter on the first Sunday following the first full moon after March 20 (which is the vernal equinox, when the sun is directly above the earth's equator). This date allowed pilgrims to have moonlight for traveling to the great Easter festivals of that day. According to this method of reckoning, Easter could be as early as March 22 and as late as April 25.

Sundays (See CCC #s 1166–1167.)

Sunday is the day the Church celebrates the Paschal mystery, the "Lord's Day" (see Revelation 1:10), according to the apostolic tradition that the day of Jesus' resurrection from the dead was the first day of the week (Sunday). The Sundays of Advent, Lent, and the Easter Season take precedence over the permanent assignment of another celebration, with the following exceptions.

Feasts Permanently Assigned to Sunday

In the United States, the immovable feasts of Epiphany and the Body and Blood of Christ have been mobilized (and moved to this list).

Holy Family	to the Sunday after Christmas
Epiphany	to the Sunday after January 1
Baptism of our Lord	to the Sunday after January 6
Holy Trinity	to the Sunday after Pentecost
Body and Blood of Christ	to the Sunday after Holy Trinity
Christ the King	to the last Sunday of the liturgical year

Feasts

The Movable Feasts

This label is still usable. Like Easter, the movable feast upon which they depend, these feasts always fall on the same day of the week and move to whatever calendar date the day of Easter makes necessary.

Ash Wednesday	Forty days before Easter
Palm Sunday	The Sunday before Easter
Good Friday	The Friday before Easter
Ascension	Forty days after Easter
Pentecost	The Seventh Sunday after Easter
Trinity	The Eighth Sunday after Easter

The Immovable Feasts

These feasts, like birthdays, cannot move from their annual date. The first four are the traditional "quarter days"; the rest are lesser immovable feasts.

Annunciation ("Lady Day")	March 25
Nativity of John the Baptist	June 24
Michaelmas Day	September 29
Christmas	December 25
Mary, Mother of God	January 1
Epiphany	January 6
All Saints'	November 1
The Apostles' days	(See page 344.)

Latin Names

It was not uncommon before the renewal of the liturgy and the Roman calendar to give names to various Sundays. At least a couple are still well known: *Gaudete* Sunday and *Laetare* Sunday. These Latin words are the first words of what was formally called the *introit* of the Mass: *Gaudete,* on the Third Sunday of Advent, and *Laetare,* on the Fourth Sunday of Lent. Both words mean "Rejoice." Others oft repeated were *Rorate* Sunday (Fourth Sunday of Advent), *Quasimodo* Sunday (First Sunday after Easter), *Jubilate* and *Cantate* Sundays, the Third and Fourth Sundays after Easter. (Incidentally, the introit, meaning "a going in," is now called the entrance antiphon, and it is omitted if there is a hymn.)

Ordinary Time

Ordinary Time is the name given to the thirty-three or thirty-four weeks (depending upon Easter) in the course of the year apart from Advent/Christmas and Lent/Triduum/Easter. Ordinary Time is that part of the liturgical year when no particular moment or aspect of the Christian mystery is celebrated.

Ordinary Time's Two Phases

Ordinary Time has two phases, a shorter one in winter between the Season of Christmas and the Season of Lent and a longer one through the summer and fall between the Season of Easter and the Season of Advent. The pre-Lenten phase begins the Monday after the Baptism of our Lord and includes what were formerly called the Sundays after Epiphany and the suppressed Sundays of *Septua-/Sexa-/Quinquagesima*. Ordinary Time is then interrupted on the Tuesday before Ash Wednesday for the Seasons of Lent, Triduum, and Easter. It resumes the Monday after Pentecost and continues until the end of the Church year. This second phase includes Trinity Sunday (the Sunday after Pentecost), the Body and Blood of Christ (the Sunday after Trinity Sunday), and Christ the King (the last Sunday of the Church year).

Advent (See CCC #524.)

Advent is the season of expectation of the Christ, and it is somewhat penitential in tone. It is four weeks long, or slightly less, the first two focusing on Jesus' final coming as Lord and judge. The final eight days anticipate his coming in history (Christ-mas). Since the tenth century, the first Sunday of Advent has marked the beginning of the Church year in the West. (The Third Sunday of Advent, traditionally named *Gaudete* Sunday, expresses a joyful note of anticipation in the season.)

The Advent wreath marks the four weeks of preparation for Christmas.

Christmas Season (See CCC #s 525–526.)

Date and Time of Christ's Birth

Originally, Jesus' birth was celebrated as part of the feast of Epiphany. Around the year 330, however, the Church in Rome assigned the celebration of Christmas to December 25. There were some early Church leaders and writers who claimed that December 25 was Christ's actual birth date, although there was never an official reason given for the ecclesiastical decision. Church scholars contend that the date was chosen to counteract the Roman feast of the "Birthday of the Sun" which took place on December 25. The tradition of a midnight Mass on Christmas originated in the pious belief that Christ was born at that hour. Don't look for historical evidence.

The Christmas Season is the celebration of Jesus' birth and epiphany (manifestation). It is second in significance only to the Easter Season. Its feasts include:

Christmas	December 25
Holy Family	The Sunday after Christmas
Mary, Mother of God	January 1
Epiphany	The Sunday after January 1
Baptism of our Lord	The Sunday after Epiphany

When Is a Christmas Carol Not a Christmas Carol?

When it's "Good King Wenceslaus"! He "look'd out, on the feast of Stephen, when the snow lay all about, deep and crisp and even," and that date was enough to enshrine this popular English carol of the last century as a Christmas favorite. The story, however, isn't about Christ's birth so much as it is about the good king, Wenceslaus, doing the work of Christmas. The words were written by a nineteenth-century hymn writer to fit a thirteenth-century air, using a miracle attributed in medieval legend to St. Wenceslaus.

Its five verses tell of the good king noticing a poor man gathering fuel. Determining from a page who the man was and where he came from, the king said, "Bring me flesh, and bring me wine, bring me pine logs hither; thou and I will see him dine, when we bear them thither. Forth they went, page and king, against the bitter weather."

On the way, the page's heart failed, threatening his life as well as the mission of mercy. "Mark my footsteps, my good page, tread thou in them boldly; thou shalt find the winter's rage freeze thy blood less coldly." The last verse earns its popular place in people's hearts as a most worthy Christian, if not Christmas, carol: "In his master's steps he trod, where the snow lay dinted; heat was in the very sod which the saint had printed. Therefore, Christian men, be sure, wealth or rank possessing, ye who now will bless the poor, shall yourselves find blessing."

What earns Wenceslaus his favored place as patron and hero is not legend but history: He was an effective ruler in difficult times, faced with factionalism within and the threat from Bavaria without, as well as the task of reconciling the Christian and non-Christian parts of Bohemia. When a son was born to Wenceslaus and his wife, his brother Boleslav lost his hopes of succession—as well as all sense of right and wrong—and he murdered Wenceslaus as the king was on his way to church.

Russian Babushka

"Grandmother" in Russian, and in Russia, was the Christmas gift-bringer. When the magi inquired their way to Bethlehem, she is said to have misdirected them. If this was not her sin, then it was her refusal of hospitality to the Holy Family during the flight into Egypt. Talk about misdirection—from Palestine through Russia to Egypt! Whichever nasty version of Babushka's past you chose, it's her repentance and reparation that explains Christmas Eve gift-giving: She goes about the world on that night looking for the Christ Child and giving gifts to children.

Mexican Bunuelos

Christmas cakes were and are a tradition in most countries. Baked on the eve of the feast and eaten during the season, they were thought to bring special blessings of health and good luck. *Bunuelos*, in Central and South America, is an unusual pastry baked of white flour, very crisp and brittle, and eaten with honey or syrup.

Getting Ready for Lent

The three Sundays before Lent, once upon a time, amounted to a pre-Lenten season which prepared for Lent, which in turn prepared for Easter, and so they were "dropped" because of their redundancy. *Septuagesima, Sexagesima,* and *Quinquagesima* could not literally be the seventieth, sixtieth, and fiftieth Sundays before Easter. The titles were used presumably to correspond with the older term *Quadragesima* (fortieth), the First Sunday of Lent.

Shrovetide, the three days before Ash Wednesday, got its name from Shrove Tuesday, which got its name from the reconciliation sought before Lent: To shrive is to hear confession, assign penance, and give absolution. One is shriven of guilt through repentance, making these days of glad tidings, sport, and merriment before the rigors of Lent. *Hall Sunday, Hall Monday,* and *Hall Night* were names used for the same time and same reason: Hall is a contraction of hallow, which means holy, festive. Still others would speak of *Merry Monday*. This preparation is partly play.

Feasting—food and drink—became the staples of the play, preparing a person as well as a pantry for the fasting. And so the names came: *Carling Sunday,* from the custom, especially in northern Europe, of eating parched peas fried in butter (carlings) and the quite unpuritanical *Blue Monday,* a day supposedly spent in dissipation, which, some say, gives a blue tinge to everything. For others, these two days were *Callop Monday* and *Pancake Day,* because of the foods specially prepared and served then. The practice originated in the effort to use up eggs, milk, and lard before Lent, with its strict conditions for fasting. And finally on *Fat Tuesday, Mardi Gras* in French, the carnival celebration, people feasted on rich foods and pastries in anticipation of the rigors of Lent and in order to use up certain foods that were not even kept in the house during the fast.

Lenten Season

This penitential season of six Sundays and forty weekdays prepares for the high feast of Easter. Lent begins on Ash Wednesday and ends with the beginning of the Mass of the Lord's Supper in the evening on Holy Thursday (not Holy Saturday noon, as formerly).

Historically, Lent was the retreat-like final preparation period for catechumens, those being initiated into the Church and into the Paschal mystery at the Easter Vigil. Naturally enough, it became in time a renewal period for the already baptized faithful, the sponsoring community being inspired by the conversion of the catechumens. It was also a time of penance for those enrolled in the order of penitents, an early form of the Sacrament of Penance, limited to serious sinners. The whole Church came to adapt Lent as a penetential season whereby the faithful initiated both catechumens and serious sinners in doing penance.

The word *Lent* is from the Anglo-Saxon *lencten* (spring). *Lenctentid* (springtide) was the Saxon name for March because March is the month in which days begin to lengthen (also a root of "lent"). The Great Fast, falling as it does largely in the month of March, adopted and adapted the term.

The Fourth Sunday of Lent

This Sunday has had many aliases:

Laetare Sunday

The word *Laetare* comes from the first words of the introit: *Laetare, Jerusalem* ("Rejoice with Jerusalem," Isaiah 66:10). This halfway point and respite in the penitential season is marked by rose vestments instead of violet. There is a joyful note at this point in Lent because of the ancient practice of "handing over" the Apostles' Creed to catechumens, the last and decisive step for those preparing for Baptism.

Mothering Sunday

The sponsoring community of the Church would have been deeply conscious of its own spiritual birth and life. Not surprisingly, the ancient and indulgenced custom of visiting one's mother church or cathedral developed on this same day of

Laetare Sunday. Small countryside chapels served as the weekly gathering places for liturgy, but on this Sunday all would go with their offerings to the mother church of the parish, where they had been baptized.

In a natural evolution of this pilgrimage, children would also return home to spend the day with mother and parents, with "mother cakes" and simnel cakes having been prepared especially for the occasion. Naturally, roses were the traditional flowers for the day, because rose was the color of the vestments and the decoration on the altar. After Mass, the roses were taken to mothers. One tradition presents Mothering Sunday as an honor to St. Anne, the Blessed Mother's mother, when children would "go a'mothering" and bring flowers, gifts, and sweets to their mother. Long before Anna Jarvis held her service to honor all mothers or Woodrow Wilson in 1914 proclaimed the second Sunday in May Mothers' Day, folks were honoring mothers, spiritual and natural, and this mid-Lent Sunday had become a day of family reunion and festivity.

Refection (Latin: refreshment, repast) Sunday

The Sunday is so named because the Scripture included the story of Joseph feeding his brothers (first reading) and Jesus feeding the multitude (gospel). On this day in certain locales, it was traditional to serve rich "simnel" cakes. Ornamented with scallops, they commemorated the food spoken of in the readings.

Rose Sunday

This name comes from the papal blessing of the golden rose, a symbol of spiritual joy. The floral spray was blessed by the pope on the Fourth Sunday of Lent and sent to some notable person or institution to acknowledge and honor special service or loyalty. There is a small container of musk and balsam in the heart of the spray's principal rose.

The Fifth Sunday of Lent

Once upon a time it was the tradition to cover all crucifixes, statues, and pictures in purple cloth from two Sundays before Easter until Good Friday. Those were the days when the Fifth Sunday of Lent, one week before Palm Sunday, was called *Passion Sunday* or *Judica Sunday* after the first word of the introit "Judge me, O Lord . . ." (from Psalm 43). The veiling referred to the closing words of the Sunday's gospel, "They picked up stones to throw at him, but Jesus hid himself, and went out of the temple" (John 8:59). The Lenten veil also expressed the sorrow of the Church at this time. As a matter of fact, the Roman Missal still says, in a note about the Saturday of the fourth week of Lent, that this tradition may be observed, continuing the veiling until the beginning of the vigil. Also, the unveiling of the cross prior to veneration on Good Friday is still an optional part of the liturgy.

Holy Week

Holy Week is a term that is still used, even with the renewal of the Triduum (see below), and it refers to the week beginning with Palm (Passion) Sunday and ending with "Holy Saturday." It includes the last days of Lent.

Fig Sunday

This was a name for Palm Sunday because figs were eaten that day, memorializing the fig tree cursed by Christ after his entry into Jerusalem (Mark 11:12–14).

> ### Slavic Ritual of Petition and Palms
>
> In various places, but especially in Slavic countries, it was customary to use the blessed palms of Passion Sunday in a domestic ritual. The whole farm family walked through their buildings and fields on that Sunday afternoon, praying and singing the ancient hymns. A palm piece was placed in each plot of ground, pasture, and plowland, in every outbuilding, barn, and stable as petition was made for protection from bad weather and disease and for blessing on produce and property.

Spy Wednesday

This name for Wednesday of Holy Week alludes to Judas agreeing with the Sanhedrin to betray Jesus (Matthew 26:3–5, 14–16).

Maundy Thursday

This is an ancient name for Holy Thursday that come from Jesus' words that day and a former antiphon of the day: in Latin, *Mandatum novum da nobis* ("I give you a new commandment . . ." John 13:34). That phrase began the ancient footwashing ceremony.

Shear Thursday

This name for Holy Thursday came about because of an ancient practice of trimming hair and beard that day as a sign of spiritual preparation for Easter.

Tre Ore (Italian: "Three Hours")

The name refers to Christ's three hours on the cross and to the noon-to-three o'clock Good Friday service. *Tre Ore* was traditionally a series of homilies on the seven last words, along with song, silence, and stations.

> ### The Tre Ore, From Lima
>
> The very well-known Good Friday devotion of the Three Hours (*Tre Ore*) was introduced in Lima, Peru, by the Jesuit priest Alphonso Messia in 1732. From there it circulated quickly in Latin-speaking countries. It was then adopted with enthusiasm by Italy, and from there it migrated to England and then to the United States where it became popular in Protestant circles. It consists of a series of sermons on the seven last words of Christ, alternating with hymns and prayers.

The Mass of the Pre-Sanctified

This is not a Mass at all but an old name for the Good Friday service which includes Communion "pre-sanctified" (consecrated the night before). Good Friday remains the only day of the year without a celebration of the Eucharist ("The Eucharist—Jesus—has died").

The Great Service of Light

Although not the heart of the Easter Vigil, this service is symbolically rich and a favorite prelude for the *Exultet*, readings, and the glorious Eucharist that follow it. Celebrated in the Middle Ages, it may even go back to the fourth century. The light of the Paschal candle represents the light Christ brought to a darkened world. It was all the more powerful as a symbol in the days when fire was struck from flint—of necessity, reminding the believer of the flame of faith which is struck from Christ, the cornerstone of the Church.

Tenebrae

The term means "darkness" in Latin. It refers to a public singing of Matins (a night office) and Lauds (a morning office), part of the old form of the Liturgy of the Hours. During the evenings of Holy Thursday, Good Friday, and Holy Saturday, the Liturgy had a tone of mourning and a ceremony of light, which used a triangular stand with fifteen candles. One by one these candles were extinguished until, after the last candle was put out, a prayer was offered in darkness, one candle was relit, and the assembly dispersed in silence.

Judas Greeting Countered

There is an impressive practice among the Syrian and Chaldean Christians (those using the East Syrian Rite, mostly in Syria, Iraq, and Iran). They put aside their customary *Shlama* ("Peace be with you") greeting on Good Friday and Holy Saturday because that's how Judas Iscariot greeted Christ when he betrayed him. Instead, for these two days they substitute the salute, "The light of God be with your departed ones."

Veneration in Old Russia

The Good Friday veneration of the cross was done with special solemnity in Russia: A silver coffin, bearing a cross and surrounded with candles and flowers, was displayed in the middle of the church. The faithful, creeping on their knees, then came to kiss the cross and venerate the image of Christ's body painted on the "winding sheet."

The Triduum

The ancient Great Three Days, to which all leads and from which all flows, celebrate the heart of Christian faith: Jesus' redemptive death and resurrection. Related to the Church year as Sunday is related to each week, the Triduum **begins** with the evening Mass of the Lord's Supper, **continues** through Good Friday and Holy Saturday, **culminates** in the Easter Vigil, and **concludes** with Evening Prayer of Easter Sunday.

With the renewal of the Triduum:

- Lent is observed until the Mass of the Lord's Supper.
- The Great Three Days are celebrated.
- The Great Feast (Easter) is sustained for fifty days.

(Easter Sunday is both the final hours of the Triduum and the first hours of The Great Fifty Days.)

The first day of the Triduum, the Christian Passover, is from Holy Thursday sunset until Good Friday sunset; it is the day of Jesus' death, and has been likened to the sixth day of creation, when God formed us from clay and breath. It includes the liturgies of "The Evening Mass of the Lord's Supper" and "The Celebration of the Lord's Passion."

The second day of the Triduum, from Good Friday sunset until Holy Saturday sunset, is the Paschal Sabbath, the day of rest. In burial, the Lord rested, and we rest in him (even from liturgy).

The third day of the Triduum, beginning Holy Saturday at sunset, is the great surprise, the Easter surprise. This third day begins with the holiest night of the year, the vigil of Easter, leading into the day of days, the queen of feasts. Its liturgy is the queen of the royal liturgical family.

According to the Roman Missal:

- Holy Thursday's service is "The Evening Mass of the Lord's Supper."
- Good Friday's service is "The Celebration of the Lord's Passion."
- Easter Sunday's services are the Easter Vigil, Easter Sunday's services during the night, and Easter Sunday.

Even though the Roman Missal does not call for a "Sunrise Service," as it does a Mass at Dawn on Christmas, the sunrise service, a relatively recent innovation, has become popular in the US. Some credit the origin of this practice to Moravians. These Czechoslovakian immigrants brought the custom to the US in the late eighteenth century.

The Egg Roll

In 1873 President and Mrs. Hayes had an Easter Monday egg roll on the White House lawn for their eight children. They could not have known that they were starting a tradition and may not have known that the egg roll was originally more than a game. Historically, the rolling egg imitated the rolling away of the stone from Christ's tomb.

The Easter Season

The Easter Season refers to the Great Fifty Days from Easter Sunday to Pentecost Sunday, a celebration of our participation in Christ's resurrection which brings us from the death of sin to a life of grace. Its last ten days (Ascension Thursday through Pentecost) focus on the promise of the presence and power of the Holy Spirit. The fiftieth day (*pente-*) is seven (the perfect number) squared plus one (the first day of the New Life). The word *Easter* probably has roots in the Norse term *Eostur*, the season of the rising sun, or the time of the new birth of spring. Both these meanings lent themselves well to Christian symbolism for the new life of the risen Christ, the eternal light.

Bright Week

The eight-day week beginning with Easter and ending the following Sunday is one of the octaves kept by the Church. It is traditional to consider the octave day as belonging to the feast, so that Easter would last eight days, including two Sundays: Easter itself (the high feast) and the following Sunday (the "low" one, thus *Low Sunday*). It was once common practice for those who had been baptized during the year, especially those initiated at the Easter Vigil, to wear white clothes to Mass during the octave. In fact, this symbolic clothing of the neophytes inspired all members of the faith community, clothed in Christ, to celebrate this grace by wearing new clothes at Easter. With everyone called to rise and shine, it is no wonder that the Easter octave was called Bright Week.

Low Sunday

The first Sunday after Easter Sunday (which is the Second Sunday of the Easter Season) was called "low" to distinguish it from the other Sunday in Easter's octave, the high feast of Easter itself.

Sundays *of* (not *after*) Easter

The renewal of liturgical seasons requires the preposition "of" instead of "after" when referring to the Sundays between Easter and Pentecost, in order to recognize Easter as a season as well as a Sunday: Sundays of Easter. (So the first Sunday after Easter and the Second Sunday of Easter are the same day, from different points of view.)

Ascension Thursday

Formerly, the Christ candle was extinguished on Ascension Thursday, representing the physical departure of Christ from the earth; now, the Christ candle remains lit through Pentecost, for the entire Easter Season. In some areas, this feast is now celebrated on the following Sunday, the Seventh Sunday of Easter.

Expectation Week

This old term designates the culmination of the Easter Season: the days between Ascension Thursday and Pentecost when the apostles prayed with expectant faith for the Paraclete. The novena prayer form originated with this advent of the Holy Spirit: the nine (Latin: *novem*) days between Christ's ascent and the Spirit's descent.

Whitsunday

This antique name for Pentecost comes from the neophytes' white (*whit*), worn for the fifty-day Easter feast, from their initiation at the Easter Vigil until the commemoration of the gift of the Spirit.

Holidays and Anniversaries

In the course of the year, the Church:

Celebrates the mystery of the risen Christ

Honors Mary

Venerates other saints as examples for the living

Holy Days of Obligation

There are ten holy days of obligation listed by Rome. In the United States six, besides Sundays, are celebrated. The number varies from country to country because conferences of bishops are free to set their country's holy days—with the Vatican's approval. Current practice is to retain at least two: Christmas and one feast honoring Mary. (In the United States, as noted by the italics below, Epiphany and The Body and Blood of Christ are transferred to the nearest Sunday; and the obligation is removed from the feasts of St. Joseph and Saints Peter and Paul.)

1. Christmas
2. *Epiphany*
3. Ascension
4. *The Body and Blood of Christ*
5. Mary, Mother of God
6. Immaculate Conception
7. Assumption
8. *St. Joseph*
9. *Saints Peter and Paul*
10. All Saints

The Hierarchy of Eucharistic Liturgies

Each is abbreviated by capitalizing and using its initial letter on the lists and calendars that follow.

Solemnities (S) celebrate events, beliefs, and personages of greatest importance and universal significance in salvation history. (Their observance begins with Evening Prayer I of the preceding day.)

Feasts (F) are of lesser significance.

Memorials (M for obligatory, blank for optional) are of the least significance. (Those important only to a local country, Church, or religious community are called optional memorials.)

Masses Celebrating the Mystery of Jesus

1. Christmas (his nativity)	December 25 (S)
2. Holy Family	Sunday after Christmas (F)
3. Epiphany	Sunday after Holy Family (S)
4. Baptism of our Lord	Sunday after Epiphany (F)
5. Presentation	February 2 (F)
6. Annunciation	March 25 (S)
7. Easter (his resurrection)	First Sunday in spring (S)
8. Ascension	Forty days after Easter (S)
9. The Body and Blood of Christ	Sunday after Trinity Sunday (S)
10. Sacred Heart	Friday after Body and Blood of Christ (S)
11. Transfiguration	August 6 (F)
12. Triumph of the Cross	September 14 (F)
13. Dedication of St. John Lateran	November 9 (F)
14. Christ the King	Last Sunday in Ordinary Time (S)

Masses Honoring Mary, the Mother of God (See CCC #1172.)

The term "Lady Day" originally referred to the feast of the Annunciation, March 25, but it later came to mean any Marian feast. Like Candlemas Day, the Annunciation is primarily a feast honoring Jesus (and the incarnation). Secondarily, it is a Marian feast.

1. Immaculate Conception	December 8 (S)
2. Our Lady of Guadalupe	December 12 (M)
3. Mary, Mother of God	January 1 (S)
4. Our Lady of Lourdes	February 11
5. Visitation	May 31 (F)
6. Immaculate Heart	Saturday after Sacred Heart
7. Our Lady of Mt. Carmel	July 16
8. Dedication of St. Mary Major	August 5
9. Assumption	August 15 (S)
10. Queenship	August 22 (M)
11. Birth	September 8 (F)
12. Our Lady of Sorrow	September 15 (M)
13. Our Lady of the Rosary	October 7 (M)
14. Presentation	November 21 (M)

Masses Honoring the Apostles

Celebrated monthly during the longer phase of Ordinary Time

May 3	Sts. Philip and James
June 29	Sts. Peter and Paul
July 3	St. Thomas
July 25	St. James
August 24	St. Bartholomew
September 21	St. Matthew
October 28	Sts. Simon and Jude
November 18	St. Andrew
December 27	St. John

Solemnities of the Church Year

Notice that, of the seventeen, ten primarily commemorate events or celebrate truths of the Lord, or the Holy Spirit, or the Holy Spirit, three are for Mary, and four are for other saints (John the Baptist, Joseph, Peter and Paul, and All Saints').

1.	Immaculate Conception	December 8
2.	Christmas (with an octave)	December 25
3.	Mary, Mother of God	January 1
4.	Epiphany	Sunday after January 1
5.	Joseph, husband of Mary	March 19
6.	Annunciation	March 25
7.	Easter (the resurrection)	First Sunday in spring
8.	Ascension	Forty days after Easter
9.	Pentecost	Fifty days after Easter
10.	Trinity	Sunday after Pentecost
11.	Body and Blood of Christ	Sunday after Trinity Sunday
12.	Sacred Heart	Friday after Second Sunday after Pentecost
13.	Birth of John the Baptist	June 24
14.	Peter and Paul, apostles	June 29
15.	Assumption	August 15
16.	All Saints'	November 1
17.	Christ the King	Last Sunday in Ordinary time

Two Footnotes

Mases are Masses

There is an ancient practice of adding the suffix "-mas" to feast days, meaning "mass of ": Christmas, Candlemas, Michaelmas, Martinmas, Childermas (an old English name for the feast of Holy Innocents, December 28).

Ferial Days

A lot of days are ferial days, an old term for a weekday with no special feast, even though the word itself means "pertaining to a holiday" (because just being alive makes any day feast day enough and reason for a holiday?).

General Roman Calendar

(See CCC #s 957, 1173.)

Italic print indicates feasts proper to the calendar of the United States. Lowercase abbreviation after some names indicates:

abbot, ab	martyr, m
apostle, ap	pope, po
bishop, b	priest, pr
doctor, d	religious, r
evangelist, e	virgin, v

Capital letter in parentheses after some of the entries indicates: Solemnities (S), Feasts (F), and memorials (M). No letter indicates an optional memorial.

January

1: Octave of Christmas; Solemnity of Mary, Mother of God (S)

2: Basil the Great and Gregory Nazianzen, b/d (M)

4: *Elizabeth Ann Seton, r (M)*

5: *John Neumann, b (M)*

6: Bl. Andrew Bessette, r

7: Raymond of Peñyafort, pr

13: Hilary of Poitiers, b/d

17: Anthony of Egypt, ab (M)

20: Fabian, po/m; Sebastian, m

21: Agnes, v/m (M)

22: Vincent, deacon/m

24: Francis de Sales, b/d (M)

25: Conversion of Paul, ap (F)

26: Timothy and Titus, b (M)

27: Angela Merici, v

28: Thomas Aquinas, pr/d (M)

31: John Bosco, pr (M)

Sunday between January 2 and January 8: Epiphany (S)

Sunday after Epiphany: Baptism of the Lord (F)

St. Agnes Flowers

Is this an honor for Agnes? "St. Agnes' flowers" are not roses in December, like those of Juan Diego at Tepeyac, but only plain old snowflakes, called St. Agnes flowers by some of the old-timers who were making the best of it in winter, as well as remembering Agnes on her cold January feast.

February

2: Presentation of the Lord (F)

3: Blaise, b/m; Anskar, b

5: Agatha, v/m (M)

6: Paul Miki and companions, m (M)

8: Jerome Emiliani

10: Scholastica, v (M)

11: Our Lady of Lourdes

14: Cyril, monk, and Methodius, b (M)

17: Seven Founders of the Order of Servites

21: Peter Damian, b/d

22: Chair of Peter, ap (F)

23: Polycarp, b/m (M)

Candlemas Day

Although now overshadowed on the revised liturgical calendar, February 2 bore a weather folklore long before the shadowy groundhog. Farmers found the day a good time to make weather predictions, applying the theory that the rest of the winter would be the opposite of that on Candlemas. There is an old English song about this.

If Candlemas be fair and bright,
Come, Winter, have another flight;
If Candlemas bring clouds and rain,
Go, Winter, and come not again.

This means if the sun casts a shadow on Candlemas, you can expect more winter, but if there is no shadow, the end of winter is close at hand. If it sounds like the old groundhog story, it's because this is where that story comes from, except that the one about the groundhog originated only about a hundred years ago. (A groundhog? That's what people in some parts used to call a woodchuck, which is the largest member of the squirrel family.)

March

  4: Casimir

  7: Perpetua and Felicity, m (M)

  8: John of God, r

17: Patrick, b

18: Cyril of Jerusalem, b/d

19: Joseph, husband of Mary (S)

23: Turibius de Mongrovejo, b

25: Annunciation (S)

The Return of the Swallows

It is the eaves of Mission San Juan Capistrano (if not the nearby shopping mall) to which the swallows return to nest each March 19. It's on October 23 that they head south, as punctually as they came six months earlier.

April

2: Francis of Paola, hermit

4: Isidore of Seville, b/d

5: Vincent Ferrer, pr

7: John Baptist de la Salle, pr (M)

11: Stanislaus, b/m (M)

13: Martin I, po/m

21: Anselm, b/d

23: George, m

24: Fidelis of Sigmaringen, pr/m

25: Mark, e (F)

28: Peter Chanel, pr/m

29: Catherine of Siena, v/d (M)

30: Pius V, po

> ### Legend of the Cuckoo
>
> There is an old rhyme, "The cuckoo sings from St. Tibertius's Day to St. John's Day." That's April 14 to June 24.

> ### April Fools!
>
> Tradition has it that April 1 is April Fools' Day because it was on this day that Noah sent doves from the ark to check for dry land before the flood had completely abated. (Actually, it was the first of Nisan, the first month of the Jewish year and roughly equivalent to our April.) This first dispatch, of course, was a wild goose chase, to use a fowl metaphor. Even though Noah might object to the implication that he was just fooling, the doves' frustrated mission is commemorated in the April Fools' tricks of today.

May

1: Joseph the Worker

2: Athanasius, b/d (M)

3: Philip and James, ap (F)

12: Nereus and Achilleus, m; Pancras, m

14: Matthias, ap (F)

15: *Isidore the Farmer*

18: John I, po/m

20: Bernardino of Siena, pr

25: Bede the Venerable, pr/d; Gregory VII, po; Mary Magdalene de' Pazzi, v

26: Philip Neri, pr (M)

27: Augustine of Canterbury, b

31: Visitation (F)

Sunday after Pentecost: Holy Trinity (S)

Sunday after Holy Trinity: The Body and Blood of Christ (S)

Friday after Trinity Sunday: Sacred Heart (S)

Saturday after Trinity Sunday: Immaculate Heart of Mary

June

1: Justin, m (M)

2: Marcellinus and Peter, m

3: Charles Lwanga and companions, m (M)

5: Boniface, b/m (M)

6: Norbert, b

9: Ephraem, deacon/d

11: Barnabas, ap (M)

13: Anthony of Padua, pr/d (M)

19: Romuald, ab

21: Aloysius Gonzaga, r (M)

22: Paulinus of Nola, b; John Fisher, b/m, and Thomas More, m

24: Birth of John the Baptist (S)

27: Cyril of Alexandria, b/d

28: Irenaeus, b/m (M)

29: Peter and Paul, ap (S)

30: The Martyrs of Rome under Nero

St. John's Wort (wort, *plant, especially an herb*)

These little sunbursts—*hypericum perforatum*—are full of legend, "enlightened" legend, not surprisingly. The herb appears around the midsummer feast of St. John the Baptist, June 24. Six months from this night, one of the shortest of the year, is Christmas Eve, one of the longest and the birthday of the Light of the World, Jesus Christ (six months younger than his forerunner, John the Baptist). It is said that these little flowers first opened on John's feast, to catch and reflect the glorious sun. Daylight and the sun at this time of the year are in triumph over the night, proclaiming, even as John himself did, the advent of Christ, the rising sun.

St. John's Wort is one of the world's treasured wildflowers with natural beauty and plenty of legend, such as: how it will stop a witch in her tracks, according to the English ("Trefoil, vervain, John's Wort, dill, / Hinder witches of their will"); how it will give protection, according to the German tradition of tossing a wreath of St. John's wort up on the housetop; how it will ward off witches and wickedness when hung in the house, according to the Swedes and the Norwegians; how, when dipped in olive oil and preserved, it is a balm for the wounded, according to the Sicilians; how it will neutralize hydrophobia (water fear) according to the Russians; and how its predawn dew, rubbed on the eyelids, will preserve the eyes, the body's source of light. And, today, a natural help for those suffering depression. Enough? Happy feast of St. John the Baptist!

July

3: Thomas, ap (F)

4: Elizabeth of Portugal; *U.S. Independence Day*

5: Anthony Zaccaria, pr

6: Maria Goretti, v/m

11: Benedict of Nursia, ab (M)

13: Henry

14: Bl. Kateri Tekakwitha, v

15: Bonaventure, b/d (M)

16: Camillus de Lellis, pr; Our Lady of Mount Carmel

21: Lawrence of Brindisi, pr/d

22: Mary Magdalene (M)

23: Bridget of Sweden, r

25: James, ap (F)

26: Joachim and Anne, parents of Mary (M)

29: Martha (M)

30: Peter Chrysologus, b/d

31: Ignatius of Loyola, pr (M)

Grandparents' Day

Saints Joachim and Anne are beloved in the Church, though nothing is said of them in the Bible. Not even their names are recorded. According to ancient tradition Anne and her husband Joachim were married for decades without having a child. In answer to their prayers, an angel appeared and told them they would soon receive a child who "shall be spoken of in all the world." They had a little girl and named her Mary. For centuries the Eastern Churches have honored this sainted couple on September 9, the day after Mary's birthday. On the revised Roman calendar, this "feast of grandparents" is July 26.

August

1: Alphonsus Liguori, b/d (M)

2: Eusebius of Vercelli, b

4: John Vianney, pr (M)

5: Dedication of St. Mary Major

6: Transfiguration (F)

7: Sixtus II, po/m and companions, m; Cajetan, pr

8: Dominic, pr (M)

10: Laurence, deacon/m (F)

11: Clare, v (M)

13: Pontian, po/m, and Hippolytus, pr/m

14: Maximilian Mary Kolbe, pr/m (M)

15: Assumption (S)

16: Stephen of Hungary

19: John Eudes, pr

20: Bernard, ab/d (M)

21: Pius X, po (M)

22: Queenship of Mary (M)

23: Rose of Lima, v

24: Bartholomew, ap (F)

25: Louis; Joseph Calasanz, pr

27: Monica (M)

28: Augustine, b/d (M)

29: Beheading of John the Baptist, m (M)

St. Grouse's Day

In old England August 12 was a holy day of obligation: the first day of grouse season!

Hiroshima Transfigured

A Day of Tragedy, A Day of Peace: Hiroshima Day

On August 6, 1945, an American bomber dropped an atomic bomb on the city of Hiroshima, Japan, killing over 300,000 people, burning the city to the ground, and contaminating it for future generations. In the late 1940s the city was rebuilt, preserving the signs of destruction as a memorial. It was declared a Peace City to remind the world that atomic weapons must never be used again. August 6 is a memorial day for the people of Hiroshima, dedicated to those who died in the tragedy and to world peace.

One victim of the Hiroshima bomb, Sadako Sasiki, was exposed to radiation at age two, and at eleven developed leukemia as a result. Sadako revived the ancient Japanese tradition which holds that if you fold 1000 paper cranes, you will be protected from illness. Cranes are associated with the mythological phoenix, a bird which rises from its own ashes to new life. As a matter of fact, people making the cranes tend to forget their worries and experience greater relaxation and health. Sadako made 600 paper cranes before she became too tired to continue. In 1957, at age 14 she died. Her classmates completed the remaining cranes and buried them with her. They then raised $20,000 for a Children's Monument in Hiroshima Peace Park, an oval, granite hill representing the Japanese holy mountain, Mt. Horai. On the hill is a statue of Sadako, lifting a gigantic golden crane to the sky, with the inscription, "This is our cry, this is our prayer, peace in the world."

The Gossamer Legend

This delicate, filmy cobweb, prevalent in the air and on the grass and bushes, especially in autumn, is explained in a fine legend. It is the delicate thread unraveling from the Blessed Virgin's winding sheet, falling to earth in her assumption. The word itself, however, comes from "goose summer" which was a name for St. Martin's summer because of the goose legend, which is another story!

The Falling Asleep of the Mother of God

Mary's assumption into heaven has been formally celebrated in all Christian countries from the beginning of the Middle Ages up to the Reformation and is consistent with the faith of the Church from the beginning. In one of his sermons, St. John Damascene (who died in 749) expressed the general belief of all Christianity: "Your sacred and happy soul, as nature will have it, was separated in death from your most blessed and immaculate body; and although the body was duly interred, it did not remain in the state of death, neither was it dissolved by decay. . . . Your most pure and sinless body was not left on earth but you were transferred to your heavenly throne, O Lady, Queen, and Mother of God in truth" (page 287, Weiser).

The belief has become interwoven with legend, the most famous of which comes from an interpolated passage (that is, added by an unknown author) in the sermons of St. John Damascene. It tells of a request to the bishop of Jerusalem at the Council of Chalcedon (451) by the East Roman Emperor Marcian (who died in 457) to have the relics of Mary brought to Constantinople. The bishop is said to have answered, "Mary died in the presence of the apostles; but her tomb, when opened later on the request of St. Thomas, was found empty, and thus the apostles concluded that the body was taken up to heaven."

Since the Church understands death to be a consequence of the first sin and believes that Mary was conceived without original sin, some theologians have wondered if Mary died or simply was assumed into heaven without dying. The *Catechism of the Catholic Church* doesn't answer the question, but says, "The Most Blessed Virgin Mary, when the course of her earthly life was completed, was taken up body and soul into the glory of heaven . . ." (#974; see also #966).

September

3: Gregory the Great, po/d (M)

8: Birth of Mary (F)

9: Peter Claver, pr (M)

13: John Chrysostom, b/d (M)

14: Triumph of the Cross (F)

15: Our Lady of Sorrows (M)

16: Cornelius, po/m and Cyprian, b/m (M)

17: Robert Bellarmine, b/d

19: Januarius, b/m

20: Andrew Kim Taegon, pr/m, Paul Chong Hasang, companions, m (M)

21: Matthew, ap/e (F)

25: Cosmas and Damian, m

27: Vincent de Paul, pr (M)

28: Wenceslaus, m; *Lawrence Ruiz and companions, m*

29: Michael, Gabriel, and Raphael, archangels (F)

30: Jerome, pr/d (M)

October

1: Thérèse of Lisieux, v (M)

2: Guardian Angels (M)

4: Francis of Assisi (M)

6: Bruno, pr; Bl. Marie Rose Durocher, v

7: Our Lady of the Rosary (M)

9: Denis, b/m, and companions, m; John Leonardi, pr

14: Callistus I, po/m

15: Teresa of Ávila, v/d (M)

16: Hedwig, r; *Margaret Mary Alacoque, v*

17: Ignatius of Antioch, b/m (M)

18: Luke, e (F)

19: Isaac Jogues and John de Brebeuf, pr/m, and companions, m (M); Paul of the Cross, pr

23: John of Capistrano, pr

24: Anthony Claret, b

28: Simon and Jude, ap (F)

> ## *Halloween*
>
> "Hallows' Eve" sounds like "Halloween," and it should, because that's where it came from: the eve, or vigil, of All Hallows, which is All Saints'. On All Souls' Day (which is actually the day after All Saints' Day) the poor begged for food and promised to pray for the dead in return. They called the little cakes they received "soul cakes"—not the biggest stretch from today's trick-or-treat spoils. Masks and costumes? Maybe these disguises will confuse the evil spirits. Candy has displaced the true soul cake, the doughnut (the cake with the hole in the center making a circle, representing eternity). There are still cultures with people who visit a cemetery on All Hallows, not for spooky reasons, but for the same reason others do on Memorial Day, except that they have picnics, with the last flowers of the year.

November

1: All Saints' (S)

2: All Souls'

3: Martin de Porres, r

4: Charles Borromeo, b (M)

9: Dedication of St. John Lateran (F)

10: Leo the Great, po/d (M)

11: Martin of Tours, b (M)

12: Josaphat, b/m (M)

13: *Frances Xavier Cabrini*, v (M)

15: Albert the Great, b/d

16: Margaret of Scotland; Gertrude, v

17: Elizabeth of Hungary, r (M)

18: Dedication of the Churches of Peter and Paul, ap

21: Presentation of Mary (M)

22: Cecilia, v/m (M)

23: Clement I, po/m; Columban, ab

30: Andrew, ap (F)

Last Sunday in Ordinary Time: Christ the King (S)

Fourth Thursday: *Thanksgiving Day*

The Church's Memorial Day

On the liturgical calendar, Memorial Day, it could be said, comes not in May but on November 1. It is prolonged through the month, the time in the natural cycle for harvest and dying. We have long called it the "month of the poor souls," but many today prefer the "month of all saints," or "holy souls," or even "memorial month." Actually for Catholics Memorial Day is plural, since it includes both All Saints' Day, November 1, and All Souls' Day, November 2. We distinguish between our loved ones in heaven—"all saints," who pray for us— and our loved ones who have died and for whom we are moved to pray. These are "the poor souls" who still may be undergoing the purging process of death-to-self that follows repentance. In this month of harvest and dying, the Church memorializes the dead and recognizes Jesus as Lord of the living and the dead.

El Dia de los Muertos

"The Day of the Dead" is a rich Mexican tradition celebrated on November 2, All Souls' Day. An outing to the graveyard may sound like no picnic, but that's where the event is held, complete with candy skulls. What a scathing satire which makes death, the enemy conquered by the dying and rising Jesus, into a child's playmate!

Philippino Memorial Day

The Church at large observes its "Memorial Day" on November 2, the feast of All Souls, at least in theory. In practice, such a memorial day is nowhere observed with more dedication and tradition than among the faithful in the Philippines. A novena for the holy souls culminates on November 2. Candles are brought and burned at the tombs, and prayers are said every night in those cemeteries close to town. The nine days are also the time for people to maintain and decorate their family graves. Crosses and tomb niches are repainted, flowers planted, weeding done, and shrubbery trimmed. On the eve of All Souls' (the evening of All Saints' Day), party-goers travel from door to door, requesting gifts in the form of cookies, candy, and pastries, while singing a traditional verse in which they represent the holy souls who are finally purged and now on their way to heaven.

Hungarian Hospitality

The "Day of the Dead" (*Halottak Napja*) is kept in Hungary on November 2 with the traditional customs common to faithful everywhere. There is an additional practice of hospitality in Hungary, however, as orphan children are invited into the family for All Saints' and All Souls' Days, served generous meals, and given new clothes and toys.

The Return of the Dead in Poland

In many cultures, superstition gave rise in the past to the belief that the spirits of the dead return for All Souls' Day. An especially charming legend used to be repeated in the rural sections of Poland, that at midnight on All Souls' Day, a great light could be seen in the parish church. It was the holy souls of all departed parishioners, still being purged for the glories of heaven and the beatific vision, gathering to pray for their completion before the very altar where they used to receive the Eucharist during their lifetime. Afterward the souls were said to pay a visit to the scenes of their earthly life and labors, especially their homes. As an external sign of welcome, people would leave doors and windows ajar on All Souls' Day.

December

3: Francis Xavier, pr (M)
4: John Damascene, pr/d
6: Nicholas, b
7: Ambrose, b/d (M)
8: Immaculate Conception (S)
11: Damasus I, po
12: *Our Lady of Guadalupe* (M); Jane Frances de Chantal, r
13: Lucy, v/m (M)
14: John of the Cross, pr/d (M)
21: Peter Canisius, pr/d
23: John of Kanti, pr
25: Christmas (S)
26: Stephen, first martyr (F)
27: John, ap/e (F)
28: Holy Innocents, m (F)
29: Thomas Becket, b/m
31: Sylvester I, po
Sunday within the octave of Christmas or on December 30: Holy Family (F)

The Shrine of the Immaculate Conception

Mary is the patroness of the United States, especially honored in this monument which is the second largest church in the country and seventh largest in the world. Like the medieval cathedrals, it is constructed entirely of masonry, with no steel structure. Begun in 1920 and dedicated in 1959, the Shrine was funded by millions of Catholics and is situated by the campus of the Catholic University in Washington, DC. Its sixty chapels feature the Church's rich Marian devotion, including Queen of Peace, Our Lady of Czestochowa, Our Mother of Sorrows, and Our Lady of Hope.

Posada

Like its German counterpart *Herbergsuchen* (Search for an Inn), the Spanish *Posada* (Inn) is an Advent play, dramatically rendering—and reversing—the Holy Family's fruitless efforts to find shelter in Bethlehem. People of Mexico and Hispanics in communities everywhere give the holy couple a much better reception than the couple received in Bethlehem. Soon after dark on the evenings between December 16 and 24, participants make candle-lit and song-full procession through the streets, bearing the figures of Mary and Joseph to the home selected to host the Holy Family for the night. In glad reparation for the old refusal, the family welcomes the pilgrims, "Come into my humble home, and welcome! May the Lord give shelter to my soul when I leave this world."

Ukrainian Christmas

It's not surprising that in this "breadbasket of Europe," the dual origin of many Christmas customs is most clearly represented: the pre-Christian thanksgiving festivals of the fertility of the earth, and the Christian celebration of the incarnation of the Son of God. To a Ukrainian peasant, Christmas was and still is a day to give thanks for a good harvest and to invoke blessings on the fields for the coming year.

From an American point of view, the celebration is more like Thanksgiving Day. The father of the Ukrainian family brings into the home on Christmas Eve a wheat sheaf from the barn and stands it in a corner of the room. This sheaf is named "Forefather" and represents the ancestors who were the first tillers of the soil. Hay and straw are strewn over the floor, even on the table on which two fragrant loaves of bread are then placed, one on top of the other. A candle is stuck in the upper loaf, and the main dish of the solemn Christmas Eve dinner is served: *Kutya* (boiled wheat with honey and poppy seed). After blessing the dish, the head of the family throws a spoonful of it against the ceiling, a thanksgiving ritual surviving since pre-Christian days.

Saints on the General Roman Calendar

Achilleus, May 12

Agatha, Feb. 5

Agnes, Jan. 21

Albert the Great, Nov. 15

Aloysius Gonzaga, June 21

Alphonsus Liguori, Aug. 1

Ambrose, Dec. 7

Andrew Bessette, Jan. 6

Andrew, Nov. 30

Andrew Kim Taegon, Sept. 20

Angela Merici, Jan. 27

Anne, July 26

Anselm, Apr. 21

Anskar, Feb. 3

Anthony, abbot, Jan. 17

Anthony Claret, Oct. 24

Anthony of Padua, June 13

Anthony of Zaccaria, July 5

Athanasius, May 2

Augustine, Aug. 28

Augustine of Canterbury, May 27

Barnabas, June 11

Bartholomew, Aug. 24

Basil the Great, Jan. 2

Bede, Venerable, May 25

Benedict, July 11

Bernard, Aug. 20

Bernardino of Siena, May 20

Blaise, Feb. 3

Bonaventure, July 15

Boniface, June 5

Bridget, July 23

Bruno, Oct. 6

Cajetan, Aug. 7

Callistus I, Oct. 14

Camillus de Lellis, July 14

Casimir, Mar. 4

Catherine of Siena, Apr. 29

Cecilia, Nov. 22

Charles Borromeo, Nov. 4

Charles Lwanga, June 3

Clare, Aug. 11

Clement I, Nov. 23

Columban, Nov. 23

Cornelius, Sept. 16

Cosmas, Sept. 26

Cyprian, Sept. 16

Cyril, monk, Feb. 14

Cyril of Alexandria, June 27

Cyril of Jerusalem, Mar. 18

Damasus I, Dec. 11

Damian, Sept. 26

Denis, Oct. 9

Dominic, Aug. 8

Elizabeth Seton, Jan. 4

Elizabeth of Hungary, Nov. 17

Elizabeth of Portugal, July 4

Ephrem, June 9

Eusebius of Vercelli, Aug. 2

Fabian, Jan. 20

Felicity, Mar. 7

Fidelis of Sigmaringen, Apr. 24

Frances of Rome, Mar. 9

Frances Xavier Cabrini, Nov. 13

Francis of Assisi, Oct. 4

Francis of Paola, Apr. 2

Francis de Sales, Jan. 24

Francis Xavier, Dec. 3

Gabriel (archangel), Sept. 29

George, Apr. 23

Gertrude, Nov. 16

Gregory the Great, Sept. 3

Gregory Nazianzen, Jan. 2

Gregory VII, May 25

Hedwig, Oct. 6

Henry, July 13

Hilary, Jan. 13

Hippolytus, Aug. 13

Ignatius of Antioch, Oct. 17

Ignatius Loyola, July 31

Irenaeus, June 28

Isaac Jogues, Oct. 19

Isidore of Seville, Apr. 4

Isidore the Farmer, May 15

James, apostle, July 25

James, apostle, (and Philip), May 3

Jane Frances de Chantal, Dec. 12

Januarius, Sept. 19

Jerome, Sept. 30

Jerome Emiliani, Feb. 8

Joachim, July 26

John I, May 18

John, apostle, Dec. 27

John Baptist, birth, June 24

John Baptist, beheading, Aug. 29

John Baptist de la Salle, Apr. 7

John Bosco, Jan. 31

John de Brebeuf, Oct. 19

John of Capistrano, Oct. 23

John Chrysostom, Sept. 13

John of the Cross, Dec. 14

John Damascene, Dec. 4

John Eudes, Aug. 19

John Fisher, June 22

John of God, Mar. 8

John of Kanti, Dec. 23

John Leonardi, Oct. 9
John Neumann, Jan. 5
John Vianney, Aug. 4
Josaphat, Nov. 12
Joseph, Mar. 19
Joseph the Worker, May 1
Joseph Calasanz, Aug. 25
Jude, Oct. 28
Justin, June 1

Kateri Tekakwitha, July 14

Lawrence, Aug. 10
Lawrence Brindisi, July 21
Leo the Great, Nov. 10
Louis of France, Aug. 25
Lucy, Dec. 13
Luke, Oct. 18

Marcellinus, June 2
Margaret Mary Alacoque, Oct. 16
Margaret of Scotland, Nov. 16
Maria Goretti, July 6
Maria Rose Durocher, Oct. 6
Mark, Apr. 25
Martha, July 29
Martin I, Apr. 13
Martin de Porres, Nov. 3
Martin of Tours, Nov. 11
Mary Magdalene, July 22
Mary Magdalene de Pazzi, May 25
Matthew, Sept. 21
Matthias, May 14
Maximilian Kolbe, Aug. 14
Methodius, Feb. 14
Michael (archangel), Sept. 29
Monica, Aug. 27

Nereus, May 12
Nicholas, Dec. 6
Norbert, June 6

Pancras, May 12
Patrick, Mar. 17
Paul, apostle, June 29
Paul, conversion, Jan. 25
Paul of the Cross, Oct. 19
Paul Chong, Sept. 20
Paul Miki, Feb. 6
Paulinus of Nola, June 22
Perpetua, Mar. 7
Peter, apostle, June 29
Peter, chair of, Feb. 22
Peter (and Marcellinus), June 2
Peter Canisius, Dec. 21
Peter Chanel, Apr. 28
Peter Chrysologus, July 30
Peter Claver, Sept. 9
Peter Damian, Feb. 21
Philip, apostle, May 3
Philip Neri, May 26
Pius V, Apr. 30
Pius X, Aug. 21
Polycarp, Feb. 23
Pontian, Aug. 13

Raphael (archangel), Sept. 29
Raymond of Peñyafort, Jan. 7
Robert Bellarmine, Sept. 17
Romuald, June 19
Rose of Lima, Aug. 23

Scholastica, Feb. 10
Sebastian, Jan. 20
Servites, Seven Founders, Feb. 17

Simon, apostle, Oct. 28

Sixtus II, Aug. 7

Stanislaus, Apr. 11

Stephen, Dec. 26

Stephen of Hungary, Aug. 16

Sylvester I, Dec. 31

Teresa of Ávila, Oct. 15

Thérèse of Lisieux, Oct. 1

Thomas, apostle, July 3

Thomas Aquinas, Jan. 28

Thomas Becket, Dec. 29

Thomas More, June 22

Timothy, Jan. 26

Titus, Jan. 26

Turibius of Mongrovejo, Mar. 23

Vincent, Jan. 22

Vincent de Paul, Sept. 27

Vincent Ferrer, Apr. 5

Wenceslaus, Sept. 28

Autumn's Summers

After the equinox, the calendar calls it "fall," but some days we say are still summer. Some may say "Indian summer," but the pilgrims didn't, and the *Farmer's Almanac* didn't. It was St. Augustine's summer when September was clear and balmy. Similarly, the golden sun, robin's-egg-blue-sky October days, usually after the first killing frost, were St. Luke's summer. And the fair, warm days of early November were St. Martin's summer. The *Farmer's Almanac* has long said: "If All Saints' day brings out winter, St. Martin's feast day brings out Indian summer." (The feast of St. Augustine is August 28; St. Luke, October 18; All Saints' Day, November 1; and St. Martin, November 11.)

Saint Nicholas

Our ubiquitous, gift-bearing Santa Claus originates in that legendary gift-giving bishop, Nicholas, of Myra, Asia Minor. In the beginning, it was more a matter of justice than generosity that caused him to give the gift that started the tradition. At least according to one of many colorful legends, he supplied three bags of gold, anonymously, to three sisters who were being reduced to prostitution because their poor father was unable to provide their dowries. (His gifts, tossed in the window, landed in the girls' stockings which were hung by the mantle with care. Sound familiar?)

Throughout the centuries this generous, compassionate bishop has been a favorite in the Eastern Church, and gift-giving a favorite memorial on his feast, December 6. In an outpouring of zealous—if superficial—piety, some Protestants banished him from calendar and custom, replacing him with a secular but still gift-giving counterpart: Father Christmas being the English version, Père Noël the French. But the durable bishop survived the purge and still lives in a kind of reincarnation.

While gift-giving remains, and his name—Saint Nikolaas, Sinterklaas, Santa Claus—is still close, his image has changed. Credit (or blame) for this goes to two people—Clement Moore and Thomas Nast. Dr. Clement Moore, a theologian, authored in 1822 "A Visit from St. Nicholas" (also known as "The Night before Christmas"). That's where Bishop Nicholas gets embellished with toy bag, pipe, reindeer, sleigh, and a chimney entrance. Moore had ample resources in the Dutch immigrants who brought Sinterklaas to the New World.

What imagination lacked, Thomas Nast supplied in his *Harper's Weekly* cartoons of the 1860s and '70s. It was his pen that fleshed out the image—and the frame—of Santa Claus. But underneath it all, there is still the robed gift-giver of Myra, Nicholas.

Actual devotion to St. Nicholas is largely submerged in contemporary Santa Claus extravagance and lost among a million independent Clauses. Still, some stubbornly celebrate on Santa's original feast (December 6) with a St. Nicholas breakfast. In honor of this Byzantine bishop's justice and generosity, food and clothing are collected for people in need.

Saint's Day or What?

St. Valentine was a third-century Christian martyr whose feast day was kept on February 14. Actually, he is one of ten St. Valentines (including a ninth-century pope) and these ten are among about 40,000 recognized saints, of whom only a fraction are commemorated in the calendar! There are various explanations for the connection between his name and the current "Valentine" practices, which have little to do with his life.

St. Valentine was from Rome and was a physician and priest, possibly a bishop. He was beheaded on the fourteenth of February. It could be said that it was because of his love for the Lord and his people that his name became associated with the devotion of lovers for one another, the devotion of children toward parents, and friend toward friend. There is also the story that he got into trouble with Roman authorities for celebrating the wedding of a loving couple when Roman law forbade it.

But wait! There's more: People in medieval times believed that birds paired off on February 14 and that this was the special day, according to natural law, for love to abound and triumph. What a natural time for young men and women to do the same, or at least to send a love token. And what a natural reason for "love birds" and "valentines" to enter the vocabulary.

And finally, not to omit the dependable old Romans: In mid-February, they celebrated a festival called *Lupercalia* to honor Lupercus, their version of the Greek god Pan. As part of the festivity, young men drew names for dance partners. If a relationship developed, an engagement might follow—the next mid-February, romantically enough. These betrothals were sealed with a gift exchange.

Christianity has often baptized practices as well as people, as Valentine's Day illustrates, at least according to some theories. Pan's passion rites prompted the Church to promote a purity rite instead, memorializing St. Valentine, especially since his feast day was nearby. Part of the plan was to substitute saints' names for women's names. Such piety was no match for passion and romance. All that stuck was "Valentine's Day." Whatever origin you choose or connection you make, one thing is sure: Valentines are sent as signs of love, devotion, or affection, and they are received as a thoughtful gesture and a nice compliment.

Feasts Eliminated in the Revised Calendar

In most cases, these feasts were eliminated not because the individuals were judged nonexistent or lacking in holiness, but because in many cases all that remains certain are their names or because they lack universal significance.

January: 5—Telephorus; 6—Higinus; 19—Marius, Martha, Audifax, and Abacus; 28—Agnes (a duplicated feast)

February: 6—Dorothy; 15—Faustinus and Jorita

March: 4—Lucius; 10—Forty Holy Martyrs

April: 17—Anicetus; 22—Soter and Cajus; 26—Cletus and Marcellinas

May: 12—Domitilla; 14—Boniface of Tarsus; 25—Urban I; 26—Eleutherius; 30—Felix I

June: 12—Basilidis, Cyrinus, Nabor, and Nazarius; 15—Modestus and Crescentia

July: 10—Seven Holy Brothers; 11—Pius I; 17—Alexius; 18—Symphorosa and her seven sons; 20—Margaret of Antioch; 28—Victor I; 28—Innocent I

August: 22—Hippolytus (a duplicate feast); 26—Zephyrinus

September: 1—Twelve Holy Brothers; 16—Lucy (a duplicated feast); 16—Geminianus; 19—Companions of St. Januarius; 20—Eustace and Companions; 23—Linus; 23—Thecla; 26—Cyprianus and Justina

October: 5—Placid and Companions; 8—Sergius; 21—Ursula and Companions; 26—Evaristus

November: 10—Tryphon, Respicius, and Nympha; 25—Catherine of Alexandria

December: 4—Barbara

Christopher

There is an ancient allegory of a giant named Christopher who was approached by a child who desired to cross a river. The giant obliged but found the burden of the child increasing with every step he took in the crossing. "Chylde," he said, "thou hast put me in grete peryll. I might bere no greater burden." "Marvel thou nothing," the child responded, "for thou hast borne all the world upon thee and its sins likewise." ("Christopher" means Christ-bearer, and the river is the river of death.) In some stories this Christopher was a burly third-century youth named Offero (carrier) who "served God and man" by carrying people through a treacherous river that had taken the lives of many.

Intersections: Sacred and Secular

Some Church traditions, rituals, holy days, and anniversaries are the descendants (or counterparts) of secular versions; others—or the same ones for that matter—are the ancestors for still other secular versions. In some cases, the Church has borrowed and baptized; in others, the Church has been borrowed from and the feasts secularized.

Though motives and meanings may vary, traditional holidays and rituals are surprisingly Catholic. All Saints'/All Souls' Day, Candlemas Day, Martinmas, Mothering Sunday, Rogation Days, St. Nicholas, and Valentine's Day are all Catholic counterparts to secular celebrations. These are merely examples of the grafting, transplanting, and inheriting that are part of Catholic, if not human, history. The relationship between sacred and secular roots is not always as evasive as St. Martin's goose, as in the following example, but this one might whet the appetite for some studying of your own.

Turkey or Goose

Even though the centerpiece of contemporary Thanksgiving dinner is a turkey, goose was the required main course at the venerable Martinmas feast, and some say this November 11 tradition is the ancestor of our Thanksgiving. There is no doubt that both celebrations have the harvest in common. There is plenty of doubt, however, about the rest.

It's Martin's kindness to a beggar on a wintry day that is the best-loved story about him, but the stories about the goose, though less edifying, are certainly no less interesting. Although it was traditional to slaughter an ox—for distribution to the poor—on his feast, it is the roast goose that has become notorious. The legend behind this is that St. Martin, annoyed by a goose, ordered it to be killed and served up for dinner. After dining on the goose, Martin died. Thereafter, on the anniversary of Martin's demise—and the goose's—a goose is sacrificed in St. Martin's name.

In another story, Martin was hiding out in a barn because he didn't want to be bishop, but the honking of a goose gave him away. While that may have been enough to make him want to kill it, we know that eating a goose that day didn't kill him, because he lived on in fact to be a bishop, which didn't kill him either.

In a much more pious vein, Dr. Parsch in *The Church's Year of Grace* ignores all this and suggests that the custom simply served as a kind of Mardi Gras before the Advent fast ("St. Martin's Lent"). It prevailed during the Middle Ages and began earlier than Advent does now.

In addition to all this is the September 29 feast of Michaelmas, or St. Michael and All Angels, and one of the quarter-days (when rents were due). There is a centuries-old tradition of eating goose on this feast also, a practice which could have arisen simply because geese were in good supply and condition at this time of the year and were often presented by tenants to landlords, we are told, as a propitiation.

For all of this, Martin deserves to have a goose be one of his common symbols. As for the quest for the origin of Thanksgiving, whether in the roast goose feast of Michaelmas or Martinmas, it may all be a wild goose chase.

The Jewish Calendar
(See CCC #1164.)

The Day

In the Jewish tradition, a day is not counted from midnight to midnight but from sunset to sunset. The day ends, naturally, when the sun goes down: thus, a new day's beginning is in the womb of the night. Four watches divide the night: the first, 6:00–9:00 P.M.; the second, 9:00 P.M.–midnight; the third, midnight–3:00 A.M.; the fourth, 3:00–6:00 A.M.

The Sacred Year

Month	Equivalent	Feasts
1. Nisan (Abib)	March–April	Passover
2. Lyar (Ziv)	April–May	
3. Sivan	May–June	Pentecost
4. Tammuz	June–July	
5. Ab	July–August	
6. Elul	August–September	⎧ Trumpets
7. Tishri (Ethanim)	September–October	⎨ Atonement
8. Marcheshvan (Bul)	October–November	⎩ Tabernacles
9. Chislev	November–December	Hanukkah
10. Tebeth	December–January	
11. Shebat	January–February	
12. Adar	February–March	Purim

Sabbaths and Jubilees

Every seven days—the Sabbath/Shabbat (the seventh day)

After seven weeks—the jubilee day (the fiftieth day)

In the seventh month—Rosh Ha-Shanah (feast of Trumpets, New Year's)

In the seventh year—the sabbatical year (commemorating the Exodus)

After seven times seven years—the jubilee year (the fiftieth year), the "Sabbath of the Sabbatical Years" or "the Holy Year," commemorating the Exodus

- Fields are left fallow for this one year (Exodus 23:10–12; Leviticus 25:3–7; Deuteronomy 15:1–11).

- Land is restored to those from whom it had been dispossessed.

- Release is given to those obliged into hired service (Leviticus 25:1–34, 39–54; 27:16–24).

The Seven Set Feasts

The Three Great Festivals
When males were required to be presented to God

1. Passover (Pesah)
Or Festival of Unleavened Bread; Exodus 23:14, Leviticus 23:4–14; begun on the eve of the fourteenth Nisan; the festival of redemption and deliverance

2. Pentecost (Shavu'ot)
Or Festival of Weeks (or Harvest, or First Fruits); Exodus 23:16, Leviticus 23:15–21, Numbers 28:26, Deuteronomy 16:9; sixth Sivan (fiftieth day after Passover); spring feast of thanks; ends the weeks of the grain harvest; a covenant renewal

3. Tabernacles (Sukkot)
Or Feast of Ingathering (or Booths); Exodus 23:16, Leviticus 23:33–43; begun on the eve of fifteenth Tishri; celebrates the autumn harvest with thankfulness and merrymaking

The Two Festivals of Awe

1. Trumpets (Rosh Ha-Shanah)
Or *Day of Awe*; Numbers 29:1, Leviticus 23:23–25; first and second Tishri; Jewish New Year, contrition; begins the most solemn month on the Jewish calendar

2. Atonement (Yom Kippur)
Or *Day of Awe*; Leviticus 23:26–32, also Leviticus 10:1–2, 16; tenth Tishri; Great Day of the year, fast day, repentance; the day the scapegoat is sent into the wilderness to die for the people's sins; the high priest enters the holy of holies

The Two Lesser Festivals

1. Feast of Lights (Hanukkah)
Or Dedication; 1 Maccabees 4:36, John 10:22; twenty-fifth Chislev; lasting eight days; commemorates the revolt and victory of the Hasmoneans; celebrates religious liberty and patriotism; a Hanukkah game of chance uses a dreidel, a four-sided top, each side bearing the initial letters of the words in the saying *Nas gadol hayah shom* ("a great miracle happened here").

2. Purim
Or Mordecai Day; Book of Esther; fourteenth Adar; Jewish deliverance; celebrates with pageantry and satire the deliverance of the Jews from death by the bravery of the Persian queen, Esther.

Dreidel

A dreidel is a four-sided top; each side bears the initial letters of the words in the saying *Nas gadol hayah shom* (a great miracle happened here). The top is used for a popular Hanukkah game.

CHAPTER 7

Devotions in Catholic Tradition

An Overview

Historically

Devotions like the following, evolving historically and admitting of great pluralism depending on times, places, and people, have dotted the Catholic year and embellished private prayer. (See CCC #2684.)

Benediction	Stations of the Cross
Various novenas	St. Mark's Day procession
Nine First Fridays	May devotions
First Saturdays	May crowning
Candlemas Day	Ember/Rogation days
St. Blaise	Forty Hours
Ember days	First Communion ceremonies
St. Joseph Day	Corpus Christi procession
Lenten devotions	Sacred Heart devotions

Distinctions

There are reincarnations from one era to another and from one culture to another; the secondary elements are the particulars popular at a certain time or place, often through the efforts of certain individuals.

1. Changeless, essential elements (basic meanings)
2. Changeable, secondary elements (forms, language, images)

Currently

Devotions are "warmly commended" by Vatican II, but it is said that they "should be so drawn up that they harmonize with the liturgical seasons, accord with the sacred liturgy, are in some fashion derived from it, and lead the people to it . . ." ("Constitution on the Sacred Liturgy," #13).

Principles

Although distinct from liturgical prayer, devotional prayer is governed by the same principles:

1. Trinitarian (mediated by Christ)—to the Father, in union with the Holy Spirit

2. Ecclesial (integrating the spirit and mission of the Church)—not overly individualistic and subjective

3. Scriptural (fortified with Bible readings) (See "Constitution on the Sacred Liturgy," #35.)

4. Liturgical (associated with the sacraments)—reflect the sacramental life and liturgical calendar

Devotional Objects

It is not uncommon for devotion to Christ, Mary, and the saints to include material objects, from pictures to scapulars to relics. The "material object" has often given to the devotion its title (the Sacred Heart, for example).

Object of Devotions

It is, however, the formal object (the meaning) that gives any devotion its true significance and value. It may be a specific attribute of the person or mystery of their life, but the real point of all the devotions is always the same: the person, be it Christ, Mary, or one of the saints.

Images   (See CCC #s 477–478, 1159–1162, 2129–2132.)

The "legitimate" portraying of Jesus' face in holy images was recognized by the Church at the Council of Nicaea II in 787. The *Catechism of the Catholic Church* teaches (#s 476–477):

> *Since the Word became flesh in assuming a true humanity, Christ's body was finite. Therefore the human face of Jesus can be portrayed. . . . The individual characteristics of Christ's body express the divine person of God's Son. He has made the features of his human body his own, to the point that they can be venerated when portrayed in a holy image, for the believer "who venerates the icon is venerating in it the person of the one depicted" [Nicaea II].*

The gospel message so familiar in the words of Scripture is the same word expressed in the images of Christian iconography. In the words of the *Catechism of the Catholic Church* (#s 1159–1160):

> *The sacred image, the liturgical icon, principally represents Christ. It cannot represent the invisible and incomprehensible God, but the incarnation of the Son of God has ushered in a new "economy" of images. . . . Christian iconography expresses in images the same Gospel message that Scripture communicates by words. Image and word illuminate each other.*

Devotion to the Eucharist

Solemnity of the Body and Blood of Christ (Latin: *Corpus Christi*)

This feast to honor the Blessed Sacrament came from a movement that began in twelfth-century Belgium. It was Pope Urban IV who first established it and, most notably, commissioned the great Dominican scholar St. Thomas Aquinas to compose liturgical texts for it. Holy Thursday, commemorating the Last Supper, is *the* Eucharistic feast. In its liturgical setting, however, it could not bear the devotional practices that piety required in its love for the Body of Christ, nor could it adequately allow for the joy that wanted expression, given the sorrowful events of Holy Thursday and Good Friday.

The Eucharistic procession was an early element in Corpus Christi devotions, emphasizing Christ's real Eucharistic presence. The Blessed Sacrament was carried through the town after Mass on its feast day (beneath its festive *ombrellino*, or canopy). These processions came to include a version of the Roman stations: stops at various points and, with Eucharist exposed on a simple altar, a sung Gospel passage, hymn, harvest blessing, and benediction.

The *infiorata*, or carpet of flowers, is a monastic tradition hundreds of years old, honoring the Blessed Sacrament. There was a custom of strewing flowers in the path of the Eucharistic procession on the feast of Corpus Christi. From this practice evolved the art of designing flower panels depicting religious themes and scenes for use on Corpus Christi.

Forty Hours' Adoration

This Blessed Sacrament devotion commemorates the forty hours Jesus was entombed. It originated at Milan in 1534 and was propagated by the Jesuits under St. Ignatius. By the end of the eighteenth century, it had spread to many countries. St. John Neumann (1811–1860) is credited with establishing it in the US. Where it is more feasible, the forty hours are interrupted for the night and extended over three days: The first and third days include liturgies of the Blessed Sacrament; the second day, a liturgy for peace; the solemn closing of Forty Hours includes the Litany of the Saints, with procession and benediction of the Blessed Sacrament.

Visit to the Blessed Sacrament

This devotion has taken various forms, depending on the culture, era, and personal preference. It acknowledges the presence of Christ in the Eucharist (the Real Presence) outside of Mass (abiding presence). The genuflection (or a deep bow, common in the Eastern Church) is a traditional gesture of respect, as is a bow or tip of the hat while passing a church. Perpetual adoration means that the Blessed Sacrament is exposed and adored around the clock.

Eucharistic Devotion (See CCC #s 1378, 1418.)

A liturgically renewed "benediction," as it was formerly called:

Introductory Rite
 Call to worship
 Expression of worship (appropriate song and/or psalms)

Liturgy of the Word
 Incensation of the Scriptures (optional)
 Proclamation of the Word
 Response: prayer or song (optional)
 Homily and/or silent meditation (optional)

Liturgy of the Eucharist
 Exposition of the Blessed Sacrament on the altar (two candles sufficient)
 Incensation of the Blessed Sacrament, altar
 Song/prayer of exposition
 Blessing with the Blessed Sacrament ("Benediction")
 Reposition

Concluding Rite
 Canticle (of Zechariah, Mary, or Simeon)
 Prayers of intercession
 Concluding prayer
 Blessing and dismissal

Hymns in Honor of the Blessed Sacrament

Panis Angelicus

Panis Angelicus ("Bread of Angels") is the last verse plus the customary Trinitarian conclusion of the seven-stanza *Sacris Solemniis*. This Matins and processional hymn is one of the jubilant and celebrated Corpus Christi hymns by St. Thomas Aquinas (1225–1274).

Panis angelicus fit panis hominum;
Dat panis caelicus figuris terminum:
O res mirabilis! Manducat Dominum
Pauper, servus, et humilis.

Te, trina Deitas unaque, poscimus;
Sic nos tu visita, sicut te colimus;
Per tuas semitas Duc nos quo tendimus,
Ad lucem quam inhabitas.

The bread of angels becomes the bread of man;
The bread of heaven puts an end to symbols:
O wonder! The poor, servant, lowly man
feeds upon his Lord.

You, God, three and one,
visit us as we pray to you:
by your footsteps guide us on our way
to the light which you inhabit.

O Salutaris Hostia

O Salutaris Hostia ("O Saving Victim") is the last verse plus the customary Trinitarian conclusion of *Verbum Supernum Prodiens* ("The Divine Word Coming Forth"). This Corpus Christi Lauds hymn by St. Thomas Aquinas is based on a more ancient hymn (of the incarnation) that has the same title.

O salutaris Hostia,	*O saving Victim, open wide*
Quae caeli pandis ostium,	*The gate of heav'n to us below,*
Bella premunt hostilia,	*Our foes press on from ev'ry side;*
Da robur fer auxilium.	*Your aid supply, your strength bestow.*
Uni trinoque Domino	*To your great name be endless praise,*
Sit sempiterna gloria:	*Immortal Godhead, One in Three;*
Qui vitam sine termino	*Grant us, for endless length of days,*
Nobis donet in patria.	*In our true native land to be.*

Pange Lingua (and *Tantum Ergo*)

"Sing, O Tongue," is the name of two famous liturgical hymns. This one, whose first line continues *gloriosi corporis mysterium* (the mystery of the glorious body), is a Corpus Christi Vespers hymn by St. Thomas Aquinas. Along with many other hymns, it is modeled on the more ancient holy cross hymn *Pange Lingua*. With various translations in all modern languages, it has been used as a Blessed Sacrament hymn for Holy Thursday and Corpus Christi processionals as well as for Forty Hours' adoration. Its last two versus, *Tantum ergo*, form a traditional Benediction hymn. It has long been used to accompany the procession of the Eucharist to its repose after the Holy Thursday service.

Pange, lingua, gloriosi,	*Sing my tongue, the Savior's glory,*
Corporis mysterium,	*Of his flesh the myst'ry sing;*
Sanguinisque pretiosi,	*Of the blood all price exceeding,*
Quem in mundi pretium.	*Shed by our immortal king,*
Fructus ventris generosi	*Destined for the world's redemption,*
Rex effudit gentium	*From a noble womb to spring.*
Nobis datus, nobis natus	*Of a pure and spotless virgin,*
Ex intacta Virgine,	*Born for us on earth below,*
Et in mundo conversatus,	*He, as man, with man conversing,*
Sparso verbi semine,	*Stayed, the seeds of truth to sow;*
Sui moras incolatus	*Then he closed in solemn order*
Miro clausit ordine.	*Wondrously his life of woe.*

In supremae nocte caenae,
Recombens cum fratribus,
Observata lege plene
Cibis in legalibus,
Cibum turbae duodenae
Se dat suis manibus.

Verbum caro, panem verum
Verbo carnem efficit:
Fitque sanguis Christi merum,
Et si sensus deficit,
Ad firmandum cor sincerum
Sola fides sufficit.

Tantum ergo Sacramentum
Veneremur cernui:
Et antiquum documentum
Novo cedat ritui;
Praestet fides supplementum
Sensuum defectui.

Genitori, Genitoque
Laus et jubilatio,
Salus, honor, virtus quoque
Sit et benedictio:
Procedenti ab utroque
Compar sit laudatio.

On the night of that last supper
Seated with his chosen band,
He, the paschal victim eating,
First fulfills the law's command;
Then as food to all his brethren
Gives himself with his own hand.

Word made flesh, the bread of nature
By his word to flesh he turns;
Wine into his blood he changes,
What though sense no change discerns?
Only be the heart in earnest,
Faith her lesson quickly learns.

Down in adoration failing,
Lo! the sacred host we hail;
Lo! o'er ancient forms departing,
Newer rites of grace prevail;
Faith for all defects supplying
Where the feeble senses fail.

To the everlasting Father,
And the Son who reigns on high,
With the Spirit blest proceeding
Forth from each eternally,
Be salvation, honor, blessing,
Might and endless majesty.

Adoro Te

"I Adore You" is a communion song by St. Thomas Aquinas and a prayer for before or after receiving Eucharist. The English verses are a translation by Gerard Manley Hopkins (1844–1889), a British Jesuit poet.

Adoro te devote, latens Deitas,
Quae sub his figuris vere latitas:
Tibi se cor meum totum subjicit,
Quia te contemplans totum deficit.

Godhead here in hiding, whom I do adore;
Masked by these bare shadows, shape and nothing
more,
See, Lord, at thy service low lies here a heart
Lost, all lost in wonder, at the God thou art.

Visus, tactus, gustus in te fallitur;
Sed auditu solo tuto creditur.
Credo quidquid dixit Dei Filius:
Nil hoc verbo veritatis verius.

Seeing, touching, tasting are in thee deceived;
How says trusty hearing? that shall be believed:
What God's Son has told me, take for truth I do;
Truth himself speaks truly or there's nothing true.

O memoriale mortis Domini,
Panis vivus vitam praestans homini,
Praesta meae menti de te vivere,
Et te illi semper dulce sapere.

O thou our reminder of Christ crucified,
Living bread the life of us for whom he died,
Lend this life to me then: feed and feast my mind,
There be thou the sweetness we were meant to
find.

Jesu, quem velatum nunc aspicio,
Oro fiat illud quod tam sitio:
Ut te revelata cernens facie,
Visu sim beatus tuae gloriae.

Jesus whom I look at shrouded here below,
I beseech thee send me what I thirst for so,
Some day to gaze on thee face to face in light
And be blest for ever with thy glory's sight.

The Legend of the Pelican

The pelican is a favorite symbol of the Eucharist and redemption. There is an ancient belief that the female pelican would rip open her breast to feed her young with her own life blood to avert their starvation in famine. In another legend, the pelican is the enemy of the serpent whose stings bring death to the young. The mother pelican, mourning over her dead brood, incinerates herself, and her warm blood restores their lives.

Devotion to the Sacred Heart

Devotion to the Sacred Heart is a worshipful relationship to the person of Christ and his redeeming love, under the aspect or symbol of his heart (see CCC #2011).

Scriptural Origins

1. The love of God for humankind is like a mother for her infant (Isaiah 49:14–15) and like a husband for his wife (Hosea 1–2; CCC #1604).

2. The human heart, a person's deepest self, is where God has written his covenant (Jeremiah 31:31–34; CCC #s 1764–1765).

3. Jesus of John's Gospel:
   - At the Feast of Tabernacles (John 7:37–39)—"Out of his heart shall flow rivers of living water."

   - On the cross (John 19:34)—when blood and water flowed from his pierced side

   - As risen Lord (John 20:27)—with his wounds still visible

Historical Evolution

1. Between 800 and 1000, there developed the use of Jesus' heart as a symbol to focus the venerable devotion to his humanity and to the wounds of Christ.

2. St. John Eudes (1601–1680) promoted devotion to the Sacred Heart and to the Heart of Mary, prompting Pope Pius XI to call him the father of the tradition.

3. Apparitions of Christ to St. Margaret Mary Alacoque (1673–1675), tell of his concern about the indifference and coldness in the world in response to his love. He asked her to promote these practices:
   - Devotion to his heart, symbolic of his love for all

   - Frequent Communion in a spirit of reparation, especially on the first Friday of the month

   - Holy hours and other devotions

4. Promotion by the Jesuits, at first through St. Margaret Mary's Jesuit spiritual director, Claude de la Colombière, became part of their institute, notably through the Apostleship of Prayer (Sacred Heart League), which popularized the Morning Offering and widely distributed the Sacred Heart badge.

5. Pope Pius XII's encyclical in 1956 on the Sacred Heart.

The Promises of Our Lord

Part of the apparitions to St. Margaret Mary, these promises to those devoted to the Sacred Heart were implicitly approved by the Church in the 1920 canonization of St. Margaret Mary.

1. I will give them all the graces necessary in their state of life.

2. I will establish peace in their houses.

3. I will comfort them in all their afflictions.

4. I will be their strength during life and above all during death.

5. I will bestow a large blessing upon all their undertakings.

6. Sinners shall find in my heart the source and infinite ocean of mercy.

7. Tepid souls shall grow fervent.

8. Fervent souls shall quickly mount to high perfection.

9. I will bless every place where a picture of my heart shall be set up and honored.

10. I will give to priests the gift of touching the most hardened hearts.

11. Those who shall promote this devotion shall have their names written in my heart, never to be blotted out.

12. I promise you in the excessive mercy of my heart that my all-powerful love will grant to all those who communicate on the first Friday in nine consecutive months the grace of final penitence; they shall not die in my disgrace nor without receiving the sacraments; my divine heart shall be their safe refuge in this last moment.

Enthronement of the Sacred Heart (See promise nine above.)

This is the formal and communal acknowledgment of the sovereignty of the heart of Jesus over a Christian family. The "apostle" of this practice was Fr. Mateo Crawley-Boevey (1875–1960), a South American Sacred Heart priest. Approved by Pope St. Pius X, the steps of the ceremony are:

1. Blessing of the home (optional)

2. Blessing of the image/picture

3. Placing of the picture in a place of honor

4. Apostles' Creed

5. Explanation of enthronement

6. Act of consecration and prayer of thanksgiving

7. Blessing of the family

8. Signing of a certificate and report

Traditional Practices of the Sacred Heart Devotion

Act of Consecration

This devotion renews the gift of ourselves that was made in Baptism and Confirmation (as well as Marriage and Holy Orders) and implies a total surrender to Christ in gratitude, promising fidelity. A most ancient form dates from the fifteenth century, popularized by the Benedictine monks at the Abbey of St. Matthias, Trier, Germany. The practice proliferated after St. Margaret Mary and later through the Apostleship of Prayer's Morning Offering as a personal and daily consecration. It was formalized in 1925 by Pope Pius XI who ordered an annual, public consecration of the human race on the feast of Christ the King:

> Most sweet Jesus, Redeemer of the human race, look down upon us humbly prostrate before Thine altar. We are Thine, and Thine we wish to be; but to be more surely united with Thee, behold, each one of us freely consecrates himself today to Thy most Sacred Heart. Many, indeed, have never known Thee; many, too, despising Thy precepts, have rejected Thee. Have mercy on them all, most merciful Jesus, and draw them to Thy Sacred Heart. Be Thou King, O Lord, not only of the faithful who have never forsaken Thee, but also of the prodigal children who have abandoned Thee; grant that they may quickly return to their Father's house, lest they die of wretchedness and hunger. Be Thou King of those whom heresy holds in error or discord keeps aloof; call them back to the harbor of truth and the unity of faith, so that soon there may be but one fold and one Shepherd. Grant, O Lord, to Thy Church assurance of freedom and immunity from harm; give peace and order to all nations, and make the earth resound from pole to pole with one cry: Praise to the divine Heart that wrought our salvation; to it be glory and honor forever. Amen.

Acts of Reparation

This conscious turning to God, change of heart, and reconciliation with others, leads to and flows from the Sacrament of Reconciliation.

First Fridays (See promise twelve on page 375.)

These are memorials of Good Friday and a response in loving praise and gratitude for the grace flowing from the heart of the Lamb of God, who takes away the sins of the world.

Holy Hour

This special kind of vigil commemorates Jesus' agony in the garden: "Could you not stay awake with me for one hour?" (Matthew 26:40).

Morning Offering

The Morning Offering was inspired by Christ's requests to St. Margaret Mary and initiated by Jesuit Fr. Gaulrelet (1844). Popularized since 1860 by the Apostleship of Prayer (League of the Sacred Heart), it associates one's "prayers, works, joys, and sufferings" with the Church's Eucharist ("Dogmatic Constitution on the Church," no. 34; 1 Peter 2:5).

Devotion to the Passion

Devotion to Christ's passion, the heart of Christian redemption, is at the heart of Christian spirituality. Just as Eucharistic devotion and Sacred Heart devotion have their feasts, so does devotion to Christ's passion: the Triumph of the Cross (September 14). At the Good Friday service, this devotion is expressed most beautifully and solemnly in the veneration of the cross. (See CCC #s 571–573, 599–627.)

The Veneration of the Cross

The Sacramentary still suggests the ancient songs for this Good Friday ceremony. Traditionally they include:

1. Psalm 67:2

"May God be gracious and bless us . . ." (words similar to the priestly blessing of Numbers 6:22–27).

2. The Reproaches (Quoting Psalm 136)

Although they are included in the Sacramentary as an option, various groups have discouraged their use, since they are capable of inspiring an anti-Jewish spirit. The venerable trisagion ("Holy God; Holy, Mighty One . . .") is the traditional refrain for the first part of the reproaches.

Reproaches of Good Friday

"Improperia" (Complaints), recited during the veneration of the cross

V. My people, what have I done to you?

How have I offended you? Answer me!

I led you out of Egypt, from slavery to freedom,

but you led your Savior to the cross.

R. Holy is God! Holy and strong!

Holy immortal One, have mercy on us!

V. For forty years I led you safely through the desert.

I fed you with manna from heaven

and brought you into a land of plenty;

but you led your Savior to the cross.

R. Holy is God! . . .

V. What more could I have done for you?

I planted you as my fairest vine,

but you yielded only bitterness:

when I was thirsty you gave me vinegar to drink,

and you pierced your Savior with a lance.

R. Holy is God! . . .

The following reproaches are sung alter-nately by the cantors.

V. For your sake I scourged your captors and their firstborn sons,

but you brought your scourges down on me.

R. My people, what have I done to you? How have I offended you? Answer me!

V. I led you from slavery to freedom and drowned your captors in the sea,

but you handed me over to your high priests.

R. My people . . .

V. I opened the sea before you,

but you have opened my side with a spear.

R. My people . . .

V. I led you on your way in a pillar of cloud,

but you led me to Pilate's court.

R. My people . . .

V. I bore you up with manna in the desert,

but you struck me down and scourged me.

R. My people . . .

V. I gave you saving water from the rock,

but you gave me gall and vinegar to drink.

R. My people . . .

V. For you I struck down the kings of Canaan,

but you struck my head with a reed.

R. My people . . .

V. I gave you a royal scepter,

but you gave me a crown of thorns.

R. My people . . .

V. I raised you to the height of majesty,

but you have raised me high on a cross.

R. My people . . .

3. Pange Lingua

Honoring and addressing Christ's cross, this celebrated hymn (once sung at Passiontide Matins) is one of the Church's most beautiful poems and has been used for Good Friday veneration since the ninth century. It has inspired many other hymns, most notably St. Thomas Aquinas's Eucharistic hymn with the same title. Written in 602 by Venantius Fortunatus, bishop of Poitiers, it is familiar to many because of its refrain, "Faithful Cross" (*Crux Fidelis*):

Faithful cross, above all others,
One and only noble tree,
None in foliage, none in blossom,
None in fruit thy peer may be;
Sweetest wood, and sweetest iron;
Sweetest weight is hung on thee.

Sing, my tongue, the glorious battle,
Sing the last, the dread affray;
O'er the cross, the victor's trophy,
Sound the high triumphal lay,
How, the pains of death enduring,
Earth's redeemer won the day.

He, our maker, deeply grieving
That the first-made Adam fell,
When he ate the fruit forbidden
Whose reward was death and hell,
Marked e'en then this tree the ruin
Of the first tree to dispel.

Thus the work for our salvation,
He ordained to be done;
To the traitor's art opposing,
Art yet deeper than his own;
Thence the remedy procuring
Whence the fatal wound begun.

Therefore, when at length the fullness
Of the appointed time was come,
He was sent, the world's creator,
From the Father's heavenly home,
And was found in human fashion,
Offspring of the virgin's womb.

Lo! he lies, an infant weeping,
Where the narrow manger stands,
While the mother-maid his members,
Wraps in mean and lowly bands,
And the swaddling clothes is winding
Round his helpless feet and hands.

Thirty years among us dwelling,
His appointed time fulfilled,
Born for this, he meets his passion,
For that this he freely willed:
On the cross the lamb is lifted,
Where his life-blood shall be spilled.

He endured the nails, the spitting,
Vinegar, and spear, and reed;
From that holy body broken
Blood and water forth proceed:
Earth and stars, and sky and ocean,
By that flood from stain are freed.

Bend thy boughs, O tree of glory!
Thy relaxing sinews bend;
For a while the ancient rigor,
That thy birth bestowed, suspend;
And the king of heavenly beauty
On thy bosom gently tend.

Thou alone was counted worthy
This world's ransom to uphold;
For a shipwrecked race preparing
Harbor, like the ark of old;
With the sacred blood anointed
From the smitten lamb that rolled.

Vexilla Regis

Written by the sixth-century bishop, Venantius Fortunatus (see *Pange Lingua*, page 379), "Abroad the Regal Banners Fly" is one of the most famous and important hymns of the cross and the passion. It was once sung at Vespers during the Liturgy of the Hours of Passiontide, on the feast of the Holy Cross, and on Good Friday when the Eucharist was brought for communion from its repository (now a time of silence). Since the fourteenth century, it has known some fifty translations into English alone.

Abroad the regal banners fly,
Now shines the cross' mystery;
Upon it life did death endure,
And yet by death did life procure.

Who, wounded with a direful spear,
Did, purposely to wash us clear
From stain of sin, pour out a flood
Of precious water mixed with blood.

That which the prophet-king of old
Hath in mysterious verse foretold,
Is now accomplished, whilst we see
God ruling nations from a tree.

O lovely and refulgent tree,
Adorned with purpled majesty;

Culled from a worthy stock, to bear
Those limbs which sanctified were.

Blest tree, whose happy branches bore
The wealth that did the world restore;
The beam that did that body weigh
Which raised up hell's expected prey.

Hail, cross, of hopes the most sublime!
Now in this mournful passion time,
Improve religious souls in grace,
The sins of criminals efface.

Blest Trinity, salvation's spring,
May every soul thy praises sing;
To those thou grantest conquest by
The holy cross, rewards apply. Amen.

Stations of the Cross

The stations commemorate the stops along the *Via Dolorosa* (Latin: way of sorrow), Jesus' journey of about a mile from Pilate's court, the praetorium, to Calvary and the tomb. Legend has it that Mary often retraced the sorrowful way her son made on Good Friday. (The Scriptures are from the the New Revised Standard Version.)

1. **Jesus is condemned to death.**
   "For God so loved the world that he gave his only Son, so that everyone who believes in him may not perish but may have eternal life" (John 3:16).

2. **Jesus bears his cross.**
   "If any want to become my followers, let them deny themselves and take up their cross daily and follow me" (Luke 9:23).

3. Jesus falls the first time.

"All we like sheep have gone astray; we have all turned to our own way, and the Lord has laid on him the iniquity of us all" (Isaiah 53:6).

4. Jesus meets his mother.

"Is it nothing to you, all you who pass by? Look and see if there is any sorrow like the my sorrow . . ." (Lamentations 1:12).

5. Simon of Cyrene helps Jesus carry his cross.

"Truly I tell you, just as you did it to one of the least of these who are members of my family, you did it to me" (Matthew 25:40).

6. Veronica wipes the face of Jesus.

"Whoever has seen me has seen the Father" (John 14:9).

7. Jesus falls a second time.

"Come to me, all you that are weary and carrying heavy burdens, and I will give you rest" (Matthew 11:28).

8. Jesus meets the women of Jerusalem.

"Daughters of Jerusalem, do not weep for me, but weep for yourselves and for your children" (Luke 23:28).

9. Jesus falls a third time.

"For all who exalt themselves will be humbled, and these who humble themselves will be exalted" (Luke 14:11).

10. Jesus is stripped of his garments.

"None of you can become my disciple if you do not give up all your possessions" (Luke 14:33).

11. Jesus is nailed to the cross.

"For I have come down from heaven, not to do my own will, but the will of him who sent me" (John 6:38).

12. Jesus dies on the cross.

"And being found in human form, he humbled himself and became obedient to the point of death—even death on a cross" (Philippians 2:7–8).

13. Jesus is taken down from the cross.

"Was it not necessary that the Messiah should suffer these things and then enter into his glory?" (Luke 24:26).

14. Jesus is placed in the tomb.

"Unless a grain of wheat falls into the earth and dies, it remains just a single grain; but if it dies, it bears much fruit" (John 12:24).

Black Spiritual

The Negro spiritual "Were You There When They Crucified My Lord?" was first published in 1899 and has become one of the most famous modern Passion hymns and a favorite hymn in many churches. The traditional melody was arranged by the Reverend Charles Winfred Douglas in 1944 and popularized by the Black tenor Roland Hayes.

Christ's Passion in Christian Art

Ecce Homo (Latin: Behold the Man)

A name given to the Good Friday pictures of Jesus, crowned with thorns and presented to the crowds by Pilate (John 19:5). See especially Correggio, Dürer, Poussin, Rembrandt, Reni, Titian, and Van Dyck.

Crucifixion Group

The famous bronze work of the fifteenth-century Italian sculptor Donatello surmounts the main altar of the Basilica of St. Anthony in Padua, which houses the tomb of the famous Franciscan preacher.

Pietà

The "thirteenth station"; artistic representation of the dead Christ in his mother's arms. The Roman virtue of love and reverence for parents/children was *pietas* (piety); see Pius Aeneas, who rescued his father from Troy when it was burning, and Antoninus the Pius, who had his adoptive father Hadrian deified. (The most famous *Pietà* is that of Michelangelo, in St. Peter's Basilica in Rome.)

Devotion to the Infant of Prague

This is the name of a devotion that has evolved from the gift of an eighteen-inch wooden statue of the child Jesus. The figure's left hand holds a globe surmounted by a cross, and its right hand is poised in blessing. It represents both Christ's kingship and childhood. The devotion gained ecclesiastical approval from the Bishop of Prague in 1655. (See CCC #s 531–534.)

Infant of Prague

About the middle of the seventeenth century the community of Discalced Carmelite Fathers in Prague found itself reduced to a state of extreme want. A certain pious benefactress had great faith in the miraculous powers of a beautiful waxen image of the infant Jesus given her by her mother who had brought it from Spain. Desiring to aid the fathers in their distress, she presented them with this statue, saying: "As long as you honor this image, you shall never want."

The words proved prophetic. The image was given a place of honor in the oratory and the community flourished. When the monastery was pillaged and the statue lost, the fathers, when able to return, were forced to live in dire poverty until the image, found after a long search, was restored to its rightful place. So many were the favors obtained through this image that it was decided to place it in the church that the faithful might share in the blessings which the divine infant dispensed with such liberality. They came in great numbers to pray at the shrine and countless were the favors granted and even miracles worked on their behalf.

The devotion soon spread beyond the limits of Prague to all Europe and thence to all parts of the world. It has continued to increase in popularity in some parts of the world. Today thousands claim to have obtained favors of all kinds by reason of their devotion to the Infant Jesus of Prague. However, liturgical renewal has resulted in a lessening of devotions such as this one, because the liturgy is better meeting some needs the devotions met.

Veneration of Saints and Heroes

The Nature of Veneration

Distinctions: Adoration and Veneration

1. Veneration given to saints is called *dulia* (see CCC #957).

2. Higher veneration given to Mary is called *hyperdulia* (see CCC #971).

3. Supreme worship or adoration due God alone is called *latria*.

Catholic Veneration of Saints (See CCC #s 823–829.)

The *Acta Sanctorum* (*Acts of the Saints*) is the monumental collection of saints' lives, initiated by the Bollandists, a group named after the seventeenth-century Jesuit, Jean Bolland. Arranged according to the liturgical calendar, it consists now of almost seventy volumes and is growing.

Liturgically

1. The Eucharistic Prayer of the Mass celebrates the communion of saints and asks their intercession.

2. The universal liturgical calendar includes saints' feast days, sometimes including special readings (departing from the seasonal cycle) and reference in the opening prayer.

3. The Liturgy of the Hours has an Office of Readings which includes a brief biography on these feast days, plus a reading by or about the saint.

Popularly

1. The Litany of the Saints

2. Traditional public devotions and novenas

3. Private devotions, including asking saints' intercessions (see Patrons) and using specific prayers that saints have used

Devotion to Mary
(See CCC #829.)

Mary in the Bible

See Chapter 9 for the favorite Marian symbols and images. Included there are the references to Scriptures in which the symbols and images are rooted.

The Blessed Mother (See CCC #s 495, 501, 963–970.)

1. A natural motherhood: Mary, mother of Jesus (referred to often in the Gospels)

2. A divine motherhood
   - Mary, "mother of my Lord" (referred to by Elizabeth, for example, in Luke 1:43)
   - Mary, Mother of God (Greek: *Theotokos*; Council of Ephesus, 431)

3. A spiritual motherhood
   - Mary, "mother" of John (See John 19:26–27.)
   - Mary, Mother of the Church (See Romans 8:29; Revelation 12:17.)

The Blessed Virgin

1. Mary, virgin mother (see CCC #s 496–498). The Scriptures are explicit: "How can this be, since I am a virgin?"

2. Mary, ever virgin (see CCC #500). According to an Old Testament expression, *brothers* means close relatives. The Catholic Church does not regard the phrase "brothers of the Lord" as referring to other children of Mary (see Mark 3:31–35, 6:3; 1 Corinthians 9:5; Galatians 1:19). James and Joseph ("brothers of Jesus") are in fact sons of another Mary who was a disciple of Christ ("the other Mary," Matthew 13:55, 28:1; see also Matthew 27:56).

The Seven Words of Mary (See CCC #2618)

The Scriptures record Mary speaking seven times.

1. "How can this be, since I am a virgin?" (Luke 1:34—response to the annunciation)

2. "Here am I, the servant of the Lord; let it be with me according to your word." (Luke 1:38—acceptance of her vocation)

3. "[Mary] entered the house of Zechariah and greeted Elizabeth." (Luke 1:40—the visitation: Mary the Christ-bearer and guest)

4. "My soul magnifies the Lord . . ." (Luke 1:46f—joyful reflection on God's fidelity, the *Magnificat*)

5. "Child, why have you treated us like this?" (Luke 2:48—the finding of the child Jesus in the temple)

6. "They have no wine." (John 2:3—her intercession on behalf of the Cana wedding hosts)

7. "Do whatever he tells you." (John 2:5—her instruction to the waiters at the Cana wedding feast)

The House of Loreto

This is the *Santa Casa*, the reputed Nazareth house of Mary around which the town of Loreto, Italy, grew. (Loreto is some fifteen miles from Ancona down the eastern coast of Italy on the Adriatic Sea). The tradition is that around 1290 a Lady Louretta "translated" the house from Nazareth to Fiume, Illyria (today's Rijeka, Croatia), and then shortly to Recanati, and finally to property near Ancona. In the chapel there are bas-reliefs of episodes in Mary's life and an image of the virgin carved, the story goes, by St. Luke.

Seven Sorrows of Mary

1. The prophecy of Simeon
2. The flight into Egypt
3. The loss of the boy Jesus in the temple
4. Meeting Jesus on the way of the cross
5. The crucifixion of Jesus
6. The taking down of Jesus from the cross
7. The burial of Jesus

Seven Joys of Mary

1. The annunciation
2. The visitation
3. The nativity
4. The epiphany
5. The presentation of Jesus
6. The finding of Jesus in the temple
7. Mary's assumption into heaven

Our Lady of Sorrows

Mater Dolorosa

The image of the "Sorrowful Mother" is familiar in Christian art. (Any mother who has lost a child is a "sorrowful mother" like Mary, who lost her son Jesus.)

*Stabat Mater (**Dolorosa**)*

The "(Sorrowful) Mother Stands" is an anonymous Latin poem, for private devotion originally, now a common Lenten hymn.

At the cross her station keeping,
Stood the mournful Mother weeping,
Close to Jesus to the last.
Through her heart his sorrow sharing,
All his bitter anguish bearing,
Now at length the sword had passed.

O how sad and sore distressed
Was that mother highly blest
Of the sole-begotten Son.
Christ above in torment hangs,
She beneath beholds the pangs
Of her dying glorious Son.

Is there one who would not weep,
Whelmed by miseries so deep,
Christ's dear mother to behold?
Can the human heart refrain
From partaking in her pain,
In that mother's pain untold?

Bruised, derided, cursed, defiled,
She beheld her tender child
All with bloody scourges rent.
For the sins of his own nation,
Saw him hang in desolation,
Till his spirit forth he sent.

O thou mother! Fount of love,
Touch my spirit from above,
Make my heart with thine accord.
Make me feel as thou hast felt;
Make my soul to glow and melt
With the love of Christ my Lord.

Holy mother, pierce me through,
In my heart each wound renew
Of my Savior crucified.
Let me share with thee his pain,
Who for all my sins was slain,
Who for me in torment died.

Let me mingle tears with thee,
Mourning him who mourned for me
All the days that I may live:
By the cross with thee to stay;
There with thee to weep and pray,
All I ask of thee to give.

Virgin of all virgins best,
Listen to my fond request:
Let me share thy grief divine.
Let me, to my latest breath,
In my body bear the death
Of that dying Son of thine.

Wounded with his every wound,
Steep my soul till it hath swooned
In his very blood away.
Be to me, O Virgin, nigh,
Lest in flames I burn and die
In his awful judgment day.

Christ, when thou shalt call me hence
Be thy mother my defense;
Be thy cross my victory;
While my body here decays,
May my soul thy goodness praise,
Safe in paradise with thee.

Mary in Recent Catholic Teaching

1. By **definition of the doctrines** of the Immaculate Conception, in the Bull *Ineffabilis Deus* by Pope Pius IX (December 8, 1854); and the Assumption, in the Apostolic Constitution *Munificentissimus*, by Pope Pius XII (November 1, 1950).

2. By **Ecumenical Council** in "The Role of the Blessed Virgin Mary, Mother of God, in the Mystery of Christ and the Church," "Dogmatic Constitution on the Church," Chapter 8, Vatican II (1962–1965).

3. By **Pope Paul VI** in *Marialis Cultus (On Devotion to the Blessed Virgin Mary)*, 1974, and "Mary, Star of Evangelization," in *Evangelii Nuntiandi (On Evangelization in the Modern World)*, #84, apostolic exhortations (December 8, 1975).

4. By **US Bishops** in "Behold Your Mother," a pastoral letter (November 21, 1973).

5. By **Pope John Paul II** in *Redemptoris Mater (The Mother of the Redeemer)* (March 25, 1987).

6. In the ***Catechism of the Catholic Church***, Part One, Section Two, Chapter 2, #s 484–511, and Chapter 3, #s 963–975; Part Four, Section One, Chapter 1, #s 2617–2619, 2622.

Mary in the Liturgy (See CCC #s 971, 1172.)

Mary is referred to in the creeds, mentioned in the Eucharistic Prayer, alluded to in some options of the penitential rite, honored with a choice of Marian prefaces, and memorialized with fourteen feast days in the liturgical calendar (see the list in Chapter 6). In addition, there is a choice of votive Masses and common Masses of the Blessed Virgin which include a choice from among dozens of Scripture readings to provide appropriate texts and to harmonize the occasion with the liturgical season.

Titles of Mary

Marian titles are virtually countless. Many are collected in the Litany of the Blessed Virgin. Some, like "Our Lady of Guadalupe," come from apparitions through the years. All, like "Our Mother of Perpetual Help," have a story to tell. The following three begin many a list and have a special significance for many Catholics.

1. Mother of God (Greek: *Theotokos*, God-bearer; see CCC #495.)

Mary's oldest title, celebrated on the January 1 solemnity, was established in 431 by the Council of Ephesus which, in defending Mary's divine maternity, was clarifying Christ's true nature. Nestorius, the bishop of Constantinople, maintained that there were two distinct Persons in the incarnate Christ, one human and the other divine. True faith, on the other hand, believed in a "hypostatic" union of the two natures in the one Person of Jesus and thus could say, as believers still do, that the Son of God was born of Mary, that he was crucified, that he died. Even after the bishops of the whole Church clarified the truth and condemned the heresy, Nestorius and his followers continued to teach and preach in error, causing a confusion among the faithful. "Nestorianism" remained, developed a whole theology, spread through Asia Minor, and migrated to Persia. To this day, a Nestorian Church survives, namely, Assyrian Christians.

2. Our Lady

"Notre Dame" corresponds with the Italian "Madonna" and its equivalent in every language of Christendom.

3. The Immaculate Conception (See CCC #s 491–492.)

Under this title, Mary is national patroness of the United States. The title celebrates her sinless beginning, conceived without having original sin, in the womb of her mother. As a title commemorating an event, the Immaculate Conception also has a feast day on the calendar, December 8 (nine months before the traditional celebration of her birthday, September 8). The Immaculate Conception of Mary is sometimes confused with Jesus' conception in the womb of Mary, an event commemorated on March 25 with a feast called the Annunciation. This March 25th feast is nine months before the traditional celebration of Jesus' birthday, December 25.

Principal Apparitions of the Blessed Virgin Mary

Rome

Devotion to Our Lady of the Snows began on Rome's Esquiline Hill in 352 and may be the oldest of Marian devotions. In the Eternal City, an elderly couple had an apparition of Mary one hot August night during which Mary requested that a shrine be built on one of the city's celebrated hills. The next morning the city woke to find the Esquiline covered with snow. Today, St. Mary Major, "Church of St. Mary of the Snow," stands on this site as the largest and most important of all churches dedicated to the Blessed Mother. (In the United States, pilgrims can visit Our Lady of the Snows Shrine in Belleville, Illinois. Open all year, the shrine includes meditative and devotional areas. It also is the site of an annual outdoor novena, celebrated during nine nights surrounding August 5, the feast day of Our Lady of the Snows, today called the Dedication of St. Mary Major.)

Guadalupe, Mexico

Four times in 1531 to Juan Diego

Our Lady of Guadalupe

Mary the "Aztec Princess"

Many images of Mary make her appear European, because the artists were European. Many make her look Middle Eastern, Jewish, which she was. One, in Mexico City, stands alone. It appears on a man's poncho, or tilma, made of two pieces of cactus cloth. Although this kind of material rarely lasts longer than twenty years, this tilma has survived intact for centuries. In 1531, it belonged to Juan Diego, an Aztec.

Only twelve years before, the Spanish explorer Hernan Cortes had first encountered the Aztecs. He and his soldiers were Christians who, in the eyes of the Aztecs, were brutal and greedy. These explorers brought great suffering, particularly to Aztec women. Nevertheless, Juan Diego and many others had been baptized.

One December morning Juan walked by the ruins of a shrine of the Aztec corn-harvest goddess, a place destroyed by the Spanish and renamed Guadalupe. There Juan saw a vision of Mary, revealing herself as "the mother of the true God from whom all life has come." She appeared with the olive skin, black hair, and magnificently colored clothing of an Aztec princess. Around her waist was the sash worn by a woman during pregnancy. She spoke with affection to Juan, bringing a message of hope and compassion, contradicting the experience the people had had at the hands of the Spanish.

Part of Mary's message required Juan to go to his bishop to gain cooperation and participation. Not surprisingly, the bishop did not immediately believe him, but wanted more evidence—a sign. As Juan was giving up, Mary reappeared and gave him a sign. Our Lady told him to bring the bishop some roses growing there at Tepeyac, near present-day Mexico City. Although it was winter, Juan found Castillian roses growing among the rocks. He gathered them carefully inside his poncho and set off to see the bishop.

When he unfolded the garment to display the sign, there was a greater one there: a beautiful image of Mary, an image no artist conceived, but one mirroring the image Juan saw at Tepeyac. The image—and the message—was unmistakable. Mary's appearance was a consolation to the poor and a rebuke to the Spanish. Mary's visitation was not to the bishop, and it was not to the powerful Spanish, and it was not to the Franciscans who were catechizing among the Aztecs. It was to an Aztec Christian peasant. Mary brought new dignity to the Aztecs. In the seven years following her appearances, eight million Aztecs were baptized.

Our Lady of the Miraculous Medal, France

Three times in 1830 to Catherine Laboure

LaSalette, France

To two children in 1846 as sorrowing and weeping figure

Lourdes, France

Eighteen times in 1858 to fourteen-year-old Bernadette Soubirous as the Immaculate Conception

Knock, Ireland

With figures of St. Joseph and St. John the Apostle to fifteen people in 1879

Fatima, Portugal

Six times in 1917 to three children, popularizing devotion to Our Lady of the Rosary. Devotion to the Immaculate Heart of Mary on the first Saturday of five successive months originated in the revelations of Mary at Fatima. Through a series of apparitions (May 13–October 13, 1917), Mary told three shepherd children that she desired frequent recitation of the Rosary and penance done for sinners. She predicted World War II, the rise of communism, and Church persecution. She promised the conversion of Russia and peace for humankind if her wishes were followed. In particular, at the third apparition (July 13, 1917) she requested that Russia be consecrated to her Immaculate Heart and that all Catholics receive Communion in reparation for sin on the first Saturday of each month. In May of 1982, Pope John Paul II, in union with all the bishops of the world, consecrated the world to the Immaculate Heart of Mary, although Russia was not specifically mentioned. It was Our Lady of Fatima whom Pope John Paul II credited when he survived the attempt on his life in 1981.

Beauraing, Belgium

Thirty-three times in 1932–1933 to five children

Banneaux, near Liege, Belgium

Eight times in 1933 to eleven-year-old peasant girl Mariette Beco as the Virgin of the Poor

Popular Marian Devotion

Private Prayer

These are the four most ancient and venerable Marian prayers:

1. Hail Mary

2. Hail Holy Queen

3. Memorare ("Remember . . .")

4. Angelus ("The Angel . . .")

The Five First Saturdays

Devotion to the Immaculate Heart of Mary on the first Saturday of five successive months originated in the revelations of Mary at Fatima.

Our Mother of Perpetual Help

This devotion began in a story about a good mother and a bad dream, an episode, so says the legend, in young Jesus' life. One day the Christ child was frightened by the terrifying vision of two angels showing him the instruments of the passion. He ran to his mother for reassurance, almost losing his sandal on the way (as the traditional picture records). Safely enfolded in her arms, his hands are turned palms down into his mother's, illustrating that the graces of redemption are in her keeping.

This story has stayed alive thanks to its picture, icon-style, that is so familiar. The original rests on the main altar of the shrine of the same name on the Via Merulana in Rome. The five markings are names, or titles, in Greek. At the top: Mother (*Meter*, shortened to "MP"—*mu rho* in Greek) of God ("ThU"—*theta upsilon*). The marking over the M is an old sign for the Holy Spirit, or redemption. The wavy line over the ThU is an old mark for an abbreviation. Over the Christ child is "Jesus Christ." The angels are designated as the archangels Michael (capital *mu* in Greek, "M" in English) and Gabriel (capital *gamma* in Greek, "G" in English).

The odyssey of this picture is a story in itself. Explanations of its origin abound. One predictable legend has it that it was painted by

St. Luke, but its creator and its age are actually unknown. Some say it was venerated for centuries in Constantinople as a miraculous icon and that it was destroyed by the Turks in 1453.

The story continues that a copy of that work was made in tempera on hard nutwood, 17 by 21 inches. This painting came from Crete, where it had been venerated, to Rome in 1490. It was owned by a private family until a little girl of the household had an apparition in which the Blessed Mother told her that she wished to have the icon placed in a church, specifically "between my beloved church of St. Mary Major's and that of my beloved son, St. John of Lateran."

On March 27, 1499, her request was fulfilled and the icon was exposed for veneration in the Church of St. Matthew which is between St. Mary Major and St. John Lateran churches. There it remained for three centuries, becoming a pilgrimage shrine for the Christian world. In 1789, the old church was demolished in a war, but the icon was saved by the Augustinian priests in charge of St. Matthew's. They took it with them to their new quarters in the city.

In 1855, the Redemptorist priests came to Rome and built a church in honor of their founder, St. Alphonsus, on the site of the old St. Matthew's. A Redemptorist priest recalled an old Augustinian telling him during his youth of a miraculous picture in their chapel that had always been venerated in old St. Matthew's.

The Redemptorists petitioned Pope Pius IX to have the image placed in the church on the spot chosen by Our Lady herself. The pope, granting the request, said: "It is our will that this picture of the Blessed Virgin be returned to the church between St. Mary Major's and St. John Lateran's." At the same time he commanded the Redemptorists to "make her known" all over the world.

On April 26, 1866, a solemn procession carried the miraculous Madonna to her chosen spot in the Church of St. Alphonsus Maria de Liguori, one of Mary's greatest lovers and defenders. Today the original painting reposes in Rome while millions of replicas bring her and her perpetual help to people everywhere.

Consecration to Mary

This devotional act, promoted by St. Louis de Montfort (1673–1716), consists of the entire gift of self to Jesus through Mary (as her "slave"), being a habitual attitude of dependence on her.

I, _____, faithless sinner, renew and ratify today in your hands the vows of my baptism; I renounce forever Satan, his pomps and works; and I give myself entirely to Jesus Christ, the incarnate Wisdom, to carry my cross after him all the days of my life, and to be more faithful to him than I have ever been before.

In the presence of all the heavenly court I choose you this day for my mother and queen. I deliver and consecrate to you, as your slave, my body and soul, my goods, both interior and exterior, and even the value of all my good actions, past, present, and future; leaving to you the entire and full right of disposing of me and all that belongs to me without exception, according to your good pleasure, for the greater glory of God, in time and in eternity. Amen.

Marian Baptismal Names

Devotion to the Blessed Mother has inspired many baptismal names, whose bearers have Mary as their patron and a particular feast day—or any—as their name's day.

1. Mary

The name is from the Hebrew *Marah* (meaning myrrh, an incense and perfume) or *Miryam* (meaning bitter) (see Ruth 1:20).

2. Marian translations and variations, such as:

Maire (Irish), Manon (French), Manette (French), Mara, Maria (Latin, Italian, Hungarian, German, Spanish), Marie (French), Maretta, Marette, Marella, Marietta, Marilla, Marilyn, Mariquita (Spanish), Marita (Spanish), Marla (Bavarian), Marya, Maryse (French), Maureen (Irish), Marya (Slavic), Miriam, Moira or Maura (Irish), Muriel (Irish for Star of the Sea), and Marianne (Marian in Italian), a name honoring both Mary and Anne

3. Marian nicknames, such as:

Mame, Mamie, Mayme, May, Mari, Moll, Mollie, Molly, and Polly

4. Marian names from Mary's many titles, such as:

Madonna (Italian for My Lady), Regina (Latin for queen, honoring Mary's queenship), and Virginia (honoring Mary's virginity)

5. Marian masculine forms, such as:

Gilmary, Gilmore, Melmore, and Myles (all deriving from "servant of Mary," as do surnames Gilmartin and Kilmartin), and Marion

---

Mary in the Middle East

The faithful in the Chaldean and Syrian liturgical traditions (which is mostly in the present-day countries of Syria, Iran, and Iraq) show respect for Mary and call forth her virtues in their children by the bestowal of her very name, Miriam. Other names too reflect esteem for Marian qualities, such as Kamala (Mary's perfection), Jamala (Mary's beauty), 'Afifa (Mary's purity), and Farida (Mary's uniqueness).

Out of Respect

The custom of giving children the name of a Christian saint can be traced back to the first millennium. Beginning in France and Germany, the practice spread through the continent of Europe by the thirteenth century. Only the name of Jesus himself is held in reserve, with one exception: Spanish-speaking peoples, unlike the faithful in all other Christian countries, have not been too shy to use the personal name of the Savior for their children.

Ireland is an exception on the other extreme: No Christian names can be found in ancient Irish documents. Just as no pope since the leader chosen by Jesus has taken the name Peter, so no Irish parent in the early years gave the name of a saint, not even beloved Patrick, to their children. Out of piety and humility, it was considered irreverent to claim such names for ourselves. Saints' names in Ireland could be found, however, as the root of certain surnames (last names): Some Gaelic clans called themselves "servants" (or "descendants of servants") of certain saints by using prefixes gil-, kil-, and mal- as in Gilmartin (servant of St. Martin), Gilpatrick and Kilpatrick, Gilmary, Gilchrist, Gillis (servant of Jesus), and Malone (servant of St. John). With the coming of the Normans, the European practice began to prevail. An Irish piety that persisted, however, was reserving and keeping sacred the original name of Mary (Muire), never using it in this form for a daughter. Girls named for the Blessed Mother received the name in another form, mostly Maire.

Just as Spanish-speaking countries brought the name of Jesus into their families, so did they bring a veneration for Mary into their family names by using some of her liturgical titles and qualities, like Asuncion (Assumption), Concepcion or Concha (Immaculate Conception), Consuelo (Our Lady of Good Counsel), Dolores (Our Lady of Sorrows), Gracia (Our Lady of Grace), Luz (Our Lady of Light), Paz (Our Lady of Peace), Pura (Virgin Most Pure), Stella (Star of the Sea), and Victoria (Our Lady of Victory).

Mary in Art

Artists' renditions in picture and statuary are countless. The following are commonly seen.

1. Events in her life that are described in Scripture (such as the annunciation, the visitation, and the nativity of Jesus)

2. Beliefs from Catholic faith, often with symbols from Scripture (such as the assumption, coronation, and immaculate conception)

3. Images from apparitions (such as Our Lady of Guadalupe, Lourdes, and Fatima)

4. Traditional images (such as Our Lady of Grace)

5. Pictures of miraculous or unknown origin (such as Our Mother of Perpetual Help and the Black Madonna)

Devotion to St. Joseph

(See CCC, "The Communion of Saints," #s 946–962. For titles of St. Joseph, see the Litany of St. Joseph in Chapter 1.)

In Scripture

Joseph is mentioned in the earliest genealogy (Matthew 1:1–17) and in the infancy narratives of Matthew and Luke. There he is the recipient of dream-born messages like those of his Hebrew predecessor Joseph: "Joseph . . . do not be afraid to take Mary as your wife," "Flee to Egypt," "It's safe to return now." He is last mentioned at the finding in the temple: "Your father and I have been searching for you . . ." (Luke 2:48).

> ### Joseph's First Wife
>
> There is one tradition that says Joseph was Mary's "nominal" husband, an eighty-year-old widower with a grown-up family of sons when he became engaged to Mary. The story appears in the apocryphal Gospels, the earliest apparently being the second-century *Protevangelium* of James. It was quoted by the Christian teacher, writer, and theologian Origen and mentioned by the theologian and Church father Clement of Alexandria and by the Christian apologist Justin. The tradition was used by them and by Eusebius of Caesarea to explain the scriptural references to the "brethren of the Lord."

In Art

St. Joseph is often pictured as a member of the Holy Family, holding Christ, with the tools of his carpenter trade, with a budding lily stalk.

The Joseph Legend of the Budding Staff of Lily

Zechariah the high priest told Mary that in a revelation he was instructed by an angel to bring together marriageable men and have each leave his staff in the temple overnight. The Lord's choice of a husband for Mary would be revealed through a sign. In the morning, the staff of Joseph the carpenter was found to have blossomed, while those of the other suitors' were barren.

The Twelve Apostles

The names of the apostles are listed in four places. Some of them had two names, either a surname or a name given otherwise. Four were fishermen and one was a tax collector. There were two sets of brothers (Simon and Andrew, James and John) and two, Matthew and John, were traditionally considered evangelists. All were martyred except John. Judas Iscariot betrayed Jesus and was replaced in the early Church by Matthias (Acts 1:21–26). In the following lists, "Alph" is son of Alphaeus, "Zlt" is the Zealot, "Isc" is Iscariot, and "Jms" is son of James. Bartholomew has been identified by some as the Nathanael of John 21:2.

Matthew 10:2–4	Mark 3:16–19	Luke 6:12–19	Acts 1:13, 26
Simon	Simon	Simon	Peter
Andrew	James	Andrew	James
James	John	James	John
John	Andrew	John	Andrew
Philip	Philip	Philip	Philip
Bartholomew	Bartholomew	Bartholomew	Thomas
Thomas	Matthew	Matthew	Bartholomew
Matthew	Thomas	Thomas	Matthew
James, Alph	James, Alph	James, Alph	James, Alph
Thaddaeus	Thaddaeus	Simon Zlt	Simon Zlt
Simon Zlt	Simon Zlt	Judas, Jms	Judas, Jms
Judas Isc	Judas Isc	Judas Isc	Matthias

Favored Apostles

Peter, James, and John are mentioned three times as accompanying Jesus apart from the others (for the raising of Jairus's daughter, at the transfiguration, and during the agony in the garden).

The Apostles in the Scriptures

Peter

Andrew's brother—Matthew 4:18; Mark 1:16; Luke 5:1–11

From Bethsaida—John 1:44

A fisherman—Matthew 4:18; Mark 1:16; Luke 5:1–11

Partner of James and John—Luke 5:10

Called by Jesus—Matthew 4:19; Mark 1:17–18; Luke 5:11

Name changed from Simon—Matthew 16:16–18; John 1:42

Rebuked Jesus about suffering and was rebuked—Matthew 16:22–23; Mark 8:32–33

Walked on water and sank—Matthew 14:28–33

Disputed with Jesus at the Last Supper over foot-washing—John 13:5–10

Severed the ear of the high priest's slave at Jesus' arrest—John 18:10

Pledged his discipleship after which Jesus foretold his denial—Luke 22:33–34

Denied Jesus—Matthew 26:69–75; Mark 14:66–72; Luke 22:54–62

Given keys to the kingdom—Matthew 16:19

Answered Jesus, "Who do you say I am?"—Matthew 16:15–16; Mark 8:29; Luke 9:20

Approached by temple tax collectors about Jesus—Matthew 17:24–27

Present with James and John at Jairus's daughter's raising—Mark 5:35–43; Luke 8:49–56

Present with James and John at the transfiguration—Matthew 17:1–2; Mark 9:2–3; Luke 9:28–29

Present with James, John, and Andrew for end-times prophecy—Mark 13:3–37

Present with James and John at agony in the garden—Matthew 26:36–46; Mark 14:32–42

Present with others for resurrection appearance by Sea of Galilee—John 21:1–3

Told by Mary Magdalene about resurrection—Mark 16:7

Ran to empty tomb—John 20:2–10

Repented and pledged love—John 21:15–17

Charged by Jesus to lead the Church—Matthew 16:13–19; John 21:15–17

Supervised election of Judas' replacement—Acts 1:15–26

First apostle to perform a miracle in Jesus' name—Acts 3:1–10

Later life: vague references—Acts 12; 1 Corinthians 1:12

"Apostle to the Jews"—Galatians 2:7

"Pillar of the Church"—Galatians 2:9

Plus more than a dozen references in Acts to his apostolic ministry

Andrew

Peter's brother—Matthew 4:18; Mark 1:16

From Bethsaida—John 1:44

A fisherman—Matthew 4:18; Mark 1:16

Originally the Baptist's disciple—John 1:35–40

Called by Jesus—Matthew 4:18–19; Mark 1:16–17; John 1:35–40

Introduced Peter to Jesus—John 1:40–42

Brought Jesus the boy with the loaves and fishes—John 6:8–9

Introduced, with Philip, some Greek believers to Jesus—John 12:21–22

Present with Peter, James, and John for end-times prophecy—Mark 13:3–37

James and John

Parentheses below mean reference is to only this one of these two apostles.

Partners of Peter as fishermen—Luke 5:1–11

Among first apostles, "fishers of men"—Matthew 4:21; Mark 1:19

(John) Called by Jesus—John 1:35–40?

Nicknamed "Sons of Thunder" by Jesus—Mark 3:17

(John) Scolded by Jesus for refusing to let outsiders exorcise—Luke 9:51–55

Wanted to call down flames on inhospitable Samaritan town—Luke 9:52–54

Requested seats in heaven beside Jesus—Mark 10:35–40 (see Matthew 20:20–23)

Present with Peter at raising of Jairus's daughter—Mark 5:35–43; Luke 8:49–56

Present with Peter at the transfiguration—Matthew 17:1–2; Mark 9:2–3; Luke 9:28–29

Present with Peter and Andrew for end-times prophecy—Mark 13:3–37

Present with Peter at agony in the garden—Matthew 26:36–46; Mark 14:32–42

Their mother was present at crucifixion—Matthew 27:56

Witnessed Jesus' resurrection appearance by Sea of Galilee—John 21:2

(John), with Peter, first healing in Jesus' name—Acts 3:1–11

(John), with Peter, goes to Samaria on a mission—Acts 8:14

"Pillars" of the Church—Galatians 2:9

(James) First apostle martyred; by Herod Antipas, in the year 44—Acts 12:2

The Beloved Disciple (John?)

Reclined on Jesus' chest at Last Supper—John 13:23–25

Entrusted with care of Mary—John 19:26–27

Told by Mary Magdalene (with Peter) of empty tomb—John 20:2

Recognized Jesus on the shore—John 21:7

Thomas (*Didymus*, Greek for twin)

Encouraged disciples to accompany Jesus on return to Jerusalem—John 11:16

Questioned Jesus in last discourse about where Jesus was going—John 14:5

Doubted Jesus' resurrection—John 20:24–25

Made an act of faith in Jesus' presence—John 20:26–28

Witnessed Jesus' resurrection appearance at the Sea of Galilee—John 21:2

Matthew (*Levi* in Hebrew; so called by Mark and Luke)

From Capernaum, in Galilee—Mark 2:13–14

Son of Alphaeus—Mark 2:14

A tax collector—Luke 5:27

Called by Jesus (and left all)—Matthew 9:9; Mark 2:14; Luke 5:27–28

Hosted by Jesus for a meal with sinners—Matthew 9:10; Mark 2:15;
Luke 5:28–29

Bartholomew (Nathanael?)

Called by Jesus after Philip's introduction—John 1:43–51

From Cana in Galilee—John 21:2

Witnessed Jesus' resurrection appearance by Sea of Galilee—John 21:2

Philip

From Bethsaida—John 1:43

Asked by Jesus to follow him—John 1:43

Introduced Nathanael to Jesus—John 1:45–46

Advised Jesus of the impossibility of feeding the multitude—John 6:5–7

Introduced, with Andrew, some Greeks to Jesus—John 12:21–22

Asked Jesus at the Last Supper to "show us the Father"—John 14:8–14

Simon (the Zealot in Luke and Acts)

Jude (Thaddaeus)

Asked Jesus why he revealed himself to them and not to the world—John 14:22

James (son of Alphaeus)

Brother of Matthew? (who was also "son of Alphaeus")—see Mark 2:14

Judas Iscariot

Treasurer for the apostles—John 13:29

Referred to prophetically by Jesus as a betrayer, a "devil"—John 6:70–71

Advised Jesus about money better spent on the poor—John 12:5–6

Induced by the devil to betray Jesus—John 13:2

Arranged betrayal—Matthew 26:14–16, Mark 14:10–11; Luke 22:3–6

Revealed by Jesus at the Last Supper as betrayer—Matthew 26:20–25 (and parallels)

Handed over Jesus—Matthew 26:47–49 (and parallels)

Died—Matthew 27:3–5

Traditional Stories of the Apostles' Deaths

Matthias, Luke, Mark, and Paul are included here with the twelve. Although some of these stories lack reliable support, they have been commonly retold.

Andrew

Andrew was martyred in Patrae (modern-day Patras), a seaport in the Peloponnesus, in western Greece on the Gulf of Patras, in the year 70. Bound to a cross, he preached to his persecutors until he died. The X-shaped cross story arose in the Middle Ages. There is also unhistorical speculation that he was the first bishop of Byzantium (Constantinople).

St. Andrew's cross (saltire)

Bartholomew

Bartholomew was martyred in Armenia in 44 by being flayed alive. He has been associated with the spread of the gospel in Lycaonia (an ancient country in southern Asia Minor), India, and Armenia (an ancient country in western Asia, part of the Soviet Union in its time, east of Turkey and northwest of Iran).

James the Greater

James was martyred in Jerusalem by beheading. After his death in Palestine, his body was put in a boat with sails set. The next day it reached the Spanish coast. According to another legend, it was his relics that were transferred to Spain, in a marble ship from Jerusalem, where he was bishop. His body was discovered in 840 (by a divine revelation), and a church was built at Compostella to enshrine it.

Called *Mata-moros* (Moor-slayer) because he was believed to have come on a white steed to the aid of the Christians in their battle against the Moors. (Moors were the Muslims of the mixed Berber and Arab inhabitants of northwest Africa. They invaded and conquered Spain in the eighth century.)

James the Less

According to Josephus, James was martyred in Jerusalem by stoning. A century later a tradition arose that he was taken to the pinnacle of the temple and ordered to dissuade the assembly from belief in Christ. He preached Christ instead, and so was hurled to the ground and stoned where he lay. Another tradition says he was clubbed with a fuller's pole. (Fulling is a special process in the manufacture of cloth by which it is cleansed and thickened.)

John

Aristodemos, a priest of the Italian goddess Diana, challenged John to drink a chalice of poison. John blessed it, whereupon a dragon-form of Satan flew from it and John drank it without harm. In the Domitian persecution (96), he was immersed in boiling oil but delivered unharmed. He then was banished to Patmos (Revelation 1:9), an island off the southwest coast of Asia Minor, where he is said to have written the Book of Revelation (most likely this was a different John). After his return to Ephesus, he died a natural death.

Judas

The Scriptures record (Matthew 27:5) that after the betrayal of Jesus, the despondent Judas took his own life by hanging.

The Unlucky Elder Tree

This innocent tree has become a tree of evil associations because of its use by the guilty Judas. At least according to a belief incorporated by medieval fable, it was on an elder tree that Judas hanged himself. Even its growths, which resemble mushrooms, are called Judas' ears. Shakespeare mentions this legend in *Love's Labor's Lost*. In other traditions, the fig is the fateful tree.

Jude (Thaddaeus)

An apocryphal account says he evangelized in Persia (Iran today) and was shot to death there with arrows.

Luke (evangelist)

An ancient source says he labored long in Greece and died there, unmarried, at the age of eighty-four. Another tradition says his martyrdom was by hanging on an olive tree.

Mark (evangelist)

Traditionally, he became the evangelist of Alexandria, Egypt, and its first bishop. He was martyred there, during the reign of the Emperor Trajan, after being dragged through the streets.

Matthew

Matthew preached for fifteen years in Judea, then took the gospel to Ethiopia, or Persia, or elsewhere, where he was slain by a sword.

Matthias

Stoned and then beheaded

Paul

After he had converted one of Nero's favorite concubines, Paul was beheaded at Rome in the year 66, whereupon milk flowed from his veins. Tradition says the place of this martyrdom is now called *Tre Fontane*, and that his body is buried where the Church of St. Paul Outside the Walls stands.

Peter

Peter confounded Simon Magus, who was at Nero's court as a magician. He was crucified under Nero around 64 or 66, upside down because he deemed himself unworthy of a death the same as Christ. Tradition has it that his tomb is under the high altar of St. Peter's in Rome.

St. Peter's cross

Philip

Philip probably preached the gospel in Phrygia (an ancient country in central and northwest Asia Minor) and died in Hierapolis, where his grave is now claimed to be.

Simon (the Zealot)

Simon evangelized in Egypt and then Persia (Iran today) where he was martyred, some say along with Jude.

Thomas

Thomas was said to be martyred at Meliapour in south India. One account says he was run through with a lance at Coromandel in the East Indies. He is mentioned in the apocryphal *Acts of St. Thomas*.

Burial Places of Apostles and Evangelists

Seven are believed to be buried in Rome, although proof is difficult to come by.

Bartholomew, in the church so named, on the Tiber Island; James the Less, in the Church of Saints Philip and James; Jude; Matthias, in St. Peter's; Philip; Peter, in St. Peter's; Simon

Near Naples
 Andrew at Amalfi, Matthew at Salerno, Thomas at Ortona

In Ephesus: John

In Venice: Mark the evangelist

In Padua: Luke the evangelist

In Santiago de Compostella in Spain: James the Greater

Names for the Nameless in the New Testament

Casper, Melchior, and Balthasar
The magi who brought the three gifts to the Christ child

Dismas
The good thief, who died in crucifixion with Christ, according to the apocryphal *Gospel of Nicodemus*

Gestas
The impenitent thief (See Dismas.)

Ignatius
The child Jesus sat in the midst of the disciples as an example.

The three crosses represent Jesus and the two thieves.

Joachim and Anne
Parents of the Blessed Virgin Mary

John (apostle and evangelist)
There is wide acceptance of the opinion that he is "the beloved disciple" (the "disciple Jesus loved"), mentioned in the fourth Gospel on four occasions during or following Jesus' passion.

Longinus
The Roman soldier who lanced the crucified Christ, according to the apocryphal *Gospel of Nicodemus*. Stories of his spear were told and embellished in the romance of King Arthur.

Mary Magdalene
The penitent woman who washed Jesus' feet with her tears and dried them with her hair (Luke 7:36). This association is both common and mistaken because this episode is followed in Luke by a reference to a Mary Magdala "from whom seven devils had been cast." She has also been identified incorrectly with the Mary of Mary and Martha (of Bethany), because of the story of this Mary also anointing Jesus' feet (John 12:3).

> ### *Veronica*
>
> Tradition holds that a woman with this name wiped the face of Jesus as he was on his way to Calvary (the sixth station of the cross). "Veronica" is really the two Latin words, *vera* and *icon*, true image, referring to Jesus' face. The word *veronica* is used not only as a personal name, but also as the name for the veil that tradition says was used. This veil is probably second only to the Shroud of Turin among the *Volto Santo* (Holy Face) relics. Some say it was actually the centurion's wife, Seraphica, who did this work of mercy and later discovered Jesus' face on the cloth. Other legends say the woman was Martha and still others, Zacchaeus's wife, or the woman Christ healed of an issue of blood (Mark 5:25–34). No mention of an actual person named Veronica can be found earlier than the fifth century.

Church Fathers

Apostolic Fathers

The Apostolic Fathers are first- and second-century writers who are associated personally with the apostles and whose writings reflect genuine apostolic teaching.

St. Clement (died about 97)

Bishop of Rome as the third successor of St. Peter; author of the letter from the church of Rome to the church of Corinth (Clement's *First Letter*)

St. Ignatius (about 50–107)

Bishop of Antioch, the second successor of St. Peter in that church, by tradition a disciple of St. John; author of seven letters (*Ephesians, Magnesians, Trallians, Romans, Philadelphians, Smyrnaeans,* and *Polycarp,* Bishop of Smyrna)

St. Polycarp (69–155)

Bishop of Smyrna, disciple of St. John; author of a letter (*Philippians*)

Author of *The Didache* (probably second century)

A Church manual and liturgical document discovered in 1873 at Constantinople containing teaching said to reflect that of the twelve apostles (the prayer the priest says while preparing the gifts is virtually verbatim from *The Didache,* "Blessed are you, Lord, God of all creation . . .").

Author of *Epistle of Barnabas*

Other Early Christian Writers (sub-apostolic)

St. Justin Martyr (100–165)

Of Asia Minor, Rome; layman, apologist

St. Irenaeus (130–202)

Bishop of Lyons, author of *Against Heresies*, an exposition of the faith

St. Cyprian (210–258)

Bishop of Carthage, opposed Novatian heresy

Fathers of the Church

Theologians and writers of the first eight centuries, eminent in holiness and learning. They were such authoritative witnesses to the belief and teaching of the Church that their unanimous acceptance of doctrines as divinely revealed has been regarded as evidence that such doctrines were so received by the Church consistent with apostolic tradition and Sacred Scripture. Their unanimous rejection of doctrines branded the ideas as heretical. This is not to say all their writing is free of error in all respects.

The Four Main Prerogatives of the Church Fathers

Antiquity, orthodoxy, sanctity, and approval by the Church

Latin Fathers of the Church

"The Four Great Fathers" are in capital (uppercase) letters.

ST. AMBROSE (340–397), bishop of Milan

Arnobius (d. 327), apologist

ST. AUGUSTINE (354–430), bishop of Hippo

St. Benedict (480–546), father of Western monasticism

St. Caesarius (470–542), archbishop of Arles

St. John Cassian (360–435), abbot, ascetical author

St. Celestine I (d. 432), pope

St. Cornelius (d. 253), pope

St. Cyprian (d. 258), bishop of Carthage

St. Damasus I (d. 384), pope

St. Dionysius (d. 268), pope

St. Ennodius (473–521), bishop of Pavia

St. Eucherius (d. 449), bishop of Lyons

St. Fulgentius (468–533), bishop of Ruspe

St. Gregory of Elvira (died after 392)

ST. GREGORY (I) the Great (540–604), pope

St. Hilary (315–368), bishop of Poitiers

St. Innocent I (d. 417), pope

St. Irenaeus (130–200), bishop of Lyons

St. Isidore (560–636), archbishop of Seville

ST. JEROME (343–420), priest, exegete, translated Hebrew and Greek
  Scriptures into Latin (the Vulgate)

Lactantius Firmianus (240–320), apologist

St. Leo the Great (390–461), pope

Marius Mercator (early fifth century), Latin polemicist

Marius Victorinus (fourth century), Roman rhetorician

Minucius Felix (second or third century), apologist

Novatian (200–262), the Schismatic

St. Optatus (fourth century), bishop of Mileve

St. Pacian (fourth century), bishop of Barcelona

St. Pamphilus (240–309), priest

St. Paulinus (353–431), bishop of Nola

St. Peter Chrysologus (400–450), archbishop of Ravenna

St. Phoebadius (d. 395), bishop of Agen

St. Prosper of Aquitaine (390–463), theologian

Rufinus (345–410), Latin translator of Greek theology

Salvian (400–480), priest

St. Siricius (334–399), pope

Tertullian (160–223), apologist, father of Latin theology

St. Vincent of Lerins (d. 450), priest and monk

Greek Fathers of the Church

"The Four Great Fathers" are in capital (uppercase) letters.

St. Anastasius Sinaita (d. 700), apologist, monk

St. Andrew of Crete (660–740), archbishop of Gortyna

Aphraates (fourth century), Syriac monk

St. Archelaus (d. 282), bishop of Cascar

ST. ATHANASIUS (c. 297–373), archbishop of Alexandria

Athenagoras (second century), apologist

ST. BASIL the Great (329–379), archbishop of Caesarea

St. Caesarius of Nazianzus (330–369)

St. Clement of Alexandria (150–215), theologian

St. Clement I of Rome (30–101), pope

St. Cyril (315–386), bishop of Jerusalem

St. Cyril (376–444), patriarch of Alexandria

Didymus the Blind (313–398), theologian

Diodore (d. 392), bishop of Tarsus

Dionysius the Pseudo-Areopagite (fifth century), mystical theologian

St. Dionysius the Great (190–264), archbishop of Alexandria

St. Epiphanius (315–403), bishop of Salamis

Eusebius (260–340), bishop of Caesarea

St. Eustathius (fourth century), bishop of Antioch

St. Firmillian (d. 268), bishop of Caesarea

Gennadius I (d. 471), patriarch of Constantinople

St. Germanus (634–733), patriarch of Constantinople

ST. GREGORY OF NAZIANZUS (329–390), bishop of Sasima

St. Gregory of Nyssa (330–395)

St. Gregory Thaumaturgus (213–270), bishop of Neocaesarea

Hermas (second century), author of *The Shepherd*

St. Hippolytus (170–236), martyr

St. Ignatius (35–107), bishop of Antioch

St. Isidore of Pelusium (360–about 450), abbot

ST. JOHN CHRYSOSTOM (347–407), patriarch of Constantinople

St. John Climacus (579–649), monk

St. John Damascene (675–749), defender of sacred images

St. Julius I (d. 352), pope

St. Justin Martyr (100–165), apologist

St. Leontius of Byzantium (sixth century), theologian

St. Macarius the Great (300–390), monk

St. Maximus (580–662), abbot and confessor

St. Melito (d. 190), bishop of Sardis

St. Methodius (d. 311), bishop of Olympus

St. Nilus the Elder (d. 430), priest and monk

Origen (184–254), head of the Catechetical School of Alexandria

St. Polycarp (69–155), bishop of Smyrna

St. Proclus (d. 446), patriarch of Constantinople

St. Serapion (died after 362), bishop of Thmuis

St. Sophronius (560–638), patriarch of Jerusalem

Tatian the Assyrian (120–180), apologist and theologian

Theodore (350–428), bishop of Mopsuestia

Theodoret (393–458), bishop of Cyrrhus

St. Theophilus (second century), bishop of Antioch

Doctors of the Church

"Doctor of the Church" is a title given since the Middle Ages to authors of eminent holiness and learning whose work has significantly enhanced the cause of Christ in his Church (which is not to say all their writing is free of error in all respects). Originally, the four Great Doctors of the Western Church were considered the Doctors of the Church. But the Church has officially added many more; there are thirty-three, including three women, Teresa of Ávila and Catherine of Siena, named in 1970, and Thérèse of Lisieux, named in 1998. All are saints.

Albert the Great (about 1200–1280)
Doctor Universalis, Doctor Expertus; Dominican; patron of natural scientists

Alphonsus Liguori (1696–1787)
Patron of confessors, moralists; founded Redemptorists

Ambrose (about 340–397)
Influenced a development of the Liturgy ("Ambrosian"); opponent of Arianism in the West; bishop of Milan

Anselm (1033–1109)
Father of Scholasticism; archbishop of Canterbury

Anthony of Padua (1195–1231)
Evangelical Doctor; Franciscan friar

Athanasius (about 297–373)
Father of Orthodoxy; main opponent of Arianism; bishop of Alexandria

Augustine (354–430)
Doctor of Grace; bishop of Hippo

Basil the Great (about 329–379)
Father of Monasticism in the East; one of three Cappadocian fathers

Bede the Venerable (about 673–735)
Father of English History; Benedictine priest

Bernard (about 1090–1153)
Mellifluous Doctor (eloquent); Cistercian monk

Bonaventure (about 1217–1274)
Seraphic Doctor; Franciscan theologian

Catherine of Siena (about 1347–1380)
Second woman proclaimed doctor (1970); mystic

Cyril of Alexandria (about 376–444)
Patriarch; opponent of Nestorianism; contributor in Christology

Cyril of Jerusalem (about 315–387)
Eastern opponent of Arianism; bishop

Ephraem (about 306–373)
Deacon of Edessa; Harp of the Holy Spirit; Scripture exegete; author

Francis de Sales (1567–1622)
Patron of Catholic writers, press; Counter-Reformation leader; bishop

Gregory of Nazianzen (about 330–390)
The Christian Demosthenes; the Theologian (in the East); one of the three Cappadocian fathers

Gregory I, the Great (about 540–604)
Pope; defender of papal primacy; clerical, monastic reformer

Hilary of Poitiers (about 315–368)
The Athanasius of the West; bishop

Isidore of Seville (560–636)
Regarded as the most learned of his time; archbishop; theologian; historian

Jerome (about 343–420)
Father of Biblical Science; translator of the Bible

John Chrysostom (about 347–407)
The Greatest of the Greek Fathers; Golden-Tongued Orator; patron of preachers; bishop of Constantinople

John Damascene (about 675–749)
Golden Speaker; Greek theologian

John of the Cross (1542–1591)
Doctor of Mystical Theology; co-founder of Discalced Carmelites

Lawrence of Brindisi (1559–1619)
Leading preacher in Counter-Reformation

Leo I, the Great (400–461)
Pope; wrote against Nestorianism, Monophysitism, Manichaeism, and Pelagianism

Peter Canisius (1521–1597)
Counter-Reformation leader; Jesuit theologian

Peter Chrysologus (about 400–450)
"Golden Worded"; bishop of Ravenna

Peter Damian (1007–1072)
Reformer of Church and clerics; Benedictine

Robert Bellarmine (1542–1621)
A champion of orthodoxy during and after the Reformation; Jesuit

Teresa of Ávila (1515–1582)
First woman proclaimed doctor (1970); Spanish Carmelite; mystic

Thérèse of Lisieux (1873–1897)
Third woman proclaimed doctor (1998); French Carmelite

Thomas Aquinas (1225–1274)
Doctor Communis; Doctor Angelicus; The Great Synthesizer; patron of Catholic schools, education; Dominican philosopher and theologian; composer of Eucharistic hymns

The Saints

Titles of Saints

Angel of the Schools: St. Thomas Aquinas (1225–1274)

Angelic Doctor: St. Thomas Aquinas (because of the greatness and purity of his work, his expositions seem beyond the limits of the human intellect)

The Straw of a Genius

Thomas Aquinas died before he was fifty, but he left behind a towering monument of scholarship, and something greater. In 1273 he put aside his *Summa Theologica*. This work was destined to be a classic systematic exposition of theology (twenty-two volumes in translation) and has had enormous impact on Catholic theology and religion. After a deep religious experience, Thomas left it unfinished saying, "All I have written seems to me like so much straw compared with what I have seen and what has been revealed to me." It was said of him, "His wonderful learning owes far less to his genius than to the effectiveness of his prayer."

Apostle among the Armenians: St. Gregory of Armenia (257–331)

Apostle of the Gauls: St. Denis (third century)

Apostle of Germany: St. Boniface (680–750) (originally Winifred, or Winfrith)

Apostles to the Slavs: Sts. Cyril and Methodius (ninth century)

Athanasius of the West: St. Hilary of Poitiers (about 315–368)

Beloved Disciple: St. John the Apostle (see, for example, John 13:23)

Beloved Physician: St. Luke, so called by Paul (Colossians 4:14)

Bishop of Hippo: St. Augustine (354–430)

Black Pope: general of the Jesuits

Champions, the Seven Champions of Christendom (a medieval designation of national patron saints): George of England, Andrew of Scotland, David of Wales, Patrick of Ireland, James of Spain, Denis of France, and Anthony of Italy

Christian Demosthenes: Gregory of Nazianzen (about 330–390)

Desert Fathers: Sts. Anthony, Pachomius the Hermit, and Hilarion (the most noted fourth-century monks/hermits of Egypt from whom Christian monasticism evolved)

Divine, The: St. John the apostle, evangelist

Doctor:

Divine Doctor: John Ruysbroek

Doctor Angelicus: St. Thomas Aquinas (1225–1274)

Doctor Expertus: St. Albert the Great (about 1200–1280)

Doctor of Grace: St. Augustine (354–430)

Doctor of Mystical Theology: St. John of the Cross (1542–1591)

Doctor Singularis: William of Occam (about 1347), scholastic, philosopher, Franciscan

Doctor Universalis: St. Albert the Great (about 1200–1280)

Ecstatic Doctor: Jean de Ruysbroek (1294–1381), mystic

Eloquent Doctor: Peter Aureolus, fourteenth-century schoolman, archbishop of Aix

Evangelical Doctor: St. Anthony of Padua (1195–1231)

Illuminated Doctor: John Trauler (1294–1361), German mystic

Invincible Doctor: William of Occam

Irrefragable Doctor: Alexander of Hales (?–1245), English Franciscan

Mellifluous Doctor: St. Bernard (1091–1153) (his writing being "a river of Paradise")

Seraphic Doctor: St. Bonaventure (1221–1274)

Subtle Doctor: Duns Scotus (1265–1308), Scottish Franciscan

Dumb Ox: St. Thomas Aquinas (1224–74) (because his tutor, St. Albert the Great, said, "The dumb ox will one day fill the world with his lowing.")

Eagle of Divines: St. Thomas Aquinas

Father:

Father of Biblical Sciences: St. Jerome (about 343–420)

Father of Church History: Eusebius of Caesaria (about 264–340)

Father of English History: Bede the Venerable (about 673–735)

Father in Faith/of the Faithful: Abraham (Romans 4; Galatians 3:6–9)

Father of Monasticism in the East: St. Basil the Great (about 329–379)

Father of Moral Philosophy: St. Thomas Aquinas

Father of Musicians: Jubal (Genesis 4:21)

Father of Orthodoxy: St. Athanasius (about 297–373)

Father of Scholasticism: St. Anselm (1033–1109)

Seraphic Father/Saint: St. Francis of Assisi

Last of the Fathers: St. Bernard (1091–1153), abbot of Clairvaux

Golden-tongued Orator: St. John Chrysostom (d. 407), Greek father

Golden-tongued ("Chrysologus"): St. Peter (d. about 449), bishop of Ravenna

Great (There are four saints called "Great" by the Church): Basil the Great (about 329–379); Gregory the Great (about 540–604); Leo the Great (about 400–461); Albert the Great (about 1200–1280)

Greatest of the Greek Fathers: St. John Chrysostom

Great Synthesizer: St. Thomas Aquinas (1125–1274)

Hammer of the Arians: St. Hilary (d. 368), bishop of Poitiers

Harp of the Holy Spirit: St. Ephraem (about 306–373)

Holy Helpers, The Fourteen: George, Pantaleon, Denis, Eustace, Catherine, Blaise, Vitus, Cyriacus, Giles, Barbara, Erasmus, Christopher, Achatius, and Margaret (Grouping these saints, all martyred during the Church's early centuries, began in twelfth-century Germany, where saints are generally regarded as "helpers in need." They are venerated as a group because they are patrons of various nations and occupations and of the victims of many common illnesses.)

Ice (or Frost) Saints: Sts. Mamertus, Pancras, Servatius, and Boniface (because their feast days fall in "black thorn winter," the second week in May, between the eleventh and fourteenth)

Illuminator: St. Gregory of Armenia (257–331), the apostle among the Armenians

Ireland, the Three Great Saints of: Patrick, Columba, and Brigid (of Kildare; also known as Bride)

Lily of the Mohawks: Blessed Kateri Tekakwitha

Madonna (Italian: my lady): Mary

Maid of Orleans: St. Joan of Arc

Mata-moros (Spanish: Moor slayer): St. James the Greater, patron of Spain

Most Learned of his Day: St. Isidore of Seville

Myrrophores (Greek: myrrh bearers): the Marys who visited Jesus' tomb (Mark 16:1)

Oracle of the Church: St. Bernard of Clairvaux

Pope of the Eucharist: Pope St. Pius X (1903–1914)

Prince of the Church: a cardinal

Saint of Miracles: St. Anthony of Padua (1195–1231)

Spouse of Christ: St. Teresa of Ávila (1515–1582) ("spouse" is from Latin *spondere*, to promise)

Thaumaturgis (Greek: wonder worker; applied because of miracles worked): Gregory, bishop of Neo-Caesaria, Cappadocia (d. 270), and also: St. Anthony (1195–1231), Wonder-Worker of Padua; Appollonius of Tyana, Cappadocia (3–98); St. Bernard of Clairvaux (1091–1153), Thaumaturgis of the West; St. Filumena; St. Francis of Assisi (1182–1226); St. Vincent de Paul (1576-1660), founder of the Sisters of Charity

Theologian, The (in the East): St. Gregory Nazianzen (329–390)

Weeping Saint: St. Swithin

Wonder Worker of Padua: St. Anthony (1195–1231)

Worthies, The Nine (heroes often grouped together):
From the Scriptures: Joshua, David, Judas Maccabeus

From the Classics: Hector, Alexander, Julius Caesar

From the Romances: Arthur, Charlemagne, Godfrey of Bouillon

Principal Patrons (See CCC #2156.)

Not all of the following traditional patrons and patronesses (Latin: *pater*, father; see "pattern") have been included among the 173 saints of the revised Roman Missal. Included in this list are saints' days according to the revised calendar. For the saint no longer so commemorated, the date of observance according to the old calendar is included in parentheses.

ab-abbot   ap-apostle   aa-archangel   e-evangelist

Some fabled patronage was purely accidental. For example, St. Martin was the patron of "drunkards" because his feast day, November 11, coincided with the Roman Vinali, or Feast of Bacchus. Times have changed, as have language, sensitivities, and appreciation of what it means to be a patron. For a case in point, read below about Matt Talbot, patron of alcoholics.

Alcoholic Patrons

Matt Talbot (1856–1925) is a good example of why a person becomes a patron. (He has not been called a saint, but venerable, which is one of the stages of the canonization process.) He was born of a poor family in Dublin and from age twelve had problems with alcohol. By the time Talbot was twenty-eight, the problem had grown to the point that he begged for drinks. Deep in shame and finding no one to buy him a drink, he took a pledge to the Sacred Heart one night to stop drinking. Realizing his sobriety depended on more than not drinking, Matt grew in holiness as he received daily Eucharist, prayed constantly, and practiced heroic personal penances. The basic successful principles of Alcoholics Anonymous are founded on a reliance on God; these principles have been adapted by numerous other twelve-step programs.

Altar boys: John Berchmans (August 13)

Animals: Francis, October 4

Animals, domestic: Ambrose, December 7; Cornelius, September 16

Archers: Sebastian

Architects/builders: Barbara (December 4); Thomas, ap, July 3

The cross and crown symbolize the reward of those who believe in the crucified Lord.

Armorers: Sebastian, January 20

Armories: Lawrence, August 10

Art: Catherine Bologna (March 9)

Artillerymen: Barbara (December 4)

Artists: Luke, October 18; Michael, aa, September 29

Astronomers: Dominic, August 8

Athletes: Sebastian, January 20

Authors: Francis de Sales, January 29; Lucy, December 13

Aviators: Joseph of Cupertino (September 18); Thérèse of Lisieux, October 1; Our Lady of Loreto (December 10)

Bakers: Elizabeth of Hungary, November 17; Nicholas of Myra, December 6; Peter, ap, June 29

Bald people: Hedwig

Bankers: Matthew, September 21

Barbers: Cosmas and Damian, September 26; Louis of France, August 25

Barren women: Anthony of Padua, June 13; Felicity, March 7

Basket-makers: Anthony, ab, January 17

Beekeepers: Ambrose, December 7; Bernard of Clairvaux, August 20

Beggars: Elizabeth of Hungary, November 17; Giles (September 1); Alexis (July 17); Martin of Tours, November 11

Blacksmiths: Dunstan (May 19)

Blind: Dunstan (May 19); Odilia (December 13); Raphael, aa, September 29; Lucy, December 13

> ### Patrons of the Blind
>
> **St. Dunstan** is associated with work for the blind because of an institution established during World War I at St. Dunstan's House, Regent's Park, London, for the welfare and rehabilitation of blinded soldiers (and later, civilians).
>
> **St. Odilia**, in a more inspirational (and imaginative) vein, is said to have been born blind and abandoned by her family. Raised in an Alsace convent, her sight was miraculously restored when she was baptized as a twelve-year old. (She became a Benedictine abbess and died around 720.)
>
> **St. Raphael**, one of the three archangels mentioned by name in the Bible, is another patron for the blind. The Book of Tobit tells the story of his miraculous intercessions. It was Raphael's instructions that Tobit's son followed in restoring his father's sight (Tobit 11:7–14). (Legend has it he is the angel who moved the waters of the healing pool in John 5:1–9.)
>
> **St. Lucy's** patronage of the blind comes in part from her name, which derives from *lux*, Latin for light. (Hence the ill-advised custom of girls processing with candles on their heads, bringing light. Tradition has it St. Lucy's persecutors put out her eyes, which makes her patronage of the blind a natural.)

Bodily ills: Our Lady of Lourdes, February 11

Bookbinders: Peter Celestine (May 19)

Booksellers: John, e, December 27

Boy Scouts: George, April 23

Brewers: Boniface, June 5; Augustine, August 28; Luke, October 18; Nicholas of Myra, December 6

Bricklayers: Stephen, December 26

Brides: Dorothy (February 6); Nicholas of Myra, December 6

Builders: Vincent Ferrer, April 5

Butchers: Anthony, ab, January 17; Adrian (September 8); Luke, e, October 18; Peter, ap, June 29

Cab drivers: Fiacre (September 1 in Ireland)

Cabinet makers: Anne, July 26

Cancer patients: Peregrine (May 1)

Captives: Nicholas of Myra, December 6

Carpenters: Joseph, March 19; Thomas, July 3

Catholic action: Francis of Assisi, October 4

Catholic writers/press: Francis de Sales, January 24

Cattle: Cornelius, September 16

Cavalrymen: George, April 23

Charitable societies: Vincent de Paul, September 27

Children: Nicholas of Myra, December 6; Pancras, May 12

Children's choir: Holy Innocents, December 28

Chivalry: George, April 23

Church universal: Joseph, March 19

Clerics: Gabriel of the Sorrowful Mother (February 27)

Clock-makers: Peter, June 29

Cloth workers (fullers): Severus (October 22?, November 8?)

Comedians: Vitus (June 15)

Communication workers: Gabriel, September 29

Confessors: Alphonsus Liguori, August 1; John Nepomucene (May 16)

Convulsion in children: Scholastica, February 10

Cooks: Lawrence, August 10; Martha, July 29

Coppersmiths: Benedict, July 11

Dairy workers: Bridget of Sweden, July 23

Deaf: Francis de Sales, January 24

Dentists: Apollonia (February 9)

Desperate situations: Jude Thaddaeus, October 28; Gregory of Neocaesarea ("the Wonderworker") (November 17)

Disabled: Giles (September 1)

Drapers: Ursula (October 21)

Druggists: Cosmas and Damian, September 26; James the Less, ap, May 3

Dying: Joseph, March 19; Barbara (December 4)

Ecology: Francis, October 4

Elderly: Anthony of Padua, June 13

Emigrants: Frances Xavier Cabrini, November 13

Engaged couples: Agnes, January 21

Engineers: Joseph, March 19; Ferdinand III (May 30)

Expectant mothers: Raymond Nonnatus (August 31); Gerard Majella (October 16)

Eye trouble: Lucy, December 13

Falsely accused: Raymond Nonnatus (August 31)

Family: Joseph, March 19

Farmers: George, April 23; Isidore, May 15

Fire prevention: Catherine of Siena, April 29; Barbara (December 4)

First communicants: Tarcisius (August 15)

Fishermen: Andrew, November 30

Florists: Dorothy (February 6); Thérèse of Lisieux, October 1

Forest workers: John Gualbert (July 12)

Founders: Barbara (December 4)

Foundlings: Holy Innocents, December 28

Funeral directors: Joseph of Arimathea (March 17); Dismas (March 25)

Gardeners: Agnes, January 21; Dorothy (February 6); Trypho (November 10); Fiacre (September 1 in Ireland)

Geometricians: Thomas, ap, July 3

Glass workers: Luke, October 18

Glaziers (people who fit glass in windows): Mark, April 25

Goldsmiths: Dunstan (May 19)

Grave diggers and graveyards: Anthony, ab, January 17

Grace, those in need: Teresa of Ávila, October 15

Greetings: Valentine (February 14)

Grocers: Michael, aa, September 29

Guardian angels: Raphael, aa, September 29

Gunners: Barbara (December 4)

Hairdressers: Martin de Porres, November 3

Happy death: Joseph, March 19

Hatters: James the Less, ap, May 3

Haymakers: Gervase and Protase (June 19)

Headaches: Teresa of Ávila, October 15

Heart ailments: John of God, March 8

Hospitality: Julian the Hospitaller (February 12)

Hospitals: Camillus de Lellis, July 14; John of God, March 8; Jude Thaddaeus, ap, October 28

Jude the Obscure

Finding the origin of St. Jude devotion is as hopeless as the cases for which he has become the patron. Like so many of the other apostles' lives, the details of his life are very obscure. The well-known devotion to him as the patron of hopeless or difficult cases may be rooted in the tradition that he was a close relative of Jesus and that in childhood they were playmates. There is a Jude (or Judas in some translations) mentioned as Jesus' "brother" (relative) by Matthew (13:55), along with "James, Joseph, and Simon." Some have taken this to be the St. Jude in question, hence a brother of James the Less who was the son of Alphaeus. This is a long way to go.

Devotion to him is of relatively recent vintage, the late date in part owing to the similarity between his name and that of the betrayer. It did, however, flourish in the fertile soil of the medieval mind, nurtured undoubtedly by an apparition of Christ to St. Bridget of Sweden, which is another story. In that one, the Lord directed Bridget to Jude: "In accordance with his surname, Thaddaeus (the amiable, the loving), he will show himself most willing to give help."

Artistically, Jude is sometimes pictured carrying the image of Jesus. The story behind that is that Abagaro, king of Edessa and also leprous, sent word to Jesus for him to come and cure him. Along with the request, the king sent an artist who was to return with a portrait of the master. Impressed with his great faith, Jesus pressed into a cloth his image and gave it to Jude to take to the king, along with a cure. Abagaro was not only cured by Jude, but also, along with most of his subjects, converted to Christ.

Housewives: Anne, July 26; Martha, July 29

Hunters: Hubert (November 3)

Innkeepers: Martin of Tours, November 11

Interior souls: Joseph, March 19

Invalids: Roch (August 16)

Ironmongers: Sebastian, January 20

Jewelers: Eligius (December 1)

Journalists: Francis de Sales, January 24

Jurists: Catherine of Alexandria (November 25); John of Capistrano, October 23

Laborers: Isidore, May 15; James, July 25

Lawyers: Ivo of Chartres (June 17); Genesius (August 25)

Learning: Ambrose, December 7; Acca (November 27)

Librarians: Jerome, September 30

Locksmiths: Dunstan (May 19)

Lost things: Anthony, ab, January 17

St. Anthony and the Lost Manuscript

For a time in his life Brother Anthony lived in a friary in Montpellier, France, where he was a novice instructor. One of the novices was a restless and unhappy brother named Louis. Every hour away from teaching and prayer, Anthony spent in his cell working on a book of the psalms. It was a labor of love that had gone on for years. One afternoon he took a much needed respite from his work, but returned to find the manuscript gone. After a diligent search, it was left only for Anthony to pray.

At the same time it came to the attention of all in the friary that Brother Louis was gone too. What's more, an area farmer had seen him walking away from the monastery with a bundle under his arm. Anthony's prayer thus became more that Louis would find his vocation than that he, Anthony, would find his parchments. When he did pray that the book would be found and his life work salvaged, he compared his situation to a child losing a toy.

Meanwhile, Louis was making his way to Paris to sell the work in his own name and thus gain the fame and fortune he felt had eluded him in life. As he rested on the way on the bank of the river, a wild wind rose, churning the river into a frenzy. From its depths a monster came, advancing on Louis with a frightening aspect and a warning for him to restore the manuscript, lest he be destroyed. Frightened and repentant, Louis returned the work to Anthony, who counseled and tutored Louis in his vocation.

Anthony's intercession was credited with the find, and his prayer was requested throughout the monastery whenever anything was lost. His reputation spread through the area, especially later as he fulfilled a preaching vocation. He was a preacher of power, whose petition was heard. Always it was said, "This is the friar who finds lost objects."

Lovers: Raphael, aa, September 29

Maidens: Agnes, January 21; Margaret (July 20); Ursula (October 21)

Mail carriers: Gabriel, September 29

Marble workers: Clement I (November 23)

Mariners: Michael, aa, September 29; Nicholas of Tolentino (September 10)

Mentally ill: Dymphna (May 15)

Merchants: Francis of Assisi, October 4; Nicholas of Myra, December 6

Metalworkers: Eligius (December 1)

Millers: Victor (July 21)

Miners: Barbara (December 4)

Missions: Francis Xavier, December 3; Thérèse of Lisieux, October 1

Missions, Home: Leonard of Port Maurice (November 26)

Missions, Black: Peter Claver, September 9; Benedict the Moor (April 4)

Moral theologians: Alphonsus Liguori, August 1

Mothers: Monica, August 27; Anne, July 26

Motorcyclists: Our Lady of Grace (May 31)

Motorists: Christopher (July 25)

Mountaineers: Bernard of Menthon (May 28)

Musicians: Cecilia, November 22; Gregory the Great, September 3; Paul, June 29

Musical Patron

St. Cecilia was a third-century Roman martyr. We are left with little more than enduring legends about her life. While still a young girl, Cecilia dedicated her virginity to God. When forced by her family to marry, she converted her husband, and the two vowed celibacy. One legend tells of "pipes" played at her wedding. Although these pipes were probably the bagpipes common throughout Europe, ancient translations rendered the word "organ pipes." Consequently, St. Cecilia has often been portrayed near a pipe organ. Another legend calls her "the inventor of the organ," while another says an angel fell in love with her because of her musical skill. This heavenly visitant gave both her and her husband a crown of martyrdom, brought from heaven. With such ample fable and long-standing tradition, she is considered the patron of music and musicians.

Notaries: Mark, April 25; Luke, October 18

Nurses: Agatha, February 5; Alexis (July 17); Camillus de Lellis, July 14; Raphael, September 29; John of God, March 8; Margaret of Scotland (November 16)

Orphans: Jerome Emiliani (July 20)

Painters: John the Evangelist, December 27; Luke, October 18

St. Luke the Artist

Legend has it that Luke painted a portrait of the Blessed Mother, the icon of Our Lady of Czestochowa, also known as the Black Madonna. According to this tradition, he painted it on a board from the table St. Joseph built for the Holy Family. Historical studies, however, place the icon's origin between the fifth and eighth centuries. Today it can be seen at Poland's Jasna Gora monastery, where it has been a symbol of Polish spirituality and a place of pilgrimage since 1382. It is said to have traveled from Palestine to Byzantium, then to Hungary, and on to Ruthenia, and finally to Poland. (One legend says that angels finished a picture of Christ that was outlined by St. Luke; another, that Luke is the anonymous painter of Our Mother of Perpetual Help.)

Pawnbrokers: Nicholas of Myra, December 6

Peasants: Margaret (July 20)

Penitents: Mary Magdalene, July 22

Pharmacists: Cosmas and Damian, September 26

Philosophers: Catherine of Alexandria (November 25); Justin, June 1

Physicians: Cosmas and Damian, September 26; Luke, October 18; Raphael, September 29

Pilgrims: Alexis (July 17); James, July 25

Plague-stricken: Roch (August 16)

Plasterers: Bartholomew, August 24

Poets: Cecilia, November 22

Poisoning: Benedict, July 11

Policemen: Michael, September 29

Poor: Lawrence, August 10; Anthony of Padua, June 13

Porters: Christopher (July 25)

Possessed: Bruno, October 6; Denis, October 9

Postal workers: Gabriel, September 29

Potters: Sebastian, January 20

Preachers: John Chrysostom, September 13

Priests: John Vianney, August 4; Paul, June 29

Printers: Augustine, August 28; John the Evangelist, December 27; Genesius of Arles (August 25); John of God, March 8

Prisoners: Dismas (March 26); Barbara (December 4)

Prisoner Patron

Traditionally, the patron of prisoners is Dismas, the name tradition (and the apocryphal *Gospel of Nicodemus*) has given to the penitent thief who suffered crucifixion on the same day Jesus did.

Prisons: Joseph Cafasso (June 23)

Publishers: John the Evangelist, December 27; Francis de Sales, January 24

Radiologists: Michael, aa, September 29

Retreats: Ignatius of Loyola, July 31

Rheumatism: James the Greater, July 25

Saddlers: Crispin and Crispinian (October 25)

Sailors: Cuthbert (March 20); Erasmus (June 2); Nicholas of Tolentino, (September 10); Brendan (May 16); Eulalia (December 10); Christopher (July 25); Peter Gonzales (April 15)

Scholars: Bridget of Sweden, July 23

Schools: Thomas Aquinas, January 28

School children: Benedict, July 11; Lawrence, August 10

Scientists: Albert the Great, November 15

Sculptors: Luke, October 18; Claude (November 8)

Secretaries: Genesius of Arles (August 25)

Seminarians: Charles Borromeo, November 4

Servants, domestic: Zita (April 27); Martha, July 29

Shepherds: Cuthbert (March 20)

Shoemakers: Crispin and Crispinian (October 25)

Sick: Michael, September 29; John of God, March 8; Camillus de Lellis, July 14; Philomena (August 11)

Silversmiths: Andronicus (October 11)

Singers: Gregory, September 3; Cecilia, November 22

Singles: Andrew, November 30

Skaters: Ledwina (April 14)

Skiers: Bernard of Menthon (May 28)

Smiths: Eliguis (December 1)

Soldiers: George, April 23; Adrian (September 8); Michael, aa, September 29; Ignatius of Loyola, July 31; Sebastian, January 20; Martin of Tours, November 11; Joan of Arc (May 30)

Sore throat: Blaise, February 3

Spinsters: Catherine of Alexandria (November 25)

Stenographers: Genesius (August 25); Cassian (December 3)

Stonecutters: Clement, November 23

Stonemasons: Stephen, December 26; Barbara (December 4)

Students: Catherine of Alexandria (November 25); Jerome, September 30; Thomas Aquinas, January 28

Surgeons: Cosmas and Damian, September 26

Swineherds: Anthony, June 13

Tailors: Boniface, June 5; Martin of Tours, November 11; Homobonus (November 13)

Tanners: Crispin and Crispinian (October 25); Lawrence, August 10

Tax collectors: Matthew, September 21

Teachers: Catherine of Alexandria (November 25); Gregory the Great, September 3; Ursula (October 21); John Baptist de La Salle, April 7

Telegraph/Telephone/Television workers: Gabriel, aa, September 29; Clare, August 11

Television: St. Clare, August 11

Patron Saint of Television

The ability to see far-off places and events is called *bilocal sight*. In 1958, St. Clare (1194–1253), founder of the Poor Clares, was named the patron of television. She never watched TV, but she did have the gift of bilocal sight.

Tentmakers: Paul, June 29

Tertiaries: Louis of France, August 25; Elizabeth of Hungary, November 17

Theologians: Augustine, August 28

Travelers: Christopher (July 25); Julian the Hospitaller (February 12); Gertrude, November 16; Raphael, aa, September 29

Vocations: Alphonsus, August 1

Watchmen: Peter of Alcantara (October 19)

Weavers: Paul the Hermit (January 15); Anastasia (December 25)

Wheelwrights: Catherine of Alexandria (November 25)

Wine growers: Vincent, January 22

Wine merchants: Amand (February 6)

Women in labor: Anne, July 26

Women's Army Corps: Genevieve (January 3)

Workers: Joseph, May 1

Young girls: Agnes, January 21

Youth: Aloysius Gonzaga, June 21; John Berchmans (August 13); Gabriel Possenti (February 27)

Patron Saints of Countries

Mary and the Americas

This patroness of Mexico, with her appearance there in 1531, has also been declared patroness of Latin America (in 1910) and of the whole of the Americas (1945). Other devotions are still treasured, however, like Our Lady of Lujan in Argentina, Our Lady of Charity in Cuba, the Immaculate Conception in Brazil, and Our Lady of Sorrows in Ecuador.

St. Emeric

The Americas are named after the cartographer Amerigo Vespucci, whose name derives from Emeric, which makes St. Emeric a secondary patron of the nations of the Americas.

Argentina: Our Lady of Lujan

Armenia: Gregory Illuminator (October 1)

Australia: Francis Xavier, December 3

Belgium: Joseph, March 19

Bohemia: Wenceslaus, September 28; Ludmilla, grandmother of Wenceslaus (September 16); John Nepomucene (May 16)

St. John Neumann

This native of Bohemia was an immigrant to America in 1836. He was subsequently ordained. After serving in the New York Diocese, he was named Bishop of Philadelphia in 1852. Throughout his life, he used his knowledge of eight languages to help many immigrants in the United States. He organized the first system of parochial schools on a diocesan level. In 1860, Bishop Neumann died. In 1921 he was declared venerable by Pope Benedict XV, in 1963 he was beatified by Pope Paul VI, and in 1977 he became the third American canonized. His feast day is January 5.

Borneo: Francis Xavier, December 3

Brazil: Immaculate Conception, December 8

Canada: Joseph, March 19; Anne, July 26

Chile: James the Greater, July 25; Our Lady of Mt. Carmel, July 16

China: Joseph, March 19

Colombia: Peter Claver, September 9; Louis Bertrand (October 9)

Czechoslovakia: Wenceslaus, September 28; John Nepomucene (May 16); Procopius (July 8)

Denmark: Anskar, February 3; Canute IV (January 19)

Dominican Republic: Our Lady of High Grace (April 4); Dominic, August 8

East Indies: Thomas, ap, July 3

Ecuador: Sacred Heart

England: George, April 23

Europe (co-patrons): Benedict, July 11; Cyril and Methodius, February 14

Finland: Henry, July 13

France: Joan of Arc (May 30); Denis, October 9

Germany: Boniface, June 5

Greece: Nicholas of Myra, December 6

Holland: Willibrord (November 7)

Hungary: Stephen of Hungary (king), August 16

India: Our Lady of Assumption, August 15

Ireland: Patrick, March 17; Brigid of Kildare (February 1); Columba (June 9)

Italy: Francis of Assisi, October 4; Catherine of Siena, April 29

Japan: Peter Baptist (February 5)

Lithuania: Casimir, March 4; Cunegunda (March 3)

Mexico: Our Lady of Guadalupe, December 12

Norway: Olaf (July 29)

Paraguay: Our Lady of Assumption, August 15

Philippines: Sacred Heart of Mary (August 22)

Poland: Casimir, March 4

Portugal: Immaculate Conception, December 8; Francis Borgia (October 10); Anthony of Padua, June 13

Russia: Andrew, November 30; Nicholas, December 6

Scotland: Andrew, November 30

Slovakia: Our Lady of Sorrows, September 15

Spain: James the Greater (July 25); Teresa, October 15

Sweden: Bridget, July 23; Eric (May 18)

Union of South Africa: Our Lady of Assumption, August 15

United States: Immaculate Conception, December 8

Uruguay: Our Lady of Lujan

Wales: David (March 1)

Canonization (See CCC #828.)

The Practice

Originally, only martyrs were so honored and "recommended" in this way to the faithful, but by the fourth century various forms of unbloody witness to Christ were added. From St. Peter until the fourth century, all popes were referred to as saints (with a few minor, and likely, exceptions). Local bishops would decide which candidates should have such honorable mention and a feast day on the liturgical calendar.

Over the years local bishops came to defer the responsibility and privilege to the Bishop of Rome to review cases submitted and make the final decision. By the sixth century this became formalized to the point of inscribing names of the canonized on a roll of saints—the occasion being Boniface IV dedicating the Roman pantheon to St. Mary the Martyrs. It was not until 993 that a saint was formally and universally canonized in the way we know today. Pope John XV elevated Ulric of Augsburg, Germany (890–973), renowned for his relief work among Germans devastated by the Magyar invasion. It was Pope Alexander III (1159–1181) who restricted the prerogative of canonization to the Holy See.

The Process

Changes in this process were announced in 1983. They included reducing the length of the process to ten years. An interested party or group approaches their bishop. Working with the advocates of the candidate, he or she sends in a report on the person to the Congregation for the Causes of Saints.

Venerable (Ven.)

The congregation researches the candidate's virtues to verify if the person practiced virtue to a heroic degree, or died a martyr's death. The congregation either does or does not recommend his or her cause. When the pope accepts the report, the candidate is termed "venerable."

Blessed (Bl.)

This second (apostolic) process continues the first, which was initiated and accomplished in the Church proper (not the Curia). Now is a very lengthy process of scrutiny by an *advocatus Dei* (advocate of God). This "promoter of the cause" (or prosecuting attorney) is authorized to examine the person's life, virtues, writings, reputation for holiness, and reported miracles. Sometimes called *promoter of the faith* or *devil's advocate (advocatus diaboli)*, he is required to raise objections. Customarily two miracles must be credited to the candidate's intercession with God. The venerable candidate is then "beatified" by the pope at a ceremony in St. Peter's Basilica, including the declaration as a *beatus (beata, f)*, unveiling of a photo or painting, and recommendation to a city or region or religious order for veneration.

Saint (St.)

The criteria has not always remained constant (for example, the requirements regarding miracles), but canonization means being "raised to the full honors of the altar." In the ceremonies, the name of the saint is mentioned in the Eucharistic Prayer of the Mass. (Beatification allows veneration; canonization requires it. The beatified are not "recommended" to the whole Church; the canonized are.)

Examples

St. Frances Xavier Cabrini

Canonized in 1946 by Pope Pius XII, Frances was the first US citizen declared a saint.

St. Elizabeth Ann Seton

Elizabeth was the first native-born US citizen canonized. In 1774 she was born and baptized; in 1805 she joined the Catholic Church. She died in 1821, and in 1882 the Church began a study of her sanctity. In 1959 she was declared venerable by Pope John XXIII, in 1963 she was beatified by Pope John XXIII, and in 1975 she was canonized by Pope Paul VI.

Bl. Kateri Tekakwitha

Kateri was the first Native American and lay person beatified. She died in 1680. In 1932 the Church opened her cause for sanctity, in 1943 she was declared venerable by Pope Pius XII, and in 1980 she was beatified by Pope John Paul II.

St. Maximilian

Maximilian Kolbe, in 1982, became the first victim of the Nazi concentration camps to be canonized. Fr. Kolbe was sent to Auschwitz after refusing involvement in the Nazi movement. He volunteered to take the place of a father of several children who was scheduled for execution at the death camp. He died in 1941; his feast day is August 14. Another martyr, Fr. Titus Brandsma, O.Carm., was beatified about the same time. Fr. Titus, a native of the Netherlands, was arrested for urging newspaper editors to refuse to accept Nazi propaganda. While in concentration camps at Amersfoort and Dachau, he led prayers, heard confessions, and ministered to the sick and dying. He was executed July 26, 1942.

Sts. Andrew Kim, Paul Chong, and their companions

These saints were canonized on May 6, 1984, during Pope John Paul II's visit to Korea, making it the first canonization in modern Church history to take place outside Rome.

Saintly Signs and Memorabilia

Hagiography is the writing and study of the lives of the saints.

Relics

Relics are objects associated with saints:

- **First class** designates an actual body or part of a body (for example, the tongue of St. Anthony, preserved at his shrine in Padua).

- **Second class** is an article of clothing or some other article used by a saint.

- **Third class** is any object touched to a first class relic.

Respecting these material things has been more or less popular since the early Church, varying according to era and culture. Mystique, exaggeration, and legend are common, and the Church is slow to offer official guarantees of authenticity; when it is established, the Church offers warm approbation. If a relic is notable in size, a bishop's permission is required for it to be kept in a private home.

The Great Relics

The three main legendary relics of Christ's passion, preserved in St. Peter's and given special veneration during the Triduum, include a piece of the true cross, a point of the spear with which Christ was lanced, and the veil offered by Veronica on the way of the cross.

Shroud of Turin

The winding sheet of Jesus' burial (presumably). It was long venerated in Turin, Italy, where, it has been argued, it was enshrined in 1578. Before that it was in France where a clear tradition of authenticity was traced to the seventh century. It has produced a whole science, *sindonology* (Latin: *sindo*, shroud), dedicated to its study and theological interpretation. It is a strip of linen, fourteen feet, three inches long and three feet, seven inches wide, seeming to bear the front and back imprints of a crucified human body. The seeming stains of sweat and blood constitute a photographic phenomenon whose nature and preservation have not been explained naturally.

Nativity Relics

The Roman Basilica of St. Mary Major has been known as "St. Mary at the Manger" since the seventh century. It has long contained legendary nativity relics: five small Levantine sycamore boards, said to be part of Christ's original crib (no matter that Jerome, according to a fifth-century Christmas homily of his, believed that it was made of clay, a pottery "trough" that would actually be more in keeping with Palestine custom of the day).

The Holy Coat of Treves (Trier, Germany)

Many legends have grown out of relics like the chalice of the Last Supper, the cross of the crucifixion, and the seamless garment of which Christ was stripped (John 19:23–24). Of the latter, it is claimed that the Empress Helena discovered and preserved it in the fourth century. It is also claimed by the cathedral of Treves that the garment is now in their possession. (A sixth-century tablet as well as a twelfth-century document are put forward as substantiation.) A "Holy Coat of Argenteuil" has a similar claim made about it, with a story just as likely, this one counting Charlemagne as its hero. This French city has a twelfth-century document mentioning the *cappa pueri Jesu* (garment of the child Jesus). From this legend has arisen the story that the coat was woven by the Blessed Virgin Mary and that it grew with Jesus as he grew. Both relics are objects of popular pilgrimage.

An Extraordinary Glossary

Bilocation

The apparition of a saint in two different places at the same time, as in the reported appearance of St. Anthony at the same time in the pulpit and in a distant friary choir.

Ecstasy

Mystical enrapture of the body and soul

Incorruptibility

The failure of the body of a saint to decay is a sign of the person's spirituality and a clear allusion to an incorruptibility that is absolute (as with God, wholly unchangeable by nature) or natural (as with angels and souls, indestructible because of their basic spirituality).

Levitation

Floating above the ground, referred to in the life of St. Francis

Liquefaction

Solids, like congealed blood, miraculously liquefying is reported about relics of some saints, as with St. Januarius's blood: This is a renowned relic of the cathedral of Naples. Januarius was the bishop of Benevento, beheaded in 304 during the Diocletian persecution. The cathedral still treasures his head and two vials of his blood. The solid red substance liquefies many times a year, usually after a time of prayer by the thousands of Neapolitans who flock to the cathedral on those days, especially September 19, the feast of St. Januarius. The cruets are removed from their silver case beneath the altar and exposed near the saint's head. This is a very famous liquefication and has been recorded since 1329. A scientific explanation has never been given. Neapolitans believe that when the blood liquefies, it portends blessings for the city.

Locution

Supernatural communication to the sense of hearing

Odor of Sanctity

A pleasant odor that was emitted from the body of a saint, especially after death or disinterment, was believed by medieval people to be evidence of sanctity: a symbol of the fragrance of extraordinary virtue. St. Francis's stigmata reportedly emitted a sweet perfume on occasion. The water in which the body of St. Teresa of Ávila was bathed as she was prepared for burial retained a pleasing fragrance; for nine months a mysterious perfume arose from her grave. See St. Paul's use of an aromatic metaphor in 2 Corinthians 2:15.

Oil of the Saints

This term refers to the oily substances believed to flow from relics or graves of certain saints as well as to the oil of their shrine lamps and water from sources near their graves. These substances are said to have curative powers for the faithful. These are three notable examples: Oil was noticed flowing periodically from the relics of St. Walburga, abbess of Heidenheim, Bavaria, beginning in 893 at Eichstadt where her body was brought after her death in 870; oil is seen to exude from the relics of St. Nicholas of Myra in his shrine at Bari, Italy; oil has come from a holy well near the national shrine of St. Menas at Mareotis in the Libyan desert.

Prolonged Abstinence

The miraculous survival without nourishment for many years is a phenomenon often associated with stigmatics who have lived on the Eucharist alone for long periods. In verifying this as supernatural, the Church has rigorously scrutinized such fasting for its authenticity, including whether the person continues attending to customary responsibilities. The following cases are examples: Angela of Foligno for twelve years, Catherine of Siena about eight years, Elizabeth of Reute over fifteen years, Lidwina for twenty-eight years, and Catherine Racconigi for ten years.

Stigmata (Latin: *stigma*, the brand on a slave or criminal)

These are marks on a body that correspond to some or all of the wounds of Christ: marks of Jesus' passion and crucifixion, or, as in specific cases, the mark of the spear or the crown of thorns. No one is required to believe in stigmatism's divine origin, but it remains a special sign of oneness with Christ's sacrificial suffering (see St. Paul, Galatians 6:17) and is for some an aid to piety. The first known stigmatic is St. Francis of Assisi, who developed bleeding sores on his palms. Others include St. Catherine of Siena, Nicholas of Ravenna, Anne Girling (foundress of an English sect of the Shakers), and—in the twentieth century—Padre Pio (beatified May 2, 1999) and Theresa Neumann.

The Good News Meets Polytheism

St. Paul appeared in the Areopagus in Athens, Greece, the cultural center of the ancient world. There he preached his climactic sermon to the Gentiles, beginning, "You Athenians, I see that in every respect you are very religious" (Acts 17:22), noting an altar inscribed "To an Unknown God." Paul appeals for a new examination of polytheism and idolatry.

The Twelve Major Greek and Roman Deities

	Greek	Roman
King	Zeus	Jupiter
Sun (and music)	Apollo	Apollo
War	Aries	Mars

	Greek	Roman
Home life	Hestia	Vesta
Messenger	Hermes	Mercury
Sea	Poseidon	Neptune
Smith (artist)	Hephaistos	Vulcan
Queen	Hera	Juno
Tillage	Demeter	Ceres
Moon (and hunting)	Artemis	Diana
Wisdom (and weaving)	Athena	Minerva
Love (and beauty)	Aphrodite	Venus

Minor Greek and Roman Deities

	Greek	Roman
Love	Eros	Cupid
Underworld	Pluto	Pluto
Pluto's wife	Persephone	Prosepine
Time	Kronos	Saturn
Wife of Kronos/Saturn	Rhea	Cybele
Wine	Dionysus	Bacchus

The Day the Great Pan Died

"Great Pan is dead" is what was heard by many, tradition says, at the moment of the crucifixion. This cry was to have swept over the ocean, as a sort of Greek version of the rending of the temple veil, whereupon the oracles ceased for good. Pan (Greek: all, everything), the god of forest, flocks, and pastures, was also the personification of the deity who imbued all of creation. (Elizabeth Barrett Browning wrote a poem entitled "Great Pan Is Dead.")

A Mythical Glossary

Ambrosia is the food of the gods.

Elysian Fields is the heaven for mortals favored by the gods.

Ichor is the blood of the gods.

Mt. Olympus is the dwelling of the gods (in Thessaly).

Nectar is the drink of the gods.

Tartarus is the place of the titan's imprisonment after their fall.

A Cosmogony

Chaos is the origin of heaven and earth.

Heaven and Earth are the parents of the titans.

Saturn and Rhea, titans, are the parents of Jupiter, supreme deity.

Atlas, a titan, was condemned to bear the earth on his shoulders.

Prometheus, a titan, supervised human creation.

Pre-Christian Deity Patronage

Roman names are used for classical deities.

Air: Ariel, elves

Beauty and charm: the Graces (to enhance the enjoyment of life): Aglaia (brilliance), Thalia (blooming), and Euphrosyne (joy)

Caves, caverns: Pixies

Commerce: Mercury

Crops: Ceres

Dawn: Aurora

Eloquence: Mercury

Evening: Vesper

Fairies: various, Oberan in Shakespeare (Greek)

Fate: the Three Fates determine the course of human life: Clotho who spun the thread of life, Lachesis who held it and fixed its length, and Atropos who cut it off

Fields: Faunus

Fire: Vulcan, Vesta, Mulciber

Flowers: Flora

Gardens: Vertummus and Pomona, his wife

Hills: Pixies, trolls (there are also wood trolls and water trolls)

Home life: Vesta

House: Penates, Lares

Hunting: Diana

Justice: Themis; Astraea (Themis's daughter); Nemesis (called the goddess of retributive justice because of her persecution of the excessively rich or proud); the Furies Tisiphone, Alecto, and Megaera (In Greek these avengers of wrong that were outside the reach of human justice were called by the euphemism *Eumenides,* meaning "good tempered.")

Laughter: Momus

Love: Cupid

Marriage: Hyman

Medicine: Aesculapius

Memory: Mnemosyne

Messenger of the gods: Mercury

Moon: Luna

Morning: Aurora

Mountains: Oreads, trolls

Poetry and music: Apollo; the Nine Muses: Calliope (chief), Clio (history and heroics), Euterpe (Dionysian music, double flute), Thalia (gaity, comedy, pastoral life), Melpomene (song, harmony, tragedy), Terpsichore (choral dance, song), Erato (erotic poetry, the lyre), Polymnia (inspired hymns), and Urania (astronomy, the celestial)

Rainbow: Iris

Rivers and streams: Fluviales, naiads, nymphs

Sea: Neptune; Triton (his son), mermaids, nereids, oceanides

Shepherds and flocks: Pan, satyrs

Sleep and dreams: Morpheus

Time: Saturn

Trees: Dryads, wood-trolls

Underworld: Pluto

War: Mars, Bellona

Wealth: Plutus

Wind: Aeolus

Wine: Bacchus

Wisdom: Minerva

Wrestling: Mercury

Youth: Hebe

Catholic Symbols

Cross
(See CCC #s 613–618.)

The cross is the distinctive, though not exclusive, Christian symbol, because it was the instrument of Christ's death.

The Four Basic Forms of the Cross

Traditionally, these are the four basic forms of the cross:

| Latin | Greek | St. Andrew | Tau |

1. Latin cross; *Crux Immissa; Crux Ordinaria*
   Upright extending above transom.
2. Greek cross; *Crux Immissa Quadrata*
   Used by the Red Cross.
3. St. Andrew's cross; *Crux Decussata; Saltire*
   His martyrdom.
4. Tau cross; *Crux Commissa*
   St. Anthony's cross; Old Testament cross; prophecy, anticipation, Advent.

Various Forms of the Cross (Descriptions on pages 442–443.)

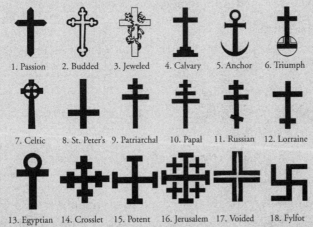

1. Passion 2. Budded 3. Jeweled 4. Calvary 5. Anchor 6. Triumph

7. Celtic 8. St. Peter's 9. Patriarchal 10. Papal 11. Russian 12. Lorraine

13. Egyptian 14. Crosslet 15. Potent 16. Jerusalem 17. Voided 18. Fylfot

1. **Passion cross**

   Ends pointed, like the nails of the passion

2. **Budded cross**

   Trefoil ends (for the Trinity); often topping a Christian flagpole

3. *Crux Gemmata* (jeweled cross)

   Suggesting a living tree, flourishing with leaf and flower

4. **Calvary cross, Graded cross**

   Steps (grises) represent faith, hope, and love (see 1 Corinthians 13:13)

5. **Anchor cross**

   Seen in catacombs; Egyptian in origin; a concealed cross (see Hebrews 6:19)

6. **Cross of Triumph, Cross of Victory, Cross of Conquest**

   The orb was originally a separate symbol (though with vertical line running down from horizontal). The segments of the orb represented Asia, Africa, and Europe. In early Christian art, Christ was pictured holding this orb. Later it was altered to a ball with a cross upon it, to represent the sovereignty of the spiritual over the temporal.

7. **Celtic cross, Cross of Iona**

   Taken by Columba to Isle of Iona, sixth century; circle represents eternity.

8. **St. Peter's cross**

   Represents his martyrdom

9. **Patriarchal cross, Archepiscopal cross**

   Part of heraldic arms of an archbishop, carried before him in procession

10. **Papal cross, Triple cross of the Western peoples**

    The two upper bars represent the two crucified with Jesus.

11. **Russian cross, Eastern cross**

    Cross of Russian Orthodox Church; footrest either slant or straight; upper bar represents the inscription; the cross of early Christianity.

12. **Cross of the Lorraine**

    Lorraine was a medieval kingdom in Western Europe along the Moselle, Meuse, and Rhine Rivers.

13. **Egyptian cross, *Crux Ansata* ("having a handle")**

    Key of the Nile; Ankh ("life"); sign of immortality; predates Christianity

14. **Cross crosslet, Holy cross, German cross**

    Composed of four Latin crosses; symbolizes evangelization

15. **Potent cross** (French: *potence*, crutch)

    Composed of four Tau crosses; its name and symbolism (healing) comes from the resemblance of each cross to the top of an old-fashioned crutch.

16. **Jerusalem cross, Crusader's cross**

Composed of four Tau and four Greek crosses; symbolizes both Christ's five wounds and evangelization (earth's four corners)

17. **Voided cross,** *Gammadia* (because of its four *gammas*, the letter "g" in Greek)

18. **Fylfot cross, Swastika** (Sanskrit: good fortune)

Gammadion charm (Greek capital *gammas*), to dispel evil; Hitler's Nazi Germany

St. Helena and the True Cross

A cruce salus: "Salvation (comes) from the cross."

The Church used to speak of the "invention" of the cross, using the word in its original sense, "to come upon, to discover" (Latin: *invenire*). An inventor is a discoverer. The discovery of the true cross used to be celebrated on May 3: "The Invention of the Cross." According to tradition, the mother of Constantine, Helena, was the inventor. She was an innkeeper's daughter, from Asia Minor, whose marriage to a Roman general, Constantius Chlorus, ended in divorce. Her son Constantine became emperor in 306 and in 313 (after his vision at the Mulvian Bridge) issued the historic Edict of Milan that granted freedom of worship to Christians. His sixty-three-year-old mother gladly converted. The likes of the historian Eusebius document her devotion as a Christian.

According to tradition, Helena is credited with finding the true cross in 326. She engineered an arduous dig in the vicinity of the Holy Sepulcher and was allegedly rewarded with the buried remains of the three crosses used the day Christ died. This wood was declared to be wood of the true cross when a woman experienced a cure when it was applied to her. The Empress Helena enshrined the relics in a silver casket within a church built for the purpose on that spot and also delivered a portion of it to Rome.

St. Helena is depicted in art with various symbols of the crucifixion and was commemorated by the Church on August 18. An incidental note: Because it was on this feast day that the Portuguese discovered an island in the south Atlantic in 1501, it was given her name. It was after a six-year exile on St. Helena's Island that Napoleon died in 1821.

The Wood of the Cross

The crucifixion has been a most fertile soil for the growth of legends and customs, as they germinate in the mystique of the cross. One says that the Savior's cross was constructed from four different woods: palm, cedar, cypress, and olive, representing the four corners of the earth. Here are some others.

The Quaking Aspen

The leaf of the aspen trembles, it is said, because of the tree's horror and shame. It is the tree that furnished the wood for the Lord's cross. As a matter of fact, the leaf stem of the "trembling poplar" is flat, which gives the tree a unique sound in a slight breeze.

The Legend of the Dogwood Tree

In the days before the crucifixion of Christ, legend has it, the dogwood tree matched the oak in stature and strength. Because of these qualities, it was chosen to provide the wood of the cross. This cruel purpose greatly distressed the noble dogwood. Sensing this sympathy, Jesus smiled upon the tree. He transformed it into a slender, twisted shrub, so that it could never again be used ignobly. Escaping destruction, the dogwood would be cherished as a reminder of the Savior's sacrifice. Furthermore, he designed its blossoms to be in the form of a cross, with two long petals and two short, each bearing nail prints, brown with rust and stained with blood. At the flower's center he enshrined an image of his crown of thorns.

Hollywood

Holly has had a host of holy associations. There are stories about its Christmas symbolism. There is also the story that the holly, like the dogwood, was once a full-sized tree, but now allowed to grow no larger than a shrub, for its role in the crucifixion. In this story, holly's stature is deemed a punishment, whereas that of the dogwood is called a protection and a sign of our Savior's sacrifice.

San Damiano Cross

This is the cross which St. Francis was praying before when the Lord commissioned him to "rebuild the Church." (The original hangs in Santa Chiarra—St. Clare—Church in Assisi, Italy.) It is an icon cross because of the style of the images that it includes. With its detail, it teaches more fully the meaning of the crucifixion.

Jesus is portrayed as both wounded and strong, regal and suffering. Note the halo and Jesus' prominence. There are also color contrasts.

The major witnesses are the second largest figures: the Blessed Mother and the Beloved Disciple, Mary and John, on the left; and on the right, Mary Magdalene, Mary, mother of James (wife of Cleopas—Mark 15:40), and the centurion of Mark's Gospel (15:39—"Truly this is the Son of God"), with an onlooker at his shoulder. His hand gesture, a classic position of Christian witness, is a traditional sign for "I am speaking."

The minor witnesses include the soldier who pierced Jesus' side (John 19:34), traditionally known as Longinus. He is the smaller figure below Mary, holding the spear and standing beneath the droplets of precious blood. (In some art, he is shown with the blood dropping in his eye, which was then healed, so says one tradition, of its blindness.) The miniature opposite is "Stephaton" (faulty derivation of the Greek word for sponge), whom Umbrian art pairs with Longinus as the soldier who offered Jesus the vinegar-soaked sponge (John 19:28–30).

At each end of the crossbar, six angels marvel at this event, their hands representing awe, discussion, and invitation.

The six figures at the bottom, typical of this Umbrian art form, are the patrons of the area: Sts. John, Michael, Rufino, John the Baptist, Peter, and Paul.

The rooster at Jesus' left calf represents Peter's denial (John 18:25–27).

The resurrection and ascension are portrayed at the top: Jesus in royal garb, brandishing the cross like a scepter, welcomed by ten angels, alive by the power of God (right hand).

Franciscan · Glory · Adorned · Quadrate · Coptic · Maltese

St. Chad · St. Julian · St. James · Chain · Paternoster · Canterbury

Pattée · Pattée formée · Alisee pattée · Pattée fitched · Pattée fitched (foot) · Crosslet fitched

Barbee · Bottony · Cercelée · Cleché · Millrine · Moline

Fitchy · Fleurée · Fleurette · Entrailed · Masely · Frettee

Trononnee · Aiguisee · Patonce · Avellane · Four ermine spots · Four pheons

Crenellé · Ragulée · Wavy · Nebulé · Demi sarcelled · Degraded

Bezant · Lambeau · Fimbriated · Cantonee · Triparted · Parted and fretty

Other Symbols

Old Testament Figures

Adam: spade, pickax, apple

Eve: spindle, distaff

Cain: plow, ox goad, yoke

Abel: shepherd's staff and lamb

Noah: ark, dove with olive branch, vine

Abraham: altar, stars

Isaac: bundles of wood in the form of a cross

Jacob: ladder, sun and full moon encircled with twelve stars (Jacob, wife, and twelve sons)

Joseph: multicolored coat, star, sheaf of wheat, Egyptian column, scepter and chain

Moses: tablets of stone, basket of bulrushes, burning bush, rod and serpent, rays of light from brow, water from rock

David: young lion, sling, five stones, head of Goliath, crown, horn of oil, tower, key

Solomon: temple

Isaiah: saw (traditional means of his death)

Jeremiah: stone (reputed means of his death)

Ezekiel: a closed gate (4:3, old translation)

Elijah: burning chariot

Daniel: ram with four horns (8:8)

The Trinity

Equilateral triangle
Three circles
Interwoven triangle and circle
Two interwoven triangles
Two triangles and a circle

Trefoil (with triangle)
Triquetra (with circle, triangle)
Shield
Three fishes
Shamrock

The Father

    All-seeing eye

    Creator's star

    Hand of God (*Manus Dei*) (Psalm 98:1)

    Souls of the righteous (in hand) (Wisdom 3:1)

    Two yods (tenth letter of the Hebrew alphabet)

Jesus

    Lamb of God (*Agnus Dei*) (Isaiah 53:7; John 1:29; Revelation 5:6–14)

    Branch (Zechariah 3:8; Jeremiah 23:5)

    Butterfly

    Cornerstone (Ephesians 2:20; 1 Peter 2:6)

    Cross and orb

    Crown (James 1:12; 1 Peter 5:4; Revelation 2:10, 3:11)

    Crucifix

    Daystar (2 Peter 1:19)

    Door (John 10:9)

    Fish (with rebus)

    Fountain (Zechariah 13:1)

    Good Shepherd (John 10:1–30)

    Lion (Revelation 5:5)

    Ox (Matthew 11:30)

    Rock (1 Corinthians 10:4; Psalm 18:3; Exodus 17:6; Matthew 7:24, 16:18)

    Scepter

    Serpent of brass (John 3:14)

    Star (Numbers 24:17; Revelation 22:16)

    Sun (Malachi 3:20)

    Tree of Jesse (Isaiah 11:1)

    Vine (John 15:1)

See also "Myth and Folklore" listing, "Christological Titles," and "Litany of the Holy Name of Jesus."

Jesus' Threefold Office

    Priest: alb, chasuble, stole

    Prophet: long robe

    King: jeweled crown

The Passion

Agony in the Garden
Chalice and rising cross (Luke 22:42)

Betrayal
Lantern, torch, sword and staff crossed, purse, kiss, Peter's sword (with Malchus's ear), rope

Trial and Condemnation
Pillar, two scourges, scarlet robe and reed, crown of thorns, basin and ewer (vase-shaped pitcher), reed, rooster crowing

Crucifixion
Latin cross, five wounds, INRI scroll, ladder, hammer and nails, vinegar-gall, reed and hyssop, seamless coat, veiled sun and moon, passion flower, pierced heart, stigmata (wounds) in hands

Descent from the cross/burial
Ladder and sheet, pincers, myrrh and aloes, shroud, tomb

The Pike's Curiosity

There is a German legend of a fish that closely resembles the legend of the passion flower (see page 482). The fishes of the sea were all terrified at the moment of crucifixion and dived deep in the water, except for the curious pike who alone emerged in order to see the spectacle. This explains why, even to this day, the pike's head is distinctively marked with the scene of the crucifixion, complete with cross, nails, and sword.

The Holy Spirit

Descending dove, flame, seven lamps, scroll with seven gifts, mystic star (seven points)

Angels

Michael: shield with symbol of Trinity

Raphael: staff, pouch, fish

Gabriel: fleur-de-lis

The Blessed Virgin

Often holding a rosary (St. Dominic; Lourdes and Fatima apparitions)

The Virgin

With flowering tresses

Queen of Heaven and Earth (glorified Madonna)

Crowned with twelve stars (Revelation 12:1), with scepter, orb with cross, robed and surrounded by angels, crescent moon underfoot

Mother of Sorrows

(Latin: *Mater Dolorosa*) Older, seated, clothed in mourning (as in the Pietà), head draped, heart pierced

The Immaculate Conception

With the crescent moon underfoot (Revelation 12:1)

Our Lady of Mercy

With arms extended, spreading out a mantle gathering sinners

Mother of God

With snake underfoot (Genesis 3:15)

Mysteries of the Rosary

Joyful: green leaves or white rosettes

Sorrowful: thorns or red rosettes

Glorious: roses or gold rosettes

Midnight Blue, Lifeblood Red

In traditional Eastern Orthodox art, Mary's robe is often a midnight blue, since she is the wise virgin, wrapped in deepest night, anxiously awaiting the bridegroom's coming. Legend has it that she laid her blue cloak on a rosemary plant to let it dry, thus transmitting the lovely blue color to that flower. (Another version linking her to the rosemary has it that she hid behind a rosemary bush when she fled with the infant Jesus to Egypt.)

If not in blue, she is robed in bloody red, since the mother of the crucified is also mother of the living, robed in the risen Spirit and Christ's own lifeblood, giving birth as queen to royal children, the children of God.

Other Marian Symbols

(See also the "Litany of the Blessed Virgin.")

Apple

Ark of the covenant (Luke 1:39–41; 2 Samuel 6)

Balsam

Book of wisdom

Closed gate

Crescent moon (Revelation 12:1)

Crown of twelve stars (Revelation 12:1)

Cypress

Enclosed garden (Song of Solomon 4:12)

Fleur-de-lis

Flowering almond (Numbers 17:23)

Gilly flower

Hawthorn

Lily (of the King)

Lily of the Valley

Myrtle

Olive

Palm

Pierced heart (Luke 2:35)

Stump (rod) of Jesse (Isaiah 11:1)

Rose (Song of Solomon 2:1; Sirach 24:14)

Sealed book

Sealed fountain (Song of Solomon 4)

Snake-encircled globe

Snow-drop

Speculum (mirror)

Star ("Miriam")

Starry crown (Revelation 12:1)

Sun and moon (Revelation 12:1)

Tower of David (Song of Solomon 4:4)

Woman treading serpent

Apostles' Symbols

Including Matthias and Paul. See "Scriptures of the Apostles," as well as stories of their deaths, which symbols often reflect.

Andrew

According to tradition, Andrew was crucified on an X-shaped (saltire) cross; he is sometimes pictured as an old man with long white hair and beard, holding the Gospel and leaning on a saltire.

Bartholomew (Nathanael?)

The flaying knives represent the manner of Bartholomew's death; he was flayed alive.

James the Great (of Compostella)

The scallop shells are pictured because the Spanish coast was said to abound in them; they represent pilgrimage and James's missionary zeal. He is also represented by a pilgrim's staff (as a patron of pilgrims) and gourd bottle.

James the Less (Son of Alphaeus)

One legend said that James the Lesser suffered a terrible martyrdom by being sawed apart; see the alternate story on page 405; another symbol is the fuller's pole (struck in the head).

John

An early story told of John drinking from a poisoned chalice and coming to no harm.

Judas Iscariot

Judas is represented with a bag (he held the common purse, from which he would steal, John 12:6).

Jude (Thaddeus)

Jude probably traveled by ship on his missionary journeys with Simon; he is variously represented with a club, staff, and carpenter's square (his trade).

Matthew (Levi)

The three purses represent Matthew's work as a tax collector before Jesus called him (Matthew 10:3). He is also represented with a hatchet or halberd and is pictured as a bearded old man, accompanied by an angel dictating the Gospel.

Matthias

Matthias, chosen to take the place of Judas, is symbolized by a battle-ax, with which he was said to be beheaded, and an open Bible.

Paul

Paul is represented by an open Bible (the new Law he preached) and the sword of the Spirit; he is pictured as being short and bald with a bushy beard.

Peter

The crossed keys represent Peter's authority (given by Christ). He is also represented with a rooster (betrayal, Matthew 26:69–75; Mark 14:66–72; Luke 22:54–62; John 18:15–18, 25–27). At times he is pictured as a bald old man with flowing beard, clad in white mantle and blue tunic, holding Scripture.

Philip

The loaves of bread on either side of the cross remind us of Philip's comment at the multiplication of the loaves and fishes (John 6:5–7). Another representation is a staff (upon which he was suspended by the neck from a pillar), surmounted with a cross.

Simon

A fish (occupation) rests on a book; in a similar way, Simon became a great fisher of people through the message of the gospel.

Thomas

The carpenter's square stands for the church Thomas is said to have built with his own hands in India; the spear or lance is a sign of the purported manner of his death.

Quo Vadis?

An interesting legend about Peter led to a book and, decades later, a movie. As Peter was fleeing Rome during Nero's persecution, the story goes, he met Christ going to Rome. *"Quo vadis?"* Peter asked him (Latin for "Where are you going?"). Christ replied, "I am coming to be crucified again." Peter, ashamed, took this as a rebuke and returned to Rome. He was crucified on a cross planted upside down in the earth. This legendary question was used by the Polish Henryk Sienkiewicz as the title for a novel (1895) on the life of the early Christians in Rome during Nero's persecution.

The Church

Ark (Matthew 24:37–39; Hebrews 11:7; 1 Peter 3:20; 2 Peter 2:5), ark of the covenant, bride of Christ, candlestick, dragnet, flock, hill, house on a rock, leaven, mustard seed, ship (Matthew 8:23–27), vine, vineyard, wheat and tares, woman and the dragon, woman crowned

Sacraments

Baptism
Shell with water, baptismal font, font with dove, running water

Confirmation
Dove, lamp with oil, bishop's staff and miter

Eucharist
Host and chalice, wheat and grapes, bread and wine, basket of loaves, wine, flowing water, vineyard, pelican

Reconciliation
Keys, scourge, closed door

Anointing of the Sick
Olive branch

Marriage
Strands tied in a knot, linked rings

Holy Orders
Keys, chalice, host, book, stole

Denominations

Symbols associated with selected Churches

1. The nine crosses of the **Episcopal Church** shield commemorate the nine original dioceses represented at the First General Convention (1789).

2. **Lutheran Church**: The well-known emblem of Martin Luther consists of a black cross on a red heart against the Marian rose on a heavenly blue background within a gold circle (symbolizing eternity). Luther adopted it as his own coat of arms to express his trust in God: "The Christian's heart / Is resting on roses / E'en while beneath the cross / It reposes."

3. The cross and flame of the **Methodist Church**.

4. The **Presbyterian Church** logo incorporates cross, open book, dove, and flames (representing the burning bush and Pentecost).

Liturgical Feasts and Seasons

Solemnities and Feasts

Annunciation (S)

Budding fleur-de-lis, lily, dove, two interlocked circles

Presentation (F)

Fifteen steps

Ascension (S)

Elijah's fiery chariot, broken chain, open gates, clouds, palms of victory (Revelation 7:9), birds flying homeward, fishnet, ball and cross

Pentecost (S)

Descending dove, flames, beehive, Blessed Virgin, any symbol of the Church (ark, for example), censor, circle, city, fishnet, lighthouse, mountain, rock

Trinity Sunday

Triangle, three interlocked circles or fish, shamrock, hand, dove, *Chi-Rho*

The Body and Blood of Christ (S)

Pelican, altar bread, chalice, fish, grapes, peacock feeding on grapes, vine, wheat, wine

Assumption (S)

Empty tomb, lily, palm and two lilies crossed, clouds, crown, angels

Seven Sorrows

Heart pierced with seven swords, Marian monogram

All Saints' (S)

Sheaf of wheat, crown, symbols of beatitudes, rayed *Manus Dei* ("the souls of the righteous are in the hand of God," Wisdom 3:1)

Christ the King (S)

Crown, stole, sheaf of wheat, scepter, throne, ball and cross

> ### Soul Cakes
>
> Doughnuts, "soul cakes," are a special November food. Their circular form symbolizes the cycle of life, death, and rebirth: Seed springs to life, grows, matures, produces its seed-bearing fruit, and dies and rises again as its seeds spring to life again, germinate, and emerge, closing the circle of life.

> ### Biblical Christmas Tree
>
> The story of the Jesse tree—or rather its inspiration—comes from Isaiah's prophecy, "There shall come forth a shoot from the stump of Jesse" (Isaiah 11:1). Jesse is King David's father and so an ancestor of Jesus ("of the House of David"). Tradition has taken Isaiah's suggestion of Jesus' "family tree" and decorated it with ornaments or pictures representing various ancestors (like Noah, Jacob, Moses, Ruth, Jesse himself, and David, of course). Jesus' spiritual heritage is thus illustrated and celebrated.

Symbols of the Seasons

Advent

Empty throne, dew falling from heaven, rising sun, fleece, anchor of hope, violet color, O Antiphons, scroll of prophecy

Immaculate Conception

Shield with Marian monogram or symbol, Mary treading a serpent, moon

Christmas

Crib, star, two interlocked circles, Trinity, tree, lambs, angels, trumpet, Holy Family symbols, three steps, candies, crook, throne, shepherds, hand of God, dove, hawthorn, Glastonbury thorn in blossom

Holy Innocents

Lily buds, sword, palms (Revelation 7:9), hoops and halos

Epiphany

Three crowns, three gifts, wise men, five-pointed star

Holy Name

Chalice, tablets of stone, Jesus' name or monogram

Purification

Candies, sword, two drinking doves

Christmas Symbols

The significance of most Christmas symbols is obvious; others, although commonplace, have deeper meaning not immediately apparent, and some represent stories no longer remembered.

Candy cane

The shepherd's crook, representing the nativity's first witnesses and Christ the Good Shepherd, inspired the candy cane. Its alternating white and red stripes represent the Lord's purity and sacrifice, even as the same colors do liturgically. Its lively peppermint flavor stands for the royal gift of spice. Finally, like the Body of Christ itself, the candy cane is given to be broken and shared.

Carnation

The carnation is known as a flower of rejoicing because of the legend that it first appeared at the birth of Christ.

Christmas holly

The bright green leaves and red berries, well into the cold season, make holly right for Christmas. Its symbolism, however, is much deeper. For the early Christian it was not only reminiscent of the burning bush seen by Moses, but prophetic as well: In the face of Christmas sentimentality, it foretells, with its prickly points and drops of blood-like berries, Christ's crown of thorns. According to ancient legend, its berries were once yellow, but were stained permanently red by Christ's blood, since it was used to fashion the Savior's crown of thorns. (Maybe this is the reason for the superstition that holly, if brought into the house before Christmas Eve, would provoke family fights.)

Holly's symbolic roots go deeper still, into the subsoil of the Roman culture. The Romans would send holly to friends, in a gesture of friendliness and good will during the mid-winter feasts. Later, Northern Europeans hung it on doors as a symbol of shelter for the wood spirits.

Poinsettia—the Mexican "Flower of the Holy Night"

Dr. Joel Poinsett was U.S. ambassador to Mexico in the early 1800s. In 1829 when he returned home, he brought with him a plant called by the Mexicans the "flower of the Holy Night." We call it the poinsettia, after Joel, and use it as a favorite Christmas plant.

It has a fabled origin: Long ago, on Christmas Eve, a poor child made his way to church in great sadness because he had no gift to offer the Christ child. Not daring to enter the church, he knelt humbly on the ground outside and prayed, tearfully telling the Lord of his great desire to offer a gift. Unwilling to approach with empty hands, he finally rose only to behold springing up at his feet a plant with dazzling red, spectacular blooms. This was the answer to his prayers. These blossoms he took to the feet of the Christ child.

Since then, the "flower of the Holy Night" spread through the whole country, blooming each year at Christmas with such glorious abandon that the very sight of it filled believers with the spirit of this season of the savior's birth.

St. Boniface and the Christmas Tree

St. Boniface was an eighth-century missionary (praised by Pope Gregory II) who brought Christianity to Germany. Returning to Germany later, he found that Christianity had not taken hold. On Christmas Eve he came upon the eldest son of the chieftain Gundhar being readied for sacrifice to the gods. The place was under the giant oak tree, sacred to their patron Thor. Boniface, in order to prove these gods powerless, felled the tree with the stroke of an ax, to the astonishment of the onlookers.

When he was then asked for the word of God, Boniface proclaimed, "This is the word, and this is the counsel. Not a drop of blood shall fall tonight, for this is the birth-night of the Saint Christ, son of the all-Father and savior of the world." Pointing to a nearby evergreen he continued, "This little tree, a young child of the forest, shall be a home tree tonight. It is the wood of peace, for your houses are built of fir. It is the sign of endless life, for its branches are ever green. See how it points toward heaven. Let this be called the tree of the Christ child. Gather about it, not in the wild woods but in your homes. There it will shelter no deeds of blood, but loving gifts and lights of kindness."

Martin Luther and the Christmas Tree

A popular legend tells how Martin Luther, during a Christmas Eve walk, was inspired with the beauty of the starlit night sky. To reproduce this celestial wonder and to commemorate Christ's birth under the starry Bethlehem sky, Martin brought a fir tree to his home, decorated it with candles, and arranged beneath it the nativity scene. This story has interesting resemblances to St. Boniface (the tree) and St. Francis (the first nativity scene with living people and animals).

Symbols of Lent and Holy Week

Lent

Fish, money bag and incense, praying hands, cross, violet color, lamp and oil, pitcher, two scourges, saltire, pretzel

Palm Sunday

Palms

Holy Thursday

Chalice and Eucharistic symbols, oil containers (Chrism liturgy)

Good Friday

Latin cross, crown of thorns and passion symbols, hot cross buns

Hot Cross Buns

Hot cross buns, a European staple on Good Friday, are made of sweet, spiced dough with icing shaped in the form of a cross. They were commonly distributed to the poor and were even considered a blessing against sickness and house fires. In some locales they were baked and distributed the day before Ash Wednesday, a kind of last celebration before the fast. One example of a comic verse is:

Hot cross buns. Hot cross buns.

One a penny, two a penny. Hot cross buns.

If your daughter won't eat them, give them to your son.

But if you have one of those little elves,

Then you must eat them all yourselves.

Another tradition is that the buns were to be made of dough kneaded for the altar host and marked, accordingly, with the cross. They were then to remain mold-resistant for twelve months:

Good Friday comes this month: the old woman runs

With one-a-penny, two-a-penny, hot cross buns.

Whose virtue is, if you believe what's said,

They'll not grow moldy like the common bread.

With such a characteristic and with such a holy association, some believed this humble bun qualified as a charm against evil, and it was superstitiously hung in the house.

Symbols of the Easter Season

Why wouldn't the season most powerful in faith be also the most prolific in symbol?

Resurrection gardens

Jesus said, "Unless a grain of wheat falls into the earth and dies, it remains just a single grain; but if it dies, it bears much fruit" (John 12:24). There is an old Paschal custom of tucking red-dyed eggs into sprouting seedlings. The "Easter grass"—rye grass or wheat—is started early and kept moist in a bowl of perlite. Come the Pasch, a few of the dyed eggs are nestled in, reminders of the baptized who "have washed their robes and made them white in the blood of the Lamb" (Revelation 7:14b). Like the egg itself, a believer can open into the white and gold of risen life. (Boiling the eggs good and long in a container stuffed with yellow onion skins gives them a beautiful bloody, mahogany color. Tying tiny ferns and flowers to the egg with thread before boiling gives it a tracery effect. Eggs can be rubbed with butter for a shine.)

The Proud Lily

Lily lore abounds. It would be enough for it to be a spring flower, representing life's renewal and the spirit's rebirth—but there's more. According to legend, the lily lost its self-respect on the night of Christ's agony in the garden: The other flowers bowed their heads in sorrow in Christ's presence, but not the lily. How could it, being the most fragrant and beautiful flower in the garden (according to its own estimation)? Upon Christ's display of humility, however, the lily belatedly hung its head in shame, and has humbly remained so ever since. (As a matter of fact, our Easter lily is not native to Palestine, but was imported in the 1880s from Bermuda. "Croft's Lily" is grown mainly in the Pacific Northwest and California.)

Easter caskets

Easter eggs symbolize not only spring's rebirth, but also Christ's resurrection. Like his tomb, the egg is the hard, cold casket from which new life finally and triumphantly breaks forth. The Roman proverb *Omne vivum ex ovo* (All life comes from an egg) took on a new, religious significance.

Lent's over

In Germany, eggs became part of the Easter decoration and celebration of the nineteenth century. If it was not its tempting symbolism that gave the egg a place in the Church, it was simply the food that it was: Eggs were prohibited during Lent, and allowed again at Easter, so at very least they symbolized the end of the fast!

Colored eggs

According to a Ukrainian folktale, a poor peddler went to the marketplace one day to sell a basket of eggs. He encountered a crowd mocking a man who was staggering under a heavy cross on which he was about to be crucified. Running to his aid, the peddler left the basket by the roadside. Upon his return, he found the eggs wondrously transformed with exquisite designs of bright colors. The man was Christ; the peddler, Simon of Cyrene; and the eggs were to become the symbol of rebirth for all humankind. Even today in the Ukraine, decorating *pysanky*, as the native eggs are called, is a treasured craft and custom.

"Gilding the lily" may be unnecessary, but gilding the egg is almost essential at Easter, bringing beauty and added significance to one of nature's fruits. Literal gilding—with actual gold leaf—was the privilege of the wealthy and none was more extravagant than the great nineteenth-century goldsmith Peter Carl Fabergé who gilded eggs for Czar Alexander III of Russia. Plainer folks merely dyed their eggs.

Easter bunnies

Though it's now a secular symbol, the rabbit was originally a religious symbol for non-Christians. It begins with the legend of "Eastre," the European goddess of spring. While this season of rebirth erupted with abundant new life, Eastre's pet bird would lay eggs in baskets and hide them in unlikely places. On a whim, Eastre transformed her bird into a rabbit but its egg-laying ways remained unchanged from its feathered past! Whether fowl or hare, Eastre's pet and its profligate produce represented abundant new life and earth reborn. Even back to the sixteenth century there is reference to an egg-laying rabbit.

Easter baskets

Easter baskets have become a fixture, and presume eggs and candy. Originally, however, the baskets held fresh, wholesome foods. In a day when reliance on the soil and its produce was more immediate and apparent, people would bring to church the fruits of the earth as an analogy of Easter's new life. So in the beginning, Easter baskets were a more graphic life-sign and were brought for blessing on Easter Saturday. In the days when the new water was blessed at Holy Saturday's morning service, holy water too added to the spiritual significance of nature's food and life.

Sacred Monograms

It has been a practice since the early days of the Church to use certain letters, mostly derived from Greek and Latin words, as symbols, slogans, and abbreviations.

A and Ω (*alpha* and *omega*)—the first and last letters of the Greek alphabet signify the eternity and the infinity of God (Revelation 1:8, 17; 21:6; 22:13) and Christ who is the beginning and the end

AM—Latin: *Ave Maria* (Hail Mary)

AMDG—Latin: *Ad Majorem Dei Gloriam* (For the greater glory of God); see also "Mottoes"

AMGPDT—Latin: *Ave Maria, gratia plena, Dominus tecum* (Hail Mary, full of grace, the Lord is with you.)

AMR—Latin: *Ave Maria, regina* (Hail Mary, queen)

BVM—Blessed Virgin Mary

DG—Latin: *Deo gratia* (By the grace of God)

DOM—Latin: *Datur omnibus mori* (It is destined that all die); also Latin: *Deo optimo maximo* (To God who is the best and the greatest); see also "Mottoes"

DV—Latin: *Deo volente* (God willing; by God's will)

ICHTHYS

The letters of this word are an acronym spelling "fish" in Greek. From the many titles of Jesus, three emerged as the favorites of believers: Christ (Greek: *Christos*, anointed), Son of God, and Savior. These three easily combined, becoming a creed and a prayer (see the Jesus Prayer). In Greek, the holy name of Jesus plus these three titles read: *Iesous Christos Theou Yos Soter* (Jesus Christ, Son of God, Savior). The initial letters of these five words form the Greek word *ichthys* (fish). For this reason Christ is often pictured as a fish, a rebus (a pictorial representation of a word) which became an early Christian secret symbol for the Redeemer.

IHS (or IHC)

First three letters of the name/title of Jesus Christ in Greek capital letters: IHCOUC (the older form of the Greek *sigma*, S, resembles our C). In art St. Ignatius Loyola is sometimes pictured with this monogram, alluding to his fabled miraculous knowledge of the Trinity. As IHS it has various interpretations:

1. *Iesus Hemeteros Soter* (Greek): Jesus our Savior, common early Christian inscription

2. *Iesus Hominum Salvator* (Latin): Jesus Savior of Humankind, common phrase on early Christian monuments; popularized by St. Bernadine of Siena in the fourteenth century

3. *In Hoc Salus* (Latin): In this (cross) is salvation.

4. *In Hoc Signo (Vinces)* (Latin): In this sign (you will conquer), from the vision and promise said to have been received by Constantine before his victory at the Mulvian Bridge (313).

5. I have suffered.

ICXC—*Iota sigma chi sigma*; first and last letters of Jesus and Christ in Greek (IHCOYC XPICTOC)

IES—*Iota eta sigma*; same as IHS, but in lowercase: first three letters of Jesus in Greek

INI—Latin abbreviation of *In nomine Jesu* (In the name of Jesus); often used at the close of letters

INRI—Latin abbreviation of *Iesus Nazarenus Rex Iudaeorum* (Jesus of Nazareth, the King of the Jews) over Jesus' cross (John 19:19). (A slightly curved horizontal line over the letters indicates abbreviation.)

IX—*Iota chi*, initial letters of Jesus Christ in Greek

JMJ—Jesus Mary Joseph

M, Maria, Marian—Mary

NIKA—A Greek word meaning victor or conquers, usually combined with ICXC

UIOGD—A Latin abbreviation for *Ut in omnibus glorificetur Deus* (That God may be glorified in all things); St. Benedict's admonition to followers

XP

The capitalized Greek letters *chi* and *rho* are equivalent to CH and R in Latin or English. It is a monogram for Christ, consisting of the first two Greek letters of that title. Hence called the *Chi-Rho* ("Key Row"). Also called a *chrisma* (Greek: ointment). Arranged artistically in a variety of ways. This abbreviation or monogram also explains the origin of "Xmas," another expression of the ubiquitous *Chi-Rho*.

In This Sign

There is a well-known story of Constantine's vision of the cross. In the year 312 this non-Christian leader was marching on Rome to engage Maxentius. At the Mulvian bridge over the Tiber, he met the foe who stood between him and  Rome. He reported that the night before, in a dream Constantine had seen a luminous cross and heard the words *In hoc signo vinces* (In this sign you will conquer). He inscribed the cross and motto on his soldiers' shields. On October 28, 312, there occurred one of the decisive military engagements of history, in which Maxentius lost the battle and his life. The West was Constantine's. The Christian God, he believed, had given him the victory. Christianity was given a legal place with any religion in the Roman Empire. The age of persecution was over.

Because of this story, some interpret the Greek letters *iota, eta, sigma* (IHS, the first three letters of the name *Jesus* in Greek) to be Latin *ihs (in hoc signo)*. That's probably better than the attempted English version of *ihs*, "I have suffered."

The story itself has been called a standing legend, for there are other such cross and victory stories, with interchangeable parts. In a Spanish version the hero is Don Alonzo, and the battle is against the Moors at Ourique in 1139. In a vision of the crucifix in the eastern sky, the crucified Christ promised the Christian king a total victory. In Denmark it was a victory for Waldermar II over the Estonians (1219) that was promised by the sturdy old vision. (The Dannebrog, the Danish national flag, is a white cross on a red field.)

Numbers and Their Significance

In many cases in the Scriptures, a number is used not so much for its numerical value (literally), but because of its symbolic meaning and the associations it has (figuratively). Sometimes the use of a number serves both purposes. Any number squared emphasizes its significance. Three, five, and nine have been called the mystical numbers.

One

One is for unity. One refers to God.

Three

The numerical signature of the Trinity leads to the celebrated "three symbolism," which reflects the old adage, *Omne trinum est perfectum* (Everything in threes is perfect). It's represented in a person's three elements (body, soul, spirit), theological virtues (see the three altar steps), elements of faith, evangelical counsels, notable duties, sons of Noah, angels who visited Abraham, branches of the vine in the butler's dream, baskets in the baker's dream, cities, witnesses, companies of soldiers, arrows, darts, sons, years, days, months, rows of stones, pillars, cubits, prayers, Hebrew children, days of Jonah in fish's belly, days of Jesus in tomb, times which God's voice was heard acknowledging his Son, three-fold punishments, blessings, denials, Peter's confessions, persons at the Transfiguration, favored disciples, days of Saul's blindness, temptations of Jesus, and men who came seeking Peter. And that's only for starters!

Four

Four is the numerical signature of nature (the four seasons) and creation (the four corners of the earth). It's the number of the evangelists, Latin/Greek fathers, rivers of paradise (Pison, Gihon, Tigris, Euphrates), beasts of the Apocalypse, living creatures of Ezekiel, horsemen of the Apocalypse (conquest, war, pestilence, death), cardinal virtues, last things, Gospel versions, winds of heaven, soldiers at foot of cross, and virgin daughters of St. Philip, for example.

Six

Seven minus one is the imperfect number, being one short of seven.

Seven

The perfect number, three plus four, the signature of totality, is the first of the symbolic numbers. Every seventh day is a Sabbath, every seventh year a sabbatical year, every seventh sabbatical year is followed by a jubilee year. There are seven weeks between Passover and Pentecost; the Passover and Tabernacle feasts last seven days, during which time twice seven lambs were offered daily. It's noticed also in the days of creation, days of the week, patriarchs, Jacob's years of service, ears of corn and oxen in pharaoh's dream, trumpets of Jericho, baths of Naaman, penitential psalms, Jewish festivals, gifts of the Holy Spirit, works of mercy, joys and sorrows of Mary, last words on the cross, deacons in the apostolic Church, Churches of Asia Minor, lamps, spirits before the throne of God, candlesticks and stars and trumpets of

Revelation, seals on the Book of Life, sacraments, great councils of the early Church, champions of Christendom, deadly sins, Christian virtues, seas, ages of man, and the stars in the Pleiades (supposed by the ancients to be heaven), for example.

Eight

The number of regeneration, Baptism, and completion is found in the octagonal baptismal font. It's the number of people saved in the ark, the Beatitudes, the day of circumcision, and the sons of Jesse, for example.

Nine

The number of mystery, the trinity of trinities, the perfect plural (thrice three, which is the perfect unity) is the number of choirs of angels, and there are the nine crosses, for example.

Ten

The complete number, signifying order and worldly power, is the number of the Commandments, plagues of Egypt, faithful disciples, wicked brothers of Joseph, sons of Haman, servants of Joshua, virgins, lepers, and pieces of silver, for example. Any number multiplied by ten or tens signifies the highest possible, as in the 144,000 in the New Jerusalem (see below).

Twelve

Three times four is the universal number, the signature of God's people. Twelve symbolizes maturity and totality. The Book of Revelation has much imagery built around this number. It is the number of the sons of Jacob, tribes of Israel, apostles, stones of the altar, pillars, months, signs of the zodiac, minor prophets, sibyls, gates of Jerusalem, fruits of the tree of life (Revelation 22:2), men and stones of Joshua, oxen–bullocks–lambs–goats of the sacrifice, cities, princes of Israel, baskets of bread at the feast of the five thousand, thrones, legions of angels, stars in the woman's crown, and foundations of the Holy City, for example.

Fifteen

Fifteen signifies ascent and progression, as seen in the number of steps of the temple, the gradual psalms, and the mysteries of the Rosary, for example.

Forty

This well-known symbolic number indicates one generation, as well as a great many or a long time. This biblical number for trial, testing, and waiting represents the Church militant. Forty is the number of days of the flood, years of Israel's wandering, days of Moses on Mt. Sinai, days of Elijah's fasting, days of Nineveh's probation, days of Jesus' temptation in the wilderness, and days of Jesus' post-resurrection ministry, for example.

Fifty

Seven times seven plus one equals fifty. Pentecost is the fiftieth day (*pentekoste* in Greek), Easter's jubilee. Fifty represents the fulfillment of divine promise.

One hundred

Alone or as multiple, one hundred symbolizes plenitude, as when Jesus spoke of a hundredfold harvest, and a hundredfold reward.

666

Perfect imperfection is symbolized by 666, falling three times short of seven. In Revelation 13:18 the number is called a person (a beast), meaning possibly a set of people, or an institution headed by a person or a group of people. It seems to mean a name, the letters of which, when regarded as numerals, total 666. In both Hebrew and Greek, letters are used for numbers, the value corresponding to the place in the alphabet; by adding up the number values in a word, a name or word may be obtained. St. Irenaeus interpreted 666 to mean *Lateinos*. Others have interpreted it to mean popes (like Leo X), emperors, generals (like Napoleon), religious reformers (like Knox or Luther), and of course Hitler. The most common interpretation is Nero Caesar, determined by using the Hebrew consonants for that name along with their traditional number values.

One thousand

This definitely large number symbolizes an indefinitely large number, too large to be counted, even symbolizes eternity ("with the Lord, one day is like a thousand years, and a thousand years are like one day"—2 Peter 3:8).

144,000

This is the population of the Church militant, according to the Book of Revelation (7:4, 14:1). This number in the Church (the New Israel, the first fruits of the gospel) at any given moment represents a totality. The number is derived by adding up the traditional twelve tribes of Israel, with each digit magnified one thousand times (or similarly 12 X 12 X 1000).

The Rainy Saint

This is the story of a man who was canonized by popular aclaim. Legend has it that a ninth-century Bishop of Winchester, Swithin, desired to be buried not inside, but outside, in the cathedral's churchyard, so the "sweet rain of heaven might fall upon his grave." So it was. But upon his canonization the good monks determined to honor his sainthood (if not his wishes) by enshrining this body in the choir. And so they did, on July 15. Forthwith it began to rain, and it continued for forty days, biblically enough, until the monks gathered that the saint was averse to their desire and reversed their position—and his.

This story has given birth to the saying, "If it rains on St. Swithin's Day, there will be rain for forty days." This story has also given birth to a Scottish version (St. Martin Bullions, July 4), French (St. Gervais, and St. Medard, June 8) and Flemish (St. Godelieve). In any event (or locale), this watery folklore has provided a "weeping saint" whose feast day betokens forty days' rain or dry weather.

Creatures of Myth and Fable

Basilisk (Cockatrice)

This is a winged reptile from classical and European mythology with a horn-like growth on its rooster head and the body of a reptile. Hatched from an egg laid on a dunghill, it was said to repel serpents and possess a glance lethal for humans. Its body could split a rock. To slay it one had to look into a mirror (symbolizing the gospel) in order to reflect its venom—all provided the slayer saw the creature before it saw him.

Centaur

This pre-Christian personification of humanity's evil inclinations is the mythical creature in the form of a horse with a human head, arms, and chest. It can be found on many ancient fonts symbolizing the baptismal transformation of the old Adam into a new creation.

Chimera

This symbol of fright and destruction is the fire-breathing monster of Greek mythology, with the head and chest of a woman, forepaws of a lion, body of a goat, and tail of a dragon.

Griffin

The griffin represents the human and divine natures, as well as omnipotence and omniscience. It is a monster from Greek mythology with a lion's body and an eagle's head and wings and sometimes a serpent's tail. It pulled the chariot of the sun.

Harpy

This fabled monster, with a woman's head and bust and a vulture's body, symbolizes evil and rapacity.

Hydra

This venomous serpent of Greek mythology, which sprouted two extra heads whenever one was cut off, represents the cancerous nature of sin and heresy.

Remora

According to ancient folklore this little fish of disproportionate strength is able to adhere to a ship's keel and prevent its rolling or pitching even in the most violent storm. It is a symbol of Jesus, protector of the Church.

Satyr

Mentioned in Isaiah ("goat-demon" in the NRSV, 13:21) and Leviticus (17:7), this fabled monster with a human head and a goat's legs symbolizes immorality and the children of evil.

Wyvern

This medieval winged monster has a dragon's head, two legs with clawed feet, and a barbed tail tied in a knot.

A Glossary of Common Symbols

A symbol is something visible with hidden meaning thrown in (Greek: *em*, in; *ballein*, to cast; hence "emblems").

Acorn

Latent strength, potential greatness

Agate

Health and long life, June

Almond

The favor of God (Numbers 17:8), Mary

Alpha* and *omega

See "Sacred Monograms" and "Abbreviations."

Altar

Christ, Eucharist, sacrifice, Abraham, worship, God's presence; two: Cain and Abel

Amethyst

Repentance, sincerity, February

> *Anniversaries*
>
> Fanciful names representing worth, durability, and common symbolism; being material suitable for gifts on those occasions:
>
> | First: cotton (wedding) | Fifteenth: crystal |
> |---|---|
> | Second: paper | Twentieth: china |
> | Third: leather | Twenty-fifth: silver |
> | Fifth: wood | Thirtieth: pearl |
> | Seventh: wool | Fortieth: ruby |
> | Tenth: tin | Fiftieth: gold |
> | Twelfth: silk; fine linen | Seventy-fifth: diamond |

Ant

Religious industry (Proverbs 6:6), frugality, foresight

Anchor

Christ, hope (Hebrews 6:19), salvation, the annunciation, St. Clement of Rome (cast into the sea while bound to an anchor), Nicholas of Bari (patron of sailors)

Ape

Levity, lust, cruelty, fraud

Apple

Original sin, Eve, capital sins (seven on tree of knowledge)

Arch

Triumph, broken, untimely death

Argent

In heraldry the tincture (color) silver

Ark

Church, Mary, Noah

Ark of the covenant

Mary, presence of God (Exodus 25:10–22)

Arm

Might, protection

Armor

Security, resistance to evil

Arrows

Fortune, persecution, martyrdom, Sts. Edmund, Sebastian, Ursula

Ashes

Repentance, grief

Aspergillum

Purity, holiness

Ass

Humility, patience, service, peace, burden bearing (see Matthew 21:1–11), St. Anthony of Padua

---

The Ass's Stripe

This beast was honored by Christ, tradition says, for his triumphant ride into Jerusalem. The dark stripe running down its back and crossed by another at its shoulders was said to be bestowed by Jesus, prophetic of the crucifixion, as an honorable badge for its part in redemption.

Aureola

Latin: *aurum*, gold, + *corna*, crown; wreath; halo of gold; an elongated nimbus surrounding the entire body, signifying the holiness of Jesus in glory; often seen with Madonna and Child. Traditionally, its use has signified the heavenly reward over and above the beatific vision itself for the conquerors of the enemies of human salvation: virgins, for victory over the flesh (Revelation 14:4–5); martyrs, for victory over the world (Matthew 5:11–12); faithful teachers of the truth (Matthew 5:19), for victory over the devil, the father of lies (Daniel 12:3). See halo.

Azure

In heraldry the tincture (color) blue

Bag of money

Almsgiving, the betrayal by Judas

Balances

Justice

Ball and cross

Power of Christ encircling world, Church's mission

Balsam

Mary

Banner

Victory, resurrection

Basin and ewer

Passion (see Pilate), service

Bat

Night, desolation, death

Bay (wreath)

Death, grief

Bear

Self-restraint, solitary life, martyrdom, Satan

Beaver

The sacrifice of anything that interferes with the spiritual quest. It was believed that the beaver has a sack with a treasured medicinal fluid in it. When endangered, however, it would sacrifice this treasure by biting off the sack, thereby avoiding further pursuit.

Bees

Resurrection, tireless activity, chastity, fertility; hive: the faithful, eloquence, Sts. John Chrysostom, Ambrose, Bernard, Isidore

---

Sweet Talk

The story is told that when Saint John Chrysostom was an infant, bees came to light on his lips, prophesying his sweet speech. The same story is told of Plato, Sophocles, Pindar, and St. Ambrose (whose symbol is a beehive).

Bell

Call to worship

Birch

Authority

Birds

The faithful; caged: soul in body; released: soul's flight at death (Psalm 124:7)

Black

Death, mourning, despair, Benedictines, Augustinians, Jesuits, Cowley Fathers; formerly common at funeral liturgies

Black and white

Humility, purity of life

Black over white

Dominicans

Blood

Death, redemption, martyrdom, sacrifice

Bloodstone

Courage, March

Boar

Ferocity, sensuality

Blue

Firmament, heaven, heavenly love, fidelity, wisdom, truth, Mary Book: priest's and deacon's teaching power, prophet, wisdom, revelation, St. Anne; open: book of life (Philippians 4:3)

Brazen serpent

Jesus

Bread

Eucharist, Jesus; loaf in hand: St. Anthony

Briars

Sin, temptation, cares of the world

Bridge

Christ

Brown

Renunciation of the world (Franciscans), spiritual death, degradation

Budding rod

St. Joseph

Bullock

Sacrifice, atonement

Burning bush unconsumed

Mary's virginity; with stone tablets: Old Law given to Moses (Exodus 3:2)

Butterfly

Resurrection

Camel

Submission

Candle

Christ (John 1:9), human life, resurrection, Baptism; burning: baptismal birth

Candle, Paschal

Five incense grains: five wounds

Candlestick

Seven-branched (menorah): Old Testament

Carnation

The flower of rejoicing because of the legend that it first appeared at the birth of Christ

Carnelian

Contentment, July

Cat

Cruelty, self-indulgence, witchcraft

Caterpillar

Earthly man

Cedar tree

Steadfastness in the faith, prosperity, longevity

Censer

Worship, prayer, priesthood

Chain

Slavery, imprisonment, might

Chalice

Eucharist, worship, faith, Gethsemane, St. John the Evangelist

Chariot, fiery

Elijah

Chrism

Baptism, Confirmation, Holy Orders, anointing

Chrysolite

Antidote to madness, September

Circle

Perfection, eternity, wholeness

City on a hill

Church, Mary

When a C is Not a C

Those who read music are familiar with the C that may appear after the clef sign. It's often thought that this designation for 4/4 time stands for "common." Not true. This C is not even a C. The most common time, in the morning of music, was "perfect" time, having three beats to the bar. This trinity of beats was considered analogous to the three Persons of the Trinity. Naturally—or symbolically—a complete circle, with the connotations of God's completeness and perfection, was used as its sign. 4/4 time, on the other hand, was not perfect and complete, and so its symbol was an incomplete circle . . . the C that is not a C.

Cloak

Love, righteousness

Cloud

Divine presence, covenant

Clover leaf

Trinity, St. Patrick

Columbine

The Spirit's seven gifts

Corn ears

Eucharist

Cornerstone

Jesus

Cornucopia

God's providence, liberality, thanksgiving

Corona

See halo.

Crescent (sickle) **moon**

Mary, purity

Crocodile

Hypocrisy

Crosier (*baculum pastorale*)

Episcopal authority

Cross

Atonement, redemption, Christ, Christianity

Crow

The devil's temptings, because the call "caw, caw" was likened to *cras, cras*, Latin for "tomorrow, tomorrow" (the temptation to procrastination), bad luck (like ravens and owls)

Crown (tiara)

Saints in heaven (Revelation 2:10; 4:4), victory; of twelve stars: Mary (Revelation 12:1)

Cypress

Immortality, death, grief, heaven

Daisy

Innocence, youth

Dates

The faithful

Diamond

Purity, happiness, innocence, April

Dice (three–throw of 18)

Great reward

Dog

Fidelity, loyalty, orthodoxy, watchfulness; at the feet of: Sts. Bernard, Benignus, Wendelin; licking the wounds of: St. Rock; carrying burning torch near: St. Dominic

Dolphin

Baptism, love, society, Jesus bearing the souls to heaven

Dove

Holy Spirit (Matthew 3:16), gifts of the Spirit, the soul, peace, humility, divine inspiration, enlightenment, creation; on a vine: souls in Christ; carrying a ring: St. Agnes; on the shoulder of: St. David; at the ear of: Sts. Dunstan and Gregory; bringing chrism to: St. Remigius

Door

Jesus (John 10:9), salvation

Dragon

A winged crocodile, with serpent's tail (sometimes the same as a serpent). As a metaphor of evil and paganism, see Revelation 12:3.

Duck (over church doors)

Enter quietly and pray

Eagle

Christians and their flight to God, Jesus, Baptism, the Gospel, St. John the Evangelist, Augustine, Gregory the Great, Prisca

Earthen vessels

Mortality, humanity (Isaiah 64:8; Jeremiah 18:1–4)

Easterly direction

The resurrection and the journey to Christ (hence bodies traditionally have been buried with feet to the east)

Egg

Resurrection, hope, creation, spring

Elephant

Chastity (because it was thought to be without passion), the fall of man (because the elephant was thought to be without knee joints so, if it fell, it needed help to get up)

Emerald

Life, growth, hope, success in love, May

Escallop (the fan-shaped shell of the scallop)

Baptism, pilgrimage

Evergreen

Immortality

Eye

The Trinity (Proverbs 22:12; Psalm 33:18), God's omniscience

Fig tree

Fruitfulness, faithfulness

Fire

Spirit, Pentecost, martyrdom, fervor, temperance (Psalm 66:10)

Fish

Jesus, Christians, Baptism, Eucharist; St. Peter; see Monograms

Fleur-de-lis

This ancient and beautiful symbol, thought to derive from the iris, is a heraldic device representing a lily. A classic symbol of Mary (also the Trinity), it has varied greatly in style through various periods and countries.

Fountain

Salvation, grace (Isaiah 12:3)

Fox

Deceit, trickery, lust, cruelty, wisdom (There is folklore saying it would bury itself in sand with only its red tongue showing. Birds, attempting to consume the apparent delicacy, would be quickly dispatched.)

Frankincense

"True," "pure" incense: Old Testament priesthood

Frog

Resurrection (because of its reappearance after winter hibernation)

Fruit

Fruits of the Holy Spirit, St. Dorothea

Garden, enclosed

Mary (Song of Solomon 4:12)

Gargoyle

Evil exorcised by the gospel

Garnet

Constancy, January

Gate, closed

Chastity, Mary, Ezekiel (4:3)

Gladiolus

The incarnation

Globe

The world of God's creation

Goat

Sacrifice, fraud, Old Testament, lust, cruelty

Gold

Royalty, wealth, providence, glory

Grapes

Eucharist, Church

Grapevine

Eucharist, autumn

Gray

Ashes, humility, mourning, Franciscans (dark brown if it is the reformed branch)

Green

Hope, growth, increase, life, immortality, fidelity; as a liturgical color: Sundays in Ordinary Time

Gridiron

Martyrdom; St. Lawrence

Gules

In heraldry the tincture (color) red

Halo: Holiness of Persons of the Trinity, Angels, and Saints

Christians began using the halo as a symbol of holiness and the soul's immortality about 400. A thousand years prior, however, it already existed as a popular symbol in Indian, Egyptian, Greek, and Asian cultures. The following words are sometimes used interchangeably, although they are technically distinguishable:

1. *Halo* (Greek): originally a circular threshing floor; the luminous circle around the sun or moon when mist refracts the light, hence a circle or disk
2. *Nimbus* (Greek): cloud; an aura
3. *Aureole* (Latin, Greek): golden, gold; a radiance; see heaven
4. *Corona* (Latin): crown; white or colored circle or concentric circles of light wreathing the sun or moon

There are three common forms:

1. *Vesica piscis* (Latin: bladder, fish; so, "fish form"): The oval glow or ornamentation that twelfth-century artists commonly used to frame pictures of Mary and Christ. It symbolized the fish (see ichthus for fish significance). Also called an *aureole*, an elliptical halo of light.
2. Circular (halo)
3. Radiated, star-like

There are several developments:

1. With rays diverging triangularly, for Deity
2. With a cross, for Jesus
3. With a circle of stars, for Mary
4. Encircled with rays, including quatrefoils (an ornament with four lobes radiating from a common center) for other personages

---

Hand

God the Father (Proverbs 1:24; Sirach 10:4; 2 Maccabees 7:31), protection, creativity, possession; often emerging from a cloud (mystery) and in the Latin form (thumb and first two fingers extended; see Benedictions); with human figures within: God involved with humanity whom God protects (Psalm 139:10; Isaiah 49:2); with three-rayed halo (*nimbus*): holiness of the Trinity; open and above: blessing

Harp

David, praise, St. Alfred, St. Cecilia

Hare

Christians haste to receive grace and the kingdom.

Hart (See stag.)

Solitude, purity of life, piety, religious desire (Psalm 42:2), Sts. Hubert, Julian, Eustace

Hawk

Watchfulness, predaciousness

Hawthorn

Jesus' birth, good hope (end of winter, beginning of spring)

Heart

Love, devotion; with arrows through: Sts. Augustine, Thérèse; flaming (charity): St. Augustine

Hen and chickens

God's providence (Matthew 23:37)

Heron

Resistance to the ugliness of sin and heresy (because it was said to abhor all dead and decaying things)

Hind

See stag.

Holly

Jesus' birth, Mary's love, resurrection, immortality, foresight

Honey (with milk)

Promised land, purity, sweetness

Horn (empty)

Vow of poverty, horn of salvation

Horse

Courage, generosity, war; ridden: conqueror (Jeremiah 22:4); Sts. Martin, Maurice, George, Victor, Leon

Hourglass

End of time, death

Hyacinth

Peace, might

Ichthys

See halo; also Monograms.

Idol

Apostasy, the world

Incense

Faithful's prayer (Psalm 141:2; Revelation 5:8), thanksgiving

Ivory tower

Mary

Ivy

Memory, fidelity, eternal life (because it remains continually green); wreath: conviviality

Keys

Penance, St. Peter (Matthew 16:19), priesthood, David (Isaiah 22:22), papal authority (saltire-wise, one gold, one silver), entrance into the kingdom

Knife

Martyrdom, sacrifice, St. Bartholomew

Lamb

Christ (John 1:29), suffering servant, meekness, an apostle, a believer (John 10:1–6), Sts. Agnes, Genevieve, Catherine, Regina; with banner: resurrection; with cross: suffering Christ (three-rayed for holiness, and reclining to signify the wounded Christ); carrying one: John the Baptist

Lamp

Word of God (Psalm 119:105), saints, human soul, knowledge; with oil pitcher: a virgin; seven: Holy Spirit (Revelation 4:5); sanctuary: the Real Presence

Lantern

Betrayal by Judas

Laurel

Victory, good news; wreath: artistic achievement

Lightning

Divine justice, God's power and majesty

Lily

Innocence, Mary, Joseph, the annunciation, Gabriel; Easter: the resurrection, immortality; buds: Holy Innocents, serenity, trust (Matthew 6:28)

Lily of the Valley

Humility

Lion

Jesus (lion of Judah), strength, fortitude, royalty, Samson, Satan (1 Peter 5:8), Sts. David, Mark, Jerome

Lizard

The transforming power of the gospel, healer of spiritual blindness (because it was believed of old that when the lizard is old and blind he can regain his sight by stretching his head toward the rising sun)

Loaf

Charity to the poor, Sts. Philip the Apostle, Osyth, Joanna, Nicholas, Godfrey

Magpie

Bad luck

Mandala

A circular design radiating outward from a center point; nature's examples include a tree's cross section and flowers opening out: wholeness, organic oneness, healing, growth, all finding their source in the life-giving center, the "still point of the turning world" ("Burnt Norton," by T.S. Eliot); see the mandala in the Jesus of the Eucharist.

Marigold

Mary

Mistletoe

Immortality

Moon

Mary in her Immaculate Conception ("Who is she that comes forth as the morning rising, fair as the moon," Song of Solomon); often a crescent, under her feet (". . . a woman clothed with the sun and the moon under her feet," Revelation 12:1); purity; eclipsed at the crucifixion, on one side of the cross, opposite the sun; in creation and judgment scenes. Used in one of its forms:

1. New (or invisible)
2. Crescent, or waxing (with horns upward)
3. Decrescent, or waning (with horns sinister, or leftward)
4. First, last quarter, or half moon
5. Gibbous, or more than half
6. Full

Mountain

Church, prayer, aspiration

Myrrh

Epiphany, mortification (in vases on the heads of the Myrrophores, the three Marys who visited the sepulcher with myrrh and spices, Mark 16:1)

Myrtle

Virginity

Nails

Passion; three: evangelical counsels

Net, fisherman's

Church

Nimbus

See halo.

Nymphs

Temptation, worldly pleasure

Oak

Strength, mercy, virtue; wreath: hospitality

Oil

Healing, Confirmation, anointing

Olive

Peace (Genesis 8:11), prosperity, healing, harmony, winter

Olive branch

Peace, end of God's wrath (Genesis 8:11), gesture of conciliation (for example, the US symbol of the eagle clutching arrows, signifying power, and the olive branch)

Olive tree

Gethsemane

Opal

Hope, October

Organ

See Harp.

Orange blossom

Virginity

Orpheus

Christ, Christian teaching, compelling grace (The ancient Roman myth of Orpheus, who made such beautiful music that even wild animals were tamed and trees swayed in harmony, has long been applied to Jesus, whose immortal teachings and amazing grace can harmonize the sinful passions of humans.)

Otter

Christ's descent among the dead

Owl

Mourning, desolation, wisdom, bad luck (like ravens and crows), a "funeral bird" (screeching before bad weather)

Ox

Patience (Matthew 11:30), fortitude, sacrifice, priesthood, Sts. Luke, Frideswide, Leonard, Sylvester, Medard, Julietta, Blandina

Palm

Victory, resurrection, triumph (Revelation 7:9); tree: Joseph, destiny of the just (Psalm 92:13)

Pansy

The Trinity, meekness

Panther

Grace (In ancient folklore, the panther was said to have a sweet smelling breath, pleasing to all animals except the dragon. The sweet aroma of Jesus' grace attracts the faithful and repels Satan and evil ones.)

Partridge

Satan (There was a saying that the partridge seeks to gather the young of other birds. This is one of the many symbols adapted by St. Jerome.)

Passion Flower

Jesus' passion

- Central column: column of the scourging
- Ovary: hammer
- Three styles: nails
- Five stamens: wounds
- Tendrils: whips
- Rays within the flower forming a nimbus: Jesus' divinity and power
- Leaf shape: spear
- Ten petals: the ten apostles—twelve minus traitorous Judas and faithful John, who never abandoned Jesus; it's said to stay open three days, representing the burial of Jesus and his three days in the tomb, and also Jesus' three-year ministry
- White tint: purity
- Blue tint: heaven

Peacock
The resurrection (See Peacock story.)

Pelican
Jesus, Eucharist, charity (See Pelican story.)

Phoenix
Resurrection (See Phoenix story.)

Pillar
Scourging of Jesus, passion

Plow
Work, diligence

Poinsettia
Star of Bethlehem; red: love of Christ

Pomegranate
Resurrection, Church unity, fertility

Potter's wheel
Life and its shaping by the Lord

Pulpit
Word of God

Purple
Sorrow, penitence, preparation; as a liturgical color: Advent and Lent

Purpura
In heraldry the tincture (color) purple

Pyramid
Holy Family's flight into Egypt

Quail
Divine providence (Exodus 16:12–13)

Quill
Divine inspiration

Rain
Grace, divine impartiality (Matthew 5:45)

Rainbow
Peace between God and humanity, hope, covenant of God's fidelity

Rake
St. Barnabas (because his feast is June 11, the time of the hay harvest)

Ram
Daniel

> ### *Raven*
>
> - Restlessness, Noah, death (because their sense of smell enables them to locate from afar dead and decaying bodies), the indifferent and unrepentant sinner (the raven did not return to the ark of Noah)
> - With owls and crows: bad luck (swallows and storks being good luck); but also: divine providence (alluding to the ravens which fed Elijah)
> - With a ring in its mouth in the hand of: St. Oswald; at the feet of: St. Augustine; bringing a loaf of bread to: St. Paul the Hermit

Rays (emanations)

Holy Spirit, God's activity and presence, grace; from a dove: guidance of the Holy Spirit

Red

Sacrifice, particularly the sacrifice of the life (blood), charity, zeal, Holy Spirit; as a liturgical color: commemorations of our Lord's passion, and of the apostles and martyrs for the faith, Pentecost, and liturgies honoring Holy Spirit; sandy red (see "Yellowish" on page 492).

Reed

Passion

Ring, marriage

Although now a common part of the wedding ceremony, it is not part of the sacrament; St. Catherine of Siena.

Ring, bishop's

Worn on the third finger right hand, gold, formerly kissed by one on bended knee out of respect for the office, formerly with a stone: sapphire (cardinal), amethyst (bishop, abbot), cameo, emerald, or ruby (pope)

Ring, nun's

Worn on the third finger of the right hand, plain gold assumed on the day of her profession

Ring of the Fisherman

Bestowed on a pope upon his election; a seal (inscribed with St. Peter fishing from a boat) used for sealing papal documents; at his death it is ceremoniously broken by the papal chamberlain.

Ring, spouse's

Worn on the third finger, left hand (the third finger of the right hand signifying engagement); the common symbol of permanence; the "ring-finger ring" indicates love and affection (it once was believed that a nerve, or a vein of blood, ran from this finger to the heart); a ring on the index finger symbolizes a haughty, bold spirit, while one on the middle finger, prudence, dignity, and discretion.

Robe, white

Baptismal innocence

Rock

Christ (1 Corinthians 10:4), Church, St. Peter, stability, Jeremiah (his martyrdom)

Rood (screen)

Gates of heaven

Rose

Love, one without peer, messianic

- Of Sharon: Jesus (Song of Solomon 2:1)
- Mystic: Mary
- Red: martyrdom
- White: purity, incorruption
- In the basket of: St. Dorothea
- In the hands or caps of: Sts. Casilda, Elizabeth of Portugal, Rose of Viterbo
- Being scattered by: St. Thérèse of Lisieux
- In a crown on: Sts. Rosalia, Angelus, Rose of Lima, Aeschylus, and Victoria
- Over a confessional (sixteenth-century origin): the sacramental seal

---

Rose (color)

Subdued joy, relieved repentance (formerly common on Gaudete Sunday, the Third Sunday of Advent, and Laetare Sunday, the Fourth Sunday of Lent)

Rooster

Watchfulness, vigilance, call to prayer, Peter's denial (Matthew 26:69–75; Mark 14:66–72; Luke 22:54–62; John 18:15–18, 25–27); with flopping wings: mortification (1 Corinthians 9:27); with palm near or held in his bill: victory gained; on tomb: resurrection; on tower: the preaching office; when fighting: Christians

Sable

In heraldry the tincture (color) black

Salamander

The graced Christian resisting temptation (because this lizard-like reptile was thought to be resistant to fire)

Salt

Wisdom, truth (Matthew 5:13; Mark 9:50; Luke 14:34)

Sapphire

Heavenly reward, truth

Sardonyx

Conjugal felicity, August

Saw

Martyrdom, St. Joseph

Scales

Judgment, justice (Leviticus 19:36), Sts. Joseph and Michael

Scepter

Majestic authority, a messianic symbol

Scorpion

Satan, sin, rebuke, remorse

Scroll

Pentateuch, prophets, petition

Scythe (sickle)

Death, end of the world

Serpent

Satan, sin, original sin, wisdom (Matthew 10:16), Sts. Cecilia, Euphemia, Patrick; bruised: Mary; with staff: Moses and Aaron; brazen on a cross: crucifixion (John 3:14–15); there is an opposite serpent symbolism, surprisingly.

Shamrock

Trinity; St. Patrick

St. Patrick's Shamrock

The mysteries of the faith are difficult to teach. Legend has it that St. Patrick used a shamrock to help explain the Trinity to the king's two daughters. Its three leaflets on one stem represent the three Persons in one God. Some say the occasion was his sermon to Laoghaire, chief of the Irish clans who had come to seize the saint for daring to ignite the Easter fire on the Hill of Slane.

Sheaf
Abundance, providence

Ship
Church

Shell
John the Baptist

Shepherd
Christ (John 10:11), care, protection

Shield
Faith, protection

Shovel
Human labor

Silver
Chastity, eloquence

Skeleton (skull)
Death, a *memento mori* (a reminder of the inevitability of death: "Remember that you must die.")

Snow
Purity

Spear
Martyrdom

Sphinx
The fabled creature with a woman's head and chest and a lion's body, feet, and tail: silence, mystery, Egypt

Spider
Patience

Squirrel
Anticipation, Christian attitude in the face of eternity

Staff
The Good Shepherd (John 10:11), apostle, bishop

Stag
Jesus' power (in ancient folklore the stag with his breath could kill the serpent or dragon), Sts. Aidan, Eustace, Hubert; drinking: Baptism (See Psalm 42.)

> ### *Star*
> David, house of Jesus' family, the faithful Christians (Revelation 2:26–28), Lucifer (Isaiah 14:12), Sts. Bruno, Dominic
> - "Day-star, morning star": Christ (2 Peter 1:19; Revelation 22:16)
> - Six-pointed: Creator's star, the six days of creation
> - The six in the Pleiades: heaven, according to the ancients

Steps to the altar (three)

Faith, hope, and charity

Stole

Reconciliation, priesthood

Stone

St. Stephen

Stork

Filial piety, birth, good luck (like swallows)

Sun

Jesus (overcoming sin in death), Mary; with moon and twelve stars: Jacob, wife, and sons (Genesis 37:9–11)

Sunflower

Obedience (because it looks to the sun from dawn to dusk; see Psalm 123:2)

Swallow

Resurrection (because it was believed by some to sleep in the water all winter and emerge in spring), good luck (like the stork)

Swine

Impurity, filth, unbelievers, abomination

Sword

Fortitude, war, justice, might; *Spiritus Gladius* (sword of the Spirit): God's word; flaming: expulsion from Eden

Tabernacle

Old Testament worship

Tablets

The Law

Teardrops

Mary's seven sorrows

Temple

God's dwelling place

Tetramorph
The four-faced creatures of Ezekiel 10 with eight wings and fiery wheels underneath: the four evangelists

Thorns
Sorrow, passion, atonement

Thistle
Original sin

Tiger
Cruelty, treachery, martyrdom

Topaz
Fidelity, November, in heraldry the tincture (color) gold

Torch
The Word of God, enlightenment, fervor

Tower
Strength, God, defense; with three windows: St. Barbara

Tree
Life (Genesis 2:9), faith

St. Adam and St. Eve

Greek, Syrian, and Coptic Christians, representing the Eastern Churches in Greece, the Middle East, and Africa (Egypt), commemorate our first parents on Christmas Eve. This devotion brought a veneration of Adam and Eve into the West by the end of the first millennium. Although the Latin Church never officially introduced a feast day for them, their popular veneration was never prohibited either. This sign of Catholicism's multiculturalism is still sometimes seen in statues of Adam and Eve among the statues of the saints. A fir tree decorated with apples—the paradise tree, precursor of our Christmas tree—is another sign in the West of the influence of the East.

Trefoil
The design with three leaf-like parts: the Trinity

Triangle
The Trinity

Trumpet
Judgment day, resurrection, call to worship

Turquoise

Prosperity, December

Unicorn

Christ

The Unicorn

The word itself means one horn (*unum cornu*). The creature represents the sinlessness of God's Son and the incarnation itself—the Son of God whom the heavens could not contain humbled himself and was born of a virgin. The unicorn is a graceful creature of fable, with a horse's head, goat's beard, antelope's legs, lion's tail, and, of course, the distinguishing great spiral horn rising from its forehead. According to medieval writers, this great horn is white at the base, black in the middle, and red at the tip (which is able to detect poison with one touch). The unicorn has a white body, a red head, and blue eyes.

The oldest description we have is one by Ctesias (400 B.C.). The following thirteenth-century account represents well the popular medieval belief: "It is the only animal that ventures to attack the elephant; and so sharp is the nail of its foot that with one blow it can rip the belly of that beast. Hunters can catch the unicorn only by placing a young virgin in his haunts. No sooner does he see the damsel than he runs toward her and lies down at her feet and so suffers himself to be captured by the hunters. The unicorn represents Jesus Christ, who took upon himself our nature in the virgin's womb, was betrayed, and delivered into the hands of Pontius Pilate. Its one horn signifies the gospel of truth."

Vase (pottery)

Humanity

Veil

Modesty, flight from the world

Vert

In heraldry the tincture (color) green

Vesica pisces

See halo.

Vine

Jesus, Christian life

Vine and branches

Christ and the Church (John 15:5)

Violet

Humility; see purple

Volcano

God's retribution

Vulture

Evil

Water

Grace, divine life, eternal life (John 4:1–15)

Water lily

Love

Weather vane

Instability

Well

The word of God, refreshment, eternal life (John 4:1–15)

Whale

Satan

Wheat

Eucharist, summer; with tares: the faithful and the wicked (Matthew 13:24–30)

Whip

Repentance, penance

White

White stands for purity, simplicity, candor, truth, hope, innocence, virginity, joy.

- As a liturgical color: joyful and glorious mysteries of our Lord (like Christmas and Easter), of Mary (like the Annunciation), of angels, and of saints who were not martyrs
- Traditionally used at celebrations honoring John the Baptist, the Chair of Peter, and the Conversion of St. Paul
- As the color of a habit: reformed branch of the Benedictines, Cistercians, Praemonstratensians, the Order of the Holy Cross

White over brown

Carmelites

Willow

Grief, death

Wine

Eucharist

Wine press

God's wrath, Jesus (Revelation 19:15–16), joy

Wings

A divine mission, human aspiration

Wolf

Satan, false prophet (Matthew 7:15), hypocrisy, famine, cruelty, lust, tribe of Benjamin

Yellow

Infidelity, deceit, treason

Yellowish

Treason (Cain and Judas are often shown in ancient art with yellowish or sandy red, or "cane" colored, beards, hence "Judas colored" means fiery red.)

Yew

Immortality

Yoke

Redemption, slavery, meekness

Word and Phrase Origins

Words and Phrases with a Biblical Origin or Allusion

Some of these terms do not appear in all translations.

Abomination of desolation ("desolating sacrilege")
An abominable thing, an idol, a pollution; quoting Jesus (Matthew 24:15)

Abraham's bosom ("to be with Abraham")
The rest of the blessed in death, alluding to Luke 16:22, and the custom of a friend reclining on one's bosom, as John on Jesus'

Abyss ("a great abyss fixed," "a great chasm")
An unsurmountable barrier, alluding to Lazarus and Dives (Luke 16:26)

Adam's ale
Water (the only drink in Eden)

Adam's apple
The remnant of Adam's sin, a piece of the forbidden fruit stuck in his throat

(The) Adversary ("Opponent")
The devil (1 Peter 5:8)

Agur's wish
"Give me neither poverty nor riches" (Proverbs 30:8).

Ahithophel
A treacherous counselor and friend. This man was David's advisor, but joined the revolt of Absalom, advising him "like the oracle of God" (see 2 Samuel 16:20–23).

All things to all people
Indispensable; the effort to relate to all; what St. Paul said of himself (1 Corinthians 9:22)

Alpha and Omega ("the beginning and the end")
The beginning and the end A biblical reference to a divine title, being actually the first and last letters of the Greek alphabet (Revelation 1:8)

Apple of one's eye ("apple of the eye")

Something or someone precious (quoting Psalm 17:8)

Armageddon ("Harmaged'on")

A slaughter, or great battle; according to Revelation 16:16, the site of the last great battle on judgment day; geographically, the mountainous district near Megiddo

Ashes to ashes, dust to dust

Complete finality; an old English burial service phrase, alluding to the creation of humans from the dust of the ground (Genesis 2:7). See also "Remember man that you are dust . . ." (Genesis 3:19).

Babel

All-out confusion, unintelligibility; allusion to the confusion of tongues at Babel (Genesis 11:1–9)

Balm ("Is there no balm in Gilead?")

"Where is consolation?" (Jeremiah 8:22, balm being comfort)

Benjamin

The youngest, a favorite; allusion to Jacob's youngest son of this name (Genesis 35:18)

Benjamin's portion (or mess)

The largest; allusion to Joseph's banquet for his brothers in Egypt, and the fact that Benjamin's share was five times the others (Genesis 43:34)

Beulah Land

A paradise, promised land, far away dream-come-true land; Isaiah 62:4 reference to Israel being called not "Forsaken" but "Married" ("Beulah" in Hebrew)

Bird ("A little bird told me.")

A caution against speaking privately what one would not want known publicly (Ecclesiastes 10:20)

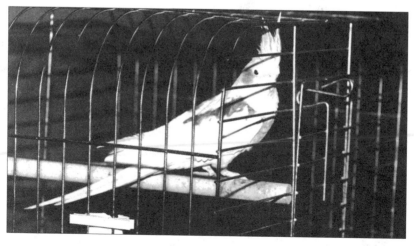

Birthright (to sell one's birthright for a mess of pottage)

To exchange one's heritage for a trifle; alluding to Esau selling his birthright for Jacob's pottage (Genesis 25:29–34)

Blind leading the blind ("blind guides of the blind")

Allusion to Matthew 15:14, Jesus confronting the Pharisees

Bosom friend (". . . it used to . . . lie in his bosom, and it was like a daughter to him.")

In 2 Samuel 12:3, Nathan tells David a parable in which he describes a poor man's ewe lamb in those terms; see also Lazarus on Abraham's bosom (Luke 16:22) and John on Jesus' (John 13:25) in some translations.

Bowing the knee to Rimmon

Temporizing; knowingly doing wrong in order to save face; allusion to 2 Kings 5:18: Naaman the Syrian getting Elisha's permission to worship Rimmon when with his master

Bread ("Ask for bread and receive a stone.")

Spoken of a rebuff, a denied request; from Matthew 7:9 where Jesus teaches about the power of prayer

Bread (break bread)

Eat together; perhaps also what today's Catholics call the Eucharist (for example, Acts 2:44–47)

Bread (Cast one's bread upon the water; send out your bread upon the water.)

". . . for after many days you will get it back" (Ecclesiastes 11:1). Be adventuresome, take a chance, be generous, don't expect immediate recognition. (The waters of the ocean sometimes bear lost treasures to the shore.)

Bricks (to make bricks without straw)

Trying to do a job without ability or materials; allusion to Hebrew forced labor under Egyptian taskmasters (Exodus 5:6–14)

Build on sand

Working with poor planning or unsure beginning; from a parable of Jesus' (Matthew 7:24–27)

Burden ("Bear the burden and heat of the day.")

To do all the hard work; the complaint of those in Jesus' parable who got paid no more than those who came on at the eleventh hour (Matthew 20:1–16)

Cain (the curse [brand, mark] of Cain)

Said of one with nowhere to go or no place to call his or her own; the stigma of murder; blood guilt that cannot be expiated; allusion to God's judgment after Cain murdered Abel (Genesis 4:1–16)

Calf ("Kill the fatted calf.")

Let's celebrate. To welcome with the best; allusion to the parable of the prodigal son (Luke 15:1–32)

Charity ("Charity begins at home.")

In 1 Timothy 5:4, Paul teaches about the true piety for the widow's children.

Citizens of no mean city ("a citizen of an important city")

A recommendation because of background; quoting Paul who referred to Tarsus as he solicited a hearing in Jerusalem (Acts 21:39)

Clay feet

A surprising flaw in one esteemed; from the clay feet of the image in Nebuchadnezzar's dream (Daniel 2:31–33) and an allusion to the standard composition of ancient idols

---

Cloud of witnesses

Quoting Hebrews 12:1, the reference to the witness of the faith of the ancients

Coals ("Heap burning coals on one's head.")

Using kindness to melt another's animosity; turning the other cheek; repaying good for evil: an effective reproach (Proverbs 25:21, 22; also Romans 12:20)

Come to pass (take place)

Happen; a phrase made popular by old translations of Christ's words regarding what would happen before the end (Matthew 24:6)

Cover a multitude of sins

A compensating virtue; a pleasing cover of good over the bad that can't be seen; quoting St. Peter when he spoke of love, the ultimate virtue (1 Peter 4:8)

Crumbs from the rich man's table ("what fell from the rich man's table")

A pittance for the poor; a phrase from a parable of Christ: all that Lazarus said he wanted from Dives (Luke 16:19–31)

Cup ("Let this cup pass from me.")

May I not have to go through this; from Christ's agony in the garden (Matthew 26:39).

Cup ("My cup runneth over; my cup overflows.")

I am richly blessed (Psalm 23:5).

Dan (from Dan to Beersheba)

From one end (of the kingdom) to the other; coast to coast; all over. These two cities were the farthest north and south in Israel.

Dead ("Let the dead bury the dead [their own dead].")

Against temporizing; quoting Matthew 8:22—the conditions for following Jesus. Let bygones be bygones. Break with the past.

De Profundis (Latin: out of the depths)

Said of a bitter cry; first Latin words of Psalm 130; common in burial services

Delilah ("There is no leaping from Delilah's lap into Abraham's bosom.")

One cannot live and die in grave sin and expect salvation. Referring to the lovely betrayer of Samson (Judges 16), and to the patriarch whose bosom represented reward and rest (see Luke 16:22).

Doubting Thomas

A skeptic; Thomas doubted when told of the resurrected Christ (John 20:24–29).

Eat, drink, and be merry. ("Eat, drink, and enjoy.")

In Ecclesiastes 8.15 it is pessimistically recommended to enjoy life while we have it, since this is the best we can do in the world. In Isaiah 22:13, in another context, there is a similar phrase, with the added "for tomorrow we shall die."

Eleventh hour

Just in time; an allusion to the day laborers parable Matthew 20:1–16, and the ones hired last.

Entertain an angel unawares (". . . some have entertained angels without knowing it.")

Encountering a virtual saint; surprised by virtue; from Hebrews 13:2 exhortation on hospitality

Eye for an eye, tooth for a tooth

The *Lex Talionis* (law of reciprocal punishment in kind: Deuteronomy 19:21)

Eye of a needle

A difficult task, if not a human impossibility; from Matthew 19:24: "It's easier for a camel to go through . . ."

Flesh (remembering the fleshpots of Egypt)

Fantasizing over, glorifying the (perceived) good things of the past when they are no longer available (Exodus 16:3)

Fly in the ointment (". . . one good bungler destroys much good.")

A little thing that spoils everything, or at least detracts from its attractiveness (Ecclesiastes 9:18)

Forbidden fruit

Anything stolen, but especially illicit love; alluding to the fruit stolen by the first humans in the garden

Fruit ("By their fruits you shall know them.")

Judging by one's actions, not words; results, not intentions; from Matthew 12:33 (also translated "A tree is known by its fruits.") where Jesus exposes the legalistic, externalized perversion of religion by some of the Pharisees.

Gall and wormwood

Extremely distasteful, a bitter pill; quoting Lamentations 3:18–19

Gird your loins

Roll up your sleeves; hitch up your figurative belt for vigorous action; common biblical exhortation (See 1 Kings 18:46; Job 38:3; Jeremiah 1:17; 1 Peter 1:13.)

Giving ("There is more joy in giving than in receiving.")

Words of Jesus, although not in the Gospels; Paul ends his farewell address to the elders of Ephesus by recalling these words of Jesus (Acts 20:35).

Giving up the ghost (only in the King James Version)

Death; expression used by Job (Job 14:10), by the psalmist (Psalm 31:6; Luke 23:46), and by John for Jesus' death (John 19:30), for example.

Gladden (to gladden the hearts of men; "to gladden the human heart")

Allusion to Psalm 104:15; the purpose of the gift of wine

Glory (in his glory)

In one's natural, truest element; Jesus was seen in his glory only in transfiguration (Mark 9:2–10); used of those who are at their best, in their natural habitat, doing what is their destiny

Goads (to kick against the goad)

Competing against odds, especially authority or fate, or in Saul's case, grace (Acts 9:5)

Good Samaritan

A good neighbor, helper of the distressed; alluding to Jesus' parable involving the priest, the Levite, and the Samaritan (Luke 10:30–37)

Grapes of wrath

Potential recipients of just punishment; used by John Steinbeck as the title of a novel and occurring in the first stanza of the "Battle Hymn of the Republic"; allusion to the winepress image of Revelation 14:19–20 which teaches about the harvest of the earth and the impending doom of the ungodly

Greater love than this no one has. ("No one has greater love than this.")

From Jesus' last discourse (John 14–17, specifically 15:13), where he teaches about the extent to which love will take the followers: martyrdom for the beloved; applied to the unbloody martyrdom of unrecognized service, especially when *agape* (sacrificial/divine love) and *philia* ("brotherly"/sisterly love) are united in one person

Green wood ("If they do these things in the green wood, what will they do in the dry?")

"If the innocent (green wood) suffers so, what will come of the wicked (dry wood)?" quoting Jesus meeting the Jerusalem women on the way of the cross (Luke 23:31).

Handwriting on the wall

The all but obvious being revealed; the announcement of the imminent fulfillment of some doom. At Belshazzar's party (Daniel 5), it was right there on the wall: "Your days are numbered."

Hewers of wood and drawers of water

Drudges; humble workers; quoting Deuteronomy 29:10 ("Those who cut your wood and those who draw your water") where Moses, in his final discourse, is summoning all Israel, from least to greatest, to a renewal of the covenant. In Joshua 9:21 it is also used as a phrase for the slaves of the community.

House built on rock

Someone or something with a sure foundation; allusion to Jesus' parable on the practice of religion (Matthew 7:24–27)

House divided

When some said that Jesus was casting out devils by the power of the prince of devils (Luke 11:14f), Jesus said that Satan in that case would be divided against himself, and that such a house divided falls; but God's kingdom lasts.

Howling wilderness

Suggesting dreariness and savagery (wind and wild beasts); from Moses' song of deliverance (Deuteronomy 32:10)

Jacob's ladder

Steps that are high and steep; also "jacob" for a ladder; an allusion to the ladder of Jacob's dream on which God's messengers were going up and down (Genesis 28:12); the flaw in a stocking where only the ladder-like weft is left

Jeremiad

A doleful complaint, lamentation. Jeremiah contains warnings of disaster for Israel. His words reveal his own inner conflicts and personal feelings about God and his job (Jeremiah 15:10–21, 18:18–23, 20:7–18).

Jericho

Used to give a specific name to an indefinite place; allusion to the "Stay in Jericho until your Beards Grow Back" story in 2 Samuel 10:1–5 (in other words, "Stay away for a while.")

Jeroboam

One who is of great promise, but who ends up in perversion; allusion to the mighty man of valor "who made Israel sin" (1 Kings 11:28; 14:16)

Jeroboam, Rehoboam

The first king of Israel and the first king of Judah

Jesse tree

A genealogical tree, sometimes taking the form of a vine (sometimes arising from Jesse himself, recumbent), or a branched candlestick, tracing the ancestry of Jesus (if in a window, a "Jesse window"); from Isaiah 11:1, "A shoot . . . from the stump of Jesse."

Jezebel (a painted Jezebel)

A depraved and seductive person; a flaunting woman, bold in manner and morally loose; said about ninth-century B.C. Phoenician wife of King Ahab of Israel who fostered worship of other gods in Israel and who arranged the murder of Naboth (1 Kings 16:31–32, 18:1–19:3, 21; 2 Kings 9:7–37)

Job
Personification of patience, poverty (Book of Job)

Job's comforter
An ineffectual empathizer or pretender who only worsens the situation; Job's friends concluded that he must have somehow caused his own grief (Job 16:2).

Jonathan's arrows
A warning, not meant to hurt; allusion to 1 Samuel 20:18–23 and the story of the arrows Jonathan shot to signal to David according to a prearranged code

Jordan (bathing seven times in the Jordan)
A remedy; an action (sacramental), not necessarily understood, and not therapeutic in itself, but efficacious; alluding to the directions Elisha gave Naaman the Syrian to heal his leprosy (2 Kings 5:1–27)

Jordan (crossing Jordan; Jordan passed)
Dying; like the mythical River Styx, the Jordan formed the boundary of the Promised Land, and crossing it ended the journey in the wilderness ("the world"; Joshua 1:1f).

Joseph
One unsuccessfully seduced, unwavering in constancy; allusion to the wife of Potiphar trying to seduce Joseph (Genesis 39)

Jot or tittle (not one jot or tittle)

The absolute minimum, the smallest possible amount or degree. Alluding to Jesus referring to letter of the law, which would not pass away until the laws were fulfilled (Matthew 5:18). In older translations, "the smallest letter" was more literally rendered "jot," which is from the Latin *jota*, which is from the Greek *iota*, which is the ninth—and smallest—letter of the Greek alphabet. Hence the saying "not one iota." *Tittle* is rendered "part of a letter." It is an old name for the diacritical marks used in Hebrew, marks that furnished a vowel sound for a word; hence, not even a letter.

Kedar's tents
This world; unpeaceful and nomadic; allusion to Psalm 120:5, the cry of one longing for peace and a home (Kedar, in Genesis 25:15, a nomad)

Kill the fatted calf
Prepare to celebrate! Especially, warm hospitality for a homecoming; the father gave these instructions upon the return of the prodigal son (Luke 15:23).

Kiss of Judas

Pretended affection; betrayal; an obvious reference to Judas and Jesus (Matthew 26:49)

Labor of love

Work engaged in because of affection for, or desire to please another; probably alluding to Paul (1 Thessalonians 1:3) and the Letter to the Hebrews (6:10) where the believers are commended for the way they live

Laborer is worth his wage. (". . . laborer deserves to be paid.")

Be fair. With these words Jesus assured the seventy-two he was sending on mission that they could "stay in one house eating and drinking what they have" (Luke 10:7).

Land of the living

Life; a phrase Jeremiah used in quoting his enemy's evil intents (Jeremiah 11:19); also Psalm 27:13, meaning that while still here "I shall see the Lord's bounty."

Land of (flowing with) milk and honey

Paradisal; heaven; in Exodus 3:8, this was the phrase used to describe the destiny of the enslaved Hebrews whom Moses was called to lead (see also Joel 2:18–29).

Laodicean

One indifferent about religion, because the Christians of that city in the Book of Revelation were indifferent about their religion. (Revelation 3:14–18)

Lazar

Victim of a repulsive disease; any poor beggar; from Lazarus, the leper lay daily at the rich man's gate, a story Jesus told (Luke 16:19–31)

Legion ("My name is Legion.")

Many; hydra-headed; more than one would want or guess; it was the name given by the Gerasene demoniac in Mark 5:9.

Leopard changing its spots

An impossibility; this is how Jeremiah described the ability of disgraced Jerusalem to change from evil to good (Jeremiah 13:23).

Light (to hide your light under a bushel basket)

Modesty, to the point of "depriving" others; concealing abilities or merit; from Christ's Sermon on the Mount (Matthew 5:14–16)

(The) lines have fallen to me in pleasant places

My portion, destiny, is good; quoting Psalm 16:6, meaning the lines drawn for the portion of a tribe.

(The) lion shall lie down with the lamb. ("The wolf and the lamb shall feed together.")

Harmony; quoting Isaiah 65:25 and the prophesy of a new world

Lip service

Just talk; from Jesus' discussions with some Pharisees (Matthew 15:8; see also Isaiah 29:13.)

Live by the sword, die by the sword.

Harm set, harm get. Jesus' use is recorded in Matthew 26:52; Mark 14:47; Luke 22:49–51; John 18:10–11, when he was being arrested and a follower drew a sword. (In John's Gospel, it was Peter.)

Loaves (with an eye to loaves and fish)

Poor motive; camouflaged desire for material gain; allusion to Jesus' teaching and feeding the multitude, and his knowledge of their motive (John 6:26)

(The) Lord loves a cheerful giver.

So says Paul as he teaches stewardship and generosity (2 Corinthians 9:7).

Lord of Creation

Human; an allusion to the divine gift to humanity of care over the world (Genesis 1:28–29)

(The) love of money is the root of all evil.

According to Paul (1 Timothy 6:10)

Magdalene

A reformatory for prostitutes; allusion to the great sinner of Luke 8:1–3, falsely identified with Mary of Magdala, out of whom Jesus cast seven devils

Magnificat

Mary's song of praise: "My soul magnifies *(magnificat)* the Lord . . ." (Luke 1:46–55).

Mammon of righteousness

Money; an old translation of Luke 16:9 in which Jesus is counseling on the right use of this world's goods

Man proposes, God disposes. ("The human mind plans the way, but the Lord directs the steps.")

The scriptural version of this ancient proverb is in Proverbs 16:9.

Many are called but few are chosen.

A warning about the need for ongoing conversion and growth, especially in the face of apathy and self-assurance; being the last line of Jesus' wedding banquet parable (Matthew 22:1–14)

Mark of the beast

Anything so designated is branded evil, unorthodox, from Revelation 16:2 and 19:20, and the references to the personification or focus of evil in the world.

Maudlin

Sickeningly sentimental; the word is derived from from Mary Magdalene (Luke 8:1–3), whose face and eyes according to some ancient artists had that kind of look.

Miserere (or *misericord*)

The underside of a folding choir stall seat, called this because in its folded-up position it is comfortable for the aged in a kneeling position; named from the Latin title (first word) of Psalm 51, David's prayer of repentance

Money ("The love of money is the root of all evil.")

See 1 Timothy 6:10.

Mouths (out of the mouths of babes)

"Out of the mouths of babes the greatest wisdom comes," which, according to Psalm 8:2 and Matthew 21:16, is praise.

Naboth's vineyard

A vulnerable holding; another's possession that one could take; Ahab did take Naboth's (1 Kings 21).

Name ("Their name lives on.")

Popular memorial saying; from the famous "Praise of the Ancestors" in Sirach 44:14

Nazareth ("Can anything good come from Nazareth?")

A not very indirect put-down; doubting greatness because of humble origin, as Nathanael was skeptical about Christ (John 1:46)

New Jerusalem

Paradise; heaven; allusion to John's vision of the new creation (Revelation 21)

New wine in new skins

Brand new, not a re-make; in Matthew 9:17, Jesus expounds on the need for a recreated spirit, not just a remodeled religion.

Nimrod

A distinguished, daring hunter; Nimrod was "a mighty hunter before the Lord" (Genesis 10:9).

No respecter of persons ("God shows no partiality.")

Indiscriminate, ignoring distinctions; quoting St. Peter (Acts 10:34, old translation) explaining that God doesn't play favorites

No rest for the wicked

Isaiah's observation (Latin: *Nemo malus felix*, No bad man is happy.)

Nothing new under the sun

(Latin: *Nil novi sub sole*); from Ecclesiastes 1:9, "That which has been is that which shall be, and that which has been done is that which shall be done; there is nothing new under the sun."

Numbered ("Your days are numbered.")

Doom saying; what Daniel saw in the handwriting on the wall (Daniel 5:26)

Nunc dimittis

To receive (or sing) one's *nunc dimittis* is to receive permission for a leave-taking, and to take satisfaction in a leave-taking; from the opening words of Simeon on the occasion of the presentation of the child Jesus, "Now you may dismiss (*nunc dimittis*) your servant" (Luke 2:29).

Olive branches

A lighthearted term for one's children; the psalmist (Psalm 128:3) calls them that, and the wife a fruitful vine.

Ox ("You shall not muzzle the ox that treads out the corn.")

Do not begrudge a laborer his little compensations; quoting Deuteronomy 25:4 and applying it to the laborer and the privileges that could be allowed him regarding the circumstances and products of his work. (See Paul's use, 1 Corinthians 9:9, 1 Timothy 5:18.)

Patience of Job

Maximum long-suffering and forbearance; from the Book of Job, though no particular line in it speaks exactly those words

Patmos

A hermitage; exile; in Revelation 1:9 it says John retired or was exiled there.

Pearls ("Casting pearls before swine.")

Giving what is precious to the unappreciative; to waste; allusion to Matthew 7:6—Jesus' acknowledgment that the good news will not be accepted by all, and that responsibility for this belongs to the one who "tramples it underfoot."

Philistine

A boorish, uncultured person; Israelite neighbor and long-standing enemy. Their name came to be used because they believed in Canaanite religion and because they stole the ark of the covenant.

Physician, heal thyself. ("Doctor, cure yourself.")

The advice, recorded by St. Luke (4:23), for those who should take the advice they give, *Medice, cura te ipsum.*

Plow ("Put one's hand to the plow.")

Commencing in earnest; quoting Luke 9:62, where Jesus preaches the cost of discipleship, and the temptation to temporize

Poor as Job

The man dispossessed through the devil's testings (Book of Job)

Poor as Lazarus

A beggar by this name lay daily at the gate of the rich Dives (Luke 16:19–31)

Potters' Field

A cemetery for the poor; originally the land in the infamous Valley of Hinnom (Gehenna) called Ha·kel'·da·ma (Field of Blood, Acts 1:19) which was bought with Judas' betrayal money (Matthew 27:7) as a cemetery for foreigners. Called "Potter's field" possibly because it was once used for clay; or because it was where potsherds were discarded (see Jeremiah 19), the land being good for nothing else.

Prodigal son

The wastrel who returns, repentant, after dissipation; from a parable in which Jesus taught about the nature of God (Luke 15:11–32)

Promised land

The place of one's dreams, referring originally to Canaan, promised to Abraham by God (Exodus 12:25, Deute-ronomy 9:28)

(A) prophet is not without honor, except in his native place.

Admiration and fame is greater the farther one is from home; proverbial in the Scriptures (See Matthew 13:57, Mark 6:6.)

Race ("The race is not to the swift, nor the battle to the strong.")

Adapting Ecclesiastes 9:11, the pessimistic original

Raise Cain

Raise a ruckus, make noise, cause trouble; Cain, Abel's brother and the first murderer (Genesis 4), being a euphemism for the devil

Reed   (a bruised reed)

Unstable, in a weakened condition, untrustworthy; allusion to Egypt as an ally for the Jews against Assyria (2 Kings 18:21; Isaiah 36:6)

Reed shaken in the wind

One who goes where the wind goes; Jesus said John the Baptist was not one, but that he was a man with firm conviction (Matthew 11:7).

Remember, man, that you are dust, and to dust you shall return.

God's words to Adam (see Genesis 3:19); also Ezekiel 28:18 refers to returning to ashes (dust); an option for the wording for the Ash Wednesday conferral of ashes

Render unto Caesar what is Caesar's (and unto God what is God's).

Jesus' quote allowing the just claims of the state; from a discussion on tribute to the emperor (Mark 12:17)

Return to one's vomit

Backsliding; return to sin; 2 Peter 2:22 cites a dog's disgusting habit (See also Proverbs 26:11.)

Right mind (in one's right mind)

Sane; serenity following agitation; this is how the townsfolk found a demoniac whom Jesus had exorcized (Mark 5:15—old translation).

Root of the matter

Basic issue; quintessence; Job (19:28) wondered if the problem's cause was within him.

Sabbatical

Time free from teaching allowing a teacher or professor time for study or travel; from the practice of leaving land fallow every seventh year (Exodus 23:10, Leviticus 25:2–7; Deuteronomy 15:1–11)

Sackcloth and ashes

Penitence, strictly speaking; common scripturally (see Matthew 11:21)

St. Peter's fingers

The fingers of a thief ("A thief has a fish hook on every finger."), alluding to the fish Peter caught that had a coin in its mouth (Matthew 17:24–27)

St. Stephen's loaves

Stones; allusion to the stoning of St. Stephen (Acts 7:54–60)

Salt (covenant of salt)

An unbreakable bond; from 2 Chronicles 13:5, referring to God's covenant with Israel; salt being a symbol of incorruption and perpetuity

Salt of the earth

Good people, for their sanctifying effect on others, "preservers of civilization"; used by Jesus of his disciples in the Sermon on the Mount (Matthew 5:13)

Samson

An exceptionally strong person; referring to the Hebrew hero (Judges 13–16)

Sanctum sanctorum

A private place, holy ground, intimacy; Latin for "holy of holies," properly the inner chamber of the Jewish temple entered only by the high priest on the high feast of atonement.

(Is) Saul also among the prophets?

Of one who now espouses a cause or idea he hitherto assailed; 1 Samuel 10:9–12 tells of the origin of this proverb. It may have been used of another Saul (or is it Paul?) in Acts 9:21.

Scapegoat

An innocent one bearing responsibility for the guilty; one paying the price for another; from the Old Testament atonement ritual (Leviticus 16) in which two goats were brought to the temple: One was sacrificed to the Lord, the other "heard" the confession of the high priest and was taken into the wilderness with the transferred sins of the people.

See how the land lies

To check out; make preliminary investigations; to test the water; an old translation of Numbers 13:16 ("reconnoiter"), where Moses is readying to enter Canaan

Semitic

Pertaining to the Jews; referring to those thought to be the descendants of Shem, the eldest son of Noah (Genesis 10). That is, the Hebrews, Arabs, Assyrians, Aramaeans, and others.

Seventy is the sum of our years, or eighty if we are strong.

Our allotted span, our natural life; frequently used scripturally (as in Psalm 90:10)

Shake off the dust from your feet.

Leave an inhospitable place; implying judgment, or at least determination and finality; alluding to Jesus' advice to disciples in the event they were not received well (Mark 6:11; Luke 9:5)

Sheep ("Separate the sheep from the goats.")

The good from the bad; alluding to the last judgment (Matthew 25:32)

Shibboleth

A catchword, slogan or test word; the criterion for distinguishing insiders. Differences in the pronunciation of this word's initial sound betrayed rival tribal affinities and became the basis for discovering and exterminating outsiders (Judges 12:4–6).

Simony

Buying and selling sacred things and Church offices; from the magician Simon Magus's offer to buy the power to bestow the Holy Spirit (Acts 8:18)

Skin (by the skin of one's teeth)

Just barely; Job thus described his hold on life (19:20).

Slow to anger

How Nehemiah, for example, describes God (Nehemiah 9:17); equanimity

Sounding brass or tinkling cymbal (". . . noisy gong or a clanging cymbal.")

A lot of talk; words without sense; allusion to a traditional translation of 1 Corinthians 13:1, Paul's description of a loveless person

Sow ("As you sow, so shall you reap.")

An old translation of Galatians 6:7

Sow the wind, reap the whirlwind.

Causing trouble, and getting more than you bargained for; starting something you can't finish; so Hosea fumes (8:7) about Israel's perversity

Spare the rod and spoil the child. ("Those who spare the rod hate their children.")

"It's folly to allow childish faults to go unreproved;" a version of Proverbs 13:24.

Spirit ("The spirit is willing, but the flesh is weak.")

Good idea, poor execution; the will, but no power. It is the caution of Jesus from Matthew 26:41, human nature being what it is.

Stars in their courses

Destiny; alluding to Judges 5:20: The enemy of Sisera in battle

Still, small voice (". . . and after the fire a sound of sheer silence.")

Conscience; an insight after a lot of huffing and puffing; allusion to 1 Kings 19:12, the sound Elijah finally heard by which he found God after not finding God in the earthquake and the fire

Stolen sweets are always sweeter.

Illegality charms, making such ill-gotten gains the more palatable; an old translation of an Old Testament proverb (Proverbs 9:17)

Stone (". . . to cast the first stone.")

To lead in fault-finding; quoting Jesus' challenge to the crowd in his defense of the woman caught in adultery (John 8:7)

Straight and narrow

Path of virtue; probably alluding to Matthew 7:14 where Jesus describes the path to eternal life

Strain ("Strain the gnat and swallow the camel.")

Fussing about peccadilloes while committing serious offenses; not allowing a small point, all the while blithely accepting a difficult one. From Matthew 23:24, and the practice of straining wine; in this instance Jesus is criticizing Pharisees.

Stranger in a strange land

A foreigner, or feeling like one. This is an allusion to the explanation Moses gave for the name ("Gershom") he bestowed on his son, who was born in Midian when he was taking refuge there from the pharaoh (Exodus 2:22).

Strength (to go from strength to strength)

To improve work, reputation, and so on; so the psalmist proclaims the progress of the just (Psalm 84:7).

Suffer fools gladly

Be patient, because you have the consolation of knowing that you are wise. Quoting one old translation of 1 Corinthians 11:19, where Paul acknowledges factions in the community, and teaches that the good will stand out by contrast.

Sun ("Don't let the sun go down on your anger.")

Quoting Ephesians 4:26

Sweat (by the sweat of your brow)

By hard manual labor; the injunction of God to Adam after the fall (Genesis 3:19)

Sweating blood

Anxiety, if not anguish; from Christ's experience in the garden the night before his death (Luke 22:44)

Swords ("They shall beat their swords into plowshares.")

Changing from war-mongering to peace-seeking (quoting Isaiah 2:4; see also Micah 4:3).

Taking your life in your hands

Risking your life; a common scriptural expression (for example, Jephthah in Judges 12:3; David in 1 Samuel 19:5; Job in 13:14)

Talent

Gift, ability; reference to Jesus' parable of Matthew 25:14–30; this was the name of a weight or piece of money in the ancient world (Greek: *talanthon*, a balance).

Teeth set on edge

Grating; experience difficulty or revulsion. When Jeremiah (31:29) and Ezekiel (18:2) teach about the consequences of sin and our personal responsibility for it, they quote a proverb with this phrase.

Tell it not in Gath.

"Don't publicize this, lest my enemies rejoice." "Don't tell anybody or they'll laugh at me"; quoting David (2 Samuel 1:20) lamenting the death of Saul, aware that the Philistines (in Gath) would rejoice.

Thirty pieces of silver

Blood money, a bribe; Judas Iscariot's payment for betraying Christ (Matthew 27:3)

Thorn in the flesh

God used this phrase in describing for Moses the inhabitants of Canaan, should they be allowed to remain after the Hebrews took over (Numbers 33:55). However, it usually alludes to St. Paul's reference to some personal cross of his (2 Corinthians 12:7).

Tongue, a two-edged sword

When words wound, as in an argument cutting both ways, addressing both the pro and the con; alluding to Hebrews 4:12 describing the word of God; also Revelation 1:16 and the sword out of the mouth of the Son of Man, with one edge to convict, the other to redeem

Touch-me-not

Name given to an impatiens plant, from the post-resurrection words of the Lord to Mary Magdalene in John 20:17, "Do not touch me" (in Latin, *Noli me tangere*).

Tried and found wanting

Or "weighed in the balance" or "on the scales . . ."; tested and proven false; translations of a phrase from Daniel's interpretation of Belshazzar's dream (Daniel 5:27)

Turn the other cheek.

Advice against retaliation, and an allusion to Jesus' mandate to love one's enemy (Luke 6:29)

(In the) twinkling of an eye

Quickly; this is how St. Paul describes how quickly the bodies of believers who are alive at the end of the world will be changed (1 Corinthians 15:52).

Uriah (letter of Uriah)

A treacherous message; a death warrant in the guise of a friendly letter; alluding to the letter by David to General Joab that Uriah should be sent to the front (2 Samuel 11:15)

Vanity of vanities, all is vanity.

The opening words of the book of Ecclesiastes; in Latin, *Vanitas vanitatum, omnis vanitas* ("vanity" being fruitlessness; the sense being, "Everything people do is in vain.")

(A) voice crying in the wilderness

Prophetic voice, precursive word and warning; John the Evangelist thus described John the Baptizer (John 1:23)

(The) wages of sin is death.

Sin results in death; so Paul teaches (Romans 6:23).

Wars and rumors of wars

Bad news; Jesus cautions that these are not signs of an imminent end (Matthew 24:6).

Washing one's hands

To back out of, to disdain responsibility after initial involvement; an allusion to Pilate with Jesus' death on his hands (Matthew 27:24)

(The) way of all flesh

To die, including demise and burial; a common scriptural phrase (See Joshua 23:14; 1 Kings 2:2.)

Weathercock

A person always changing his mind; one not living up to his own words. A weather vane in the form of a rooster; it was a medieval tradition to adorn church steeples with this symbol of St. Peter (an allusion to St. Peter's denial of Christ after Christ predicted it, Matthew 26:31–35, 69–75).

Widow's cruse

Any small supply that—managed well, or merely spent—becomes adequate and apparently inexhaustible; from Elisha's miracle with the cruse (or cruet) of oil (2 Kings 4:1–7)

Widow's mite

A small amount at great sacrifice; the offering praised by Christ (Mark 12:42)

Wine ("Good wine gladdens a person's heart.")

This Latin phrase (*Bonum vinum laetificat cor hominis*) makes a proverb of Psalm 104:15: "Wine (God's providence) that makes glad the heart of man." (See also Judges 9:13.)

Wings of the wind

Swiftly; alluding to Psalm 18:11 describing omnipresence, divine mobility

---

Wisdom of Solomon

Proverbial wisdom; great wisdom. Referring to the Hebrew king; see Solomon's prayer for wisdom (Wisdom 9:1–12). Jesus recalled that the Queen of the South came to hear the wisdom of Solomon, and was said to have proclaimed that "something greater than Solomon is here" (Luke 11:31).

Wise as serpents, gentle as doves

Quoting Jesus in his mission to the twelve; a modern translation renders this as "clever" and "innocent," pointing to two virtues that are not mutually exclusive (Matthew 10:16).

Youth renewed like the eagle's

From Psalm 103:5, and the ancient belief that every ten years an eagle would fly into the "fiery regions," thence to the ocean depths, and then rise, molted, to a new life

Words and Phrases with a Church Origin or Allusion

Bartholomew pig

An obese person; one of the principal attractions at the St. Bartholomew fair was the pig, roasted whole and served up hot.

Bead

Our word for prayer comes from the Anglo-Saxon word *bede*, which is derived from *bidden*, "to ask." Prayers in some forms were counted or kept track of using a string of bean-like articles. Eventually, each was called a bead (a "prayer") and the whole device was called a string of beads. (The word *rosary* may come from the French word for bead, *rosaire*.)

Bean ("He's found a bean in the cake.")

"He was lucky, he won something, he came into unexpected good fortune." An allusion to the cake of Twelfth Night in which a bean is hidden, awaiting a finder who thereby becomes Twelfth Night King

Bell, book, and candle

Used in connection with a reprimand in terms of rejection, closing a case. It has overtones of laying down or upholding the law, and originated in an ancient ceremonial excommunication in which the bell was rung, the book closed, and the candle extinguished.

Braid (to braid St. Catherine's tresses)

Living as a virgin

Carnival

Shrovetide, originally; the little season before Lent ending on Shove Tuesday: a time of merriment and excess before the spartan Season of Lent; good eating before the abstinence; through Italian *carnevale*, from Latin *carnilevanem* (*carnem*, flesh; *levare*, to lift), to remove meat

---

Catherine wheel

A firework, twirled by its explosions; named because of its shape, which is similar to the instrument of her martyrdom

Catherine-wheel window

A circular window, like a rose window, because of the method of St. Catherine's torture and death

Cloistered

Reclused; withdrawn from the world; a cloister is the covered walk, usually around three sides of a quadrangle of a monastery.

Cruet

Salt, pepper, and mustard containers; specifically, the containers for water and wine to be used at Eucharist

Devil's advocate *(Advocatus diaboli)*

The person fond of taking the opposing view in any discussion, for the sake of argument; from the role of "devil's advocate" in the canonization process; this role no longer exists as such

Ex cathedra

(Latin: from the chair) Authoritative; a dogmatic assertion, self-sufficient mandate; from the papal pronouncement made "from the chair" of St. Peter's successors (that is, authoritative and binding) which fulfills certain criteria and is binding for the universal Church

Filbert

The nut, so called because it is ripe by August 20, the feast day of St. Philibert, a seventh-century abbot.

Good-bye

Contraction of "God be with you." (Like *adieu*, French: *a' Dieu*, "I commend you to God.")

Grange

A national farm organization; from Latin: *granum* (granary), the monastery's farm and its corn storage; derivatively, a lone farm or house attached to a monastery on which rent was paid in grain; more loosely, a country house on the grand side

Magnificat (to correct *Magnificat* before one has learned *Te Deum*)

Presumptuous criticism; performing above station (the former being more difficult than the latter)

Magnificat (to sing the *Magnificat* at Matins)

Doing things in the wrong order; *Magnificat* is a Vespers (evening) and not a Matins (morning) canticle.

Martin

A bird of the swallow family, maybe associated with St. Martin (and the legend about the goose), or maybe because it comes upon the scene (for some) in March (the Martian month) and departs around Martinmas (November 11)

Martinmas ("His Martinmas will come, as it does to every hog.")

"Death is inevitable." November and St. Martin's tide was prime time among the Anglo-Saxons for butchering.

Mumpsimus

That's what a person is who knows he's wrong but refuses to change, stubbornly adhering to error (which is also called a *mumpsimus*). This because of *sumpsimus*, a word in the Latin Mass meaning "we have received" (which is beside the point). Centuries ago, a certain aged priest would mumble "*mumpsimus*" for *sumpsimus*, and a certain young priest would correct him, without effect. Furthermore, in some kind of justice, what made the wrong one a *mumpsimus* made the right one a *sumpsimus,* or one who officiously insists on using a technically correct term or form instead of what's popular but incorrect. So there!

Odor ("[He's died] in the odor of sanctity.")

As a saint; because it was believed in the Middle Ages that sometimes a pleasant odor was given off by the body of a saint at death (or disinterment, if the remains were moved)

Orientation (oriented)

Referring generally to getting one's bearings, learning the ropes; from the custom of facing the east (orient) in prayer, already a practice before Christ; christianized as (1) the direction to Israel, where Christ lived on earth, and (2) the direction of the sunrise, and the east whence he will come to judge the living and the dead.

Poor as a church mouse

Where could a mouse find even a crumb in a building with no cupboard or pantry?

Red-letter day

Lucky day, memorable; on calendars and in daybooks, saints' days and holidays were printed in red ink (days which have special prayers in liturgical books).

Repenter curls

A woman's tresses; a repentant woman (confused with Mary Magdalene) washed Jesus' feet with tears and dried them with her hair.

Robbing Peter to pay Paul

Debt shifting; borrowing money from one to pay off another; impoverishing one church to improve another. Commonly related to an English fable: Property of St. Peter's Abbey Church, Westminster, was used to help defray repair expenses on St. Paul's Cathedral, London. (The phrase, however, predates these churches.)

Rose, *Sub rosa* (Latin: under the rose)

See "Under the Rose," page 304.

Rubric

Law, directive, heading; red ochre, *rubrica* in Latin, was the color in which the Romans wrote laws (rubrics). Following this practice, monks and printers after them used red ink in manuscripts and Church books for heading, directions, titles, and such. They're still rubrics today, even when they're in black.

St. Anthony's fire

The pestilential disease *erysipelas* ("the sacred fire"), because of the cures experienced in the eleventh-century plague through the intercession of St. Anthony, the Franciscan friar

St. Anthony's pig (Tantony Pig)

The runt of the litter, and one that becomes a pet is so called because proctors of a St. Anthony's hospital would protect pigs that were unfit for food by tying bells around them. Hence St. Anthony the Hermit, the fourth-century founder of a society of ascetics, is the patron of swineherds and often pictured with a little pig at his side.

St. Bernard dogs

Bred and trained for tracking and helping snowbound travelers by the Augustinian Canons who staffed the hospice of St. Bernard in Switzerland's Great St. Bernard Pass

St. Bernard Passes

Two passes in the Alps into Italy: the Great St. Bernard from Switzerland and the Little St. Bernard from France. On the Great Pass stands the great hospice of St. Bernard of Menthon (923–1008).

St. Crispin's holiday

Monday, for those whose work week begins on Tuesday; because Monday is the day off for a shoemaker, whose patron saint is Crispin, the shoemaker

St. Cuthbert's duck

The eider duck, because its breeding grounds are in the Farne Islands, which is also the locale of that saint and legends about him

St. Dunstan and blindness

Associated with him because of a World War I era institution for the blind at St. Dunstan's House, Regents Park; for the care and rehabilitation of blinded soldiers, and later for all

---

St. Elmo's Fire

The "corposant" (Portuguese: *corpo santo*; body, holy), or fireball sometimes seen around masts and rigging of ships in a storm; a brush discharge, electrically speaking; a luminous electrical field, reddish when positive, bluish when negative. There is no such saint. Perhaps the name is a corruption of Anselm of Lucca, or Erasmus (patron saint of Neapolitan sailors), or Helena (sister of Castor and Pollux, the twins whose names are also associated with the corposant).

St. Francis's distemper

Poverty, impecuniosity, because of the Franciscan's vows of poverty, and the rule which disallowed carrying money

St. Lawrence (fiery tears of St. Lawrence)

A name for the shooting stars of the prolific Perseid meteor shower which is at its height between August 11 and 13. Legend has it that ever since 258 when he was burned to death (on August 10), the deacon Lawrence weeps from his place in heaven over the cruelty of humanity, and that his tears glisten through the dark sky like drops of gold.

St. Martin's beads

Trinket jewelry; St. Martin-le-Grand once had a reputation as a place for imitation jewelry.

St. Monday

Any Monday, facetiously so called by those who take a long weekend by making it a holiday (or holy day); when idle workmen spend Saturday's paycheck in amusement or dissipation

St. Vitus's Dance

Chorea, the disease. In Medieval Germany it was believed that an annual dance around a statue of St. Vitus on his feast day (June 15) would secure the gift of good health for that year. The near mania that evolved came to be compared to, if not confused with, the symptoms of chorea, and vice versa; the saint himself became an intercessor for those with the disease.

Scot-free

Exempt from payment, penalty or punishment; a *scot* (from early Saxon silver coin *sceat*) was an ancient Anglo-Saxon tax levied to support the clergy. The payment, originally in corn, was made on St. Martin's (November 11).

Sic transit gloria mundi.

Old phrase addressed to a newly elected pope on the occasion of his enthronement: "So passes the glory of the world." (See the story in Chapter 4.)

Sinecure (Latin: *sine cure*, without cure or without care)

Salary and position with responsibility; a benefice with salary but no pastoral duties

Sunday saint

A practicing Church person and churchgoer who doesn't practice faith the other six days

Supererogation (works of supererogation)

Service beyond the call of duty; an archaic term theologians gave to things done but not enjoined on believers (Latin: *super*, above; *erogare*, to pay out)

Tawdry

Corrupted from St. Audrey, which is in turn a corruption of Etheldrida; originally referring to the ostentatious low-quality lace and jewelry at the annual St. Audrey fair in the Isle of Ely

---

Tiffany

A sheer, woven fabric like gauze, originally silken; a corruption of *theophany* (Greek: *Theos*, God; *ephainein*, to show), a divine manifestation (an epiphany); applied to the material because it was a common costume fabric for the Twelfth Night (Epiphany) revels

Index

A

Aaron, 39, 161, 185; blessing, 42

abbey, 237, 273

abbot, 237, 312

Abel, 447

abomination of desolation, 493

abortion, and excommunication, 306

Abraham, 131,132, 158, 174, 175, 183, 190, 447

Abraham's bosom, 493

absolution, 302, 305; general, 305

abstinence, 101, 103

abyss, 127

abyss, 127, 493

Acca, St., 423

access prayers, 100

Act of Contrition, 8

Act of Faith, Hope, Love, 7

Acts of Consecration to the Sacred Heart, 376

Acts of Reparation to the Sacred Heart, 376

actual sin, 109–110

Ad Limina, 222*, 222**

Adam, 208, 447

Adam's ale, 493; apple, 493

Adam's Grave, 208*

Adonai, 172

Adoramus te, Christe, 294

Adoration of the Magi, 67**

Adoro Te, 373

Adrian, St., 428

* Story
** Picture

Advent, 333; symbols of, 456; wreath, 333**

adversary, The, 493

Aetatus Suae, 115

African Epiphany Water Blessing, 324*

Agatha, St., 425

Agnes, St., 346*, 421, 422, 424, 429, 479

Agnus Dei, 7

agony in the garden, symbol of, 449

Agur's wish, 493

Ah-Choo, 60*

Ahithopel, 493

Aidan, St., 319*

alb, 298

Albert the Great, St., 412, 416, 417, 427

Albrecht Dürer and the Praying Hands, 98*

Alcoholic Patrons, 418*

Alexis, St., 419, 425, 426

All Saints, Litany, 26–30; symbols of, 455

All Souls' Day, 122*, 354

All things to all people, 493

alleluia, 294

almsgiving, 103, 199

Aloysius Gonzaga, St., 429

alpha and omega, 192, 461, 468, 493

Alphonsus Liguori, St., 396, 412, 421, 425, 429

altar stone, 268

altar, 468; candles, 322; in the Old Testament, 178; symbolism, 267

Always go forward . . . , 237

Amand, St., 429

Ambrose, St., 10, 102, 409, 412, 419, 423, 470

ambry, 268

amen, 294

amice, 298

amillennialism (chart), 128

amphora, 295

ampullae, 295

Anastasia, St., 429

anathema, 231

anchor, 468

anchorites, 244

Ancient Folklore and Christian Analogy, 126*

Ancient of Days, title, 172

And the Word Made His Dwelling Among Us, 58*

Andrew Kim, St., 433

Andrew, St., 400, 402, 403, 404, 407, 422, 428, 431, 452**

Andronicus, St., 427

angels, 8**, 117–120; fallen, 105–106; in Scriptures, 120; nine choirs of, 118, 465; rebellious, 105–106; symbols of, 118, 450, 497**

Angelus, the, 9

Anima Christi, 34

Anne, St., 262, 277, 278, 309, 337, 350*, 407, 420, 423, 425, 429, 430, 471

anniversaries, Silver/Golden Wedding Blessing, 58; symbols of, 468

annulment, 320

annunciation, 185, symbols of, 455

Anointing of the Sick, 112, 277, 278; as sacrament, 276; effects of, 307; elements of, 306; recipient of, 307; symbol of, 454

Anselm, St., 413, 416

Anskar, St., 430

Ante Mortem, 112

antependium, 268

Anthony, St., 84, 97, 262, 382, 413, 415, 417, 418, 419, 420, 421, 422, 424*, 426, 428, 431, 471

anti-Christ, 124

Apocalyptic, 134

Apocrypha, 133

Apollonia, St., 421

Apologia Pro Vita Sua, 282*

Apostles' Creed, 3

apostles' symbols, 452–453

apostolic brief, 231

apostolic bull, 231

apostolic succession, 215, 227

apparitions, 129, 262, 374–375, 391–394

apple of one's eye, 494

April Fools! 348*

apse, 268

Aquinas, Thomas, see Thomas Aquinas

Arabic, language, 135; alphabet, 136

archangels, 8**, 118; the seven, 119

archbishop, 223, 237; coats of arms, 236**; 239**

archdiocese, 237

architecture, church, 263–267

ark, 469; of the covenant, 177

Armageddon, 127, 128, 494

armed resistence, 86

Ars Moriendi, 112

Arthur, King, 296

Ascension, 101, 190, 217; symbols of, 455; Thursday, 18, 342; window, 212**

Ascetic St. Giles, The, 244*

ashes, 324; to ashes, 494

aspergillum, 295

aspiration prayer, 100

Ass's Stripe, The, 469*

Assumption of Mary, 300, 352*; symbols of, 455

Assyrian Empire (map), 166

Athanasian Creed, 4–5

Athanasius, St., 4–5, 411, 413, 416

Atonement (Yom Kippur), 366

Audrey, St., 520*

Augustine, St., 10, 64, 82, 102, 108, 141, 246, 248, 360, 409, 413, 415, 416, 420, 427, 429, 478; prayers, 31, 33

Augustinian canons, 246

Augustinians, 248, 471

Autumn's Summers, 360*

auxiliary bishop, 224; coats of arms, 236**

Ave Maria, the, 2

B

Babel, 494

Babylonian Empire (map), 166

Bacon, Francis, 64

Baldacchino, 268

balm, 494

Balthasar, 407

Baltimore, Council of, 90; Catechism, 62

banns of marriage, 309

Baptism, 275**, 281–283; as sacrament, 276–279; candle, 322; Old Testament prefigurements, 190, 278; principle effects, 278; symbols of, 454; three valid methods of, 281

baptistry, 268

Barbara, St., 309, 419, 421, 422, 425, 427, 489

Barnabas, St., 483

Bartholomew, St., 400, 403, 404, 406, 426, 452**; Bartholomew's pig, 515

Basil, St., 26, 245, 246, 411, 413, 416, 417

Basilians, 246

Basilica of Dormition, 390

basilicas, names of, 259

basilisk, 467

"Battle for Purity," 89

bead, 515

bean, 515

bearing witness, 88

Beatae Memoriae, 115

Beatific Vision, 116

Beatitudes, 93; symbol of, 93**, 465

Beelzebub, 124

belfry, 266

Beliar, 124

bell, book, and candle, 515

bells, 319–320, 470

Beloved Disciple, 403

Benedict the Black, 91*

Benedict, St., 238, 245, 262, 409, 421, 426, 427, 430

Benedictines, 245, 316, 471, 477

Benediction, 13, 100; liturgical gesture, 300

Benedictus, 7, 45

Benjamin, 492, 494; Benjamin's portion, 494

Bernadette Soubirous, St., 129

Bernard of Menthon, St., 425, 428

Bernard, St., 15, 17, 245, 413, 416, 417, 419, 470

Bernardine, St., 20

Beulah Land, 494

Beware the Ides of March, 328*

Bible lands before Jesus
(map), 132

*Bible on the End and Eternity,
The* (chart), 111

Bible, books, 133–134;
choices of, 139; on the
end and eternity, 111; eras
of translation, 140–152;
languages of, 135–136;
principals of translation,
139; vernacular, 138–141;
versions of, 141–152

Biblical Christmas Tree, 456*

bier, 268

bilocation, 435

bird, 347, 471; 494; *Birds at
the Crucifixion,* 210*, 210**

biretta, 298

birthright, 495

Bishop of Rome, 229

bishop, 222–225, 310–313;
coats of arms, 236**;
239**; insignia, 239–240

Black Spiritual, 382*

black, 471; liturgical
significance of, 299

Blaise, St., 428

blessed candles, 322

Blessed Sacrament, hymns in
honor of, 370–373; visit
to the, 369

Blessed Virgin, symbols of,
450

Blessed, in canonization
process, 432

blessings, 93; New
Testament, 55–57; Old
Testament, 42; of St. Paul,
55–56; other blessings,
58–60

blind leading the blind, 495

Blue Monday, 335

Body and Blood of Christ,
symbols of, 455

Bonaventure, St., 84, 413,
415

Boniface, St., 415, 417, 420,
430, 458*

Book of the Living, 127

bosom friend, 495

bowing, liturgical posture,
300; the knee to Rimmon,
495

braid, 515

brass, 268

bread, 495

Brendan, St., 427

bricks, 495

Bridget of Swedan, St., 427,
431

Bright Week, 341

Brigid of Kildare, St., 431

brother, 242

Bruno, St., 426

build on sand, 495

burden, 495

buttress, 266

By the Dark of the Moon,
330*

C

Cain, 447, 496, 507

calf, 496

California Missions, The, 246*

Calvary cross, 188**, 441**,
442

Camillus de Lellis, St., 422,
425, 427

campanile, 266

Canaan, 175

Candlemas Day, 322–323;
347*

candles, 295, 321–323,
472**

canonization, 431–433

canons, 242

Canterbury cross, 256**

Canticle of Brother Sun, 32

canticles, New Testament,
43–46; Old Testament,
39–40

Canute IV, St., 430

capital sins, 110

capsula, 295

Cardinal Hugo de Sancto-
Caro, 153

cardinal, 223; coats of arms,
236**

carillon, 266

Carling Sunday, 335

Carmelites, 247*

carnival, 515

Carthusians, 245

Casimir, St., 431

casket orientation, 114

Casper, St., 407

Cassian, St., 428

cassock, 298

Castel Gandolfo, 233

catechesis, four pillars of, 63

Catechisms, 62, 63, 89, 256;
references throughout

cathedra, 269

Catherine of Alexandria, St.,
423, 426, 428, 429

Catherine of Siena, St., 412,
413, 422, 431, 479

Catherine wheel, 515, window, 515

Catholic Church is apostolic,
215

Catholic Worker, The, 349*

catholic, 215–217

Catholic, becoming one,
282–283; symbols,
441–492; tradition (lan-
guages of), 294; word
defined, 216

Catholicism in Mary's Land,
258*

Cecilia, St., 425*, 426, 427,
478, 486

celebrant, 313

celebret, 315

celestial hierarchy, three
triads of, 117

Celtic cross, 441**, 442

*Cenacle of St. Mark's Mother,
The,* 207*

cenacle, 207

Cenobites, 245

censer, 295

censures, 306

centaur, 467

cerecloth, 269

chalice veil, 296

chalice, 22**; 295, 472

chamael, 119

chancel, 269

chapel, 260

chapelle ardente, 114

chaplain, 313

Chapter and Verse on Horseback, 153*

characteristics of the Church, 213

charisms, 80

charity, 496

Charles Borromeo, St., 427

chastity, fruits of, 87; sins against, 87; three forms of, 87

chasuble, 298**

cherubim, 118

Chi Rho, 134, 460, 463**

chimera, 467

Chinese Rites Controversy, Ancestor Worship or Veneration? 386*

chrism, 319, 472

Christ as Divine Guru, Missionary as Sannyasi, 68*

Christ, candle, 321**; date and time of birth, 333; four manifestations of, 66; the King, symbols of, 455; passion in Christian art, 382; three-fold belief in, 68; three-fold birth of, 67; three-fold office of, 67; titles, 190–195; The Trinity crowning Mary, 9**

Christianity, 131; chief mysteries of, 64; evolution of (map), 226; roots and grafts, 132; unity, gift of and call to, 257

Christmas Among the Hurons, 66*

Christmas Tree, Fruit Tree, 286*; *St. Boniface and the,* 458*; *Martin Luther and the,* 458*

Christmas, Season of, 333–334; symbols of, 456–457

Christological confessions, 68

Christopher, St., 363*, 425, 426, 427, 429

Church fathers, 408–412, 464; apostolic, 408

Church of the Acts of the Apostles, the (map), 220

Church, 190, 213–274; apostolic stories of, 217; architecture, 263–273; characteristics of, 213; outline chronology of, 218–219; four marks of, 215; as house of God, 259; mission of, 213; periods of architecture (graph), 263; rites, of, 249–250; symbols of, 454, 466, 481; three states of, 216

Church's Memorial Day, The, 355*

ciborium, 296

cincture, 298

Cistercians, 245

Cities of Refuge, 176

citizens of no mean city, 496

Clare, St., 247**

clay feet, 496

Clement, St., 408, 424, 428

cleric, 313

clerical glossary, 315

Clerical Haircut, A, 311*

cloister, 273, -ed, 516

clothing the dead for burial, 114

cloud of witnesses, 496

coadjutor bishop, 225; coats of arms, 236**

coals, 496

coats of arms, 236–237

Columba, St., 12, 327, 431

come to pass, 496

Come, Holy Spirit, 13

Commandments, the Great, 89; the Ten, 81–89

common prayers, 1–2

common symbols, a glossary of, 468–492

communion of saints, 216

Communion, names for, 284

concupiscence, 107

confession, 302, 305

confessional, 271

Confirmation, 277–280; name, 280; as sacrament, 276, 282–283; symbols of, 454, 481

Confiteor, 6

Consecration of a Church, 260*

consecration, 100

consequence of sin, 109

Consolation at La Vang: A Vietnamese Guadalupe, 393*

Constantine's Vision of the Cross, 463**, 463*

contrition, 302; four qualities of, 304; three elements of, 304

convent, 273

conversion, 70–73; Paul's, 72; process, 71–72; stages of, 70

cooperating in the sin of another, 109

cope, 298

corporal, 296; works of mercy, 76

Cosmos and Damien, Sts., 419, 421, 426

Councils, 3, 18, 62, 68, 73, 235

Covenant of Salt, A, 283*

covenant, 173–174, 177

cover a multitude of sins, 496

Coverdale, Miles (Coverdale's Bible), 143

covetousness, St. John's, 89

creatures of myth and fable, 467

credence table, 269

Creeds, 3–5, 73

crescelle, 297

Crispin and Crispinian, Sts., 427, 428

crosier, 239, 474

cross and crown, symbol, 419**

cross, 208, 474; doctrine of the, 200; forms of, 441–443; sign of, 300; stations of, 380–382; examples of**, 31, 34, 48, 93, 152, 188, 189, 209, 237, 253, 256, 269, 404, 407, 419, 441–443, 446; San Damiano, 445*, 445**; veneration of, 377; wood of the, 444*

crucifix, 12**, 269, 448; Prayer Before a, 12

Crucifixion group, 378**, 382

crucifixion, symbol of, 449

cruets, 297, 516

crumbs from a rich man's table, 496

crypt, 270

cuius regio eius religio, 256

Cunegunda, St., 431

cup, 496–497

curate, 313

Cuthbert, St., 427

Cyprian, St., 409

Cyril, St., 251*, 251**, 413, 415, 430

Czech's Cherry Blossoms, 309*

D

dalmatic, 298

Dan, 497

Daniel, 39, 40, 169, 181, 189, 447

David, 39, 156, 158, 162–163, 175, 177, 181, 183, 191, 447

David, St., 431

Day of the Lord, 127

Day the Great Pan Died, The, 437*

Dayenu, 41

De Carne Christi, 69

de Nobili, Roberto, 68

De Profundis, 497

deacon, 217, 310, 313

dead, 497

Dear Pope, 230*

death, 111–115; second, 128

death, meaning of, 111; talk, 112

Defender of the Faith, 232*

defense, legitimate, 86

deities, Greek and Roman, 436–437; Old Testament neighbors, 173

Delilah, 497

deliverance miracles, 204

Denis, St., 415, 426, 430

denominations, symbols of, 454–455**

Deo gratias, 217, 294

Deuterocanonical, 133

devil, 124–126

devil's advocate, 516

devil's door, 266

Devil's Funeral, The, 66

devotion to St. Joseph, 399–400

devotion to the Eucharist, 369–373

devotion to the Infant of Prague, 383–384

devotion to the Passion, 377–382

devotion to the Sacred Heart, 374–376

devotions in Catholic tradition, 367–368; devotional objects, 368; images, 368; object of devotions, 368; principles of, 368;

Didache, The, 1, 281, 408

Dies Irae, 114

dignity of persons, 86, 87

diocese, 237

directions, symbolic in church, 267

Discalced Carmelites, 248

Dismas, St., 407, 422, 427

Distinct Pope, A, 228*

Divided Kingdom, 163–167, 180

Divine Ambassadors, 78

Divine Choice, 158*

divine names and titles, 171–173

Divine Praises, 13

doctors of the Church, 412–414, 416

Documents of Vatican II, 235–236

dolphin, 112**, 474

Dom, 313

Dominations, 118

Dominic, St., 247, 262, 419, 430

Dominican Rosary, 15

Dominicans, 246–247

Dominus vobiscum, 294

door, symbolism, 266

Dorothea, St., 117

Dorothy, St., 422

dossal, 270

Doubting Thomas, 497

dove, 474

Doxology, the greater, 6; the lesser, 2

dreams, in Scripture, 130

Dunstan, St., 125, 419, 420, 422, 424

Dürer, Albrecht, 98

duties, of parents, 85; political community's to honor the family, 85; three notable, 94

Dymphna, St., 424

E

Easter, 331; cross, 189**; Season, 341–342; Sundays of, 341; symbols of, 459–461

Eastern Rites, 223, 225, 226, 250–253

Eat, drink, and be merry, 497

Ecce Homo, 382

ecstasy, 435

ecumenical councils, 235

Ecumenical Movement and Topics of Discussion (chart), 257

Edict of Milan, 221

egg roll, symbolic meaning of, 341, 341**

Ehyeh-asher-ehyeh, 172

eight, significance of, 464

eight-pointed star, 190**

El Camino de Santiago, 261*

El Dia de los Muertos, 355*

El Shaddai, 172

El, 171

eleventh hour, 497

Eligius, St., 423, 425, 428

Elijah, 104, 163, 181, 190, 447

"*Elijah's Melons*," 104*

Elizabeth Ann Seton, St., 432

Elizabeth of Hungary, St., 419, 428

Elohim, 172

Ember Days, 327

Emmaus, 189

Enchiridion of Indulgences, 122

encyclical, 231

end times (glossary), 127–128

entertain an angel unawares, 497

Enthronement of the Sacred Heart, 375

ephod, 179

epigonation, 241

Epiphany, 186; symbols of, 456

episcopacy, 222–225

Erasmus, St., 427

eschatology, 127

Estienne, Robert (Stephanus), 153

Eternal Rest Prayer, 12

eternity, 111, 115–117

Eucharist, 190, 277, 278, 372**; as sacrament, 276; changes in, 287; devotion, 369–370; fast, 102; fruits of, 293; gestures and postures, 300–301; liturgies, hierarchy of, 342; names for, 283–284; objects and vessels, 295–297; parts of, 287–293; prayer, 292–293; readings at, 289–291; sacrifice, 285; symbols of, 454; vesture, 298–299

Eulalia, St., 427

eulogia, 100

European Co-Patrons, 251*

evangelical counsels, 76

evangelists, four, 196

evangelization cross, 152**

Eve, 447; *Eve's Tears*, 108*

ex cathedra, 231, 516

excardination, 315

excommunication, 306

exeat, 315

Exile, 156, 167

Exodus, 40, 156, 177; The Route of the (map), 176

exorcism, 100

Expectation Week, 342

expression of piety, 318–319

eye for an eye, 497

eye of a needle, 498

Ezekiel, 39, 158, 167, 447

F

Fabergé eggs, 460

fable, creatures of, 467

faculties, 316

fair linen, 270

faith, Act of, 7; elements of, 76; in one God, 63; qualities of, 76

fald stool, 270

Falling Asleep of the Mother of God, The, 352*

Fast of the Ninevites, The, 165*

fasting, 101–103, 199

Fat Tuesday, 335

Father of lies, 124

Father, symbols of God the, 448; title, 172, 313

Fathers of the Church, 409–412, 416–417; four main prerogatives of, 409; Desert Fathers, 11; Greek Fathers, 411–412; Latin Fathers, 409–410

Fatima, 15, 393**, 393–394; Invocation, 15

fear of the Lord, 80

Fearful Thomas, 134*

Feast of Lights (Hanukkah), 366

feasts, eliminated in revised calendar, 363; Eucharistic liturgy, 342; movable and immovable, 332; symbols of, 455

Ferial Days, 345

Fiat voluntas tua, 294

fiery pool of sulphur, 127

fifteen marks of the Church, 215

fifteen, significance of, 465

fifty, significance of, 465

Fig Sunday, 338

filbert, 516

finger bowl and towel, 297

first resurrection, 127

fish, ICHTHYS, 192**

flesh, 498

floor, symbolic in church, 270

Flowers in the Garden of Eden, 108*

Flowers on Calvary, 209*

flowers, 108*, 209*, 211*; the Little Flower, 248*, 248**

fly in the ointment, 498

folded hands, liturgical gesture, 300

"For My Yoke Is Easy," 198*

For the greater glory of God, 237

Forty Hours' Adoration, 369

forty, significance of, 465

Four Horsemen of the Apocalypse, The, 106

four last things, 111

four, significance of, 464

Frances Xavier Cabrini, St., 262, 432

Francis Borgia, St., 431

Francis de Sales, St., 413, 419, 421, 423

Francis of Assisi, St., 31–32, 42, 67, 76, 247, 262, 417, 419, 421, 425, 431, 445

Francis Xavier, St., 425, 429, 430

Franciscan Crown, the (or Seraphic Rosary), 17

Franciscans, 246–247, 471, 476

friars, 247

friary, 273

Fridays, First, 376

Friend as Far as to the Altars, A, 83*

frontal, 270

frontlet, 270

fruit, 498; forbidden, 498

fruits of the Holy Spirit, 81

fruits of the Mass, 293

funeral, rites, 113; tradition and terminology, 114

G

Gabriel Possenti, St., 429

Gabriel, archangel, 119, 421, 426, 428, 479

Gabriel's hounds, 116

Galileo, 272*

gall and wormwood, 498

garb, 312

gargoyle, 266

Gehenna, 123

Geneology of Christian Churches/Nationalities/ Liturgies (chart), 252

general absolution, 305

Genesius, St., 423, 427, 428

Genevieve, St., 429

genuflection, liturgical posture, 301

George, St., 126*, 126**, 420, 421, 428, 430, 478

Gerard, St., 422

Gertrude, St., 286*, 429

Gervase and Protase, Sts., 422

Gestas, 407

Gideon Bible, The, 146*

gifts of the Holy Spirit, 79, 464, 474

Giles, St., 244*, 419

gird your loins, 498

giving, 498; up the ghost, 498

gladden, 498

Gloria in excelsis Deo, 294

glorified body, properties of, 115

Glorious Mysteries, 17

Glory to the Father, 2

glory, 498; of Jesus, 211

goads, 498

God willing, 237

God wills it, 237*

God, 63; flowchart, 214; names/titles of, 171–173

God's Irresistible Call, 221*

Godspeed, 58

Gog and Magog, 127, 128

Going to the Table, Not Confession, 303*

Golgotha, 208

Good Friday, symbols of, 458

Good Luck and Amazing Grace, 327*

"Good Manners and Self-Defense," 125*

Good Samaritan, 499**

good-bye, 516

gospel, 291; the last, 291

Gospels, 219, number of, 464; three stages in the formation of, 196; resurrection and the, 210–211

Gossamer Legend, The, 352*

Gothic style, 264**

Grace Builds on Nature, 75*

grace, 73; of marriage, 309

graded cross, 188**

Grandparents' Day, 350*

grange, 516; 516**

grapes of wrath, 499

Great Commandment, 89

Great Promise, 112

Great Service of Light, 339

Greater and Lesser Evils, 109*

Greater love than this no one has, 499

Greek cross, 253**, 265**, 441**

Greek, language, 135; alphabet, 136

green wood, 499

green, liturgical significance of, 299

Gregorian calendar, 325
Gregorian chant, 100
Gregory of Armenia, St., 415, 417
Gregory of Nazianzus, St., 411, 413, 415
Gregory the Great, St., 60, 100, 232*, 410, 413, 417, 425, 427
griffin, 467
Guadalupe, 392*
"Gypsies," 78*

H

Hades, 123
hagiography, 433
Hail Mary, 2
Hail, Holy Queen, 15–16
Hall Sunday/Monday/Night, 335
Halloween, 354*
Halo: Holiness of Persons of the Trinity, Angels, and Saints, 477*
hand, symbol, 477
handwriting on the wall, 499
Harmaged'on, 127
harpy, 467
"He descended into hell," 123*, 123**
healing miracles, 203–204
heart, symbol, 478
heaven, 116, 117
Hebrew, language, 135; alphabet, 136
Helena, St., 443*
hell, 116, 123
Henry, St., 430
heraldic cross pattée, 237**
heresy, 63, 75
Heritage Blessing, 59
hermits, 244
hewers of wood and drawers of water, 499
Hic iacet, 115

Hiroshima Transfigured, 351*
history of the Church, 218–221; early Church, 218–220; persecutions, 221
holidays and anniversaries, 342–345
Holy Coat of Treves, 434*
holy days of obligation, 342
"Holy God, We Praise Thy Name," 10
Holy Grail, definition of, 296,
holy hour, 376
Holy Innocents, symbols of, 456
Holy Land, 175
Holy Name, Litany, 20–21; Society, 84; symbols of, 456
holy oils, 318–319, 319**
Holy Orders, as sacrament, 276, 310–316; clerical glossary, 315–316; degrees, 320; garb, 312; minor orders, 311; symbols of, 454; titles, 312–315
Holy See, 222
Holy Sleeping, 390*
Holy Spirit, 14**; and the Seven Flames, 79**; gifts of, 79, 464, 473; Gospel of the, 212; prayer, 14, 31; symbols of, 69**, 449**; titles of, 69
Holy Thursday, symbols of, 458
holy water, 324
Holy Week, 337–339; symbols of, 458
Hope, Act of, 7
Horned Moses, A, 160*
Hosanna, 294
hospitality, in Scriptures, 77–78
Hot Cross Buns, 459*
Hounds of the Lord, 247*

house built on rock, 500
house divided, 500
House of Loreto, The, 387*
How Great Thou Art, 157*
howling wilderness, 500
Hubert, St., 72, 423
humeral veil, 299
Hungarian Hospitality, 355*
Huron carolers, 66
hydra, 467

I

I.N.R.I., 208, 462
ICHTHYS, 192**, 462, 478
icon, 270
Ignatius of Antioch, St., 222*, 407, 408, 411
Ignatius of Loyola, St., 34, 100, 248, 427, 428
IHS, 462, 463*, 463**
Immaculate Conception, 480, symbols of, 456, 480
Imprimatur, 75
In articulo mortis, 112
In giving we receive, 104*
In memoriam, 114
In petto, 231
In This Sign, 463*
incarnation, 185
incense, 320–321; procedure (graph), 321; symbolism, 321
incorruptibility, 435
Indians are Truly Human, 249*
indulgences, 121–122
indult, 231
Infant of Prague devotion, 383**–384
insignia, 239
interdicts, 306
interior conversion, 303
intersections, sacred and secular of calendar, 364
invocation, 100; liturgical gesture, 301

Irenaeus, St., 409

Irish blessings, 60

Isaac, 158, 159, 174, 447

Isaiah, 39, 40, 41, 168, 447

Isidore of Seville, St., 414, 417

Isidore, St., 423

Islam, 131

Israel, 156, 160–171; holy women of, 175; name, 174–175; sanctuaries in, 177; territory of twelve tribes of (map), 180; twelve tribes of, 179, 465

It is better to light . . . , 238

itinerarium, 101

Ivo, St., 423

J

Jacob, 130, 159–160, 174, 189, 190, 447; Jacob's ladder, 500

James and John, 402–403

James the Great, St., 400, 401, 402, 404–405, 407, 417, 423, 426, 427, 430, 431, 452**

James the Less, St., 400, 404, 405, 406, 422, 452**

"Japanese Tempura," 92*

Jehovah, 172

jeremiad, 500

Jeremiah, 39, 40, 41, 158, 165, 447

Jericho, 500

Jeroboam, 500, and Rohoboam, 500

Jerome Emiliani, St., 425

Jerome, St., 137*, 137**, 410, 414, 416, 424, 482

Jerusalem cross, 152**, 441**, 443

Jerusalem of Jesus (map), 205

Jesse tree, 500

Jesuits, 248, 471

Jesus Prayer, 11, 94

Jesus, 131, 158; descent among the dead, 123**, 124; discourses, 199–200; glory of, 211; and the Jews, 199; lamb, 479**; Litanies, 19–23; miracles, 203–204; parables, 201; passion of, 207, 449; post-resurrection appearances of, 212; prayers of, 47–48, 94–95; prophecy fulfillment, 183–185; resurrection of, 210–211; seven last words, 208; similitudes and allegories used, 202; symbols of, 448; temptations of, 464, 465; the Nazorean, 190; threefold office of, 191, 448; titles, 190–195; typology, 185–190

Jew(s) (Judaism), 131, 174; opposition to Jesus, 199

Jewish calendar, 365–366; seven set feasts, 366, 464

Jezebel, 500

Joachim and Anne, 407

Joachim, St., 350*

Joan of Arc, St., 417, 428, 430

Job, 40, 501, 506; Job's comforter, 501

John Berchmans, St., 419, 429

John Capistran, St., 20

John Chrysostom, St., 411, 414, 417, 426, 470*

John Damascene, St., 98, 352*, 412, 414

John Eudes, St., 374

John Henry Cardinal Newman, 282*

John Nepomucene, St., 430

John Neumann, St., 430

John of Capistrano, St., 423

John of God, St., 422, 425, 427

John of the Cross, St., 248*, 414, 416

John the Apostle and Evangelist, St., 196**, 210, 400–403, 405, 407, 415, 420, 425, 427, 452**, 482

John the Baptist, 187, 198, 200, 513**

John Vianney, St., 34, 313, 427

John's "Book of Signs," 206

Jonathon's arrows, 501

Jophiel, 119

Jophkiel, 119

Jordan, 501

Joseph (OT), 130, 159, 174, 189, 190, 447

Joseph Cafasso, St., 427

Joseph Legend of the Budding Staff of Lily, The, 400*, 400**

Joseph of Cupertino, St., 419

Joseph, St., 25**, 79*, 130, 158, 262, 349*, 399–400, 420–423, 429, 430, 471, 479, 486; Litany, 25

Joseph's First Wife, 399*

Jot or Tittle, 501*

Joyful/Sorrowful Mysteries, 16

Judah, 174, 175

Judas Greeting Countered, 339*

Judas Iscariot, 404; symbol of, 452**

Judas, 400, 405, 452, 482, 501

Jude the Obscure, 423*

Jude, St., 262, 400, 405, 406, 421, 422, 423*, 452**

Judge, title of Jesus, 191

Julian Calendar, 325

Julian the Apostate, 74*

Julian the Hospitaller, St., 422, 429

Juniper, The, 281*

justice, three forms of, 88; demands of social, 92–93

Justin Martyr, St., 286, 409, 426

K

Kateri Tekakwitha, Blessed 417, 433

Kedar's tents, 501

kerygmatic sermons in Acts, 218

keys, 479

Kill the fatted calf, 501

kingdom of God, 117

Kingdom of Israel, 162–163

Kingdom, Divided, 163–167, 180

Kings, Three, 67

kiss of Judas, 502

Knights of the Holy Sepulcher and Knights of St. Gregory, 210*

Kyrie Eleison, 6, 294

L

labor of love, 502

laborer is worth his wage, 502

Lady of the Lake, The 2*

Laetare Sunday, 336

Lamb of God, 7, 191, 194, 198, 240, 479

Lamed Vav, The, 399*

Land of Milk and Honey, 175, 502

Languages of the Bible, 135*

Laodicean, 502

Last Blessing, 112

Last Gospel, 291

last judgment, 116, 128, 200

Last Rites, 278

Last Supper, 187–188, 198, 200, 206

last things, 111

Lateran Palace, 233

Latin cross, 263, 265**, 441**

*Latin Inscriptions, 115**

*Latin Names, 332**

Latin, language, 135

lavabo dish, 297

Lawrence, St., 221*, 419, 421, 426, 427, 428, 477

Lazar(us), 204, 502, 506

lectern, 270

Lectio Prayer, 99

Lectionary, 291; general principles of the new, 291

Ledwina, St., 428

Legacy of St. Maron, 251*

Legend of St. Gertrude, The, 286*

Legend of the Cuckoo, 348*

Legend of the Pelican, The, 373*; 373**

legion, 502

legitimate armed resistance to oppression, 86

legitimate defense by military force, conditions of, 86

Lenctentid, 336

Lent, fast and abstinence, 101; Fifth Sunday of, 337; Fourth Sunday of, 336; penitential observance of, 103; preparing for, 335; Season of, 336; symbols of, 458

Leo the Great, St., 417

Leonard of Port Maurice, St., 425

Leonine Prayers, 8

leopard changing its spots, 502

leper window, 266

letters, New Testament, 49–57, 219

levitation, 435

Liber Usualis, 297

life everlasting, 111, 116–117

Life of a Day, The, 330*

Lift up your hearts, 238

light, 503

Lilith, 124

lily, 460**, 479

limbo, 117

lines have fallen to me in pleasant places, The, 503

lion shall lie down with the lamb, The, 503

lip service, 503

liquefaction, 435

Litanies, 18–30; of St. Joseph, 25; of the Blessed Virgin (Loreto), 23–24; of the Holy Name of Jesus, 20–21; of the Sacred Heart, 19–20; of the Saints, 26–30

Litany of the Dying, 112

Little Flower, The, 248*

liturgical year, 325–366; calendar, 325; seasons, months, days, 327–330; two kinds of time, 325; the year, 326–327;

liturgical, colors, 299–300; feasts and seasons, 455–461; gestures and postures, 300–301; objects and vessels, 295–297; prayer, 275; purple, 483; vesture, 298–299; year, 325–366

Liturgy of the Hours, 39, 316–317, 385; elements, 317

liturgy, 96; angels in the, 120; elements of (listing), 317; funeral, 113

Live by the Sword, Die by the Sword, 503*

loaves, 503

locution, 435

Longinus, 407

Lord is my light, The, 238

Lord loves a cheerful giver, The, 503

Lord of Creation, 503

Lord, title of Jesus, 191

Lord's Day requirements, 84

Lord's Prayer, 1, 109; comparing Scripture translations, 153–155; seven petitions of, 95

Lost Tribes, The, 181*

Louis Bertrand, St., 430

Louis de Montfort, St., 396

Louis of France, St., 428

love of money is the root of all evil, The, 503

Love, Act of, 7

Low Sunday, 341

Lucifer, 125

Lucy, St., 419, 420, 422

Ludmilla, St., 430

Luke, St., 196**, 210, 212, 405, 407, 420, 422, 425, 426*, 426**, 482

Luke's banqueting scenes, 206

luna, 297

Luther, Martin, 248, 254, 255, 458

M

"M" of the Archbishop, The, 237*

Magdalene, 503

Magi, 130, 186; Adoration of the, 67**

Magnificat, 44, 503, 517

Malek, 173

Maltese cross, 93**

mammon of righteousness, 504

man of the cloth, title, 313

Man proposes, God disposes, 504

maniple, 299

manse, 273

Many are called but few are chosen, 504

Many Dwelling Places, 78*

maps, 132, 166, 176, 180, 197, 205, 220, 225, 226, 256

Marana tha, 294

Mardi Gras, 335–336

Margaret Mary, St., 129, 374–376

Margaret of Scotland, St., 425

Margaret, St., 126, 424, 426

Marian apparitions, 129, 262, 374–375, 391–394

mark of the beast, 504**

Mark, St., 196**, 207, 210, 406, 407, 422, 425

marks of the Church, 215–217

Maron, St., 251*

Marriage, as metaphor, 309; banns, 309; bond, 308; elements of, 308; exchange of rings, 308; grace of, 309; recognizing those that are unsacramental, 310; Sacrament of, 276, 308–310; symbols of, 454

Martha, St., 47, 126, 427

Martin de Porres, St., 422

Martin Luther, 248, 254*, 255; and the Christmas Tree, 458*

Martin of Tours, St., 77, 313, 364*, 419, 423, 428, 478, 517

Mary and the Americas, 429*

Mary at Fatima, 393**

Mary in the Middle East, 397*

Mary Magdalene, 209–211, 401, 407, 426

Mary the "Aztec Princess," 392*

Mary, in art, 398; 451**; baptismal names, 280, 397, 398; in the Bible, 158, 386; Blessed Virgin, 387; canticle, 44; consecration to, 396–397; devotion to, 23–24, 386–389, 395–396; in liturgy, 390; Mount Carmel, 243; Litany, 23–24; Our Lady of Sorrows, 388; principle apparitions of the Blessed Virgin, 391–394; in recent Catholic teaching, 389; Mystical Rose, 24; patron, 429–431; seven sorrows/joys of, 388, 464, 488; seven words of, 387; symbols, 330, 451, 473–476, 479–480, 485, 488; titles of, 390–391, 417, 421, 426

Mass in the Year 150, The, 286*

Mass, celebrating the mystery of Jesus, 343; chronology of changes, 287; honoring the apostles, 344; honoring Mary, mother of God, 343; parts of, 287; of the Pre-Sanctified, 339

Mata-moros, 405

Mater Dolorosa, 388

Matt Talbot, 418*

Matt Talbot, St., 418

Matthew, St., 210, 400, 403, 406, 407, 419, 428, 196**, 452**

Matthias, St., 400, 406, 453**

maudlin, 504

Maundy Thursday, 338

maxima culpa, 6

Maximilian, St., 433

Mea Culpa, 6, 294

medals, 324

Melchior, 407

Memorare, 17

Memorial Acclamation, three tenses of, 285

Memorials, Eucharistic Liturgy, 342

Mendicants, 246–247

menorah, 179**

mensa, 270

Methodius, St., 251*, 251**, 415, 430

metropolitan, 224

Mexican Bunuelos, 335*

Michael the Archangel, 8**, 106, 119, 119**, 419, 424, 426, 427, 428

Michaelmas Day, 120*

Michelangelo and the Image Asleep, 383*

Michelangelo, 160, 208, 233, 382, 383

Midnight Blue, Lifeblood Red, 450*

millennium, 127–128

minister, 313

miracles of Jesus, 203–204

Miserere, 504

mission of the Church 213

Missionaries in Statuary Hall, 258*

miter, 239

Mizpah Blessing, 42

monastery at New Melleray, IA, 274**

monastery, 274

money, 504

Monica, St., 102, 309*, 425

monograms, sacred, 461–463

monsignor, 314

monstrance, 297

month's mind, 114

months, dedication of, 329; names of, 328

moon, 330*, 473, 480*

morality, sources of, 75

Mordecai Nathan, Rabbi, 153

Morning Offering, 11, 376

mortal sin, 110

Moses, 39, 42, 129, 131, 132, 158, 160–161, 172, 174, 175, 185–187, 465, 447, 486; final blessing of the people, 42

mosque, 261

motherhouse, 274

Mothering Sunday, 336–337

Mothers' Patrons, 309*

mottoes, 237–238

Motu proprio, 231

mouths, 504

movement of the celebration, 288

Ms. Wisdom, 171*

Muhammad, 131

Multiculturalism at the Crèche, 186*

Mumpsmus, 517

Musical Patron, 425*

Muslims, 131

My Breastplate Prayer (St. Patrick), 33

Mysteries of the Rosary, 15–17; symbols of, 450

mystery plays, 286*

Mystical Rose, 24

myth, creatures of, 467; Orpheus, 481

mythical glossary, 437–440

N

Naboth's vineyard, 504

Nagasaki, 65

name, 505; naming, 280

narthex, 270

Nativity Scenes, 67*, 182, 186

nativity, of Jesus, 67, 185; gifts, 67; relics, 434*

nature miracles, 203

nave, 270

Nazareth, 505

new heaven and new earth, 116, 128

New Jerusalem, 505

New Testament, blessings, 55–60; books of (chart), 134; canticles, 43–46; fulfilling Old Testament, 182; glossary of titles of Christ, 193–195; names for the nameless, 407; prayerful greetings, 51–52; prayers, 46–51; symbols of, 215; table of contents, 198

new wine in new skins, 505

Newman, John Henry Cardinal, 34, 282*

Nicene Creed, 3–4

Nicholas of Tolentino, St., 424, 427

Nicholas, St., 361*, 361**, 419, 420, 421, 426, 430, 431, 480

Nihil Obstat, 75

Nihil Obstat Quominus Imprimatur, 75*

Nimrod, 505

Nine Crosses, The, 269*

nine, significance of, 464

No Pope Peter, 223*

no respecter of persons, 505

No Rest for the Wicked, 209*

Noah, 447

Noli me tangere, 211*

Non possumus, 232

Norbert, St., 246

nothing new under the sun, 505

novena, 101, 342, 391

numbers, significance of, 464–466; numbered, 505

nun (sister), 242

Nunc Dimittis, 46, 505

O

O Blessed Tongue . . . , 84*

O Salutaris Hostia, 371

obit, 115

Odilia, St., 419, 420

odor of sanctity, 435, 517

oil(s), holy, 318–319; of catechumens, 319; of the saints, 436; of the sick, 319

Olaf, St., 431

Old Bendy, 125

Old Harry, 125

Old Nick, 125

Old Scratch, 125

Old Testament, books of (chart), 133; canticles, 39–40; covenant in, 173–174; deities in, 173; figures, symbols of, 447; fulfilled in New Testament, 182; historical outline, 156; places and things of worship, 177–179; poems and songs, 41; prayers, 39–41; symbols, 447; table of contents, 159–171; terms, 174–175

olive branches, 505

ombrellino, 270

omnipotence, 63

One Day While Hunting, 72*

One Greeting in a Diversity of Tongues, 217*

one hundred, significance of, 466

one thousand, significance of, 466

one, significance of, 464

one-hundred forty-four thousand, significance of, 466

Oplatki, 285*

orans, liturgical gesture, 301

oratory, 260

Order of St. Gregory the Great, 232*

Ordinary Time, 333

Ordo, 297

orientation, 517; church, 265

original justice, 107

original sin, 106–108, 156, 159

orphrey, 299

Orthodox faith, 225–226, 253

Orthodoxy, 73–75

Our Lady of Guadalupe, 391**, 392, 431

Our Lady of Mount Carmel, 243*

Our Mother of Perpetual Help, 395–396*, 395**, 426

Out of Respect, 398*

overview of the faith to be known by heart, 61

ox, 506

P

Palestine of Jesus, The (map), 197

Palestine, name for land, 175

pall, 114, 297

pallium, 240*, 299

Palm Sunday, symbols of, 458

palms, 324

Pange Lingua, 371–372, 379

Panis Angelicus, 370

papacy, 222, 227–234; coats of arms, 227**, 234**, 236**; election, 227; insignia, 241; places, 232–233; statements, 231; things, 234

parables of Jesus, 201

paradise, 117

parament, 271

parents, duties of, 85

parochial vicar, 314

parousia, 127, 128

parson, 314

parsonage, 274

particular judgment, 116

passing bell, 112

Passion cross, 48**, 188**, 441**, 442

Passion Flower, 482*, 482**

Passion Sunday, 337

Passion, 188–189, 198, 207–210, 263; symbols of, 449

Passover, 366

pastor, 314

paten, 297

patience of Job, 506

Patmos, 506

patriarch(s), 156, 159, 174, 223, 229; cross, 253**; of the West, 229; rights and role of, 253; sanctuaries, 177; seven, 174

patriarchates, the five, 225; five Christian patriarchates (map), 225

Patrick, St., 33**, 70*, 121*, 262, 431, 473, 486*

Patron Saint of Television, 428*

Paul Chong, St., 433

Paul, Missionary Journeys (map), 220; symbol, 453**

Paul, St., 49–56, 79, 108, 109, 158, 212, 217, 218, 219, 220, 225, 240, 406, 425, 428, 436, 453, 508

Paul the Hermit, St., 429

Peace Prayer of St. Francis, 31

pearls, 506

pectoral cross, 239

pelican, 373*, 373**

Penance, effects of the Sacrament of, 304; major forms of, 303–304; names, 301–302; outline, 305; parts, 302; see Reconciliation

Pentecost, 14**, 101, 128, 190, 218; Jewish, 366; symbols of, 455, 464, 465

Peregrine, St., 302*, 420

persecutions, 221

Persian Empire (map), 166

Peter Baptist, St., 431

Peter Canisius, St., 62, 414

Peter Claver, St., 425, 430

Peter Gonzales, St., 427

Peter of Alcantara, St., 429

Peter, 401–402, 406, 453*, 464; symbol of, 453**

Peter, St., 46–48, 200, 207, 211, 217, 218, 223, 225, 227, 228, 240, 241, 400–402, 406, 421, 445, 453*, 453**, 475, 479, 485, 508

Peter's Pence, 234*

Philip, 403, 406; symbol of, 453**

Philip, St., 217, 400, 403, 406, 453, 480

Philippino Memorial Day, 355*

Philistine, 506

Philomena, St., 427

Physician, heal thyself, 506

Pietà, 382, 383, 450

Pike's Curiosity, The, 449*

Pilate's wife, 130

Pilgrimage of the Way of the Cross, The, 263*

pilgrimage, 261; shrines, 262

Pius X, St., 417

plow, 506

poems and songs in the Old Testament, 41

Poinsettia—the Mexican "Flower of the Holy Night," 457*; 483

Polish Emmaus Walk, 189*

Polycarp, St., 408

polytheism, 436–437

pontifical letter, 231

Poor Friday, 330*

poor, as a church mouse, 517; as Job, 506; as Lazarus, 506

pope, 222, 223, 229; first and twentieth centuries, 228; titles, 229–230

Posada, 356*

postmillennialism (chart), 128

post-resurrection appearances of Jesus, 212

Potter's Field, 506

"Pouring the Ocean Down a Hole," 64*

powers, 118

Praise God always, 238

Pray and work, 238

Prayer of the Curé of Ars, St. John Vianney, 34

prayer, 1–55, 94–101, 199; before a crucifix, 12; difficulties in, 99; forms of, 97; to the Guardian Angel, 11; kinds of, 1–16, 96–97; *Lectio,* 99; motive for, 99; forms of, 97; from the New Testament, 46–51; from the Old Testament, 39–41; of Jesus, 94; of the Church, 96; Paul's of Thanksgiving, 52–55; process of, 99; saints', 31–34; sequence of Christian prayer, 98–99; sources of, 98; three notable definitions of, 98

prayerful glossary, 100–101; greetings, 51–52

Praying Hands, 98

preacher, 314

preaching, 292

precepts of the Church, the, 90–91

Precious Blood of Jesus, Litany of the, 22–23

predella, 271

prelate, 314

Premillennialism (chart), 128

Premonstratensians, 246

presbyter, 314

Presentation in the Temple, The, 45**; symbols of, 455

preternatural gifts, 107

Pretzels, 300*

Prie-dieu, 271

priest, 314; see Holy Orders

priesthood, baptismal, 310

Priest, Prophet, King, title of Jesus, 191

primate, 224, 229; of Italy, 229

principalities, 118

prior, 314

priory, 274

Prisoner Patron, 427*

Pro Defunctis, 114

processional cross, 297

prodigal son, 507

prolonged abstinence, 436

Promised Land, 507; names for the, 175

promises of Our Lord, 375

prophecy fulfillment in Jesus, 183–185

prophets, 181–182, 507

prostration, liturgical posture, 301

Protestantism, 254–257; denominationalism (chart), 255; mid-sixteenth century (map), 256; Reformation, 254*

Proud Lily, The, 460*, 460**

provincial, 314

psalms, 160; categories, 37–38; classification, 36; notable, 35; numbering, 36

Psalter of Mary, 15, 36

pulpit, 271

purgatory, 116, 121

Purification, symbols of, 456

purificator, 297

Purim, 366

purity, requirements, 89

Purvey, John, 142

pyx, 297

Q

Queen of Heaven Prayer, 9

Quo Vadis?, 453*

R

R.I.P., 115

Rabbi, title of Jesus, 191

Raccolta, 122

race, 507

Rainy Saint, The, 466*

Raising Cain, 507

Raphael, archangel, 78, 119, 419, 420, 422, 424, 425, 426, 429

rapture, 128

Raymond Nonnatus, St., 422

Real Presence, The, 284*

Reconciliation and Healing, 302*

Reconciliation, four traditional parts of, 302; as sacrament, 276; symbols of, 454

rector, 315

rectory, 274

red, liturgical significance of, 299; -letter day, 518

Redemptive Dolphin, 112*

reed, 507; shaken in the wind, 507

Refection Sunday, 337

Reformation, The, 254*; 254–257

Regina Caeli, 9

Relationship between Old Testament and New Testament, 182

relics, 433–434

religion, virtue of, 82

religions, in the Western world, 131; major world, 131

religious life, traditional, 244–249

religious order, a glossary of, 241–243

religious rule, 242; world (chart), 131

reliquary, 271

Remember, man . . . , 507

remora, 467

renaming, 281

Render unto Caesar . . . , 507

repenter curls, 518

repository, 271

Reproaches of Good Friday, 377

reredos, 271

Resigning Pope, 228*

respect for the dignity of persons, meaning of, 86

resurrection, 115–116, 128, 210–211; first, 127; gardens, 459; of the body, 115; symbol of, 116**

resuscitation miracles, 204

Return of the Dead in Poland, The, 355*

Return of the Swallows, The, 347*

return to one's vomit, 507

revelation, 214; definitions of, 129

Revelation, Book of, 49, 93, 106, 181

reverence, the four forms, 315

Reverend, 315

right mind, 508

ring of the Fisherman, 241, 484**

ring, as a symbol, 308; papal, 241, symbolic meaning, 239, 484

Rite of Christian Initiation of Adults, the, 279–280

Rite of Committal, 113

Rite of Penance, outline of, 305

Rite of Reception of Baptized Christians into Full Communion, 283

rites, funeral, 113

robbing Peter to pay Paul, 518

Robert Bellarmine, St., 62, 414

Robert Molesme, St., 245

Roch, St., 308*, 423, 426

Rogation Days, 18

Rogers, John (Thomas Matthew), 143

Roman calendar, general, 345–356; saints on, 357–359

Roman Collar, The, 312*

Roman Missal, 297

Romanesque style, 264**

rood screen, 271**

root of the matter, 508

Rosary, 15**–17, 450

Rose of Paradise, The, 108*

Rose Sunday, 337

rose window, 271, 515

rose, 24, 108, 117, 248, 304, 337, 392, 450, 451, 454, 455, 485, 515, 518; liturgical significance of, 299; under the, 304

Route of the Exodus (map), 176

rubric, 518

Russian Babushka, 335*

Russian cross, 189**, 253**, 441**, 442

Russian Reconciliation, 72*

S

Sabbath, 91, 199, 200, 465; requirements, 84

sabbatical, 508

sackcloth and ashes, 508

Sacrament of Holy Orders, 310–316; essential rite of, 311; minor orders, 311; three degrees of ministerial priesthood, 310; titles, 312–315

sacramental sacrifice, three meanings of, 285

sacramental seal, 304

sacramentals, 318–324; purpose of, 318; elements of, 318

Sacramentary, 289–290

Sacraments of Healing, 301

Sacraments of Mission, 308–310

sacraments, defined, 275; listed, 276–277; symbols of, 454

sacrarium, 271

Sacred College, 224

Sacred Heart, 19–20, 430; Devotion, 374**, 374–376; traditional practices, 376

sacred monograms, 461–463

sacred places, 258–261

sacrifice, significance of, 285

sacrificial giving, 104–105

sacristan, 295

sacristy, 272, 295

saint, in canonization process, 432; on the general Roman calendar, 357–359; patrons of the blind, 420; patrons of countries, 429–431; principle patrons, 418–429; titles of, 415–418

St. Adam and St. Eve, 489*

St. Agnes' Flowers, 346*; symbol of, 346**

St. Aidan's Cruse of Oil, 319*

St. Andrew's cross, 209**, 393**, 404, 441**, 452**

St. Anthony and the Child Jesus, 97*

St. Anthony and the Lost Manuscript, 424*

St. Anthony's fire, 518

St. Bernard dogs, 518, 474**

St. Bernard Passes, 518

St. Boniface and the Christmas Tree, 458*

St. Chad's cross, 209**

St. Crispin's holiday, 519

St. Cuthbert's duck, 519

St. Distaff's Day, 346*

St. Dorothea's Roses, 117*

St. Dunstan and blindness, 519

St. Elmo's Fire, 519

St. Emeric, 429*

St. Francis and Lady Poverty, 76*

St. Francis's distemper, 519

St. George and the Dragon, 126*, 126**

St. Grouse's Day, 351*

St. Helena and the True Cross, 443*, 443**

St. Jerome and the Lion, 137*, 137**

St. John Neumann, 430*

St. John's Wort, 349*

St. Joseph Table, 79*

St. Julian's cross, 209**

St. Lawrence, fiery tears of, 519

St. Luke the Artist, 426*, 426**

St. Martin and the Shirt off his Back, 77*

St. Martin's beads, 519

St. Monday, 519

St. Patrick's Purgatory, 121*

St. Patrick's Shamrock, 486*

St. Peter's Basilica, 222**, 231, 259, 265, 268, 382, 406

St. Peter's fingers, 508; cross, 209**, 406**

St. Stephen's loaves, 508

St. Thomas the Builder, 265*

St. Vitus's Dance

Saint's Day or What? 362*

saintly signs and memorabilia, 433–435

Saints, Litany of the, 26–30

salt, 508; of the earth, 508

Salve, Regina, 16

Samson, 508

San Damiano Cross, 31**; 445*; symbol, 445**

Sanctuaries in Israel before the temple, 177

sanctuary, 272; candle, 322; lamp, 272*, 272**; screen, 272

sanctum sanctorum, 508

Sanctus, 294

Sand Dollar, The Legend of the, 62

santa casa, 387

Satan, 125; bound, 128; chained, 128

satisfaction, 302

satyr, 467

Saul also among the prophets? Is, 508

Savior, title of Jesus, 191

Scala Sancta, 233

scapegoat, 509

scapular, 242–243, 324, 368**

schism, 75

Scholastica, St., 421

scot-free, 520

scriptural evangelizers (ten), 70

Scripture, two senses of, 130

Sebastian, St., 419, 423, 426, 428

second death, 128

Second Order, 242

Secret of Fatima, The, 394*

sedia gestatoria, 241

sedilia, 272

see how the land lies, 509

Semitic, 509

Septuagint, 133

sequence, 292

seraphim, 118

sermons in Acts, 218

serpent (devil), 125

Serra, Miguel, 281*

Servant of the servants of God, 230

Servites, 248

seven heavens, 117

seven hills of Rome, 233

Seven Holy Founders, 248, 359

Seven Last Words, 208, 464

seven sacraments, 277–278, 465

seven signs from St. John, 206

Seven Sorrows, symbols of, 455

seven, significance of, 464–465

seven-pointed star, 190**

Seventy is the sum of your years, 509

Shake off the dust from your feet, 509

Shear Thursday, 338

sheep, 509

Shekinah, 178

sheol, 123

Shibboleth, 509

Shlama, 339

shofar, 179

Shrine of the Immaculate Conception, 356*

shrine, 260, 302, 319, 356, 390, 391; pilgrimage, 262

Shroud of Turin, 434*

Sic transit gloria mundi, 227, 520

Sign of the Cross, 300

Silver/Golden Wedding Anniversary Blessing, 58–59

Simeon Stylites, St., 244*

Simeon's Canticle, 46, 323

similitudes and allegories Jesus used, 202

Simon Stock, St., 247

Simon, St., 400, 404, 406, 453**

simony, 509

Simple Harmonic Motion of a Sanctuary Lamp, The, 272*

sin, 105–110; actual, 109–110; against chastity, 87; against faith, 82; against fifth commandment, 86; against God's love, 82; against Holy Spirit, 110; against honor due to God, 83; against hope, 82; mortal, 110; original, 106–108; seven capital (deadly, 110, 465; against seventh commandment, 87; against truth, 88–89; against the name of God, 84; of irreligion, 83; that cry to heaven for vengence, 110; venial, 109

sinecure, 316, 520

Sistine Chapel, 227, 233

sitting, liturgical posture, 301

six points of ritualism, 298

six, significance of, 464

six-sixty-six, significance of, 466

skin, 509

Slave of the Slaves, 230*

Slavic Bells, 320*

Slavs' Memorial Day, The, 114*

slow to anger, 509

Snakes and Healing, 307*

snakes, symbols of, 307**

social justice, 92–93; demands of, 92; principles of, 93

solemnities, 342; of the Church year, 344; symbols of, 455

Solomon, 39, 40, 132, 156, 158, 163, 177, 264, 447; Solomon's blessing, 42

Solomon, I have Surpassed You, 264*

Solomon's Cedar, 163*

Son of David, title of Jesus, 191

Son of God, title of Jesus, 191

Son of Man, title of Jesus, 191

Sophia (Wisdom), 309

Soul Cakes, 456*

Soul of Christ Prayer, 34

Soul, bell, 112; likeness to God, 64

sounding brass, 509

South American Last Supper, 188*

Sovereign of Vatican City, 230

sow, 510; the wind, 510

Spare the rod . . . , 510

spire, 266

spirit, 310

spiritual, life dynamic, 95–96; works of mercy, 77

sponsor, 280

Spy Wednesday, 338

squint, 266

Stabat Mater, 388

standing, liturgical posture, 301

star, of Bethlehem, 483; of David (Magen David), 156**; of the Epiphany, 186**; seven- and eight-pointed, 190**; six-pointed, 488; twelve-pointed, 179**

stars in their courses, 510

states of the Church, 216

steeple, 266

Stephen Harding, St., 245

Stephen of Hungary, St., 430

Stephen, St., 48, 217, 219, 420, 508

steps, symbolic, 273, 488

stewardship, 103

stewardship, 103

stigmata, 436

still, small voice, 510

stole, 299, 488

Stolen sweets are always sweater, 510

stone, 510

"Stone Soup," 104*

straight and narrow, 510

strain, 510

stranger in a strange land, 511

Straw of a Genius, The, 415*

Straw under the Tablecloth, 185*

strength, 511

Stylites or Pillar Ascetics, 244*

stylites, 244

sub rosa, 304

Successor of St. Peter, 229

Suffer fools gladly, 511

Suffering Servant, title of Jesus, 191

suffragan bishop, 224

sun, 511

Sunday saint, 520

Sundays of Easter, 341

Sundays, 331

supererogation, 520

superfrontal, 273

superior, 315

Supreme Pontiff, 229

surplice, 299

Suspice, 34

sweat, 511; sweating blood, 511

Sweet Talk, 470*

Swiss Guards and Designer Clothes, 233*

swords, 511, 512

Sylvester, St., 126, 482

symbols, Christmas, 457–458; dolphin, 112**, 474; general glossary of, 468–492; numbers,

464–466; of angels, 450; of denominations, 454–455; of God the Father, 448; of Jesus, 448; of Jesus' threefold office, 448; of Lent and Holy Week, 458–459; of Mary, 450–451; of Old Testament figures, 447; of the Easter Season, 459–461; of the apostles, 452–453; of the Church, 215, 454; of the Holy Spirit, 69**, 449**; of the Passion, 449; of the sacraments, 454; of the season, 456–461; of solemnities and feasts, 455–456; of the Trinity, 65**, 300**, 447**; of the virtues of faith, hope, and love, 5**

synagogue, 261

T

tabernacle, 273; Jewish, 366

taking your life in your hands, 511

talent, 511

Tarcisius, St., 422

Tau cross, 209**, 441**

tawdry, 520

Te Deum, 10

Tears of St. Lawrence, The, 221*

teeth set on edge, 511

Tell it not in Gath, 512

Temple of Jerusalem, 175, 177–178, 205 (map), 261, 465, 488

temptation(s), threatening prayer, 99

Ten Great Persecutions, 221

ten, significance of, 464

Tenebrae, 339

tent of the Exodus, 177

Teresa of Ávila, St., 248, 412, 414, 417, 422, 431

Territory of the Twelve Tribes of Israel, The (map), 180

Thanks be to God, 238

"That's Impossible," 69*

The Atonement of Nagasaki? 65*

The Devil and the Horseshoe, 125*

The Devil's Funeral, 66*

The Doubting Monk and the Singing Bird, 97*

The Fast of Adam, 102*

The Fast of the Ninevites, 165*

The Gideon Bible, 146*

The Good-Friday Born, 118*

The Legend of the Pelican, 373*, 373**

The Legend of the Sand Dollar, 62*

The Man in the Moon and the Sabbath Breaker, 91*

The Otter and the Crocodile, 124*

The Peacock on the Tomb, 116*

The Phoenix of the Resurrection, 116*

The Proud Lily, 460*, 460**

The Rose of Paradise, 108*

The Serpent's Fast, 102*

The Three Kings, 67*, 67**

Theotokos, 386, 390

There is nothing without God, 238

Thérèse Martin, St., 98, 248*, 248**, 262, 412, 414, 419, 422, 425, 478, 485

"They Have Pierced My Hands and My Feet," 208*

They Reclined at Table, 207*

Third Order, 242

thirty pieces of silver, 512

Thomas à Kempis, 109

Thomas Aquinas, St., 108, 134*, 247, 369, 370, 371, 373, 379, 414, 415*, 416, 417, 427, 428

Thomas the Builder, St., 265*

Thomas, St., 186, 190, 221*, 265, 400, 403, 406–407, 415–416, 420, 422, 430, 452, 453**, 497

Thorn in the flesh, 512

three crosses, symbol, 407**

three expressions of the moral law, 81

three, significance of, 464; symbolism, 67–68, 81

thrones, 118

thurible, 297

tiara, 241

tide, 327*

tiffany, 520

tithing, 104

titles of Christ, 193–195

titular bishop, 224

To consecrate life to truth, 238

To God who is the best . . . , 238

To restore all things in Christ, 238

"Too Late Have I Loved You" (from St. Augustine), 33

tongue, a two-edged sword, 512

tonsure, 312

Totally Yours, 238

Touch-me-not, 512

traditional prayer, 7

Trappists, 245

tre ore, 338

Tre Ore, From Lima, The, 338*

tribulation, 128

Trick or Treat, 122*

Triduum, the, 340

tried and found wanting, 512

Trinity Sunday, symbols of, 455

Trinity, the, dogma of, 64, 173; symbols of**, 65, 173, 300, 447; as title, 173

trisagion, 101

trumpets (Rosh Ha-Shanah), 366

truth shall make you free, The, 238

Turkey or Goose, 364*

Turn the other cheek, 512

Twelve Apostles, burial places of, 406–407; deaths (stories of), 404–406; list, 400; in Scripture, 401–404

Twelve Apostles; 158 Teach All Nations (map), 220

Twelve Tribes of Israel, 179; *The Territory of the* (map), 180

twelve, significance of, 464

twelve-pointed star of the Twelve Tribes of Israel, 179**

twinkling of an eye, In the, 512

Tyndale, William (Tyndale's Bible), 140–142

typology, 185–190

U

Ukrainian Christmas, 357*

Under the Rose, 304*

Unicorn, The, 490*

universal hierarchy, 222

Unlucky Elder Tree, The, 405*

unorthodoxy, types of, 74

Urbi et orbi, 231

Uriah, 512

Uriel, 119

urim and thummin, 179

Ursula, St., 424

V

Valentine, St., 422

vanity of vanities, 513

Vatican City, 232; seal, 234**

Vatican, 232–233

Venerable, in canonziation process, 432

Veneration in Old Russia, 339*

veneration, of saints and heroes, 385

Veni, Sancte Spiritus, 14, 294

venial sin, 109

Veronica, 408*, 382**

vestibule, 273

Vexilla Regis, 380

Via Dolorosa, 380

vicar, 315; apostolic, 224; of Christ, 229

Victor, St., 425

victories over hostile wills, miracles of, 204

vigil lights, 322

vigil, funeral, 113

Vincent de Paul, St., 421

Vincent Ferrer, St., 420

Vincent, St., 74, 421, 429

Vincentian Canon, 74*

vine and branches, 202, 490

violet, 491; liturgical significance of, 299

virtue(s), 75–76, 118; balanced by truth, 88; of religion, 82; the seven Christian, 76, 464

visions, 129; see apparitions

vitandus, 306

Vocation in a Dream, A, 70*

voice crying in the wilderness, A, 513

vows, religious, 242

W

wages of sin is death, The, 513

wars and rumors of war, 513

Watch Thou, Dear Lord (St. Augustine), 31

Watchful Ostrich, The, 43*

water, 491

way of all flesh, the, 513

weathercock, 513

week, dedication of, 330; names of days, 329

Wenceslaus, St., 430

west front, 267

What do you know? 64*

"*What name do you give your child?*" 280*

Wheat of St. Ignatius, The, 222*

When a C is Not a C, 473*

When Blackberries Turn Tasteless, 120*

When in Rome, 102*

When Is a Christmas Carol Not a Christmas Carol? 334*

white, liturgical significance of, 299, 491

Whitsunday, 342

Why Seven? 329*

Why the Robin's Breast Is Red, 12*

widow's cruse, 513

widow's mite, 513

Willibrord, St., 430

wine, 514

wings of the wind, 514

Wisdom of Solomon, 514

Wisdom, 170–171

Wise as serpents . . . , 514

With God's favor, 238

With God's help, 238

Womb of the Baptistry, The, 268*

Wonders of the world, 157

Wood of the Cross, The, 444*

word and phrase origins, biblical, 493–514; Church, 515–520

Word, The, title of Jesus, 191

works of mercy, 76–77

World Religions, Major (chart), 132

Wounded Healer, A, 308*

Wycliffe, John, 140–142, 153

wyvern, 467

X

XP, 463**

Y

Yahweh (YHWH), 172, 173, 190

year, Church, 331–334; months of, 328; numbering, 326–327

YHWH Sebaoth, 173

youth renewed like the eagle's, 514**

Z

Zadkiel, 119

Zebaot, 172

Zechariah's Canticle, 45

Zion, 175

Photo List

Gene Plaisted, OSC/The Crosiers—8, 14, 22, 25, 33, 67, 69, 115, 119, 123, 126, 135, 212, 222, 251, 265, 275, 298, 319, 360, 361, 372, 374, 383, 393, 400, 426, 460, 472, 502, 510, 519; James L. Shaffer—12, 79, 211, 248, 274, 333, 341, 391, 395, 439, 443, 445, 471, 491, 494, 514, 516